THE ENCYCLOPÆDIA
BRITANNICA
VOLUME V SLICE V

Cat to Celt

CAT,1 properly the name of the well-known domesticated feline animal usually termed by naturalists *Felis domestica*, but in a wider sense employed to denote all the more typical members of the family *Felidae*. According to the *New English Dictionary*, although the origin of the word "cat" is unknown, yet the name is found in various languages as far back as they can be traced. In old Western Germanic it occurs, for instance, so early as from A.D.400 to 450; in old High German it is *ŏchazza* or *catero*, and in Middle German *kattaro*. Both in Gaelic and in old French it is *cat*, although sometimes taking the form of *chater* in the latter; the Gaelic designation of the European wild cat being *cat fiadhaich*. In Welsh and Cornish the name is *cath*. If Martial's *cattae* refer to this animal, the earliest Latin use of the name dates from the 1st century of our era. In the work of Palladius on agriculture, dating from about the year A.D. 350, reference is made to an animal called *catus* or *cattus*, as being useful in 488granaries for catching mice. This usage, coupled with the existence of a distinct term in Gaelic for the wild species, leaves little doubt that the word "cat" properly denotes only the domesticated species. This is confirmed by the employment in Byzantine Greek of the term κάττος or κάττα to designate domesticated cats brought from Egypt. It should be added that the αἴλουρος of the Greeks, frequently translated by the older writers as "cat," really refers to the marten-cat, which appears to have been partially domesticated by the ancients and employed for mousing.

As regards the origin of the domesticated cats of western Europe, it is well known that the ancient Egyptians were in the habit of domesticating (at least in some degree) the Egyptian race of the African wild cat (*Felis ocreata maniculata*), and also of embalming its remains, of which vast numbers have been found in tombs at Beni Hasan and elsewhere in Egypt. These Egyptian cats are generally believed by naturalists to have had a large share in the parentage of the European breeds, which have, however, in many cases been crossed to a greater or less extent with the European wild cat (*F. catus*).

One of the features by which the Egyptian differs from the European wild cat is the longer and less bushy tail; and it has been very generally considered that the same feature is characteristic of European domesticated cats. According, however, to Dr E. Hamilton, "the measurement of a number of tails of the [European] wild cat and of the domestic cat gives a range between 11 in. and 14½ in., the longer length being quite as often found in the wild cats as in the domestic. The bushy appearance depends entirely on the length of the fur, and accords with the thick fur of the rest of the body of the wild cat, while in the domestic race the fur both on the body and tail is thinner and softer."

Possibly those domesticated cats with unusually short and bushy tails may have a larger share of European wild-cat blood; while, conversely, such wild cats as show long tails may have a cross of domesticated blood.

More importance was attached by Dr A. Nehring of Berlin (*SB. Ges. Naturfor.*, Berlin, 1887) to the colour of the soles of the hind-feet as a means of determining the relationship of the domesticated cat of Europe. According to his observations, in the Egyptian wild cat the pads of the toes are wholly black, while the black extends back either continuously or in long stripes as far as the calcaneum or heel-bone. In the European wild cat, on the other hand, the black is limited to a small round spot on the pads, while the colour of the hair as far back as the heel-bone is yellowish or yellowish-grey. Since in all domesticated cats retaining the colouring of the wild species the soles of the hind-feet correspond in this particular with the Egyptian rather than with the European wild cat, the presumption is in favour of their descent from the former rather than from the latter.

Later, Dr Nehring (*op. cit.* 1889) came to the conclusion that the domesticated cat has a dual parentage, one stock coming from south-eastern Asia and the other from north-eastern Africa; in other words, from a domesticated Chinese cat (itself derived from a wild Chinese species) on the one hand, and from the Egyptian cat on the other. The ordinary domesticated cats of Europe are, however, mainly of African origin, although they have largely crossed, especially in Germany (and probably also in Great Britain), with the wild cat. The same author was likewise of opinion that the domestication or taming of various species of wild cats took place chiefly among nationalities of stationary or non-nomadic habits who occupied themselves with agricultural pursuits, since it would be of vital importance that their stores of grain should be adequately protected from the depredations of rats and mice.

The foregoing opinion as to the dual parentage of our domesticated cats receives support from observations made many years ago by E. Blyth, which have recently been endorsed and amplified by R.I. Pocock (*Proc. Zool. Soc. London*, 1907). According to these observations, two distinct types of so-called tabby cats are recognizable. In the one the pattern consists of narrow vertical stripes, and in the other of longitudinal or obliquely longitudinal stripes, which, on the sides of the body, tend to assume a spiral or sub-circular arrangement characteristic of the blotched tabby. This latter type appears to be the true "tabby"; since that word denotes a pattern like that of watered silk. One or other of these types is to be found in cats of almost all breeds, whether Persian, short-haired or Manx; and there appear to be no intermediate stages between them. Cats of the striped type are no doubt descended from the European and North African wild cats; but the origin of cats exhibiting the blotched pattern appears to be unknown. As it was to a cat of the latter kind that Linnaeus gave the name of *Felis catus*, Pocock urges that this title is not available for the European wild cat, which he would call *Felis sylvestris*. Without accepting this proposed change in nomenclature, which is liable to lead to confusion without any compensating advantage, it may be suggested that the blotched tabby type represents Dr Nehring's presumed Chinese element in the cat's parentage, and that the missing wild stock may be one of the numerous phases of the leopard-cat (*F. bengalensis*), in some of which an incipient spiral arrangement of the markings may be noticed on the shoulder.

As to the introduction of domesticated cats into Europe, the opinion is very generally held that tame cats from Egypt were imported at a relatively early date into Etruria by Phoenician traders; and there is decisive evidence that these animals were established in Italy long before the Christian era. The progeny of these cats, more or less crossed with the indigenous species, thence gradually spread over Europe, to become mingled at some period, according to Dr Nehring's hypothesis, with an Asiatic stock. The earliest written record of the introduction of domesticated cats into Great Britain dates from about A.D. 936, when Hywel Dda, prince of South Wales, enacted a law for their protection. "The Romans," writes Dr Hamilton, "were probably the original introducers of this cat, and as the final evacuation of Britain by that nation took place under the emperor Valentinian about A.D. 436, the period of its introduction may certainly be dated some 500 years previous to the Welsh chronicle and even much earlier." It is added that the remains of cats from Roman villas at Silchester and Dursley are probably referable to the domesticated breed.

Before proceeding to notice some of the different types of domesticated cats, a few lines may be devoted to the wild European species, *F. catus*. Beyond stating that in colour it conforms very closely to the striped phase of domesticated tabby, it will be unnecessary to describe the species. Its geographical range was formerly very extensive, and included Great Britain, France, the Netherlands, Switzerland, Germany, Bohemia, Hungary, Poland, Transylvania, Galicia, the Caucasus as far as the Caspian, southern Russia, Italy, Spain, Greece, Rumania, Bulgaria, Servia, and portions of central and northern Asia. "At the present time," observes Dr Hamilton, "the wild cat has become almost extinct in many of the above districts. Examples may perhaps occasionally still be found in the uninhabited forests of Hungary and Transylvania, and occasionally in Spain and Greece, as well as in the Caucasus and in some of the Swiss cantons, but the original race has in most countries interbred with the domestic cat wherever the latter has penetrated." In Great Britain wild cats survive only in some of the Scottish forests, and even there it is difficult to decide whether pure-bred specimens are extant. Remains of the wild cat occur in English caverns; while from those of Ireland (where the wild species has apparently been unknown during the historic period) have been obtained jaws and teeth which it has been suggested are referable to the Egyptian rather than to the European wild cat. Such a determination is, however, extremely hazardous, even if it be admitted that the remains of cats from the rock-fissures of Gibraltar pertain to *Felis ocreata*.

PLATE I.

FIG. 1.—SKINS OF THE BLOTCHED DOMESTIC CAT, SHOWING SOME OF THE VARIATIONS TO WHICH THE PATTERN IS LIABLE. (Cf. Fig. 5 on Plate II.)

FIG. 2.—SKINS OF THE STRIPED DOMESTIC CAT, GIVING THE "TICKED" BREED AND A PARTIALLY ALBINO SPECIMEN. (Cf. Fig. 4 on Plate II.)

FIG. 3.—SKINS OF THE EUROPEAN WILD CAT, FROM ROSS-SHIRE, SCOTLAND. (Cf. Fig. 1 on Plate II.)

Note—Of the two types of colouration found in modern domestic cats, the striped type obviously corresponds to the original wild cat as seen in various parts of North Europe to-day. The origin of the blotched as a special type is wholly unknown.

(Photos from Plates VIII., IX., and X., *P.Z.S.*, 1907, by permission of the Zoological Society of London.)

PLATE II.

Photo, W.G. Berridge.
FIG. 1.—EUROPEAN WILD CAT.

Photo, W.G. Berridge.
FIG. 2.—PALLAS'S CAT.

Photo, R.C. Ryan.
FIG. 3.—ROYAL SIAMESE CAT.

Photo, Topical Press Agency.
FIG. 4.—STRIPED DOMESTIC CAT.

Photo, Topical Press Agency
FIG. 5.—BLOTCHED DOMESTIC CAT.

Photo, R.C. Ryan
FIG. 6.—TAIL-LESS CAT.

Photo, Topical Press Agency.
FIG. 7.—WHITE PERSIAN

Photo, Topical Press Agency.
FIG. 8.—BLUE PERSIAN

3

Photo, Topical Press Agency.
FIG. 9.—BLACK PERSIAN KITTEN.

The favourite haunts of the wild cat are mountain forests where masses or rocks or cliffs are interspersed with trees, the crevices in these rocks or the hollow trunks of trees affording sites for the wild cat's lair, where its young are produced and reared. In the Spanish plains, however, the young are often produced in nests built in trees, or among tall bamboos in 489cane-brakes. "To fight like a wild cat" is proverbial, and wild cats are described as some of the most ferocious and untamable of all animals. How far this untamable character lends support to the view of the origin of our domesticated breeds has not yet been determined. Hares, rabbits, field-mice, water-rats, rats, squirrels, moles, game-birds, pigeons, and small birds, form the chief food of the wild cat.

Apart from the above-mentioned division of the striped members of both groups into two types according to the pattern of their markings, the domesticated cats of western Europe are divided into a short-haired and a long-haired group. Of these, the former is the one which bears the closest relationship to the wild cats of Africa and of Europe, the latter being an importation from the East. The striped (as distinct from the blotched) short-haired tabby is probably the one most nearly allied to the wild ancestors, the stripes being, however, to a great extent due to the European wild cat. In one direction the tabby shows a tendency to melanism which culminates in complete blackness, while in the other direction there is an equally marked tendency to albinism; grey cats, which may be regarded as tabbies whose stripes have disappeared, forming the connecting link between the tabby and the white cat. A mixture of the melanistic with the albinistic type will of course give rise to parti-coloured cats. A third colour-phase, the "erythristic" or red, is represented by the sandy cat, the female of which takes the form of the "tortoise-shell," characterized, curiously enough, by the colour being a blend of black, white, and sandy. The so-called orange tabby is one phase of the erythristic type.

As to long-haired cats, there appear originally to have been two closely-allied strains, the Angora and the Persian, of which the former has been altogether replaced in western Europe by the latter. That these long-haired cats have an ancestry, to some extent at any rate distinct from the ordinary short-haired breeds, is practically certain, and it has been suggested that they are derived from the "manul" cat, or Pallas's cat (*Felis manul*), of the deserts of central Asia, which is a long-haired and bushy-tailed species with comparatively slight striping. The fact that in tabby Persians the body-markings are never so strong as in the short-haired breeds is in some degree confirmatory of this, as suggesting descent from a nearly whole-coloured type. At the present day, however, Persians exhibit nearly all the colour and pattern types of the short-haired breeds, the "orange Persian" representing the erythristic phase.

Turning to the tailless or so-called Manx cats, in which the tail should be represented merely by a tuft of hair without any remnant of bone, it seems that the strain is to be met with in many parts of Russia, and there is a very general opinion that it originally came from Japan or some other far eastern country. Throughout Japan, China, Siam, and the Malay countries, normal long-tailed cats are indeed seldom seen. Instead of these are cats with more or less abbreviated tails, showing in greater or less degree a decided kink or bend near the tip. In other cases the tail is of the short curling type of that of a bulldog; sometimes it starts quite straight, but divides in a fork-like manner near the tip; and in yet other instances it is altogether wanting, as in the typical Manx cats. These kink-tailed or tailless cats are moreover smaller in size than the ordinary short-tailed breeds, with rather longer hair, whose texture approaches that of rabbit-fur, and a cry said to be like that of the jungle-cat (*F. chaus*)

4

of India and Africa, and more dog-like habits. Unless the jungle-cat, which is a nearly whole-coloured species, can claim the position, the ancestry of these Manx-Malay cats is still unknown. Kink-tailed cats, it should be added, are also known from Madagascar.

Among the domesticated cats of India a spotted type of colouring, with a more or less decided tendency for the spots to coalesce into stripes, is very noticeable; and it is probable that these cats are derived from the spotted Indian desert-cat (*F. ornata*), with a certain amount of crossing from other species. The so-called *F. torquata* of India is probably based on cats of this type which have reverted to the wild state. Other Indian cats with a tawny or fulvous type of colouring are probably the more or less modified descendants of the jungle-cat. From the same stock may be derived the Abyssinian breed, in which the ears are relatively large and occasionally tipped with long hairs (thus recalling the tufted ears of the jungle-cat). The colour is typically reddish-brown, each individual hair being "ticked" like that of a wild rabbit, whence the popular name of "bunny cat." Another African breed is the Mombasa cat, in which the hair is reported to be unusually short and stiff.

By far the most remarkable of all the Old World domesticated breeds is, however, the royal Siamese cat, which almost certainly has an origin quite distinct from that of the ordinary European breeds; this being rendered evident not only by the peculiar type of colouring, but likewise by the cry, which is quite unmistakable. Siamese cats may have the tail either straight or kinked, but whether the latter feature belongs of right to the breed, or has been acquired by crossing with the ordinary black and tabby kink-tailed cats of the country, is not known. In the royal Siamese breed the head is rather long and pointed, the body also elongated with relatively slender limbs, the coat glossy and close, the eyes blue, and the general colour some shade of cream or pink, with the face, ears, feet, under-parts, and tail chocolate or seal-brown. There is however a wholly chocolate-coloured strain in which the eyes are yellow. The most remarkable feature about the breed is that the young are white. "The kittens," observes a lady writer, "are born absolutely white, and in about a week a faint pencilling comes round the ears, and gradually all the points come. At four or five months they are lovely, as generally they retain their baby whiteness, which contrasts well with their almost black ears, deep-brown markings, and blue eyes." In constitution these cats are extremely delicate. The blue eyes and the white coat of the kitten indicate that the Siamese breed is a semi-albino, which when adult tends towards melanism, such a combination of characters being apparently unknown in any other animal. If the frequent presence of a kink in the tail be an inherent feature, the breed is evidently related to the other kink-tailed Malay cats which, as already stated, have a cry differing from that of European cats. Should this be so, then if the ordinary Malay cats are the descendants of the jungle-cat, we shall have to assign the same ancestry to the Siamese breed.

Although definite information on this point is required, it seems probable that the southern part of North America and South America possessed certain native domesticated breeds of cats previous to the European conquest of the country; and if this be so, it will be obvious that these breeds must be derived from indigenous wild species. One of these breeds is the Paraguay cat, which when adult weighs only about three pounds, and is not more than a quarter the size of an ordinary cat. The body is elongated, and the hair, especially on the tail, short, shiny and close. This small size and elongated form suggest origin from the jaguarondi (*F. jaguarondi*), a chestnut-coloured wild species; but information appears to be lacking with regard to the colouring of the domesticated breed. Another South American breed is said to be free from the hideous "caterwauling" of the ordinary cat. In old days New Mexico was the home of a breed of hairless cats, said to have been kept by the ancient Aztecs, but now well-nigh if not completely extinct. Although entirely naked in summer, these cats developed in winter a slight growth of hair on the back and the ridge of the tail.

LITERATURE.—St George Mivart, *The Cat* (London, 1881); R. Lydekker, "Cats," in *Allen's Naturalists' Library* (1888); F. Hamilton, *The Wild Cat of Europe* (London. 1896); Frances Simpson, *The Book of the Cat* (London, 1903).

(R. L.*)

1The word "cat" is applied to various objects, in all cases an application of the name of the animal. In medieval siegecraft the "cat" (Med. Lat. *chattus* or *gattus, chatta* or *gatta*, in Fr.*chat* or *chat-chasteil*) was a movable pent-house used to protect besiegers when approaching a wall or gateway, for the purpose of sapping, mining or direct attack, or to cover a ram or other battering-engine. The word is also sometimes applied to a heavy timber fitted with iron spikes or projections to be thrown down upon besiegers, and to the large work known as a "cavalier." "Cat" or "cat-head," in nautical usage, is the projecting beam on the bows of a ship used to clear the anchor from the sides of the vessel when weighed. The stock of the anchor rests on the cat-head when hung outside the ship. The name is also used of a type of a vessel, now obsolete, and formerly used in the coal and timber trade on the north-east coast of England; it had a deep waist and narrow stem; it is still applied to a small rig of sailing boats, with a single mast stepped far forward, with a fore and aft sail. Among other objects also known by the name of "cat" is the small piece of wood pointed at either end used in the game of tip-cat, and the instrument of punishment, generally known as the "cat o' nine tails." This consists of a handle of wood or rope, about 18 in. long, with nine knotted cords or thongs. The multiplication of thongs for purposes of flogging is found in the old Roman*flagellum*, a scourge, which had sometimes three thongs with bone or bronze knots fastened to them. The "cat" was the regular instrument with which floggings were performed in the British army and navy. Since the abolition of flogging in the services, the use of the cat is now restricted to certain classes of offenders in military prisons (Army Act 1881, § 133). In the English criminal law, where corporal punishment is ordered by the court for certain criminal offences, the "cat" is used only where the prisoner is over sixteen years of age. It may not be used except when actually ordered in the sentence, and must be of a pattern approved by a secretary of state. Further floggings are inflicted with the "cat" upon convicted prisoners for breaches of discipline in prison. They must be ordered by the visitors of the prison and confirmed by the home secretary.

CATABOLISM, or KATABOLISM (Gr. κατά, down, βολή, a throw), the biological term for the reverse of anabolism, namely the breaking down of complex into simpler substances, destructive metabolism (see PHYSIOLOGY).

CATACLYSM (Gr. κατακλυσμός, a deluge), a great flood or deluge (*q.v.*). The term is used in geology to denote an 490overwhelming catastrophe which has produced sudden changes in the earth's surface; and also, figuratively, of any great and violent change which sweeps away the existing social or political order.

CATACOMB, a subterranean excavation for the interment of the dead or burial-vault. In this sense the word "catacomb" has gained universal acceptance, and has found a place in most modern languages. The original term, *catacumbae*, however, had no connexion with sepulture, but was simply the name of a particular locality in the environs of Rome. It was derived from the Greek κατά and κύμβη, "a hollow," and had reference to the natural configuration of the ground. In the district that bore this designation, lying close to the Appian Way, the basilica of San Sebastiano was erected, and the extensive burial-vaults beneath that church—in which, according to tradition, the bodies of the apostles St Peter and St Paul rested for a year and seven months previous to their removal to the basilicas which bear their names—were, in very early times, called from it *coemeterium ad catacumbas*, or*catacumbas* alone. From the celebrity of this cemetery as an object of pilgrimage its name became extensively known, and in entire forgetfulness of the origin of the word, *catacumbae*came to be regarded as a generic appellation for all burial-places of the same kind. This extension of the term to Christian burial-vaults generally dates from the 9th century, and obtained gradual currency through the Christian world. The original designation of these places of sepulture is *crypta* or *coemeterium*.

The largest number of Christian catacombs belong to the 3rd and the early part of the 4th centuries. The custom of subterranean interment gradually died out, and entirely ceased with the sack of Rome by Alaric, A.D. 410. "The end of the catacomb graves," writes

Mommsen (*Cont. Rev.*, May 1871), "is intimately connected with the end of the powerful city itself.... Poverty took the place of wealth, ... the traditions of the Christian tomb-architects sank into utter insignificance, and the expanse of the wasted Campagna now offered room enough to bury the few bodies, without having to descend as once far down below the surface of the earth." The earliest account of the catacombs, that of St Jerome narrating his visits to them when a schoolboy at Rome, about A.D. 354, shows that interment in them was even then rare if it had not been altogether discontinued; and the poet Prudentius's description of the tomb of the Christian martyr Hippolytus, and the cemetery in which it stood, leads us to the same conclusion. With the latter part of the 4th century a new epoch in the history of the catacombs arose—that of religious reverence. In the time of Pope Damasus, A.D. 366-384, the catacombs had begun to be regarded with special devotion, and had become the resort of large bands of pilgrims, for whose guidance catalogues of the chief burial-places and the holy men buried in them were drawn up. Some of these lists are still extant.1 Pope Damasus himself displayed great zeal in adapting the catacombs to their new purpose, restoring the works of art on the walls, and renewing the epitaphs over the graves of the martyrs. In this latter work he employed an engraver named Furius Philocalus, the exquisite beauty of whose characters enables the smallest fragment of his work to be recognized at a glance. This gave rise to extensive alterations in their construction and decoration, which has much lessened their value as authentic memorials of the religious art of the 2nd and 3rd centuries. Subsequent popes manifested equal ardour, with the same damaging results, in the repair and adornment of the catacombs, and many of the paintings covering their walls, which have been assigned to the period of their original construction, are really the work of these later times. The catacombs shared in the devastation of Rome by the Goths under Vitiges in the 6th century and by the Lombards at a later period; and partly through the spoliation of these barbarian invaders, partly through the neglect of those who should have been their guardians, they sank into such a state of decay and pollution that, as the only means of preserving the holy remains they enshrined from further desecration, Pope Paul I., in the latter part of the 8th century, and Pope Paschal, at the beginning of the 9th, entered upon the work of the translation of the relics, which was vigorously carried on by successive pontiffs until the crypts were almost entirely despoiled of their dead. The relics having been removed, the visits of pilgrims naturally ceased, and by degrees the very existence of those wonderful subterranean cemeteries was forgotten. Six centuries elapsed before the accidental discovery of a sepulchral chamber by some labourers digging for *pozzolana* earth (May 31, 1578) revealed to the amazed inhabitants of Rome "the existence," to quote a contemporary record, "of other cities concealed beneath their own suburbs." Baronius, the ecclesiastical historian, was one of the first to visit the new discovery, and his *Annals* in more than one place evidence his just appreciation of its importance. The true "Columbus of this subterranean world," as he has been aptly designated, was the indefatigable Antonio Bosio (d. 1629), who devoted his life to the personal investigation of the catacombs, the results of which were given to the world in 1632 in a huge folio, entitled *Roma sotterranea*, profusely illustrated with rude but faithful plans and engravings. This was republished in a Latin translation with considerable alterations and omissions by Paolo Aringhi in 1651; and a century after its first appearance the plates were reproduced by Giovanni Bottari in 1737, and illustrated with great care and learning. Some additional discoveries were described by Marc Antonio Boldetti in his *Osservazioni*, published in 1720; but, writing in the interests of the Roman Church with an apologetic, not a scientific object, truth was made to bend to polemics, and little addition to our knowledge of the catacombs is to be gained from his otherwise important work. The French historian of art, Seroux d'Agincourt, 1825, by his copious illustrations, greatly facilitated the study of the architecture of the catacombs and the works of art contained in them. The works of Raoul Rochette display a comprehensive knowledge of the whole subject, extensive reading, and a thorough acquaintance with early Christian art so far as it could be gathered from books, but he was not an original investigator. The great pioneer in the path of independent research, which, with the intelligent use of documentary and historical evidence, has led to so vast an increase in our acquaintance with the Roman Catacombs, was Padre Marchi of the Society of Jesus. His work, *Monumenti delle arti christiane primitive*, is the first in which the strange misconception, received with unquestioning faith by earlier writers, that the catacombs were exhausted sand-pits adapted by the Christians to the purpose of interment, was dispelled, and the true history of their formation demonstrated. Marchi's line of investigation was followed by the Commendatore De Rossi, and his brother Michele, the former of whom was Marchi's fellow-labourer during the latter part of his explorations; and it is to them that we owe the most exhaustive scientific examination of the whole subject. The Catacombs of Rome are the most extensive with which we are acquainted, and, as might be expected in the centre of the Christian world, are in many respects the most remarkable. No others have been so thoroughly examined and illustrated. These may, therefore, be most appropriately selected for description as typical examples.

Our description of the Roman Catacombs cannot be more appropriately introduced than by St Jerome's account of his visits to them in his youth, already referred to, which, after the lapse of above fifteen centuries, presents a **Catacombs of Rome.** most accurate picture of these wonderful subterranean labyrinths. "When I was a boy," he writes, "receiving my education in Rome, I and my schoolfellows used, on Sundays, to make the circuit of the sepulchres of the apostles and martyrs. Many a time did we go down into the catacombs. These are 491 excavated deep in the earth, and contain, on either hand as you enter, the bodies of the dead buried in the wall. It is all so dark there that the language of the prophet (Ps. lv. 15) seems to be fulfilled, 'Let them go down quick into hell.' Only occasionally is light let in to mitigate the horror of the gloom, and then not so much through a window as through a hole. You take each step with caution, as, surrounded by deep night, you recall the words of Virgil—

"Horror ubique animos, simul ipsa silentia terrent."2

In complete agreement with Jerome's vivid picture the visitor to the Roman Catacombs finds himself in a vast labyrinth of narrow galleries, usually from 3 to 4 ft. in width, interspersed with small chambers, all excavated at successive levels, in the strata of volcanic rock subjacent to the city and its environs, and constructed originally for the interment of the Christian dead. The galleries are not the way of access to the cemeteries, but are themselves the cemeteries, the dead being buried in long low horizontal recesses, excavated in the vertical walls of the passages, rising tier above tier like the berths in a ship, from a few inches above the floor to the springing of the arched ceiling, to the number of five, six or even sometimes twelve ranges. These galleries are not arranged on any definite plan, but, as will be seen from the plan (fig. 1), they intersect one another at different angles, producing an intricate network which it is almost impossible to reduce to any system. They generally run in straight lines, and as a rule preserve the same level. The different storeys of galleries lie one below the other (fig. 2) to the number of four or five (in one part of the cemetery of St Calixtus they reach seven storeys), and communicate with one another by stairs cut out of the living rock. Light and air are introduced by means of vertical shafts (*luminaria*) running up to the outer air, and often serving for several storeys. The drawing (fig. 3) from Northcote gives a very correct idea of these galleries, with the tiers of graves pierced in the walls. The doorways which are seen interrupting the lines of graves are those of the family sepulchral chambers, or *cubicula*, of which we shall speak more particularly hereafter.

FIG. 1.—Plan of part of the Cemetery of Sant' Agnese. (From Martigny.)

A. Entrance from the Basilica of St Agnes.

1, 2. Ancient staircases leading to the first storey.

3. Corridors from the staircases.

4. Two ruined

6. Air-shafts, or luminaria.

7. Ruined vault.

8. Blind ways.

9. Passages built up or ruined.

10. Passages obstructed by landslips.

13. Narrow apertures between adjoining galleries.

14-17. Arcosolia.

18-32. Cubicula.

33. Chapel with vestibule and apse, and two chairs.

staircases leading to the lower storey.	11. Unfinished passage.	34. Double chapel with three chairs.
5. Steps of the rock.	12. Passages destitute of tombs.	35. Large chapel in five divisions.

The graves, or *loculi*, as they are commonly designated, were, in the Christian cemeteries, with only a few exceptions (Padre Marchi produces some from the cemetery of St Ciriaca,*Monum. primitiv.* tav. xiv. xliii. xliv.), parallel with the length of the gallery. In the pagan cemeteries, on the other hand, the sepulchral recess as a rule entered the rock like an oven at right angles to the corridor, the body being introduced endways. The plan adopted by the Christians saved labour, economized space, and consulted reverence in the deposition of the corpse. These *loculi* were usually constructed for a single body only. Some, however, were formed to contain two, three, or four, or even more corpses. Such recesses were known respectively as *bisomi, trisomi, quadrisomi*, &c., terms which often appear in the sepulchral inscriptions. After the introduction of the body the *loculi* were closed with the greatest care, either with slabs of marble the whole length of the aperture, or with huge tiles, three being generally employed, cemented together with great exactness so as to prevent the escape of the products of decomposition (fig. 4). Where any epitaph was set up—an immense number are destitute of any inscription at all—it is always painted or engraved on these slabs or tiles. In the earlier interments the 492epitaph is usually daubed on the slab in red or black paint. In later examples it is incised in the marbles, the letters being rendered clearer by being coloured with vermilion. The enclosing slab very often bears one or more Christian symbols, such as the dove, the anchor, the olive-branch, or the monogram of Christ (figs. 5, 6). The palm branch, which is also of frequent occurrence, is not an indisputable mark of the last resting-place of a martyr, being found in connexion with epitaphs of persons dying natural deaths, or those prepared by persons in their lifetime, as well as in those of little children, and even of pagans. Another frequent concomitant of these catacomb interments, a small glass vessel containing traces of the sediment of a red fluid, embedded in the cement of the *loculus* (fig. 7), has no better claim. The red matter proves to be the remains of wine, not of blood; and the conclusion of the ablest archaeologists is that the vessels were placed where they are found, after the eucharistic celebration or *agape* on the day of the funeral or its anniversary, and contained remains of the consecrated elements as a kind of religious charm. Not a few of the slabs, it is discovered, have done double duty, bearing a pagan inscription on one side and a Christian one on the other. These are known as *opisthographs*. The bodies were interred wrapped in linen cloths, or swathed in bands, and were frequently preserved by embalming. In the case of poorer interments the destruction of the body was, on the contrary, often accelerated by the use of quicklime.

FIG. 2—Section of Galleries at different levels. (From Seroux d'Agincourt.)

FIG. 3—View of a Gallery.

FIG 4.—Loculi. (From de Rossi.)

FIGS. 5 and 6.—Loculi. (From de Rossi.)

Interment in the wall-recess or *loculus*, though infinitely the most common, was not the only mode employed in the catacombs. Other forms of very frequent recurrence are the *table tomb* and *arched tomb*, or *arcosolium*. From the annexed woodcuts it will be seen that these only differ in the form of the surmounting recess. In each case the arched tomb was formed by an oblong chest, either hollowed out of the rock, or built of masonry, and closed with a horizontal slab. But in the table-tomb (fig. 8) the recess above, essential for the introduction of the corpse, is square, while in the arcosolium (fig. 9), a form of later date, it is semicircular. Sarcophagi are also found in the catacombs, but are of rare occurrence. They chiefly occur in the earlier cemeteries, and the costliness of their construction confined their use to the wealthiest classes—*e.g.* in the cemetery of St Domitilla, herself a member of the imperial house. Another unfrequent mode of interment was in graves like those of modern times, dug in the floor of the galleries (Marchi, *u.s.*, tav. xxi. xxvi.). Table-tombs and arcosolia are by no means rare in the corridors of the catacombs, but they belong more generally to the *cubicula*, or family vaults, of which we now proceed to speak.

FIG. 7—Glass Bottles. (From Bosio.)

FIG. 8.—Table-tomb.

These *cubicula* are small apartments, seldom more than 12 ft. square, usually rectangular, though sometimes circular or polygonal, opening out of the main corridors. They are not unfrequently ranged regularly along the sides of the galleries, the doors of entrance, as may be seen in a previous illustration (fig. 3), following one another in as orderly succession as the bedchamber doors in the passage of a modern house. The roof is sometimes 493flat, but is more usually vaulted, and sometimes rises into a cupola. Both the roof and the walls are almost universally coated with stucco and covered with fresco paintings—in the earlier works merely decorative, in the later always symbolical or historical. Each side of the cubiculum, except that of the entrance, usually contains a recessed tomb, either a table-tomb or an arcosolium. That facing the entrance was the place of greatest honour, where in many instances the remains of a martyr were deposited, whose tomb, according to primitive usage, served as an altar for the celebration of the eucharist. This was sometimes, as in the Papal crypt of St Calixtus (fig. 10), protected from irreverence by lattice work (*transennae*) of marble. The cubiculum was originally designed for the reception of a very limited number of dead. But the natural desire to be buried near one's relatives caused new tombs to be cut in the walls, above and around and behind the original tombs, the walls being thus completely honeycombed with *loculi*, sometimes as many as seventy, utterly regardless of the paintings originally depicted on the walls. Another motive for multiplying the number of graves operated when the cubiculum contained the remains of any noted saint or martyr. The Christian antiquary has cause continually to lament the destruction of works of art due to this craving. One of the most perfect examples of early Christian pictorial decoration, the so-called "Dispute with the Doctors," in the catacomb of Calixtus, the "antique style of beauty" of which is noticed by Kugler, has thus suffered irreparable mutilation, the whole of the lower part of the picture having been destroyed by the excavation of a fresh grave-recess (Bottari, vol. ii. tav. 15). The plates of De Rossi, Ferret, and, indeed, all illustrations of the catacombs, exhibit frequent examples of the same destructive superstition. The illustrations (figs. 11 and 12), taken from De Rossi's great work, representing two of the cubicula in the cemetery of St Calixtus, show the general arrangement of the loculi and the character of the frescoes which ornament the walls and roof. These paintings, it will be seen, are simply decorative, of the same style as the wall-paintings of the baths, and those of Pompeii.

FIG. 9—Arcosolia. (From Bosio.)

FIG. 10—Restoration of the Papal Crypt, Cemetery of St Calixtus. (From de Rossi.)

FIG. 11.—Cubiculum in Cemetery of St Calixtus. (From de Rossi.)

FIG. 12.—Cubiculum in the Cemetery of St Calixtus. (From de Rossi.)

FIG. 13.—Plan of a supposed Church, Catacomb of Sant' Agnese. (From Marchi.)

FIG. 14.—Bishop's Chair.
Catacomb of Sant' Agnese.

Each *cubiculum* was usually the burying-place of some one family, all the members of which were interred in it, just as in the chantry-chapels connected with medieval churches. In them was celebrated the funeral-feast on the day of burial and on its anniversary, as well as the eucharist, which was the invariable accompaniment of funerals in the primitive church (Bingham, *Orig. Eccl.* bk. xxiii. c. iii. 12). The funeral-banquet descended to the Christian church from pagan times, and was too often profaned by heathen licence. St Augustine, in several passages, inveighs against those who thus by "gluttony and insobriety buried themselves over the buried," and "made themselves drunk in the chapels of the martyrs, placing their excesses to the score of religious reverence for the dead." (August., *De Mor. Eccl. Cathol.*, c. 34, *Contr. Faust*, lib. xx. c. 21, *Confess.*, lib vi. c. 2) Some curious frescoes representing these funeral-feasts, found in the *cubicula* which were the scene of them, are reproduced by Bosio (pp. 355, 391) and others. A romantic air has been thrown over these burial chapels by the notion that they were the places of worship used by the

Christians in times of persecution. This to a certain extent is doubtless true, as in the case of the chapel of Santa Priscilla, where the altar or stone coffin of a martyr remains, with a small platform behind it for the priest or bishop to stand upon. But that they can have been so used to any large extent is rendered impossible by their limited dimensions, as none of them could hold more than fifty or sixty persons. In some of the catacombs, however, there are larger halls and connected suites of chapels which may possibly have been constructed for the purpose of congregational worship during the dark periods when the public exercise of the Christian religion was made penal. The most remarkable of these is in the cemetery of Sant' Agnese (see plan, fig. 13). It consists of five rectangular compartments, three on one side of the corridor and two on the other, connected by a passage intersecting the gallery at right angles. Two of the five compartments are supposed to have been assigned to male, and two to female worshippers, the fifth, at the extremity of the whole, being reserved for the altar and its ministers. In the centre of the end-wall stands a stone chair (fig. 14), considered to have been the episcopal cathedra, with a bench for the clergy on each side. There is no trace of an altar, which may, Marchi thinks, have been portable. The walls of the compartments are occupied by arched sepulchral recesses, above and below which are tiers of ordinary graves or *loculi*. The arrangements are certainly such as indicate a congregational purpose, but the extreme narrowness of the suite, and still more of the passage which connects the two divisions, must have rendered it difficult for any but a small number to take any intelligent part in the services at the same time. Although the idea of the use of the catacombs for religious worship may have been pressed too far, there can be no doubt that the sacred rites of the church were celebrated within them. We have already spoken of the eucharistic celebrations of which the *cubicula* were the scene; and still existing baptisteries prove that the other sacrament was also administered there. The most remarkable of these baptisteries is that in the catacomb of San Pontianus (fig. 15). Ten steps lead down to a basin of sufficient depth for immersion, supplied by a spring. Some of the subterranean chambers contain armed seats and benches cut out of the tufa rock. These are supposed by Marchi and others to indicate schoolrooms, where the catechumens were instructed by the bishop or presbyters. But this theory wants verification. It is impossible not to be struck with the remarkable analogy between these rock-hewn chairs and those discovered in the Etruscan tombs, of the purpose of which no satisfactory explanation has been given.

FIG. 15.—Baptistery of San Pontianus. (From Perret.)

Very exaggerated statements have been made as to the employment of the catacombs as dwelling-places by the Christians in times of persecution. We have, however, sufficient evidence that they were used as places of refuge from *Theories of the use of the catacombs.* the fury of the heathen, in which the believers—especially the bishops and clergy, who would naturally be the first objects of attack—might secrete themselves until the storm had blown over. This was a purpose for which they were admirably adapted both by the intricacy of their labyrinthine passages, in which any one not possessing the clue would be inevitably lost, and the numerous small chambers and hiding-places at different levels which might be passed unperceived in the dark by the pursuers. As a rule also the catacombs had 495more than one entrance, and frequently communicated with an *arenaria* or sand-quarry; so that while one entrance was carefully watched, the pursued might escape in a totally different direction by another. But, to quote J.H. Parker, "the catacombs were never intended, nor fit for, dwelling-places, and the stories of persons living in them for months are probably fabulous. According to modern physicians it is impossible to live many days in the caves of *pozzolana* in which many of the catacombs are excavated." Equally exaggerated are the statements as to the linear and lateral extent of the catacombs, and their intercommunication with one another. Without resorting to this exaggeration, Mommsen can speak with perfect truth of the "enormous space occupied by the burial vaults of

Christian Rome, not surpassed even by the *cloacae* or sewers of Republican Rome," but the data are too vague to warrant any attempt to define their dimensions. Marchi has estimated the united length of the galleries at from 800 to 900 m., and the number of interments at between 6,000,000 and 7,000,000; Martigny's estimate is 587 m.; and Northcote's, lower still, at "not less than 350 m." The idea of general intercommunication is negatived by the fact that the chief cemeteries are separated by low ground or valleys, where any subterranean galleries would be at once filled with water.

It now remains to speak of the history of these subterranean burial-places, together with the reasons for, and mode of, their construction. From the period of the rediscovery of the catacombs in the 16th century till comparatively recent times a gigantic fallacy prevailed, repeated by writer after writer, identifying the Christian burial-places with disused sand-pits. It was accepted as an unquestionable fact by every one who undertook to describe the catacombs, that the Christians of Rome, finding in the labyrinthine mazes of the exhausted *arenariae*, which abounded in the environs of the city, whence the sand used in building had been extracted, a suitable place for the interment of their martyred brethren, where also the sacred rites accompanying the interment might be celebrated without fear of interruption, took possession of them and used them as cemeteries. It only needed a comparison of the theory with the visible facts to refute it at once, but nearly three centuries elapsed before the independence of the *arenariae* and the catacombs was established. The discovery of this independence is due to Marchi. Starting with the firmest belief in the old traditional view, his own researches by degrees opened his eyes to the truth, now universally recognized, that the catacombs were exclusively the work of the Christians, and were constructed for the interment of the dead. It is true that a catacomb is often connected with the earlier sand-quarry, and starts from it as a commencement, but the two are excavated in different strata, suitable to their respective purposes, and their plan and construction are so completely unlike as to render any confusion between them impossible.

The igneous formation of which the greater part of the Roman Campagna is, in its superior portion, composed, contains three strata known under the common name of *tufa*,—the "stony," "granular," and "sandy" tufa,—the last being commonly known as *pozzolana*.[3] The *pozzolana* is the material required for building purposes, for admixture with mortar; and the sandpits are naturally excavated in the stratum which supplies it. The stony tufa (*tufa litoide*) is quarried as building-stone. The granular tufa is useless for either purpose, containing too much earth to be employed in making mortar, and being far too soft to be used as stone for building. Yet it is in this stratum, and in this alone, that the catacombs are constructed; their engineers avoiding with equal care the solid stone of the *tufa litoide* and the friable *pozzolana*, and selecting the stratum of medium hardness, which enabled them to form the vertical walls of their galleries, and to excavate the *loculi* and *cubicula* without severe labour and also without fear of their falling in. The annexed illustration (fig. 16) from Marchi's work, when compared with that of the catacomb of Sant' Agnese already given, presents to the eye the contrast between the wide winding irregular passages of the sand-pit, calculated for the admission of a horse and cart, and the narrow rectilinear accurately-defined galleries of the catacomb. The distinction between the two is also plainly exhibited when for some local or private reasons an ancient *arenaria* has been transformed into a cemetery. The modifications required to strengthen the crumbling walls to support the roof and to facilitate the excavation of *loculi*, involved so much labour that, as a rule, after a few attempts, the idea of utilizing an old quarry for burial purposes was abandoned.

FIG. 16.—Arenaria beneath the Cemetery of Calixtus.

Another equally erroneous idea was that these vast burial-places of the early Christians remained entirely concealed from the eyes of their pagan neighbours, and were constructed not only without the permission of the municipal authorities but without their cognizance. Nothing can be farther from the truth. Such an idea is justly stigmatized by

Mommsen as ridiculous, and reflecting a discredit as unfounded as it is unjust on the imperial police of the capital. That such vast excavations should have been made without attracting attention, and that such an immense number of corpses could have been carried to burial in perfect secrecy is utterly impossible. Nor was there any reason why secrecy should have been desired. The decent burial of the dead was a matter especially provided for by the Roman laws. No particular mode was prescribed. Interment was just as legal as cremation, and had, in fact, been universally practised by the Romans until the later days of the republic.4 The bodies of the Scipios and Nasos were buried in still existing catacombs; and if the Christians preferred to adopt that which Minucius Felix calls "the better, and more ancient custom of inhumation" (*Octavius*, c. 2), there was absolutely nothing, to quote the words of Northcote (*Roma sotterran.* pp. 56, 61), "either in their social or religious position to interfere with their freedom of action. The law left them entire liberty,... and the faithful did but use their liberty in the way that suited them best, burying their dead according to a fashion to which many of them had been long accustomed, and which enabled them at the same time to follow in death the example of him who was also their model in life." Interment in rock-hewn tombs, "as the manner of the Jews is to bury," had been practised in Rome by the Jewish settlers for a considerable period anterior to the rise of the Christian Church. A Jewish catacomb, now lost, was discovered and described by Bosio (*Rom. sott.* p. 141), and others are still accessible. They are to be distinguished from Christian catacombs only by the character of their decorations, the absence of Christian symbols and the language of their inscriptions. There would, therefore, be nothing extraordinary in the fact that a community, always identified in the popular heathen mind with the Jewish faith, should adopt the mode of interment belonging to that religion. Nor have we the slightest trace of any official interference with Christian burials, such as would render secrecy necessary or desirable. Their funerals were as much under the protection of the law, which not only invested the tomb itself with a sacred character, but included in its protection the area in which it stood, and the *cella memoriae* or chapel connected with it, as those of their heathen fellow-citizens, while the same shield would be thrown over the burial-clubs, which, as we learn from Tertullian 496(*Apolog.* c. 39), were common among the early Christians, as over those existing among the heathen population of Rome.

We may then completely dismiss the notion of there being any studied secrecy in connexion with the early Christian cemeteries, and proceed to inquire into the mode of their formation. Almost without exception, they had their origin in **Mode of formation.** small burial areas, the property of private persons or of families, gradually ramifying and receiving additions of one subterranean storey after another as each was required for interments. The first step would be the acquisition of a plot of ground either by gift or purchase for the formation of a tomb, Christians were not beyond the pale of the law, and their faith presented no hindrance to the property being secured to them in perpetuity. To adapt the ground for its purpose as a cemetery, a gallery was run all round the area in the tufa rock at a convenient depth below the surface, reached by staircases at the corners. In the upright walls of these galleries *loculi* were cut as needed to receive the dead. When these first four galleries were full others were mined on the same level at right angles to them, thus gradually converting the whole area into a net-work of corridors. If a family vault was required, or a burial chapel for a martyr or person of distinction, a small square room was excavated by the side of the gallery and communicating with it. When the original area had been mined in this way as far as was consistent with stability, a second storey of galleries was begun at a lower level, reached by a new staircase. This was succeeded by a third, or a fourth, and sometimes even by a fifth. When adjacent burial areas belonged to members of the same Christian confraternity, or by gift or purchase fell into the same hands, communications were opened between the respective cemeteries, which thus spread laterally, and gradually acquired that enormous extent which, "even when their fabulous dimensions are reduced to their right measure, form an immense work."5 This could only be executed by a large and powerful Christian community unimpeded by legal enactments or police regulations, "a living witness of its immense development corresponding to the importance of the capital." But although, as we have said, in ordinary times there was no necessity for secrecy, yet when the peace of the Church was broken by the fierce and often protracted persecutions of the heathen emperors, it became essential to adopt precautions to conceal the entrance to the cemeteries, which became the temporary hiding-places of the Christian fugitives, and to baffle the search of their pursuers. To these stormy periods we may safely assign the alterations which may be traced in the staircases, which are sometimes abruptly cut off, leaving a gap requiring a ladder, and the formation of secret passages communicating with the *arenariae*, and through them with the open country.

When the storms of persecution ceased and Christianity had become the imperial faith, the evil fruits of prosperity were not slow to appear. Cemetery interment became a regular trade in the hands of the *fossores*, or grave-diggers, who appear to have established a kind of property in the catacombs, and whose greed of gain led to that destruction of the religious paintings with which the walls were decorated, for the quarrying of fresh *loculi*, to which we have already alluded. Monumental epitaphs record the purchase of a grave from the fossores, in many cases during the lifetime of the individual, not unfrequently stating the price. A very curious fresco, found in the cemetery of Calixtus, preserved by the engravings of the earlier investigators (Bottari, tom. ii. p. 126, tav. 99), represents a "fossor" with his lamp in his hand and his pick over his shoulder, and his tools lying about him. Above is the inscription, "Diogenes Fossor in Pace depositus."

FIG. 17.—Fresco Ceiling. (From Bosio.)

The subjects, beginning at the top and going to the right, are—

(1) The paralytic carrying his bed.
(2) The seven baskets full of fragments.
(3) Raising of Lazarus.
(4) Daniel in the lions' den.

(5) Jonah swallowed by the fish.
(6) Jonah vomited forth.
(7) Moses striking the rock.
(8) Noah and the dove. In the centre, the Good Shepherd.

It is unnecessary to enter on any detailed description of the frescoes which cover the walls and ceilings of the burial-chapels in the richest abundance. It must suffice to say that the earliest examples are only to be distinguished from the mural decorations employed by their pagan contemporaries (as seen at Pompeii and elsewhere) by the absence of all that was immoral or idolatrous, and that it was only very slowly and timidly that any distinctly *Decoration.* religious representations were introduced. These were at first purely symbolical, meaningless to any but a Christian eye, such as the Vine, the Good Shepherd, the Sheep, the Fisherman, the Fish, &c. Even the personages of ancient mythology were pressed into the service of early Christian art, and Orpheus, taming the wild beasts with his lyre, symbolized the peaceful sway of Christ; and Ulysses, deaf to the Siren's song, represented the Believer triumphing over the allurements of sensual pleasure. The person of Christ appeared but rarely, and then commonly simply as the chief personage in an historical picture. The events depicted from the life of Christ are but few, and always conform rigidly to the same traditional type. The most frequent are the miracle at Cana, the multiplication of the loaves and fishes, the paralytic carrying his bed, the healing of the woman with the issue of blood, the raising of Lazarus, Zacchaeus, and the triumphal entry into Jerusalem. The Crucifixion, and subjects from the Passion, are never represented. The cycle of Old Testament subjects is equally limited. The most common are the history of Jonah as a type of the Resurrection, the Fall, Noah receiving the dove with the olive branch, Abraham's sacrifice of Isaac, Moses taking off his shoes, David with the sling, Daniel in the lions' den, and the Three Children in the fiery furnace. The mode of representation is always conventional, the treatment of the subject no less than its choice being dictated by an authority to which the artist was compelled to bow. All the more valuable of these paintings have been produced in J.H. Parker's series of photographs taken in the catacombs by the magnesium light.6 Wilpert's great work, in which these frescoes are reproduced in colours, now enables the student even better to distinguish the styles of different centuries and follow the course of artistic development or decay.

FIG. 18.—Fresco Ceiling. (From Bosio.)

The subjects, beginning at the bottom and going to the right, are—

(1) Moses striking the rock.
(2) Noah and the dove.
(3) The three children in the furnace.

(4) Abraham's sacrifice.
(5) The miracle of the loaves.

Beyond Rome and its suburbs the most remarkable Christian catacombs are those in the vicinity of Naples, described by Pelliccia (*De Christ. Eccl. Polit.* vol. iv. Dissert. 5), and in separate treatises by Bellerman and Schultze. Plans of them are also given by Agincourt in his great work on Christian art. These 497 catacombs differ materially from those of Rome. They were certainly originally stone-quarries, and the hardness of the rock **Catacombs of Naples.** has made the construction practicable of wide, lofty corridors and spacious halls, very unlike the narrow galleries and contracted chambers in the Roman cemeteries. The mode of interment, however, is the same as that practised in Rome, and the *loculi* and *arcosolia* differ by little in the two. The walls and ceilings are covered with fresco paintings of different dates, in some cases lying one over the other. This catacomb contains an unquestionable example of a church, divided into a nave and chancel, with a rude stone altar and bishop's seat behind it.

FIG. 19.—Plan of the Catacombs of St John, Syracuse.

FIG. 20.—Plan of Circular Hall, Catacombs of St John, Syracuse. (From Agincourt.)

FIG. 21—Plan of Catacomb at Alexandria. (From Agincourt.)

FIG. 22.—Section of a Gallery in Catacomb at Alexandria. (From Agincourt.)

At Syracuse also there are very extensive catacombs known as "the Grottos of St John." They are also figured by Agincourt, and described by Denon (*Voyage en Sicile et Malte*) and Führer. There is an entire underground city with **Syracuse.** several storeys of larger and smaller streets, squares and cross ways, cut out of the rock; at the intersection of the cross

16

ways are immense circular halls of a bottle shape, like a glass-house furnace, lighted by air shafts. The galleries are generally very narrow, furnished on each side with arched tombs, and communicating with family sepulchral-chambers closed originally by locked doors, the marks of the hinges and staples being still visible. The walls are in many places coated with stucco adorned with frescoes, including palms, doves, labara and other Christian symbols. The ground-plans (figs. 19, 20), from Agincourt, of the catacomb and of one of the circular halls, show how widely this cemetery differs in arrangement from the Roman catacombs. The frequency of blind passages and of circular chambers will be noticed, as well as the very large number of bodies in the cruciform recesses, apparently amounting in one instance to nineteen. Agincourt remarks that this cemetery "gives an idea of a work executed with design and leisure, and with means very different from those at command in producing the catacombs of Rome."

Denon also describes catacombs at Malta near the ancient capital of the island. The passages were all cut in a close-grained stone, and are very narrow, with arched ceilings, running very irregularly, and ramifying in all directions. **Malta.** The greater part of the tombs stand on either side of the galleries in square recesses (like the table-tombs of the Roman catacombs), and are rudely fashioned to imitate sarcophagi. The interments are not nearly so numerous as in other catacombs, nor are there any vestiges of painting, sculpture or inscriptions. At Taormina in Sicily is a Saracenic catacomb, also**Taormina.** figured by Agincourt. The main corridor is 12 ft. wide, having three or more ranges of *loculi* on either side, running longitudinally into the rock, each originally closed by a stone bearing an inscription.

Passing to Egypt, a small Christian catacomb at Alexandria is described and figured by de Rossi.7 The *loculi* here also are set endways to the passage. The walls are abundantly decorated with paintings, one of a liturgical character. But the most extensive **Egypt.** catacombs at Alexandria are those of Egypto-Greek origin, from the largest of which, according to Strabo (lib. xvii. p. 795), the quarter where it is placed had the name of the Necropolis. The plan, it will be seen, is remarkable for its regularity (figs. 21, 22). Here, too, the graves run endways into the rock. Other catacombs in the vicinity of the same city are described by Pocock and other travellers, and are figured by Agincourt.

Subterranean cemeteries of the general character of those described are very frequent in all southern and eastern countries. A vast necropolis in the **Sidon.** environs of Saida, the ancient Sidon, is described in Renan's *Mission en Phénicie,* and figured in Thobois's plates. It consists of a series of apartments approached by staircases, 498the sides pierced with sepulchral recesses running lengthwise into the rock.

FIG. 23.—Plan of a Tomb at Cervetri. (From Dennis.)

FIG. 24.—Section of the Tomb of the Seats and Shields, Cervetri. (From Dennis.)

The rock-hewn tombs of Etruria scarcely come under the category of catacombs, in the usual sense, being rather independent family burial-places, grouped together in a necropolis. They are, however, far too remarkable **Rocktombs of Etruria.** to be altogether passed over. These sepulchres are usually hollowed out of the face of low cliffs on the side of a hill. They often rise tier above tier, and are sometimes all on the same level "facing each other as in streets, and branching off laterally into smaller lanes or alleys"; and occasionally forming "a spacious square or piazza surrounded by tombs instead of houses" (Dennis, *Cities and Cemeteries of Etruria,* ii. 31). The construction of the tombs commonly keeps up the same analogy between the cities of the living and those of the dead. Their plan is for the most part that of a house, with a door of entrance and passage leading into a central chamber or *atrium*, with others of smaller size opening from it, each having a stone-hewn bench or *triclinium* on three of its sides, on which the dead, frequently a pair of corpses side by side, were laid as if at a banquet. These benches are often hewn in the form of couches with pillows at one end, and the legs carved in relief. The ceilings have the representation of beams and rafters cut in the rock. In some instances arm-chairs, carved out of the living rock, stand between the doors of the chambers, and the walls above are decorated with the semblance of suspended shields. The walls are often covered with paintings in a very simple archaic style, in red and black. As a typical example of the Etruscan tombs we give the plan and section (figs. 23, 24) of the *Grotta detta Sedia* at Cervetri from Dennis (pp. 32, 35). The tombs in some instances form subterranean groups more analogous to the general idea of a catacomb. Of this nature is the very remarkable cemetery at Poggio Gaiella, near Chiusi, the ancient Clusium, of a portion of the principal storey of which the woodcut (fig. 25) is a plan. The most remarkable of these sepulchral chambers is a large circular hall about 25 ft. in diameter, supported by a huge cylindrical pillar hewn from the rock. Opening out of this and the other chambers, and connecting them together, are a series of low winding passages or *cuniculi*, just large enough for a man to creep through on all fours. No plausible suggestion has been offered as to the purpose of these mysterious burrows, which cannot fail to remind us of the labyrinth which, according to Varro's description as quoted by Pliny (*Hist.* lib. xxxvi. c. 19, § 4), was the distinguishing mark of Porsena's tomb, and which have led some adventurous archaeologists to identify this sepulchre with that of the great king of Etruria (Dennis, *u.s.*, pp. 393 ff.).

(E. V.; O. M. D.)

FIG. 25.—Plan of a portion of the principal storey in the Poggio Gajella. (From Dennis.)

Modern Discoveries.—In 1873 was discovered, near the cemetery of St Domitilla, the semi-subterranean basilica of Santi Nereo ed Achilleo, 100 ft. by 60 ft. This is now covered with a roof, and the fallen columns have been raised up. The lower part of a pillar, which once supported a baldachino over the altar, still preserves the name ACILLEUS, and beneath it a bas-relief of the martyr, with his hands bound, receiving his death-blow from the executioner. The base of a similar column has only feet in the same attitude, and probably bore the name NEREUS. In a grave in the apse was found a large fragment of an inscription, composed by Pope Damasus, but set up by his successor Siricius, which, from the note-book of a Salzburg pilgrim of the 8th century, can be completed thus:—

Militiae nomen dederant saevum Officium pariter spectantes juss Praeceptis pulsante metu servi Mira fides rerum subito posue Conversi fugiunt ducis impia castr Projiciunt clypeos faleras tel Confessi gaudent Christi portar Credite per Damasum possit quid

Nereus (see Rom. xvi. 15) and Achilleus, said to have been baptized by St Peter, refused to do the bidding of Domitian as praetorians, and entering the service of Flavia Domitilla, suffered martyrdom with their mistress Petronilla, of the Aurelian family closely connected with the Flavii, and the spiritual daughter of St Peter, who was buried in a sarcophagus with the inscription:—

AVRELIAE ·PETRONILLAE ·FIL ·DVLCISSIMAE

This is now in St Peter's, but was probably originally behind the apse of this basilica, for there is a fresco of her in an arcosolium, with a matron named Veneranda. The original entrance to the cemetery leads directly into a spacious corridor with no *loculi*, but recesses for sarcophagi, and decorations of the classical style of the 2nd century. From this a wide staircase leads directly down to a chamber, discovered in March 1881, of a very early date. Within an arcosolium is a tablet set up by "Aurelius Ampliatus and his son Gordian, to

Aurelia Bonifatia, his incomparable wife, a woman of true chastity, who lived 25 years, 2 months, 4 days, and 2 hours." The letters are of the 2nd century; but above the arcosolium was found a stone with great letters, 5 or 6 in. high: "AMPLIATI, the tomb of Ampliatus." Now Ampliatus is a servile name: how comes it to be set up with such distinction in the sepulchre of the Flavii? Romans xvi. 8 supplies the answer: "Salute Ampliatus, most beloved to me in the Lord." De Rossi thinks the identification well grounded (*Bullettino*, 1881, p. 74). Epitaphs of members of the Flavian family have been found here, and others stating that they are put up "EX INDULGENTIA FLAVIAE DOMITILLAE VESPASIANI NEPTIS." So that De Rossi did not hesitate to complete an inscription on a broken stone thus:—

De Rossi began his excavations in the cemetery of Santa Priscilla in 1851, but for thirty years nothing but what had been described by Bosio came to light. In 1880 he unearthed a portion near the Cappella Greca, and found galleries that had not been touched since they were filled in during the Diocletian persecution. The *loculi* were intact and the epitaphs still in their places, so that "they form a kind of museum, in which the development, the formulae, and the symbolic figures of Christian epigraphy, from its origin to the end of the 3rd or 4th century, can be notified and contemplated, not in artificial specimens as in the Lateran, but in the genuine and living reality of their original condition." (*Bullett.*, 1884, p. 68). Many of the names mentioned in St Paul's Epistles are found here: Phoebe, Prisca, Aquilius, Felix Ampliatus, Epenetus, Olympias, Onesimus, Philemon, Asyncritus, Lucius, Julia, Caius, Timotheus, Tychicus, Crescens, Urbanus, Hermogenes, Tryphaena and Tryphо(sa) on the same stone. Petrus, a very rare name in the catacombs, is found here several times, both in Greek and in Latin. The neighbouring *Coemeterium Ostrianum* was anciently known as "*Fons S. Petri*," "*ubi Petrus baptizavit*," "*ubi Petrus prius sedit*." This cemetery derives its name from Priscilla, mother of Pudens, who is said to have given hospitality to St Peter the Apostle. We are reminded of St Paul, and of his friends Aquila and Prisca, by a monument erected by an imperial freedman who was PRAEPOSITVS TABERNACVLORVM—chief tentmaker. In 1888 a corridor was discovered which had at one time been isolated from the rest of the cemetery. It had no *loculi*, but recesses in the wall to receive sarcophagi. At the end of the corridor there was a large chamber, 23 ft. by 13 ft., once lined with marble and the ceiling covered with mosaic, a few fragments of which still remain. The only tomb here was a sarcophagus, of which the broken front bears the letters which show it to have been the epitaph of one of the Acilian family:—

ACILIO GLABRIONI FILIO

In the vicinity are fragments of the epitaphs of Manius Acilius and Priscilla, of Quintus Acilius and Caia Acilia in Greek, another Greek inscription "Acilius Rufinus mayest thou live in God." After careful examination of the nine Acilii, who were consuls, De Rossi concludes that this was the resting-place of that Acilius Glabrio, consul with Trajan, A.D. 91, who in the year of his consulate was compelled by Domitian to fight with beasts in the arena, and then banished and put to death in 95. The question of his Christianity seems settled by the discovery of the sepulchre of these Christian Acilii. From this crypt a staircase led up to the basilica in which Pope Silvester was buried, and the whole plan of which was laid bare by De Rossi. The tomb of St Silvester could be identified, and that of Pope Siricius "at his feet," as the pilgrim noted (*Bullett.*, 1890, pp. 106-119).

Just before De Rossi's death, Mgr. Wilpert discovered in the Cappella Greca a painting of the "Fractio Panis" or eucharistic feast, which he cleansed from the dust with which it had been covered. The picture of the Blessed Virgin and Child, which De Rossi ascribed to the 2nd, if not to the 1st century, has received an unexpected proof of its antiquity. In 1890 the floor of the gallery in which it stands was excavated, and another floor was found to be 6 ft. below its supposed level. The *loculi* in this lower portion were intact, with inscriptions of the 2nd century still in their places, proving that the niche in which that picture was painted must have been considerably older than the lowering of the floor. A flight of iron steps enables the visitor now to examine this venerable specimen of early Christian art.

After the death of De Rossi, one of his pupils, H. Stevenson, since dead, discovered in 1896 a small subterranean basilica in the catacomb of Santi Pietro e Marcellino on the Via Labicana, with pious acclamations on the plaster similar to those in the Papal crypt in St Calixtus. Near the well-known subterranean chapel in the *Coemeterium Ostrianum* was discovered by Mgr. Crostarosa, in 1877, another chapel, in which Signor Armellini found traces of St Emerentiana, foster-sister of St Agnes. Near this a whole region of galleries has been brought to light with *loculi* intact.

Explorations conducted in the cemetery of Domitilla in 1897-1898 brought to light a fine double crypt with frescoes representing Christ seated between six male and female saints; also an inscription relating to a new saint (Eulalius) in a cubiculum of the 3rd century. In 1899-1900 were discovered two opposite cubicula in the catacomb of Santi Pietro e Marcellino. These were unknown to Bosio, and are both covered with frescoes, the vault being in one case decorated with the scene which represents Christ seated among the apostles and pronouncing sentence upon the defunct. An inscription discovered in 1900 on the site of the ancient cemetery of St Ciriaca, and dating from A.D. 405, states that one Euryalus bought a site *ad mensam beati martyris Laurentii* from a certain *fossor* whose name has been erased. This is interesting as an example of what was known as *memoriae damnatio* or the blotting out of a name on account of some dishonourable action. From the end of the 4th to the first half of the 5th century, the *fossores* had the privilege of selling sites, which frequently led to grave abuses. In 1901-1902 excavations in the cemetery of Santa Priscilla, near the Cappella Greca, revealed a polygonal chamber. This may have originally been the *nymphaeum* of the great villa of the Acilii Glabriones, the *hypogaeum* of which was discovered by De Rossi near this spot in 1888. It may have been used as a burial-place for martyrs, and Professor Marucchi is inclined to see in it the sepulchral chapel of Pope Marcellinus, who died in A.D.304 during the persecutions of Diocletian. In 1902, in that part of the Via Ardeatina which passes between the cemeteries of Calixtus and Domitilla, was discovered a crypt with frescoes and the sanctuary of a martyr: it is thought that this, rather than a neighbouring crypt brought to light in 1897, may prove to be the sepulchral crypt of SS. Marcus and Marcellianus. In a cubiculum leading out of a gallery in the vicinity there was also discovered an interesting impression in plaster of an inscription of the mother of Pope Damasus, beginning:

HIC DAMASI MATER POSVIT LAVREN[TIA MEMBRA].

In the same year building operations in the Via di Sant' Onofrio revealed the presence of catacombs beneath the foundations: examination of the *loculi* showed that no martyrs or illustrious persons were buried here.

In 1903 a new cemetery with frescoes came to light on the Via Latina, considered by Marucchi to have belonged to a heretical sect. In the same year the Jewish cemetery on the Via Portuense, known to Bosio but since forgotten, was rediscovered. The subterranean basilica of SS. Felix and Adauctus, discovered by Boldetti and afterwards choked up with ruins, was cleared again: the crypt, begun by Damasus and enlarged by Siricius, contains frescoes of the 6th-7th centuries.

A good plan of the catacombs at Albano (at the 15th milestone of the Appian way), discovered by Boldetti and described by De Rossi, has been published by Marucchi (*Nuovo Bulletino di archeologia cristiana*, 1902, pp. 89 ff.). In 1904 a small subterranean cemetery was discovered at Anagnia. Catacombs have also been recently discovered on the site of Hadrumetum near Sousse in Tunisia.

(W. R. B.; O. M. D.)

AUTHORITIES.—The classical work on the catacombs of Rome is G.B. De Rossi's *Roma sotterranea*, on which most of the accounts in other languages than Italian have been based. The fine volume by Mgr. Wilpert, *Le Pitture delle catacombe romane* (Rome, 1903), in which all the important frescoes are reproduced in colours, is to be regarded as an addition to the *Roma sotterranea*. All new 500discoveries made by the active*Commissione di archeologia sacra* are chronicled with as little delay as possible in the*Nuovo Bulletino de archeologia cristiana* published in Rome.

The most recent accounts of the catacombs are to be found in the following books:—Armellini, *Gli Antichi Cimiteri cristiani di Roma e d' Italia* (Rome, 1893); O. Marucchi,*Le Catacombe romane* (Rome, 1903; also translated into French), *Manuale di epigrafia cristiana* (Milan, 1904); M. Besnier, *Les Catacombes de Rome* (Paris, 1909).

Among the older works are: Bosio, *Roma sotterranea*, Severano's edition (1632), and Aringhi's edition (1651); Boldetti, *Osservazioni sopra i cimiteri dei santi martiri* (Rome, 1720); Bottari, *Sculture e pitture sagre, &c.* (Rome, 1737-1754); Seroux d'Agincourt,*Histoire de l'art par les monuments* (Paris, 1823; German ed., 1840); G. Marchi,*Monumenti delle arti cristiane primitive* (Rome, 1844); Raoul Rochette, *Tableau des catacombes de Rome* (2nd ed., Paris, 1853); Perret, *Les Catacombes de Rome* (Paris, 1855)—a sumptuous folio work, but not always accurate, Roller, *Les Catacombes de Rome* (Paris, 1881); V. Schultze, *Die Katakomben* (Leipzig, 1882).

Works written in English are: Northcote and Brownlow, *Roma sotterranea* (London, 1869; based upon De Rossi); Wharton Marriott, *The Testimony of the Catacombs*(London, 1870); J.H. Parker, *The Archaeology of Rome: the Catacombs*; Smith and Cheetham, *Dictionary of Christian Antiquities, s.v.* "Catacombs"; R. Lanciani, *Pagan and Christian Rome* (London, 1892); W. Lowry, *Christian Art and Archaeology*, ch. ii. (London, 1901; a useful introduction to the subject); H. Gee, "The Church in the Catacombs," in W. Lefroy's *Lectures in Ecclesiastical History* (1896); Th. Mommsen, in the *Contemporary Review*, May 1871.

Accounts of the catacombs will also be found in the encyclopaedias and manuals published under the following names: Martigny, Pératé, F.X. Kraus (*Realencyklopädie*and *Geschichte der christlichen Kunst*), Reusens, V. Schultze and C.M. Kauffmann, and in the large new *Dictionnaire d'archéologie chrétienne et liturgie*, published at Paris under the editorship of Dom F. Cabrol.

The catacombs at Naples are described in C.F. Bellermann, *Über die ältesten christlichen Begräbnisstätten und besonders die Katakomben zu Neapel* (Hamburg, 1839); Armellini, as above, and V. Schultze, *Die Katakomben von San Gennaro dei Poveri in Neapel* (Jena, 1877).

For the catacombs in Malta, A.A. Caruana, *Ancient Pagan Tombs and Christian Cemeteries in the Islands of Malta* (Malta, 1898), and A. Mayr, "Die altchristlichen Begräbnisstätten auf Malta," in *Römische Quartalschrift*, vol. xv. pp. 216 and 352 (Rome, 1901), may be consulted.

The fullest account of the Sicilian catacombs is given by J. Führer, *Forschungen zur Sicilia sotterranea* (Munich, 1897); and D.C. Barrecca, *Le Catacombe di San Giovanni in Siracusa* (Syracuse, 1906).

A catacomb of the 5th century, discovered at Kertch in South Russia, is described by J. Kulakovsky in *Materials for Russian Archaeology* (St Petersburg, 1896; a publication of the Russian Imperial Archaeological Commission), but it is written in Russian, as also is the account by V. Latyshev, in *Vizantieski Vremennik*, vol. vi. pp. 337 ff. (St Petersburg, 1899).

The catacombs at Hadrumetum (Sousse) are described by A.F. Leynard, *Les Catacombes d'Hadrumète, deuxième campagne de fouilles* (1904-1905). See also *Revue Tunisienne* (1905), p. 250.

For the catacombs of Alexandria, Neroutsos Bey, *L'Ancienne Alexandrie,* may be consulted in addition to De Rossi's article mentioned in the text.

(O. M. D.)

1The most important of these lists are the two Itineraries belonging to the first half of the 7th century, in the Salzburg library. One still earlier, but less complete, appears in the*Notitia Urbis Romae*, under the title *Index Coemeteriorum*. Another Itinerary, preserved at Einsiedeln, printed by Mabillon, dates from the latter half of the same century. That found in the works of William of Malmesbury (Hardy's ed. vol. ii. pp. 539-544) appears to be copied from it, or both may be from the same source. De Rossi gives a comparative table of these Itineraries and other similar lists.

2Hieron., *Comment. in Ezech.* lib xx. c. 40. The translation is Dean Burgon's.

3In Rome the three strata are known to geologists as *tufa litoide, tufa granolare* and*pozzolana.*

4Cicero is our authority for the burial of Marius, and for Sulla's being the first member of the Gens Cornelia whose dead body was burnt (*De Legg.* ii. 22).

21

5Mommsen's chosen example of an ancient burial-chamber, extending itself into a catacomb, or gathering subterranean additions round it till a catacomb was established, is that of the cemetery of St Domitilla, traditionally identified with a granddaughter of Vespasian, and the catacomb of Santi Nereo ed Achilleo on the Appian and Ardeatine way.

6Parker's invaluable series of Roman photographs may be seen at the library of the Victoria and Albert museum, at the Ashmolean museum and the Bodleian library, Oxford.

7*Bulletino di archaeologia cristiana*, November 1864, August 1865. See also *Authorities*, below.

CATAFALQUE (a word of unknown origin, occurring in various forms in many European languages, meaning a funeral scaffold or temporary stage), a movable structure of wood sometimes richly decorated, erected temporarily at funeral ceremonies in a church to receive the coffin or effigy of the deceased; also an open hearse or funeral car.

CATALANI, ANGELICA (1780-1849), Italian opera-singer, daughter of a tradesman at Sinigaglia, was educated at the convent of Santa Lucia at Gubbio, where her magnificent soprano voice, of extraordinary compass and purity, soon became famous. In 1795 she made her début on the stage at Venice, and from that moment every impresario in Europe was anxious to engage her. For nearly thirty years she sang at all the great houses, receiving very large fees; her first appearance in London being at the King's theatre in 1806. She remained in England, a prima donna without a serious rival, for seven years. Then she was given the management of the opera in Paris, but this resulted in financial failure, owing to the incapacity and extravagance of her husband, Captain Valabrègue, whom she married in 1806. But her continental tours continued to be enormously successful, until she retired in 1828. She settled at Florence in 1830, where she founded a free singing school for girls; and her charity and kindness were unbounded. She died of cholera in Paris on the 12th of June 1849.

CATALEPSY (from Gr. κατάληψις, a seizure), a term applied to a nervous affection characterized by the sudden suspension of sensation and volition, accompanied with a peculiar rigidity of the whole or of certain muscles of the body. The subjects of catalepsy are in most instances females of highly nervous temperament. The exciting cause of an attack is usually mental emotion operating either suddenly, as in the case of a fright, or more gradually in the way of prolonged depression. The symptoms presented vary in different cases, and even in the same individual in different attacks. Sometimes the typical features of the disease are exhibited in a state of complete insensibility, together with a statue-like appearance of the body which will retain any attitude it may be made to assume during the continuance of the attack. In this condition the whole organic and vital functions appear to be reduced to the lowest possible limit consistent with life, and to such a degree as to simulate actual death. At other times considerable mental excitement will accompany the cataleptic symptoms, and the patient will sing or utter passionate exclamations during the fit, being all the while quite unconscious. The attack may be of short duration, passing off within a few minutes. It may, however, last for many hours, and in some rare instances persist for several days; and it is conceivable that in such cases the appearances presented might be mistaken for real death, as is alleged to have occasionally happened. Catalepsy belongs to the class of functional nervous disorders (see MUSCLE AND NERVE: *Pathology*) in which morbid physical and psychical conditions are mixed up. Although it is said to occur in persons in perfect health, careful inquiry will usually reveal some departure from the normal state, as is shown by the greater number of the recorded cases. More particularly is this true of females, in whom some form of menstrual derangement is generally found to have preceded the cataleptic affection. Catalepsy is sometimes associated with epilepsy and with grave forms of mental disease. In ordinary cases, however, the mental phenomena bear close resemblance to those witnessed in hysteria. In many of the subjects of catalepsy there appears to be a remarkable weakness of the will, whereby the tendency to lapse into the cataleptic state is not resisted but rather in some measure encouraged, and attacks may thus be induced by the most trivial circumstances.

CATALOGUE (a Fr. adaptation of the Gr. κατάλογος, a register, from καταλέγειν, to enrol or pick out), a list or enumeration, generally in alphabetical order, of persons, things, &c., and particularly of the contents of a museum or library. A *catalogue raisonnée* is such a list classified according to subjects or on some other basis, with short explanations and notes. (See also articles BIBLIOGRAPHY AND BIBLIOLOGY, and LIBRARIES.)

CATALONIA (*Cataluña*), a captaincy-general, and formerly a province of Spain, formerly also a principality of the crown of Aragon; bounded on the N. by the Pyrenees, W. by Aragon, S. by Valencia, and E. by the Mediterranean Sea. Pop. (1900) 1,966,382; area, 12,427 sq. m. The triangular territory of Catalonia forms the north-eastern corner of the Iberian Peninsula. A full account of the physical features, and of the modern development of commerce, communications, &c., in this area is given in the articles on the four provinces Barcelona, Gerona, Lérida and Tarragona, into which Catalonia was divided in 1833.

The coast, which is partly sandy, partly rocky, extends about 240 m.; its chief harbours are those of the capital, Barcelona, of Mataró, of Rosas and of Tarragona. The surface is much broken by spurs of the Pyrenees, the direction of which is generally south. Running south-west to north-east, and united on the north with one of the offsets of the Pyrenees, is the range of the Sierra Llena, which bisects Catalonia, and forms its central watershed. The principal rivers are the Ter, the Llobrégat, and the Ebro (*q.v.*), which all run into the Mediterranean. None of them is navigable. The climate, in spite of frequent mists and rains, sudden changes of temperature, and occasional great mid-day heat, is healthy and favourable to vegetation. The dwarf-palm, orange, lime, and olive grow in the warmer tracts; and on the higher grounds the thorn-apple, pomegranate, myrtle, esparto and heaths flourish. There is much woodland, 501 but meadows and pastures are rare. Maize, millet, rye, flax, liquorice and fruits of all sorts—especially nuts, almonds, oranges, figs, walnuts and chestnuts—are produced. Wheat sufficient for one-fourth of the population is grown, and the vine is extensively cultivated. Few cattle, but numbers of sheep, goats and swine are reared. Game is plentiful, and the fisheries on the coast are excellent. The wines are for the most part rough and strong, though some are very good, especially when matured. They are much used to adulterate those of Oporto, or, after undergoing the blending operation termed *compage*, are passed off as Bordeaux wines in France. The best of them, *priorato*, is chiefly known in England, under the disguise of second or third-rate port; it was much used in the military hospitals of America during the Civil War.

The Catalonians are a frugal, sharp-witted, and industrious people, having much national pride, and a strong revolutionary spirit. They are distinct in origin from the other inhabitants of Spain, from whom they differ in their dialect and costume. In their great energy and their love of enterprise they resemble the Basques. Irrigation, careful husbandry and railroad communications have much developed the resources of their country, in themselves excellent; and there are many manufacturing towns and industrial establishments.

Catalonia was one of the first of the Roman possessions in Spain, and formed the north-eastern portion of Hispania Tarraconensis. About 470 it was occupied by the Alans and Goths. It was conquered by the Moors in 712, but these invaders were in turn dispossessed by the Spaniards and the troops of Charlemagne in 788. Catalonia was subsequently ruled by French counts, who soon, however, made themselves independent of France. By the marriage of Count Raymond Berenger IV. of Barcelona with Petronilla of Aragon, Catalonia became annexed to Aragon; but this union was frequently severed. In 1640, when Philip IV. attempted to deprive Catalonia of its rights and privileges, it gave itself up to Louis XIII. of France. It was restored to Spain in 1659, and was once more occupied by the French from 1694 to 1697. Under Philip V. Catalonia, in 1714, was deprived of its cortes and liberties. From 1808 to 1813 it was held by France. It was the scene of civil war in 1823, and of important revolutionary operations in the Carlist wars.

The history and literature of Catalonia have been closely studied, and in many cases the results of research are published in the Catalan language. See *Cataluña, sus monumentos y artes, su naturaleza e historia* (2 vols. of the illustrated series *España*), by P. Pifferrer, F. Pi Margall, and A.A. Pijoan (Barcelona, 1884); *Historia de Cataluña*, by V. Balaguer (11 vols., Madrid, 1886, &c.); *Historia de Cataluña*, by A. Bori y Fontestá (Barcelona, 1898); *Origines históricos de Cataluña*, by J. Balari y Jovany (Barcelona, 1899); *Coleccio dels monografias de Catalunya*, by J. Reig y Vilardell (Barcelona, 1890); *Historia del derecho en Catalonia, Mallorca y Valencia*, by B. Oliver (Madrid, 1876-1880); and *Antigua marina catalana*, by F. de Bofarull y Sans (Barcelona, 1898). The *Revista catalana* (Catalan Review), published at Barcelona from 1889, contains many valuable papers on local affairs. See also SPAIN: sections *Language, Literature* and *History*, and BARCELONA.

CATALPA, in botany, a genus belonging to the family *Bignoniaceae* and containing about ten species in America and eastern Asia. The best known is *Catalpa bignonioides*, a native of the eastern United States which is often cultivated in parks and gardens. It is a stately tree with large heart-shaped pointed leaves and panicles of white bell-shaped flowers streaked with yellow and brown purple.

CATALYSIS (from the Gr. κατά, down, and λύειν, to loosen), in chemistry, the name given to chemical actions brought about by a substance, termed the "catalyst," which is recovered unchanged after the action. The term was introduced by Berzelius, who first studied such reactions. It is convenient to divide catalytic actions into two groups:—(1) when the catalyst first combines with one of the reaction components to form a compound which immediately reacts with the other components, the catalyst being simultaneously liberated, and free to react with more of the undecomposed first component; and (2), when the catalyst apparently reacts by mere contact. The theory of catalysis is treated under CHEMICAL ACTION; in this article mention will be made of some of the more interesting examples.

A familiar instance of a catalytic action is witnessed when a mixture of potassium chlorate and manganese dioxide is heated to 350°, oxygen being steadily liberated, and the manganese dioxide being unchanged at the end of the reaction. The action may be explained as follows:—part of the chlorate reacts with the manganese dioxide to form potassium permanganate, chlorine and oxygen, the chlorine subsequently reacting with the permanganate to produce manganese dioxide, potassium chloride and oxygen, thus

$$2KClO3 + 2MnO2 = 2KMnO4 + Cl2 + O2 = 2KCl + 2MnO2 + 3O2.$$

This explanation is supported by the facts that traces of chlorine are present in the gas, and the pink permanganate can be recognized when little dioxide is used. Other oxides bring about the same decomposition at temperatures below that at which the chlorate yields oxygen when heated alone; but since such substances as kaolin, platinum black and some other finely powdered compounds exercise the same effect, it follows that the explanation given above is not quite general. Another example is Deacon's process for the manufacture of chlorine by passing hydrochloric acid gas mixed with air over heated bricks which had been previously impregnated with a copper sulphate solution. The nitrous gases employed in the ordinary chamber process of manufacturing sulphuric acid also act catalytically. Mention may be made of the part played by water vapour in conditioning many chemical reactions. Thus sodium will not react with dry chlorine or dry oxygen; carbon, sulphur and phosphorus will not burn in perfectly dry oxygen, neither does nitric oxide give red fumes of the peroxide. In organic chemistry many catalytic actions are met with. In the class of reaction known as "condensations," it may be found that the course of the reaction is largely dependent upon the nature of some substance which acts catalytically. One of the most important is the Friedel and Craft's reaction, in which an aromatic compound combines with an alkyl haloid in the presence of aluminium, zinc or ferric chloride. It seems in this, as in other cases, that additional compounds are first formed which subsequently react with the re-formation of the catalyst. The formation of benzoin from benzaldehyde in the presence of potassium cyanide is another example; this action has been investigated by G. Bredig and Stern (*Zeit. Elektrochem.*, 1904, 10, p. 582).

The second class of catalytic actions, viz. those occasioned by the presence of a metal or some other substance which undergoes no change, is of especial interest, and has received much attention. The accelerating influence of a clean platinum plate on the rate of combination of hydrogen and oxygen was studied by Faraday. He found that with the pure gases the velocity of reaction increased until the mixture exploded. The presence of minute quantities of carbon monoxide, carbon disulphide, sulphuretted hydrogen and hydrochloric acid inhibited the action; in the case of the first two gases, there is no alteration of the platinum surface, since the plate brings about combination when removed to an atmosphere of pure hydrogen and oxygen; with the last two gases, however, the surface is altered, since the plate will not occasion the combination when placed in the pure gases. M. Bodenstein (*Zeit. phys. Chem.*, 1904, 46, p. 725) showed that combination occurs with measurable velocity at ordinary temperatures in the presence of compact platinum. More energetic combination is observed if the metal be finely divided, as, for instance, by immersing asbestos fibres in a solution of platinum chloride and strongly heating. The "spongy" platinum so formed brings about the combination of ammonia and oxygen to form water and nitric acid, of nitric oxide and hydrogen to form ammonia (see German Patent, 1905, 157,287), and of sulphur dioxide and oxygen to form sulphur trioxide. The last reaction, which receives commercial application in the contact process of sulphuric acid manufacture, was studied by M. Bodenstein and W. Pohl (*Zeit. Elektrochem.*, 1905, 11, p. 373), who found that the equilibrium followed the law of mass-action (see also F. W. Küster, *Zeit. anorg. Chem.*, 1904, 42, p. 453, R. Lucas, *Zeit. Elektrochem.*, 1905, 11, p. 457). Other metals, such as nickel, iron, &c., can also react as catalysts. 502The use of finely divided nickel (obtained by reducing the oxide in a current of pure hydrogen at a temperature of 350°) has been carefully studied by P. Sabatier and J.B. Senderens; a summary of their results is given in the *Ann. Chim. Phys.*, 1905 (viii.) 4, pp. 319-488. Of special interest is the condensation of acetylene. If this gas mixed with hydrogen be passed over the reduced nickel in the cold, the temperature may rise to as high as 150°, the acetylene disappearing and becoming replaced by a substance like petroleum. If the nickel be maintained at 200°, and the gases circulated for twenty-eight hours, a product, condensible to a yellow liquid having a beautiful fluorescence and boiling at 45°, is obtained. This substance closely resembles ordinary Pennsylvanian petroleum. If acetylene be passed alone over nickel heated to 200°-300°, a mixture, boiling at 60°-70° and having a green colour by diffused and a red by transmitted light, was obtained. This substance closely resembles Caucasian petroleum. The decomposition of carbon monoxide according to the reaction 2CO ⇄ C + CO2 is purely catalytic in the presence of nickel and cobalt, and also in the presence of iron, so long as the amount of carbon dioxide present does not exceed a certain amount (R. Schenck and W. Heller, *Ber.*, 1905, 38, pp. 2132, 2139). It is of interest that finely divided aluminium and magnesium decompose methane, ethane, and ethylene into carbon and hydrogen in the same way as nickel. Charcoal at 350° also reacts catalytically; for example, Senderens found that ethyl alcohol was decomposed by animal charcoal into methane, ethylene, hydrogen, carbon monoxide and a little carbon dioxide, and propyl alcohol gave propylene, ethane, carbon monoxide and hydrogen, while G. Lemoine obtained from ethyl alcohol and wood charcoal a mixture of acetaldehyde and hydrogen.

CATAMARAN (a Tamil word, from *catta*, to tie, and *maram* wood), a surf-boat or raft used by the natives of Madras and along the Coromandel Coast in India. It is usually made of three tree trunks lashed together, the centre trunk being the largest and longest, and having one end bent upward to form a kind of prow. Catamarans of a larger size are in use in the West Indies and South America. The name is also given to two boats lashed together. Apparently through an erroneous connexion with cat, the name has been applied to a noisy scolding woman.

CATAMARCA, an Andean province of the Argentine Republic, lying W. of Santiago del Estero and Tucuman and extending to the Chilean frontier, with Los Andes and Salta on the N., Cordoba on the S.E., and Rioja on the S. Pop. (1895) 90,161; (1904, estimate) 103,082; area, 47,531 sq. m. The surface of the province is extremely broken, the Andes forming its western boundary, and the Aconquija, Ancaste, Ambato, Gulampaja and other ranges traversing it from north to south. It is composed very largely of high plateaus with a general slope southward broken by a few fertile valleys. The greater part of the province is arid and barren, being sheltered from the moist, eastern winds by the high mountain barriers of Aconquija and Ancaste. The rivers are small, and some of them are lost in the barren, sandy wastes. Others, especially in the foothills of the high sierras, are utilized to irrigate the fertile valleys. The climate of some of the low, sheltered valleys is extremely hot and unhealthy, but on the open plateaus it is peculiarly dry and bracing and is probably beneficial in the treatment of pulmonary diseases. The mineral resources of the province include gold, silver, copper, lead, nickel, iron, coal and malachite, but of these only copper and silver are mined, and these chiefly in the Andalgalá district. Salt deposits also exist, but are worked only to a limited extent. Cereals, alfalfa and fruit are grown. Large numbers of cattle, fattened in the alfalfa fields of Pucará, Tinogasta and Copacabana, are driven into northern Chile across the San Francisco pass (13,124 ft. above sea level) and mules are bred for the Bolivian market. Wine of an excellent quality is produced and exported. Tanning leather is another industry of the province, some of the trees growing in the Catamarca forests being rich in tannin. Catamarca is traversed by the Northern Central railway between Cordoba and the city of Catamarca, its capital, which passes around the southern extremity of the Sierra de Ancaste and makes a long detour to Chumbicha, near the Rioja frontier. The more important towns, after Catamarca, the capital, are Andalgalá and Tinogasta with populations (estimated, 1904) of 5000 to 6000 each. Belen is the oldest Spanish settlement in the province and was founded in 1550, being called Barco at first. The population is largely mixed with Indian blood.

CATAMARCA (*San Fernando de Catamarca*), capital of the above province on the Rio del Valle de Catamarca, 230 m. (318 m. by rail) N.N.W. of Cordoba. Pop. (1895) 7397; (1905, estimate) 8000, with a large percentage of mestizos. Catamarca is connected by railways with Rioja and Patquia and with Cordoba. The city stands in a narrow, picturesque valley at the foot of the Sierra de Ambato, 1772 ft. above sea level. The valley is highly fertile, partially wooded, and produces fruit in abundance, wine and some cereals. In the city are flour mills and tanneries, and among its exports are leather, fruit, wine, flour, and a curious embroidery for which the women of Catamarca have long been famous. There is a fine church, 220 by 90 ft., and a national college occupies the old Merced convent. The alameda is one of the prettiest in the Argentine Republic, having a reservoir of two acres surrounded by shrubbery and walks. Catamarca was founded in 1685 by Fernando de Mendoza because the town of Chacra, the former provincial capital, a few miles north of Catamarca, had been found unhealthy and subject to inundations. Previous to the selection of Chacra as the provincial capital, the seat of government was at San Juan de Londres, founded in 1558 and named after the capital of England by order of Philip II. in honour of his marriage with Queen Mary. The arid surroundings of Londres led to its partial abandonment and it is now a mere village. Cholla, a suburb of Catamarca, is inhabited wholly by Calchaqui Indians, a remnant of the original inhabitants of this region.

CATANIA (Gr. *Katane*, Rom. *Catina1*), a city and episcopal see of Sicily, the chief town of the province of Catania, on the east coast, 59 m. by rail S. of Messina, and 151 m. by rail S.E. of Palermo (102 m. direct). Pop. (1881) 100,417; (1905) 157,722. The principal buildings are handsome, and the main streets, meeting in the Piazzo del Duomo, are fine. The cathedral of S. Agatha, containing the relics of the saint, retains its three original Norman apses (1091), but is otherwise a large baroque edifice. The monument of Don Ferrando d'Acunea, a Spanish viceroy of Sicily, is a fine early Renaissance work (1494). In the west portion of the town is the huge Benedictine abbey of S. Nicola (now suppressed), the buildings of which occupy an area of about 21 acres and contain the museum, a library, observatory, &c. The church, dating, like the rest of the buildings, from 1693-1735, is the largest in Sicily, and the organ, built in 1760 by Donato del Piano, with 72 stops and 2916 pipes, is very fine. The university, founded in 1444, has regained some of its former importance. To the south near the harbour is the massive Castell' Ursino, erected in 1232 by Frederick II. Remains of several ancient buildings exist, belonging in the main to the Roman period. The theatre, covered by a stream of lava, and built partly of small rectangular blocks of the same material, though in the main of concrete, has been superimposed upon the Greek building, some foundations of which, in calcareous stone, of which the seats are also made, still exist. It is 106 yds. in diameter, and is estimated to have accommodated 7000 spectators. Close to it are the remains of the so-called Odeum, of similar plan to the theatre but without a stage, and to the north is the church of S. Maria Rotonda, originally a Roman domed structure, perhaps part of a bath. To the north, in the Piazza Stesicoro, is the amphitheatre, a considerable portion of which has been uncovered, including the two corridors which ran round the whole building and gave access to the seats, while a part of the arcades of the exterior has been excavated and left open; the pillars are made of blocks of lava, and the arches of brick. The external diameters of the amphitheatre are 410 and 348 ft., while the corresponding diameters of the arena are 233 and 167 ft. It is thus the third largest Roman amphitheatre known, being surpassed only by that at Verona and the Colosseum. Remains of many other Roman buildings also exist beneath the modern town, among the best preserved of which may be noted the public baths (*Thermae Achilleae*) under the cathedral, and those under the church of S. Maria dell' Indirizzo. The number of baths is remarkable, and gives some idea of the luxury of the place in Roman times. Their excellent preservation is accounted for by their burial under the lava. The majority were excavated by Prince Ignazio Biscari (1719-1786), who formed an important private collection of antiquities. Of the ancient city walls no authenticated remains exist.

Catania has a considerable export trade in sulphur, pumice stone, asphalt, oranges and lemons, almonds, filberts, cereals, wine (the total production of wine in the province amounted to 28,600,000 gallons in 1905) and oil. The total value of exports in 1905 was £1,647,075, and of imports £1,326,055, the latter including notably coal, almost entirely from the United Kingdom, and wheat, from Russian ports. The harbour is a good one, and has been considerably enlarged since 1872; £128,000 was voted in 1905 towards the completion of the harbour works by the Italian government. Sulphide of carbon is produced here; and there are large dyeworks, and a factory for making bed-stuffing from seaweed.

The ancient Catina was founded in 729 B.C. by colonists from Naxos, perhaps on the site of an earlier Sicel settlement—the name is entirely un-Greek, and may be derived from κάτινον, which in the Sicel language, as *catinum* in Latin, meant a basin, and would thus be descriptive of the situation of the town. Charondas, a citizen of Catina, is famous as its lawgiver, but his date and his birthplace are alike uncertain; the fragments preserved of his laws show that they belong to a somewhat primitive period. The poet Stesichorus of Himera died here. Very little is heard of Catina in history until 476 B.C., when Hiero I. removed its inhabitants to Leontini, repeopled it with 5000 Syracusans and 5000 Peloponnesians, and changed its name to Aetna. In 461 B.C., however, with the help of Ducetius and the Syracusans, the former inhabitants recovered possession of their city and revived the old name. Catina was, however, an ally of Athens during the Syracusan expedition (415-413 B.C.), and served as the Athenian base of operations in the early part of the war. In 403 B.C. it was taken by Dionysius of Syracuse, who plundered the city, sold the inhabitants into slavery and replaced them with Campanian mercenaries. In the First Punic War it was one of the first cities of Sicily to be taken by the Romans (263 B.C.). Marcellus constructed a gymnasium here out of the booty of Syracuse. In 123 B.C. there was an eruption of Etna so violent that the tithe on the territory of Catina payable to Rome was remitted for ten years. It appears to have been a flourishing city in the ist century B.C., but to have suffered from the ravages of Sextus Pompeius. It became a Roman *colonia* under Augustus, and it is from this period that the fertile plain, hitherto called the plain of Leontini, begins to be called the plain of Catina. It seems to have been at this time the most important city in the island, to judge from the language of Strabo and the number of inscriptions found there. In A.D. 251 a lava stream threatened the town and entered the amphitheatre, which in the time of Theodoric had fallen into ruins, as is clear from the fact that he permitted the use of its fallen stones to build the city wall. It was recovered by Belisarius in 535, sacked by the Saracens in 902 and taken by the Normans. The latter founded the cathedral; but the town was almost entirely destroyed by earthquake in 1170, and devastated by Henry VI. in 1197. It became the usual residence of the Aragonese viceroys of the 13th and 14th centuries. In 1669 an eruption of Etna partly filled up the harbour, but spared the town, which was, however, almost entirely destroyed by the earthquake of 1693. Since that catastrophe it has been rebuilt, and has not further suffered from its proximity to Etna.

See A. Holm, *Das alte Catania* (Lübeck, 1873).

(T. AS.)

1This is the form vouched for by the inscriptions.

CATANZARO, a town and episcopal see of Calabria, Italy, capital of the province of Catanzaro, 1125 ft. above sea-level. Pop. (1901) 22,799 (town); 32,005 (commune). The station for the town (Catanzaro Sala) is situated on a branch line connecting the two main lines along the east and west coasts of Calabria, 6 m. N. by W. of Catanzaro Marina on the east coast, and 20 m. E. of S. Eufemia Biforcazione, on the west coast line. The town enjoys a comparatively cool climate in summer, and commands fine views. Numerous wealthy families reside here, and the town has a trade in olive-oil, silk and velvet. The castle, built by Robert Guiscard, has been modernized, and so has the cathedral. The see was founded in 1121. The provincial museum contains antiquities and especially coins from the ancient cities of Magna Graecia, and a few pictures.

CATAPHYLL (Gr. κατά, down, φύλλον, leaf), a botanical term for the early leaf-forms produced in the lower part of a shoot, such as bud-scales, or scales on underground stems.

CATAPULT (Lat. *catapulta*, Gr. καταπέλτης) a generic name for warlike engines of the cross-bow type used by the ancients. Although engines of war appear on Assyrian remains, and are mentioned in 2 Chronicles xxvi. 15, it appears that Greek armies, even of the 5th century, did not possess them, and the first record of a large siege train in classical literature is of the year 399 B.C., when Dionysius I. of Syracuse, contemplating an expedition against Carthage, provided himself with engines. From Sicily siege engines found their way some years later into Greece; they were used by Philip of Macedon at the siege of Byzantium in 340, and thereafter, as a natural consequence of the regularizing or professionalizing of armies, artillery, as we may call it, came into prominence and called into existence technical corps to work it.

The war engines of the Romans, during the republic and early principate, are of the same type as those of Alexander's successors in Greece. They are usually classed as (a) catapults and (b) ballistae (λιθοβόλοι). The former were smaller and were used with arrows for what is now called direct fire (*i.e.* at low angles of elevation); the latter were large siege engines discharging heavy bolts or stones at a high angle of elevation, like the modern howitzer. They were, of course, principally siege engines, but the smaller natures of catapult appear in field warfare from time to time, and eventually, during the early principate, they are found as part of the regulation equipment of infantry units. Both were constructed on the same principle.

The essential parts of the catapult (see illustration) were the frame, the propelling gear, the trough (corresponding to the modern barrel) and the pedestal. The frame consisted of two horizontal beams forming top and bottom sills, and four strong upright bars mortised into them. The three open spaces or compartments, resembling narrow windows, between these four uprights carried the propelling and laying gear. The propelling gear occupied the two outer "windows." In each a thick skein of cord or sinews was fastened to the top and

28

bottom sills and tightly twisted. Two stiff wooden arms were inserted in the two skeins, and a specially strong bowstring joined the tips of these arms. In the middle compartment was the hinged fore-end of the trough, which was at right angles to the frame and at the back of it. The trough could be laid for elevation by a movable prop, the upper end of which was hinged to the trough, while the lower ran up and down a sort of trail fastened to the pedestal. The whole equipment was laid for "line" by turning the frame, and with it the trough, prop and trail by a pivot in the head of the pedestal. Sliding up and down in the trough was a block, fitted with a trigger mechanism, through which passed the middle of the bowstring. The pedestal was a strong and solid upright resting upon, and strutted to, a framework on the ground; its upper end, as mentioned above, took the pivot of the frame and the head of the trail.

504

On coming into action the machine was laid for direction and elevation. The block and with it the bowstring was next forced back against the resistance of the twisted skeins to the rear end of the trough, this being effected by a windlass attachment. The trigger being then pressed or struck with a hammer, the bowstring was released from the block, the stiff arms were violently brought back to the frame by the untwisting of the skeins, and the arrow was propelled through the centre "window" with great velocity. A small machine of the type described weighed about 85 ℔, and sent a "three-span" (26-in.) arrow weighing ½ ℔ at an effective man-killing velocity somewhat over 400 yds.

The ballista was considerably larger and more expensive than this. In Scipio's siege train, at the attack of New Carthage (Livy xxvi. 47. 5), the number of the ballistae was only one-sixth that of the catapults. In the ballista the rear end of the trough (which projected in front of the frame) always rested upon the ground, or rather was fixed to the framework of the pedestal—which was a heavy trestle construction—and the trough was thus restricted to the angle of elevation, giving the maximum range (45°). Even so the range was not appreciably greater than that of a catapult, and in the case of the largest ballistae (ninety-pounder) it was much less. These enormous engines, which, once in position, could not be laid on any fresh target, were used for propelling beams and stones rather than for shooting arrows, that is, more for the destruction of material than for man-killing effect. The skeins that supplied the motive force of all these engines were made of the sinews of animals, twisted raw hide, horsehair rope, and, in at least one celebrated case, of women's hair. In 146 B.C., the authorities of Carthage having surrendered their engines to the Romans in the vain hope of staying their advance, new ones were hurriedly constructed, and the women and virgins of the city cut off their hair to supply the needed skeins.

The modern implement known as a "catapult" is formed by a forked stick, to the forks of which are attached the ends of a piece of elastic. To the middle of this elastic a pocket is fitted to contain a bullet or small stone. In use the forked stick is held in the left hand and the pocket drawn back with the right. Aim is taken and, the pocket being released, the missile flies through the fork of the stick. Though classed as a toy, this weapon can do considerable execution among birds, &c., when skilfully used. The name of "catapult" has also been given to a bowling machine which is used for cricket practice.

CATARACT (from the Lat. form *cataracta* of the Gr. καταρράκτης, a floodgate, or waterfall, properly something which rushes down), a downpour of water, a waterfall. The earliest use in English is of a floodgate or portcullis, and this survives in the name of a disease of the eye (see EYE: *Eye Diseases*), in which the crystalline lens becomes opaque, and forms an apparent grating over the eye. The term is also used of a device to regulate the strokes in certain types of steam-engine.

CATARGIU (or CATARGI), **LASCAR** (1823-1899), Rumanian statesman, was born in Moldavia in November 1823. He belonged to an ancient Walachian family, one of whose members had been banished in the 17th century by Prince Matthew Bassaraba, and had settled in Moldavia. Under Prince Gregory Ghica (1849-1856), Catargiu rose to be prefect of police at Jassy. In 1857 he became a member of the *Divan ad hoc* of Moldavia, a commission elected in accordance with the treaty of Paris (1856) to vote on the proposed union of Moldavia and Walachia. His strongly conservative views, especially on agrarian reform, induced the Conservatives to support him as a candidate for the throne in 1859. During the reign of Prince Cuza (1859-1866), Catargiu was one of the Opposition leaders, and received much assistance from his kinsman, Barbu Catargiu (b. 1807), a noted journalist and politician, who was assassinated at Bucharest on the 20th of June 1862. On the accession of Prince Charles in May 1866, Lascar Catargiu became president of the council, or prime minister; but, finding himself unable to co-operate with his Liberal colleagues, I.C. Bratianu and C.A. Rosetti, he resigned in July. After eight more ministerial changes, culminating in the anti-dynastic agitation of 1870-1871, Catargiu formed, for the first time in Rumanian history, a stable Conservative cabinet, which lasted until 1876. His policy, which averted revolution and revived the popularity of the crown, was regarded as unpatriotic and reactionary by the Liberals, who resumed office in 1876; and a proposal to impeach the whole Catargiu cabinet was only withdrawn in 1878. Catargiu remained in opposition until 1889, when he formed another cabinet, taking the portfolio of the Interior; but this administration fell after seven months. In the Florescu ministry of March 1891 he occupied the same position, and in December he again became president of the council, retaining office until 1895. During this period he was responsible for several useful reforms, chiefly financial and commercial. He died suddenly at Bucharest on the 11th of April 1899.

CATARRH (from the Gr. καταρρεῖν, to flow down), a term principally employed to describe a state of irritation of the mucous membrane of the respiratory passages, or what is called in popular language a "cold." It is the result of infection by a micro-organism in one or more of various predisposing conditions, damp, chill, fatigue, &c. The complaint usually begins as a nasal catarrh or *coryza* (Gr. κόρυς, head), with a feeling of weight about the forehead and some degree of difficulty in breathing through the nose, increased on lying down. Fits of sneezing accompanied with a profuse watery discharge from the nostrils and eyes soon follow, while the sense of smell and to some extent that of taste become considerably impaired. There is usually present some amount of sore throat and of bronchial irritation, causing hoarseness and cough. Sometimes the vocal apparatus becomes so much inflamed (laryngeal catarrh) that temporary loss of voice results. There is always more or less feverishness and discomfort, and frequently an extreme sensitiveness to cold. After two or three days the symptoms begin to abate, the discharge from the nostrils and chest becoming thicker and of purulent character, and producing when dislodged considerable relief to the breathing. On the other hand the catarrh may assume a more severe aspect and pass into some form of pulmonary inflammation (see BRONCHITIS) or influenza (*q.v.*).

When the symptoms are first felt it is well to take a good purge, and to encourage free perspiration by a hot bath, some diaphoretic drug, as spirits of nitrous ether, being taken before retiring to bed. Some of the older school of physicians still pin their faith to a dose of Dover's powder. When the cold manifests itself by aches and pains in back and limbs, aspirin taken three or four times in the first twenty-four hours will often act like magic. Locally a snuff made of menthol 1 part, ammonium chloride 3 parts and boracic acid 2 parts will relieve the discomfort of the nose. Also, remembering the microbic origin of the disease, gargling and nasal syringing should be repeated at intervals. As soon as the attack shows signs of subsiding, a good tonic and, still better, a change of air are very helpful.

The term catarrh is used in medical nomenclature in a wider sense to describe a state of irritation of any mucous surface in the body, which is accompanied with an abnormal discharge of its natural secretion, hence the terms gastric catarrh, intestinal catarrh, &c.

See also RESPIRATORY SYSTEM: *Pathology*, and DIGESTIVE ORGANS, *Pathology of.*

CATARRHINE APE, the term used to describe those apes which have the nostrils approximated, the aperture pointing downward, and the intervening septum narrow; distinguishing features of both the lower "doglike" apes (Cynomorpha) and the higher "manlike" apes (Anthropomorpha). The Catarrhini are restricted entirely to the Old World, and include the gorilla, the chimpanzee and orang-utan.

CATASTROPHE (Gr. καταστροφή, from καταστρέφειν, to overturn), a term of the ancient Greek drama for the change in the plot which leads up to the conclusion. The word is thus used of any sudden change, particularly of a violent or disastrous nature, and in geology of a cataclysm or great convulsion of the earth's surface.

505

CATAUXI, a numerous cannibal tribe of South American Indians of the Purus river district, Brazil. They are a fine warlike race, with remarkably clear complexions and handsome features; round wrists and ankles they wear rings of twisted hair. They cultivate mandioc, and make pottery and bark canoes.

CATAWBAS (from the Choctaw for "divided"), a tribe of North American Indians of Siouan stock; formerly the dominant people of South Carolina. Some of their divisions extended into North Carolina. They are now almost extinct, but were at one time able to send nearly 2000 "braves" into battle. In the American War of Independence they furnished a valuable contingent to the South Carolina troops. They then occupied a number of small towns on the Catawba river, but they afterwards leased their land and removed to the territory of the Cherokees, with whom they had been formerly at war. There, however, they did not long remain, but returned to a reservation in their original district. Their affinities have not been very clearly made out, and by Albert Gallatin they were grouped with the Cherokees, Choctaws, Muskogees and Natchez. A vocabulary of sixty of their words was published by Horatio Hale in vol. ii. of the *Transactions of the American Ethnological Society* in 1848; and a much fuller list—about 300—collected by Oscar M. Lieber, the geologist, in 1856, made its appearance in vol. ii. of *Collections of the South Carolina Historical Society*, 1858. Of the one hundred Catawbas still said to be surviving, few, if any, can claim to be full-blooded. They are in the Catawba Reservation in York county, South Carolina. The name is familiar in connexion with the white American wine, the praises of which have been sung by Longfellow. The grape from which the wine is obtained was first discovered about 1801, near the banks of the Catawba river, and named by Major Adlum in 1828, but it is now cultivated extensively in Illinois, Ohio and New York, and especially on the shores of Lake Erie.

See also *Handbook of American Indians* (Washington, 1907).

CATCH THE TEN, sometimes Called *Scotch Whist*, a game played with a pack of 36 cards, from ace, king, queen to six in each suit, the ace being highest both in play and cutting. In trumps, however, the knave ranks highest. Any number from two to eight may play. If an even number, partners are cut for; if odd, each plays for himself. An odd number of players sit as they like; four players sit as at whist; six playing in two sides sit so that no two partners shall be next each other; six playing three sides sit so that two opponents shall divide each pair; eight are arranged in alternate pairs. After cutting, the cards are dealt according to the number of players. The last card is turned up for the trump. When five or seven play, the six of spades is usually omitted; when eight play, the four sixes are thrown out. The eldest hand leads any card he chooses and all must follow suit if able, the penalty for a revoke being the loss of the game. The tricks are not kept separate but gathered in by one player for his side. At the end of the deal there are six hands of six cards on the table. The players first play out the first two hands, next the second two and finally the last two, the trump card remaining on the table until the first four hands are played out. The game is 41 points, the object of the play being to win the cards which have a special value. These are, with their values: knave of trumps 11, ace of trumps 4, king of trumps 3, queen of trumps 2, ten of trumps 10. All other cards have no counting value. As the ten can be taken by any other honour the object is to "catch the ten."

CATECHISM (from Gr. κατηχεῖν, teach by word of mouth), a compendium of instruction (particularly of religious instruction) arranged in the form of questions and answers. The custom of catechizing, common to all civilized antiquity, was followed in the schools of Judaism and in the Early Church, where it helped to preserve the Gospel narrative (see CATECHUMEN).

The catechism as we know it is intended primarily for children and uneducated persons. Its aim is to instruct, and it differs from a creed or confession in not being in the first instance an act of worship or a public profession of belief. The first regular catechisms seem to have grown out of the usual oral teaching of catechumens, and to have been compiled in the 8th and 9th centuries. Among them the work of Notker Labeo and of Kero, both monks of St Gall, and that of Ottfried of Weissenburg in Alsace deserve mention. But it is not until the first stirrings of revolt against the hierarchy, which preceded the Reformation, that they became at all widespread or numerous. The Waldenses of Savoy and France, the *Brethren*(small communities of evangelical dissenters from the medieval faith) of Germany, and the*Unitas Fratrum* of Bohemia all used the same catechism (one that was first printed in 1498, and which continued to be published till 1530) for the instruction of their children. It was based on St Augustine's *Enchiridion*, and considers (a) Faith, *i.e.* the Creed, (b) Hope, *i.e.*the Lord's Prayer, and (c) Love, *i.e.* the Decalogue.

The age of the Reformation gave a great stimulus to the production of catechisms. This was but natural at a time when the invention of printing had thrown the Bible open to all, and carried the war of religious opinion from the schools into the streets. The adherents of the "old" and the "new" religions alike had to justify their views to the unlearned as well as to the learned, and to give in simple formulas their reasons for the faith that was in them. Moreover, in the universal unrest and oversetting of all authority, Christianity itself was in danger of perishing, not only as the result of the cultured paganism of the Renaissance, but also through the brutish ignorance of the common folk, deprived now of their traditional religious restraints. To the urgency of this peril the reformers were fully alive; and they sought its remedy in education. "Let the people be taught," said Luther, "let schools be opened for the poor, let the truth reach them in simple words in their own mother tongue, and they will believe."

Catechisms of the Chief Religious Communions.—(a) *Evangelical (Lutheran and Reformed).*—It was the ignorance of the peasantry, as revealed by the horrors of the Peasants' War of 1524-25, and his pastoral visitation of the electorate of Saxony 1525-1527, that drew the above exclamation from Luther, and impelled him to produce his two famous catechisms (1529). In 1520 he had brought out a primer of religion dealing briefly with the Decalogue, the Creed and the Lord's Prayer; and Justus Jonas, Johannes Agricola and other leaders had done something of the same kind. Now all these efforts were superseded by Luther's Smaller Catechism meant for the people themselves and especially for children, and by his Larger Catechism intended for clergy and schoolmasters. These works, which did much to mould the character of the German people, were set among the doctrinal standards of the Lutheran Church and powerfully influenced other compilations. The Smaller Catechism, with the Augsburg Confession, was made the Rule of Faith in Denmark in 1537.

In this same year (1537) John Calvin at Geneva published his catechism for children. It was called *Instruction and Confession of Faith for the Use of the Church of Geneva* (a reprint edited by A. Rilliet and T. Dufour Was published in 1878), and explained the Decalogue, the Apostles' Creed, the Lord's Prayer and the Sacraments. Though it was meant, as he said, to give expression to a simple piety rather than to exhibit a profound knowledge of religious truth, it was the work of a man who knew little of the child mind, and, though it served as an admirable and transparent epitome of his famous *Institutes*, it was too long and too minute for the instruction of children. Calvin came to see this, and in 1542, after his experience in Strassburg, drafted a new one which was much more suitable for teaching purposes, though, judged by modern standards, still far beyond the theological range of childhood. It was used at the Sunday noon instruction of children, on which Calvin laid much stress, and was adopted and similarly used by the Reformed Church of Scotland. The Reformed churches of the Palatinate, on the other hand, used the Heidelberg Catechism (1562-1563), "sweet-spirited, experiential, clear, moderate and happily-phrased," mainly the work of two of Calvin's younger disciples, Kaspar Olevianus and Zacharias Ursinus. The Heidelberg Catechism, set forth by order of the elector, is perhaps the most widely accepted symbol of the Calvinistic faith, and is noteworthy for its 506emphasis on the less controversial aspects of the Genevan theology. As revised by the synod of Dort in 1619, this catechism became the standard of most of the Reformed churches of central Europe, and in time of the Dutch and German Reformed churches of America. Other compilations were those of Oecolampadius (Basel, 1526), Leo Juda (Zürich, 1534), and Bullinger (Zürich, 1555). In France, after Calvin's day, the Reformed church used besides Calvin's book the catechisms of Louis Capell (1619), and Charles Drelincourt (1642), and at the present time Bonnefon's*Nouveau Catéchisme élémentaire* (14th ed., 1900) seems most in favour. In Scotland both Calvin's Geneva Catechism and then the Heidelberg Catechism were translated by order of the General Assembly and annotated. In 1592 these were superseded by that of John Craig, for a time the colleague of John Knox at the High Church, Edinburgh.

Since 1648 the standard Presbyterian catechisms have been those compiled by the Westminster Assembly, presented to parliament in 1647, and then authorized by the General Assembly of the Church of Scotland (July 1648) and by the Scottish parliament (January 1649). The Larger Catechism is "for such as have made some proficiency in the knowledge of the Christian religion," but is too detailed and minute for memorizing, and has never received anything like the reception accorded to the Shorter Catechism, which is "for such as are of weaker capacity." The work was done by a committee presided over first by Herbert Palmer, master of Queens', Cambridge, and then by Anthony Tuckney, master of Emmanuel. The scriptural proof texts were added at the request of the English parliament. In his negotiations with the parliament in 1648 Charles I. offered to license the printing of the catechism, but, as the negotiations were broken off, this was not done. The Shorter Catechism, after a brief introduction on the end, rule and essence of religion, is divided into two parts:—I. The doctrines we are to believe (1) concerning the nature of God, (2) concerning the decrees of God and their execution—(a) in creation and providence, (b) in the covenant of works, (c) in the covenant of grace; II. The duties we are to perform (1) in regard to the moral law, (2) in regard to the gospel—(a) inward duties, *i.e.* faith and repentance, (b) outward duties as to the Word, the sacraments and prayer. It has 107 questions and answers, while that of the Anglican Church has but 24, grouping as it does the ten commandments and also the petitions of the Lord's Prayer, instead of dealing with them singly. Though the Shorter Catechism, closely associated as this has been from the first with Scottish public elementary education, has had very great influence in forming and training the character of Presbyterians in Scotland, America and the British colonies, it is, like most other catechisms drawn up by dogmatic theologians, more admirable as an epitome of a particular body of divinity than as an instruction for the young and the unlearned. Its use is now generally preceded by something more adapted to the child-mind, and this is true also in other communions and in the case of other catechisms.

(b) *Roman Catholic.*—There was no universal catechism published by the Latin Church before the council of Trent, but several provincial councils, *e.g.* in Germany and Scotland (where Archbishop Hamilton's catechism appeared in 1552 and was ordered to be read in church by the parish priest), moved in self-defence along the lines already adopted by the reformers. The council of Trent in 1563 resolved on an authoritative work which was finally carried through by two small papal commissions, and issued in 1566 by Pius V. (Eng. trans, by Donovan, Dublin, 1829). Being uncatechetical in form and addressed to the clergy rather than to the people, it missed its intention, and was superseded by others of less exalted origin, especially by those of the Jesuit Peter Canisius, whose *Summa Doctrinae et Institutionis Christianae* (1554) and its shorter form (1556) were already in the field. The catechisms of Bellarmine (1603) and Bossuet (1687) had considerable vogue, and a summary of the former known as *Schema de Parvo* was sanctioned by the Vatican council of 1870. But the Roman Catholic Church as a whole has never had any one official catechism, each bishop being allowed to settle the matter for his own diocese. In England the Roman Catholic bishops have agreed on the use of what is known as "The Penny Catechism," which is very lucid and well constructed.

(c) *Orthodox Eastern Church.*—Peter Mogilas, metropolitan of Kiev, drew up in 1643 the*Orthodox Confession of the Catholic and Apostolic Eastern Church*. This bulwark against the encroachments of the Jesuits and the Reformed Church was standardized by the synod of

Jerusalem in 1672. A smaller catechism was drawn up by order of Peter the Great in 1723. The catechisms of Levshin Platon (1762) and V.D. Philaret (1839), each in his day metropolitan of Moscow, are bulky compilations which cannot be memorized, though there is a short introductory catechism prefaced to Philaret's volume (Eng. trans, in Blackmore's *Doctrine of the Russian Church*, 1845). These works are not to any extent in the hands of the people, but are used by the Russian clergy and schoolmasters as guides in giving instruction. The Coptic and Armenian churches also have what H. Bonar describes as "mere pretences at catechisms."

(d) *Anglican.*—The catechism of the Church of England is included in the Book of Common Prayer between the Orders for Baptism and Confirmation. It has two parts: (i.) the baptismal covenant, the Creed, the Decalogue and the Lord's Prayer, drawn up probably by Cranmer1 and Ridley in the time of Edward VI., and variously modified between then (1549) and 1661; (ii.) the meaning of the two sacraments, written on the suggestion of James I. at the Hampton Court Conference in 1604 by John Overall, then dean of St Paul's, and afterwards bishop successively of Coventry and Lichfield and of Norwich. This supplement to what had become known as the Shorter Catechism established its use as against the longer one, *King Edward VIth's Catechisme*, which had been drawn up in 1553 by John Ponet or Poynet, bishop of Winchester, and then revised and enlarged in 1570 by Alexander Nowell, Overall's predecessor as dean of St Paul's. The Anglican catechism with occasional modification, especially in the sacramental section, is used not only in the Church of England but in the Episcopal churches of Ireland, Scotland, the British dominions and the United States of America. By the rubric of the Prayer Book and by the 59th canon of 1603 the clergy are enjoined to teach the catechism in church on Sundays and holidays after the second lesson at Evening Prayer. This custom, long fallen into disuse, has largely been revived during recent years, the children going to church for a special afternoon service of which catechizing is the chief feature. Compared with the thoroughness of most other catechisms this one seems very scanty, but it has a better chance of being memorized, and its very simplicity has given it a firm hold on the inner life and conscience of devout members of the Anglican communion throughout the world.

(e) *Other Communions.*—Almost every section of the church, *e.g.* the Wesleyan Methodist, has its catechism or catechisms, but in addition to those already enumerated only a few need be mentioned. The Socinians embodied their tenets in the larger and smaller works drawn up by Fausto Sozzini and Schmalz, and published at Rakow in Poland in 1605;2modern Unitarians have modern catechisms. The Quakers or Friends possess a kind of catechism said to have been written by George Fox in 1660, in which father and son are respectively questioner and answerer, and an interesting work by Robert Barclay, in which texts of Scripture form the replies. Congregationalists for some time used Isaac Watts's *Catechisms for Children and Youth* (1730), since superseded by the manuals of J.H. Stowell, J.H. Riddette and others. In 1898 the National Council of the Evangelical Free Churches in England and Wales published 507an *Evangelical Free Church Catechism*, the work of a committee (convened by Rev. Hugh Price Hughes) comprising Congregationalists, Baptists, Methodists (Wesleyan, Primitive and others), and Presbyterians, and thus representing directly or indirectly the beliefs of sixty or seventy millions of avowed Christians in all parts of the world, a striking example of inter-denominational unity. More remarkable still in some respects is *The School Catechism*, issued in 1907 by a conference of members of the Reformed churches in Scotland, which met on the invitation of the Church of Scotland. In its compilation representatives of the Episcopal Church in Scotland co-operated, and the book though "not designed to supersede the distinctive catechisms officially recognized by the several churches for the instruction of their own children," certainly "commends itself as suitable for use in schools where children of various churches are taught together."

Catechisms have a strong family likeness. In the main they are expositions of the Creed, the Lord's Prayer and the Decalogue, and thus follow a tradition that has come down from the days when Cyril of Jerusalem delivered his catechetical Lectures. Even when (as in the Shorter Westminster Catechism and the School Catechism) the Creed is simply printed as an appendix, or where (as in the Free Church Catechism) it is not mentioned at all, its substance is dealt with. The order in which these three main themes are treated is by no means constant. The Heidelberg and Westminster Catechisms are of a more logical and independent character. The former is based on the Epistle to the Romans, and deals with the religious life as (1) Repentance, (2) Faith, (3) Love. Under these heads it discusses respectively the sin and misery of men, the redemption wrought by Christ (here are included the Creed and the Sacraments), and the grateful service of the new life (the Decalogue).

It may be noted that Sir Oliver Lodge has adopted the catechetical form in his book,*The Substance of Faith Allied with Science* (1907), which is described as "a catechism for parents and teachers."

See Ehrenfeuchter, *Geschichte des Katechismus* (1857); P. Schaff, *History of the Creeds of Christendom* (3 vols., 1876-1877); Mitchell, *Catechisms of the Second Reformation* (1887); C. Achelis, *Lehrbuch der prakt. Theologie* (2 vols., 1898); L. Pullan, *History of the Book of Common Prayer*, pp. 207-208; E.A. Knox, *Pastors and Teachers* (1902), chs. iii. and iv.; W. Beveridge, *A Short History of the Westminster Assembly* (1904), ch. x.

(A. J. G.)

1Cranmer bad published a separate and larger catechism on the basis of the work of Justus Jonas in 1548; note also *Allen's Catechisme, A Christen Instruccion of the Principall Pointes of Christes Religion* (1551).

2A Latin edition in 1609 was dedicated to James I. of England. The British Houses of Parliament passed a resolution ordering all copies of it to be publicly burned, and again in 1652 when another edition appeared. An English translation, probably by John Bidle, was printed in Amsterdam and widely circulated.

CATECHU, or CUTCH (Malay, *kachu*), an extract obtained from several plants, its chief sources being the wood of two species of acacia (*A. catechu* and *A. suma*), both natives of India. This extract is known as black catechu. A similar extract, known in pharmacy as pale catechu (*Catechu pallidum*), and in general commerce as gambir, or *terra japonica*, is produced from the leaves of *Uncaria gambir* and *U. acida*, cinchonaceous plants growing in the East Indian Archipelago. A third product to which the name catechu is also applied, is obtained from the fruits of the areca or betel palm, *Areca catechu*.

Ordinary black catechu is usually imported in three different forms. The first and best quality, known as Pegu catechu, is obtained in blocks externally covered with large leaves; the second and less pure variety is in masses, which have been moulded in sand; and the third consists of large cubes packed in coarse bags. The wood of the two species of *Acacia*yielding catechu is taken for the manufacture when the trees have attained a diameter of about 1 ft. The bark is stripped off and used for tanning, and the trunk is split up into small fragments, which are covered with water and boiled. When the extract has become sufficiently thick it is cast into the forms in which the catechu is found in commerce. Catechu so prepared is a dark brown, or, in mass, almost black, substance, brittle, and having generally a shining lustre. It is astringent, with a sweetish taste. In cold water it disintegrates, and in boiling water, alcohol, acetic acid and strong caustic alkali it is completely dissolved. Chemically it consists of a mixture of a peculiar variety of tannin termed catechu-tannic acid with catechin or catechuic acid, and a brown substance due to the alteration of both these principles. Catechu-tannic acid is an amorphous body soluble in cold water, while catechin occurs in minute, white, silky, needle-shaped crystals, which do not dissolve in cold water. A very minute proportion of quercetin, a principle yielded by quercitron bark, has been obtained from catechu.

Gambir, which is similar in chemical composition to ordinary catechu, occurs in commerce in the form of cubes of about an inch in size, with a pale brown or yellow colour, and an even earthy fracture. For the preparation of this extract the plants above mentioned are stripped of their leaves and young twigs, and these are boiled down in shallow pans. The juice is strained off, evaporated, and when sufficiently concentrated is cast into shallow boxes, where, as it hardens and dries, it is cut into small cubes.

Gambir and catechu are extensively employed in dyeing and tanning. For dyeing they have been in use in India from the most remote period, but it was only during the 19th century that they were placed on the list of European dyeing substances. Catechu is fixed by oxidation of the colouring principle, catechin, on the cloth after dyeing or printing; and treated thus it yields a variety of durable tints of drabs, browns and olives with different mordants (see DYEING). The principal consumption of catechu occurs in the preparation of fibrous substances exposed to water, such as fishing-lines and nets, and for colouring stout canvas used for covering boxes and portmanteaus under the name of tanned canvas. Black catechu is official in most pharmacopoeias except that of Great Britain, in which pale catechu is the official drug. The actions and uses of the two are similar, but black catechu is the more powerful. The dose is from five to twenty grains. The *pulvis catechu compositus* contains catechu and kino, and may be given in doses twice as large as those named. The drug has the actions and uses of tannic acid, but owing to the relative insolubility of catechu-tannic acid, it is more valuable than ordinary tannic acid in diarrhoea, dysentery and intestinal haemorrhage.

CATECHUMEN (Lat. *catechumenus*, Gr. κατηχούμενος, instructed, from κατηχεῖν, to teach orally), an ecclesiastical term applied to those receiving instruction in the principles of the Christian religion with a view to baptism. As soon as Christianity became a missionary religion, it was found necessary to make arrangements for giving instruction to new converts. At the beginning the Apostles themselves seem to have undertaken this duty, and the instruction was apparently given after baptism, for in Acts ii. 41, 42, we are told that "they that gladly received the word were baptized ... and they continued stedfastly in the Apostles' teaching." There are two instances in the New Testament where reference is made to individual instruction in this technical sense. Luke (i. 4) in dedicating the third Gospel to Theophilus tells him that his aim in writing the book was "that thou mightest have certainty in the things in which thou has been instructed" (κατηχήθης) and we are told that Apollos was instructed (κατηχημένος) "in the way of the Lord" (Acts xviii. 25).

With the development of Christianity the instruction became more definite and formal. It is probable that the duty of instructing converts was assigned to "the teachers," who are ranked by Paul immediately after the Apostles and prophets (1 Cor. xii. 28), and occupied an important position in the Christian ministry. In the *Didache*, or Teaching of the Apostles, we have an excellent illustration of the teaching which was given to candidates for baptism in early times. There can be little doubt that the *Didache* was used as a manual for catechumens for several centuries. Athanasius (*Festal Epistles*, 39), for instance, says that "it was appointed by the Fathers to be read by those who are just recently coming to us, and wish to be instructed in the word of godliness" (κατηχεῖσθαι τὸν τῆς εὐσεβείας λόγον). The instruction prescribed by the *Didache* is very largely ethical, and stands in striking contrast to the more elaborate doctrinal teaching which came into vogue in later days. The *Shepherd of Hermas* too is another book which seems to have been used for the purpose of catechesis, for Eusebius says that it "was deemed most necessary for those who have need of elementary instruction" (*Eccles. Hist.* iii. 3-6).

With the rise of theological controversy and the growth of heresy catechetical instruction became of vital importance to the Church, and much greater importance was attached to it. After the middle of the 4th century it was regarded as essential that the candidate for baptism should not only be acquainted with the spiritual truths and ethical demands which form the basis of practical Christianity, but should also be trained in theology and the interpretation of the creeds. Two books have been preserved which throw a striking light upon the transformation which had taken place in the conception of catechesis; (1) the Catechetical Lectures of Cyril of Jerusalem; (2) the *De rudibus Catechizandis* of Augustine. Cyril's Lectures may be termed the *Pearson on the Creed* of the 4th century. He takes each article separately, discusses it clause by clause, explains the meaning of each word, and justifies each statement from Scripture. Augustine's treatise was written at the request of a catechist, named Deogratias, who had asked him for advice. After replying to the question of Deogratias, and giving sundry counsels as to the best method of interesting catechumens, Augustine concludes by giving a model catechetical lecture, in which he covers the whole of biblical history, beginning from the opening chapters of

Genesis, and laying particular stress on the doctrinal parts of Scripture. Cyril and Augustine differ, as we should expect, in the doctrines which they select for emphasis, but they both agree in requiring a knowledge of sound doctrine on the part of the candidates.

In spite of the numerous references to catechumens in Patristic literature, our knowledge of the details of the system is often very deficient, and upon some points there is considerable diversity of opinion amongst experts. The following are the most important questions which come under consideration.

1. *The Classification of Catechumens.*—Bingham and many of the older writers held that there were four classes of catechumens, representing different stages in the process of instruction: (a) "The inquirers" whose interest in Christianity had been sufficiently aroused to make them desire further information, and who received private and individual instruction from the teachers before they were admitted into the second class, (b) "The hearers" (*audientes*), who were admitted into the Church for the purpose of listening to sermons and exhortations, (c) The *prostrati* or *genu flectentes*, who were allowed also to take part in the prayers, (d) The *electi* or *competentes*, who had completed the period of probation and were deemed ready to receive baptism. Modern scholars, however, for the most part, deny that there is sufficient basis to justify this elaborate classification, and think that its advocates have confused the catechumenate with the system of penance. The evidence does not seem to warrant more than two classes, (a) the *audientes*, who were in the initial stages of their training, (b) the *competentes*, who were qualified for baptism.

2. *The Relation of Catechumens to the Church.*—Catechumens were allowed of course to attend church services, but at a certain point were dismissed with the words "Ite catechumeni, missa est." The moment at which the dismissal took place cannot be exactly determined, and it is not clear whether the catechumens were allowed to remain for a portion of the Communion service, and if so, whether as spectators or as partial participants. A passage in Augustine seems to imply that in some way they shared in the Sacrament, "that which they (the catechumens) receive, though it be not the Body of Christ, is yet an holy thing and more holy than the common food which sustains us, because it is a Sacrament" (*De peccatorum meritis*, ii. 42). The explanation of these words has occasioned considerable controversy. Many scholars hold (and this certainly seems the most natural interpretation) that consecrated bread was taken from the Eucharist and given to the catechumens. Bingham, however, maintains that the reference is not to the consecrated bread, but to salt, which was given to them as a symbol "that they might learn to purge and cleanse their souls from sin."

3. *The Duration of the Training.*—Various statements with regard to the duration of the catechumenical training are found in ecclesiastical authorities. The Apostolical Constitutions, for instance, fix it at three years;1 the synod of Elvira at two.2 The references in the Fathers, however, imply that for practical purposes it was limited to the forty days of Lent. Very probably, however, the forty days of actual instruction were preceded by a period of probation.

4. *The Relation between the Catechumenate and Baptism.*—Catechetical instruction was designed as a preliminary to baptism. There were two directions, however, in which this purpose was enlarged: (a) We have no reason to suppose that when infant baptism was introduced, those who had been baptized in infancy were excluded from the catechetical training, or that instruction was deemed unnecessary in their case, though as a matter of fact we have no definite reference to their admission. The custom of postponing baptism, which was very general in the 4th and 5th centuries, probably made such cases more rare than is generally supposed, and so accounts for the absence of any allusion to them in connexion with the catechumenate. (b) We have no reason to suppose that the instruction given in the famous catechetical schools of Alexandria and Carthage was restricted to candidates for baptism. There is no doubt that "catechetical" is used in a much wider sense when applied to the lectures of Origen than when used of the addresses of Cyril of Jerusalem. The "instruction" of Origen was given to all classes of Christians, and not merely to those who were in the initial stages.

5. *Characteristics of the Catechumenical Training.*—Besides instruction there were some other important features connected with the catechumenate. (a) The duty of *confession* was

impressed on the candidates. (b) The ceremony of *exorcism* was often performed in order to free the catechumen from evil spirits. (c) At a certain point in the training the creed and the doctrine of the Sacraments were delivered to the candidates by the bishop with much impressive ceremonial. This teaching constituted the "holy secret" or "mystery" (*disciplina arcani*) of Christianity, and could only be imparted to those who were qualified to receive it. The acquisition of this arcanum was regarded as the most essential element in the catechetical discipline, and marked off its possessors from the rest of the world. There can be little doubt that this conception of the "Holy Secret" came into the Church originally from the Greek mysteries, and that much of the ceremonial connected with the catechumenate and baptism was derived from the same source.

AUTHORITIES.—Cyril, *Catecheses*; Gregory of Nyssa, *Oratio Catechetica*; Chrysostom,*Catecheses ad illuminandos*; Augustine, *De rudibus Catechizandis*; Mayer, *Geschichte des Katechumenats ... in den ersten sechs Jahrhunderten* (1868); S. Cheetham, *The Mysteries, Pagan and Christian.*

(H. T. A.)

1*Apost. Constit.* viii. 2.
2Canon 42.

CATEGORY (Gr.: κατηγορία, "accusation"), a term used both in ordinary language and in philosophy with the general significance of "class" or "group." In popular language it is used for any large group of similar things, and still more generally as a mere synonym for the word "class." The word was introduced into philosophy as a technical term by Aristotle, who, however, several times used it in its original sense of "accusation." He also used the verb κατηγορεῖν, to accuse, in the specific logical sense, to predicate; τὸ κατηγορούμενον becomes the predicate; and κατηγορικὴ πρότασις may be translated as affirmative proposition. But though the word thus received a new signification from Aristotle, it is not on that account certain that the thing it was taken to signify was equally a novelty in philosophy. In fact we find in the records of Oriental and early Greek thought something corresponding to the Aristotelian classification.

Our knowledge of Hindu philosophy, and of the relations in which it may have stood to Greek speculation, scarcely enables us to give decisive answers to various questions that naturally arise on observation of their many resemblances (see **Hindu philosophy.**an article by Richard Garbe in *Monist*, iv. 176-193). Yet the similarity between the two is so striking that, if not historically connected, they must at least be regarded as expressions of similar philosophic needs. The Hindu classification to which we specially refer is that of Kanada, who lays down six categories, or classes of existence, a seventh being generally added by the commentators. The term employed is *Padārtha*, meaning "signification of a word." This is in entire harmony with the Aristotelian doctrine, the categories of which may with truth be described as significations of simple terms, τὰ κατὰ μηδεμίαν συηπλοκὴν λεγόμενα. The six categories of Kanada are Substance, Quality, Action, Genus, Individuality, and Concretion or Co-inherence. To these is added Non-Existence, Privation or Negation. *Substance* is the permanent substance in which *Qualities* exist.*Action*, belonging to or inhering in substances, is that which produces change, *Genus*belongs to substance, qualities and actions; there are higher and lower genera.*Individuality*, found only in substance, is that by which a thing is self-existent and marked off from others. *Concretion* or Co-inherence denotes inseparable or necessary connection, such as that between substance and quality. Under these six classes, γένη τοῦ ὄντος, Kanada then proceeds to range the facts of the universe.1

Within Greek philosophy itself there were foreshadowings of the Aristotelian doctrine, but nothing so important as to warrant the conclusion that Aristotle was directly influenced by it. Doubtless the One and Many, Being and Non-Being, of the*Greek philosophy*Eleatic dialectic, with their subordinate oppositions, may be called categories, but they are not so in the Aristotelian sense, and have little or nothing in common with the later system. Their 509starting-point and results are wholly diverse. Nor does it appear necessary to do more than mention the Pythagorean table of principles, the number of which is supposed to have given rise to the decuple arrangement adopted by Aristotle. The two classifications have nothing in common; no term in the one list appears in the other; and there is absolutely nothing in the Pythagorean principles which could have led to the theory of the categories.2

One naturally turns to Plato when endeavouring to discover the genesis of any Aristotelian doctrine, and undoubtedly there are in the Platonic writings many detached discussions in which the matter of the categories is touched upon. Special *Plato.* terms also are anticipated at various times, *e.g.* ποιότης in the *Theaetetus,* ποιεῖν and πάσχειν in the *Gorgias,* and πρός τι in the *Sophist.* 3But there does not seem to be anything in Plato which one could say gave occasion directly and of itself to the Aristotelian doctrine; and even when we take a more comprehensive view of the Platonic system and inquire what in it corresponds to the widest definition of categories, say as ultimate elements of thought and existence, we receive no very definite answer. The Platonic dialectic never worked out into system, and only in two dialogues do we get anything like a list of ultimate or root-notions. In the *Sophist,* Being, Rest and Motion (τὸ ὄν αὐτὸ καὶ στάσις καὶ κίνησις) are laid down as μέγιστα τῶν γενῶν.4 To these are presently added the Same and the Other (ταὐτόν καὶ θάτερον), and out of the consideration of all five some light is cast upon the obscure notion of Non-Being (τὸ μὴ ὄν). In the same dialogue (262 seq.) is found the important distinction of ὄνομα and ῥῆμα, noun and verb. The *Philebus* presents us with a totally distinct classification into four elements—the Infinite, the Finite, the Mixture or Unity of both and the Cause of this unity (τὸ ἄπειρον, τὸ πέρας, ἡ σύμμιξις, ἡ αἰτία). It is at once apparent that, however these classifications are related to one another and to the Platonic system, they lie in a different field from that occupied by the Aristotelian categories, and can hardly be said to have anything in common with them.

The Aristotelian doctrine is most distinctly formulated in the short treatise Κατηγορίαι, which generally occupies the first place among the books of the *Organon.* The authenticity of the treatise was doubted in early times by some of the *Aristotle.* commentators, and the doubts have been revived by such scholars as L. Spengel and Carl Prantl. On the other hand, C.A. Brandis, H. Bonitz, and Ed. Zeller are of opinion that the tract is substantially Aristotle's. The matter is hardly one that can be decided either *pro* or *con* with anything like certainty; but this is of little moment, for the doctrine of the categories, even of the *ten* categories, does not stand or fall with only one portion of Aristotle's works.

It is surprising that there should yet be so much uncertainty as to the real significance of the categories, and that we should be in nearly complete ignorance as to the process of thought by which, Aristotle was led to the doctrine. On both points It is difficult to extract from the matter before us anything approaching a satisfactory solution. The terms employed to denote the categories have been scrutinized with the utmost care, but they give little help. The most important—κ. τοῦ ὄντος or τῆς οὐσίας, γένη τοῦ ὄντος or τῶν ὄντων, γένη simply, τὰ πρῶτα or τὰ κοινὰ πρῶτα, αἱ πτώσεις, or αἱ διαιρέσεις—only indicate that the categories are general classes into which Being as such may be divided, that they are *summa genera.* The expressions γένη τῶν κατηγορίων and σχήματα τῶν κ., which are used frequently, seem to lead to another and somewhat different view. κατηγορία being taken to mean that which is predicated, γένη τῶν κ. would signify the most general classes of predicates, the framework into the divisions of which all predicates must come. To this interpretation there are objections. The categories must be carefully distinguished from predicables; in the scholastic phraseology the former refer to *first intentions,* the latter to *second intentions, i.e.* the one denote real, the other logical connexion. Further, the categories cannot without careful explanation be defined as predicates; they are this and something more. The most important category, οὐσία, in one of its aspects cannot be predicate at all.

In the Κατηγορίαι Aristotle prefixes to his enumeration a grammatico-logical disquisition on homonyms and synonyms, and on the elements of the proposition, *i.e.* subject and predicate. He draws attention to the fact that things are spoken of either in the connexion known as the proposition, *e.g.* "a man runs," or apart from such connexion, *e.g.* "man" and "runs." He then proceeds, "Of things spoken of apart from their connexion in a proposition (τῶν κατὰ μηδεμίαν συμπλοκὴν λεγομένων), each signifies either Substance (οὐσία), or Quantity (ποσόν), or Quality (ποιόν), or Relation (πρός τι,) or Where (*i.e.* Place, ποῦ), or When (*i.e.* Time, ποτέ), or Position (κεῖσθαι), or Possession (ἔχειν), or Action (ποιεῖν), or Passion (πάσχειν). οὐσία, the first category, is subdivided into πρώτη οὐσία or primary substance, which is defined to be τόδε τι, the singular thing in which properties inhere, and to which predicates are attached, and δεύτεραι οὐσίαι, genera or species which can be predicated of primary substances, and are therefore οὐσία. only in a secondary sense. Nevertheless, they too, after a certain fashion, signify the singular thing, τόδε τι" (K. p. 3 b 12, 13). It is this doctrine of πρώτη οὐσία that has raised doubts with regard to the authenticity of theΚατηγορίαι But the tenfold classification, which has also been captiously objected to, is given in an acknowledged writing of Aristotle's (see *Topica*, i. 9, p. 103 b 20).5 At the same time it is at least remarkable that in two places where the enumeration seems intended to be complete (*Met.* p. 1017 a 25; *An. Pos.* i. 22, p. 83 a 21), only eight are mentioned, ἔχειν and κεῖσθαι being omitted. In other passages6 six, five, four, and three are given, frequently with some addition, such as καὶ αἱ ἄλλαι κ. It is also to be observed that, despite of this wavering, distinct intimations are given by Aristotle that he regarded his list as complete, and he uses phrases which would seem to indicate that the division had been exhaustively carried out. He admits certainly that some predicates which come under one category might be referred to another, but he declines to deduce all from one highest class, or to recognize any relation of subordination among the several classes.

The full import of the categories will never be adequately reached from the point of view taken up in the Κατηγορίαι, which bears all the marks of an early and preliminary study. For true understanding we must turn to the *Metaphysics*, where the doctrine is handled at large. The discussion of Being in that work starts with a distinction that at once gives us a clue. τὸ ὄν is spoken of in many ways; of these four are classified—τὸ ὄν κατὰ συμβεβηκός, τὸ ὄν ὡς ἀληθές, τὸ ὄν δυνάμει καὶ ἐνεργεία, and τὸ ὄν κατὰ τὰ σχήματα τῶν κατηγοριῶν. It is evident from this that the categories can be regarded neither as purely logical nor as purely metaphysical elements. They indicate the general forms or ways in which Being can be predicated; they are determinations of Being regarded as an object of thought, and consequently as matter of speech. It becomes apparent also why the analysis of the categories starts from the singular thing, for it is the primary form under which all that is becomes object of knowledge, and the other categories modify or qualify this real individual. Πάντα δὲ τὰ γιγνόμενα ὑπό τέ τινος γίγνεται καὶ ἔκ τινος καὶ τὶ. Τὸ δὲ τὶ λέγω καθ᾽ ἑκάστην κατηγορίαν· ἢ γὰρ τόδε ἢ ποσὸν ἢ ποιὸν ἢ ποῦ (*Met.* p. 1032 a 13-15).... The categories, therefore, are not logical forms, but real predicates; they are the general modes in which Being may be expressed. The definite thing, that which comes forward in the process from potentiality to full actuality, can only appear and be spoken of under forms of individuality, quality, quantity and so on. The nine later categories all denote entity in a certain imperfect fashion.

The categories then are not to be regarded as heads of predicates, the framework into which predicates can be thrown. They are real determinations of Being—*allgemeine Bestimmtheiten*, as Hegel calls them. They are not *summa genera* of existences, still less are they to be explained as a classification of namable things in general. The objections Mill has taken to the list are entirely irrelevant, and would only have significance if the categories were really—what they are not—an exhaustive division of concrete existences. Grote's view (*Aristotle*, i. 108) that Aristotle drew up his list by examining Various popular propositions, and throwing the different predicates into genera, "according as they stood in different logical relation to the subject," has no foundation. The relation of the predicate category to the subject is not entirely a logical one; it is a relation of real existence, and wants the essential marks of the prepositional form. The logical relations of τὸ ὄν are provided for otherwise than by the categories.

40

Aristotle has given no intimation of the course of thought by which he was led to his tenfold arrangement, and it seems hopeless to discover it. Trendelenburg in various essays has worked out the idea that the root of the matter is to be found in grammatical considerations, that the categories originated from investigations into grammatical functions, and that a correspondence will be found to obtain between categories and parts of speech. Thus, Substance corresponds to noun substantive, Quantity and Quality to the adjective, Relation partly to the comparative degree and perhaps to the preposition, When and Where to the adverbs of time and place. Action to the active, Passion to the passive of the verb, Position (κεῖσθαι) to the intransitive verb, ἔχειν to the peculiar Greek perfect. That there should be a very close correspondence between the categories and grammatical elements is by no means surprising; that the one were deduced from the other is both philosophically and historically improbable. Reference to the detailed criticisms of Trendelenburg by Ritter, Bonitz, and Zeller will be sufficient.

Aristotle has also left us in doubt on another point. Why should there be only *ten* categories? and why should these be the ten? Kant and Hegel, it is well known, signalize as the great defect in the Aristotelian categories the want of a principle, and yet some of Aristotle's expressions would warrant the inference that he *had* a principle, and that he thought his arrangement exhaustive. The leading idea of all later attempts at reduction to unity of principle, 510the division into substance and accident, was undoubtedly not overlooked by Aristotle, and Fr. Brentano7 has collected with great diligence passages which indicate how the complete list might have been deduced from this primary distinction. His tabular arrangements (pp. 175, 177) are particularly deserving of attention. The results, however, are hardly beyond the reach of doubt.

There was no fundamental change in the doctrine of the categories from the time of Aristotle to that of Kant, and only two proposed reclassifications are of such importance as to require notice. The Stoics adopted a fivefold arrangement of*Later Greek.*highest classes, γενικώτατα. τὸ ὄν or τὶ, Being, or somewhat in general, was subdivided into ὑποκείμενα or subjects, ποιά or qualities in general, which give definiteness to the blank subject, πὼς ἔχοντα, modes which further determine the subject, and πὼς ἔχοντα, definite relative modes. These categories are so related that each involves the existence of one higher than itself, thus there cannot be a πρός τι πὼς ἔχον which does not rest upon or imply a πὼς ἔχον, but πὼς ἔχον is impossible without ποιόν, which only exists in ὑποκείμενον, a form or phase of τὸ ὄν.8

Plotinus, after a lengthy critique of Aristotle's categories, sets out a twofold list. τὸ ἕν, κίνησις, στάσις, ταὐτότης, ἑτερότης are the primitive categories (πρῶτα γένη) of the intelligible sphere. οὐσία, πρός τι, ποιά, ποσόν, κίνησις are the categories of the sensible world. The return to the Platonic classification will not escape notice.

Modern philosophy, neglecting altogether the dry and tasteless treatment of the Aristotelian doctrine by scholastic writers, gave a new, a wider and deeper meaning to the categories. They now appear as ultimate or root notions, the metaphysical *Modern philosophy.*or thought elements, which give coherence and consistency to the material of knowledge, the necessary and universal relations which obtain among the particulars of experience. There was thus to some extent a return to Platonism, but in reality, as might easily be shown, the new interpretation was, with due allowance for difference in point of view, in strict harmony with the true doctrine of Aristotle. The modern theory dates in particular from the time of Kant, who may be said to have reintroduced the term into philosophy. Naturally there are some anticipations in earlier thinkers. The Substance, Attribute and Mode of Cartesianism can hardly be classed among the categories; nor does Leibnitz's chance suggestion of a fivefold arrangement into Substance, Quantity, Quality, Action and Passion, and Relations, demand any particular notice. Locke, too, has a classification into Substances, Modes and Relations, but in it he has manifestly no intention of drawing up a table of categories. What in his system corresponds most nearly to the modern view of these elements is the division of kinds of real predication. In all judgments of knowledge we predicate either (1) Identity or Diversity, (2) Relation, (3) Co-existence, or necessary connexion, or (4) Real existence. From this the transition was easy to Hume's important classification of *philosophical relations* into those of Resemblance, Identity, Time and Place, Quantity or Number, Quality, Contrariety, Cause and Effect.

These attempts at an exhaustive distribution of the necessary relations of all objects of knowledge indicate the direction taken by modern thought, before it received its complete expression from Kant.

The doctrine of the categories is the very kernel of the Kantian system, and, through it, of later German philosophy. To explain it fully would be to write the history of that philosophy. The categories are called by Kant Root-notions of the **Kant.**Understanding (*Stammbegriffe des Verstandes*), and are briefly the specific forms of the a priori or formal element in rational cognition. It is this distinction of matter and form in knowledge that marks off the Kantian from the Aristotelian doctrine. To Kant knowledge was only possible as the synthesis of the material or a posteriori with the formal or a priori. The material to which a priori forms of the understanding were applied was the sensuous content of the pure intuitions, Time and Space. This content could not be *known* by sense, but only by intellectual function. But the understanding in the process of knowledge makes use of the universal form of synthesis, the judgment; intellectual function is essentially of the nature of judgment or the reduction of a manifold to unity through a conception. The specific or type forms of such function will, therefore, be expressed in judgments; and a complete classification of the forms of judgments is the key by which one may hope to discover the system of categories. Such a list of judgments Kant thought he found in ordinary logic, and from it he drew up his well-known scheme of the twelve categories. These forms are the determinations of all objects of experience, for it is only through them that the manifold of sense can be reduced to the unity of consciousness, and thereby constituted experience. They are a priori conditions, subjective in one sense, but objective as being universal, necessary and constitutive of experience.

The table of logical judgments with corresponding categories is as follows:—

Judgments.		Categories.
Universal Particular Singular	I. Of Quantity	Unity. Plurality. Totality.
Affirmative Negative Infinite	II. Of Quality	Reality. Negation. Limitation.
Categorical Hypothetical Disjunctive	III. Of Relation	Inherence and Subsistence (Substance and Accident). Causality and Dependence (Cause and Effect). Community (Reciprocity).
Problematic al Assertoric Apodictic	IV. Of Modality	Possibility and Impossibility. Existence and Non-Existence. Necessity and Contingency.

Kant, it is well known, criticizes Aristotle severely for having drawn up his categories without a principle, and claims to have disclosed the only possible method by which an exhaustive classification might be obtained. What he criticized in Aristotle is brought against his own procedure by the later German thinkers, particularly Fichte and Hegel. And in point of fact it cannot be denied that Kant has allowed too much completeness to the ordinary logical distribution of propositions; he has given no proof that in these forms are contained all species of synthesis, and in consequence he has failed to show that in the categories, or pure conceptions, are contained all the modes of a priori synthesis. Further, his principle has so far the unity he claimed for it, the unity of a single function, but the specific forms in which such unity manifests itself are not themselves accounted for by this principle. Kant himself hints more than once at the possibility of a completely rational system of the categories, at an evolution from one single movement of thought, and in his *Remarks on the Table of the Categories* gave a pregnant hint as to the method to be employed. From any complete realization of this suggestion Kant, however, was precluded by one portion of his theory. The categories, although the necessary conditions under which alone an object of experience can be thrown, are merely forms of the mind's own activity; they apply only to sensuous and consequently subjective material. Outside of and beyond them lies the thing-in-itself, which to Kant represented the ultimately real. This subjectivism was a distinct hiatus in the Kantian system, and against it principally Fichte and Hegel directed criticism. It was manifest that at the root of the whole *Fichte.* system of categories there lay the synthetizing unity of self-consciousness, and it was upon this unity that Fichte fixed as giving the possibility of a more complete and rigorous deduction of the pure notions of the understanding. Without the act of the Ego, whereby it is self-conscious, there could be no knowledge, and this primitive act or function must be, he saw, the *position* or affirmation of itself by the Ego. The first principle then must be that the Ego posits itself as the Ego, that Ego = Ego, a principle which is unconditioned both in form and matter, and therefore capable of standing absolutely first, of being the *prius* in a system. Metaphysically regarded this act of self-position yields the categories of Reality. But, so far as matter is concerned, there cannot be affirmation without negation, *omnis determinatio est negatio.* The determination of the Ego presupposes or involves the Non-Ego. The form of the proposition in which this second act takes to itself expression, the Ego is not = Not-Ego, is unconditioned, not derivable from the first. It is the absolute antithesis to the primitive thesis. The category of Negation is the result of this second act. From these two propositions, involving absolutely opposed and mutually destructive elements, there results a third which reconciles both in a higher synthesis. The notion in this third is determination or limitation; the Ego and Non-Ego limit, and are opposed to one another. From these three positions Fichte proceeds to evolve the categories by a series of thesis, antithesis and synthesis.

In thus seizing upon the unity of self-consciousness as the origin for systematic development, Fichte has clearly taken a step in advance of, and yet in strict harmony with, the Kantian doctrine. For, after all that can be said as to the demonstrated character of formal logic, Kant's procedure was empirical, and only after the list of categories had been drawn out, did he bring forward into prominence what gave them coherence and reality. The peculiar method of Fichte, also, was nothing but a consistent application of Kant's own Remark on the Table of the Categories. Fichte's doctrine, however, is open to some of the objections advanced against Kant. His method is too abstract and external, and wants the unity of a single principle. The first two of his fundamental propositions stand isolated from one another, not to be resolved into a primitive unity. With him, too, the whole stands yet on the plane of subjectivity. He speaks, indeed, of the universal Ego as distinct from the empirical self-consciousness; but the universal does not rise with him to concrete spirit. Nevertheless the *Wissenschaftslehre* contains the only real advance in the treatment of the categories from the time of Kant to that of Hegel.9 This, of 511course, does not imply that there were not certain elements in Schelling, particularly in the *Transcendental Idealism*, that are of value in the transition to the later system; but on the whole it is only in Hegel that the whole matter of the Kantian categories has been assimilated and carried to a higher stage. The Hegelian philosophy, in brief, is a system of the categories; and, as it is not intended here to expound that philosophy, it is impossible to give more than a few general and quite external observations as to the Hegelian mode of viewing these elements of thought. With Kant, as has been seen, the categories were still subjective, not as being forms of the individual subject, but as having over against them the world of *noumena* to which they were inapplicable. Self-consciousness, which was, even with Kant, the *nodus* or kernel whence the categories sprang, was nothing but a logical centre,—the reality was concealed. There was thus a dualism, to overcome which is the first step in the Hegelian system. The principle, if there is to be one, must be universally applicable, all-comprehensive. Self-consciousness is precisely the principle wanted; it is a unity, an identity, containing in itself a multiplicity. The universal in absolute self-consciousness is just pure thinking, which in systematic evolution is the categories; the particular is the natural or multiform, the external as such; the concrete of both is spirit, or self-consciousness come to itself. The same law that obtains among the categories is found adequate to an explanation of the external thing which had so sadly troubled Kant. The categories themselves are moments of the universal of thought, type forms, or definite aspects which thought assumes; determinations, *Bestimmungen*, as Hegel most frequently calls them. They evolve by the same law that was found to be the essence of ultimate reality—*i.e.* of self-consciousness. The complete system is pure thought, the Universal *par excellence*.

After the Hegelian there can hardly be said to have been a philosophical treatment of the categories in Germany which is not more or less a criticism of that system. It does not seem necessary to mention the unimportant modifications introduced by Kuno Fischer, J.E. Erdmann, or others belonging to the school. In the strongly-opposed philosophy of J.F. Herbart the categories can hardly be said to hold a prominent place. They are, with him, the most general notions which are psychologically formed, and he classifies them as follows:— (1) Thing, either as product of thought or as given in experience; (2) Property, either qualitative or quantitative; (3) Relation; (4) The Negated. Along with these he posits as categories of inner process—(1) Sensation, (2) Cognition, (3) Will, (4) Action. Joh. Fr. L. George (1811-1873),10 who in the main follows Schleiermacher, draws out a table of categories which shows, in some points, traces of Herbartian influence. His arrangement by enneads, or series of nine, is fanciful, and wanting in inner principle.

The most imposing of more recent attempts at a reconstruction of the categories is that of F.A. Trendelenburg. To him the first principle, or primitive reality, is Motion, which is both real as external movement, and ideal as inner construction. **Trendelenburg.** The necessary conditions of Motion are Time and Space, which are both subjective and objective. From this point onwards are developed the mathematical (point, line, &c.) and real (causality, substance, quantity, quality, &c.) categories which appear as involved in the notion of motion. Matter cannot be regarded as a product of motion; it is the condition of motion, we must think something moved. All these categories, "under the presupposition of motion as the first energy of thought, are ideal and subjective relations; as also, under the presupposition of motion as the first energy of Being, real and objective relations."11 A serious difficulty presents itself in the next category, that of End (*Zweck*), which can easily be thought for inner activity, but can hardly be reconciled with real motion. Trendelenburg solves the difficulty only empirically, by pointing to the insufficiency of the merely mechanical to account for the organic. The consideration of Modality effects the transition to the forms of logical thought. On the whole, Trendelenburg's unique fact of motion seems rather a blunder. There is much more involved than he is willing to allow, and motion *per se* is by no means adequate to self-consciousness. His theory has found little favour.

Hermann Ulrici works out a system of the categories from a psychological or logical point of view. To him the fundamental fact of philosophy is the distinguishing activity (*unterscheidende Tätigkeit*) of thought. Thought is only possible **Ulrici.** by distinction, difference. The fixed points in the relations of objects upon which this activity turns are the categories, which may be called the forms or laws of thought. They are the aspects of things, notions under which things must be brought, in order to become objects of thought. They are thus the most general predicates or heads of predicates. The categories cannot be completely gathered from experience, nor can they be evolved a priori; but, by attending to the general relations of thought and its purely indefinite matter, and examining what we must predicate in order to know Being, we may attain to a satisfactory list. Such a list is given in great detail in the *System der Logik* (1852), and in briefer, preciser form in the *Compendium der Logik* (2nd ed., 1872); it is in many points well deserving of attention.

44

The definition of the categories by the able French logician Charles Bernard Renouvier in some respects resembles that of Ulrici. To him the primitive fact is Relation, of which all the categories are but forms. "The categories," he says, "are the *Renouvier, Cousin, Hamilton, Mill.* primary and irreducible laws of knowledge, the fundamental relations which determine its form and regulate its movements." His table and his criticism of the Kantian theory are both of interest.12 The criticism of Kant's categories by Cousin and his own attempted classification are of no importance. Of little more value is the elaborate table drawn out by Sir W. Hamilton.13 The generalized category of the *Conditioned* has but little meaning, and the subordinate categories evolve themselves by no principle, but are arranged after a formal and quite arbitrary manner. They are never brought into connexion with thought itself, nor could they be shown to spring from its nature and relations. J.S. Mill presented, "as a substitute for the abortive classification of Existences, termed the categories of Aristotle," the following as an enumeration of all nameable things:—(1) Feelings, or states of consciousness; (2) The minds which experience these feelings; (3) Bodies, or external objects which excite certain of those feelings; (4) Successions and co-existences, likenesses and unlikenesses, between feelings or states of consciousness.14 This classification proceeds on a quite peculiar view of the categories, and is here presented only for the sake of completeness.

By modern psychologists the subject has been closely investigated. Professor G.F. Stout (*Manual of Psychology*, vol. ii. pp. 312 foll.) defines categories as "forms of cognitive consciousness, universal principles or relations presupposed either in all *Modern psychologists.* cognition or in all cognition of a certain kind." He then treats External (or Physical) Reality, Space, Time, Causality and "Thinghood" from the standpoint of the perceptual consciousness; showing in what sense the categories of causality, substance and the rest exist in the sphere of perception. As contrasted with the ideational, the perceptual consciousness is concerned with practice. Perception tells the child of things as separate entities, not in their ultimate relations as parts of a coherent whole. G.T. Ladd (*Psychology Descriptive and Explanatory*, ch. xxi., on "Space, Time and Causality") defines the categories from the psychological standpoint as "those highly abstract conceptions which the mind frames by reflection upon its own most general modes of behaviour. They are our own notions resulting from co-operation of imagination and judgment, concerning the ultimate and unanalyzable forms of our own existence and development." In other words, the categories are highly abstract, have no content, and are realized as a kind of thinking which has for its object all the other mental processes.

AUTHORITIES.—Besides those quoted above, see Eduard v. Hartmann, *Kategorienlehre* (Leipzig, 1896), and "Begriff der Kategorialfunktion", in *Zeitschr. f. Philos. und phil. Krit.* cxv. (1899), pp. 9-19; E. König in the same periodical cxiii. (1889), pp. 232-279, and cxiv. (1899). pp. 78-105; F.A. Trendelenburg, *Geschichte der Kategorienlehre* (1846); P. Ragnisco *Storia critica delle categorie* (2 vols., Florence, 1871); W. Windelband *Vom System der Kategorien* (Tübingen, 1900); R. Eisler, *Wörterbuch der philosphischen Begriffe* (Berlin, 1899), pp. 400-409; S. Joda, *Studio critico su le categorie* (Naples, 1881); H. Vaihinger, *Die transcendentale Deduktion der Kategorien* (Halle, 1902); H.W.B. Joseph, *Introduction to Logic* (Oxford, 1906), ch. iii.; F.H. Bradley, *Principles of Logic* (1883); B. Bosanquet's *Knowledge and Reality* (1885, 2nd ed. 1892); histories of philosophy. For further authorities see works quoted under ARISTOTLE and KANT, and in J.M. Baldwin's *Dict. Philos. Psych.* vol. iii. pt. 2, p. 685.

(R. AD.; X.)

1For details of this and other Hindu systems see H. T. Colebrooke, *Miscellaneous Essays* (1837; new ed., E. B. Cowell, 1873); H. H. Wilson, *Essays and Lectures on the Religions of the Hindus* (1861-1862); Monier Williams, *Indian Wisdom* (4th ed., 1893); A. E. Gough's *Vaiseshika-Sutras* (Benares, 1873), and *Philosophy of the Upanishads* (London, 1882, 1891); Max Müller, *Sanskrit Literature*, and particularly his appendix to Thomson's *Laws of Thought*.

2The supposed origin of that theory in the treatise περὶ τοῦ παντός, ascribed to Archytas (*q.v.*), has been proved to be an error. The treatise itself dates in all probability from the Neo-Pythagorean schools of the 2nd century A.D.

3Prantl, *Ges. der Logik*, i. 74-75; F.A. Trendelenburg, *Kategorienlehre*, 209. n.

4*Soph.* 254 D.

5Against this passage even Prantl can raise no objection of any moment; see *Ges. der Logik*, i. 206. *n.*

6See Bonitz, *Iridex Aristotelicus, s.v.*, and Prantl, *Ges. der Logik*, i. 207.

7Brentano, *Bedeutung des Seienden nach A.*, pp. 148-178.

8For detailed examination of the Stoic categories, see Prantl, *Ges. d. Logik*, i. 428 sqq.; Zeller, *Ph. d. Griech.* iii. 1, 82, sqq,; Trendelenburg, *Kateg.* p. 217.

9It does not seem necessary to do more than refer to the slight alterations made on Kant's Table of Categories by J.G. von Herder (in the *Metakritik*), by Solomon Malmon (in the*Propadeutik zu einer neuen Theorie des Denkens*), by J.F. Fries (in the *Neue Kritik der Vernunft*), or by Schopenhauer, who desired to reduce all the categories to one—that of Causality. We should require a new philosophical vocabulary even to translate the extraordinary compounds in which K.C.F. Krause expounds his theory of the categories. Notices of the changes introduced by Antonio Rosmini-Serbati, and of Vincenzo Gioberti's remarkable theory, will be found in Ragnisco's work referred to below.

10*System der Metaphysik* (1844).

11*Logische Untersuchungen*, i. 376-377.

12*Essais de critique générale* (2nd ed.), *La Logique*, i. pp. 184, 190, 207-225.

13*Discussions*, p. 577.

14*Logic*, i. 83; cf. Bain, *Ded. Log.*, App. C.

CATENARY (from Lat. *catena*, a chain), in mathematics, the curve assumed by a uniform chain or string hanging freely between two supports. It was investigated by Galileo, who erroneously determined it to be a parabola; Jungius detected Galileo's error, but the true form was not discovered until 1691, when James Bernoulli published it as a problem in the*Acta Eruditorum*. Bernoulli also considered the cases when (1) the chain was of variable density, (2) extensible, (3) acted upon at each point by a force directed to a fixed centre. These curves attracted much attention and were discussed by John Bernoulli, Leibnitz, Huygens, David Gregory and others.

512

The mechanical properties of the curves are treated in the article MECHANICS, where various forms are illustrated. The simple catenary is shown in the figure. The cartesian equation referred to the axis and directrix is $y = c \cosh (x/c)$ or $y = \frac{1}{2}c(e^{x/c} + e^{-x/c})$; other forms are $s = c \sinh (x/c)$ and $y^2 = c^2 + s^2$, s being the arc measured from the vertex; the intrinsic equation is $s = c \tan \psi$. The radius of curvature and normal are each equal to $c \sec^2 \psi$.

The surface formed by revolving the catenary about its directrix is named the*alysseide*. It is a minimal surface, *i.e.* the catenary solves the problem: to find a curve joining two given points, which when revolved about a line co-planar with the points traces a surface of minimum area (see VARIATIONS, CALCULUS OF).

The involute of the catenary is called the *tractory, tractrix* or *antifriction* curve; it has a cusp at the vertex of the catenary, and is asymptotic to the directrix. The cartesian equation is

$$x = \sqrt{(c^2 - y^2)} + \tfrac{1}{2}c \log [\{c - \sqrt{(c^2 - y^2)}\} / \{c + \sqrt{(c^2 + y^2)}\}],$$

and the curve has the geometrical property that the length of its tangent is constant. It is named the tractory, since a weight placed on the ground and drawn along by means of a flexible string by a person travelling in a straight line, the weight not being in this line, describes the curve in question. It is named the antifriction curve, since a pivot and step

46

having the form of the surface generated by revolving the curve about its vertical axis wear away equally (see MECHANICS: *Applied*).

CATERAN (from the Gaelic *ceathairne*, a collective word meaning "peasantry"), the band of fighting men of a Highland clan; hence the term is applied to the Highland, and later to any, marauders or cattle-lifters.

CATERHAM, an urban district in the Wimbledon parliamentary division of Surrey, England, 20 m. S. of London by the South-Eastern & Chatham railway. Pop. (1901) 9486. It lies in a healthy, hilly district, and has grown in modern times from a village into a large residential town. There are large barracks in the neighbourhood, and the Metropolitan lunatic asylum is close to the town.

CATERPILLAR, the popular name of the larva of various insects, particularly of butterflies and moths (see LEPIDOPTERA, HEXAPODA, METAMORPHOSIS). The word appears first in the form *caterpyl* (*Promptorium Parvulorum,* about the middle of the 15th century). This may be the original form, with the addition of *-ar* or *-er*; if so, it represents the O. Fr.*chatepelose* or *chatepeleuse, i.e.* "hairy-cat" (*chat,* cat, and *pelouse,* hairy, Lat. *pilosus*), a name applied to the hairy caterpillar, and also according to Cotgrave to a weevil. The use of "cat" in this connexion is paralleled by the Swiss name for a caterpillar, *teufelskatz,* and the popular English name for the blossom of the willow, "catkin," somewhat resembling a caterpillar (cf. "palmer"); the modern French is *chenille,* Latin *canicula,* a little dog. The termination of the word seems to have been early connected with "piller," a robber, plunderer from the destructive habits of the larva, cf. Joel i. 4—"That which the palmer-worm hath left, hath the locust eaten." The spelling "caterpillar," a 17th century corruption, has been the usual form since Johnson.

CATESBY, ROBERT (1573-1605), English conspirator, son of Sir William Catesby of Lapworth in Warwickshire, a prominent recusant who was a descendant of Sir William Catesby, speaker of the House of Commons in 1484, executed by Henry VII. after the battle of Bosworth, was born in 1573, and entered Gloucester Hall (now Worcester College), Oxford, in 1586. He possessed a considerable estate, and was said to be wild and extravagant in his youth. In 1596 he was one of those arrested on suspicion during an illness of Queen Elizabeth. In 1601 he took part in the rebellion of Essex, was wounded in the fight and imprisoned, but finally pardoned on the payment of an enormous fine, to obtain which he was forced to sell a portion of his property. In 1602 he despatched Thomas Winter and the Jesuit Tesimond *alias* Greenway to Spain to induce Philip III. to organize an invasion of England, and in 1603, after James's accession, he was named as an accomplice in the "Bye Plot." Catesby was a man of great beauty of person, "above 2 yards high," says Father Gerard, "and though slender, yet as well-proportioned to his height as any man one should see." He possessed a clear head and unflinching courage, and with a strong determination and fascinating manner mastered the minds of his associates and overpowered all opposition. He was, however, headstrong, wilful and imprudent, fit for action, but incapable of due deliberation, and entirely wanting in foresight. Exasperated by his personal misfortunes and at the repressive measures under which his co-religionists were suffering, and blinded by a religious zeal which amounted to fanaticism, he was now to be the chief instigator of the famous Gunpowder Plot, which must in any event have brought disaster upon the Roman Catholic cause. The idea of some great stroke seems to have first entered his mind in May 1603. About the middle of January 1604 he imparted his scheme of blowing up the Parliament House to his cousin Thomas Winter, subsequently taking in Guy Fawkes and several other conspirators and overcoming all fears and scruples. But it was his determination, from which he would not be shaken, not to allow warning to be given to the Roman Catholic peers that was the actual cause of the failure of the plot. A fatal mistake had been made in imparting the secret to Francis Tresham (*q.v.*), in order to secure his financial assistance; and there is scarcely any doubt that he was the author of the celebrated letter to his brother-in-law, Lord Monteagle, which betrayed the conspiracy to the government, on the 26th of October. On receiving the news of the letter on the 28th, Catesby exhibited extraordinary coolness and fortitude, and refused to abandon the attempt, hoping that the government might despise the warning and still neglect precautions; and his confidence was strengthened by Fawkes's report that nothing in the cellar had been touched or tampered with. On the 2nd of November his resolution was shaken by Tresham's renewed entreaties that he would flee, and his positive assurance that Salisbury knew everything. On the evening of the 3rd, however, he was again, through Percy's insistence, persuaded to stand firm and hazard the great stroke. The rest of the story is told in the article GUNPOWDER PLOT. Here it need only be said that Catesby, after the discovery of the conspiracy, fled with his fellow-plotters, taking refuge ultimately at Holbeche in Staffordshire, where on the night of the 8th of November he was overtaken and killed. He had married Catherine, daughter of Thomas Leigh of Stoneleigh, Warwickshire, and left one son, Robert, who inherited that part of the family estate which had been settled on Catesby's mother and was untouched by the attainder, and who is said to have married a daughter of Thomas Percy.

CAT-FISH, the name usually applied to the fishes of the family *Siluridae*, in allusion to the long barbels or feelers about the mouth, which have been compared to the whiskers of a cat. The *Siluridae* are a large and varied group, mostly inhabitants of fresh waters; some of them by their singular form and armature are suggestive of the Devonian mailed fishes, and were placed at one time in their vicinity by L. Agassiz. Even such authorities as T.H. Huxley and E.D. Cope were inclined to ascribe ganoid affinities to the *Siluridae*; but this view has gradually lost ground, and most modern ichthyologists, if not all, have adopted the conclusions of M. Sagemehl, who has placed the *Siluridae* near the carps and Characinids in the group Ostariophysi. The Silurids and Cyprinids may be regarded as two parallel series derived from some common stock which cannot have been very different from the existing Characinids. In spite of the archaic appearance of some of its members, the family *Siluridae*does not appear to extend far back in time, its oldest known representative being the*Bucklandium diluvii* of the Lower Eocene (London Clay) of Sheppey. A great number of forms were placed by Cuvier and his successors in the family *Siluridae*, which has since been broken up by T. Gill and other American authors into several families, united under the name of Nematognathi. A middle course appears the more reasonable to the 513present writer, who has divided the *Siluridae* of Cuvier into three families, with the following definitions:—

Siluridae—ribs attached to strong parapophyses; operculum well developed.

Loricariidae—ribs sessile; parapophyses absent; operculum more or less developed.

Aspredinidae—ribs sessile; strong parapophyses; operculum absent.

These three families may be defined among the Ostariophysi by having the parietal bones fused with the supraoccipital, no symplectic, the body naked or with bony scutes, the mouth usually toothed, with barbels, and usually an adipose dorsal fin.

The *Siluridae* embrace more than one thousand species, spread over the fresh waters of all parts of the world, but mostly from between the tropics. They are absent from western Europe and north-west Africa, and from North America west of the Rocky Mountains, but this deficiency has been made good by now, the introduction of *Amiurus nebulosus* and allied species in various parts of continental Europe and California having proved a success. Only a few forms are marine (*Plotosus, Arius, Galeichthys*).

FIG. 1.—The "Wels"
(*Silurus glanis*).

The species which has given the name to the whole family is the "Wels" of the Germans,*Silurus glanis*, the largest European fresh-water fish, inhabiting the greater part of Europe from the Rhine eastwards and north of the Alps. Its head is large and broad, its mouth wide, furnished with six barbels, of which those of the upper jaw are very long. Both jaws and the palate are armed with broad bands of small closely-set teeth, which give the bones a rasp-like appearance. The eyes are exceedingly small. The short body terminates in a long, compressed, muscular tail, and the whole fish is covered with a smooth, scaleless, slippery skin. Specimens of 4 and 5 ft. in length, and of 50 to 80 ℔ in weight, are of common occurrence, and the fish grows to 10 ft., with a weight of 400 ℔, in the Danube. Its food consists chiefly of other bottom-feeding fishes, and in inland countries it is considered one of the better class of food fishes. Stories about children having been found in the stomach of very large individuals are probably inventions. An allied species (*S. aristotelis*) is found in Greece.

The *Clarias* and *Heterobranchus* of Africa and south-eastern Asia have an elongate, more or less eel-shaped body, with long dorsal and anal fins, and are known to be able to live a long time out of water, being provided with an accessory dendritic breathing organ situated above the gills. Some species live in burrows during the dry season, crawling about at night in search of food. The common Nile species, the "Harmoot" (*Clarias lazera*), occurs abundantly in the Lake of Galilee and was included in, if not chiefly aimed at, by the Mosaic law which forbade the Jews to eat scaleless fishes, a prohibition which has been extended to eels in spite of the obvious presence of minute scales in the latter.

The *Saccobranchus* of India and Ceylon, a genus more nearly related to *Silurus*, have also an accessory organ for breathing atmospheric air. It consists of a long sac behind the gill-cavity, extending far back on each side of the body under the muscles.

In the majority of the *Siluridae*, called by A. Gunther the *Proteropterae*, a section extremely numerous in species, and represented throughout the tropics, the dorsal fin consists of a short-rayed and an adipose portion, the former belonging to the abdominal vertebral column; the anal is always much shorter than the tail. The gill-membranes are not confluent with the skin of the isthmus; they have a free posterior margin. When a nasal barbel is present, it belongs to the posterior nostril. This section includes among many others the genus *Bagrus*, of which the bayad (*B. bayad*) and docmac (*B. docmac*) frequently come under the notice of travellers on the Nile; they grow to a length of 5 ft. and are eaten.

Of the "cat-fishes" of North America (*Amiurus*), locally called "bull-heads" or "horned-pouts," with eight barbels, some twenty species are known. Some of them are valued as food, especially one which is abundant in the ponds of New England, and capable of easy introduction into other localities (*A. nebulosus*). Others which inhabit the great lakes (*A. nigricans*) and the Mississippi (*A. ponderosus*) often exceed the weight of 100 ℔ *Platystoma* and *Pimelodus* people the rivers and lakes of tropical America, and many of them are conspicuous in this fauna by the ornamentation of their body, by long spatulate snouts, and by their great size.

The genus *Arius* is composed of a great number of species and has the widest distribution of all Silurids, being represented in almost all tropical countries which are drained by large rivers. Most of the species live in salt water. They possess six barbels, and their head is extensively osseous on its upper surface; their dorsal and pectoral spines are generally developed into powerful weapons. *Bagarius*, one of the largest Silurids of the rivers of India and Java, exceeding a length of 6 ft., differs from *Arius* in having eight barbels and the head covered with skin.

R. Semon has made observations in Queensland on the habits of *Arius australis*, which builds nests in the sandy bed of the Burnett river. These nests consist of circular basin-like excavations about 20 in. in diameter, at the bottom of which the eggs are laid and covered over by several layers of large stones. In the marine and estuarine species of *Arius, Galcichthys* and *Osteogeniosus*, the male, more rarely the female, carries the eggs in the mouth and pharynx; these eggs, few in number, are remarkably large, measuring as much as 17 or 18 millimetres in diameter in *Arius commusonii*, a fish 3 or 4 ft. in length.

The common North American *Amiurus nebulosus* also takes care of its eggs, which are deposited beneath protecting objects at the bottom of the water, failing which both parents join in excavating a sort of nest in the mud. The male watches over the eggs, and later leads the young in great schools near the shore, seemingly caring for them as the hen for her chickens.

FIG. 2.—*Synodonus xiphias.*

In the *Siluridae Stenobranchiae* of Gunther the dorsal fin consists of an adipose portion and a short-rayed fin which belongs to the abdominal vertebral column, and, like the adipose fin, may be sometimes absent. The gill-membranes are confluent with the skin of the isthmus. The Silurids belonging to this section are either South American or African. Among the former we notice specially the genus *Doras*, which is distinguished by having a series of bony scutes along the middle of the side. The narrowness of their gill-openings appears to have developed in them a habit which has excited the attention of all naturalists who have visited the countries bordering upon the Atlantic rivers of tropical America, viz. the habit of travelling during seasons of drought from a piece of water about to dry up to ponds of greater capacity. These journeys are occasionally of such a length that the fish have to travel all night; they are so numerous 514that the Indians fill many baskets of them. J. Hancock supposes that the fish carry a small supply of water with them in their gill-cavity, which they can easily retain by closing their branchial apertures. The same naturalist adds that they make regular nests, in which they cover up their eggs with care and defend them—male and female uniting in this parental duty until the eggs are hatched. *Synodontis* is an African genus and common in the Nile, where the various species are known by the name of "Shal." They frequently occur among the representations of animals left by the ancient Egyptians. The upper part of their head is protected by strong osseous scutes, and both the dorsal and pectoral fins are armed with powerful spines. Their mouth is small, surrounded by six barbels, which are more or less fringed with a membrane or with branched tentacles.

FIG. 3.—-*Malopterurus electricus.*

The curious fact of some species of *Synodontis* having the lower parts darker than the upper, some being whitish above and blackish beneath, appears to be connected with their habit of swimming in a reversed position, the Belly turned upwards. This habit, known to the ancient Egyptians, who have frequently represented them in that attitude, has been described by E. Geoffrey, who says they nearly constantly swim on their back, moving quite freely forwards and sidewards; but if alarmed, they revert to the normal position to escape more rapidly.

The electric cat- or sheath-fishes (*Malopterurus*) have been referred to the same section. Externally they are at once recognized by the absence of a rayed dorsal fin, of which only a rudiment remains as a small interneural spine concealed below the skin. The entire fish is covered with soft, villose skin, an osseous defensive armour having become unnecessary in consequence of the development of a powerful electric apparatus, the strength of which, however, is exceeded by that of the electric eel and the large species of *Torpedo*.

The electric organ of *Malopterurus* differs essentially from that of other fishes provided with such batteries, being part of the tegumentary system instead of being derived from the muscles. It consists of rhomboidal cells of a fine gelatinous substance immediately under the skin. It is put into action by a single ganglionic cell at the anterior extremity of the spinal cord. Contrary to what takes place in other electric fishes, the current proceeds from the head to the tail.

The electric cat-fish, which grows to a length of 3 ft. in the Congo, has a wide distribution in Africa, extending from the Nile to the Zambezi and from the Senegal to the Congo. It was well known to the ancient Egyptians, who have depicted it in their mural paintings and elsewhere, and an account of its electric properties was given by an Arab physician of the 12th century; then as now the fish was known under the suggestive name of *Raad* or *Raash*, which means "thunder."

Günther's *Siluridae Branchicolae* comprise the smallest and least developed members of the family; they are referred to two genera only from South America, *Stegophilus* and *Vandellia*, the smallest of which does not exceed the length of 2 in. Their body is soft, narrow, cylindrical and elongate; the dorsal and anal fins short; the vent far behind the middle of the length of the body; gill-membranes confluent with the skin of the isthmus. Each maxillary is provided with a small barbel; and the gill-covers are armed with short stiff spines. Their small size notwithstanding, these Silurids are well known to the Brazilians, who accuse them of entering and ascending the urethra of persons while bathing, causing inflammation and sometimes death. Some certainly live parasitically in the gill-cavity of large Silurids, and F. Silvestri has observed *Stegophilus insidiosus* to suck the blood in the gills of *Platystoma coruscans*, a Silurid growing to a length of 6 ft.

FIG. 4.—*Callichthys armatus*, from the upper Amazons.

The mailed cat-fish of the South American genus *Callichthys* builds regular nests of grass on leaves, sometimes placed in a hole scooped out in the bank, in which they cover their eggs and defend them, male and female sharing in this parental duty. In the allied *Corydoras* a lengthy courtship takes place, followed by an embrace, during which the female receives the seminal fluid in a sort of pouch formed by the folded membranes of her ventral fins; immediately after, five or six eggs are produced and received in the pouch, to be afterwards carefully placed in a secluded spot. This operation is repeated many times, until the total number of eggs, about 250, have been deposited. In accordance with these pairing habits, the pectoral spines of the male, which are used in amplexation, are larger and stronger than those of the female. These fish are monogamous, and both parents remain by the side of the nest, furiously attacking any assailant.

FIG. 5.—*Loricaria lanceolata*, from the upper Amazons.

The allied family *Loricariidae* is entirely confined to the fresh waters of Central and South America. C.T. Regan, who has recently published an elaborate monograph of them, recognizes 189 species, referred to 17 genera. Many of them are completely mailed; but all have in common a short-rayed dorsal fin, with the 5 15 ventrals below or rarely in front of it. Their gill-openings are reduced to a short slit. The first group of this section comprises alpine forms of the Andes, without any armature, and with a very broad and pendent lower lip. They have been referred to several genera (*Stygogenes, Arges, Brontes, Astroblepus*), but are collectively called "preñadillas" by th natives, who state that they live in subterranean craters within the bowels of the volcanoes of the Andes, and are ejected with streams of mud and water during eruptions. These fishes may, however, be found in surface waters at all times, and their appearance in great quantities in the low country during volcanic eruptions can be accounted for by numbers being killed by the sulphuretted gases which escape during an eruption and by their being swept down with the torrents of water issuing from the volcano. The lowland forms have their body encased in large scutes, either rough, scale-like, and arranged in four or five series (*Chaetostomus*), or polished, forming broad rings round the slender and depressed tail (*Loricaria*, fig. 5). They are mostly of small size.

FIG. 6.—Abdomen of *Aspredo batrachus*, with the ova attached; at *a* the ova are removed, to show the spongy structure of the skin, and the processes filling the interspaces between the ova.

In certain of the mailed genera the secondary sexual differences may be very pronounced, and have given rise to many nominal species. The shape of the snout may differ according to the sex, and its margin may be beset with tentacles in the male, whilst it frequently happens that the head of the latter is margined with spines or bristles which are either absent or considerably shorter in the female.

The *Aspredinidae*, which are also closely related to the *Siluridae*, are represented by four genera and eighteen species from South America. *Aspredo batrachus* (fig. 6), of the Guianas, the largest form, reaching to about a foot in length, deserves notice from the manner in which the female carries her eggs attached to the belly and paired fins, in a single layer, each egg being connected with the skin by a cup-shaped pedunculate base supplied with blood-vessels and coated with a layer of epithelium, the formation of which is still unexplained.

(G. A. B.)

CATGUT, the name applied to cord of great toughness and tenacity prepared from the intestines of sheep, or occasionally from those of the horse, mule and ass. Those of the cat are not employed, and therefore it is supposed that the word is properly *kitgut*, *kit* meaning "fiddle," and that the present form has arisen through confusion with *kit* = cat. The substance is used for the strings of harps and violins, as well as other stringed musical instruments, for hanging the weights of clocks, for bow-strings, and for suturing wounds in surgery. To prepare it the intestines are cleaned, freed from fat, and steeped for some time in water, after which their external membrane is scraped off with a blunt knife. They are then steeped for some time in an alkaline ley, smoothed and equalized by drawing out, subjected to the antiseptic action of the fumes of burning sulphur, if necessary dyed, sorted into sizes, and twisted together into cords of various numbers of strands according to their uses. The best strings for musical instruments are imported from Italy ("Roman strings"); and it is found that lean and ill-fed animals yield the toughest gut.

CATHA, the *khat* of the Arabs, a shrub widely distributed and much cultivated in Arabia and tropical Africa from, Abyssinia to the Cape. The dried leaves are used for the preparation of a kind of tea and also as tobacco. The plant is a member of the natural order *Celastraceae*, a family of shrubs and trees found in temperate and tropical climates and represented in Britain by the spindle-tree (*Euonymus europaeus*).

CATHARS (CATHARI or CATHARISTS), a widespread heretical sect of the middle ages. They were the débris of an early Christianity, scattered in the 10th to 14th centuries over East and West, having their analogues in the Mahommedan world as well. In the East they were called Bogomils (*q.v.*) and Paulicians; in the West, Patarenes, Tixerands (*i.e.* Weavers), Bulgars, Concorricii, Albanenses, Albigeois, &c.; in both, Cathars and Manicheans. This article relates to the Western Cathars, as they appear (1) in the Cathar Ritual written in Provençal and preserved in a 13th-century MS. in Lyons, published by Clédat, Paris, 1888; (2) in Bernard Gui's *Practica inquisitionis haereticae pravitatis*, edited by Canon C. Douais, Paris, 1886; and (3) in the *procès verbal* of the inquisitors' reports. Some were downright dualists, and believed that there are two gods or principles, one of good and the other of evil, both eternal; but as a rule they subordinated the evil to the good. All were universalists in so far as they believed in the ultimate salvation of all men.[1]

Their tenets were as follows:—The evil god, Satan, who inspired the malevolent parts of the Old Testament, is god and lord of this world, of the things that are seen and are temporal, and especially of the outward man which is decaying, of the earthen vessel, of the body of death, of the flesh which takes us captive under the law of sin and desire. This world is the only true purgatory and hell, being the antithesis of the world eternal, of the inward man renewed day by day, of Christ's peace and kingdom which are not of this world. Men are the result of a primal war in heaven, when hosts of angels incited by Satan or Lucifer to revolt were driven out, and were imprisoned in terrestrial bodies created for them by the adversary. But there are also celestial bodies, bodies spiritual and not natural. These the angel souls left behind in heaven, and they are buildings from God, houses not made with hands, tunics eternal. 516Imprisoned in the garment of flesh, burdened with its sin, souls long to be clothed upon with the habitations they left in heaven. So long as they are at home in the body, they are absent from the Lord. They would fain be at home with the Lord, and absent from the body, for which there is no place in heaven since flesh and blood cannot inherit the kingdom of God, nor corruption inherit incorruption. There is no resurrection of the flesh. The true resurrection is the spiritual baptism bequeathed by Christ to the *boni homines*. How shall man escape from his prison-house of flesh, and undo the effects of his fall? For mere death brings no liberation, unless a man is become a new creation, a new Adam, as Christ was; unless he has received the gift of the spirit and become a vehicle of the Paraclete. If a man dies unreconciled to God through Christ, he must pass through another cycle of imprisonment in flesh; perhaps in a human, but with equal likelihood in an animal's body. For when after death the powers of the air throng around and, persecute, the soul flees into the first lodging of clay that it finds.2 Christ was a life-giving spirit, and the *boni homines*, the "good men," as the Cathars called themselves, are his ambassadors. They alone have kept the spiritual baptism with fire which Christ instituted, and which has no connexion with the water baptism of John; for the latter was an unregenerate soul, who failed to recognize the Christ, a Jew whose mode of baptism with water belongs to the fleeting outward world and is opposed to the kingdom of God. It would be interesting to trace Bardesanes and the Syriac Hymn of the Soul in all this.

The Cathars fell into two classes, corresponding to the Baptized and the Catechumens of the early church, namely, the Perfect, who had been "consoled," *i.e.* had received the gift of the Paraclete; and the *credentes* or Believers. The Perfect formed the ordained priesthood, were women no less than men, and controlled the church; they received from the Believers unquestioning obedience, and as vessels of election in whom the Holy Spirit already dwelt, they were adored by the faithful, who were taught to prostrate themselves before them whenever they asked for their prayers. For none but the Consoled had received into their hearts the spirit of God's Son, which cries "Abba, Father." They alone were become adopted sons, and so able to use the Lord's Prayer, which begins, "Our Father, which art in heaven." The Perfect alone knew God and could address him in this prayer, the only one they used in their ceremonies. The mere *credens* could at best invoke the living saint, and ask him to pray for him.

All adherents of the sect seem to have kept three Lents in the year, as also to have fasted Mondays, Wednesdays and Fridays of each week; in these fasts a diet of bread and water was usual. But a *credens* under probation for initiation, which lasted at least one and often several years, fasted always. The life of a Perfect was so hard, and, thanks to the inquisitors, so fraught with danger, that most Believers deferred the rite until the death-bed, as in the early centuries many believers deferred baptism. The rule imposed complete chastity. A husband at initiation left his wife, committing her "to God and the gospel"; a wife her husband. A male Perfect could not lay his hand on a woman without incurring penance of a three-days' fast. All begetting of children is evil, for Adam's chambering with Eve was the forbidden fruit. It is good for a man not to touch a woman; a man's relations with his own wife are merely a means of fornication, and marriage and concubinage are indistinguishable as against the kingdom of God, in which there is no marrying or giving in marriage. Those only have been redeemed from earth who were virgins, undefiled with women. The passages of the New Testament which seem to connive at the married relation were interpreted by the Cathars as spoken in regard of Christ and the church. The Perfect must also leave his father and mother, and his children, for a man's foes are they of his own household. The family must be sacrificed to the divine kinship. He that loveth father or mother more than Christ is not worthy of him, nor he that loveth more his son or daughter. The Perfect takes up his cross and follows after Christ.

Next he must abstain from all flesh diet except fish. He may not even eat cheese or eggs or milk, for they, like meat, are produced *per viam generationis seu coitus*. Everything that is sexually begotten is impure. Fish were supposed to be born in the water without sexual connexion, and on the basis of this old physiological fallacy the Cathars equally with the Catholic framed their rule of fasting. And there was yet another reason why the Perfect should not eat animals, for a human soul might be doing time in its body. Nor might a Perfect or one in course of probation kill anything, for the Mosaic commandment applies to all life. He might not lie nor take an oath, for the precept "Swear not at all" was, like the rest of the gospel, taken seriously. This was the chief of their "anarchist doctrines."[3]

The Cathar rites, which remain to us in a manual of the sect, "recall," says the Abbé Guiraud, no too favourable a witness, "those of the primitive church with a truth and precision the more striking the nearer we go back to the apostolic age." The medieval inquisitor saw in them an aping of the rites of the Catholic church as he knew them; but they were really, says the same authority, "archaeological vestiges (*i.e.* survivals) of the primitive Christian liturgy. In the bosom of medieval society they were the last witness to a state of things that the regular development of Catholic cult had amplified and modified. They resemble the erratic blocks which lost amid alien soils recall, where we find them, the geological conditions of earlier ages. This being so, it is of the deepest interest to study the Cathar cult, since through its rites we can get a glimpse of those of the primitive church, about which want of documents leaves us too often in the dark."

The central Cathar rite was *consolamentum*, or baptism with spirit and fire. The spirit received was the Paraclete derived from God and sent by Christ, who said, "The Father is greater than I." Of a consubstantial Trinity the Cathars naturally had never heard. Infant baptism they rejected because it was unscriptural, and because all baptism with water was an appanage of the Jewish demiurge Jehovah, and as such expressly rejected by Christ.

The *consolamentum* removes original sin, undoes the sad effects of the primal fall, clothes upon us our habitation which is from heaven, restores to us the lost tunic of immortality. A Consoled is an angel walking in the flesh, whom the thin screen of death alone separates from Christ and the beatific vision. The rite was appointed by Christ, and has been handed down from generation to generation by the *boni homines*.

The long probation called "abstinence" which led up to it is a survival of the primitive catechumenate with its scrutinies. The prostrations of the *credens* before the Perfect were in their manner and import identical with the prostrations of the catechumen before the exorcist. We find the same custom in the Celtic church of St Columba. Just as at the third scrutiny the early catechumen passed a last examination in the Gospels, Creed and Lord's Prayer, so after their year of abstinence the credens receives creed and prayer; the allocution with which the elder "handed on" this prayer is preserved, and of it the Abbé Guiraud remarks that, if it were not in a Cathar ritual, one might believe it to be of Catholic origin. It is so Christian in tone, he quaintly remarks elsewhere, that an inquisitor might have used it quite as well as a heretic. In it the Perfect addresses the postulant, as in the corresponding Armenian rite, by the name of Peter; and explains to him from Scripture the indwelling of the spirit in the Perfect, and his adoption as a son by God. The Lord's Prayer is then repeated by the postulant after the elder, who explains it clause by clause; the words *panis 517 superstantialis* being interpreted not of the material but of the spiritual bread, which consists of the Words of Life.

There followed the Renunciation, primitive enough in form, but the postulant solemnly renounced, not Satan and his works and pomp, but the harlot church of the persecutors, whose prayers were more deadly than desirable. He renounced the cross which its priests had signed on him with their chrism, their sham baptisms and other magical rites. Next followed the spiritual baptism itself, consisting of imposition of hands, and holding of the Gospel on the postulant's head. The elder begins a fresh allocution by citing Matt. xxviii. 19, Mark xvi. 15, 16, John iii. 3 (where the Cathars' text must originally have omitted in v. 5

the words "of water and," since their presence contradicts their argument). Acts ix. 17, 18, viii. 14-17, are then cited; also John xx. 21-23, Matt. xvi. 18, 19, Matt. xviii. 18-20, for the Perfect one receives in this rite power to bind and loose. The Perfect's vocation is then defined: he must not commit adultery nor homicide, nor lie, nor swear any oath, nor pick and steal, nor do unto another that which he would not have done unto himself. He shall pardon his wrongdoers, love his enemies, pray for them that calumniate and accuse him, offer the other cheek to the smiter, give up his mantle to him that takes his tunic, neither judge nor condemn. Asked if he will fulfil each of these, the postulant answers: "I have this will and determination. Pray God for me that he give me his strength."

The next episode of the rite exactly reproduces the Roman *confiteor* as it stood in the 2nd century; "the postulant says: '*Parcite nobis*. For all the sins I have committed, in word or thought or deed, I come for pardon to God and to the church and to you all.' And the Christians shall say: 'By God and by us and by the church may they be pardoned thee, and we pray God that he pardon you them.'"

There follows the act of "consoling." The elder takes the Gospel off the white cloth, where it has lain all through the ceremony, and places it on the postulant's head, and the other good men present place their right hands on his head; they shall say the *parcias* (spare), and thrice the "Let us adore the Father and Son and Holy Spirit," and then pray thus: "Holy Father, welcome thy servant in thy justice and send upon him thy grace and thy holy spirit." Then they repeat the "Let us adore," the Lord's Prayer, and read the Gospel (John i. 1-17).

This was the vital part of the whole rite. The *credens* is now a Perfect one. He is girt with the sacred thread round his naked body under the breasts. Where the fear of the persecutor was absent he was also clad in a black gown. The Perfect ones present give him the kiss of peace, and the rite is over. This part of the rite answers partly to the Catholic confirmation of a baptized person, partly to the ordination of a pope of Rome or Alexandria. The latter in being ordained had the Gospel laid on their heads, and the same feature occurs in old Gallican and Coptic rites of ordaining a bishop.

Thus the Cathar ritual, like that of the Armenian dissenters (see PAULICIANS), reflects an age when priestly ordination was not yet differentiated from confirmation. "Is it not curious," says the Abbé Guiraud, "to remark that the essential rite of the *consolamentum* is in effect nothing but the most ancient form of Christian ordination?"

The Cathar Eucharist was equally primitive, and is thus described by a contemporary writer in a 13th-century MS. of the Milan Library:—"The Benediction of bread is thus performed by the Cathars. They all, men and women, go up to a table, and standing up say the 'Our Father.'4 And he who is prior among them, at the close of the Lord's Prayer, shall take hold of the bread and say: 'Thanks be to the God of our Jesus Christ. May the Spirit be with us all.' And after that he breaks and distributes to all. And such bread is called bread blessed, although no one believes that out of it is made the body of Christ. The Albanenses, however, deny that it can be blessed or sanctified, because it is corporeal" (*i.e.* material).

As Tertullian relates in his contemporaries in the 2nd century, so the Cathars would reserve part of their bread of blessing and keep it for years, eating of it occasionally though only after saying the *Benedicite*. The Perfect kept it wrapped up in a bag of pure white cloth, tied round the neck,5 and sent it long distances to regions which through persecution they could not enter. On the death-bed it could even, like the Catholic *Viaticum*, take the place of the rite of *Consolamentum*, if this could not be performed. Once a month this solemn rite of breaking bread was held, the *credentes* assisting. The service was called *apparellamentum*, because a table was covered with a white cloth and the Gospel laid on it. The Perfect were adored, and the kiss of peace was passed round.

The influence of Catharism on the Catholic church was enormous. To counteract it celibacy was finally imposed on the clergy, and the great mendicant orders evolved; while the constant polemic of the Cathar teachers against the cruelty, rapacity and irascibility of the Jewish tribal god led the church to prohibit the circulation of the Old Testament among laymen. The sacrament of "extreme unction" was also evolved by way of competing with the death-bed *consolamentum*.

AUTHORITIES—J.J I. Döllinger, *Beiträge zur Sektengeschichte* (München, 1890); Jean Guiraud, *Questions d'histoire* (Paris, 1906); F.C. Conybeare, *The Key of Truth* (Oxford, 1898);

Henry C. Lea, *History of the Inquisition* (New York, 1888); C. Douais,*L'Inquisition* (Paris, 1906), and his *Les Hérétiques du midi au XIIIe siècle* (Paris, 1891);*Les Albigeois* (Paris, 1879); also *Practica Inquisitionis* (of Bernard Gui or Guidon), (Paris, 1886); L. Clédat, *Le Nouveau Testament, traduit au XIIIe siècle en langue provençale, suivi d'un rituel cathare* (Paris, 1887); E. Cunitz in *Beiträge zu den theol. Wissensch.* (1852), vol. iv.; P. van Limborch, *Liber Sententiarum Inquis. Tholos. 1307-1323* (Amsterdam, 1692); Hahn, *Gesch. der Ketzer im M.A.* (Stuttgart, 1845); Ch. Schmidt, *Histoire et doctrine de la secte des Cathares* (Paris, 1849); A. Lombard,*Pauliciens bulgares et Bons-Hommes* (Geneva, 1879); Fredericq, *Corpus documentorum haer, pravitatis Neerlandicae* (Gent, 1889-1896); Felix Tocco, "Nuovi documenti" in *Archiv. di studi ital.* (1901), and his *L'Eresia nel media evo* (Florence, 1881); P. Flade, *Das romische Inquisitions-verfahren in Deutschland* (Leipzig, 1902); Ch. Molinier, "Rapport sur une mission en Italie," in *Archives scientifiques de Paris*, tom. 14 (1888); C.H. Haskins, "Robert le Bougre," in *American Hist. Rev.* (1902).

(F. C. C.)

1A certain Peter (*Doc. Doat.*, 22, p. 98) declared that could he but get hold of the false and perfidious God of the Catholics who created a thousand men in order to save a single one and damn all the rest, he would break him to pieces and tear him asunder with his nails and spit in his face.

2Here we have a doctrine of metempsychosis which seems of Indian origin (seeASCETICISM). But Julius Caesar (*de B.G.* vi. 13) attests this belief among the ancient Druids of Gaul.

3The Abbé Guiraud remarks that in refusing to take oaths the Cathars "contraried the social principles on which the constitutions of all states repose," and congratulates himself that society is not yet so thoroughly "laicized" as to have given up oaths in the most important acts of social life.

4Cf. S. Gregorii *Ep.* ix. 12 (26): "Mos apostolorum fuit ut ad ipsam solummodo orationem oblationis hostiam consecrarent." ("The custom of the apostles was to use no other prayer but the Lord's in consecrating the host of the offering.")

5Cf. Duchesne, *Origines*, ed. 1898, p. 177.

CATHAY, the name by which China (*q.v.*) was known to medieval Europe and is still occasionally referred to in poetry, as in Tennyson's "Better fifty years of Europe than a cycle of Cathay." It is derived from Khitāī, or Khitāt, the name which was properly that of the kingdom established by the Khitān conquerors in the northern provinces of China about A.D.907, which after the fall of this dynasty in 1125 remained attached to their former territory, and was subsequently applied by the nations of Central Asia to the whole of China. Thus "Kitai" is still the Russian name for China. The name penetrated to Europe in the 13th century with the fame of the conquests of Jenghiz Khan. After the discovery of southern China by European navigators Cathay was erroneously believed to be a country to the north of China, and it was the desire to reach it that sent the English adventurers of the 16th century in search of the north-east passage.

CATHCART, SIR GEORGE (1794-1854), English soldier, third son of the 1st Earl Cathcart, was born in London on the 12th of May 1794. He was educated at Eton and Edinburgh University. In 1810 he entered the army, and two years later accompanied his father to Russia as aide-de-camp. With him he joined the Russian headquarters in March 1813; and he was present at all the great battles of that year in Germany, and of the following year in France, and also at the taking of Paris. The fruits of his careful observation and critical study of these operations appeared in the *Commentaries* on the war in Russia and Germany 1812-1813, a plain soldier-like history, which he published in 1850. After the peace of 1814 he accompanied his father to the congress of Vienna. He was present at Quatre Bras and at Waterloo, as an aide-de-camp to the duke of Wellington, and remained on the staff till the army of occupation quitted France. 518Reappointed almost immediately, he accompanied the duke to the congresses of Aix-la-Chapelle and Verona, and in 1826 to Prussia. Promoted lieutenant-colonel in 1826, he was placed on half-pay in 1834. He was recalled to active service in 1838, and sent as commander of the King's Dragoon Guards to Canada, where he played an important part in suppressing the rebellion and pacifying the country. In 1844 he returned to England, and two years later was appointed deputy-lieutenant of the Tower, a post which he held up to the time of his promotion to major-general in 1851. In March 1852 he succeeded Sir Harry Smith as governor and commander-in-chief at the Cape, and brought the Kaffir war, then in progress, to a successful conclusion. He promulgated the first constitution of Cape Colony, and conducted operations against the Basuto. Cathcart was made a K.C.B. and received the thanks of both Houses for his services (1853). In December 1853 he was made adjutant-general of the army, but never entered upon his duties, being sent out to the Crimean War as soon as he arrived in England. He was even given a dormant commission entitling him to the chief command in case of accident to Lord Raglan, and the highest hopes were fixed on him as a scientific and experienced soldier. But these hopes were not to be fulfilled; for he fell at the battle of Inkerman (November 5, 1854). His remains, with those of other officers, were buried on Cathcart's Hill. Sir George Cathcart married in 1824 Lady Georgiana Greville, who survived him, and by whom he had a family.

See *Colburn's United Service Magazine*, January 1855; *Correspondence of the Hon. Sir George Cathcart relative to Kaffraria* (1856); A.W. Kinglake's *Invasion of the Crimea*, vol. v.

CATHCART, WILLIAM SCHAW CATHCART, 1ST EARL (1755-1843), English soldier and diplomatist, was born at Petersham on the 17th of September 1755, and educated at Eton. In 1771 he went to St Petersburg, where his father, Charles, 9th Baron Cathcart (1721-1776), a general in the army, was ambassador. From 1773 to 1777 he studied law, but after succeeding to the barony in 1776 he obtained a commission in the cavalry. Proceeding to America in 1777, he had before the close of his first campaign twice won promotion on the field of battle. In 1778 he further distinguished himself in outpost work, and at the battle of Monmouth he commanded an irregular corps, the "British Legion," with conspicuous success; for a time also he acted as quartermaster-general to the forces in America. He returned home in 1780, and in February 1781 was made captain and lieutenant-colonel in the Coldstream Guards. He was elected a representative peer for Scotland in 1788, and in 1792 he became colonel of the 29th foot. He served with distinction in the campaigns in the Low Countries, 1793-1795, in the course of which he was promoted major-general; and in 1801 he was made a lieutenant-general, having in the meanwhile received the appointments of vice-admiral of Scotland (1795), privy councillor (1798), and colonel of the 2nd Life Guards (1797). From 1803 to 1805 Lord Cathcart was commander-in-chief in Ireland, and in the latter year he was sent by Pitt in command of the British expedition to Hanover (seeNAPOLEONIC CAMPAIGNS). After the recall of this expedition Cathcart commanded the forces in Scotland until 1807, when he was placed in charge of the expedition to Copenhagen, which surrendered to him on the 6th of September. Four weeks later he was created Viscount Cathcart of Cathcart and Baron Greenock of Greenock in the peerage of the United Kingdom, resuming the Scottish command on his return from the front. On the 1st of January 1812 he was promoted to the full rank of general, and a few months later he proceeded to Russia as ambassador and military commissioner. In the latter capacity he served with the headquarters of the allies throughout the War of Liberation (1812-1814); his success in the delicate and difficult task of maintaining harmony and devotion to the common cause amongst the generals of many nationalities was recognized after the war by his elevation to the earldom (July 1814). He then went to St Petersburg, and continued to hold the post of ambassador until 1820, when he returned to England. He died at his estate near Glasgow on the 16th of June 1843.

His son, CHARLES MURRAY CATHCART, 2nd earl (1783-1859), succeeded to the title in 1843. He entered the 2nd Life Guards in 1800, and saw active service under Sir James Craig in the Mediterranean, 1805-1806. In 1807 he became known by courtesy Lord Greenock. He took part in the Walcheren expedition of 1809 as a major, and as a lieutenant-colonel served at Barossa, Salamanca and Vittoria. He had already gained staff experience, and he now served under Graham in Holland, 1814, as quartermaster-general. He was present at Waterloo, and for his services received the C.B. and several foreign orders. During the peace he became deeply interested in scientific pursuits, and a new mineral discovered by him in 1841 was named Greenockite. His later military services included the chief command in Canada during a period of grave unrest (1846-1849). He retired from active service in 1850, becoming a full general just before his death. The title passed to his son and grandson as 3rd and 4th earls.

CATHCART, a parish situated partly in Renfrewshire and partly in Lanarkshire, Scotland. The Renfrewshire portion has the larger area (2387 acres), but the smaller population (7375), the area of the Lanarkshire portion being 745 acres and the population (1901) 20,983. The industries include paper-making, dyeing and sandstone quarrying, but limestone and coal have also been worked. The parish includes the town of Cathcart (pop. 4808), and the villages of Old and New Cathcart, but much of it, though outside the city boundaries, is practically continuous with some of the southern suburbs of Glasgow, with which there is communication by electric tram and the Caledonian railway's circular line. The White Cart flows through the parish. In the 12th century Cathcart became a barony of the Cathcarts, who derived the title of their lordship (1460) and earldom (1814) from it. On the Queen's Knowe, a hillock near the ruins of Cathcart Castle, a memorial marks the spot where Queen Mary watched the progress of the battle of Langside (1568), the site of which lies within the parish.

CATHEDRAL, more correctly "cathedral church" (*ecclesia cathedralis*), the church which contains the official "seat" or throne of a bishop—*cathedra*, one of the Latin names for this, giving us the adjective "cathedral." The adjective has gradually, for briefness of speech, assumed the character of a substantive, but though an instance of this (strictly incorrect) use of the word as a substantive has been found as far back as 1587, it became common only at the end of the 18th, or first half of the 19th, century. One of the earliest instances of the term *ecclesia cathedralis* is said to occur in the acts of the council of Tarragona in 516. Another name for a cathedral church is *ecclesia mater*, indicating that it is the mother church. As being the one important church, it was also known as *ecclesia major*. This is the formal expression used by Archbishop Walter Gray of York (1216-1255), and it is preserved in modern times by the name of "*La Majeure*," by which the old cathedral church of Marseilles is popularly known. Again, as the chief house of God, the cathedral church was the *Domus Dei*, and from this name the German *Domkirche*, or *Dom*, is derived, as also the Swedish *Domkyrka*, and the Italian *Duomo*.

History and Organization.—It was early decreed that the *cathedra* of a bishop was not to be placed in the church of a village, but only in that of a city. There was no difficulty as to this on the continent of Europe, where towns were numerous, and where the cities were the natural centres from which Christianity was diffused among the people who inhabited the surrounding districts. In the British islands, however, the case was different; towns were few, and owing to other causes, instead of exercising jurisdiction over definite areas or districts, many of the bishops were bishops of tribes or peoples, as the bishops of the south Saxons, the west Saxons, the Somersaetas and others. The *cathedra* of such a bishop was often migratory, and was at times placed in one church, and then another, and sometimes in the church of a village. In 1075 a council was held in London, under the presidency of Archbishop Lanfranc, which, reciting the decrees of the council of Sardica held in 347 and that of Laodicea held in 360 on this matter, ordered the 519bishop of the south Saxons to remove his see from Selsey to Chichester; the Wilts and Dorset bishop to remove his *cathedra* from Sherborne to Old Sarum, and the Mercian bishop, whose *cathedra* was then at Lichfield, to transfer it to Chester. Traces of the tribal and migratory system may still be noted in the designations of the Irish see of Meath (where the result has been that there is now no cathedral church) and Ossory, the cathedral church of which is at Kilkenny. Some of the Scottish sees were also migratory.

By the canon law the bishop is regarded as the pastor of the cathedral church, the *parochia*of which is his diocese. In view of this, canonists speak of the cathedral church as the one church of the diocese, and all others are deemed chapels in their relation to it.

Occasionally two churches jointly share the distinction of containing the bishop's *cathedra*. In such case they are said to be con-cathedral in relation to each other. Instances of this occurred in England before the Reformation in the dioceses of Bath and Wells, and of Coventry and Lichfield. Hence the double titles of those dioceses. In Ireland an example occurs at Dublin, where Christ Church and St Patrick's are jointly the cathedral churches of that diocese. In France the bishop of Couserans (a see suppressed at the Revolution) had two con-cathedral churches at St Lizier, and the bishop of Sisteron (a see also suppressed) had a second throne in the church of Forcalquier which is still called "La Con-cathédrale." Other instances might be named. In the case of York the collegiate churches of Beverley, Ripon and Southwell were almost in the same position, but although the archbishop had a stall in each he had no diocesan *cathedra* in them, and the chapters were not united with that of the metropolitical church in the direct government of the diocese, or the election of the archbishop, nor had they those other rights which were held to denote the cathedral character of a church.

Cathedral churches are reckoned as of different degrees of dignity: (1) the simple cathedral church of a diocesan bishop, (2) the metropolitical church to which the other diocesan cathedral churches of a province are suffragan, (3) the primatial church under which are ranged metropolitical churches and their provinces, (4) patriarchal churches to which primatial, metropolitical, and simple cathedral churches alike owe allegiance. The title of "primate" was occasionally conferred on metropolitans of sees of great dignity or importance, such as Canterbury, York, Rouen, &c., whose cathedral churches remained simply metropolitical. Lyons, where the cathedral church is still known as "La Primatiale," and Lund in Sweden, may be cited as instances of churches which were really primatial. Lyons had the archbishops of Sens and Paris and their provincial dioceses subject to it till the Revolution, and Lund had the archbishop of Upsala and his province subject to it. As with the title of primate so also that of "patriarch" has been conferred on sees such as Venice and Lisbon, the cathedral churches of which are patriarchal in name alone. The cathedral church of St John Lateran, the cathedral church of the pope as bishop of Rome and patriarch of the West, alone in western Europe possesses potentially a patriarchal character. Its formal designation is *"Patriarchalis Basilica, Sacrosancta Romana Cathedralis Ecclesia Lateranensis."*

The removal of a bishop's *cathedra* from a church deprives that church of its cathedral dignity, although often the name clings in common speech, as for example at Antwerp, which was deprived of its bishop at the French Revolution.

The history of the body of clergy attached to the cathedral church is obscure, and as in each case local considerations affected its development, all that can be attempted is to give a general outline of the main features which were more or less common to all. Originally the bishop and cathedral clergy formed a kind of religious community, which, in no true sense a monastery, was nevertheless often called a *monasterium*. The word had not the restricted meaning which it afterwards acquired. Hence the apparent anomaly that churches like York and Lincoln, which never had any monks attached to them, have inherited the name of minster or monastery. In these early communities the clergy often lived apart in their own dwellings, and were not infrequently married. In the 8th century, however, Chrodegang, bishop of Metz (743-766), compiled a code of rules for the clergy of the cathedral churches, which, though widely accepted in Germany and other parts of the continent, gained little acceptance in England. According to Chrodegang's rule the cathedral clergy were to live under a common roof, occupy a common dormitory and submit to the authority of a special officer. The rule of Chrodegang was, in fact, a modification of the Benedictine rule. Gisa, a native of Lorraine, who was bishop of Wells from 1061 to 1088, introduced it into England, and imposed its observance on the clergy of his cathedral church, but it was not followed for long there, or elsewhere in England.

During the two centuries, roughly bounded by the years 900 and 1100, the cathedral clergy became more definitely organized, and were also divided into two classes. One was that of a monastic establishment of some recognized order of monks, very often that of the Benedictines, while the other class was that of a college of clergy, living in the world, and bound by no vows, except those of their ordination, but governed by a code of statutes or canons. Hence the name of "canon" given to them. In this way arose the distinction between the monastic and secular cathedral churches. In England the monastic cathedral churches were Bath, Canterbury, Carlisle, Coventry, Durham, Ely, Norwich, Rochester, Winchester and Worcester, all of them Benedictine except Carlisle, which was a church of Augustinians. The secular churches were Chichester, Exeter, Hereford, Lichfield, Lincoln, St Paul's (London), Salisbury, Wells, York, and the four Welsh cathedral churches. In Ireland all were secular except Christ Church, Dublin (Augustinian), and Down (Benedictine), and none, even in their earliest days, were ever, it is believed, churches of recognized orders of monks, except the two named. In Scotland St Andrew's was Augustinian, Elgin (or Moray), Glasgow and Aberdeen were always secular, and ordered on the models of Lincoln and Salisbury. Brechin had a community of Culdees till 1372, when a secular chapter was constituted. The cathedral church of Galloway, at Whithorn, of English foundation, was a church of Praemonstratensians. In Germany, as in England, many of the cathedral churches were monastic. In Denmark all seem to have been Benedictine at first, except Borglum, which was Praemonstratensian till the Reformation. The others were changed to churches of secular canons. In Sweden, Upsala was originally Benedictine, but was secularized about 1250, and it was ordered that each of the cathedral churches of Sweden should have a chapter of at least fifteen secular canons. In France monastic chapters were very common, but nearly all the monastic cathedral churches there had been changed to churches of secular canons before the 17th century. One of the latest to be so changed was that of Seez, in Normandy, which was Augustinian till 1547, when Pope Paul III. dispensed the members from their vows, and constituted them a chapter of secular canons. The chapter of Senez was monastic till 1647, and others perhaps even later, but the majority were secularized about the time of the Reformation.

In the case of monastic cathedral churches there were no dignitaries, the internal government was that of the order to which the chapter belonged, and all the members kept perpetual residence. The reverse of this was the case with the secular chapters; the dignities of provost, dean, precentor, chancellor, treasurer, &c., soon came into being, for the regulation and good order of the church and its services, while the non-residence of the canons, rather than their perpetual residence, became the rule, and led to their duties being performed by a body of "vicars," who officiated for them at the services of the church.

Abroad, the earliest head of a secular church seems to have been the provost (*praepositus, Probst*, &c.), who was charged, not only with the internal regulation of the church, and oversight of the members of the chapter and control of the services, but was also the steward or seneschal of the lands and possessions of the church. The latter often mainly engaged his attention, 520to the neglect of his domestic and ecclesiastical duties, and complaints were soon raised that the provost was too much mixed in worldly affairs, and was too frequently absent from his spiritual duties. This led, in many cases, to the institution of a new officer called the "dean," who had charge of that portion of the provost's duties which related to the internal discipline of the chapter and the services of the church. In some cases the office of provost was abolished, but in others it was continued, the provost, who was also occasionally archdeacon as well, remaining head of the chapter. This arrangement was most commonly followed in Germany. In England the provost was almost unknown. Bishop Gisa introduced a provost as head of the chapter of Wells, but the office was afterwards subordinated to the other dignities, and the provost became simply the steward of certain of the prebendal lands. The provost of the collegiate church of Beverley was the most notable instance of such an officer in England, but at Beverley he was an external officer with no authority in the government of the church, no stall in the choir and no vote in chapter. The provost of Eton, introduced by Henry VI., occupied a position most nearly approaching that of a foreign cathedral provost. In Germany and in Scandinavia, and in a few of the cathedral churches in the south of France, the provost was the ordinary head of the cathedral chapter, but the office was not common elsewhere. As regards France, of one hundred and thirty-six cathedral churches existing at the Revolution, thirty-eight only, and those either on the borders of Germany or in the extreme south, had a provost as the head of the chapter. In others the provost existed as a subordinate officer. There were two provosts at Autun, and Lyons and Chartres had four each, all as subordinate officers.

The normal constitution of the chapter of a secular cathedral church comprised four dignitaries (there might be more), in addition to the canons. The dean (*decanus*) seems to have derived his designation from the Benedictine dean who had ten monks under his charge. The dean, as already noted, came into existence to supply the place of the provost in the internal management of the church and chapter. In England the dean was the head of all the secular cathedral churches, and was originally elected by the chapter and confirmed in office by the bishop. He is president of the chapter, and in church has charge of the due performance of the services, taking specified portions of them by statute on the principal festivals. He sits in the chief stall in the choir, which is usually the first on the right hand on entering the choir at the west. Next to the dean (as a rule) is the precentor (*primicerius, cantor*, &c.), whose special duty is that of regulating the musical portion of the services. He presides in the dean's absence, and occupies the corresponding stall on the left side, although there are exceptions to this rule, where, as at St Paul's, the archdeacon of the cathedral city ranks second and occupies what is usually the precentor's stall. The third dignitary is the chancellor (*scholasticus, écolâtre, capiscol, magistral*, &c.), who must not be confounded with the chancellor of the diocese. The chancellor of the cathedral church is charged with the oversight of its schools, ought to read divinity lectures, and superintend the lections in the choir and correct slovenly readers. He is often the secretary and librarian of the chapter. In the absence of the dean and precentor he is president of the chapter. The easternmost stall, on the dean's side of the choir, is usually assigned to him. The fourth dignitary is the treasurer (*custos, sacrista, cheficier*). He is guardian of the fabric, and of all the furniture and ornaments of the church, and his duty was to provide bread and wine for the eucharist, and candles and incense, and he regulated such matters as the ringing of the bells. The treasurer's stall is opposite to that of the chancellor. These four dignitaries, occupying the four corner stalls in the choir, are called in many of the statutes the "*quatuor majores personae*" of the church. In many cathedral churches there were additional dignitaries, as the praelector, subdean, vice-chancellor, succentor-canonicorum, and others, who came into existence to supply the places of the other absent dignitaries, for non-residence was the fatal blot of the secular churches, and in this they contrasted very badly with the monastic churches, where all the members were in continuous residence. Besides the dignitaries there were the ordinary canons, each of whom, as a rule, held a separate prebend or endowment, besides receiving his share of the common funds of the church. For the most part the canons also speedily became non-resident, and this led to the distinction of residentiary and non-residentiary canons, till in most churches the number of resident canons became definitely limited in number, and the non-residentiary canons, who no longer shared in the common funds, became generally known as prebendaries only, although by their non-residence they did not forfeit their position as canons, and retained their votes in chapter like the others. This system of non-residence led also to the institution of vicars choral, each canon having his own vicar, who sat in his stall in his absence, and when the canon was present, in the stall immediately below, on the second form. The vicars had no place or vote in chapter, and, though irremovable except for offences, were the servants of their absent canons whose stalls they occupied, and whose duties they performed. Abroad they were often called demi-prebendaries, and they formed the *bas choeur* of the French churches. As time went on the vicars were themselves often incorporated as a kind of lesser chapter, or college, under the supervision of the dean and chapter.

There was no distinction between the monastic cathedral chapters and those of the secular canons, in their relation to the bishop or diocese. In both cases the chapter was the bishop's *consilium* which he was bound to consult on all important matters and without doing so he could not act. Thus, a judicial decision of a bishop needed the confirmation of the chapter before it could be enforced. He could not change the service books, or "use" of the church or diocese, without capitular consent, and there are many episcopal acts, such as the appointment of a diocesan chancellor, or vicar general, which still need confirmation by the chapter, but the older theory of the chapter as the bishop's council in ruling the diocese has become a thing of the past, not in England only, but on the continent also. In its corporate capacity the chapter takes charge *sede vacante* of a diocese. In England, however (except as regards Salisbury and Durham), this custom has never obtained, the two archbishops having, from time immemorial, taken charge of the vacant dioceses in their respective provinces. When, however, either of the sees of Canterbury or York is vacant, the chapters of those churches take charge, not only of the diocese, but of the province as well, and incidentally, therefore, of any of the dioceses of the province which may be vacant at the same time.

All the English monastic cathedral chapters were dissolved by Henry VIII., and, except Bath and Coventry, were refounded by him as churches of secular chapters, with a dean as the head, and a certain number of canons ranging from twelve at Canterbury and Durham to four at Carlisle, and with certain subordinate officers as minor canons, gospellers, epistolers, &c. The precentorship in these churches of the "New Foundation," as they are called, is not, as in the secular churches of the "Old Foundation," a dignity, but is merely an office held by one of the minor canons.

English cathedral churches, at the present day, may be classed under four heads: (1) the old secular cathedral churches of the "Old Foundation," enumerated in the earlier part of this article; (2) the churches of the "New Foundation" of Henry VIII., which are the monastic churches already specified, with the exception of Bath and Coventry; (3) the cathedral churches of bishoprics founded by Henry VIII., viz. Bristol, Chester, Gloucester, Oxford and Peterborough (the constitution of the chapters of which corresponds to those of the New Foundation); (4) modern cathedral churches of sees founded since 1836, viz. (a) Manchester, Ripon and Southwell, formerly collegiate churches of secular canons; (b) St Albans and Southwark, originally monastic churches; (c) Truro, Newcastle and Wakefield, formerly parish churches, (d) Birmingham and Liverpool, originally district churches. The ruined cathedral church of the diocese of Sodor (*i.e.* the Southern Isles) and Man, at Peel in the latter island, appears never to have had a chapter of clergy attached to it.

521

AUTHORITIES.—Frances, *De ecclesiis cathredralibus* (Venice, 1698); Bordenave,*L'Estat des églises cathédrales* (Paris, 1643); Van Espen, *Supplement III.*, cap. 5; Hericourt, *Les Loix ecclésiastiques de France* (Paris, 1756); *La France ecclésiastique*(Paris, 1790); Daugaard, *Om de Danske Klostre i Middelalderen* (Copenhagen, 1830); Hinschius, *Das Kirchenrecht der Katholiken u. Protestanten in Deutschland,* ii. (Berlin, 1878); Walcott, *Cathedralia* (London, 1865); Freeman, *Cathedral Church of Wells*(London, 1870); Benson, *The Cathedral* (London, 1878); Bradshaw and Wordsworth,*Lincoln Cathedral Statutes* (Camb., 1894).

(T. M. F.)

Architecture.—From the architectural point of view there is no special treatment as regards dimensions or style for a cathedral church other than that required for a church or abbey, as there are cases when the former are comparatively small buildings (like the old cathedral at Athens), and some parish churches and abbeys are larger than many cathedrals. In recent times, indeed, some English abbeys or minsters, such as those of Ripon, Manchester, St Albans and Southwell, partly on account of their dimensions, have been raised to the rank of cathedrals, in consequence of the demand for additional sees; others, such as those of Bristol, Gloucester, Oxford, Chester and Peterborough, became cathedrals only on the dissolution of the monasteries by Henry VIII.

FIG. 1.—Plan of Canterbury Cathedral.

Under the headingsNAVE, AISLE, CHOIR, APSE,CHEVET, and LADY-CHAPEL, the principal arrangements of the plan of a cathedral are dealt with, and its architectural features, such as TOWER and SPIRE, PORCH,TRIFORIUM, CLERESTORY andVAULT, are separately defined; while in the articleARCHITECTURE the evolution of the various styles in England, France, Germany, Italy and Spain, is set forth. It is only necessary here to deal with the development of the eastern end of English and foreign cathedrals, as it was in those that the greatest changes from the middle of the 11th century to the close of the 16th century took place.

The earliest extended development of the eastern end of the cathedral is that which was first set out in Edward the Confessor's church at Westminster, probably borrowed from the ancient church of St Martin at Tours; in this church, dating probably from the 10th century, two new elements are found, (1) the carrying of the choir aisle round a circular apse so as to provide a processional aisle round the eastern end of the church, and (2) five apsidal chapels, constituting the germ of the chevet, which transformed the eastern terminations of the French cathedrals in the 12th and 13th centuries. It is only within recent times that the foundations of the early church at Tours with its choir aisle and chapels have been traced under the existing church. In Edward the Confessor's church (1050) there were probably only three chapels and a processional aisle; in the next example at Gloucester (1089) were also three chapels, two of which, on the north and south sides of the aisle, still remain; the same is found in Canterbury (1096-1107) and Norwich (1089-1119), the eastern chapel in all three cases having been taken down to make way for the Lady-chapel in Gloucester and Norwich, and for the Trinity chapel in Canterbury cathedral (fig. 1). The semicircular aisle is said to have existed in the Anglo-Norman cathedral of Winchester, but the eastern end being square, two chapels were arranged filling the north and south ends, and an apsidal chapel projecting beyond the east wall. This semicircular processional aisle with chevet chapels was the favourite type of plan in the Anglo-Norman cathedrals, and was followed up to about the middle of the 12th century, when the English builders in some cases returned to the square east end instead of the semicircular apsidal termination. The earliest example of this exists in Romsey Abbey (c. 1130), where the processional path crosses behind the presbytery, there being eastern apsidal chapels in the axis of the presbytery aisle and a central rectangular chapel beyond. A similar arrangement is found in Hereford cathedral, and exists in Winchester, Salisbury (fig. 2), Durham, St Albans, Exeter, Ely, Wells and Peterborough, except that in all those cases (except Wells) the eastern chapels are square ended; in Wells cathedral the most eastern chapel (the Lady-chapel) has a polygonal termination; in Durham (fig. 3), the eastern chapels are all in one line, constituting the chapel of the nine altars, which was probably borrowed from the eastern end of Fountains Abbey. It should be noted that in some of the above the original design has been transformed in rebuilding; thus in St Albans, Durham, York and Exeter cathedrals, there was no eastern ambulatory but three parallel apses, in some cases rectangular externally. In Southwell, Rochester, Ely and Chester, there was no processional path or ambulatory round the east end; in Carlisle no eastern chapels; and in Oxford only one central apse. In Ely cathedral (fig. 4) the great central tower built by the first Norman abbot (1082-1094) fell down in 1321, carrying with it portions of the adjoining bays of the nave, transept and choir; instead of attempting to rebuild the tower, 522Alan of Walsingham conceived the idea of obtaining a much larger area in the centre of the cathedral, and instead of rebuilding the piers of the tower he took as the base of his design a central octagonal space, the width of which was equal to that of nave and aisles, with wide arches to nave, transepts and choir, and smaller arches across the octagonal sides; from shafts in the eight pier angles, ribs in wood project forward and carry a smaller octagon on which the lantern rests. Internally the effect of this central octagon is of great beauty and originality, and it is the only instance of such a feature in English Gothic architecture. (See ARCHITECTURE, Plate VIII., fig. 82.)

FIG. 2.—Plan of Salisbury
Cathedral.

From Rickman's *Styles of
Architecture.*

63

FIG. 3.—Plan of Durham
Cathedral.

FIG. 4.—Plan of Ely Cathedral.

The earliest example of the chevet is probably to be found in the church of St Martin at Tours; this was followed by others at Tournus, Clermont-Ferrand, Auxerre, Chartres, Le Mans and other churches built during the great church-building period of the 11th century. In the still greater movement in the 12th century, when the episcopacy, supported by the emancipated communes, undertook the erection of cathedrals of greater dimensions and the reconstruction of others, in some cases they utilized the old foundations, as in Chartres (fig. 5), Coutances and Auxerre cathedrals, while in others (as at Le Mans) they extended the eastern termination, much in the same way as in many of the early examples in England, with this important difference, that when the apsidal east end was given up (about the middle of the 12th century) in favour of the square east end in England, the French, on the other hand, developed it by doubling the choir aisles and adding to the number of extra chapels; thus in Canterbury, Norwich and Gloucester, there were only three apsidal chapels in the chevet, whereas in Noyon (1150), Soissons (1190), Reims (1212), Tours, Seez, Bayeux (1230), Clermont (1275), Senlis, Limoges, Albi and Narbonne cathedrals there were five; in Amiens, Le Mans and Beauvais, there were seven apsidal chapels, and in Chartres cathedral nine. Double aisles round the choir, of which there are no examples in England, are found in the cathedrals of Paris, Bourges and Le Mans; the cathedral of Sens (fig. 6) (1144-1168) possesses one feature which is almost unique, viz. the coupled columns of the alternate bays of nave and choir and of the apse; and these were introduced into the chapel of the Trinity in Canterbury cathedral, probably from the designs of William of Sens, by his successor William the Englishman. The square east end found no favour in France—Laon, Poiters and Dol being the only cathedral examples; and of the triapsal arrangement, viz. with apses in the axes of the choir aisle and a central apse, the only example is that of the cathedral of Autun. The immense development given to the eastern limb of the French cathedrals was sometimes obtained at the expense of the nave, so that, notwithstanding the much greater dimensions compared with English examples, in the latter the naves are much longer and consist of more bays than those in France.

FIG. 5.—Plan of Chartres Cathedral.

In one of the French cathedrals, Bourges, there is no transept; on the other hand there are many examples in which this part of the church is emphasized by having aisles on each side, as at Laon, Soissons, Chartres, Reims, Amiens, Rouen and Clermont cathedrals. Transept aisles in England are found in Ely, York, Wells and Winchester cathedrals, in the last being carried round the south and north ends of the transept; aisles on the east side of the transept only, in some cases probably for 523additional altars, exist in Durham, Salisbury, Lichfield, Peterborough and Ripon cathedrals; and on the north side only in Hereford cathedral. In Rouen cathedral, east of the transept aisles, there are apsidal chapels, which with the three chapels in the chevet make up the usual number. The cathedral of Poitiers has been referred to as an example of a square east end, but a sort of compromise has been made by the provision of three segmental apses, and there are no windows in the east front; the most remarkable divergence from the usual design is found here in the absence of any triforium or clerestory, owing to the fact that the vault of the aisles is nearly as high as that of the nave, so that it constitutes an example of what in Germany (where there are many) are called *Hallen Kirchen*; the light being obtained through the aisle windows only gives a gloomy effect to the nave. Another departure from the usual plan is that found in Albi cathedral (1350), in which there are no aisles, their place being taken by chapels between the buttresses which were required to resist the thrust of the nave vault, the widest in France. The cathedral is built in brick and externally has the appearance of a fortress. In the cathedrals of the south-west of France, where the naves are covered with a series of domes—as at Cahors, Angoulême and St Front de Périgueux— the immense piers required to carry them made it necessary to dispense with aisles. The cathedral of Angoulême (fig. 7) consists of a nave covered with three domes, a transept of great length with lofty towers over the north and south ends, and an apsidal choir with four chevet chapels. In St Front de Périgueux (1150), based on St Mark's at Venice, the plan consists of nave, transept and choir, all of equal dimensions, each of them, as well as the crossing, vaulted over with a dome, while originally there was a simple apsidal choir.

FIG. 6.—Plan of Sens Cathedral.

FIG. 7.—Plan of Angoulême Cathedral.

FIG. 8.—Perspective of Amiens Cathedral.

Returning now to the great cathedrals in the north of France, we give an illustration (fig. 8) of Amiens cathedral (from Viollet le Duc's *Dictionnaire raisonné*) which shows the disposition of a cathedral, with its nave-arches, triforium, clerestory windows and vault, the flying buttresses which were required to carry the thrust of the vault to the outer buttresses which flanked the aisle walls, and the lofty pinnacles which surmounted them. In this case there was no triforium gallery, owing to the greater height given to the aisles. In Notre Dame at Paris the triforium was nearly as high as the aisles; in large towns this feature gave increased accommodation for the congregation, especially on the occasion of great fêtes, and it is found in Noyon, Laon, Senlis and Soissons cathedrals, built in the latter part of the 12th century; later it was omitted, and a narrow passage in the thickness of the wall only represented the triforium; at a still later period the aisles were covered with a stone pavement of slight fall so as to allow of loftier clerestory windows.

The cathedrals in Spain follow on the same lines as those in France. The cathedral of Santiago de Compostela is virtually a copy of St Sernin at Toulouse, consisting of nave and aisles, transepts and aisles, and a choir with chevet of five chapels; at Leon there is a chevet with five apsidal chapels, and at Toledo an east end with double aisles round the apse with originally seven small apsidal chapels, two of them rebuilt at a very late period. At Leon, Barcelona and Toledo the processional passage round the apse with apsidal chapels recalls the French disposition, there being a double aisle around the latter, but in Leon and Toledo cathedrals the east end is masked externally by other buildings, so that the beauty of the chevet is entirely lost. At Avila and Salamanca (old cathedral) the triapsal arrangement is adopted, and the same is found in the German cathedrals, with one important exception, the cathedral of Cologne, which was based on that of Amiens, the comparative height of the former, however, being so exaggerated that scale has been lost, and externally it has the appearance of an overgrown monster.

Under   the   headings VAULT, FLYING BUTTRESS, PINNACLE, CLERESTORY and TRIFORIUM, definitions are given of these chief components of a cathedral or church; but as their design varies materially in almost every example, without a very large number of drawings it would be impossible to treat them more in detail. The perspective view, taken from Viollet le Duc's dictionary, of the interior of the nave of Amiens cathedral illustrates the principal features, viz. the vault (in this case quadripartite, with flying buttresses and pinnacle), the triforium (in this case limited to a narrow passage in the thickness of the wall), and the nave-arches, with the side aisles, beneath the windows of which is the decorative arcade.

(R. P. S.)

CATHELINEAU, JACQUES (1759-1793), French Vendean chieftain during the Revolution, was born at Tin-en-Manges, in the country now forming the department of Maine-et-Loire. He became well known in the country of Anjou, over which he travelled as a pedlar and dealer in contraband goods. His physical strength and his great piety gave him considerable ascendancy over the peasants, who surnamed him "the saint of Anjou." In the first years of the Revolution, Cathelineau listened to the exhortations of Catholic priests and royalist *émigrés*, and joined the insurrection provoked by them against the revolutionary government. Collecting a band of peasants and smugglers, he took the chateau of Gallais, where he captured a cannon, christened by the Vendeans the "Missionary"; he then took the towns of Chemillé, Cholet, Vihiers and Chalonnes (March 1793). His companions committed atrocities which brought upon them terrible reprisals on the part of the 524Republicans. Meanwhile Cathelineau's troops increased, and he combined with the other Vendean chiefs, such as N. Stofflet and Gigot d'Elbée, taking the towns of Beaupréau, Fontenay and Saumur. The first successes of the Vendeans were due to the fact that the Republicans had not expected an insurrection. When the resistance to the insurgents became more serious, differences arose among their leaders. To avoid these rivalries, it is thought that Cathelineau was named generalissimo of the rebels, though his authority over the undisciplined troops was not increased by the new office. In 1793 all the Royalist forces tried to capture Nantes. Cathelineau entered the town in spite of the resistance of General J.B.C. Canclaux, but he was killed, and the Vendean army broke up. Numerous relatives of Cathelineau also perished in the war of La Vendée. His grandson, Henri de Cathelineau, figured in the war of 1870 between France and Germany (see also VENDÉE; CHOUANS).

See C. Port, *Vie de J. Cathelineau* (1882); "La Légende de Cathelineau" in the review*La Révolution française,* vol. xxiv.; *Les Origines de la Vendée* (Paris, 1888, 2 vols.);*Dictionnaire historique de Maine-et-Loire*; Cretineau-Joly, *Histoire de la Vendée militaire,* Th. Muret, *Vie populaire de Cathelineau* (1845).

(R. A.*)

CATHERINE, SAINT. The Roman hagiology contains the record of six saints of this name. 1. ST CATHERINE OF ALEXANDRIA, Virgin and Martyr, whose day of commemoration recurs on the 25th of November, and in some places on the 5th of March. 2. ST CATHERINE OF SWEDEN, a daughter of St Bridget, who died abbess of Watzen in March 1381, and is commemorated on the 22nd of that month. 3. ST CATHERINE OF SIENA, 1347-1380, whose festal day is observed on the 30th of April. 4. ST CATHERINE OF BOLOGNA, 1413-1463, a visionary, abbess of the convent of the Poor Clares in Bologna, canonized by Pope Benedict XIII., and commemorated throughout the Franciscan order on the 9th of March. 5. ST CATHERINE OF GENOA,1 who belonged to the noble family of Fieschi, was born about 1447, spent her life and her means in succouring and attending on the sick, especially in the time of the plague which ravaged Genoa in 1497 and 1501, died in that city in 1510, was beatified by Clement V. in 1675 and canonized by Clement XII. in 1737; her name was placed in the calendar on the 22nd of July by Benedict XIV. 6. ST CATHERINE DE' RICCI, of Florence, daughter of a wealthy merchant prince, was born in 1522, became a nun in the convent of the Dominicans at Prato in 1536, and died in 1589. She was famous during her life-time for the weekly ecstasy of the Passion, during which in a trance she experienced the sufferings of the Holy Virgin contemplating the Passion of her Son. She was canonized in 1746 by Benedict XIV., who fixed her festal day on the 13th of February. In Celtic and English martyrologies (November 25) there is also commemorated St Catherine Audley (c. 1400), a recluse of Ledbury, Hereford, who was reputed for piety and clairvoyance.

Of two of these saints, St Catherine of Alexandria, *the* St Catherine *par excellence,* and St Catherine of Siena, something more must be said. Of the former history has little or nothing to tell. The Maronite scholar, Joseph Simon **St Catherine, virgin and martyr.** Assemani (1687-1768), first identified her with the royal and wealthy lady of Alexandria (Eusebius, *Hist. Eccl.* viii. 14) who, for refusing the solicitations of the emperor Maximinus, was deprived of her property and banished. But Rufinus (*Hist. Eccl.* viii. 17) called this lady Dorothea, and the old Catherine legend, as recorded in the Roman martyrology and by Simeon Metaphrastes, has quite other features. According to it Catherine was the daughter of King Konetos, eighteen years old, beautiful and wise. During the persecution under Maximinus she sought an interview with the emperor, upbraided him for his cruelties, and adjured him to give up the worship of false gods. The angry tyrant, unable to refute her arguments himself, sent for pagan scholars to argue with her, but they were discomfited. Catherine was then scourged and cast into prison, and the empress was sent to reason with her; but the dauntless virgin converted not only the empress but the Roman general and his soldiers who had accompanied her. Maximinus now ordered her to be broken on the wheel; but the wheel was shattered by her touch. The headsman's axe proved more fatal, and the martyr's body was borne by angels to Mount Sinai, where Justinian I. built the famous monastery in her honour. Another development of the legend is that in which, having rejected many offers of marriage, she was taken to heaven in vision and betrothed to Christ by the Virgin Mary.

Of all these marvellous incidents very little, by the universal admission of Catholic scholars, has survived the test of modern criticism. That St Catherine actually existed there is, indeed, no evidence to disprove; and it is possible that some of the elements in her legend are due to confusion with the story of Hypatia (*q.v.*), the neo-platonic philosopher of Alexandria, who was done to death by a Christian mob. To the men of the middle ages, in any case, St Catherine was very real; she was ranked with the fourteen most helpful saints in heaven, and was the constant theme of preachers and of poets. Her festival was celebrated in many places with the utmost splendour, and in certain dioceses in France was a holy day of obligation as late as the beginning of the 17th century. Numberless chapels were dedicated to her, and in nearly all churches her statue was set up, the saint being represented with a wheel, her instrument of torture, and sometimes with a crown and a book. The wheel being her symbol she was the patron saint of wheelwrights and mechanics; as the confounder of heathen sophistry she was invoked by theologians, apologists, preachers and philosophers, and was chosen as the patron saint of the university of Paris; as the most holy and illustrious of Christian virgins she became the tutelary saint of nuns and virgins generally. So late as the 16th century, Bossuet delivered a panegyric upon her, and it was the action of Dom Deforis, the Benedictine editor of his works, in criticizing the accuracy of the data on which this was based, that first discredited the legend. The saint's feast was removed from the Breviary at Paris about this time, and the devotion to St Catherine has since lost its earlier popularity. See Leon Clugnet's article in the *Catholic Encyclopaedia*, vol. iii. (London, 1908).

St Catherine of Siena was the youngest of the twenty-five children of Giacomo di Benincasa, a dyer, and was born, with a twin-sister who did not survive her birth, on the 25th of March 1347. A highly sensitive and imaginative **St Catherine of Siena.** child, she very early began to practise asceticism and see visions, and at the age of seven solemnly dedicated her virginity to Christ. She was attracted by what she had heard of the desert anchorites, and in 1363-1364, after much struggle, persuaded her parents to allow her to take the habit of the Dominican tertiaries. For a while she led at home the life of a recluse, speaking only to her confessor, and spending all her time in devotion and spiritual ecstasy. Her innate humanity and sound sense, however, led her gradually to return to her place in the family circle, and she began also to seek out and help the poor and the sick. In 1368 her father died, and she assumed the care of her mother Lapa. During the following years she became known to an increasingly wide circle, especially as a peacemaker, and entered into correspondence with many friends. Her peculiarities excited suspicion, and charges seem to have been brought against her by some of the Dominicans to answer which she went to Florence in 1374, soon returning to Siena to tend the plague-stricken. Here first she met the Dominican friar, Raimondo of Capua, her confessor and biographer.

The year 1375 found Catherine entering on a wider stage. At the invitation of Piero Gambacorti, the ruler of the republic of Pisa, she visited that city and there endeavoured to arouse enthusiasm for the proposed crusade, urging princes and presidents, commanders and private citizens alike to join in "the holy passage." To this task was added that of trying to keep Pisa and Lucca from joining the Tuscan League against the pope. It was at Pisa, in the church of Santa Cristina, on the fourth Sunday in Lent (April 1), while rapt in ecstasy after the communion, that Catherine's greatest traditional glory befell her, viz. the *stigmata* or impression on her hands, feet and heart, of the wounds corresponding with those received by Christ at his 525crucifixion. The marks, however, were at her prayer not made visible. There is no need to doubt the reality of Catherine's exaltation, but it should be remembered that she and her circle were Dominicans, and that the stigmata of St Francis of Assisi were considered the crowning glory of the saint, and hitherto the exclusive boast of the Franciscans. The tendency observable in many of the austerities and miracles attributed to St Catherine to outstrip those of other saints, particularly Francis, is especially remarkable in this marvel of the stigmata, and so acute became the rivalry between the two orders that Pope Sixtus IV., himself a Franciscan, issued a decree asserting that St Francis had an exclusive monopoly of this particular wonder, and making it a censurable offence to represent St Catherine receiving the stigmata.

In the year 1376, the 29th of Catherine's life, Gregory XI. was living and holding the papal court at Avignon. He was the last of seven French popes in succession who had done so, and had perpetuated for seventy-three years what ecclesiastical writers are fond of terming "the Babylonian captivity of the church." To put an end to this absenteeism, and to bring back the papacy to Italy was the cherished and anxious wish of all good Italians, and especially of all Italian churchmen. Petrarch had urgently pressed Urban V., Gregory's immediate predecessor, to accomplish the desired change; and Dante had at an earlier date laboured to bring about the same object. But these and all the other influences which Italy had striven to bring to bear on the popes had hitherto failed to induce them to return. In these circumstances Catherine determined to try her powers of persuasion and argument, attempting first by correspondence to reconcile Gregory and the Florentines, who had been placed under an interdict, and then going in person as the representative of the latter to Avignon, where she arrived on the 18th of June. Gregory empowered her to treat for peace, but the Florentine ambassadors were first tardy and then faithless. Nothing daunted, Catherine herself besought Gregory, who, indeed, was himself so minded, to return, and he did so, in September (taking the sea route from Marseilles to Genoa), though perhaps intending only to make a temporary stay in Italy. Catherine went home by land and stayed for a month in Genoa with Madonna Orietta Scotti, a noble lady of that city, at whose house Gregory had a long colloquy with her, which encouraged him to push on to Rome. To this year, 1376, belongs the admission to Catherine's circle of disciples of Stefano di Corrado Maconi, a Sienese noble distinguished by a character full of charm and purity, and her healing of the bitter feud between his family and the Tolomei. Another family quarrel, that of the Salimbeni at Rocca D'Orcia, was ended by her intervention in 1377. This year also she turned the castle of Belcaro, which had been given to her, into a monastery.

Meanwhile the returned pope was not having an easy time. Besides perpetuating the strife with his enemies he was alienating his friends, and finding it increasingly difficult to pay his mercenaries. He vented his anger upon Catherine, who reproved him for minding temporal rather than spiritual things, but in the beginning of 1378 sent her on an embassy to Florence and especially to the Guelph party. While she was urging the citizens to make peace with the pope there came the news of his death. During the troubles that ensued in Florence Catherine nearly lost her life in a popular tumult, and sorely regretted not winning her heart's desire, "the red rose of martyrdom." Peace was signed with the new pope, Urban VI., and Catherine, having thus accomplished her second great political task, went home again to Siena. Thence on the outbreak of the schism Urban summoned her to Rome, whither, somewhat reluctantly, she journeyed with her now large spiritual family in November. Once arrived she gave herself heartily to Urban's cause, and wore her slender powers out in restraining his impatient temper, quieting the revolt of the people of Rome, and trying to win for Urban the support of Europe. After prolonged and continual suffering she died on the 29th of April 1380.

Catherine of Siena lived on not only in her writings but in her disciples. During her short course she gathered round her a devoted company of men and women trained to labour for the reformation of the individual, the church and the state. Her death naturally broke up the fellowship, but its members did not cease their activity and kept up what mutual correspondence was possible. Among them were Fra Raimondo, who became master-general of the Dominicans, William Flete, an ascetically-minded Englishman from Cambridge, Stefano Maconi, who joined the Carthusians and ultimately became prior-general, and the two secretaries, Neri di Landoccio and Francesco Malavolti. The last of her band, Tommaso Caffarini, died in 1434, but the work was taken up, though in other shape, by Savonarola, between Francis of Assisi and whom Catherine forms the connecting link.

Catherine's works consist of (1) a treatise occupying a closely-printed quarto volume, which Fra Raimondo describes as "a dialogue between a soul, which asked four questions of the Lord, and the same Lord, who made answer and gave instruction in many most useful truths," (2) letters, and (3) prayers. The dialogue is entitled, *The Book of Divine Doctrine, given in person by God the Father, speaking to the mind of the most glorious and holy virgin Catherine of Siena, and written down as she dictated it in the vulgar tongue, she being the while entranced, and actually hearing what God spoke in her.* The work is declared to have been dictated by the saint in her father's house in Siena, a little before she went to Rome, and to have been completed on the 13th of October 1378. The book opens with a passage on the essence of mysticism, the union of the soul with God in love, and the bulk of it is a compendium of the spiritual teachings scattered throughout her letters. There is more monologue than dialogue. The book has a significant place in the history of Italian literature. "In a language which is singularly poor in mystical works it stands with the *Divina Commedia* as one of the two supreme attempts to express the eternal in the symbolism of a day, to paint the union of the soul with the supra-sensible while still imprisoned in the flesh." The prayers (twenty-six in all) are mostly mystical outpourings repeating the aspirations found in her other writings. Of more interest are the letters, nearly four hundred in number, and addressed to kings, popes, cardinals, bishops, conventual bodies, political corporations and private individuals. Their historical importance, their spiritual fragrance and their literary value combine to put their author almost on a level with Petrarch as a 14th century letter-writer. Her language is the purest Tuscan of the golden age of the Italian vernacular, and with spontaneous eloquence she passes to and fro between spiritual counsel, domestic advice and political guidance.

AUTHORITIES.—The sources for the personal life of Catherine of Siena are (1) the *Vita*or *Legenda*, Fra Raimondo's biography written 1384-1395, first published in Latin at Cologne, 1553, and widely translated; (2) the *Processus*, a collection of testimonies and letters by those of her followers who survived in 1411, and had to justify the reverence paid to the memory of one yet uncanonized; (3) the *Supplementum* to Raimondo's *Vita*, compiled by Tommaso Caffarini in 1414; (4) the *Legenda abbreviata*, Caffarini's summary of the *Vita*, translated into beautiful Italian by Stefano Maconi; (5) the *Letters*, of which the standard edition is that of Girolamo Gigli (2 vols., Siena, 1713, Lucca, 1721). A selection of these has been published in English by V.D. Scudder (London, 1905). A complete bibliography is given in E.G. Gardner's *Saint Catherine of Siena*(London, 1907), a monumental study dealing with the religion, history and literature of the 14th century in Italy as they centre "in the work and personality of one of the most wonderful women that have ever lived."

1See the study in Baron Fr. von Hügel's *Mystical Element in Religion* (1909).

CATHERINE I. (1683-1727), empress of Russia. The true character and origin of this enigmatical woman were, until quite recently, among the most obscure problems of Russian history. It now appears that she came of a Lithuanian stock, and was one of the four children of a small Catholic yeoman, Samuel Skovronsky; but her father died of the plague while she was still a babe, the family scattered, and little Martha was adopted by Pastor Glück, the Protestant superintendent of the Marienburg district. Frau Glück finally rid herself of the girl by marrying her to a Swedish dragoon called Johan. A few months later, the Swedes were compelled by the Russians to evacuate Marienburg, and Martha became one of the prisoners of war of Marshal Sheremetev, who sold her to Prince Menshikov, at whose house, in the German suburb of Moscow, Peter the Great first beheld and made love to her in his own peculiar fashion. After the birth of their first daughter Catherine, Peter made no secret of their relations. He had found, at last, the woman he wanted, and she soon became so indispensable to him that it was a torment to be without her. The situation was regulated by the reception of Martha into the Orthodox Church, when she was rechristened under the name of Catherine Alekseyevna, the tsarevich Alexius being her godfather, by the bestowal upon her of the title *Gosudaruinya* or sovereign (1710), 526and, finally (1711), by her public marriage to the tsar, who divorced the tsaritsa Eudoxia to make room for her. Henceforth the new tsaritsa was her husband's inseparable companion. She was with him during the campaign of the Pruth, and Peter always attributed the successful issue of that disastrous war to the courage and sang-froid of his consort. She was with him, too, during his earlier Caspian campaigns, and was obliged on this occasion to shear off her beautiful hair and wear a close-fitting fur cap to protect her from the rays of the sun.

By the *ukaz* of 1722 Catherine was proclaimed Peter's successor, to the exclusion of the grand-duke Peter, the only son of the tsarevich Alexius, and on the 7th of May 1724 was solemnly crowned empress-consort in the Uspensky cathedral at Moscow, on which occasion she wore a crown studded with no fewer than 2564 precious stones, surmounted by a ruby, as large as a pigeon's egg, supporting a cross of brilliants. Within a few months of this culminating triumph, she was threatened with utter ruin by the discovery of a supposed*liaison* with her gentleman of the bedchamber, William Mons, a handsome and unscrupulous upstart, and the brother of a former mistress of Peter. A dangerously familiar but perfectly innocent flirtation is, however, the worst that can fairly be alleged against Catherine on this occasion. So Peter also seemed to have thought, for though Mons was decapitated and his severed head, preserved in spirits, was placed in the apartments of the empress, she did not lose Peter's favour, attended him during his last illness, and closed his eyes when he expired (January 28, 1725). She was at once raised to the throne by the party of progress, as represented by Prince Menshikov and Count Tolstoy, whose interests and perils were identical with those of the empress, before the reactionary party had time to organize opposition, her great popularity with the army powerfully contributing to her success. The arch-prelates of the Russian church, Theodosius, archbishop of Novgorod, and Theophanes, archbishop of Pskov, were also on her side for very much the same reason, both of them being unpopular innovators who felt that, at this crisis, they must stand or fall with Tolstoy and Menshikov.

The great administrative innovation of Catherine's reign was the establishment of the*Verkhovny Tainy Sovyet*, or supreme privy council, by way of strengthening the executive, by concentrating affairs in the hands of a few persons, mainly of the party of Reform (*Ukaz*ofFebruary 26, 1726). As to the foreign policy of Catherine I. (principally directed by the astute Andrei Osterman), if purely pacific and extremely cautious, it was, nevertheless, dignified, consistent and independent. Russia, by the mere force of circumstances, now found herself opposed to England, chiefly because Catherine protected Charles Frederick, duke of Holstein, and George I. found that the Schleswig-Holstein question might be reopened to the detriment of his Hanoverian possessions. Things came to such a pass that, in the spring of 1726, an English squadron was sent to the Baltic and cast anchor before Reval. The empress vigorously protested, and the fleet was withdrawn, but on the 6th of August Catherine acceded to the anti-English Austro-Spanish league. Catherine died on the 16th of May 1727. Though quite illiterate, she was an uncommonly shrewd and sensible woman, and her imperturbable good nature under exceptionally difficult circumstances, testifies equally to the soundness of her head and the goodness of her heart.

See Robert Nisbet Bain, *The Pupils of Peter the Great*, chs. ii.-iii. (London, 1897);*The First Romanovs*, ch. xiv. (London, 1905).

(R. N. B.)

CATHERINE II. (1729-1796), empress of Russia, was the daughter of Christian Augustus, prince of Anhalt-Zerbst, and his wife, Johanna Elizabeth of Holstein-Gottorp. The exact date and place of her birth have been disputed, but there appears to be no reason to doubt that she was right in saying that she was born at Stettin on the 2nd of May 1729.

Her father, who succeeded to the principality of Anhalt-Zerbst in 1746 and died in 1747, was a general in the Prussian service, and, at the time of her birth, was military commandant at Stettin. Her baptismal name was Sophia Augusta Frederica. In accordance with the custom then prevailing in German princely families, she was educated chiefly by French governesses and tutors. In 1744 she was taken to Russia, to be affianced to the grand-duke Peter, the nephew of the empress Elizabeth (*q.v.*), and her recognized heir. The princess of Anhalt-Zerbst was the daughter of Christian Albert, bishop of Lübeck, younger brother of Frederick IV., duke of Holstein-Gottorp, Peter's paternal grandfather. The choice of her daughter as wife of the future tsar was the result of not a little diplomatic management in which Frederick the Great took an active part, the object being to strengthen the friendship between Prussia and Russia, to weaken the influence of Austria and to ruin the chancellor Bestuzhev, on whom Elizabeth relied, and who was a known partisan of the Austrian alliance. The diplomatic intrigue failed, largely through the flighty intervention of the princess of Anhalt-Zerbst, a clever but very injudicious woman. But Elizabeth took a strong liking to the daughter, and the marriage was finally decided on. The girl had spared no effort to ingratiate herself, not only with the empress, but with the grand-duke and the Russian people. She applied herself to learning the language with such zeal that she rose at night and walked about her bedroom barefoot repeating her lessons. The result was a severe attack of congestion of the lungs in March 1744. During the worst period of her illness she completed her conquest of the good-will of the Russians by declining the religious services of a Protestant pastor, and sending for Simon Todorskiy, the orthodox priest who had been appointed to instruct her in the Greek form of Christianity. When she wrote her memoirs she represented herself as having made up her mind when she came to Russia to do whatever had to be done, and to profess to believe whatever she was required to believe, in order to be qualified to wear the crown. The consistency of her character throughout life makes it highly probable that even at the age of fifteen she was mature enough to adopt this worldly-wise line of conduct. Her father, who was a convinced Lutheran, was strongly opposed to his daughter's conversion, and supplied her with books of controversy to protect her Protestantism. She read them, and she listened to Todorskiy, and to other advisers who told her that the Russian crown was well worth a mass, or that the differences between the Greek and Lutheran churches were mere matters of form. On the 28th of June 1744 she was received into the Orthodox Church at Moscow, and was renamed Catherine Alexeyevna. On the following day she was formally betrothed, and was married to the archduke on the 21st of August 1745 at St Petersburg.

At that time Catherine was essentially what she was to remain till her death fifty-one years later. It was her boast that she was as "frank and original as any Englishman." If she meant that she had a compact character, she was right. She had decided on her line in life and she followed it whole-heartedly. It was her determination to become a Russian in order that she might the better rule in Russia, and she succeeded. She acquired a full command of all the resources of the language, and a no less complete understanding of the nature of the Russian people. It is true that she remained quite impervious to religious influences. The circumstances of her conversion may have helped to render her indifferent to religion, but their influence need not be exaggerated. Her irreligion was shared by multitudes of contemporaries who had never been called upon to renounce one form of Christianity and profess belief in another in order to gain a crown. Her mere actions were, like those of other and humbler people, dictated by the conditions in which she lived. The first and the most important of them was beyond all question the misery of her married life. Her husband was a wretched creature. Nature had made him mean, the smallpox had made him hideous, and his degraded habits made him loathsome. And Peter had all the sentiments of the worst kind of small German prince of the time. He had the conviction that his princeship entitled him to disregard decency and the feelings of others. He planned brutal practical jokes, in which blows had always a share. His most manly taste did not rise above the kind of military interest which has been defined as "corporal's mania," the passion for uniforms, pipeclay, buttons, the "tricks of parade and the froth of discipline." He detested the Russians, and surrounded himself with Holsteiners. For ten years the marriage was barren, and the only reason for supposing that the future tsar Paul (*q.v.*), who was born on the 2nd of October 1754, was the son of Peter, is the strong similarity of their characters. Living in the grossly animal court of the empress Elizabeth, bound to a husband whom she could not but despise and detest, surrounded by suitors, and entirely uninfluenced by religion, Catherine became and remained perfectly immoral in her sexual relations to men. The scandalous chronicle of her life was the commonplace of all Europe. Her male favourites were as openly paraded as the female favourites of King Louis XV. It may be said once and for all that her most trusted agents while she was still grand-duchess, and her chief ministers when she became empress, were also her lovers, and were known to be so.

For some time after the marriage, the young couple were controlled by the empress Elizabeth, who appointed court officials to keep a watch on their conduct; but before long these custodians themselves had become the agents of Catherine's pleasures and ambition. After the birth of Paul she began to take an active part in political intrigues. Her abilities forced even her husband to rely on her judgment. When in difficulty he ran to her and flattered her with the name of Madame La Ressource—Madame Quick Wit—which did not prevent him from insulting and even kicking her when the immediate need of her help was over. In 1758 he endeavoured to turn the empress Elizabeth against her, and for a time Catherine was in danger. She faced the peril boldly, and reconquered her influence over the sovereign, but from this time she must have realized that when the empress was dead she would have to defend herself against her husband. That Peter both hated and dreaded her was notorious. The empress Elizabeth died on the 5th of January 1762. The grand duke succeeded without opposition as Peter III. His behaviour to his wife continued to be brutal and menacing, and he went on as before offending the national sentiment of the Russian people. In July he committed the insane error of retiring with his Holsteiners to Oranienbaum, leaving his wife at St Petersburg. On the 13th and 14th of that month a "pronunciamiento" of the regiments of the guard removed him from the throne and made Catherine empress. The history of this revolt is still obscure. It has naturally been said that she organized the mutiny from the first, and some plausibility is conferred on this belief by the fact that the guards were manipulated by the four Orlov brothers. The eldest, Gregory, was her recognized chief lover, and he was associated with his brother Alexis in the office of favourite. On the other hand, there does not appear to have been any need for organization. The hatred felt for Peter III. was spontaneous, and Catherine had no need to do more than let it be known that she was prepared to profit by her husband's downfall. Peter, who behaved with abject cowardice, was sent to a country house at Ropcha, where he died on the 15th or 18th of July of official "apoplexy." The truth is not known, and Frederick the Great at least professed long afterwards to believe that Catherine had no immediate share in the murder. She had no need to speak. Common-sense must have shown the leaders of the revolt that they would never be safe while Peter lived, and they had insults to avenge.

The mere fact that Catherine II., a small German princess without hereditary claim to the throne, ruled Russia from 1762 to 1796 amid the loyalty of the great mass of the people, and the respect and admiration of her neighbours, is sufficient proof of the force of her character. Her title to be considered a great reforming ruler is by no means equally clear. Voltaire and the encyclopaedists with whom she corresponded, and on whom she conferred gifts and pensions, repaid her by the grossest flattery, while doing their best to profit by her generosity. They made her a reputation for "philosophy," and showed the sincerity of their own love of freedom by finding excuses for the partition of Poland. There is a very great difference between Catherine II. as she appears in the panegyrics of the encyclopaedists and Catherine as she appears in her correspondence and in her acts. Her foreign admirers amused her, and were useful in spreading her reputation. The money they cost her was a small sum in comparison to the £12,000,000 she lavished on her long series of lovers, who began with Soltykov and Stanislaus Poniatowski (q.v.) before she came to the throne, and ended with the youthful Platon Zubov, who was tenant of the post at her death. She spent money freely on purchasing works of art and curios. Yet she confessed with her usual candour that she had no taste for painting, sculpture or music. Her supposed love of literature does not appear to have amounted to more than a lively curiosity, which could be satisfied by dipping into a great number of books. She had a passion for writing, and produced not only a mass of letters written in French, but pamphlets and plays, comic and serious, in French and Russian. One on the history of Oleg, the more or less legendary Varangian, who was guardian to the son of Rurik, was described by her as an "imitation of Shakespeare." The scheme is not unlike that of a "chronicle play." Her letters are full of vivacity, of colour, and at times of insight and wit, but she never learnt to write either French or German correctly. The letters to Voltaire attributed to her are not hers, and were probably composed for her by Andrei Shuvalov. The philosophers and encyclopaedists who, by the mouth of Diderot, complimented Catherine on being superior to such female affectations as modesty and chastity, flattered her to some extent even here. She enforced outward decency in her household, was herself temperate in eating and drinking, and was by no means tolerant of disorderly behaviour on the part of the ladies of her court. They flattered her much more when they dwelt on her philanthropy and her large share of the enlightenment of the age. She was kind to her servants, and was very fond of young children. She was rarely angry with people who merely contradicted her or failed to perform their service in her household. But she could order the use of the knout and of mutilation as freely as the most barbarous of her predecessors when she thought the authority of the state was at stake, and she did employ them readily to suppress all opinions of a heterodox kind, whether in matters of religion or of politics, after the beginning of the French Revolution. Her renowned toleration stopped short of allowing the dissenters to build chapels, and her passion for legislative reform grew cold when she found that she must begin by the emancipation of the serfs. There were exceptions even to her personal kindness to those about her. She dropped her German relations. She kept a son born to her shortly before the palace revolution of 1762, whose paternity could not be attributed to Peter, at a distance, though she provided for him. He was brought up in a private station under the name of Bobrinski. She was a harsh mother to her son Paul. It seems highly probable that she intended to exclude him from the succession, and to leave the crown to her eldest grandson Alexander, afterwards the emperor Alexander I. Her harshness to Paul was probably as much due to political distrust as to what she saw of his character. Whatever else Catherine may have been she was emphatically a sovereign and a politician who was in the last resort guided by the reason of state. She was resolved not to allow her authority to be disputed by her son, or shared by him.

As a ruler, Catherine professed a great contempt for system, which she said she had been taught to despise by her master Voltaire. She declared that in politics a capable ruler must be guided by "circumstances, conjectures and conjunctions." Her conduct was on the surface very unstable. In a moment of candour she confessed that she was a great *commenceuse*—that she had a mania for beginning innumerable enterprises which she never pursued. This, however, is chiefly true of her internal administration, and even there it should be qualified. Many of her beginnings were carried on by others and were not barren. Her foreign policy was as consistent as it could be considering the forces she had to contend against. It was steadily aimed to secure the greatness and the safety of Russia. There can be no question, that she loved her adopted country sincerely, and had an affection for her people, and an opinion of their great qualities which she did not hesitate to express in hyperbolical terms. Her zeal for the reputation of the Russians 528was almost comically shown by the immense trouble she took to compile an answer to the *Voyage en Sibérie* of the French astronomer Chappe d'Auteroche. The book is in three big quartos, and Catherine's answer—which was never finished—is still larger. Chappe d'Auteroche had discovered that Siberia was not a paradise, and had observed that the Russians were dirty in their habits, and that masters whipped their servants, male and female. Her patriotism was less innocently shown by her conquests. Yet it may be doubted whether any capable ruler of Russia could have abstained from aggressions at the expense of the rights of the Saxon family in Courland, of Poland, and of Turkey (seeRUSSIA: *History*). It does seem now to be clearly proved that the partition of Poland was not suggested by her, as has been frequently asserted. Catherine would have preferred to control the country through a vassal sovereign of the type of Stanislaus Poniatowski, the old lover whose election she secured in 1763. Poland was incapable of maintaining its independence at the time of the first partition (1772), and the division of the unhappy country was forced on by Austria and Prussia. In the case of the second partition in 1793, she did show herself to be very unscrupulous. Her opposition to the reform of the Polish government was plainly due to a wish to preserve an excuse for further spoliation, but her conduct was less cruel and base than that of Prussia.

Catherine had adhered to her husband's policy of a Prussian alliance. While Frederick the Great lived she was impressed by his ability. But the Prussian alliance became hateful to her, and her later correspondence with Grimm overflows with contempt of his successor Frederick William II., who is always spoken of by her as "Brother Gu." Her exasperation with the affectations of the Prussian king was unquestionably increased by her discovery that he would not be induced to apply himself to a crusade against the French Revolution, which by employing all his forces would have left Russia free to annex the whole of what remained of Poland. But at least she did not enter into a solemn engagement to defend the Poles who were engaged in reforming their constitution, and then throw them over in order to share in the plunder of their country.

Catherine's Turkish policy was at first marked by a certain grandiosity. When the Turks declared war in 1768 in order to support Poland, which they looked upon as a necessary buffer state, she retaliated by the great Greek scheme. For a time it was a pet idea with her to revive the Greek empire, and to plant the cross, with the double-headed Russian eagle, at Constantinople. She formed a corps of Greek cadets, caused her younger grandson to be christened Constantine, and began the policy of presenting Russia to the Christian subjects of the Porte as their deliverer. In pursuit of this heroic enterprise, which excited the loud admiration of Voltaire, she sent a fleet under Alexis Orlov into the Mediterranean in 1770. Orlov tempted the Greeks of the Morea to take up arms, and then left them in the lurch. When Catherine found herself opposed by the policy of France and England, and threatened by the jealousy of Prussia and Austria, she dropped the Greek design, observing to Voltaire that the descendants of the Spartans were much degenerated. The introduction into the treaty of Kuchuk-Kainarji of 1774 of a clause by which the Porte guaranteed the rights of its Christian subjects, and of another-giving Russia the right to interfere on behalf of a new Russian church in Constantinople, advertised the claim of the tsars to be the natural protectors of the Orthodox in the Ottoman dominions; but when she took up arms again in 1788 in alliance with Joseph II. (*q.v.*), it was to make a mere war of conquest and partition. The Turkish wars show the weak side of Catherine as a ruler. Though she had mounted the throne by a military revolt and entered on great schemes of conquest, she never took an intelligent interest in her army. She neglected it in peace, allowed it to be shamefully administered in war, and could never be made to understand that it was not in her power to improvise generals out of her favourites. It is to her credit that she saw the capacity of Suvarov, yet she never had as much confidence in him as she had in Potemkin, who may have been a man of genius, but was certainly no general. She took care never to have to deal with a disciplined opponent, except the Swedes, who beat her, but who were very few.

It was the misfortune of Catherine that she lived too long. She disgraced herself by living with her last lover, Zubov, when she was a woman of sixty-seven, trusting him with power and lavishing public money on him. The outbreak of the French Revolution stripped off the varnish of philosophy and philanthropy which she had assumed in earlier years. She had always entertained a quiet contempt for the French writers whom she flattered and pensioned, and who served her as an advertising agency in the west. When the result of their teaching was seen in Paris, good-natured contempt was turned to hatred. She then became a persecutor in her own dominions of the very ideas she had encouraged in former years. She scolded and preached a crusade, without, however, departing from the steady pursuit of her own interests in Poland, while endeavouring with transparent cunning to push Austria and Prussia into an invasion of France with all their forces. Her health began to break down, and it appears to be nearly certain that towards the end she suffered from hysteria of a shameful kind. It is plain that her intellect had begun to fail just before her death, for she allowed the reigning favourite, Platon Zubov, to persuade her to despatch his brother Valerian, with the rank of field marshal and an army of 20,000 men, on a crack-brained scheme to invade India by way of Persia and Tibet. The refusal of the king of Sweden to marry into her family unless the bride would become a Lutheran is said to have thrown her into a convulsion of rage which hastened her death. On the 9th of November 1796, she was seized by a fit of apoplexy, and died on the evening of the 10th.

All other accounts of Catherine II. have been superseded by Waliszewski's two volumes, *Le Roman d'une impératrice* (Paris, 1893) and *Autour d'un Trône: Catherine II., ses collaborateurs, ses amis, ses favoris* (Paris, 1894). The original sources for the history of her policy and her character are to be found in the publications of the Imperial Russian Historical Society, vols. i.-cix. (St Petersburg), begun in 1867; her private and official correspondence will be found in vols. i., ii., iv., v., vi., vii., viii., ix., x., xiii., xiv., xv., xvii., xx., xxiii., xxxii., xxxiii., xxxvi., xlii., xliii., xlvii., xlviii., li., lvii., lxvii., lxviii., lxxxvii., xcvii., xcviii., cvii., cxv., cxviii.

CATHERINE DE' MEDICI (1519-1589), queen of France, the wife of one French king and the mother of three, was born at Florence in 1519. She was a daughter of Lorenzo II. de' Medici and a French princess, Madeleine de la Tour d'Auvergne. Having lost both her parents at an early age, Catherine was sent to a convent to be educated; and she was only fourteen when she was married (1533) at Marseilles to the duke of Orléans, afterwards Henry II. It was her uncle, Pope Clement VII., who arranged the marriage with Francis I. Francis, still engaged in his lifelong task of making head against Charles V., was only too glad of the opportunity to strengthen his influence in the Italian peninsula, while Clement, ever needful of help against his too powerful protector, was equally ready to hold out a bait. During the reign of Francis, Catherine exercised no influence in France. She was young, a foreigner, a member of a state that had almost no weight in the great world of politics, had not given any proof of great ability, and was thrown into the shade by more important persons. For ten years after her marriage she had no children. In consequence, a divorce began to be talked of at court; and it seemed not impossible that Francis, alarmed at the possible extinction of the royal house, might listen to such a proposal. But Catherine had the happiness of bringing him grandchildren ere he died. During the reign of her husband, too (1547-1559), Catherine lived a quiet and passive, but observant life. Henry being completely under the influence of his mistress, Diane de Poitiers, she had little authority. In 1552, when the king left the kingdom for the campaign of Metz, she was nominated regent, but with very limited powers. This continued even after the accession of her son Francis II. Francis was under the spell of Mary Stuart, and she, little disposed to meddle with politics on her own account, was managed by her uncles, the cardinal of Lorraine and the duke of Guise. The queen-mother, however, soon grew weary of the domination of the Guises, and entered upon a course of secret opposition. On the 1st of April 1560 she placed in the 529chancellorship Michel de l'Hôpital (*q.v.*), who advocated the policy of conciliation.

On the death of Francis (5th of December 1560), Catherine became regent during the minority of her second son, Charles IX., and now found before her a career worthy of the most soaring ambition. She was then forty-one years old, but, although she was the mother of nine children, she was still very vigorous and active. She retained her influence for more than twenty years in the troubled period of the wars of religion. At first she listened to the moderate counsels of l'Hôpital in so far as to avoid siding definitely with either party, but her character and the habits of policy to which she had been accustomed, rendered her incapable of any noble aim. She had only one virtue, and that was her zeal for the interests of her children, especially of her favourite third son, the duke of Anjou. Like so many of the Italians of that time, who were almost destitute of a moral sense, she looked upon statesmanship in particular as a career in which finesse, lying and assassination were the most admirable, because the most effective weapons. By habit a Catholic, but above all things fond of power, she was determined to prevent the Protestants from getting the upper hand, and almost equally resolved not to allow them to be utterly crushed, in order to use them as a counterpoise to the Guises. This trimming policy met with little success: rage and suspicion so possessed men's minds, that she could no longer control the opposing parties, and one civil war followed another to the end of her life. In 1567, after the "Enterprise of Meaux," she dismissed l'Hôpital and joined the Catholic party. But, having failed to crush the Protestant rebellion by arms, she resumed in 1570 the policy of peace and negotiation. She conceived the project of marrying her favourite son, the duke of Anjou, to Queen Elizabeth of England, and her daughter Margaret to Henry of Navarre. To this end she became reconciled with the Protestants, and allowed Coligny to return to court and to re-enter the council. Of this step she quickly repented. Charles IX. conceived a great affection for the admiral and showed signs of taking up an independent attitude. Catherine, thinking her influence menaced, sought to regain it, first by the murder of Coligny, and, when that had failed, by the massacre of St Bartholomew (*q.v.*). The whole of the responsibility for this crime, therefore, rests with Catherine; unlike the populace, she had not even the excuse of fanaticism. This responsibility, however, weighed but lightly on her; while her son was overwhelmed with remorse, she calmly enjoyed her short-lived triumph. After the death of Charles in 1574, and the succession of Anjou under the name of Henry III., Catherine pursued her old policy of compromise and concessions; but as her influence is lost in that of her son, it is unnecessary to dwell upon it. She died on the 5th of January 1589, a short time before the assassination of Henry, and the consequent extinction of the House of Valois. In her taste for art and her love of magnificence and luxury, Catherine was a true Medici; her banquets at Fontainebleau in 1564 were famous for their sumptuousness. In architecture especially she was well versed, and Philibert de l'Orme relates that she discussed with him the plan and decoration of her palace of the Tuileries. Catherine's policy provoked a crowd of pamphlets, the most celebrated being the *Discours merveilleux de la vie, actions et déportemens de la reine Catherine de Médicis*, in which Henri Estienne undoubtedly collaborated.

See *Lettres de Catherine de Médicis*, edited by Hector de la Ferrière (Paris, 1880, seq.), in the *Collection de documents inédits sur l'histoire de France*; A. von Reumont,*Die Jugend Caterinas de' Medici* (1854; French translation by A. Baschet, 1866); H. Bouchot, *Catherine de Médicis* (Paris, 1899). For a more complete bibliography see Ernest Lavisse, *Histoire de France* (vol. v., by H. Lemonnier, and vol. vi., by J.H. Mariéjol, 1904-1905). See also Miss E. Sichel's books, *Catherine de' Medici and the French Reformation* (1905), and *The Later Years of Catherine de' Medici* (1908).

CATHERINE OF ARAGON (1485-1536), queen of Henry VIII. of England, daughter of Ferdinand and Isabella of Spain, was born on the 15th or 16th of December 1485. She left Spain in 1501 to marry Arthur, prince of Wales, eldest son of King Henry VII., and landed at Plymouth on the 2nd of October. The wedding took place on the 14th of November in London, and soon afterwards Catherine accompanied her youthful husband to Wales, where, in his sixteenth year, the prince died on the 2nd of April 1502. On the 25th of June 1503, she was formally betrothed to the king's second son, Henry, now prince of Wales, and a papal dispensation for the alliance was obtained. The marriage, however, did not take place during the lifetime of Henry VII. Ferdinand endeavoured to cheat the English king of the marriage portion agreed upon, and Henry made use of the presence of the unmarried princess in England to extort new conditions, and especially to secure the marriage of his daughter Mary to the archduke Charles, grandson of Ferdinand, and afterwards Charles V. Catherine was thus from the first the unhappy victim of state politics. Writing to Ferdinand on the 11th of March 1509, she describes the state of poverty to which she was reduced, and declares the king's unkindness impossible to be borne any longer.1 On the old king's death, however, a brighter prospect opened, for Henry VIII. decided immediately on marrying her, the wedding taking place on the 11th of June and the coronation on the 24th. Catherine now enjoyed a few years of married happiness; Henry showed himself an affectionate husband, and the alliance with Ferdinand was maintained against France. She was not without some influence in state affairs. During Henry's invasion of France in 1513 she was made regent; she showed great zeal and ardour in the preparations for the Scottish expedition, and was riding towards the north to put herself at the head of the troops when the victory of Flodden Field ended the campaign. The following year an affectionate meeting took place between the king and queen at Richmond on the return of the former. Ferdinand's treachery, however, in making a treaty with France roused Henry's wrath, and his angry reproaches fell upon his unfortunate wife; but she took occasion in 1520, during the visit of her nephew Charles V. to England, to urge the policy of gaining his alliance rather than that of France. Immediately on his departure, on the 31st of May 1520, she accompanied the king to France, on the celebrated visit to Francis I., called from its splendour the Field of the Cloth of Gold; but in 1522 war was declared against France and the emperor again welcomed to England. In 1521 she is represented by Shakespeare as pleading for the unfortunate duke of Buckingham.

These early years of happiness and of useful influence and activity had, however, been gradually giving way to gloom and disappointment. Between January 1510 and November 1518 Catherine gave birth to six children (including two princes), who were all stillborn or died in infancy except Mary, born in 1516, and rumour did not fail to ascribe this series of disasters to the curse pronounced in Deuteronomy on incestuous unions. In 1526 the condition of Catherine's health made it highly improbable that she would have more children. No woman had ever reigned in England, alone and in her own right, and to avoid a fresh dispute concerning the succession, and the revival of the civil war, a male heir to the throne was a pressing necessity. The act of marriage, which depended for its validity on the decision of the ecclesiastical courts, had, on account of the numerous dissolutions and dispensations granted, not then attained the security since assured to it by the secular law. For obtaining dissolutions of royal marriages the facilities were especially great. Pope Clement VII. himself permitted such a dissolution in the case of Henry's own sister Margaret, in 1528, proposed later as a solution of the problem that Henry should be allowed two wives,2 and looked not unfavourably, with the same aim, on the project for marrying the duke of Richmond to Mary, a brother to a sister.3 In Henry's case also the irregularity of a union, which is still generally reprobated and forbidden in Christendom, and which it was very doubtful that the pope had the power to legalize, provided a moral justification for a dissolution which in other cases did not exist. It was not therefore the immorality of the plea which obstructed the papal decree in 530Henry's favour, but the unlucky imprisonment at this time of Clement VII at the hands of Charles V., Catherine's nephew, which obliged the pope, placed thus "between the hammer and the anvil," to pursue a policy of delay and hesitation. Nor was the immorality of Henry's own character the primary cause of the project of divorce. Had this been so, a succession of mistresses would have served as well as a series of single wives. The real occasion was the king's desire for a male heir. But, however clear this may be, the injustice done to Catherine was no less cruel and real. Rumours, probably then unfounded, of an intended divorce had been heard abroad as early as 1524. But the creation in 1525 of the king's illegitimate son Henry, as duke of Richmond—the title borne by his grandfather Henry VII—and the precedence granted to him over all the peers as well as the princess Mary, together with the special honour paid at this time by the king to his own half-sister Mary, were the first real indications of the king's thoughts. In 1526, and perhaps earlier, Wolsey had been making tentative inquiries at Rome on the subject. In May 1527 a collusive and secret suit was begun before the cardinal, who, as legate, summoned the king to defend himself from the charge of cohabitation with his brother's wife; but these proceedings were dropped. On the 22nd of June Henry informed Catherine that they had been living in mortal sin and must separate. During Wolsey's absence in July at Paris, where he had been commissioned to discuss vaguely the divorce and Henry's marriage with Renée, daughter of Louis XII., Anne Boleyn is first heard of in connexion with the king, his affection for her having, however, begun probably as early as 1523, and the cardinal on his return found her openly installed at the court. In October 1528 the pope issued a commission to Cardinal Campeggio and Wolsey to try the cause in England, and bound himself not to revoke the case to Rome, confirming his promise by a secret decretal commission which, however, was destroyed by Campeggio. But the trial was a sham. Campeggio was forbidden to pronounce sentence without further reference to Rome, and was instructed to create delays, the pope assuring Charles V. at the same time that the case should be ultimately revoked to Rome.4

The object of all parties was now to persuade Catherine to enter a nunnery and thus relieve them of further embarrassment. While Henry's envoys were encouraged at Rome in believing that he might then make another marriage, Henry himself gave Catherine assurances that no other union would be contemplated in her lifetime. But Catherine with courage and dignity held fast to her rights, demanded a proper trial, and appealed not only to the bull of dispensation, the validity of which was said to be vitiated by certain irregularities, but to a brief granted for the alliance by Pope Julius II. Henry declared the latter to be a forgery, and endeavoured unsuccessfully to procure a declaration of its falsity from the pope.

The court of the legates accordingly opened on the 31st of May 1529, the queen appearing before it on the 18th of June for the purpose of denying its jurisdiction. On the 21st both Henry and Catherine presented themselves before the tribunal, when the queen threw herself at Henry's feet and appealed for the last time to his sense of honour, recalling her own virtue and helplessness. Henry replied with kindness, showing that her wish for the revocation of the cause to Rome was unreasonable in view of the paramount influence then exercised by Charles V. on the pope. Catherine nevertheless persisted in making appeal to Rome, and then withdrew. After her departure Henry, according to Cavendish, Wolsey's biographer, praised her virtues to the court. "She is, my lords, as true, as obedient, as conformable a wife as I could in my phantasy wish or desire. She hath all the virtues and qualities that ought to be in a woman of her dignity or in any other of baser estate." On her refusal to return, her plea was overruled and she was adjudged contumacious, while the sittings of the court continued in her absence. Subsequently the legates paid her a private visit of advice, but were unable to move her from her resolution. Finally, however, in July 1529, the case was, according to her wish, and as the result of the treaty of Barcelona and the pope's complete surrender to Charles V., revoked by the pope to Rome: a momentous act, which decided Henry's future attitude, and occasioned the downfall of the whole papal authority in England. On the 7th of March 1530 Pope Clement issued a brief forbidding Henry to make a second marriage, and ordering the restitution of Catherine to her rights till the cause was determined; while at the same time he professed to the French ambassador, the bishop of Tarbes, his pleasure should the marriage with Anne Boleyn have been already made, if only it were not by his authority.5The same year Henry obtained opinions favourable to the divorce from the English, French and most of the Italian universities, but unfavourable answers from Germany, while a large number of English peers and ecclesiastics, including Wolsey and Archbishop Warham, joined in a memorial to the pope in support of Henry's cause.

Meanwhile, Catherine, while the great question remained unsolved, was still treated by Henry as his queen, and accompanied him in his visits in the provinces and in his hunting expeditions. On the 31st of May 1531 she was visited by thirty privy councillors, who urged the trial of the case in England, but they met only with a firm refusal. On the 14th of July Henry left his wife at Windsor, removing himself to Woodstock, and never saw her again. In August she was ordered to reside at the Moor in Hertfordshire, and at the same time separated from the princess Mary, who was taken to Richmond. In October she again received a deputation of privy councillors, and again refused to withdraw the case from Rome. In 1532 she sent the king a gold cup as a new year's gift, which the latter returned, and she was forbidden to hold any communication with him. Alone and helpless in confronting Henry's absolute power, her cause found champions and sympathizers among the people, among the court preachers, and in the House of Commons, while Bishop Fisher had openly taken her part in the legatine trial. Subsequently Catherine was removed to Bishops Hatfield, while Henry and Anne Boleyn visited Francis I. Their marriage, anticipating any sentence of the nullity of the union with Catherine, took place after their return about the 25th of January 1533, in consequence of Anne's pregnancy. On the 10th of May Cranmer, for whose consecration as archbishop of Canterbury Henry had obtained bulls from Rome, opened his court, and declared on the 23rd the nullity of Catherine's marriage and the validity of Anne's. On the 10th of August the king caused proclamation to be made forbidding her the style of queen; but Catherine refused resolutely to yield the title for that of princess-dowager. Not long afterwards she was removed to Buckden in Huntingdonshire. Here her household was considerably reduced, and she found herself hemmed in by spies, and in fact a prisoner. In July she had refused Henry the loan of a certain rich cloth, which had done service at the baptism of her children, for the use of Anne Boleyn's expected infant; and on the birth of Elizabeth and the refusal of Mary to give up the title of princess, the latter's household was entirely dismissed and she herself reduced to the position of attendant in Elizabeth's retinue. A project for removing Catherine from Buckden to Somersham, an unhealthy solitude in the isle of Ely, with a still narrower maintenance, was only prevented by her own determined resistance. The attempt in November to incriminate the queen in connexion with Elizabeth Barton failed. She passed her life now in religious devotions, taking strict precautions against the possibility of being poisoned. On the 23rd of March 1534 the pope pronounced her marriage valid, but by this time England had thrown off the papal jurisdiction, the parliament had transferred Catherine's jointure to Anne Boleyn, and the decree had no effect on Catherine's fortunes. She refused to swear to the new act of succession, which declared her marriage null and Anne's infant the heir to the throne, and soon afterwards she was removed to Kimbolton, where she was well treated. On the 21st of May she was visited by the archbishop of York and Tunstall, bishop of Durham, who threatened her with death if she persisted in her refusal, but only succeeded in confirming her resolution. She was kept in strict seclusion, separated from Mary 5[3]and from all outside communications, and in December 1535 her health gave way, her death taking place on the 8th of January 1536, not without suspicions of poison, which, however, may be dismissed. She was buried by the king's order in Peterborough cathedral. Before her death she dictated a last letter to Henry, according to Polydore Vergil, expressing her forgiveness, begging his good offices for Mary, and concluding with the astounding assurance—"I vow that mine eyes desire you above all things." The king himself affected no sorrow at her death, and thanked God there was now no fear of war.

Catherine is described as "rather ugly than otherwise; of low stature and rather stout; very good and very religious; speaks Spanish, French, Flemish, English; more beloved by the islanders than any queen that has ever reigned." She was a woman of considerable education and culture, her scholarship and knowledge of the Bible being noted by Erasmus, who dedicated to her his book on *Christian Matrimony* in 1526. She endured her bitter and undeserved misfortunes with extraordinary courage and resolution, and at the same time with great womanly forbearance, of which a striking instance was the compassion shown by her for the fallen Wolsey.

BIBLIOGRAPHY.—See the article in *Dict. of Nat. Biog.* by J. Gairdner, and those on Henry VIII. and Wolsey, where the case is summed up very adversely to Henry, and*The Divorce of Catherine of Aragon*, by J.A. Froude (1891), where it is regarded from the contrary aspect; *Henry VIII.*, by A. F. Pollard (1905); *Cambridge Mod. History*(1903), ii. 416 et seq. and bibliographies, p. 789; *The Wives of Henry VIII.*, by M. Hume (1905).

(P. C. Y.)

1*Cat. of State Pap., England and Spain*, i. 469.
2*Letters and Papers*, iv. 6627, 6705, and app. 261.
3*Ib.* iv. 5072.
4*Cal. of State Pap., England and Spain*, iii. pt. ii. 779.
5*Cal. of State Pap., Foreign and Dom.*, iv. 6290.

CATHERINE OF BRAGANZA (1638-1705), queen consort of Charles II. of England, daughter of John IV. of Portugal, and of Louisa de Gusman, daughter of the duke of Medina Sidonia, was born on the 15/25 of November 1638 at Villia Viçosa. She was early regarded as a useful medium for contracting an alliance with England, more necessary than ever to Portugal after the treaty of the Pyrenees in 1659 whereby Portugal was ostensibly abandoned by France. Negotiations for the marriage began during the reign of Charles I., were renewed immediately after the Restoration, and on the 23rd of June, in spite of Spanish opposition, the marriage contract was signed, England securing Tangier and Bombay, with trading privileges in Brazil and the East Indies, religious and commercial freedom in Portugal and two million Portuguese crowns (about £300,000); while Portugal obtained military and naval support against Spain and liberty of worship for Catherine. She reached England on the 13th of May 1662, but was not visited by Charles at Portsmouth till the 20th. The next day the marriage was solemnized twice, according to the Roman Catholic and Anglican usages. Catherine possessed several good qualities, but had been brought up in a conventual seclusion and was scarcely a wife Charles would have chosen for himself. Her personal charms were not potent enough to wean Charles away from the society of his mistresses, and in a few weeks after her arrival she became aware of her painful and humiliating position as the wife of the selfish and licentious king. On the first presentation to her of Lady

Castlemaine, Charles's mistress *en titre*, whom he insisted on making lady of her bedchamber, she fainted away. She withdrew from the king's society, and in spite of Clarendon's attempts to moderate her resentment, declared she would return to Portugal rather than consent to a base compliance. To overcome her resistance nearly the whole of her Portuguese retinue was dismissed. She was helpless, and the violence of her grief and anger soon changed to passive resistance, and then to a complete forbearance and complaisance which gained the king's regard and favour. In the midst of Charles's debauched and licentious court, she lived neglected and retired, often deprived of her due allowance, having no ambitions and taking no part in English politics, but keeping up rather her interest in her native country.

As the prospect diminished of her bearing children to Charles, several schemes were set on foot for procuring a divorce on various pretexts. As a Roman Catholic and near to the king's person Catherine was the special object of attack by the inventors of the Popish Plot. In 1678 the murder of Sir Edmund Berry Godfrey was ascribed to her servants, and Titus Oates accused her of a design to poison the king. These charges, of which the absurdity was soon shown by cross-examination, nevertheless placed the queen for some time in great danger. On the 28th of November Oates accused her of high treason, and the Commons passed an address for her removal and that of all the Roman Catholics from Whitehall. A series of fresh depositions were sent in against her, and in June 1679 it was decided that she must stand her trial; but she was protected by the king, who in this instance showed unusual chivalry and earned her gratitude. On the 17th of November Shaftesbury moved in the House of Lords for a divorce to enable the king to marry a Protestant and have legitimate issue; but he received little support, and the bill was opposed by Charles, who continued to show his wife "extraordinary affection." During the winter the calumnies against the queen were revived by Fitzharris, who, however, before his execution in 1681 confessed to their falsity; and after the revival of the king's influence subsequent to the Oxford parliament, the queen's position was no more assailed.

During Charles's last illness in 1685 she showed great anxiety for his reconciliation with the Romish Church, and it was probably effected largely through her influence. She exhibited great grief at his death. She afterwards resided at Somerset House and at Hammersmith, where she had privately founded a convent. She interceded with great generosity, but ineffectually, for Monmouth the same year. On the 10th of June 1688 she was present at the birth of the prince of Wales and gave evidence before the council in favour of the genuineness of the child. She was still in England at the Revolution, having delayed her return to Portugal to prosecute a lawsuit against the second earl of Clarendon, formerly her chamberlain. She maintained at first good terms with William and Mary; but the practice of her religion aroused jealousies, while her establishment at Somerset House was said to be the home of cabals against the government; and in 1691 she settled for a short time at Euston. She left England finally with a train of one hundred persons in March 1692, travelling through France and arriving at Lisbon on the 20th of January 1693. She took up her residence at the palace of Bemposta, built by herself, near Lisbon. In 1703 she supported the Methuen Treaty, which cemented still further the alliance between Portugal and England, and in 1704 she was appointed regent of Portugal during the illness of her brother King Pedro II., her administration being distinguished by several successes gained over the Spaniards. She died on the 31st of December 1705, bequeathing her great wealth, the result of long hoarding, after the payment of divers charitable legacies, to King Pedro; and was buried with great ceremony and splendour at Belem.

See L. C. Davidson, *Catherine of Braganza* (1908).

CATHERINE OF VALOIS (1401-1437), queen of Henry V. of England, daughter of Charles VI. of France by his wife Isabel of Bavaria, was born in Paris on the 27th of October 1401. The lunacy of her father and the depravity of her mother were serious drawbacks to Catherine, and her only education was obtained in a convent at Poissy. About 1408 a marriage was suggested between the princess and Henry, prince of Wales, afterwards Henry V., who renewed this proposal after he became king in March 1413. In addition to the hand of Catherine, however, the English king asked for a large dowry both in money and lands, and when these demands were rejected war broke out. Once or twice during short intervals of peace the marriage project was revived, and was favoured by Queen Isabel. When peace was eventually made at Troyes in May 1420 Henry and Catherine were betrothed, and the marriage took place at Troyes on the 2nd of June 1420. Having crossed to England with Henry, the queen was crowned in Westminster Abbey on the 23rd of February 1421, and in the following December gave birth to a son, afterwards King Henry VI. She joined Henry in France in May 1422, returning to England after his death in the succeeding August. Catherine's name soon began to be coupled with that of Owen Tudor, a Welsh gentleman, and in 1428 Humphrey, duke of Gloucester, secured the passing of an act to prevent her from marrying without the 532consent of the king and council. It appears, however, that by this time Catherine and Tudor were already married. They lived in obscurity till 1436, when Tudor was imprisoned, and Catherine retired to Bermondsey Abbey, where she died on the 3rd of January 1437. Her body was buried in the Lady chapel of Westminster Abbey, and when the chapel was pulled down during the reign of Henry VII., was placed in Henry V.'s tomb. It lay afterwards under the Villiers monument, and in 1878 was re-buried in Henry V.'s chantry. By Tudor Catherine had three sons and a daughter. Her eldest son by this marriage, Edmund, was created earl of Richmond in 1452, and was the father of Henry VII.

See Agnes Strickland, *Lives of the Queens of England*, vol. iii. (London, 1877).

CATHETUS (Gr. κάθετος, a perpendicular line), in architecture the eye of the volute, so termed because its position is determined, in an Ionic or voluted capital, by a line let down from the point in which the volute generates.

CATHOLIC (Gr. καθολικός, general, universal), a designation adopted in the 2nd century by the Christian Church to indicate Christendom as a whole, in contrast with individual churches. With this idea went the notions that Christianity had been diffused throughout the whole earth by the apostles, and that only what was found everywhere throughout the church could be true. The term thus in time became full of dogmatic and political meaning, connoting, when applied to the church, a universal authoritative and orthodox society, as opposed to Gnostic and other "sects" (cf. the famous canon of Vincent of Lerins A.D. 434; *quod ubique, quod semper, quod ab omnibus creditum est*). The term "Catholic" does not occur in the old Roman symbol; but Professor Loofs includes it in his reconstruction, based on typical phrases in common use at the time of the ante-Nicene creeds of the East. In the original form of the Nicene creed itself it does not occur; but in the creed of Jerusalem (348), an amplification of the Nicene symbol, we find "one Holy Catholic Church," and in the revision by Cyril of Alexandria (362) "Catholic and Apostolic Church" (see CREEDS). Thus, though the word "Catholic" was late in finding its way into the formal symbols of the church, it is clear that it had long been in use in the original sense defined above. It must be borne in mind, however, that the designation "Catholic" was equally claimed by all the warring parties within the church at various times; thus, the followers of Arius and Athanasius alike called themselves Catholics, and it was only the ultimate victory of the latter that has reserved for them in history the name of Catholic, and branded the former as Arian.

With the gradual development and stereotyping of the creed it was inevitable that the term "Catholic" should come to imply a more narrowly defined orthodoxy. In the Eastern churches, indeed, the conception of the church as the guardian of "the faith once delivered to the saints" soon overshadowed that of interpretation and development by catholic consent, and, though they have throughout claimed the title of Catholic, their chief glory is that conveyed in the name of the Holy Orthodox Church. In the West, meanwhile, the growth of the power of the papacy had tended more and more to the interpretation of the word "catholic" as implying communion with, and obedience to, the see of Rome (see PAPACY); the churches of the East, no less than the heretical sects of the West, by repudiating this allegiance, had ceased to be Catholic. This identification of "Catholic" with "Roman" was accentuated by the progress of the Reformation. The Reformers themselves, indeed, like other dissidents and reformers before them, did not necessarily repudiate the name of Catholic; they believed, in fact, in Catholicism, *i.e.* the universal sanction of their beliefs, as firmly as did the adherents of "the old religion"; they included the Catholic creeds, definitions formulated by the universal church, in their service books; they too appealed, as the fathers of Basel and Constance had done, from the papal monarchy to the great ecclesiastical republic. The Church of England at least, emphasizing her own essential catholicity, retained in her translations of the ancient symbols the word "catholic" instead of replacing it by "universal." But the appeal to the verbally inspired Bible was stronger than that to a church hopelessly divided; the Bible, and not the consent of the universal church, became the touchstone of the reformed orthodoxy; in the nomenclature of the time, "evangelical" arose in contradistinction to "Catholic," while, in popular parlance, the "protest" of the Reformers against the "corruptions of Rome" led to the invention of the term "Protestant," which, though nowhere assumed in the official titles of the older reformed churches, was early used as a generic term to include them all.

"Catholic" and "Catholicism" thus again changed and narrowed their meaning; they became, by universal usage, identified definitely with "Romanist" and the creed and obedience of Rome. Even in England, where the church retained most strongly the Catholic tradition, this distinction of "Protestant" and "Catholic" was clearly maintained, at least till the "Catholic revival" in the Church of England of the 19th century. On the continent of Europe the equivalent words (*e.g.* Ger. *Katholik, Katholizismus*; Fr. *catholique, catholicisme*) are even more definitely associated with Rome; they have lost the sense which they still convey to a considerable school of Anglicans. The dissident "Catholic" churches are forced to qualify their titles: they are "Old Catholics" (*Alt-Katholiken*) or "German Catholics" (*Deutsch-Katholiken*). The Church of Rome alone, officially and in popular parlance, is "the Catholic Church" (*katholische Kirche, église catholique*), a title which she proudly claims as exclusively her own, by divine right, by the sanction of immemorial tradition, and by reason of her perpetual protest against the idea of "national" churches, consecrated by the Reformation (see CHURCH HISTORY, and ROMAN CATHOLIC CHURCH). The additional qualification of "Roman" she tolerates, since it proclaims her doctrine of the see of Rome as the keystone of Catholicism; but to herself she is "the Catholic Church," and her members are "Catholics."

Yet to concede this claim and surrender without qualification the word "Catholic" to a connotation which is at best only universal in theory, is to beg several very weighty questions. The doctrine of the Catholic Church, *i.e.* the essential unity and interdependence of "all God's faithful people scattered throughout the world," is common to all sections of Christians. The creed is one; it is the interpretation that differs. In a somewhat narrower sense, too, the Church of England at least has never repudiated the conception of the Catholic Church as a divinely instituted organization for the safe-guarding and proclamation of the Christian revelation. She deliberately retained the Catholic creeds, the Catholic ministry and the appeal to Catholic antiquity (see ENGLAND, CHURCH OF). A large section of her members, accordingly, laying stress on this side of her tradition, prefer to call themselves "Catholics." But, though the invention of the terms "Roman Catholic" and "Roman Catholicism" early implied the retention by the English Church of her Catholic claim, her members were never, after the Reformation, called Catholics; even the Caroline divines of the 17th century, for all their "popish practices," styled themselves Protestants, though they would have professed their adherence to "the Catholic faith" and their belief in "the Holy Catholic Church."

Clearly, then, the exact meaning of the term varies according to those who use it and those to whom it is applied. To the Romanist "Catholic" means "Roman Catholic"; to the high Anglican it means whatever is common to the three "historic" branches into which he conceives the church to be divided—Roman, Anglican and Orthodox; to the Protestant pure and simple it means either what it does to the Romanist, or, in expansive moments, simply what is "universal" to all Christians. In a yet broader sense it is used adjectivally of mere wideness or universality of view, as when we speak of a man as "of catholic sympathies" or "catholic in his tastes."

The name of *Catholic Epistles* is given to those letters (two of Peter, three of John, one of James, one of Jude) incorporated in the New Testament which (except 2 and 3 John) are not, like 533those of St Paul, addressed to particular individuals or churches, but to a larger and more indefinite circle of readers. (See BIBLE: *New Testament, Canon.*)

The title of *Catholicus* (καθολικός) seems to have been used under the Roman empire, though rarely, as the Greek equivalent of *consularis* and *praefectus*. Thus Eusebius (*Hist. eccl.* viii. 23) speaks of the catholicus of Africa (καθολικὸν τῆς Ἀφρικῆς). As an ecclesiastical title it was used to imply, not universal (ecumenical), but a great and widespread jurisdiction. Thus the bishop of the important see of Seleucia (Bagdad), though subordinate to the patriarch of Antioch, had the title of Catholicus and power to consecrate even archbishops; and on the division of the see there were two *Catholici* under the patriarch of Antioch. In Ethiopia, too, there were *Catholici* with less extensive powers, subject to the patriarch of Alexandria. The title now survives, however, only as that of the head of the Armenian Church (*q.v.*). A bishop's cathedral church is, however, in Greek the *Catholicon*.

An isolated use of the word "catholic" as a secular legal term survives in Scots law; a *catholic creditor* is one whose debt is secured over several or over all of the subjects belonging to the debtor.

CATHOLIC APOSTOLIC CHURCH, THE, a religious community often called "Irvingites," though neither actually founded nor anticipated by Edward Irving (*q.v.*). Irving's relation to this community was, according to its members, somewhat similar to that of John the Baptist to the early Christian Church, *i.e.* he was the forerunner and prophet of the coming dispensation, not the founder of a new sect; and indeed the only connexion which Irving seems to have had with the existing organization of the Catholic Apostolic body was in "fostering spiritual persons who had been driven out of other congregations for the exercise of their spiritual gifts." Shortly after Irving's trial and deposition (1831), certain persons were, at some meetings held for prayer, designated as "called to be apostles of the Lord" by certain others claiming prophetic gifts. In the year 1835, six months after Irving's death, six others were similarly designated as "called" to complete the number of the "twelve," who were then formally "separated," by the pastors of the local congregations to which they belonged, to their higher office in the universal church on the 14th of July 1835. This separation is understood by the community not as "in any sense being a schism or separation from the one Catholic Church, but a separation to a special work of blessing and intercession on behalf of it." The twelve were afterwards guided to ordain others—twelve prophets, twelve evangelists, and twelve pastors, "sharing equally with them the one Catholic Episcopate," and also seven deacons for administering the temporal affairs of the church catholic. The apostles were the channels of the Holy Ghost and the mysteries of God, and the authoritative interpreters of "prophetic utterance"; their teaching was brought home to the people by the "evangelists." The function of the prophets was to explain scripture and exhort to holiness, that of the "pastors" is explained by their title. The central episcopacy of forty-eight was regarded as "indicated by prophecy," being foreshown in the forty-eight boards of the Mosaic tabernacle. For ecclesiastical purposes the church universal is under their charge in twelve tribes; for Christendom is considered to be divided into twelve portions or tribes, each tribe being under the special charge of an apostle and his co-ministers, and the seat of the Apostolic College being at Albury, near Guildford. This is an ideal outline which has never been fulfilled. There has never been a "central episcopacy" of forty-eight. The "apostles" alone always held the supreme authority, though, as their number dwindled, "coadjutors" were appointed to assist the survivors, and to exercise the functions of the "apostolate." The last "apostle" died on the 3rd of February 1901.

For the service of the church a comprehensive book of liturgies and offices was provided by the "apostles." It dates from 1842 and is based on the Anglican, Roman and Greek liturgies. Lights, incense, vestments, holy water, chrism, and other adjuncts of worship are in constant use. The ceremonial in its completeness may be seen in the church in Gordon Square, London, and elsewhere. The daily worship consists of "matins" with "proposition" (or exposition) of the sacrament at 6 A.M., prayers at 9 A.M. and 3 P.M., and "vespers" with "proposition" at 5 P.M. On all Sundays and holy days there is a "solemn celebration of the eucharist" at the high altar; on Sundays this is at 10 A.M. On other days "low celebrations" are held in the side-chapels, which with the chancel in all churches correctly built after apostolic directions are separated or marked off from the nave by open screens with gates. The community has always laid great stress on symbolism, and in the eucharist, while rejecting both transubstantiation and consubstantiation, holds strongly to a real (mystical) presence. It emphasizes also the "phenomena" of Christian experience and deems miracle and mystery to be of the essence of a spirit-filled church.

Each congregation is presided over by its "angel" or bishop (who ranks as angel-pastor in the Universal Church), under him are four-and-twenty priests, divided into the four ministries of "elders, prophets, evangelists and pastors," and with these are the deacons, seven of whom regulate the temporal affairs of the church—besides whom there are also "sub-deacons, acolytes, singers, and door-keepers." The understanding is that each elder, with his co-presbyters and deacons, shall have charge of 500 adult communicants in his district; but this has been but partially carried into practice. This is the full constitution of each particular church or congregation as founded by the "restored apostles," each local church thus "reflecting in its government the government of the church catholic by the angel or high priest Jesus Christ, and His forty-eight presbyters in their fourfold ministry (in which apostles and elders always rank first), and under these the deacons of the church catholic." The priesthood is supported by tithes; it being deemed a duty on the part of all members of the church who receive yearly incomes to offer a tithe of their increase every week, besides the free-will offering for the support of the place of worship, and for the relief of distress. Each local church sends "a tithe of its tithes" to the "Temple," by which the ministers of the Universal Church are supported and its administrative expenses defrayed; by these offerings, too, the needs of poorer churches are supplied. It claims to have among its clergy many of the Roman, Anglican and other churches, the orders of those ordained by Greek, Roman and Anglican bishops being recognized by it with the simple confirmation of an "apostolic act." The community has not changed recently in general constitution or doctrine. It does not publish statistics, and its growth during late years is said to have been more marked in the United States and in certain European countries, such as Germany, than in Great Britain. There are nine congregations enumerated in *The Religious Life of London* (1904).

For further details of doctrines, ritual, &c., see R. N. Bosworth, *Restoration of Apostles and Prophets, Readings on the Liturgy, The Church and Tabernacle,* and *The Purpose of God in Creation and Redemption* (6th ed., 1888); G. Miller, *History and Doctrines of Irvingism* (1878).

CATILINE [LUCIUS SERGIUS CATILINA] (c. 108-62 B.C.), a member of an ancient but impoverished patrician family of Rome, the prime mover in the conspiracy known by his name. He appears in history first as a supporter of Sulla, and during the proscription he was conspicuous for his greed and cruelty. He slew his inoffensive brother-in-law with his own hand, and tortured and mutilated the much-loved Marius Gratidianus. He was believed to have made away with his wife and his son to win the profligate and wealthy Aurelia Orestilla; it was even suspected that he had been guilty of an intrigue with the Vestal Fabia. In 77 he was quaestor, in 68 praetor, and in 67-66 governor of Africa. His extortions and subsequent impeachment by P. Clodius Pulcher having disqualified him as a candidate for the consulship, he formed a conspiracy, in which he was joined by young men of all classes, even Crassus and Caesar, according to rumour, being implicated. The new consuls were to be murdered on the 1st of January; but the plot—the execution of which was deferred till the 5th of February—failed in consequence of the impatience of Catiline, who gave the signal too hastily. Soon after, Catiline, having bribed both judges and accuser, was acquitted in the trial for extortion. His scheme was forthwith immensely widened. The city was to be fired, and those who opposed the revolution were to be slain; all debts were to be cancelled; and there was to be a proscription of all the wealthy citizens. Among the conspirators were many men of the first rank and influence. Arms and money were collected, soldiers were enlisted, and the assistance of the slaves was sought. But Catiline's hopes were again disappointed; once more he failed to obtain the consulship (64); and, moreover, it soon became apparent that one of the new consuls, Cicero, was mysteriously able to thwart all the schemes of the conspirators. He was, in fact, informed of every detail, through Fulvia, the mistress of Curius, one of the plotters, who was himself soon persuaded to turn informer.

The other consul, C. Antonius, in whom Catiline hoped to find a supporter, was won over and got out of the way by Cicero, who resigned the province of Macedonia in his favour. Before the next *comitia consularia* assembled, the orator had given so impressive a warning of the danger which was impending, that Catiline was once more rejected (63), and the consuls were invested with absolute authority. Catiline now resolved upon open war; preparations were set on foot throughout Italy, especially in Etruria, where the standard of revolt was raised by the centurion C. Manlius (or Mallius), one of Sulla's veterans. A plan to murder Cicero in his own house on the morning of the 7th of November was frustrated. On the next day Cicero attacked Catiline so vigorously in the senate (in his first Catilinarian oration) that he fled to his army in Etruria. Next day Cicero awoke the terror of the people by a second oration delivered in the forum, in consequence of which Catiline and Manlius were declared public enemies, and the consul Antonius was despatched with an army against them. Meanwhile the imprudence of the conspirators in Rome brought about their own destruction. Some deputies from the Allobroges, who had been sent to Rome to obtain redress for certain grievances, were approached by P. Lentulus Sura, the chief of the conspirators, who endeavoured to induce them to join him. After considerable hesitation, the deputies decided to turn informers. The plot was betrayed to Cicero, at whose instigation documentary evidence was obtained, implicating Lentulus and others. They were arrested, proved guilty, and on the 5th of December condemned to death and strangled in the underground dungeon on the slope of the Capitol. This act, which was opposed by Julius Caesar and advocated by Cato Uticensis (and, indirectly, by Cicero), was afterwards vigorously attacked as a violation of the constitution, on the ground that the senate had no power of life and death over a Roman citizen. Thus a heavy blow was dealt to the cause of Catiline, who, in the beginning of 62, saw his legions, only partially armed and diminished by desertion, shut in between those of Metellus Celer and C. Antonius. Near Pistoria he hazarded battle with the forces of the latter, but was completely defeated in a desperate encounter. He himself, fighting with the utmost bravery, rushed into the ranks of the enemy and met his death.

Such was the conspiracy of Catiline and the character of its author, as we find them in the speeches of Cicero, and the histories of Sallust and Dio Cassius (see also Plutarch, *Cicero*; Vell. Pat. ii. 35; Florus iv. 1; Appian, *B.C.* ii. 6; Eutropius vi. 15). It must not be forgotten, however, that our authorities were all members of the aristocratic party. Some of the incidents given as facts by Dio Cassius are manifest absurdities; and Cicero paid more regard to the effect than to the truthfulness of an accusation. We find him at one time admitting that Catiline had almost persuaded him of his honesty and merit, and even seeking a political union with him; at another, when his alliance had been rejected and an election was at hand, declaiming against him as a murderer and a profligate. Lastly, though Sallust's vivid narrative is consistent throughout, it is obvious that he cherished very bitter feelings against the democratic party. Nevertheless, we cannot regard Catiline as an honest enemy of the oligarchy, or as a disinterested champion of the provincials. It is held by some historians that there was at the time on the part of many of the Roman nobles a determination to raise themselves to power, despite the opposition of the senate: others with greater probability maintain that Catiline's object was simply the cancelling of the huge debts which he and his friends had accumulated. Catiline, by his bravery, his military talents, his vigorous resolution, and his wonderful power over men, was eminently qualified as a revolutionary leader. He is the subject of tragedies by Ben Jonson and P. Crébillon, and of the *Rome sauvée* of Voltaire.

See P. Mérimée, *Études sur la guerre sociale et la conjuration de Catiline* (1844); E. Hagen, *Catilina* (1854), with introductory discussion of the authorities; E.S. Beesley, "Catiline as a Party Leader" (*Fortnightly Review*, June 1865), in defence of Catiline; C. John, *Die Entstehungsgeschichte der catilinarischen Verschwörung* (1876), a critical examination of Sallust's account; E. von Stern, *Catilina und die Parteikämpfe in Rom* 66-63 (1883), with bibliography in preface; C. Thiaucourt, *Étude sur la conjuration de Catiline* (1887), a critical examination of Sallust's account and of his object in writing it; J.E. Blondel, *Histoire économique de la conjuration de Catiline* (1893), written from the point of view of a political economist; Gaston Boissier, *La Conjuration de Catiline* (1905), and *Cicero and his Friends* (Eng. trans.); Tyrrell and Purser's ed. of Cicero's *Letters* (index vol. *s.v.* "Sergius Catilina"); J.L. Strachan

Davidson, *Cicero* (1894), ch. v.; Warde Fowler's *Caesar* (1892); see also art. <u>ROME</u>: *History, The Republic.*

CATINAT, NICOLAS (1637-1712), marshal of France, entered the Gardes Françaises at an early age and distinguished himself at the siege of Lille in 1667. He became a brigadier ten years later, *maréchal de camp* in 1680, and lieutenant-general 1688. He served with great credit in the campaigns of 1676-1678 in Flanders, was employed against the Vaudois in 1686, and after taking part in the siege of Philipsburg at the opening of the War of the League of Augsburg, he was appointed to command the French troops in the south-eastern theatre of war. In 1690 he conquered Savoy, and in 1691 Nice; the battle of Staffarda, won by him over the duke of Savoy in 1690, and that of Marsaglia in 1693, were amongst the greatest victories of the time. In 1696 Catinat forced the duke to make an alliance with France. He had in 1693 been made a marshal of France. At the beginning of the war of the Spanish Succession, Catinat was placed in charge of operations in Italy, but he was much hampered by the orders of the French court and the weakness of the forces for their task. He suffered a reverse at Carpi (1701) and was soon afterwards superseded by Villeroy, to whom he acted as second-in-command during the campaign of Chiari. He died at St Gratien in 1712. His memoirs were published in 1819.

See E. de Broglie, *Catinat, 1637-1712* (Paris, 1902).

CATLIN, GEORGE (1796-1872), American ethnologist, was born at Wilkes-Barre, Pennsylvania, in 1796. He was educated as a lawyer and practised in Philadelphia for two years; but art was his favourite pursuit, and forsaking the law he established himself at New York as a portrait painter. In 1832, realizing that the American Indians were dying out, he resolved to rescue their types and customs from oblivion. With this object he spent many years among the Indians in North and South America. He lived with them, acquired their languages, and studied very thoroughly their habits, customs and mode of life, making copious notes and many studies for paintings. In 1840 he came to Europe with his collection of paintings, most of which are now in the National Museum, Washington, as the Catlin Gallery; and in the following year he published the *Manners, Customs and Condition of the North American Indians* in two volumes, illustrated with 300 engravings. This was followed in 1844 by *The North American Portfolio*, containing 25 plates of hunting scenes and amusements in the Rocky Mountains and the prairies of America, and in 1848 by *Eight Years' Travels and Residence in Europe.* In 1861 he published a curious little volume, in "manugraph," entitled *The Breath of Life*, on the advantage of keeping one's mouth habitually closed, especially during sleep; and in 1868, *Last Rambles amongst the Indians of the Rocky Mountains and the Andes.* He died in Jersey City, New Jersey, on the 22nd of December 1872.

535

CATO, DIONYSIUS, the supposed author of the *Dionysii Catonis Disticha de Moribus ad Filium.* The name usually given is simply Cato, an indication of the wise character of the maxims inculcated, but Dionysius is added on the authority of a MS. declared by Scaliger to be of great antiquity. This MS. also contains Priscian's translation of the Periegesis of the geographer Dionysius Periegetes; this has probably led to the *Disticha* also being attributed to him. In the middle ages the author on the *Disticha* was supposed to be Cato the Elder, who wrote a *Carmen de Moribus*, but extracts from this in Aulus Gellius show that it was in prose. Nothing is really known of the author or date of the *Disticha*; it can only be assigned to the 3rd or 4th century A.D. It is a small collection of moral apophthegms, each consisting of two hexameters, in four books. They are monotheistic in character, not specially Christian. The diction and metre are fairly good. The book had a great reputation in the middle ages, and was translated into many languages; it is frequently referred to by Chaucer, and in 1483 a translation was issued from Caxton's press at Westminster.

Editions by F. Hauthal (1869), with full account of MSS. and early editions, and G. Némethy (1895), with critical notes; see also F. Zarncke, *Der deutsche Cato* (1852), a history of middle age German translations; J. Nehab, *Der altenglische Cato* (1879); E. Bischoff, *Prolegomena zum sogenannten Dionysius Cato* (1893), in which the name is discussed; F. Plessis, *Poésie latine* (1909), 663; for medieval translations and editions see Teuffel, *Hist. of Roman Lit.* § 398, 3.

CATO, MARCUS PORCIUS (234-149 B.C.), Roman statesman, surnamed "The Censor," *Sapiens, Priscus,* or *Major* (the Elder), to distinguish him from Cato of Utica, was born at Tusculum. He came of an ancient plebeian family, noted for some military services, but not ennobled by the discharge of the higher civil offices. He was bred, after the manner of his Latin forefathers, to agriculture, to which he devoted himself when not engaged in military service. But, having attracted the notice of L. Valerius Flaccus, he was brought to Rome, and became successively quaestor (204), aedile (199), praetor (198), and consul (195) with his old patron. During his term of office he vainly opposed the repeal of the lex Oppia, passed during the Second Punic War to restrict luxury and extravagance on the part of women. Meanwhile he served in Africa, and took part in the crowning campaign of Zama (202). He held a command in Sardinia, where he first showed his strict public morality, and again in Spain, which he reduced to subjection with great cruelty, and gained thereby the honour of a triumph (194). In the year 191 he acted as military tribune in the war against Antiochus III. of Syria, and played an important part in the battle of Thermopylae, which finally delivered Greece from the encroachments of the East. His reputation as a soldier was now established; henceforth he preferred to serve the state at home, scrutinizing the conduct of the candidates for public honours and of generals in the field. If he was not personally engaged in the prosecution of the Scipios (Africanus and Asiaticus) for corruption, it was his spirit that animated the attack upon them. Even Africanus, who refused to reply to the charge, saying only, "Romans, this is the day on which I conquered Hannibal," and was absolved by acclamation, found it necessary to retire self-banished to his villa at Liternum. Cato's enmity dated from the African campaign when he quarrelled with Scipio for his lavish distribution of the spoil amongst the troops, and his general luxury and extravagance.

Cato had, however, a more serious task to perform in opposing the spread of the new Hellenic culture which threatened to destroy the rugged simplicity of the conventional Roman type. He conceived it to be his special mission to resist this invasion. It was in the discharge of the censorship that this determination was most strongly exhibited, and hence that he derived the title (the Censor) by which he is most generally distinguished. He revised with unsparing severity the lists of senators and knights, ejecting from either order the men whom he judged unworthy of it, either on moral grounds or from their want of the prescribed means. The expulsion of L. Quinctius Flamininus for wanton cruelty was an example of his rigid justice. His regulations against luxury were very stringent. He imposed a heavy tax upon dress and personal adornment, especially of women, and upon young slaves purchased as favourites. In 181 he supported the lex Orchia (according to others, he first opposed its introduction, and subsequently its repeal), which prescribed a limit to the number of guests at an entertainment, and in 169 the lex Voconia, one of the provisions of which was intended to check the accumulation of an undue proportion of wealth in the hands of women. Amongst other things he repaired the aqueducts, cleansed the sewers, prevented private persons drawing off public water for their own use, ordered the demolition of houses which encroached on the public way, and built the first basilica in the forum near the curia. He raised the amount paid by the publican for the right of farming the taxes, and at the same time diminished the contract prices for the construction of public works.

From the date of his censorship (184) to his death in 149, Cato held no public office, but continued to distinguish himself in the senate as the persistent opponent of the new ideas. He was struck with horror, along with many other Romans of the graver stamp, at the licence of the Bacchanalian mysteries, which he attributed to the fatal influence of Greek manners; and he vehemently urged the dismissal of the philosophers (Carneades, Diogenes and Critolaus), who came as ambassadors from Athens, on account of the dangerous nature of the views expressed by them. He had a horror of physicians, who were chiefly Greeks. He procured the release of Polybius, the historian, and his fellow-prisoners, contemptuously asking whether the senate had nothing more important to do than discuss whether a few Greeks should die at Rome or in their own land. It was not till his eightieth year that he made his first acquaintance with Greek literature. Almost his last public act was to urge his countrymen to the Third Punic War and the destruction of Carthage. In 157 he was one of the deputies sent to Carthage to arbitrate between the Carthaginians and Massinissa, king of Numidia. The mission was unsuccessful and the commissioners returned home. But Cato was so struck by the evidences of Carthaginian prosperity that he was convinced that the security of Rome depended on the annihilation of Carthage. From this time, in season and out of season, he kept repeating the cry: "Delenda est Carthago."

To Cato the individual life was a continual discipline, and public life was the discipline of the many. He regarded the individual householder as the germ of the family, the family as the germ of the state. By strict economy of time he accomplished an immense amount of work; he exacted similar application from his dependents, and proved himself a hard husband, a strict father, a severe and cruel master. There was little difference apparently, in the esteem in which he held his wife and his slaves; his pride alone induced him to take a warmer interest in his sons. To the Romans themselves there was little in this behaviour which seemed worthy of censure; it was respected rather as a traditional example of the old Roman manners. In the remarkable passage (xxxix. 40) in which Livy describes the character of Cato, there is no word of blame for the rigid discipline of his household.

Cato perhaps deserves even more notice as a literary man than as a statesman or a soldier. He was the first Latin prose writer of any importance, and the first author of a history of Rome in Latin. His treatise on agriculture (*De Agricultura*, or *De Re Rustica*) is the only work by him that has been preserved; it is not agreed whether the work we possess is the original or a later revision. It contains a miscellaneous collection of rules of good husbandry, conveying much curious information on the domestic habits of the Romans of his age. His most important work, *Origines*, in seven books, related the history of Rome from its earliest foundations to his own day. It was so called from the second and third books, which described the rise of the different Italian towns. His speeches, of which as many as 150 were collected, were principally directed against the young free-thinking and loose-principled nobles of the day. He also wrote a set of maxims for the use of his son (*Praecepta ad Filium*), and some rules for everyday life in verse (*Carmen de Moribus*). The collection of proverbs in hexameter verse, 536extant under the name of Cato, probably belongs to the 4th century A.D. (See CATO, DIONYSIUS.)

AUTHORITIES.—There are lives of Cato by Cornelius Nepos, Plutarch and Aurelius Victor, and many particulars of his career and character are to be gathered from Livy and Cicero. See also F.D. Gerlach, *Marcus Porcius Cato der Censor* (Basel, 1869); G. Kurth, *Caton l'ancien* (Bruges, 1872); J. Cortese, *De M. Porcii Catonis vita, operibus, et lingua* (Turin, 1883); F. Marcucci, *Studio critico sulle Opere di Catone il Maggiore*(1902). The best edition of the *De Agricultura* is by H. Keil (1884-1891), of the fragments of the *Origines* by H. Peter (1883) in *Historicorum Romanorum Fragmenta*, of the fragments generally by H. Jordan (1860); see also J. Wordsworth, *Fragments and Specimens of Early Latin* (1874); M. Schanz, *Geschichte der römischen Litteratur*(1898); article in Smith's *Dictionary of Greek and Roman Biography*, Mommsen, *Hist. of Rome* (Eng. trans.), bk. iii. ch. xi and xiv.; Warde Fowler, *Social Life at Rome* (1909).

CATO, MARCUS PORCIUS (95-46 B.C.), Roman philosopher, called *Uticensis* to distinguish him from his great-grandfather, "the Censor." On the death of his parents he was brought up in the house of his uncle, M. Livius Drusus. After fighting with distinction in the ranks against Spartacus (72 B.C.), he became a military tribune (67), and served a campaign in Macedonia, but he never had any enthusiasm for the military profession. On his return he became quaestor, and showed so much zeal and integrity in the management of the public accounts that he obtained a provincial appointment in Asia, where he strengthened his reputation. Though filled with disgust at the corruption of the public men with whom he came in contact, he saw much to admire in the discipline which Lucullus had enforced in his own eastern command, and he supported his claims to a triumph, while he opposed the inordinate pretensions of Pompey. When the favour of the nobles gained him the tribuneship, he exerted himself unsuccessfully to convict L. Licinius Murena (2), one of their chief men, of bribery. Cicero, who defended Murena, was glad to have Cato's aid when he urged the execution of the Catilinarian conspirators. Cato's vote on this matter drew upon him the bitter resentment of Julius Caesar, who did his utmost to save them.

Cato had now become a great power in the state. Though possessed of little wealth and no family influence, his unflinching resolution in the cause of the ancient free state rendered him a valuable instrument in the hands of the nobles. He vainly opposed Caesar's candidature for the consulship in 59, and his attempt, in conjunction with Bibulus, to prevent the passing of Caesar's proposed agrarian law for distributing lands amongst the Asiatic veterans, proved unsuccessful. Nevertheless, although his efforts were ineffectual, he was still an obstacle of sufficient importance for the triumvirs to desire to get rid of him. At the instigation of Caesar he was sent to Cyprus (58) with a mission to depose its king, Ptolemy (brother of Ptolemy Auletes), and annex the island. On his return two years later he continued to struggle against the combined powers of the triumvirs in the city, and became involved in scenes of violence and riot. He succeeded in obtaining the praetorship in 54, and strenuously exerted himself in the hopeless and thankless task of suppressing bribery, in which all parties were equally interested. He failed to attain the consulship, and had made up his mind to retire from the arena of civic ambition when the civil war broke out in 49. Feeling that the sole chance for the free state lay in conceding an actual supremacy to Pompey, whom he had formerly vigorously opposed, he did not scruple to support the unjust measures of the nobles against Caesar. At the outset of the war he was entrusted with the defence of Sicily, but finding it impossible to resist the superior forces of C. Scribonius Curio, who had landed on the island, he joined Pompey at Dyrrhachium. When his chief followed Caesar to Thessaly he was left behind in charge of the camp, and thus was not present at the battle of Pharsalus. After the battle, when Pompey abandoned his party, he separated himself from the main body of the republicans, and conducted a small remnant of their forces into Africa. After his famous march through the Libyan deserts, he shut himself up in Utica, and even after the decisive defeat at Thapsus (46), in spite of the wishes of his followers, he determined to keep the gates closed till he had sent off his adherents by sea. While the embarkation was in progress he continued calm and dignified; when the last of the transports had left the port he cheerfully dismissed his attendants, and soon afterwards stabbed himself.

He had been reading, we are told, in his last moments Plato's dialogue on the immortality of the soul, but his own philosophy had taught him to act upon a narrow sense of immediate duty without regard to the future. He conceived that he was placed in the world to play an active part, and when disabled from carrying out his principles, to retire gravely from it. He had lived for the free state, and it now seemed his duty to perish with it. In politics he was a typical doctrinaire, abhorring compromise and obstinately blind to the fact that his national ideal was a hopeless anachronism. From the circumstances of his life and of his death, he has come to be regarded as one of the most distinguished of Roman philosophers, but he composed no works, and bequeathed to posterity no other instruction than that of his example. The only composition by him which we possess is a letter to Cicero (*Ad Fam.* xv. 5), a polite refusal of the orator's request that he would endeavour to procure him the honour of a triumph. The school of the Stoics, which took a leading part in the history of Rome under the earlier emperors, looked to him as its saint and patron. It continued to wage war against the empire, hardly less openly than Cato himself had done, for two centuries, till at last it became actually seated on the imperial throne in the person of Marcus Aurelius. Immediately after his death Cato's character became the subject of discussion; Cicero's panegyric *Cato* was answered by Caesar in his *Anticato*. Brutus, dissatisfied with Cicero's work, produced another on the same subject; in Lucan Cato is represented as a model of virtue and disinterestedness.

See *Life* by Plutarch, and compare Addison's tragedy. Modern biographies by H. Wartmann (Zürich, 1859), and F.D. Gerlach (Basel, 1866); C.W. Oman, *Seven Roman Statesmen of the Later Republic, Cato* ... (1902); Mommsen, *Hist. of Rome* (Eng. trans.), bk. v. ch. v.; article in Smith's *Dictionary of Classical Biography*; Gaston Boissier,*Cicero and his Friends* (Eng. trans., 1897), esp. pp. 277 foll.; Warde Fowler, *Social Life at Rome* (1909).

CATO, PUBLIUS VALERIUS, Roman poet and grammarian, was born about 100 B.C. He is of importance as the leader of the "new" school of poetry (*poetae novi*, νεώτεροι, as Cicero calls them). Its followers rejected the national epic and drama in favour of the artificial mythological epics and elegies of the Alexandrian school, and preferred Euphorion of Chalcis to Ennius. Learning, that is, a knowledge of Greek literature and myths, and strict adherence to metrical rules were regarded by them as indispensable to the poet. The νεώτεροι were also determined opponents of Pompey and Caesar. The great influence of Cato is attested by the lines:—

"Cato   grammaticus,
Latina Siren,
       Qui solus legit ac facit
poetas."1

Our information regarding his life is derived from Suetonius (*De Grammaticis*, 11). He was a native of Cisalpine Gaul, and lost his property during the Sullan disturbances before he had attained his majority. He lived to a great age, and during the latter part of his life was in very reduced circumstances. He was at one time possessed of considerable wealth, and owned a villa at Tusculum which he was obliged to hand over to his creditors. In addition to grammatical treatises, Cato wrote a number of poems, the best-known of which were the *Lydia* and *Diana*. In the *Indignatio* (perhaps a short poem) he defended himself against the accusation that he was of servile birth. It is probable that he is the Cato mentioned as a critic of Lucilius in the lines by an unknown author prefixed to Horace, *Satires*, i. 10.

Among the minor poems attributed to Virgil is one called *Dirae* (or rather two, *Dirae* and *Lydia*). The *Dirae* consists of imprecations against the estate of which the writer has been deprived, and where he is obliged to leave his beloved Lydia; in the *Lydia*, on the other hand, the estate is regarded with envy as the possessor of his charmer. Joseph Justus Scaliger was the first to attribute the poem (divided into two by F. Jacobs) to Valerius Cato, on the ground 537 that he had lost an estate and had written a *Lydia*. The question has been much discussed; the balance of opinion is in favour of the *Dirae* being assigned to the beginning of the Augustan age, although so distinguished a critic as O. Ribbeck supports the claims of Cato to the authorship. The best edition of these poems is by A.F. Näke (1847), with exhaustive commentary and excursuses; a clear account of the question will be found in M. Schanz's *Geschichte der römischen Litteratur*, for the "new" school of poetry see Mommsen, *Hist. of Rome*, bk. v. ch. xii.; F. Plessis, *Poésie latine* (1909), 188.

1 "Cato, the grammarian, the Latin siren, who alone reads aloud the works and makes the reputation of poets."

CATS, JACOB (1577-1660), Dutch poet and humorist, was born at Brouwershaven in Zeeland on the 10th of November 1577. Having lost his mother at an early age, and being adopted with his three brothers by an uncle, Cats was sent to school at Zierikzee. He then studied law at Leiden and at Orleans, and, returning to Holland, he settled at the Hague, where he began to practise as an advocate. His pleading in defence of a wretched creature accused of witchcraft brought him many clients and some reputation. He had a serious love affair about this time, which was broken off on the very eve of marriage by his catching a tertian fever which defied all attempts at cure for some two years. For medical advice and change of air Cats went to England, where he consulted the highest authorities in vain. He returned to Zeeland to die, but was cured mysteriously by a strolling quack. He married in 1602 a lady of some property, Elisabeth von Valkenburg, and thenceforward lived at Grypskerke in Zeeland, where he devoted himself to farming and poetry. His best works are: *Emblemata* or *Minnebeelden* with *Maegdenplicht* (1618); *Spiegel van den ouden en nieuwen Tijt* (1632); *Houwelijck* ... (1625); *Selfstrijt* (1620); *Ouderdom, Buitem leven ... en Hofgedachten op Sorgvliet* (1664); and *Gedachten op slapelooze nachten* (1661). In 1621, on the expiration of the twelve years' truce with Spain, the breaking of the dykes drove him from his farm. He was made pensionary (stipendiary magistrate) of Middelburg; and two years afterwards of Dort. In 1627 Cats came to England on a mission to Charles I., who made him a knight. In 1636 he was made grand pensionary of Holland, and in 1648 keeper of the great seal; in 1651 he resigned his offices, but in 1657 he was sent a second time to England on what proved to be an unsuccessful mission to Cromwell. In the seclusion of his villa of Sorgvliet (Fly-from-Care), near the Hague, he lived from this time till his death, occupied in the composition of his autobiography (*Eighty-two Years of My Life*, first printed at Leiden in 1734) and of his poems. He died on the 12th of September 1660, and was buried by torchlight, and with great ceremony, in the Klooster-Kerk at the Hague. He is still spoken of as "Father Cats" by his countrymen.

Cats was contemporary with Hooft and Vondel and other distinguished Dutch writers in the golden age of Dutch literature, but his Orangist and Calvinistic opinions separated him from the liberal school of Amsterdam poets. He was, however, intimate with Constantin Huygens, whose political opinions were more nearly in agreement with his own. For an estimate of his poetry see DUTCH LITERATURE. Hardly known outside of Holland, among his own people for nearly two centuries he enjoyed an enormous popularity. His diffuseness and the antiquated character of his matter and diction, have, however, come to be regarded as difficulties in the way of study, and he is more renowned than read. A statue to him was erected at Brouwershaven in 1829.

See Jacob Cats, *Complete Works* (1790-1800, 19 vols.), later editions by van Vloten (Zwolle, 1858-1866; and at Schiedam, 1869-1870); Pigott, *Moral Emblems, with Aphorisms, &c., from Jacob Cats* (1860); and P.C. Witsen Gejisbek, *Het Leven en de Verdiensten van Jacob Cats* (1829). Southey has a very complimentary reference to Cats in his "Epistle to Allan Cunningham."

CAT'S-EYE, a name given to several distinct minerals, their common characteristic being that when cut with a convex surface they display a luminous band, like that seen by reflection in the eye of a cat. (1) Precious cat's-eye, oriental cat's-eye or chrysoberyl cat's-eye. This, the rarest of all, is a chatoyant variety of chrysoberyl (*q.v.*), showing in the finest stones a very sharply defined line of light. One of the grandest known specimens was in the Hope collection of precious stones, exhibited for many years at the Victoria and Albert Museum. (2) Quartz cat's-eye. This is the common form of cat's-eye, in which the effect is due to the inclusion of parallel fibres of asbestos. Like the chrysoberyl, it is obtained chiefly from Ceylon, but though coming from the East it is often called "occidental cat's-eye"—a term intended simply to distinguish it from the finer or "oriental" stone. It is readily distinguished by its inferior density, its specific gravity being only 2.65, whilst that of oriental cat's-eye is as high as 3.7. A greenish fibrous quartz, cut as cat's-eye, occurs at Hof and some other localities irr Bavaria. (3) Crocidolite cat's-eye, a beautiful golden brown mineral, with silky fibres, found in Griqualand West, and much used in recent years as an ornamental stone, sometimes under the name of "South African cat's-eye." It consists of fibrous quartz, coloured with oxide of iron, and results from the alteration of crocidolite (*q.v.*). It is often distinguished as "tiger's-eye" (or more commonly "tiger-eye"), whilst a blue variety, less altered, is known as "hawk's-eye." By the action of hydrochloric acid the colour of tiger's-eye may to a large extent be removed, and a greyish cat's-eye obtained. (4) Corundum cat's-eye. In some asteriated corundum (see ASTERIA) the star is imperfect and may be reduced to a luminous zone, producing an indistinct cat's-eye effect. According to the colour of the corundum the stone is known as sapphire cat's-eye, ruby cat's-eye, topaz cat's-eye, &c.

(F. W. R.*)

CATSKILL, a village and the county-seat of Greene county, New York, U.S.A., on the W. bank of the Hudson river, 33 m. S. of Albany. Pop. (1890) 4920; (1900) 5484; of whom 657 were foreign-born; (1910) 5206. It is served by the West Shore railway, by several lines of river steamboats, and by the Catskill Mountain railway, connecting it with the popular summer resorts in the Catskill mountains. A ferry connects with Catskill station (Greendale) on the east side of the Hudson. The village is in a farming country, and manufactures woollen goods and bricks, but it is best known as a summer resort, and as the principal gateway to the beautiful Catskill Mountain region. The *Recorder*, a weekly newspaper, was established here in 1792 as the *Packet*. The first settler on the present site of

Catskill was Derrick Teunis van Vechten, who built a house here in 1680. The village was not incorporated until 1806.

See J.D. Pinckney, *Reminiscences of Catskill* (Catskill, 1868).

CATSKILL (formerly KAATSKIL) **MOUNTAINS,** a group of moderate elevation pertaining to the Alleghany Plateau, and not properly included in the Appalachian system of North America because they lack the internal structures and the general parallelism of topographic features which characterize the Appalachian ranges. The group contains many summits above 3000 ft. elevation and half a dozen approaching 4000, Slide Mountain (4205 ft.), and Hunter Mountain (4025 ft.), being the only ones exceeding that figure. The bottom lands along the creeks which drain the mountains, together with rolling uplands rising to elevations of from 1500 to 2000 ft., are under cultivation, the mountain slopes being forested or devoted to grazing. The pure and cool atmosphere attracts summer visitors, for whose accommodation many hotels have been built, some of which have become celebrated. Stoney Clove and Kaaterskill Clove are picturesque gorges, the former being traversed by a rail way, and the latter containing three cascades having a total fall of about 300 ft. The growing need of New York City for an increased water-supply has driven her engineers to the Catskills, where several great reservoirs have been projected to supplement those of the Croton watershed.

CATTANEO, CARLO (1801-1869), Italian philosopher and patriot. A republican in his convictions, during his youth he had taken part in the Carbonarist movement in Lombardy. He devoted himself to the study of philosophy, hoping to regenerate the Italian people by withdrawing them from romanticism and rhetoric, and turning their attention to the positive sciences. He expounded his ideas in a review founded by him at Milan in 1837, called *Il Politecnico*. But when the revolution of 1848 broke out he threw himself heart and soul into the fray, and became one of the leading spirits of the insurrection against the Austrians, known as the Five Days of Milan (March 18-22, 1848). Together with Terzaghi, Cernuschi and Clerici he formed a 538council of war which, having its headquarters at Casa Taverna, directed the operations of the insurgents. He was second to none in self-sacrificing energy and heroic resolution. When on the 18th of March Field Marshal Radetzky, feeling that the position of the Austrian garrison was untenable, sounded the rebels as to their terms, some of the leaders were inclined to agree to an armistice which would give time for the Piedmontese troops to arrive (Piedmont had just declared war), but Cattaneo insisted on the complete evacuation of Lombardy. Again on the 21st, Radetzky tried to obtain an armistice, and Durini and Borromeo were ready to grant it, for it would have enabled them to reorganize the defences and replenish the supplies of food and ammunition, which could only last another day. But Cattaneo replied: "The enemy having furnished us with munitions thus far, will continue to furnish them. Twenty-four hours of victuals and twenty-four hours of hunger will be many more hours than we shall need. This evening, if the plans we have just arranged should succeed, the line of the bastions will be broken. At any rate, even though we should lack bread, it is better to die of hunger than on the gallows." On the expulsion of the Austrians the question arose as to the future government of Milan and Italy. Cattaneo was an uncompromising republican and a federalist; so violent was his dislike of the Piedmontese monarchy that when he heard that King Charles Albert had been defeated by the Austrians, and that Radetzky was marching back to reoccupy Milan, he exclaimed: "Good news, the Piedmontese have been beaten. Now we shall be our own masters; we shall fight a people's war, we shall chase the Austrians out of Italy, and set up a Federal Republic." When the Austrians returned Cattaneo had to flee, and took refuge at Lugano, where he gave lessons, wrote his *Storia della Rivoluzione del 1848*, the *Archivio triennale delle cose d' Italia* (3 vols., 1850-1855), and then early in 1860 he started the *Politecnico* once more. He bitterly attacked Cavour for his unitarian views, and for the cession of Nice and Savoy. In 1860 Garibaldi summoned him to Naples to take part in the government of the Neapolitan provinces, but he would not agree to the union with Piedmont without local autonomy. After the union of Italy he was frequently asked to stand for parliament, but always refused because he could not conscientiously take the oath of allegiance to the monarchy. In 1868 the pressure of friends overcame his resistance, and he agreed to stand, but at the last moment he drew back, still unable to take the oath, and returned to Lugano, where he died in 1869. As a writer Cattaneo was learned and brilliant, but far too bitter a partisan to be judicious, owing to his narrowly republican views; his ideas on local autonomy were perhaps wise, but, at a moment when unity was the first essential, inopportune.

BIBLIOGRAPHY.—A. and J. Mario, *Carlo Cattaneo* (Florence, 1884); E. Zanoni, *Carlo Cattaneo nella vita e nelle opere* (Rome, 1898); see also his own *Opere edite ed inedite*(7 vols., Florence, 1881-1892), *Scritti politici ed epistolari* (3 vols., Florence, 1892-1901), *Scritti storici, letterari* (Milan, 1898, &c.).

CATTARO (Serbo-Croatian *Kotor*), the chief town of an administrative district in Dalmatia, Austria. Pop. (1900) of town, 3021; of commune, 5418. Cattaro occupies a narrow ledge between the Montenegrin Mountains and the Bocche di Cattaro, a winding and beautiful inlet of the Adriatic Sea. This inlet expands into five broad gulfs, united by narrower channels, and forms one of the finest natural harbours in Europe. Teodo, on the outermost gulf, is a small naval port. Cattaro is strongly fortified, and about 3000 troops are stationed in its neighbourhood. On the seaward side, the defensive works include Castelnuovo (*Erceg Novi*), which guards the main entrance to the Bocche. On the landward side, the long walls running from the town to the castle of San Giovanni, far above, form a striking feature in the landscape; and the heights of the Krivoscie or Crevoscia (*Krivošije*), a group of barren mountains between Montenegro, Herzegovina and the sea, are crowned by small forts. Cattaro is divided almost equally between the Roman Catholic and Orthodox creeds. It is the seat of a Roman Catholic bishop, with a small cathedral, a collegiate church and several convents. The transit trade with Montenegro is impeded by high tariffs on both sides of the frontier. Foreign visitors to Montenegro usually land at Cattaro, which is connected by steamer with Trieste and by road with Cettigne. The railway from Ragusa terminates at Zelenika, near Castelnuovo.

There are many interesting places on the shores of the Bocche. Castelnuovo is a picturesque town, with a dismantled 14th-century citadel, which has, at various times, been occupied by Bosnians, Turks, Venetians, Spaniards, Russians, French, English and Austrians. The orthodox convent of St Sava, standing amid beautiful gardens, was founded in the 16th century, and contains many fine specimens of 17th-century silversmiths' work. There is a Benedictine monastery on a small island opposite to Perasto (*Perast*), 8 m. east of Castelnuovo. Perasto itself was for a time an independent state in the 14th century. Rhizon, the modern hamlet of Risano, close by, was a thriving "Illyrian" city as early as 229 B.C., and gave its name to the Bocche, then known as *Rhizonicus Sinus*. Rhizon submitted to Rome in 168 B.C., and about the same time Ascrivium, or Ascruvium, the modern Cattaro, is first mentioned as a neighbouring city. Justinian built a fortress above Ascrivium in A.D. 535, after expelling the Goths, and a second town probably grew up on the heights round it, for Constantine Porphyrogenitus, in the 10th century, alludes to "Lower Cattaro" τὸ κάτω Δεκάτερα. The city was plundered by the Saracens in 840, and by the Bulgarians in 1102. In the next year it was ceded to Servia by the Bulgarian tsar Samuel, but revolted, in alliance with Ragusa, and only submitted in 1184, as a protected state, preserving intact its republican institutions, and its right to conclude treaties and engage in war. It was already an episcopal see, and, in the 13th century, Dominican and Franciscan monasteries were established to check the spread of Bogomilism. In the 14th century the commerce of Cattaro rivalled that of Ragusa, and provoked the jealousy of Venice. The downfall of Servia in 1389 left the city without a guardian, and, after being seized and abandoned by Venice and Hungary in turn, it passed under Venetian rule in 1420. It was besieged by the Turks in 1538 and 1657, visited by plague in 1572, and nearly destroyed by earthquakes in 1563 and 1667. By the treaty of Campo-Formio in 1797 it passed to Austria; but in 1805, by the treaty of Pressburg, it was assigned to Italy, and was united in 1810 with the French empire. In 1814 it was restored to Austria by the congress of Vienna. The attempt to enforce compulsory military service, made and abandoned in 1869, but finally successful in 1881, led to two short-lived revolts among the Krivoscians, during which Cattaro was the Austrian headquarters.

See G. Gelcich (Gelčić), *Memorie storiche sulle Bocche di Cattaro* (Zara, 1880).

CATTEGAT, or KATTEGAT (Scand. "cat's-throat"), a strait forming part of the connexion between the Baltic and the North Seas. It lies north and south between Sweden and Denmark, and connects north with the Skagerrack and south through the Sound, the Great Belt and the Little Belt with the Baltic Sea. Its length is about 150 m. and its extreme breadth about 90 m.

CATTERMOLE, GEORGE (1800-1868), English painter, chiefly in water-colours, was born at Dickleburgh, near Diss, Norfolk, in August 1800. At the age of sixteen he began working as an architectural and topographical draughtsman; afterwards he contributed designs to be engraved in the annuals then so popular; thence he progressed into water-colour painting, becoming an associate of the Water-Colour Society in 1822, and a full member in 1833. In 1850 he withdrew from active connexion with this society, and took to painting in oil. His most fertile period was between 1833 and 1850. At the Paris exhibition of 1855 he received one of the five first-class gold medals awarded to British painters. He also enjoyed professional honours in Amsterdam and in Belgium. He died on the 24th of July 1868. Among his leading works are "The Murder of the Bishop of Liége" (15th century), "The Armourer relating the Story of the Sword," "The Assassination of the Regent Murray by Hamilton of Bothwellhaugh," and (in oil) "A Terrible Secret." 539He was largely employed by publishers, illustrating the *Waverley Novels* and the *Historical Annual* of his brother the Rev. Richard Cattermole (his scenes from the wars of Cavaliers and Roundheads in this series are among his best engraved works), and many other volumes besides. Cattermole was a painter of no inconsiderable gifts, and of great facility in picturesque resource; he was defective in solidity of form and texture, and in realism or richness of colour. He excelled in rendering scenes of chivalry, of medievalism, and generally of the romantic aspects of the past.

CATTLE (Norman Fr. *catel*, from Late Lat. *capitate*, wealth or property, a word applied in the feudal system to movable property and particularly to live stock, and surviving in its wider meaning as "chattel" or "chattle"), a general term for the cows and oxen of agricultural use. For the zoological account, see BOVIDAE, and the subordinate articles there referred to; for details concerning dairy-farming, see DAIRY.

Oxen appear to have been among the earliest of domesticated animals, as they undoubtedly were among the most important agents in the growth of early civilization. They are mentioned in the oldest written records of the Hebrew and Hindu peoples, and are figured on Egyptian monuments raised over 3000 years B.C.; while remains of domesticated specimens have been found in Swiss lake-dwellings along with the stone implements and other relics of Neolithic man. In infant communities a man's wealth was measured by the number and size of his herds—Abraham, it is said, was rich in cattle—and oxen for a long period formed, as they still do among many savage or semi-savage tribes, the favourite medium of exchange between individuals and communities. After the introduction of a metal coinage into ancient Greece, this method of exchange was commemorated by stamping the image of an ox on the new money; while the connexion between cattle and coin as symbols of wealth has left its mark on the languages of Europe, as is seen in the Latin word *pecunia* and the English "pecuniary," derived from *pecus*, cattle. The value attached to cattle in ancient times is further shown by the Bull figuring among the signs of the zodiac; in its worship by the ancient Egyptians under the title of Apis; in the veneration which has always been paid to it by the Hindus, according to whose sacred legends it was the first animal created by the three divinities directed by the supreme Deity to furnish the earth with animated beings; and in the important part it played in Greek and Roman mythology. The Hindus were not allowed to shed the blood of the ox, and the Egyptians could only do so in sacrificing to their gods. Both Hindus and Jews were forbidden to muzzle it when treading out the corn; to destroy it wantonly was a crime among the Romans, punishable with exile.

Breeds.—There exist in Britain four interesting remnants of what were at one time numerous enclosed herds of ancient forest cattle,1 with black or red points, in parks at Chillingham, Cadzow, Vaynol (near Bangor, North Wales) and Chartley. A few of the last have been removed to Woburn. Other representatives of old stock are a resuscitated white Welsh breed with black points, derived from white specimens born of black Welsh cows; several herds of a white polled breed with black points; a herd of the ancient Polled Suffolk Dun, an excellent milking breed; a White Belted Galloway and a White Belted Welsh breed; the old Gloucester breed at Badminton, with a white rump, tail and underline, related to the now extinct Glamorgan breed; the Shetland breed; and a few herds of Dutch cattle preserved for their superior milking powers.

The prominent breeds of cattle in the British Isles2 comprise the Shorthorn, Lincolnshire Red Shorthorn, Hereford, Devon, South Devon, Sussex, Welsh, Longhorn, Red Polled, Aberdeen-Angus, Galloway, West Highland, Ayrshire, Jersey, Guernsey, Kerry and Dexter.

The Shorthorn, Lincolnshire Red Shorthorn, Hereford, Devon, South Devon, Sussex, Longhorn and Red Polled breeds are native to England; the Aberdeen-Angus, Galloway, Highland and Ayrshire breeds to Scotland; and the Kerry and Dexter breeds to Ireland. The Jersey and Guernsey breeds—often spoken of as Channel Islands cattle—belong to the respective islands whose names they bear, and great care is taken to keep them isolated from each other. The term Alderney is obsolete, the cattle of Alderney being mainly a type of the Guernsey breed.

Among breeds well known in the United States2 and not mentioned above, the more important are the Holsteins, large black and white cattle highly valued for their abundant milk production, and the Dutch Belted breed, black with a broad white band round the body, also good milkers.

The *Shorthorn*3 is the most widely distributed of all the breeds of cattle both at home and abroad. No census of breeds has ever been taken in the United Kingdom, but such an enumeration would show the Shorthorn far to exceed in numbers any other breed, whilst the great majority of cross-bred cattle contain Shorthorn blood. During the last quarter of the 18th century the brothers Charles Colling (1751-1836) and Robert Colling (1749-1820), by careful selection and breeding, improved the cattle of the Teeswater district in the county of Durham. If the Shorthorn did not originate thus, it is indisputable that the efforts of the Collings4 had a profound influence upon the fortunes of the breed. It is still termed the Durham breed in most parts of the world except the land of its birth, and the geographical name is far preferable, for the term "shorthorn" is applicable to a number of other breeds. Other skilled breeders turned their attention to the Shorthorns and established famous strains, the descendants of which can still be traced. By Thomas Booth, of Killerby and Warlaby in Yorkshire (1777), the "Booth" strains of Shorthorns were originated; by Thomas Bates, of Kirklevington in Yorkshire, the "Bates" families5 (1800).

The Shorthorn is sometimes spoken of as the ubiquitous breed, its striking characteristic being the ease with which it adapts itself to varying conditions of soil, climate and management. It is also called the "red, white and roan." The roan colour is very popular, and dark red has its supporters, as in the case of the *Lincolnshire Red Shorthorns*; white is not in favour, especially abroad. The Shorthorn breed is more noted for its beef-making than for its milk-yielding properties, although the non-pedigree milking Shorthorn of the north of England is an excellent cow with dual-purpose qualifications of the first order. An effort is being made to restore milking qualities to certain strains of pedigree blood.

The culmination of what may be termed the Booth and Bates period was in the year 1875, when the sales took place of Lord Dunmore's and William Torr's herds, which realized extraordinary prices. In that black year of farming, 1879, prices were declining, and they continued to do so till within the last few years of the close of the 19th century, when there set in a gradual revival, stimulated largely by the commercial prosperity of the country. The result of extremely high prices when line-bred animals were in fashion was a tendency to breed from all kinds of animals that were of the same tribe, without selection. A deterioration set in, which was aggravated by the overlooking of the milking properties. Shorthorn breeders came to see that change of blood was necessary. Meanwhile, for many years breeders in Aberdeenshire had been holding annual sales of young bulls and heifers from their herds. The late Amos Cruickshank began his annual sales in the 'forties, and the late W.T. Talbot-Crosbie had annual sales from his Shorthorn herd in the south-west of Ireland for a number of years. Many Aberdeen farmers emigrated to Canada, and bought Shorthorn calves in their native county to take with them. The Cruickshanks held their bull sales at that time, and many of their animals were bought by the small breeders in Canada. This continued until 1875, when the Cruickshanks had so much private demand that they discontinued their public sales. Subsequently, when Cruickshank sold his herd privately 540to James Nelson & Sons for exportation, the animals could not all be shipped, and W. Duthie, of Collynie, Aberdeenshire, bought some of the older cows, whilst J. Deane Willis, of Bapton Monar, Wilts, bought the yearling heifers. Duthie thereupon resumed the sales that the Cruickshanks had relinquished, his averages being £30 in 1892, about £50 in 1893-1894, and £80 in 1895. These prices advanced through English breeders requiring a little change of blood, and also through the increasing tendency to exhibit animals of great substance, or rather to feed animals for show. The success of this movement strengthened the demand, whilst an inquiry for his line of blood arose in the United States and Canada. A faithful contemporary history of the Shorthorn breed is to be found in *Thornton's Circular*, published quarterly since 1868; see also J. Sinclair, *History of Shorthorn Cattle* (1907); R. Bruce, *Fifty Years among Shorthorns* (1907); A.H. Sanders, *Shorthorn Cattle* (Chicago, 1901).

The *Lincolnshire Red Shorthorns* are the best dual-purpose cattle—for milk and meat—that possess a pedigree record, in the United Kingdom, and their uniform cherry red colour has brought them into high favour in tropical countries for crossing with the native breeds.

The *Hereford* breed is maintained chiefly in Herefordshire and the adjoining counties. Whilst a full red is the general colour of the body, the Herefords are distinguished by their white face, white chest and abdomen, and white mane. The legs up to the knee or hock are also often white. As a protection against the sun in a hot climate dark spots on the eyelids or round the orbits are valuable. The horns are moderately long. Herefords, though they rear their own calves, have acquired but little fame as dairy cattle. They are very hardy, and produce beef of excellent quality. Being docile, they fatten easily and readily, and as graziers' beasts they are in high favour.

When the Bates' Shorthorn bubble burst in America about 1877, the Hereford gradually replaced the Shorthorn of the western ranches, and it is now the most numerous ranch animal in the United States and Canada. The bulls beat the bulls of all other breeds in "rustling" capacity.

In America the ranch-bred Herefords have got too small in the bone in recent years, and Shorthorns, chiefly of the Scottish type, are being introduced to increase their size by crossing. In the "feed lot" a well-bred Hereford steer feeds more quickly than either a Shorthorn or an Aberdeen-Angus.

In Queensland, Hereford cattle bred from the "Lord Wilton" strain by Robert Christison of Lammermoor have for years been triumphant as beef-producers in competition with the Shorthorn. When these are quartered in the ordinary butchers' fashion, the hind-quarters outweigh the fore-quarters, which is a reversal of the prevailing rule.

North Devons.—The "Rubies of the West," as they are termed from their hue, are reared chiefly in Devon and Somerset. The colour is a whole red, its depth or richness varying with the individual, and in summer becoming mottled with darker spots. The Devons stand somewhat low; they are neat and compact, and possess admirable symmetry. Although a smaller breed than the Shorthorn or the Hereford, they weigh better than either. The horns of the female are somewhat slender, and often curve neatly upwards. Being fine-limbed, active animals, they are well adapted for grazing the poor pastures of their native hills, and they turn their food to the best account, yielding excellent beef. They have not yet attained much celebrity as milch kine, for, though their milk is of first-class quality, with a few notable exceptions, its quantity is small. Latterly, however, the milking qualities have received more attention from breeders, whose object is to qualify the Devon as a dual-purpose breed.

The *South Devon* or *South Hams* cattle are almost restricted to that southern part of the county of Devon known as the Hams, whence they are also called "Hammers." With a somewhat ungainly head, lemon-yellow hair, yellow skin, and large but hardly handsome udder, the South Devon breed more resembles the Guernsey, with which it is supposed to be connected, than the trim-built cattle of the hills of North Devon. The cows are large, heavy milkers, and produce excellent butter. They are rarely seen outside their locality except when they appear in the showyards.

The *Sussex* breed resembles the North Devon in many respects, but it is bigger, less refined in appearance, less graceful in outline, and of a deeper brown-chestnut colour than the "dainty Devon," as the latter may well be called when compared with them. As a hardy race, capable of thriving on poor rough pastures, the Sussex are highly valued in their native districts, where they were rapidly improved before the end of the 19th century. They are essentially a beef-producing breed, the cows having little reputation as milkers. By stall-feeding they can be ripened for the butcher at an early age. Sussex cattle are said to "die well," that is, to yield a large proportion of meat in the best parts of the carcase.

In the *Welsh* breed of cattle black is the prevailing colour, and the horns are fairly long. They do not mature very rapidly, but some of them grow eventually into great ponderous beasts, and their beef is of prime quality. The cows often possess considerable reputation as milkers. As graziers' beasts Welsh cattle are well known in the midland counties of England, where, under the name of "Welsh runts," large herds of bullocks are fattened on the pastures or "topped up" in the yards in winter.

All the remaining strains of Welsh cattle were recognized as one breed in 1904, when the Welsh Black Cattle Society united into one register the Herd Books of North and South Wales.

The *Longhorn* or "Dishley" breed of cattle is one of the most interesting historically. It was with Longhorns that Robert Bakewell, of Dishley, Leicestershire (1726-1795), showed his remarkable skill as an improver of cattle in the middle of the 18th century.6 At one period Longhorns spread widely over England and Ireland, but, as the Shorthorns extended their domain, the Longhorns made way for them. They are big, rather clumsy animals, with long drooping horns, which are very objectionable in these days of cattle transport by rail and sea. They are slow in coming to maturity, but are very hardy. The bullocks feed up to heavy weights, and the cows are fair milkers. No lover of cattle can view these quaint creatures without a feeling of satisfaction that the efforts made to resuscitate a breed which has many useful qualities to commend it have been successful, and that the extinction which threatened it in the 'eighties of last century is no longer imminent. In 1907 there were twenty-two Longhorn herds containing about four hundred registered cattle located mainly in the English midlands and Man.

The *Red Poll* breed, though old, has only come into prominence within recent years. They were known as the East Anglian Polls, and later as the Norfolk and Suffolk Polled cattle, being confined chiefly to these two counties. They are symmetrically built, of medium size, and of uniformly red colour. They have a tuft of hair on the poll. As dairy cattle, they are noted for the length of the period during which they continue in milk. Not less are they valued as beef-producers, and, as they are hardy and docile, they fatten readily and mature fairly early. Hence, like the Lincolnshire Red Shorthorn, they may claim to be a dual-purpose breed. As beef cattle they are always seen to advantage at the Norwich Christmas cattle show, held annually in November.

The *Aberdeen-Angus*, a polled, black breed, the cows of which are often termed "Doddies," belongs to Aberdeenshire and adjacent parts of Scotland, but many herds are maintained in England and some in Ireland. The steers and heifers fed for the butcher attain great weight, make first-class show beasts, and yield beef of excellent quality. The cross between the Shorthorn and the Aberdeen-Angus is a favourite in the meat markets and at fat-stock competitions.

The *Galloways* are named from the district, Kirkcudbright and Wigtonshire, in the south-west of Scotland, to which they are native. Like the Aberdeen-Angus cattle, they are hornless, and normally of a black colour. But, with a thicker hide and shaggy hair, suited to a wet climate, they have a coarser appearance than the Aberdeen-Angus, the product of a less humid region, though 541it approaches the latter in size. Galloways yield superior beef, but mature less rapidly than the Aberdeen-Angus. They make admirable beasts for the grazier, and the cross between the Galloway and the white Shorthorn bull, known as a "Blue Grey," is much sought after by the grazier and the butcher.

PLATE I.

BREEDS OF ENGLISH CATTLE.

SHORTHORN
BULL.

DEVON BULL.

HEREFORD
BULL.

SOUTH DEVON
BULL.

PLATE II.

BREEDS OF ENGLISH AND WELSH CATTLE.
(From photographs by F. Babbage.)

LONGHORN
BULL.

RED POLLED
BULL.

WELSH BULL.

SUSSEX BULL.

BREEDS OF SCOTCH CATTLE.

ABERDEEN-ANGUS
BULL.

GALLOWAY BULL.

AYRSHIRE COW.

HIGHLAND BULL.

BREEDS OF IRISH AND CHANNEL ISLANDS CATTLE.
(From photographs by F. Babbage.)
The comparative sizes of the animals are indicated by the scale of reproduction of the
photographs.

DEXTER
BULL.

KERRY
COW.

GUERNSEY
COW.

JERSEY
COW.

The *West Highland* or Kyloe breed are perhaps the most hardy and picturesque of British cattle. Their home is amidst the wild romantic scenery of the Highlands and the Western Isles of Scotland, though Highland bullocks with long, spreading curved horns may be seen in English parks. They have not made much progress towards early maturity, but their slowly ripened beef is of the choicest quality. The colour of their thick shaggy hair varies from white and light dun to tawny yellow of many shades, and black.

The *Ayrshires* are the dairy breed of Scotland, where they have considerably overstepped the limits of the humid western county whence they take their name. They are usually of a white and brown colour, the patches being well defined. The neat, shapely, upstanding horns are characteristic. The Ayrshires are under medium size and move gracefully, and the females display the wedge-shape typical of dairy cows. They are a hardy breed, and, even from poor pastures, give good yields of milk, especially useful for cheese-making purposes. The milking powers of the breed are being improved under a system of milk-testing and records supported by the Highland and Agricultural Society.

The *Jerseys* are graceful, deer-like cattle, whose home is in the island of Jersey, where, by means of stringent regulations against the importation of cattle, the breed has been kept pure for many generations. As its milk is especially rich in fat (so rich that it requires to be diluted with a little water before it can be safely fed to calves), the Jersey has attained a wide reputation as a butter-producing breed. It is a great favourite in England, where many pure-bred herds exist. The colours most preferred are "whole" fawns of many shades. The light silver-grey, which was in high repute in England in the early 'seventies of the 19th century, is out of favour. Browns and brindles are rarely seen. The grey zone surrounding the black muzzle gives the appearance designated "mealy-mouthed." The horns are short, and generally artificially curved inwards; the bones are fine. The best milch cows have a yellowish circle round the eye, and the skin at the extremity of the tail is of a deep yellow, almost orange colour. The cows are gentle and docile when reared in close contact with human beings, but the bulls, despite their small size, are often fierce.

Guernsey cattle are native to the islands of Guernsey, Alderney, Sark and Herm. They are kept pure by importation restrictions. Herds of pure-bred Guernseys also exist in the Isle of Wight and in various counties of England and Scotland. They have not the refined and elegant appearance of the Jerseys, which, however, they exceed in size. They are usually of a rich yellowish-brown colour, patched with white, in some cases their colour almost meriting the appellation of "orange and lemon." The yellow colour inside the ears is a point always looked for by judges. The cows, large-bellied and narrow in front, are truly wedge-shaped, the greatly developed udder adding to the expanse of the hinder part of the body. They yield an abundance of milk, rich in fat, and are excellent butter-producers. The horns are yellow at the base, curved, and not coarse. The nose is flesh-coloured and free from black markings.

The *Canadian* breed, black with a narrow brown stripe down the back and a light ring round the muzzle, are descended from old Brittany cattle imported into Canada by French settlers three hundred years ago, and are in consequence related to the Channel Islands cattle. They are remarkably hardy and good milkers, and it is claimed they produce butter fat at 2 c. a ℔ less cost than any other breed.

The *Kerry* is a breed of small black cattle belonging to the south-west of Ireland, whence they have spread into many parts, not only of their native land, but of England as well. Although they are able to subsist on the roughest and scantiest of fare, and are exceedingly hardy, the cows are, nevertheless, excellent milkers, and have acquired celebrity as a dairy breed. The colour is black, but the cows sometimes have a little white on the udder. The horns are white, with black tips, and are turned upwards. The Kerry is active and graceful, long and lithe in body, and light-limbed. On the rich pastures of England it has increased considerably in size.

The *Dexter* breed is reputed to take its name from one Dexter, agent of Maude, Lord Hawarden, who is credited with having established it by selection and breeding from the best mountain types of the Kerry. Until recently it was called the Dexter-Kerry. It is smaller and more compact than the Kerry, shorter in the leg, and intoed before and behind. Whilst valuable as a beef-making animal, it is equally noted for its milk-producing capacity. Black is the usual colour, but red is also recognized, with, in either case, a little white. When of a red colour, the appearance of the animal has been aptly compared to that of a grand Shorthorn viewed through the wrong end of a telescope. The Kerry and the Dexter are readily distinguishable. The Kerry has a gay, light, deer-like head and horn, light limbs and thin skin. The Dexter has coarser limbs, a square body, flat back, thick shoulder, short neck, and head and horn set on low.

A herd of *Dexter-Shorthorns* was founded by Major Barton at Straffan, Ireland, in 1860, in which prominent characteristics of the two breeds have been permanently blended so that they breed true to type.

As milk-producers, and therefore as dairy cattle, certain strains of the Shorthorn (registered as well as non-pedigree), the Lincolnshire Red Shorthorn, South Devon, Longhorn, Red Polled, Ayrshire, Jersey, Guernsey, Kerry and Dexter breeds have acquired eminence. Such breeds as the Shorthorn, Lincolnshire Red Shorthorn, South Devon, Welsh, Red Polled and Dexter are claimed as useful beef-makers as well as milk-producers, and are classified as dual-purpose animals. The others belong to the beef-producers. As regards colour, red is characteristic of the Lincolnshire Shorthorn, the Hereford, Devon, Sussex and Red Polled. Black is the dominating colour of the Welsh, Aberdeen-Angus, Galloway, Kerry and Dexter. A yellowish hue is seen in the West Highland, Guernsey and South Devon breeds. Various shades of fawn colour are usual in Jersey cattle and also appear among Highlanders. The Herefords, though with red bodies, have white faces, manes, and dewlaps, whilst white prevails to a greater or less extent in the Shorthorn, Longhorn and Ayrshire breeds. The Shorthorn breed is exceedingly variable in colour; pure-bred specimens may be red, or white, or roan, or may be marked with two or more of these colours, the roan resulting from a blending of the white and red. Black is not seen in a pure-bred Shorthorn. The biggest and heaviest cattle come from the beef-making breeds, and are often cross-bred. Very large or heavy beasts, if pure-bred, usually belong to one or other of the Shorthorn, Hereford, Sussex, Welsh, West Highland, Aberdeen-Angus and Galloway breeds. The Devon, Red Polled and Guernsey are medium-sized cattle; the Ayrshires are smaller, although relatively the bullocks grow larger than bulls or cows. The Jerseys are small, graceful cattle, but the smaller type of Kerries, the Dexters and the Shetlanders furnish the smallest cattle of the British Isles.

See generally the *Herd Books* of the various breed societies.

(W. Fr.; R. W.)

*Rearing and Feeding.*7—A calf at birth scales from one-twelfth to one-fourteenth the weight of the dam. A sucking calf of one of the large breeds should gain 3 ℔ per day for the first month, 2.5 ℔ for the second, and 2 ℔ during the later calf period. Colostrum, or first-day milk after calving, contains more than five times the albuminoid compounds found in average cows' milk. In the course of three or four days it gradually becomes normal in composition, although the peculiar flavour remains a few days longer. Nature has specially prepared it for the young 542calf with extremely nourishing and also laxative properties, and it is of practically no value for any other purpose. Normal cows' milk has an albuminoid ratio slightly narrower than 1 : 4—colostrum 1 : .71. [The ratio is arrived at by adding to the percentage of milk-sugar, possessing about the food equivalent of starch, the fat multiplied by 2.268, and dividing by the total albuminoids—all digestible.]

Common nutrient ratios for older animals are stated in the following table of food standards by Dr Emil Wolff:—

| | Food Consumed per Day. | | | | | |
| | Dry. | | | | Digestible. | |
	Live Weight	Organic Matter	Albuminoid	Fats	Carbo-Hydrates	Albuminoid Ratio.
	℔	℔	℔		℔	℔

Calves, growing, 2 to 3 months	150	3.3	.6	.30	2.1	1 : 4.7
Young cattle " 3 to 6 "	300	7.0	1.0	.30	4.1	1 : 5
" " 6 to 12 "	500	12.0	1.2	.30	6.8	1 : 6
" " 12 to 18 "	700	16.8	1.4	.28	9.1	1 : 7
" " 18 to 24 "	850	20.4	1.4	.26	10.3	1 : 8
Oxen in complete rest	1000	27.5	.7	.15	8.0	1 : 12
" fattening, 1st period	1000	27.0	2.5	.50	15.0	1 : 65
" " 2nd period	1000	26.0	3.0	.70	14.8	1 : 5.5
" " 3rd period	1000	25.0	2.7	.60	14.8	1 : 6
Milch cows	1000	24.0	2.5	.40	12.5	1 : 5.4

Digestible albuminoid nitrogen is the scarcest and consequently the costliest ingredient in food-stuffs, but, since the introduction of vegetable proteid made by Mitchell's process from the castor bean, an easy and inexpensive means of balancing cattle food ratios is available. By this means the manurial value of the excrement is increased. The calculations necessary in arriving at a ratio are simplified by the employment of Jeffers's calculator (Plainsboro, N.J.).

There are three common methods of rearing calves, (1) The calf sucks its mother or foster-mother. This is the natural method and the best for the show-yard and for early fattening purposes; but it is the most expensive, and the calves, if not handled, grow up wild and dangerous. Store stock may be also raised by putting two calves to one cow and weaning at three months old; a second pair in turn yielding place to a single calf. (2) Full milk from the cow at about 90° F. is given alone until the latter part of the milk period; then the calf is trained to eat supplementary foods to preserve the calf-fat after weaning. A large calf at first receives daily three quarts of milk at three meals. The amount is increased to 2 gallons by the end of the fourth week, and to 2½ gallons at 3 months, when gradual weaning begins. Linseed cake meal is specially suitable for such calves. (3) The calf receives full milk from the mother for one to two weeks, or better, for three to four weeks; then it is slowly transferred to fortified separated milk or milk substitutes. Cod-liver oil, 2 oz. daily, is a good substitute for butter fat. In America cotton-seed oil, ½ oz. to the quart of milk, or an equivalent of oleomargarine heated to 110° F. and churned with separated milk, has produced a live-weight-increase of 2 ℔ daily. Linseed simmered to a jelly and added to separated milk gives good results. Moderate amounts are easily digested. Oatmeal or maize meal containing 10% of linseed meal does well, later, at less cost. Milk substitutes and calf meals require close attention in preparation, and would not fetch the prices they do if feeders possessed the technical knowledge necessary to select and mix common foods. Ground cake or linseed meal is, after a time, better given dry than cooked, being then better masticated and not so liable to produce indigestion.

Grass or fine hay in racks is provided when the calf can chew the cud. As cattle get older, live-weight-increase grows less. Smithfield weights[8] show that a good bullock up to a year old will increase 2 ℔ daily, a two-year-old 1¾ ℔, and a three-year-old a little over 1½ ℔

Cattle feeding on a farm consume crude produce that is inconvenient to market, and make farmyard manure; but there is frequently no profit left. To secure the balance on the right side the inlaid price per live cwt. requires to be 5s. less than the sale price—say 32s. per cwt. for lean cattle, and 37s. per cwt. for the animal when sold fat and capable of producing 60% of dressed beef. The ordinary animal yields only about 57%. A well-bred fattening bullock begins with 2 ℔ of cake and meal per day, increasing to 8 ℔ at the end of five months (6 ℔ on an average), and receives ¾ cwt. of roots and 12 ℔ of straw; at an average cost of about 4s. 3d. per imperial stone or 50s. per cwt. of dressed carcase. Heifers feed faster than bullocks, and age tells on the rate at which an animal will mature: a three-year-old will develop into prime beef more quickly and easily than a two-year-old. It is difficult to produce "baby beef" at a profit, and it can only be done with picked animals of the best flesh-producing breeds, which cannot be bought at a price per cwt. below the finished sale price, for animals producing baby beef must from start to finish (under two years old) be at all times fit to go to the fat market. It is true that a very young animal can give a better account of food than an older one, but this advantage is counterbalanced by the tendency to grow rather than to fatten. (See also AGRICULTURE.)

In cold and stormy districts cattle thrive best in covered courts, but in a mild climate they do equally well in open yards with shelter-sheds. The more air they get the less liable they are to tuberculosis—example Lincolnshire and the drier south-eastern counties. The ideal method of house-feeding cattle is singly in boxes 10 ft. square, where they are undisturbed, and where the best manure is made because it is not washed by rain.

On the finest British grazing lands two lots of cattle are fed in one season. The first is finished early in July, having, without artificial feeding, laid on eight to nine stones of beef. The second lot requires three or four pounds of undecorticated cotton cake each towards the end of September and in October when grass begins to fail.

(R. W.)

1Rev. J. Storer, *The Wild White Cattle of Great Britain* (1879).

2See Wallace's *Farm Live Stock of Great Britain* (1907), Low's *Breeds of the Domestic Animals of the British Isles* (1842, illustrated, and 1845), and E.V. Wilcox's *Farm Animals* (1907), an American work.

3Shorthorn Society of Great Britain and Ireland (1822). Sec. E.J. Powell, 12 Hanover Square, London, W.

4C.J. Bates, "The Brothers Colling," *Jour. Roy. Agric. Soc.* (1899).

5C.J. Bates, *Thomas Bates and the Kirklevington Shorthorns: a Contribution to the History of Pure Durham Cattle* (Newcastle-upon-Tyne, 1897).

6Housman, "Robert Bakewell," *Jour. Roy. Agric. Soc.* (1894).

7See E. Wolff, *Farm Foods,* by H.H. Cousins (1895); A.D. Hall, *Rothamsted Experiments* (1905); R. Warington, *Chemistry of the Farm* (15th ed., 1902); W.A. Henry, *Feeds and Feeding* (1907); H.W. Mumford, *Beef Production* (1907); H.P. Armsby, *Animal Nutrition* (2nd ed., 1906); T. Shaw, *Animal Breeding* (1903); R. Wallace, *Farm Live Stock of Great Britain* (4th ed., 1907).

8E. J. Powell, *History of the Smithfield Club from 1798 to 1900* (1902).

CATULLUS, GAIUS VALERIUS (?84-54 B.C.), the greatest lyric poet of Rome. As regards his names and the dates of his birth and death, the most important external witness is that of Jerome, in the continuation of the Eusebian *Chronicle*, under the year 87 B.C., "Gaius Valerius Catullus, scriptor lyricus Veronae nascitur," and under 57 B.C., "Catullus xxx. aetatis anno Romae moritur." There is no controversy as to the gentile name, *Valerius*. Suetonius, in his *Life of Julius Caesar* (ch. 73), mentions the poet by the names "Valerium Catullum." Other persons who had the *cognomen* Catullus belonged to the Valerian gens, *e.g.* M. Valerius Catullus Messalinus, a *delator* in the reign of Domitian, mentioned in the fourth satire of Juvenal (l. 113):—

"Et cum mortifero prudens Veiento Catullo."

Inscriptions show, further, that *Valerius* was a common name in the native province of Catullus, and belonged to other inhabitants of Verona besides the poet and his family (Schwabe, *Quaestiones Catullianae*, p. 27). Scholars have been divided in opinion as to whether his *praenomen* was *Gaius* or *Quintus*, and in the best MSS. the volume is called simply *Catulli Veronensis liber*. For *Gaius* we have the undoubted testimony, not only of Jerome, which rests on the much earlier authority of Suetonius, but also that of Apuleius. In support of *Quintus* a passage was quoted from the *Natural History* of Pliny (xxxvii. 6, 81). But the *praenomen* Q. is omitted in the best MSS., and in other passages of the same author the poet is spoken of as "Catullus Veronensis." The mistake may have arisen from confusion with Q. Catulus, the colleague of Marius in the Cimbric War, himself also the author of lyrical poems. Allusions in the poems show that the date of his death given by Jerome (57B.C.) is wrong, and that Catullus survived the second consulship of Pompey (55 B.C.) (cf. lv. 6, cxiii. 2), and was present in August of the 543following year at the prosecution of Vatinius by Licinius Calvus (cf. liii.). The allusion in lii. 3—

"Per consulatum peierat Vatinius,"

does not prove that Catullus must have lived to see the consulship bestowed on Vatinius in the end of 47 B.C. but only that Vatinius, after being praetor in 55 B.C., was in the habit of boasting of the certainty of his attaining the consulship, as Cleopatra was in the habit of confirming her most solemn declarations by appealing to her hope of one day administering justice in the Capitol (cf. Haupt, "Quaestiones Catullianae," *Opuscula*, vol. i. 1875). There is then nothing to prove that Catullus lived beyond the month of August 54 B.C. Some of the poems (as xxxvii. and lii.) may have been written during his last illness. If he died in 54 B.C.or early in 53 B.C., Catullus must either have been born later than 87 B.C., or have lived to a greater age than thirty. Catullus is described by Ovid as "hedera iuvenalia cinctus Tempora" (*Amor.* iii. 9. 61),—a description somewhat more suitable to a man who dies in his thirtieth year than to one who dies three or four years later. Further, the age at which a man dies is more likely to be accurately remembered than the particular date either of his death or of his birth, and the common practice of recording the age of the deceased in sepulchral inscriptions must have rendered a mistake about this less likely to occur. It seems, therefore, on the whole, most likely that Jerome's words "xxx. aetatis anno" are correct, and that Catullus was born in 84 B.C.

The statement that he was born at Verona is confirmed by passages in Ovid and Martial. Pliny the elder, who was born at Como, speaks of Catullus in the preface to his *Natural History*, as his "countryman" (*conterraneus*), and the poet speaks of Verona as his home, or at least his temporary residence, in more than one place. His occasional residence in his native place is further attested by the statement of Suetonius (*Julius Caesar*, 73), that "Julius Caesar accepted the poet's apology for his scurrilous verses upon him, invited him to dine with him on the same day, and continued his intimacy with his father as before." As this incident could only have happened during the time that Julius Caesar was pro-consul, the scene of it must have been in the Cisalpine province, and at the house of the poet's father, in or near Verona. The verses apologized for were those contained in poems xxix. and lvii., the former of which must have been written after Caesar's invasion of Britain, so that this interview probably took place in the winter of 55-54 B.C. The fact that his father was the host of the great pro-consul, and lived on terms of intimacy with him, justifies the inference, that he was, in wealth and rank, one of the principal men of the province. The only other important statement concerning the poet's life which rests on external authority is that of Apuleius, that the real name of the Lesbia of the poems was Clodia. Another, which concerns the reputation which he enjoyed after his death, is given in the *Life of Atticus* by Cornelius Nepos (12. 4). It is to the effect that he regarded Lucretius and Catullus as the two greatest poets of his own time.

The poems of Catullus consist of 116 pieces, varying in length from 2 to 408 lines, the great mass of them being, however, short pieces, written in lyric, iambic or elegiac metre. The arrangement cannot be the poet's; it is neither chronological nor in accordance with the character of the topics. The shorter poems, lyric or iambic, are placed first, next the longer epithalamia, (most being written in hexameters) amongst which the *Attis* is inserted and then those written in the elegiac metre. But, though no chronological order is observed, yet internal evidence enables us to determine the occasions on which many of the poems were written, and the order in which they followed one another. They give a very vivid image of various phases of the poet's life, and of the strong feelings with which persons and things affected him. They throw much light also on the social life of Rome and of the provincial towns of Italy in the years preceding the outbreak of the second civil war. In this respect they may be compared with the letters of Cicero.

The poems extend over a period of seven or eight years, from 61 or 62 till 54 B.C. Among the earliest are those which record the various stages of the author's passion for Lesbia. It is in connexion with this passion that he is generally mentioned, or alluded to, by the later Roman poets, such as Propertius, Ovid, Juvenal and Martial. Her real name, as we learn from Apuleius, was Clodia. The admiration of Catullus for Sappho, the Lesbian poetess, which is clearly indicated by the imitation of her language in his fifty-first and sixty-second poems, affords an obvious explanation of the Greek name which he gave to his Roman mistress. Clodia was the notorious sister of Publius Clodius Pulcher, and in the year 56 she charged M. Caelius Rufus, after tiring of him, as she had of Catullus, with an attempt to poison her. It was in defence of Rufus that Cicero described the spell she exercised over young men, in language which might have been applied to her previous relations with the youthful poet, as well as those with the youthful orator and politician.

Poems concerning Lesbia occur among both the earliest and the latest of those contained in the series. They record the various stages of passion through which Catullus passed, from absolute devotion and a secure sense of returned affection, through the various conditions of distrust and jealousy, attempts at renunciation, and short-lived "amoris integrationes," through the "odi et amo" state, and the later state of savage indignation against both Lesbia and his rivals, and especially against Caelius Rufus, till he finally attains, not without much suffering and loss, the last state of scornful indifference. Among the earliest of the poems connected with Lesbia, and among those written in the happiest vein, are ii. and iii., and v. and vii. The 8th, "Miser Catulle, desinas ineptire," perhaps the most beautiful of them all, expresses the first awakening of the poet to a sense of her unworthiness, before the gentler have given place to the fiercer feelings of his nature. His final renunciation is sent in a poem written after his return from the East, with a union of imaginative and scornful power, to his two butts, Furius and Aurelius (xi., "Furi et Aureli, comites Catulli"), who, to judge by the way Catullus writes of them, appear to have been hangers-on upon him, who repaid the pecuniary and other favours they received by giving him grounds for jealousy, and making imputations on his character (cf. xv., xvi., xviii., xxiii.).

The intrigue of Caelius Rufus with Lesbia began in 59 or 58 B.C. It was probably in the earlier stages of this liaison that the 68th poem was written, from which it appears that Catullus, at the time living at Verona, and grieving for the recent death of his brother in the Troad, had heard of Lesbia's infidelity, and, in consideration of her previous faithlessness in his favour, was not inclined to resent it very warmly. Two other poems in the series express the grief which Catullus felt for the death of his brother,—one, the 65th, addressed to the orator Hortensius, who is there, as in some of Cicero's letters, called Hortalus or Ortalus, and sent to him along with the *Coma Berenices* (lxvi.), a translation of a famous elegy of Callimachus. The other poem referring to this event (ci.) must have been composed some years later, probably in 56 B.C., when Catullus visited his brother's tomb in the Troad, on his return from Bithynia. Between 59 and 57 B.C. most of the lampoons on Lesbia and her numerous lovers must have been written (*e.g.* xxxvii., xxxix., &c.). Some, too, of the poems expressive of his more tender feelings to her, such as viii. and lxxvi. belong also to these years; and among the poems written either during this period or perhaps in the early and happier years of his liaison, some of the most charming of his shorter pieces, expressing the affection for his young friends Verannius and Fabullus (ix., xii., xiii.), may be included.

In the year 57 the routine of his life was for a short time broken by his accompanying the propraetor C. Memmius, the friend to whom Lucretius dedicates his great poem, as one of his staff, to the province of Bithynia. His object was probably to better his fortunes by this absence from Rome, as humorous complaints of poverty and debt (xiii., xxvi.) show that his ordinary means were insufficient for his mode of life. He frankly acknowledges the disappointment of these hopes, and still more frankly his disgust with his chief (x., xxviii.). Some of the most charming and perfect among the shorter poems express the delight with which the poet changed the dulness and sultry climate of the 544province for the freedom and keen enjoyment of his voyage home in his yacht, built for him at Amastris on the

Euxine, and for the beauty and peace of his villa on the shores of Lake Benacus, which welcomed him home "wearied with foreign travel." To this period and to his first return to Rome after his visit to his native district belong the poems xlvi., ci., iv., xxxi. and x., all showing by their freshness of feeling and vivid truth of expression the gain which the poet's nature derived from his temporary escape from the passions, distractions and animosities of Roman society. Two poems, written in a very genial and joyous spirit, and addressed to his younger friend Licinius Calvus (xiv. and l.), who is ranked as second only to himself among the lyrical poets of the age, and whose youthful promise pointed him out as likely to become one of the greatest of Roman orators, may, indeed, with most probability be assigned to these later years (xiv.). From the expression "Odissem te odio Vatiniano," in the third line of xiv., it may be inferred that the poem was written not earlier than December (the "Saturnalia") of the year 56B.C., as it was early in that year, as we learn from a letter of Cicero to his brother Quintus (ii. 4. 1), that Calvus first announced his intention of prosecuting Vatinius. The short poem numbered liii. would be written in August 54 B.C. The poems which have left the greatest stain on the fame of Catullus—those "referta contumeliis Caesaris," the licentious abuse of Mamurra, and probably some of those personal scurrilities addressed to women as well as men, or too frank confessions, which posterity would willingly have let die, may well have been written in the last years of his life, under the influence of the bitterness and recklessness induced by his experience. It cannot be determined with certainty whether the longer and more artistic pieces, which occupy the middle of the volume—the *Epithalamium* in celebration of the marriage of Manlius Torquatus, the 62nd poem, written in imitation of the Epithalamia of Sappho, "Vesper adest: iuvenes, consurgite"; the *Attis*, and the Epic Idyll representing the marriage festival of Peleus and Thetis—belong to the earlier or the later period of the poet's career. If the person addressed in the first part of the 68th is the Manlius of the *Epithalamium*, and the lines from 3 to 8—

"Naufragum ut eiectum ... pervigilat,"

refer to the death of Vinia, it would follow that the first Epithalamium was written some time before that poem, and thus belongs to the earlier time. While the translations of Sappho,—

"Ille mi par esse deo videtur,"

and of Callimachus (lxvi.),—

"Omnia qui magni dispexit lumina mundi,"

belong to the earlier period, the *Attis* and the *Peleus and Thetis*, although perhaps suggested by the treatment of the same or similar subjects in Greek authors, are executed with such power and originality as declare them to be products of the most vigorous stage in the development of the poet's genius. That his genius came soon to maturity is a reason for hesitation in assigning any particular time between 62 and 54 B.C. for the composition of the *Attis* and of that part of the *Epithalamium* ("Peliaco quondam prognatae vertice pinus") which deals with the main subject of the poem. But the criticism of Munro in his edition of Lucretius, which shows similarities of expression that cannot be mere casual coincidences, between the Ariadne-episode in the *Epithalamium* of Catullus (from line 52 to 266) and the poem of Lucretius, leaves little doubt that that portion at least of the poem was written after the publication of the *De rerum natura*, in the winter of 55-54 B.C.

No ancient author has left a more vivid impression of himself on his writings than Catullus. Coming to Rome in early youth from a distant province, not at that time included within the limits of Italy, he lived as an equal with the men of his time of most intellectual activity and refinement, as well as of highest social and political eminence. Among those to whom his poems are addressed, or who are mentioned in them, we find the names of Hortensius, Cicero, Cornelius Nepos, Licinius Calvus, Helvius Cinna and Asinius Pollio, then only a youth (xii. 8). Catullus brought into this circle the genius of a great poet, the social vivacity of a vigorous nature, the simplicity and sincerity of an unambitious, and the warmth of an affectionate disposition. He betrays all the sensitiveness of the poetic temperament, but it is never the sensitiveness of vanity, for he is characterized by the modesty rather than the self-confidence which accompanies genius, but the sensitiveness of a heart which gives and expects more sympathy and loyalty in friendship than the world

106

either wants or cares to give in return. He shows also in some of his lighter pieces the fastidiousness of a refined taste, intolerant of all boorishness, pedantry, affectation and sordid ways of life. The passionate intensity of his temperament displays itself with similar strength in the outpourings of his animosity as of his love and affection. It was, unfortunately, the fashion of the time to employ in the expression of these animosities a licence of speech and of imputation which it is difficult for men living under different social conditions to understand, still more difficult to tolerate. Munro has examined the 29th poem—

"Quis hoc potest videre, quis potest pati,"

the longest and most important of the lampoons on Caesar and Mamurra, and shown with much learning and acuteness the motives and intention of Catullus in writing them. Had Julius Caesar really believed, as Suetonius, writing two hundred years afterwards, says he did, that "an eternal stigma had been cast upon him by the verses concerning Mamurra," we should scarcely apply the word magnanimity to his condonation of the offence. But these verses survive as a memorial not of any scandal affecting Julius Caesar which could possibly have been believed by his contemporaries, but of the licence of speech which was then indulged in, of the jealousy with which the younger members of the Roman aristocracy, who a little later fought on the side of Pompey, at that time regarded the ascendancy both of the "father-in-law and the son-in-law," and the social elevation of some of their instruments, and also, to a certain extent, of the deterioration which the frank and generous nature of Catullus underwent from the passions which wasted, and the faithlessness which marred his life.

The great age of Latin poetry extends from about the year 60 B.C. till the death of Ovid in 17 A.D. There are three marked divisions in this period, each with a distinct character of its own: the first represented by Lucretius and Catullus, the second by Virgil and Horace, the last by Ovid. Force and sincerity are the great characteristics of the first period, maturity of art of the second, facility of the last. The educating influence of Greek art on the Roman mind was first fully experienced in the Ciceronian age, and none of his contemporaries was so susceptible of that influence as Catullus. With the susceptibility to art he combined a large share of the vigorous and genial qualities of the Italian race. Like most of his younger contemporaries, he studied in the school of the Alexandrine poets, with whom the favourite subjects of art were the passion of love, and stories from the Greek mythology, which admitted of being treated in a spirit similar to that in which they celebrated their own experiences. It was under this influence that Catullus wrote the *Coma Berenices*, the 68th poem, which, after the manner of the Alexandrines, interweaves the old tale of Protesilaus and Laodamia with the personal experiences of the poet himself, and the *Epithalamium* of Peleus and Thetis, which combines two pictures from the Greek mythology, one of the secure happiness of marriage, the other of the passionate despair of love betrayed. In this last poem Catullus displays a power of creative pictorial imagination far transcending that displayed in any of the extant poetry of Alexandria. We have no means of determining what suggested the subject of the *Attis* to Catullus, whether the previous treatment of the subject by some Greek writer, some survival of the myth which he found still existing during his residence among the "Phrygii Campi," or the growth of various forms of Eastern superstition and fanaticism, at Rome, in the last age of the Republic. Whatever may have been its origin, it is the finest specimen we possess, in either Greek or Latin literature, of that kind of short poem more common in modern than ancient times, in which some situation or passion entirely alien to the writer, and to his own age, is realized with dramatic intensity. 545But the genius of Catullus is, perhaps, even happier in the direct expression of personal feeling than in artistic creation, or the reproduction of tales and situations from mythology. The warmth, intensity and sincerity of his own nature are the sources of the inspiration in these poems. The most elaborate and one of the finest of them is the *Epithalamium* in honour of the marriage of a member of the old house of Manlius Torquatus with Vinia Aurunculeia, written in the glyconic in combination with the pherecratean metre. To this metre Catullus imparts a peculiar lightness and grace by making the trochee, instead of the spondee as in Horace's glyconics and pherecrateans, the first foot in the line. His elegiac metre is constructed with less smoothness and regularity than that of Ovid and Tibullus or even of Propertius, but as employed by him it gives a true echo to the serious and plaintive feelings of some of his poems, while it adapts itself, as it did later in the hands of Martial, to the epigrammatic terseness of his invective. But the perfection of the art of Catullus is seen in his employment of those metres which he adapted to the Latin tongue from the earlier poets of Greece, the pure iambic trimeter, as in iv.—

"Phaselus ille quem videtis hospites,"

the scazon iambic, employed in viii. and xxxi.—

"Paeninsularum, Sirmio, insularumque,"

and the phalecian hendecasyllabic, a slight modification of the Sapphic line, which is his favourite metre for the expression of his more joyful moods, and of his lighter satiric vein. The Latin language never flowed with such ease, freshness and purity as in these poems. Their perfection consists in the entire absence of all appearance of effort or reflection, and in the fulness of life and feeling, which gives a lasting interest and charm to the most trivial incident of the passing hour. In reference to these poems Munro has said with truth and force: "A generation had yet to pass before the heroic attained to its perfection; while he (Catullus) had already produced glyconics, phalecians and iambics, each 'one entire and perfect chrysolite,' 'cunningest patterns' of excellence, such as Latium never saw before or after,—Alcaeus, Sappho, and the rest then and only then having met their match."

The work of Catullus has not come down to us intact, as is shown by lacunae and quotations in ancient writers which cannot now be found in his poems. Out of the MSS. only three have claims to intrinsic importance. The oldest and best appears to be the Bodleian (Canon. 30). But little inferior is the *Sangermanensis* (Par. 14137). Of the third, the *Romanus*, we shall be better able to judge when its discoverer, Prof. W.G. Hale, has published his collation. None of these MSS. are older than the 14th century. One poem, 62, is, however, preserved in a MS. of the 9th century (the *Thuaneus*, Par. 8071). Prof. R. Ellis's discovery of the Bodleian MS. and E. Baehrens's recognition of its value opened a new chapter in the history of the text. Ellis's contributions comprise an indispensable commentary (ed. 2, 1889), an elaborate critical edition (ed. 2, 1878) and an English translation (1871) in the metres of the original. The text in the Oxford series, published in 1905, is inferior to those specified below. Baehrens's edition, 2 volumes (text 1876, the second edition by K.P. Schulze is a misnomer; and Latin commentary 1885) is still of value. Amongst other editions with critical or explanatory notes or both may be mentioned those of A. Riese (1884), L. Schwabe (1886, with*index verborum*), B. Schmidt (1887), J.P. Postgate (1889, text differing little from that in the new *Corpus Poetarum*), E. Benoist and E. Thomas, with French translation by Rostand (2 vols., 1882-1890), S.G. Owen (1893, an *édition de luxe*), W.T. Merrill (1893, Boston, U.S.A., with succinct English notes), A. Palmer (1896, one of the best of this scholar's works); M. Haupt's text of the three poets Catullus, Tibullus and Propertius, edited by J. Vahlen, reached its sixth edition in 1904. Of the numerous contributions to the textual and literary criticism of the poems may be named the papers in M. Haupt's *Opuscula*, L. Schwabe's *Quaestiones Catullianae* (1862), B. Schmidt's*Prolegomena*, H.A.J. Munro's *Criticisms and Elucidations of Catullus* (1878; second edition by J.D. Duff, 1905). Translations into English verse by J. Cranstoun (1867), Sir T. Martin (1861, 1876), R. Ellis (above); a recent version in prose with the Latin text by F.W. Cornish (1904). For further information see Teuffel's *History of Roman Literature*(tr. by Warre), § 214, or the more recent accounts by M. Schanz, *Geschichte der römischen Litteratur*, i. §§ 102-106, and Frédéric Plessis, *La Poésie latine* (1909), pp. 143-173.

(W. Y. S.; X.)

CATULUS, the name of a distinguished family of ancient Rome of the gens Lutatia. The following are its most important members.

1. GAIUS LUTATIUS CATULUS, Roman commander during the First Punic War, consul 242B.C. He was sent with a fleet of 200 ships to Sicilian waters, and almost without opposition occupied the harbours of Lilybaeum and Drepanum. A hurriedly equipped fleet sent out from Carthage under Hanno was intercepted by the praetor Publius Valerius Falto and totally defeated (battle of the Aegates Islands, March 10, 241). Catulus, who had been wounded at Drepanum, took no part in the operations, but on his return to Rome was

accorded the honour of a triumph, which against his will he shared with Valerius. (See PUNIC WARS: First, ad fin.).

2. QUINTUS LUTATIUS CATULUS, Roman general and consul with Marius in 102 B.C. In the war against the Cimbri and Teutones he was sent to defend the passage of the Alps but found himself compelled to retreat over the Po, his troops having been reduced to a state of panic (see MARIUS, GAIUS). In 101 the Cimbri were defeated on the Raudine plain, near Vercellae, by the united armies of Catulus and Marius. The chief honour being ascribed to Marius, Catulus became his bitter opponent. He sided with Sulla in the civil war, was included in the proscription list of 87, and when Marius declined to pardon him, committed suicide. He was distinguished as an orator, poet and prose writer, and was well versed in Greek literature. He is said to have written the history of his consulship and the Cimbrian War after the manner of Xenophon; two epigrams by him have been preserved, one on Roscius the celebrated actor (Cicero, *De Nat. Deorum*, i. 28), the other of an erotic character, imitated from Callimachus (Gellius xix. 9). He was a man of great wealth, which he spent in beautifying Rome. Two buildings were known as "Monumenta Catuli": the temple of *Fortuna hujusce diei*, to commemorate the day of Vercellae, and the Porticus Catuli, built from the sale of the Cimbrian spoils.

See Plutarch, *Marius, Sulla*; Appian, *B.C.* i. 74; Vell. Pat. ii. 21; Florus iii. 21; Val. Max. vi. 3, ix. 13; Cicero, *De Oratore*, iii, 3. 8, *Brutus*, 35.

3. QUINTUS LUTATIUS CATULUS (c. 120-61 B.C.), sometimes called Capitolinus, son of the above, consul in 102. He inherited his father's hatred of Marius, and was a consistent though moderate supporter of the aristocracy. In 78 he was consul with Marcus Aemilius Lepidus, who after the death of Sulla proposed the overthrow of his constitution, the re-establishment of the distribution of grain, the recall of the banished, and other democratic measures. Catulus vigorously opposed this, and a temporary compromise was effected. But Lepidus, having levied troops in his province of Transalpine Gaul, returned to Rome at the head of an army. Catulus defeated him at the Mulvian bridge and near Cosa in Etruria, and Lepidus made his escape to Sardinia, where he died soon afterwards. In 67 and 66 Catulus unsuccessfully opposed, as prejudicial to constitutional freedom, the Gabinian and Manilian laws, which conferred special powers upon Pompey (*q.v.*). He consistently opposed Caesar, whom he endeavoured to implicate in the Catilinarian conspiracy. Caesar, in return, accused him of embezzling public money during the reconstruction of the temple on the Capitol, and proposed to obliterate his name from the inscription and deprive him of the office of commissioner for its restoration. Catulus's supporters rallied round him, and Caesar dropped the charge. Catulus was the last *princeps senatus* of republican times; he held the office of censor also, but soon resigned, being unable to agree with his colleague Licinius Crassus. Although not a man of great abilities, Catulus exercised considerable influence through his political consistency and his undoubted solicitude for the welfare of the state.

See Sallust, *Catilina*, 35. 49; Dio Cassius xxxvi. 13; Plutarch, *Crassus*; Suetonius, *Caesar*, 15.

CAUB, or KAUB, a town of Germany, in the Prussian province of Hesse-Nassau, on the right bank of the Rhine, 28 m. N.W. from Wiesbaden, on the railway from Frankfort-on-Main to Cologne. Pop. 2200. It has a Roman Catholic and an Evangelical church, and a statue of Blücher. The trade mainly consists of the wines of the district. On a crag above the town stands the 546imposing ruin of Gutenfels, and facing it, on a rock in the middle of the Rhine, the small castle Pfalz, or Pfalzgrafenstein, where, according to legend, the Palatine countesses awaited their confinement, but which in reality served as a toll-gate for merchandise on the Rhine.

Caub, first mentioned in the year 983, originally belonged to the lords of Falkenstein, passed in 1277 to the Rhenish Palatinate, and attained civic rights in 1324. Here Blücher crossed the Rhine with the Prussian and Russian armies, on New Year's night 1813-1814, in pursuit of the French.

CAUCA, a large coast department of Colombia, South America, lying between the departments of Bolivar, Antioquia, Caldas and Tolima on the E., and the Pacific Ocean and

Panama on the W., and extending from the Caribbean Sea S. to the department of Nariño. Pop. (1905, estimate) 400,000; area 26,930 sq. m. Although Cauca was deprived of extensive territories on the upper Caquetá and Putumayo, and of a large area bordering on Ecuador in the territorial redistribution of 1905, it remained the largest department of the republic. The Western Cordillera, traversing nearly its whole length from south to north, and the Central Cordillera, forming a part of its eastern frontier, give a very mountainous character to the region. It includes, besides, the fertile and healthful valley of the upper Cauca, the hot, low valley of the Atrato, and a long coastal plain on the Pacific. The region is rich in mines and valuable forests, but its inhabitants have made very little progress in agriculture because there are not adequate transportation facilities. The capital of the department is Popayán at its southern extremity, with an estimated population in 1905 of 10,000, other important towns are Cali (16,000), Buga, Cartago and Buenaventura.

CAUCASIA, or CAUCASUS, a governor-generalship of Russia, occupying the isthmus between the Black Sea and the Sea of Azov on the west and the Caspian Sea on the east, as well as portions of the Armenian highlands. Its northern boundary is the Kuma-Manych depression, a succession of narrow, half-desiccated lakes and river-beds, only temporarily filled with water and connecting the Manych, a tributary of the Don, with the Kuma, which flows into the Caspian. This depression is supposed to be a relic of the former post-Pliocene connexion between the Black Sea and the Caspian, and is accepted by most geographers as the natural frontier between Europe and Asia, while others make the dividing-line coincide with the principal water-parting of the Caucasus mountain system. The southern boundary of Caucasia is in part coincident with the river Aras (Araxes), in part purely conventional and political. It was shifted several times during the 19th century, but now runs from a point on the Black Sea, some 20 m. south of Batum, in a south-easterly and easterly direction to Mt. Ararat, and thence along the Aras to within 30 m. of its confluence with the Kura, where it once more turns south-east, and eventually strikes the Caspian at Astara (30° 35′ N.). This large territory, covering an area of 180,843 sq. m., and having in 1897 9,248,695 inhabitants (51 per sq. m.), may be divided into four natural zones or sections:—(i.) the plains north of the Caucasus mountains, comprising the administrative division of Northern Caucasia; (ii.) the Caucasus range and the highlands of Daghestan; (iii.) the valleys of the Rion and the Kura, between the Caucasus range and the highlands of Armenia; and (iv.) the highlands of Armenia.

(i.) The *plains of Northern Caucasia*, which include most of the provinces of Kuban and Terek and of the government of Stavropol, slope gently downwards from the foot of the Caucasus range towards the Kuma-Manych depression. It is only in their centre that they reach altitudes of as much as 2000-2500 ft. *e.g.* in the Stavropol "plateau," which stretches northwards, separating the tributaries of the Kuban from those of the Terek and the Kuma. Towards the foothills of the Caucasus they are clothed with thick forests, while in the west they merge into the steppes of south Russia or end in marshy ground, choked with reeds and rushes, in the delta of the Kuban. In the north and east they give place, as the Manych and the coasts of the Caspian are approached, to arid, sandy, stony steppes. The soil of these plains is generally very fertile and they support a population of nearly 2,800,000 Russians, composed of Cossacks and peasant immigrants, settled chiefly along the rivers and grouped in large, wealthy villages. They carry on agriculture—wheat-growing on a large scale—with the aid of modern agricultural machines, and breed cattle and horses. Vines are extensively cultivated on the low levels, and a variety of domestic trades are prosecuted in the villages. The higher parts of the plains, which are deeply trenched by the upper tributaries of the rivers, are inhabited by various Caucasian races—Kabardians and Cherkesses (Circassians) in the west, Ossetes in the middle, and several tribal elements from Daghestan, described under the general name of Chechens, in the east; while nomadic Nogai Tatars and Turkomans occupy the steppes.

(ii.) The *Caucasus range* runs from north-west to south-east from the Strait of Kerch to the Caspian Sea for a length of 900 m., with a varying breadth of 30 to 140 m., and covers a surface of 12,000 sq. m. The orographical characteristics of the Caucasus are described in detail under that heading.

(iii.) The combined *valleys of the Rion and the Kura*, which intervene between the Caucasus and the Armenian highlands, and stretch their axes north-west and south-east respectively, embrace the most populous and most fertile parts of Caucasia. They correspond roughly with the governments of Kutais, Tiflis, Elisavetpol and Baku, and have a population of nearly 3,650,000. The two valleys are separated by the low ridge of the Suram or Meskes mountains.

Spurs from the Caucasus and from the Armenian highlands fill up the broad latitudinal depression between them. Above (*i.e.* west of) Tiflis these spurs so far intrude into the valley that it is reduced to a narrow strip in breadth. But below that city it suddenly widens out, and the width gradually increases through the stretch of 350 m. to the Caspian, until in the Mugan steppe along that sea it measures 100 m. in width. The snow-clad peaks of the main Caucasus, descending by short, steep slopes, fringe the valley on the north, while an abrupt escarpment, having the characteristics of a border ridge of the Armenian highlands, fronts it on the south. The floor of the valley slopes gently eastwards, from 1200 ft. at Tiflis to 500 ft. in the middle, and to 85 ft. *below*normal sea-level beside the Caspian. But the uniformity of the slope is interrupted by a plateau (2000-3000 ft. in altitude) along the southern foothills of the east central Caucasus, in the region known as Kakhetia, drained by the Alazan, a left-hand tributary of the Kura. The deep, short gorges and glens which seam the southern slopes of the Caucasus are inhabited by Ossetes, Tushes, Pshavs and Khevsurs in the west, and by various tribes of Lesghians in the east. In these high and stony valleys every available patch of ground is utilized for the cultivation of barley, even up to altitudes of 7000 and 8000 ft. above the level of the sea; but cattle-breeding is the principal resource of the mountaineers, whose little communities are often separated from one another by passes, few of which are lower than 10,000 ft. The steppes along the bottom of the principal valley are for the most part too dry to be cultivated without irrigation. It is only in Kakhetia, where numerous mountain streams supply the fields and gardens of the plateau of Alazan, that wheat, millet and maize are grown, and orchards, vineyards and mulberry plantations are possible. Lower down the valley cattle-breeding is the chief source of wealth, while in the small towns and villages of the former Georgian kingdom various petty trades, exhibiting a high development of artistic taste and technical skill, are widely diffused. The slopes of the Armenian highlands are clothed with fine forests, and the vine is grown at their base, while on the wide-stretching steppes the Turko-Tatars pasture cattle, horses and sheep. The lower part of the Kura valley assumes the character of a dry steppe, the rainfall not reaching 14 in. annually at Baku, and it is still less in the Mugan steppe, though quite abundant in the adjacent region of Lenkoran. The vegetation of the steppe is on the whole scanty. Trees are generally absent, except for thickets of poplars, dwarf oaks and tamarisks along the course of the Kura, the delta of which is smothered under a jungle of reeds and rushes. The Mugan steppe is, however, in spite of its dryness, a more fertile region in virtue of the irrigation practised; but the Kura has excavated its bed too deeply to admit of that being done along its course. The Lenkoran district, sometimes called Talysh, on the western side of the Kizil-Agach bay, is blessed with a rich vegetation, a fertile soil, and a moist climate.

The inhabitants of the Kura valley consist principally of Iranian Tates and Talyshes, of Armenians and Lesghians, with Russians, Jews and Arabs. This conjoint valley of the Rion-Kura was in remote antiquity the site of several Greek colonial settlements, later the seat of successive kingdoms of the Georgians, and for centuries it has formed a bulwark against hostile invasions from the south and east. It is still inhabited chiefly by Georgian tribes—Gurians, Imeretians, Mingrelians, Svanetians—in the basin of the Rion, and by Georgians intermingled with Armenians in the valley of the Kura, while the steppes that stretch away from the lower course of the latter river are ranged over by Turko-Tatars. Mingrelia and Imeretia (valley of Rion) are the gardens of Caucasia, but the high valleys of Svanetia, farther north on the south slopes of the Caucasus mountains, are wild and difficult of access. In the cultivated parts the land is so exceedingly fertile and productive that it sells for almost fabulous prices, and its value is still further enhanced by the discovery of manganese and copper mines in the basin of the Rion, and of the almost inexhaustible supplies of naphtha and petroleum at Baku in the Apsheron peninsula. The principal products of the soil are mentioned lower down, while the general 547character of the vegetation is indicated under CAUCASUS: *Western Caucasus*. In the basin of the Rion, in that of the Chorokh (which runs off the Pontic highlands into the Black Sea south of Batura), and on the Black Sea littoral from Batum northwards to Sukhum-kaleh, and beyond, the climate is extremely hot and the rainfall heavy (see under *Climate* below). It is in this valley that the principal towns (except Vladikavkaz at the north foot of the Caucasus) of Caucasia are situated, namely, Baku (179,133 inhabitants in 1900), Tiflis (160,645 in 1897), Kutais (32,492), and the two Black Sea ports of Batum (28,512) and Poti (7666).

(iv.) The *highlands of Armenia* are sometimes designated the Minor Caucasus, Little Caucasus and Anti-Caucasus. But to use such terms for what is not only an independent, but also an older, orographical formation than the Caucasus tends to perpetuate confusion in geographical nomenclature. The Armenian highlands, which run generally parallel to the Caucasus, though at much lower elevations (5000-6000 ft.), are a plateau region, sometimes quite flat, sometimes gently undulating, clothed with luxuriant meadows and mostly cultivable. From it rise double or triple ranges connected by cross-ridges and spined with outer spurs. These double and triple ranges, which have a general elevation of 8500-10,000 ft., stretch from the south-east angle of the Black Sea, 400 m. south-eastwards to the Kara-dagh and Salavat mountains in north Persia, and the latter link them on to the Elburz mountains that skirt the southern end of the Caspian Sea. Various names are given to the different parts of the constituent ranges, or, perhaps more correctly, elongated groups of mountains. The Ajar, Akhalt-sikh and Meskes or Trialety groups in the west are succeeded farther east by the Somkhet, Murguz, Ganji and Karabakh sections, forming the southern rim of the Kura basin, while parallel with them, but farther south, run the Mokry, Miskhan, Akmangan and Paltapin ranges, marking the northern edge of the Aras drainage area. These two sets of parallel ranges are linked together transversely by the cross-ridges of Bezobdal, Pambak, Shah-dagh and Gok-cha. From this last branches off the highest range in the entire series, namely, the Zangezur, which soars up to 10,000 ft. above the left bank of the Aras. From it again there shoot away at right angles, one on each side, the ranges of the Dar-alagöz and Bergushet. These highlands exhibit very considerable evidences of volcanic activity both in remote geological periods and also since the Tertiary epoch. Large areas are overlain with trachyte, basalt, obsidian, tuff and pumice. The most conspicuous features of the entire region, Mount Ararat (16,930 ft.) and Mount Alagöz (13,440 ft.), are both solid masses of trachyte; and both rise above the limits of perpetual snow. Extinct volcanoes are numerous in several of the ranges, *e.g.*Akmangan, Mokry, Karabakh and Egri-dagh (see below). It is in this region of the Armenian highlands that the largest lakes of Caucasia are situated, namely, the Gok-cha or Sevanga (540 sq. m. in area) at an altitude of 6340 ft., the Chaldir-gol (33 sq. m.) at 6520 ft., and several smaller ones, such as the *gols* of Khozapin, Khopchalu, Arpa, Toporavan and Tabiztskhur, all situated between 6500 and 7000 ft. above sea-level. The principal water-divide in this highland region is, however, the range of Egri-dagh (Ararat), which just south of 40° S. forms for 100 m. the boundary between Russian and Turkish Armenia, having Ararat at its eastern extremity and the extinct volcano of Kessa-dagh (11,260 ft.) at its western. Its importance lies in the fact that it divides the streams which flow into the Black Sea and Caspian from those which make their way into the Persian Gulf. The Egri-dagh possesses a sharply defined crest, ranges at a general elevation of 8000 ft., is bare of timber, scantily supplied with water, and rugged and deeply fissured.

The transverse water-parting between the Black Sea and the Caspian begins on the south side of the main range of the Caucasus, at Mount Zikara (12,560 ft.), a little south-west of Kasbek, and runs south-west along the sinuous crests of the Racha, Suram or Meskes (3000-5000 ft.), Vakhan (10,000-11,000 ft.), Arzyan (7000-10,000 ft.), and its continuation the Soganluk, thus linking the Caucasus ranges with those of the Armenian highlands. This line of heights separates the basins of the Chorokh and the Rion (Black Sea) from those of the Aras and the Kura (Caspian Sea). North of the Caucasus ranges the water-divide between these two seas descends from Mount Elbruz along the Sadyrlar Mountains (11,000 ft.), and finally sinks into the Stavropol "plateau" (1600 ft.). But the main axis of the transverse upheavals would appear to be continued in a north-eastern direction in the Andi and other parallel ranges of Daghestan, as stated under CAUCASUS.

The population in this region consists principally of Armenians, Tatars, Turks, Kurds, Ossetes, Greeks, with Persians, Tates and a few Russians (see particulars below).

Climate.—Owing in part to the great differences in altitude in different regions of Caucasia and in part to the directions in which the mountain ranges run, and consequently the quarters towards which their slopes face, the climate varies very greatly according to locality. Generally speaking, it may be characterized as a climate of extremes on the Armenian highlands, in the Kura valley and in northern Caucasia, and as maritime and genial in Lenkoran, on the Black Sea coastlands, and in the valley of the Rion. The greatest recorded range of temperature is at Erivan (altitude 3230 ft.), namely, of 64° between a January average of 14.9° and an August average of 78.8° F. At Sukhum-kaleh, on the Black Sea, the corresponding range is only 27.3°, between a January average of 48.8° and an August average of 76.1°. The highest mean temperatures for the whole year are those of Lenkoran (60.3°) and of Sukhum-kaleh and Poti (about 58°), and the lowest at Ardahan (5840 ft.), in the province of Kars, namely, 37.9°, and at Gudaur (7245 ft.), a few miles south of Kasbek, namely, 38.6°. The following table gives particulars of temperature averages at a few typical places:—

Place.	Altitude.	Annual Mean.	January Mean.	July Mean.
Stavropol	2030	47.0°	24.0°	70.0°
Vladikavkaz	2345	47.3°	23.4°	68.0°
Gudaur	7245	38.6°	20.3°	57.2°
Baku	on Caspian	58.0°	38.0°	80.0°
Tiflis	1490	55.0°	32.0°	76.5°
Batum	on Black Sea	59.0°	42.0°	75.0°
Sochi	on Black Sea	56.3°	40.3°	76.1°
Lenkoran	on Caspian	60.3°	39.0°	80.6°
Erivan	3170	51.0°	51.0°	75.0°

In respect of precipitation the entire region of Caucasia may be divided into two strikingly contrasted regions, a wet and a dry. To the former belong the Black Sea littoral, where the rainfall averages 59 to 93 in. annually, and the valleys that open upon it or are exposed to winds blowing off it, in which the rainfall varies, however, from 20 in. (Abbastuman, Borzhom) to 60 (Kutais). In Lenkoran also the rainfall averages 40 to 50 in. in the year. Between 16 and 40 in. fall as a rule at the northern foot of the Caucasus (Mozdok, Pyatigorsk) and in the Kura valley (Tiflis, Novo-bayazet). On the Armenian highlands and on the steppes north of Pyatigorsk the rainfall is less than 12 in. annually, and even in some places less than 8 in., *e.g.* at the foot of Ararat. Most rain falls at Batum and at Lenkoran in the autumn, in northern Caucasia and in Transcaucasia in spring and summer, but in the vicinity of the Sea of Azov in winter.

Flora and Fauna.—Plant-life, in such a mountainous country as Caucasia, being intimately dependent upon aspect and altitude, is treated under CAUCASUS. The wild animals of Caucasia are for the most part the same as those which frequent the mountainous parts of central Europe, though there is also an irruption of Asiatic forms, *e.g.* the tiger (in Lenkoran only), panther, hyaena and jackal. The more important of the carnivores which haunt the forests, valleys and mountain slopes are the bear (*Ursus arctos*), wolf, lynx, wild cat and fox (*Vulpes melanotus*). The wild boar occurs around Borzhom. The aurochs (*Bos urus*) appears to exist still in the forests of the western Caucasus. Of interest for sportsmen, as well as serving as prey for the carnivores, are red deer, goats (*Capra pallasit* and *C. aegagrus*), chamois, roebuck, moufflon (*Ovis musimon*), argali or Asiatic wild sheep (*O. Amman*), another species of sheep in *O. gmelini*, and fallow deer (*Capreolus pigargns*) in northern Caucasus only. Rodents are numerous, the mouse (*Mus sylvaticus*) is very destructive, and beavers are met with in places. The birds of prey are the same as these of central Europe, and include the sea eagle, alpine vulture (*Gyps fulvus*), buzzard, kites (*Gypaëtus barbatus* and*Milvus ater*), hawks (*e.g. Astur nisus*), goshawk (*A. palumbarius*), fish-hawk (*Pandion haliaëtus*) and owls. Among the smaller birds may be enumerated finches, the siskin, bullfinch, pipit, titmouse, wagtail, lark, fine-crested wren, hedge-sparrow, corn-wren, nut-hatch, starling, swallow, martin, swift, thrush, butcher bird, shrike, dipper, yellow-hammer, ortolan and a warbler (*Accentor alpinus*). The game birds consist of grouse, blackcock, moorhen, quail and partridge. The pheasant derives its name from the ancient name (*Phasis*) of the Rion.

In the seas and rivers about 190 species of fishes have been enumerated. Of these, 115 species are Mediterranean, 30 are common to the Caspian Sea, and the remaining species are peculiar to the Black Sea. The most useful economically are several species of sturgeon and of herring, trout, barbel, chubb, bream, ray, sea-dace, 548carp, anchovy. Insects abound, especially Coleoptera. Flies, lice, gadflies and mosquitoes are the worst of the insect plagues. There are several snakes, including the viper (*Pelias berus*).

Ethnology.—The population of Caucasis is increasing rapidly. In 1897 it numbered 9,291,090, of whom 4,886,230 were males and 4,404,867 were females. The most densely-peopled provinces were Kutais and Tiflis, each with 80 inhabitants to the square mile; the thinnest the Black Sea government (20½ per sq. m.), Terek (31), and Kars (39). Of the total population 3,725,543 lived in northern Caucasia and 5,564,547 in Transcaucasia (including Daghestan). In the latter territorial division there exists a great disproportion between the sexes, namely, to every 100 males only 86 females; indeed in the Black Sea government there are only 65.5 females to every 100 males. Ethnologically the population belongs to a great variety of races. The older authorities asserted that these numbered as many as 150, or even 300; the more recent researches of Baron P.V. Uslar, F. Anton, von Schiefner, Zagursky, and others have greatly reduced this number; but even then there are not less than fifty represented.

According to the languages spoken the populations of Caucasia admit of being classified as follows,1 according to Senator N. Trointsky, president of the Russian Census Committee for 1897.

ARYANS	4,901,412	
Slavs	3,183,870	
Great Russians		1,829,793
Little Russians		1,305,463
White Russians		19,642
Poles		25,117
Germans	47,391	
Greeks	10,0,299	

114

Rumanians	7,232	
French and Italians	1,435	
Lithuanians	6,687	
Lithuanians proper		5,121
Letts		1,511
Iranians	31 5,695	
Persians		13 ,929
Talyshes		34 ,994
Tates		95 ,056
Ossetes		17 1,716
Kurds	99 ,836	
Armenians	1,116,461	
Gypsies	3,041	
SEMITES	46 ,739	
Jews	40 ,498	
Chaldaeans (Aisors)	5,353	
URAL-ALTAIANS	1,902,142	
Finns	7,422	
Esthonians		4,281
Turko-Tatars	1,879,908	
Tatars		1,509,785
Osmanli Turks		13 9,419
Nogai Tatars		64 ,048
Turkomans		24 ,522
Bashkirs		95 3
Chuvashes		41

	1
Kirghiz	98
Sarts	158
Karachais	27,222
Kumyks	83,408
Kara-papaks	29,902
Kalmucks	14,409
CAUCASIANS	2,439,071
Georgians (including Imeretians, Gurians, Svanetians, Lazes, Mingrelians, &c.)	1,352,455
Circassians	
Cherkesses (Adigheh) and Kabardians	144,847
Abkhasians	72,103
Chechens	274,318
Chechens proper	226,496
Ingushes[2]	47,409
Kistines	413
Lesghians	600,514
Avaro-Andians	212,692
Darghis	130,209
Kurins	159,213
Udins	7,100
Others	91,300

Religion.—Most of the Russians and the Georgians belong to the Orthodox Greek Church (over 4,000,000 in all); but considerable numbers (estimated at nearly 122,000, though in reality probably a good many more) are Nonconformists of different denominations. The Georgian Lazes are, however, Mussulmans. The Armenians are Christians, mostly of the national Gregorian Church (979,566), though 34,000 are Roman Catholics. The Caucasian races (except the Gregorians), together with the Turks and Tatars, are Mussulmans of the Sunnite sect (2,021,300), and the Iranian races mostly Mussulmans of the Shiite sect (884,100). The Kalmucks and other Mongolic tribes are Lamaists (20,300), and some of the Kurds profess the peculiar tenets of the Yezids.

Industries.—The principal occupation of the settled inhabitants is agriculture and of the nomadic the breeding of live stock, including camels. The cultivation of the soil is, however, attended in many parts with great difficulties owing to the scanty rainfall and the very primitive implements still in use, and in the valley of the Kura heavy losses are frequently incurred from depredations by locusts. But where irrigation is employed the yield of crops is excellent. Rye and wheat are the most important crops harvested in northern Caucasia, but oats, barley and maize are also cultivated, whereas in Transcaucasia the principal crops are maize, rice, tobacco and cotton. The rice is grown chiefly in the valley of the Kura and in Lenkoran; the tobacco in the Rion valley and on the Black Sea coastlands, also to some extent in Kuban; and the cotton in the eastern provinces. Various kinds of fodder crops are grown in Transcaucasia, such as hay, rye-grass and lucerne. It is estimated that nearly 54,000 acres are under vineyards in northern Caucasia and some 278,000 acres in Transcaucasia, the aggregate yield of wine being 30 million gallons annually. The best wine grows in Kakhetia, a district lying north-east and east of Tiflis; this district alone yields nearly 8 million gallons annually. Large numbers of mulberry trees are planted for rearing silkworms, especially in Kutais, Erivan, Elisavetpol (Nukha) and Baku (Shemakha); the groves occupy nearly 150,000 acres, and the winding of the silk gives employment to large numbers of the population. Melons and water-melons are also important objects of cultivation. Sunflowers are very extensively grown for oil in the government of Kuban and elsewhere, and also some flax. Liquorice is an article of export. Many varieties of fruit are grown, especially good being the apricots, peaches, walnuts and hazel nuts. A limited area (not more than 1150 acres) of the Black Sea coast between Sukhum-kaleh and Batum is planted with the tea-shrub, which succeeds very well. In the same district bamboos, ramie-fibre and attar (otto) of roses are cultivated.

The *mining* industry is growing rapidly in importance in spite of costly and deficient means of communication, want of capital, and lack of general initiative. So far the principal developments of the industry have been in the governments of Kutais, Batum, Elisavetpol and Kuban. Copper ore is extracted above the Murgul river (some 30 m. south of Batum), at Akhtala south of Tiflis, and at Kedabek in Elisavetpol; manganese to a considerably greater extent (over 400,000 tons annually) at Chiaturi in the Kvirila valley in Kutais. Steam coal of good quality is reported to exist about 30 m. inland from the open roadstead of Ochemchiri in Kutais, but it is not mined. About 50,000 tons of coal of very poor quality are, however, extracted annually, and the same quantity of salt in the Armenian highlands and in Kuban. Small quantities of quicksilver, sulphur and iron are obtained. But all these are insignificant in comparison with the mineral oil industry of Baku, which in normal times yields annually between ten and eleven million tons of crude oil (naphtha). A good deal of this is transported by gravitation from Baku to Batum on the Black Sea by means of a pipe laid overland. The refined oil is exported as kerosene or petroleum, the heavier refuse (*mazut*) is used as fuel. Naphtha is also obtained, though in much smaller quantities, in Terek and Kuban, in Tiflis and Daghestan. Numerous mineral springs (chalybeate and sulphurous) exist both north and south of the Caucasus ranges, *e.g.* at Pyatigorsk, 549Zhelesnovodsk, Essentuki, and Kislovodsk in Terek, and at Tiflis, Abbas-tuman and Borzhom in the government of Tiflis.

Manufacturing industry is confined to a few articles and commodities, such as cement, tea, tin cans (for oil), cotton goods, oil refineries, tobacco factories, flour-mills, silk-winding mills (especially at Shusha and Jebrail in the south of Elisavetpol), distilleries and breweries. On the other hand, the domestic industries are extensively carried on and exhibit a high degree of technical skill and artistic taste. Carpets (especially at Shusha), silk, cotton and woollen goods, felts and fur cloaks are made, and small arms in Daghestan and at Tiflis, Nukha and Sukhum-kaleh; silversmiths' work at Tiflis, Akhaltsikh and Kutais; pottery at Elisavetpol and Shusha; leather shoe-making at Alexandropol, Nukha, Elisavetpol, Shusha and Tiflis; saddlery at Sukhum-kaleh and Ochemchiri on the Black Sea and at Temirkhan-shura in Daghestan; and copper work at Derbent and Alexandropol. But industries of every description were most seriously crippled by the spirit of turbulence and disorder which manifested itself throughout Transcaucasia in the years 1904-1906, accentuated as they were further by the outbreak of the long-rooted racial enmities between the Armenians and the Tatars, especially at Baku in 1905.

Commerce.—The exports through the Black Sea ports of Batum, Poti and Novorossiysk average in value a little over £10,000,000 annually, though showing a tendency to increase slightly. By far the most important commodity is petroleum, fully one-half of the total value. In addition large quantities are shipped at Baku direct for the Volga and the Transcaspian port of Krasnovodsk. The export that comes next in value is silk, and after it may be named wheat, barley, manganese ore, maize, wool, oilcake, carpets, rye, oats, liquorice and timber. The import trade reaches nothing like the same value, and what there is is confined almost entirely to Batum. The annual average vahie may be put at not quite £2,000,000, machinery and tin-plate being a long way the most important items. There is further a small transit trade through Transcaucasia from Persia to the value of less than half a million sterling annually, and chiefly in carpets, cocoons and silk, wool, rice and boxwood; and further a sea-borne trade between Persia and Caucasian ports (Baku and Petrovsk) to the value of over 1½ millions sterling in all. The very extensive internal trade with Russia can only be mentioned.

Railways.—The principal approach to Caucasia from Russia by rail is the line that runs from Rostov-on-Don to Vladikavkaz at the foot of the central Caucasus range. Thence, or rather from the junction of Beslan, 14 m. north of Vladikavkaz, the main line proceeds east of Petrovsk on the Caspian, and from Petrovsk skirts the shore southwards as far as Baku, the distance from Vladikavkaz to Baku being 414 m. This railway, together with the driving roads over the Caucasus mountains via the Mamison pass (the Ossetic military road) and the Darial pass (the Georgian military road), and the route across the Black Sea to Poti or Batum are the chief means of communication between southern Russia and Transcaucasia. Baku and Batum (also Poti) are connected by another main line, 560 m. long, which traverses the valleys of the Kura and the Rion, south of the Caucasus. From Tiflis, nearly midway on this last line, a railway proceeds south as far as Erivan (234 m.), with a branch to Kars (48 m.). The Erivan line is being continued into Persia, namely, to Tabriz via Julfa on the Aras.

History.—To the ancient Greeks Caucasia, and the mighty range which dominates it, were a region of mystery and romance. It was there that they placed the scene of the sufferings of Prometheus (*vide* Aeschylus, *Prometheus Vinctus*), and there, in the land of Colchis, which corresponds to the valley of the Rion, that they sent the Argonauts to fetch the golden fleece. Outside the domain of myth, the earliest connexion of the Greeks with that part of the world would appear to have been through the maritime colonies, such as Dioscurias, which the Milesians founded on the Black Sea coast in the 7th century B.C. For more than two thousand years the most powerful state in Caucasia was that of Georgia (*q.v.*), the authentic history of which begins with its submission to Alexander the Great in 323 B.C. The southern portion of Transcaucasia fell during the 1st century B.C. under the sway of Armenia, and with that country passed under the dominion of Rome, and so eventually of the Eastern empire. During the 3rd century A.D. Georgia and Armenia were invaded and in great part occupied by the Khazars, and then for more than a thousand years the mountain fastnesses of this borderland between Europe and Asia were the refuge, or the resting-place, of successive waves of migration, as people after people and tribe after tribe was compelled to give way to the pressure of stronger races harassing them in the rear. The Huns, for instance, and the Avars appeared in the 6th century, and the Mongols in the 13th. In the 10th century bands of Varangians or Russified Scandinavians sailed out of the Volga and coasted along the Caspian until they had doubled the Apsheron peninsula, when they landed and captured Barda, the chief town of Caucasian Albania.

But, apart from Georgia, historical interest in Caucasia centres in the long and persistent attempts which the Russians made to conquer it, and the heroic, though unavailing, resistance offered by the mountain races, more especially the Circassian and Lesghian tribes. Russian aggression began somewhat early in the 18th century, when Peter the Great, establishing his base at Astrakhan on the Volga, and using the Caspian for bringing up supplies and munitions of war, captured Derbent from the Persians in 1722, and Baku in the following year. But these conquests, with others made at the expense of Persia, were restored to the latter power after Peter's death, a dozen years later. At that period the

Georgians were divided into various petty principalities, the chief of which were Imeretia and Georgia (Kharthlia), owing at times a more or less shadowy allegiance to the sultan of the Ottoman Turks at Constantinople. In 1770, during the course of a war between Russia and Turkey, the Russians crossed over the Caucasus and assisted the Imeretians to resist the Turks, and from the time of the ensuing peace of Kuchuk-kainarji the Georgian principalities looked to their powerful northern neighbour as their protector against the southern aggressors the Turks. In 1783 George XIII., prince of Georgia and Mingrelia, formally put himself under the suzerainty of Russia, and after his death Georgia was converted (1801) into a Russian province. The same fate overtook Imeretia, nine years later. Meanwhile the Russians had also subdued the Ossetes (1802) and the Lesghian tribes (1803) of the middle Caucasus. By the peace of Gulistan in 1813 Persia ceded to Russia several districts in eastern Caucasia, from Lenkoran northwards to Derbent. Nevertheless the mountain tribes who inhabited the higher parts of the Caucasus were still independent, and their subjugation cost Russia a sustained effort of thirty years, during the course of which her military commanders were more than once brought almost to the point of despair by the tenacity, the devotion and the adroitness and daring which the mountaineers displayed in a harassing guerilla warfare. The animating spirit of their resistance was Shamyl (Samuel), a chief and priest of the Lesghians, who, a Mahommedan, proclaimed a "holy war" against the "infidel" aggressors. At first the Russians were able to continue their policy of conquest and annexation without serious check. After acquiring the northern edge of the Armenian plateau, partly from Persia in 1828 and partly from Turkey in 1829, Russia crushed a rising which had broken out in the Caspian coast districts of Daghestan on the north of the Caucasus. This took place during the years 1831-1832. The next seven years were occupied with the subjugation of the Abkhasians along the Black Sea coast, and of other Circassian tribes in the west. Meanwhile Shamyl had roused the Lesghian tribes farther east and begun his twenty years' struggle for freedom, a struggle which called forth the sympathy and admiration of nearly the whole of Europe. More than once he escaped, in a manner that seemed little short of marvellous, out of the hands of the Russians when they held him closely invested in some mountain fastness, as at Himry in 1831, at Akhulgo in 1839, and again at the same stronghold in 1849. 550The general who at last broke the back of the long opposition of the prophet-chief of the Lesghians was Prince Baryatinsky, who after three years of strenuous warfare succeeded in capturing Shamyl's stronghold of Weden, and then in surrounding that chieftain himself on the inaccessible rocky platform of Gunib in the heart of Daghestan. There the hitherto indomitable champion of Caucasian independence was forced to surrender to the Russians on the 6th of September 1859. Nevertheless the spirit of resistance in these stubborn mountaineers was not finally broken until 1864, when the Russians eventually stifled all opposition in the difficult valleys and glens of the western Caucasus. But this was followed, during the next fourteen years, by the wholesale emigration of thousands upon thousands of Circassians, who sought an asylum in Turkish territory, leaving their native region almost uninhabited and desolate, a condition from which it has not recovered even at the present day. During the Russo-Turkish War of 1877-78 the self-exiled Circassians and other Caucasian mountaineers, supported by a force of 14,000 Turks, made a determined attempt to wrest their native glens from the power of Russia; but, after suffering a severe defeat at the hands of General Alkhazov, the Turks withdrew, and were accompanied by some 30,000 Abkhasians, who settled in Asia Minor. A few months later the Lesghians in Daghestan, who had risen in revolt, were defeated and their country once more reduced to obedience. By the ensuing peace of Adrianople, Russia still further enlarged her Transcaucasian territories by the acquisition of the districts of Kars, Batum and Ardahan. After a peaceful period of a quarter of a century the Armenian subjects of Russia in Transcaucasia were filled with bitterness and discontent by the confiscation of the properties of their national (Gregorian) church by the Russian treasury. Nor were their feelings more than half allayed by the arrangement which made their ecclesiastics salaried officers of the Russian state. This ferment of unrest, which was provoked in the years 1903-1904, was exacerbated in the winters that followed by the renewed outbreak of the century-long racial feud between the Tatars and the Armenians at Baku and other places. In fact, nearly the whole of the region between the Caucasus and the Perso-Turkish frontier on the south, from the Caspian Sea on the one side to the Black Sea on the other, was embroiled in a civil war of the most sanguinary and ruthless character, the inveterate racial animosities of the combatants being in both cases inflamed by religious fanaticism. Complete anarchy prevailed at the worst centres of disorder, as Baku and Batum, the imperial authorities being more powerless to preserve even the semblance of order than they were in the interior of Russia. Many of the oil wells at Baku were burned, and massacres took place at that town, at Shusha, at Erivan, at Tiflis, at Batum, at Jebrail and at other places. An end was put to these disorders only by the mutual agreement of the two contestants, alike horrified and exhausted by the fierce outburst of passion, in September 1905.

(J. T. BE.)

1 *Premier Recensement général de la population de l'empire de Russie*, ed. N. Trointsky (St Petersburg, 1905, 2 vols.), in Russian and French.
2 Although the Ingushes speak a Chechen dialect, they have recently been proved to be, anthropologically, quite a distinct race.

CAUCASUS, a mountain range of Asia, wholly within the Russian empire, stretching north-west to south-east from the Strait of Kerch (between the Black Sea and Sea of Azov) to the Caspian Sea, over a length of 900 m., with a breadth varying from 30 to 140 m. In its general character and conformation the Caucasus presents a closer analogy with the Pyrenees than with the Alps. Its general uniformity of direction, its comparatively narrow width, and its well-defined limits towards both south and north are all features which it has in common with the former. The range of the Caucasus, like that of the Pyrenees, maintains for considerable distances a high average elevation, and is not cleft by deep trenches, forming natural passes across the range, such as are common in the Alps. In both ranges, too, some of the highest summits stand on spurs of the main range, not on the main range itself; as Mont Perdu and Maladetta lie south of the main backbone of the Pyrenees, so Mount Elbruz and Kasbek, Dykh-tau, Koshtan-tau, Janga-tau and Shkara—all amongst the loftiest peaks of the Caucasus—stand on a subsidiary range north of the principal range or on spurs connecting the two. On the other hand, it is interesting to compare the arrangement of the drainage waters of the Caucasus with those of the Alps. In both orographical systems the principal rivers start nearly all together from a central nucleus, and in both cases they radiate to opposite quarters of the compass; but whereas in the Alps the Rhone and the Rhine, flowing south-west and north-east respectively, follow longitudinal valleys, and the Aar and the Ticino, flowing north-west and south-east respectively, follow transverse valleys, in the Caucasus the streams which flow south-west and north-east, namely, the headwaters of the Rion and the Terek, travel along transverse valleys, and those of the Kura and the Kuban, flowing south-east and north-west respectively, traverse longitudinal valleys. For purposes of description it is convenient to consider the range in four sections, a western, a middle with two subsections, and an eastern.

1. WESTERN CAUCASUS. This section, extending from the Strait of Kerch to Mount Elbruz in 42° 40′ E., is over 420 m. long, and runs parallel to the north-east coast of the Black Sea and at only a short distance from it. Between the main range and the sea there intervene at least two parallel ranges separated by deep glens, and behind it a third subsidiary parallel range, likewise separated by a deep trough-like valley, and known as the Bokovoi Khrebet. All these ranges are shorn through transversely by numerous glens and gorges, and, the rainfall being heavy and the exposure favourable, they are densely clothed with vegetation. Many of the spurs or broken segments of ranges thus formed abut steeply upon the Black Sea, so that this littoral region is on the whole very rugged and not readily accessible, especially as the general elevations are considerable. The seaward flanking ranges run up to 4000 ft. and more, and in many places shoot out cliffs which overhang the coast some 2000-3000 ft. sheer, while the main range gradually ascends to 10,000-12,000 ft. as it advances eastwards, the principal peaks being Fisht (8040 ft.), Oshten (9210 ft.), Shuguz (10,640 ft.), and Psysh (12,425 ft.). And whereas the main range is built up of hard eruptive or crystalline rocks, the subsidiary chains are composed of softer (Cretaceous and Tertiary)

laminated formations, which easily become disintegrated and dislocated. The snow-line runs here at about 9000 ft. on the loftiest summits, and east of Oshten the crest of the main range is capped with perpetual snow and carries many hanging glaciers, while larger glaciers creep down the principal valleys. The passes lie at relatively great altitudes and are few in number, so that although the northern versants of the various ranges all have a tolerably gentle slope, communication between the Black Sea and the valley of the Kuban, and the low steppe country beyond, is the reverse of easy. The more important passes, proceeding from west to east, are Pshekh (5435 ft.) west of Oshten, and Shetlib (6060 ft.) east of Oshten, Pscashka (6880 ft.) east of Shuguz, Sanchar (7990 ft.) west of Psysh; and between the last-named mountain and Elbruz, facilitating communication between Sukhum-Kaleh (and the coast as far as Potī) and the upper valley of the Kuban, are the passes of Marukh (11,500 ft.), Klukhor (9450 ft.) and Nakhar (9615 ft.).

Flora.—The southern exposure of this littoral region, the shelter afforded against the bitter winds of the north by the lofty Caucasus range, and the copious rainfall all combine to foster a luxuriant and abundant vegetation. The most distinguishing feature of the flora of this region is the predominance of arborescent growths; forests cover in fact 56% of the area, and are not only dense but laced together with climbing and twining plants. The commonest species of trees are such as grow in central Europe, namely, ash, fir, pine, beech, acacia, maple, birch, box, chestnut, laurel, holm-oak, poplar, elm, lime, yew, elder, willow, oak. The common box is especially prevalent, but the preponderating species are *Coniferae*, including the Caucasian species *Pinus halepensis* and *P. insignis*. The commonest firs are *Abies nordmannia* and *A. orientalis*. There are two native oaks, *Quercus ponticus* and *Q. sessiliflora*. A great variety of shrubs grow on these slopes of the western Caucasus, chiefly the following species, several of which are indigenous—*Rhododendron ponticum, Azalea pontica, Aristotelia maqui, Agave* 551 *americana, Cephalaria tatarica, Coloneaster pyracantha, Citrus aurantium, Diospyros ebenum, Ficus carica, Illicium anisatum, Ligustrum caucasicum, Punica granatum, Philadelphus coronarius, Pyrus salicifolia, Rhus cotinus* and six species of *Viburnum*. Aquatic plants thrive excellently and occur in great variety. The following purely Caucasian species also grow on the coast—five species of spearwort, three of saxifrage, *Aster caucasica, Dioscorea caucasica, Echinops raddeanus, Hedera colchica, Helleborus caucasica* and *Peucedanum caucasicum*. Here too are found many of the more beautiful open-air flowering plants of a shrubby character, *e.g.* magnolia, azalea, camellia, begonia and paulownia. Among the cultivated trees and shrubs the most valuable economically are the vine, peach, pomegranate, fig, olive (up to 1500 ft. above sea-level), chestnut, apricot, apple, pear, plum, cherry, melon, tea (on the coast between Sukhum-Kaleh and Batum), maize (yielding the staple food of the inhabitants), wheat (up to 6000 ft.), potatoes, peas, currants, cotton, rice, colza and tobacco. Before the Russian conquest the native inhabitants of this region were Kabardians, Circassians (Adigheh) and Abkhasians, also a Circassian race. But half a million of these people being Mahommedans, and refusing to submit to the yoke of Christian Russia, emigrated into Turkish territory between 1864 and 1878, and the country where they had lived remained for the most part unoccupied until after the beginning of the 20th century. Then, however, the Russian government held out inducements to settlers, and these have been responded to by Russians, Greeks, Armenians and Rumanians, but the process of repeopling the long deserted territory is slow and difficult. The coast-line is remarkably regular, there being no deep bays and few seaports. The best accommodation that these latter afford consists of more or less open roadsteads, *e.g.* Novo-rossiysk, Gelenjik, Anapa, Sukhum-Kaleh, Poti and Batum. Along the coast a string of summer bathing resorts is springing up similar to those that dot the south-east coast of the Crimea. The most promising of these little seaside places are Anapa, Gelenjik and Gagry.

2. MIDDLE CAUCASUS: (a) *Western Half.*—This sub-section, with a length of 200 m., reaches from Mount Elbruz to Kasbek and the Pass of Darial. It contains the loftiest summits of the entire range, fully a dozen exceeding Mont Blanc in altitude (see table below).

List of Peaks in the west central Caucasus, with their altitudes, names and dates of mountaineers who have climbed them.

Name of Peak.	A	By whom ascended.

	ltitude in Feet.		ate
Elbruz, E. peak	1 8,345	D.W. Freshfield, A.W. Moore and C. Tucker	868
Elbruz, W. peak	1 8,465	F.C. Grove, H. Walker and F. Gardiner	874
„ „	„	H. Woolley	889
Donguz-orun	1 4,600	G. Merzbacher and L. Purtscheller	890
„	„	Donkin and H. Fox	888
„	„	Helbling, Reichert and Weber	903
Shtavler	1 3,105	Ficker, W.R. Rickmers, Scheck and Wigner	903
Ledosht-tau	1 2,580	Schuster and Wigner	903
Hevai	1 3,055	Schuster and Wigner	903
Lakra-tau	1 2,185	Rolleston and Longstaff	903
Ushba, N.E. peak	1 5,400	Cockin	888
Ushba, S.W. peak	1 5,410	Helbling, Schulze, Reichert, Schuster and Weber	903
Ushba, both peaks	„	Distel, Leuchs and Pfann	903
Sultran-kol-bashi	1 2,495	Grove, Walker and Gardiner	874
Bak	1 1,739	Collier, Solly and Newmarch	894
Gulba	1 2,500	Freshfield	887
Salynan-bashi	1 4,700	Cockin and H.W. Holder	888
Shikildi-tau	1 4,170	Helbling, Reichert, Schulze and Weber	903
Bshedukh	1 4,010	Distel, Leuchs and Pfann	903
Ullu-tau-chana	1 3,800	Rolleston and Longstaff	903
Adyr-su-bashi	1 4,335	Holder, Cockin and Woolley	896
Sullu-kol-bashi	1 3,970	Merzbacher and Purtscheller	890
Tikhtengen	1 5,135	Rolleston and Longstaff	903
Gestola	1 5,940	C.T. Dent and Donkin	886

122

Tetnuld	1 5,920	Freshfield	887
„	„	Merzbacher and Purtscheller	890
Adish or Katuyn-tau	1 6,295	Holder and Woolley	888
Janga-tau, E. peak	1 6,525	Cockin	888
„ „	„	Merzbacher and Purtscheller	890
Janga-tau, E. and W. peaks	1 6,660	Helbling, Reichert, Schulze and Weber	903
Shkara	1 7,040	Cockin	888
Ailama	1 4,855	Woolley	889
Ullu-auz	1 5,350	V. Sella	888
Dykh-tau *	1 7,050	Cockin, Holder and Woolley	888
Koshtan-tau **	1 6,875	Woolley	888
Mishirghi-tau, E. peak	1 6,350	Woolley	889
Laboda	1 4,170	Dent and Woolley	895
Tsikhvarga, E. peak	1 3,575	V. Sella	890
" W. peak	1 3,575	Holder and Cockin	890
Karagom-khokh or Burdshula	1 4,295	Holder and Cockin	890
Adai-khokh	1 5,275	Holder and Cockin	890
Tepli	1 4,510	V. Sella	896
Kasbek	1 6,545	Freshfield, Moore and Tucker	868
„	„	Woolley	889
„	„	Merzbacher	890
„	„	V. Sella	896
Gimarai-khokh	1 5,670	Merzbacher	890
Laila, N. peak	1 3,045	Freshfield and Powell	889
Laila, middle peak	1 3,155	V. Sella	889
Laila, S. peak	1	Merzbacher and Purtscheller	

	3,105		890
Khamkhakhi-khokh	1	M. de Déchy	
	4,065		884

* Formerly the Koshtan-tau.

** Formerly the Dykh-tau.

In addition to the peaks enumerated in the table, the following also exist between Elbruz and Kasbek all exceeding 13,000 ft. in altitude: Dong-osenghi, 14,265 ft.; Kurmychi, 13,310 ft.; Ullu-kara-tau, 14,070 ft.; Jailyk, 17,780 ft.; Sarikol-bashi, 13,965 ft.; Dumala-tau, 14,950 ft.; Sugan-tau, 14,730 ft.; Tiutiu-bashi, 14,500 ft.; Nuamkuam, 13,975 ft.; Zurungal, 13,915 ft.; Mala-tau, 14,950 ft.; Tiutiun-tau, 15,115 ft.; Khrumkol-tau, 14,653 ft.; Bubis-khokh, 14,500 ft.; Giulchi, 14,680 ft.; Doppakh, 14,240 ft.; Nakhashbita-khokh, 14,405 ft.; Shan-khokh, 14,335 ft.; Mishirghi-tau (W. peak), 16,410 ft.; Fytnargyn-tau, 13,790 ft.; Gezeh-tau, 14,140 ft.; and Kaltber, 14,460 ft.

The crest of the main range runs continuously at an altitude exceeding 10,000 ft., but even it is surpassed in elevation by the secondary range to the north, the Bokovoi Khrebet. These two ranges are connected by more than half a dozen short transverse spurs or necks, inclosing as many cirques or high cauldron glens. Besides the Bokovoi Khrebet several other short subsidiary ranges branch off from the main range at acute angles, lifting up high montane glens between them; for instance, the two ranges in Svanetia, which divide, the one the river (glen) Ingur from the river (glen) Tskhenis-Tskhali, and the other the river (glen) Tskhenis-Tskhali from the rivers (glens) Lechkhum and Racha. Down all these glens glacier streams descend, until they find an opportunity to pierce through the flanking ranges, which they do in deep and picturesque gorges, and then race down the northern slopes of the mountains to enter the Terek or the Kubań, or down the southern versant to join the Rion or the Kura. Amongst all these high glens there is a remarkable absence of lakes and waterfalls; nor are there down in the lower valleys at the foot of the mountains, as one would naturally expect in a region so extensively glaciated, any sheets of water corresponding to the Swiss lakes. In this section of the Caucasus the loftiest peaks do not 552as a rule rise on the main range, but in many cases on the short spurs that link it with the Bokovoi Khrebet and other subsidiary ranges.

"The central chain of the Caucasus," writes Mr Douglas W. Freshfield,[1] "consists of a number of short parallel or curved horseshoe ridges, crowned with rocky peaks and enclosing basins filled by the *névés* of great glaciers.... On either side of the main chain the same succession is repeated, with one important difference. On the north the schists come first, sometimes rising into peaks and ridges in a state of ruin ... but more often worn to rolling downs; then the limestone range—writing-desk mountains that turn their steep fronts to the central snows; lastly low Cretaceous foothills, that sink softly into the steppe. But on the south side the crystalline rocks are succeeded by a broad belt of slates, as to the age of which the evidence is at present conflicting and the opinion of geologists divided. East of Adai-khokh, by what seems a strange freak of nature, the granitic [main] range is rent over and over again to its base by gorges, the watershed being transferred to the parallel chain of clay slates ... which has followed it from the Black Sea, attaining on its way the height of 13,400 ft. in the Laila, and limiting the great parallel basins of the Rion, Ingur and Skenis Shali [= Tskhenis-Tskhali]...." "At the base of the central core of the chain spread (to the north) broad, smooth, grassy downs, the pastures of the Turk and the Ossete.... Their ridges attain to 9000 to 10,000 ft. They are composed of friable crystalline schists.... Beyond these schists rises a broken wall of limestone, cleft to the base by gorges, through which flow the mountain torrents, and capped by pale precipitous battlements, which face the central chain at a height of 11,000 to 12,000 ft. Beyond, again, lies a broad furrow, or 'longitudinal fold,' as geologists call it, parallel to the ridges, and then rises the last elevation, a belt of low calcareous hills, on which, here and there among the waves of beech forest, purple or blue with distance, a white cliff retains its local colour and shines like a patch of fresh snow. Beyond, once more beyond, spreads the Scythian steppe, not the dead level of Lombardy, but an expanse of long low modulations, which would be reckoned hills in our home counties, seamed by long shining ribbons, which mark the courses of the tributaries of the

Terek.... Southwards too, immediately under the snows, we find 'crystalline schists,' smooth grassy heights, separated by shallow trenches, which form the lesser undulations of the three basins, the *drei Langenhochthäler Imeritiens* of Dr Radde. These basins or 'longitudinal folds' are enclosed on the south by the long high ridge of dark slates, which extends parallel to the crystalline [main] chain from the neighbourhood of Sukhum-Kale to the Krestovaya Gora [pass of Darial.] Behind this slate crest spreads a confused multitude of hills, Jurassic and Cretaceous in their formation.... Their outer edge, distant some 30 to 40 m. from the snows, is marked by a limestone belt, lower and less continuous than that on the north, which frames the gorges of the Rion, and rises in the Kuamli (6352 ft.) and Nakarala (4774 ft.) near Kutais, its best known elevations."2 It may be added that, south of the central watershed, the strata, both Mesozoic and Palaeozoic, are compressed, crumpled, faulted and frequently overfolded, with their apices pointing to the south.

Glaciers.—As a rule the snow-line runs at 9500 to 10,000 ft. on the northern face and 1000 ft. higher on the southern face. It is estimated that there are in all over nine hundred glaciers in this section of the range, and although they often rival those of the Alps in size, they do not descend generally to such low altitudes as the latter. The best known are the Bezingi or Ullu, between Dykh-tau and Janga-tau, 10½ m. long, covering an area of 31 sq.m., and descending to 6535 ft. above sea-level; Leksyr, situated south of Adyr-su-bashi, 7½ m. long, 19 sq.m. in area, and creeping down to as low as 5690 ft., this being the lowest point to which any glacier descends on the south side of the range; Tseya or Zea, descending 6 m. from the Adai-khokh to an altitude of 6730 ft.; Karagom, from the same mountain, 9½ m. long, 14 sq.m. in area and reaching down to 5790 ft., the lowest on the north side; Dyevdorak or Devdorak, from Kasbek, 2½ m. long, its lower end at 7530 ft.; Khaldeh or Geresho 4¼ m. long, from Shkara and Janga-tau; Tuyber from Tetnuld, 6½ m. long, area 21 sq.m., and reaching down to 6565 ft.; Tsanner or Zanner, the same length and the same area, but stopping short 240 ft. higher, likewise given off by Tetnuld; while between that peak, Adish and Gestola originates the Adish or Lardkhat glacier, 5 m. long and terminating at 7450 ft. The total area covered by glaciers in the central Caucasus is estimated at 625 to 650 sq.m., the longest being the Maliev on Kasbek, 36 m. long; but according to the investigations of M. Rossikov several of the largest glaciers are shrinking or retreating, the Tseya at the rate of something like 40-45 ft. per annum.

Passes.—It is in this section that the entire mountain system is narrowest, and here it is that (apart from the "gate" at Derbent close beside the Caspian) the principal means of communication exist between north and south, between the steppes of southern Russia and the highlands of Armenia and Asia Minor. These means of communication are the passes of Darial and Mamison. Over the former, which lies immediately east of Kasbek, runs the Georgian military road (made 1811-1864) from Vladikavkaz to Tiflis, cutting through the mountains by a gorge (8 m. long) of singular beauty, shut in by precipitous mountain walls nearly 6000 ft. high, and so narrow that there is only just room for the carriage-road and the brawling river Terek side by side. The pass by which this road crosses the main range, farther south, is known as the Krestovaya Gora (Mountain of the Cross) and lies 7805 ft. above sea-level. The Mamison Pass, over which runs the Ossetic military road (made passable for vehicles in 1889) from the Terek (below Vladikavkaz) to Kutais in the valley of the Rion, skirting the eastern foot of the Adai-khokh, lies at an altitude of 9270 ft. and is situated a little south of the main range. Scarce any of the remaining passes in this west-central region are better than mountain paths; horses can traverse the best of them only during a few weeks in the height of summer. They mostly range at altitudes of 9000-12,500 ft., and between the pass of Nakhar in the west and that of Mamison in the east there is not a single pass below 10,000 ft. The best known in this section are the three Baksan passes of Chiper (10,800 and 10,720 ft.), Bassa (9950 ft.) and Donguz-orun (10,490 ft.), south of Elbruz; those of Becho (11,070 ft.), Akh-su (12,465 ft.), Bak (10,220 ft.), Adyr-su (12,305 ft.) and Bezingi (10,090 ft.), between Elbruz and Dykh-tau; and those of Shari-vizk (11,560 ft.), Edena, Pasis-mta or Godivizk (11,270 ft.), Shtulu-vizk (10,860 ft.), Fytnargyn (11,130 ft.), between Dykh-tau and Adai-khokh; the Bakh-fandak (9570 ft.), between Adai-khokh and Kasbek; and the two Karaul passes (11,680 and 11,270 ft.) and Gurdzi-vizk (10,970 ft.), connecting the valley of the Urukh with that of the Rion. The most frequented pass in Svanetia is that of Latpari

(9260 ft.), situated in the first of the southern subsidiary ranges mentioned above, and thus connecting the valley of the Ingur with the valley of the Tskhenis-Tskhali.

Flora.—In this section of the range again the southern slopes are clothed with vegetation of remarkable luxuriance and richness, more especially in the region of Svanetia (42°-43° E.). Not only are the plants bigger than they grow in the Alps, but the blossoms are more abundant. Here again forests of *Coniferae* predominate, especially on the northern and eastern slopes; and the other distinguishing features of the flora are gigantic male ferns (*Aspidium filix-mas*), *Paris incompleta* (a member of the Trilliaceae), *Usnea* or tree-moss, box, holly (*Ilex aquifolium*), *Lilium monadelphum* and many of the familiar herbaceous plants which flower in English gardens, though here they grow to an altogether extraordinary size— "monkshoods, *Cephalaria*, *Mulgedia* and groundsels, among which men on horseback might play at hide and seek without stooping" (E. Levier). Other prominent species are *Campanula*, *Pyrethrum*, aconite, *Cephaelis*, speedwell, *Alchemilla sericea*, *Centaurea macrocephala*, *Primula grandis* and a species of primrose. And the great height (13,000 ft.) at which the flowering plants blossom is not less remarkable than the great beauty and abundance of the flowers. Species which grow on both the northern and the southern slopes ascend 2000 ft. higher on the latter than on the former. Walnuts grow up to an altitude of 5400 ft., the vine and mulberry up to 3250 ft., the lime and ash to 4000 ft. The forests extend to the upper end of the limestone gorges. Above that the crystalline schists are bare of tree vegetation. The upper limit of arborescent vegetation is considered to run at 7000-7500 ft., of shrubs such as rhododendrons at 8500 ft., and of pasture-lands up to 9000 ft. The principal cultivated varieties of plants in this section are wheat, rye, oats, barley, beans, millet and tobacco.

3. MIDDLE CAUCASUS: (b) *Eastern Part.*—In this sub-section, which stretches from Kasbek and the Darial gorge eastwards to 553the Baba-dagh in 48° 25′ E., a distance of 230 m., the Caucasus attains its greatest breadth. For the whole of that distance the main range keeps at an average elevation of 10,000 ft., though the peaks in many instances tower up 2000 to nearly 5000 ft. higher, the altitudes increasing towards the east. As the main range approaches the Caspian its granite core gradually disappears, giving place to Palaeozoic schists, which spread down both the northern and the southern slopes. The glaciers too decrease in the same proportion both in magnitude and in extent. Here the principal peaks, again found for the most part on the spurs and subsidiary ranges, are the Tsmiakom-khokh (13,570 ft.), Shan-tau (14,530 ft.), Kidenais-magali (13,840 ft.), Zilga-khokh (12,645 ft), Zikari (12,565 ft.), Choukhi (12,110 ft.), Julti-dagh (12,430 ft.), Alakhun-dagh (12,690 ft.) and Maghi-dagh (12,445 ft.). On the main range itself stand Borbalo (10,175 ft.), Great Shavi-kildeh (12,325 ft.), Murov (11,110 ft.), Ansal (11,740 ft.), Ginor-roso (11,120 ft), while farther east come Trfan-dagh (13,765 ft.) and Bazardyuz or Kichen (14,727 ft.). In the same direction, but again outside the main range, lie Shah-dagh (13,955 ft.), Shalbuz (13,675 ft.) and Malkamud (12,750 ft.).

But the most noteworthy feature of this section is the broad *highland region of Daghestan*, which flanks the main range on the north, and sinks down both eastwards to the Black Sea and northwards to the valley of the Terek. On the north-west this rugged highland region is well defined by the distinctive transverse ridge of Andi, which to the east of Kasbek strikes off from the Caucasus range almost at right angles. The rest of the Daghestan region consists of a series of roughly parallel folds, of Jurassic or Cretaceous age, ranging in altitudes from 7500 up to 12,500 ft., separated from one another by deep gorge-like river glens which cut it up into a number of arid, treeless plateaus which have something of the appearance of independent ranges, or rather elongated tablelands of a mountainous character. The most prominent of these tablelands is Bash-lam, which stretches east and west between the Chanti Argun and the Andian Koisu, both tributaries of the Terek. Upon it rise the conspicuous peaks of Tebulos-mta (14,775 ft.), Tugo-mta (13,795 ft.), Komito-tavi or Kachu (14,010 ft.), Donos-mta (13,560 ft.), Diklos-mta (13,740 ft.), Kvavlos-mta or Kolos-mta (13,080 ft.), Motshekh-tsferi (13,140 ft.) and Galavanas-tsferi (13,260 ft.). Farther east come the Bogos tableland, stretching from south-south-west to east-north-east between the Andian Koisu and the Avarian Koisu and rising to over 13,400 ft. in several peaks, *e.g.* Antshovala (13,440 ft.), Botshokh-meër (13,515 ft.), Kosara-ku (13,420 ft.) and Addala-shuogchol-meër (13,580 ft.); and the Dyulty tableland, reaching 12,400 ft. between the Kara Koisu and the Kazikumukh Koisu. On some of these peaks again there is a considerable amount of glaciation, more particularly on the slopes of Diklos-mta, where the glaciers descend to 7700 ft. on the north side and to 8350 ft. on the south side. In this section of the Caucasus the passes run somewhat lower than those between Elbruz and Kasbek, though still at appreciable heights, fully equal to those that lead up from the Black Sea to the valley of the Kuban in the western section of the range. The best known are the Krestovaya Gora (7805 ft.) on the Georgian military road, south of Darial; Kodor (9300 ft.) and Satskheni, leading up from Telav in the upper valley of the Alazan; and Gudur (10,120 ft.) and Salavat (9280 ft.), carrying the Akhty military road from the valley of the Samur up past the Shah-dagh and the Bazar-dyusi to the valley of the Alazan.

The *flora* of this section bears a general resemblance to that farther west. Ample details will be found in Dr G. Radde's (1831-1903) monographs on Daghestan, quoted at the end of the present article.

4. The EASTERN SECTION of the Caucasus gradually dies away east of Baba-dagh (11,930 ft.) towards the Caspian, terminating finally in the peninsula of Apsheron. It is, however, continued under the waters of the Caspian, as stated in the article on that sea, and reappears on its eastern side in the Kopet-dagh, which skirts the north-east frontier of Persia. In this section of the Caucasus no peak exceeds 9000 ft. in altitude and the crest of the main range retains no snow. The most frequented pass, that of Alty-agach, necessitates a climb of not more than 4355 ft.

Slopes of Range.—Between the northern and the southern sides of the range there is quite as great a difference in climate, productions and scenery as there is between the Swiss and the Italian sides of the Alps. In the south-western valleys and on the south-western slopes of the Caucasus, where a heavy rainfall is combined with a warm temperature, magnificent forests clothe the mountain-sides and dip their skirts into the waters of the Black Sea. There not only the littoral from (say) Sukhum-Kaleh to Batum but the inland parts of the basin of the Rion will bear comparison with any of the provinces of Italy in point of fertility, and in richness and variety of products. But farther inland, upon proceeding eastwards towards Tiflis, a great change becomes noticeable on the other side of the transverse ridge of the Suram or Meskes mountains. Arid upland plains and parched hillsides take the place of the rich verdure and luxuriant arborescent growth of Imeretia, Svanetia and Mingrelia, the districts which occupy the valleys of the Ingur and Rion and the tributaries of the latter. A very similar change likewise becomes noticeable in the higher regions of the Caucasus Mountains upon proceeding north of the pass of Mamison, which separates the head-waters of the Rion from those of the Ardon, an important tributary of the Terek. The valleys of the two streams last mentioned, and of others that flow in the same direction, are almost wholly destitute of trees, but where the bare rock does not prevail, the mountain slopes are carpeted with grass. Freshfield's description of the valley of the Terek above Kasbek will apply pretty generally to all the valleys that descend on that face of the range: "treeless valleys, bold rocks, slopes of forbidding steepness (even to eyes accustomed to those of the Alps), and stonebuilt villages, scarcely distinguishable from the neighbouring crags." But, austere and unattractive though these valleys are, the same epithets cannot be applied to the deep gorges by which in most cases the streams make their escape through the northern subsidiary range. These defiles are declared to be superior in grandeur to anything of the kind in the Alps. That of Darial (the Terek) is fairly well known, but those of the Cherek and the Urukh, farther west, are stated to be still more magnificent. And not only do the snow-clad ranges and the ice-panoplied peaks which tower up above them surpass the loftiest summits of the Alps in altitude; they also in many cases excel them in boldness and picturesqueness of outline, and equal the most difficult of them in steepness and relative inaccessibility.

Hydrography.—Nearly all the larger rivers of Caucasia have their sources in the central parts of the Caucasus range. The short, steep, torrential streams of Mdzimta, Pzou, Bzyb and Kodor drain the country west of Elbruz. The Ingur, Tskhenis-Tskhali, Rion and its tributaries (*e.g.* the Kvirila) are longer, but also in part torrential; they drain the great glacier region between Elbruz and Kasbek. The Rion is the *Phasis* of the ancients and flows through the classic land of Colchis, associated with the legends of Medea and the Argonauts. The Lyakhva and Aragva, tributaries of the Kura, carry off the waters of the main range south of Kasbek, and other tributaries, such as the Yora and the Alazan, collect the surplus drainage of the main Caucasus range farther east. The other large river of this region, the Aras, has its sources, not in the Caucasus range, but on the Armenian highlands a long way south-west of Ararat. The rivers which go down from the central Caucasus northwards have considerably longer courses than those on the south side of the range, partly as a consequence of the gentler versant and partly also because of the great distances to which the steppes extend across which they make their way to the sea. The most important of these are the Kubañ and the Terek; but it is the latter that picks up most of the streams which have their sources among the central glaciers, *e.g.* the Malka, Baksan, Chegem, Cherek, Urukh, Ardon, all confined to deep narrow glens until they quit the mountains. The Kuma, which alone pursues an independent course through the steppes, farther north than the 554Terek, has its sources, not in the main ranges of the Caucasus, but in an outlying group of mountains near Pyatigorsk, the highest summit of which, Besh-tau, does not exceed 4600 ft. But its waters become absorbed in the sands of the desert steppes before they reach the Caspian. Of the streams that carve into chequers the elevated plateau or highland region of Daghestan four are known by the common name of the Koisu, being distinguished *inter se* as the Andian Koisu, the Avarian Koisu, the Kara Koisu and the Kazikumukh Koisu, which all unite to form the Sulak. The only other stream deserving of mention in this province is the Samur. Both rivers discharge their waters into the Caspian; as also does the Zumgail, a small stream which drains the eastern extremity of the Caucasus range in the government of Baku.

Volcanic Evidences.—Ancient, but now extinct, volcanic upheavals are pretty common at the intersections of the main range with the transverse ranges; of these the most noteworthy are Elbruz and Kasbek. The town of Shemakha, near the eastern end of the system, was the scene of volcanic outbreaks as late as 1859, 1872 and 1902; while in the adjacent peninsula of Apsheron mud volcanoes exist in large numbers. All along the northern foot of the system hot mineral springs gush out at various places, such as Pyatigorsk, Zheleznovodsk, Essentuki and Kislovodsk; and the series is continued along the north-eastern foot of the highlands of Daghestan, *e.g.* Isti-su, Eskiendery, Akhta. In this connexion it may also be mentioned that similar evidences of volcanic activity characterize the northern border of the Armenian highlands on the southern side of the Rion-Kura depression, in the mountains of Ararat, Alagöz, Akmangan, Samsar, Godoreby, Great and Little Abull, and in the mineral springs of Borzhom, Abbas-tuman, Sleptzov, Mikhailovsk and Tiflis.

(J. T. BE.; P. A. K.)

Geology.—The general structure of the Caucasus is comparatively simple. The strata are folded so as to form a fan. In the centre of the fan lies a band of crystalline rocks which disappears towards the east. Beneath it, on both sides, plunge the strongly folded Palaeozoic and Jurassic schists. On the northern flank the folded beds are followed by a zone of Jurassic and Cretaceous beds which rapidly assume a gentle inclination towards the plain. On the south the corresponding zone is affected by numerous secondary folds which involve the Sarmatian or Upper Miocene deposits. In the eastern part of the chain the structure is somewhat modified. The crystalline band is lost. The northern Mesozoic zone is very much broader, and is thrown into simple folds like those of the Jura. The southern Mesozoic zone is absent, and the Palaeozoic zone sinks abruptly in a series of faulted steps to the plain of the Kura, beneath which no doubt the continuation of the Mesozoic zone is concealed.

The geological sequence begins with the granite and schists of the central zone, which form a band extending from Fisht on the west to a point some distance beyond Kasbek on the east. Then follow the Palaeozoic schists and slates. Fossils are extremely rare in these beds; *Buthotrephis* has long been known, and doubtful traces of *Calamites*and ferns have been found, but it was not until 1897 that undoubted Palaeozoic fossils were obtained. They appear to indicate a Devonian age. Upon the Palaeozoic beds rest a series of Mesozoic deposits, beginning with the Lias and ending with the Upper Cretaceous. Whether the series is continuous or not is a matter of controversy. F. Loewinson-Lessing states that there is a more or less marked discordance between the Lias and the Upper Jurassic and between the latter and the Cretaceous; E. Fournier asserts that there exists a very strongly marked unconformity at the base of the Tithonian, and other writers have expressed other views. In general the Upper ajurassic beds are much more calcareous on the north flank of the chain than they are on the south. The Mesozoic beds are followed by the Tertiary deposits, which on the north are nearly horizontal but on the south are in part included in the folds—the Eocene and Miocene being folded, while the later beds, though sometimes elevated, are not affected by the folding. The final folding of the chain undoubtedly occurred at the close of the Miocene period. That there were earlier periods of folding is almost equally certain, but there is considerable difference of opinion as to their dates. The difference in character of the Jurassic beds on the two sides of the chain appears to indicate that a ridge existed in that period. The last phase in the history of the Caucasus was marked by the growth of the great volcanoes of Elbruz and Kasbek, which stand upon the old rocks of the central zone, and by the outflow of sheets of lava upon the sides of the chain. The cones themselves are composed largely of acid andesites, but many of the lavas are augite andesites and basalts. There seem to have been two periods of eruption, and as some of the lavas have flowed over Quaternary gravels, the latest outbursts must have been of very recent date.

Near the northern foot of the Caucasus, especially in the neighbourhood of the hot mineral springs of Pyatigorsk, a group of hills of igneous rocks rises above the plain. They are laccolites of trachytic rock, and raised the Tertiary beds above them in the form of blisters. Subsequent denudation has removed the sedimentary covering and exposed the igneous core.

(P. LA.)

BIBLIOGRAPHY.—Of the older works the following are still useful: A. von Haxthausen,*Transkaukasia* (2 vols., Leipzig, 1856); A. Petzholdt, *Der Kaukasus* (2 vols., Leipzig, 1866-1867); M.G. von Thielmann, *Travels in the Caucasus* (Eng. trans., 2 vols., London, 1875); F.C. Grove, *The Frosty Caucasus* (London, 1875); G. Radde, *Reisen im mingrelischen Hochgebirge* (Tiflis, 1866) and *Vier Vorträge uber den Kaukasus*(Gotha, 1874); E. Favre, *Recherches géologiques dans la partie centrale de la chaîne du Caucase* (Geneva, 1875); Batsevich, Simonovich and others,*Mat. dlya geologiy Kavkaza* (Tiflis, 1873 seq.); O. Schneider, *Naturwissenschaftliche Beitrage zur Kenntnis der Kaukasuslander* (Dresden, 1879), and J. Bryce, *Transcaucasia* (London, 1878). The more important amongst the more recent books are D.W. Freshfield, *Exploration of the Caucasus* (2nd ed., 1902, 2 vols., London); A.F. Mummery, *My Climbs in the Alps and Caucasus* (London, 1895); H. Abich, *Geologische Forschungen in den kaukasischen Landern* (3 vols., Vienna, 1878-1887), *Aus kaukasischen Landern* (2 vols., Vienna, 1896), and "Vergleichende Grundzuge des Kaukasus wie der armenischen und nordpersischen Gebirge," in *Mém. Acad. Sc. St-Pétersb.* (sér. 6, *Math. et Phys.*, vii. 359-534); R. von Erckert, *Der Kaukasus und seine Volker* (Leipzig, 1887); E. Chantre, *Recherches anthropologiques dans le Caucase* (4 vols., Lyons and Paris, 1885-1887); C. von Hahn, *Aus dem Kaukasus* (Leipzig, 1892), *Kaukasische Reisen und Studien* (Leipzig, 1896), and *Bilder aus dem Kaukasus* (Leipzig 5551900); V. Sella and D. Vallino, *Nel Caucaso Centrale* (Turin, 1890); K. Koch, *Der Kaukasus* (Berlin, 1882); C. Phillipps Woolley, *Savage Svanetia* (2 vols., London, 1883); E. Levier, *À travers le Caucase* (Paris, ed. 1905), especially valuable for botany; G. Merzbacher, *Aus den Hochregionen des Kaukasus* (2 vols., Leipzig, 1901); A. Fischer, *Zwei Kaukasische Expeditionen* (Berne, 1891); E. Fournier, *Description géologique du Caucase central*(Marseilles, 1896); G. Radde, *Reisen an der persisch-russischen Grenze. Talysch und seine Bewohner* (Leipzig, 1886), *Die Fauna und Flora des südwestlichen Kaspigebiets*(Leipzig,

1886), *Karabagh* (Gotha, 1890), and *Aus den daghestanischen Hochalpen*(Gotha, 1887); and Count J. Zichy, *Voyages au Caucase* (2 vols., Budapest, 1897). F. Loewinson-Lessing has an account of the geology of the district along the military road from Vladikavkaz to Tiflis in the *Guide des Excursions du VIIe Congrès géol. internat.* (St Petersburg, 1897). N.Y. Dinnik writes on the fauna in *Bull. Soc. Impériale des Naturalistes de Moscou* (1901); J. Mourier on the folk-tales in *Contes et légendes du Caucase* (1888); and on modern history G. Baumgarten, *Sechzig Jahre des kaukasischen Krieges* (Leipzig, 1861). But a very great amount of most valuable information about the Caucasus is preserved in articles in encyclopaedias and scientific periodicals, especially the *Izvestia* and *Zapiski* of the Russian and Caucasian geographical societies, in P.P. Semenov's *Geographical Dictionary* (in Russian, 5 vols., St Petersburg, 1863-1884), and in the *Russkiy encyklopedicheskiy slovar* (1894), and in the *Kavkazskiy kalendar* (annually at Tiflis). See also G. Radde and E. Koenig, "Der Nordfuss des Daghestan und das vorlagernde Tiefland bis zur Kuma" (Ergänzungsheft No. 117 to *Petermanns Mitteilungen*), and "Das Ostufer des Pontus und seine kulturelle Entwickelung im Verlaufe der letzten 30 Jahre" (Ergänzungsheft No. 112 of the same); by V. Dingelstedt in *Scot. Geog. Mag.*—"Geography of the Caucasus" (July 1889); "The Caucasian Highlands" (June 1895); "The Hydrography of the Caucasus" (June 1899); "The Riviera of Russia" (June 1904), "The Small Trades of the Caucasus" (March 1892); and "Caucasian Idioms" (June 1888). The best map is that of the Russian General Staff on the scale of 1 : 210,000 (ed. 1895-1901).

(J. T. BE.; P. A. K.)

1*Exploration of the Caucasus* (2nd ed., 1902), i. 30-31.
2Op. cit. i. 35-36.

CAUCHOIS-LEMAIRE, LOUIS FRANÇOIS AUGUSTE (1789-1861), French journalist, was born in Paris on the 28th of August 1789. Towards the end of the First Empire he was proprietor of the *Journal de la littérature et des arts*, which he transformed at the Restoration into a political journal of Liberal tendencies, the *Nain jaune*, in which Louis XVIII. himself had little satirical articles secretly inserted. After the return from Elba the *Nain jaune* became Bonapartist and fell into discredit. It was suppressed at the second Restoration. Cauchois-Lemaire then threw himself impetuously into the Liberal agitation, and had to take refuge in Brussels in 1816, and in the following year at the Hague, whence he was expelled for publishing an *Appel à l'opinion publique et aux États Généraux en faveur des patriotes français*. Returning to France in 1819, he resumed the struggle against the ultra-royalist party with such temerity that he was condemned to one year's imprisonment in 1821 and fifteen months' imprisonment in 1827. After the revolution of July 1830 he refused a pension of 6000 francs offered to him by King Louis Philippe, on the ground that he wished to retain his independence even in his relations with a government which he had helped to establish. He made a bitter attack upon the Périer ministry in his journal *Bon sens*, and in 1836 was one of the founders of a new opposition journal, the *Siècle*. He soon, however, abandoned journalism for history and, having no private means, in 1840 accepted the post of head of a department in the Royal Archives. Of a *Histoire de la Révolution de Juillet*, which he then undertook, he published only the first volume (1842), which contains a historical summary of the Restoration and a preliminary sketch of the democratic movement. He died in Paris on the 9th of August 1861.

CAUCHON, PIERRE (d. 1442), French bishop, was born near Reims in the latter half of the 14th century. We find him rector of the university of Paris in October 1397. In 1413 he joined the Burgundian faction, and was exiled by the parlement of Paris. But on the triumph of his party this decree was annulled, and Philip the Good, duke of Burgundy, gave him a canonry at Beauvais, sent him to the council of Constance, procured him the post of *maître des requêtes* in 1418, and finally in 1420 had him made bishop of Beauvais. But the people were hostile to him, and he was driven from his bishopric in 1429; whereupon he attached himself to the English court, and in 1431 endeavoured to procure the surrender of Reims to the English, so that Henry VI. might be crowned there. In this he failed, and Henry was crowned in Paris on the 17th of December 1431 by Henry Beaufort, cardinal bishop of

Winchester, assisted by the bishops of Beauvais and Noyon. On the 24th of May 1430, Joan of Arc having been taken prisoner at Compiègne, within the limits of his diocese, Cauchon acted as her accuser, and demanded the right of judging her. Joan was taken to Rouen, whither Cauchon followed her, having been driven from Beauvais. He conducted the trial with marked partiality and malevolence, condemned the maid to imprisonment for life, and then, under pressure from the populace and the English, had recourse to fresh perfidies, declared Joan a relapsed heretic, excommunicated her, and handed her over to the secular arm on the 30th of May 1431. As, in consequence of this, it was impossible for him to return to his own diocese, he obtained the bishopric of Lisieux in 1432 by favour of the king of England. He assisted at the council of Basel in 1435, and died suddenly on the 18th of December 1442. Excommunicated posthumously by Pope Calixtus IV., his body was exhumed and thrown in the common sewer.

See Cerf, "Pierre Cauchon de Sommièvre, chanoine de Reims et de Beauvais, évêque de Beauvais et de Lisieux, son origine, ses dignités, sa mort et sa sépulture," in the*Transactions* of the Academy of Reims (1896-1898).

CAUCHY, AUGUSTIN LOUIS, BARON (1789-1857), French mathematician, was born at Paris on the 21st of August 1789, and died at Sceaux (Seine) on the 23rd of May 1857. Having received his early education from his father Louis François Cauchy (1760-1848), who held several minor public appointments and counted Lagrange and Laplace among his friends, Cauchy entered École Centrale du Panthéon in 1802, and proceeded to the École Polytechnique in 1805, and to the École des Ponts et Chaussées in 1807. Having adopted the profession of an engineer, he left Paris for Cherbourg in 1810, but returned in 1813 on account of his health, whereupon Lagrange and Laplace persuaded him to renounce engineering and to devote himself to mathematics. He obtained an appointment at the École Polytechnique, which, however, he relinquished in 1830 on the accession of Louis Philippe, finding it impossible to take the necessary oaths. A short sojourn at Freiburg in Switzerland was followed by his appointment in 1831 to the newly-created chair of mathematical physics at the university of Turin. In 1833 the deposed king Charles X. summoned him to be tutor to his grandson, the duke of Bordeaux, an appointment which enabled Cauchy to travel and thereby become acquainted with the favourable impression which his investigations had made. Charles created him a baron in return for his services. Returning to Paris in 1838, he refused a proffered chair at the Collège de France, but in 1848, the oath having been suspended, he resumed his post at the École Polytechnique, and when the oath was reinstituted after the *coup d'état* of 1851, Cauchy and Arago were exempted from it. A profound mathematician, Cauchy exercised by his perspicuous and rigorous methods a great influence over his contemporaries and successors. His writings cover the entire range of mathematics and mathematical physics.

Cauchy had two brothers: ALEXANDRE LAURENT (1792-1857), who became a president of a division of the court of appeal in 1847, and a judge of the court of cassation in 1849; andEUGÈNE FRANÇOIS (1802-1877), a publicist who also wrote several mathematical works.

The genius of Cauchy was promised in his simple solution of the problem of Apollonius, *i.e.* to describe a circle touching three given circles, which he discovered in 1805, his generalization of Euler's theorem on polyhedra in 1811, and in several other elegant problems. More important is his memoir on wave-propagation which obtained the *Grand Prix* of the Institut in 1816. His greatest contributions to mathematical science are enveloped in the rigorous methods which he introduced. These are mainly embodied in his three great treatises, *Cours d'analyse de l'École Polytechnique* (1821);*Le Calcul infinitésimal* (1823); *Leçons sur les applications du calcul infinitésimal à la géométrie* (1826-1828); and also in his courses of mechanics (for the École Polytechnique), higher algebra (for the Faculté des Sciences), and of mathematical physics (for the Collège de France). His treatises and contributions to scientific journals (to the number of 789) contain investigations on the theory of series (where he developed with perspicuous skill the notion of convergency), on the theory of numbers and complex quantities, the theory of groups and 556substitutions, the theory of functions, differential equations and determinants. He clarified the principles of the calculus by developing them with the aid of limits and continuity, and was the first to prove Taylor's theorem rigorously, establishing his well-known form of the remainder. In mechanics, he made many researches, substituting the notion of the continuity of geometrical displacements for the principle of the continuity of matter. In optics, he developed the wave theory, and his name is associated with the simple dispersion formula. In elasticity, he originated the theory of stress, and his results are nearly as valuable as those of S.D. Poisson. His collected works, *OEuvres complètes d'Augustin Cauchy*, have been published in 27 volumes.

See C.A. Valson, *Le Baron Augustin Cauchy: sa vie et ses travaux* (Paris, 1868).

CAUCUS, a political term used in America of a special form of party meeting, and in Great Britain of a system of party organization. The word originated in Boston, Massachusetts, in the early part of the 18th century, when it was used as the name of a political club, the "Caucus" or "Caucas" club. Here public matters were discussed, and arrangements made for local elections and the choosing of candidates for offices. The first mention of the club in contemporary documents occurs in the diary of John Adams in 1763, but William Gordon (*History of the Independence of the United States of America*, 1788) speaks of the Caucus as having been in existence some fifty years before the time of writing (1774), and describes the methods used for securing the election of the candidates the club had selected. The derivation of the word has been much disputed. It was early connected with "caulkers," and it was supposed referred to meetings of the caulkers in the dockyard at Boston in 1770, to protest against the action of the British troops, or with a contemptuous allusion to the lower class of workmen frequenting the club. This is, however, a mere guess, and does not agree with the earlier date at which the club is known to have existed, nor with the accounts given of it. That it was a fanciful classical name for a convivial club, derived from the late Greek καῦκος, a cup, is far-fetched, and the most plausible origin is an Algonquin word *kaw-kaw-was*, meaning to talk. Indian words and names have been popular in America as titles for societies and clubs; cf. "Tammany" (see *Notes and Queries*. sixth series, vols. xi. and xii.). In the United States "caucus" is used strictly of a meeting either of party managers or of party voters. Such might be a "nominating caucus," either for nominating candidates for office or for selecting delegates for a nominating convention. The caucus of the party in Congress nominated the candidates for the offices of president and vice-president from 1800 till 1824, when the convention system was adopted, and the place of the local "nominating caucus" is taken by the "primaries" and conventions. The word is used in America of the meetings of a party in Congress and other legislative bodies and elsewhere which decide matters of policy and plan campaigns. "Caucus" came first into use in Great Britain in 1878. The Liberal Association of Birmingham (see LIBERAL PARTY) was organized by Mr Joseph Chamberlain and Mr F. Schnadhorst on strict disciplinary lines, more particularly with a view to election management and the control of voters on the principle of "vote as you are told." This managing body of the association, known locally as the "Six Hundred," became the model for other Liberal associations throughout the country, and the Federation of Liberal Associations was organized on the same plan. It was to this supposed imitation of the American political "machine" that Lord Beaconsfield gave the name "caucus," and the name came to be used, not in the American sense of a meeting, but of a closely disciplined system of party organization, chiefly used as a stock term of abuse applied by opponents to each other's party machinery.

CAUDEBEC-EN-CAUX, a town of France, in the department of Seine-Inférieure, 27 m. W.N.W. of Rouen by the Ouest-État railway. Pop. (1906) 2141. It is situated on the right bank of the Seine, the tidal wave of which (*mascaret*) can be well seen at this point. The chief interest of the town lies in its church, a building of the 15th and the early 16th centuries. Round its top run balustrades formed of Gothic letters, which read as part of the Magnificat. Its west portal, the decoration of the spire of the tower, and its stained glass are among the features which make it one of the finest churches of the Rouen diocese. The town also possesses several old houses. Its industries include tanning and leather-currying, and there is trade in grain. The port has a small trade in coal, live-stock and farm produce.

CAUDINE FORKS (*Furculae Caudinae*), a pass in Samnium, famous for the disaster which befell the Roman army in the second Samnite War (321 B.C.). Livy (ix, 2) describes it as formed by two narrow wooded gorges, between which lay a plain, grassy and well-watered, but entirely enclosed by mountains. Through this plain the road (later the Via Appia) led. The Romans, marching from Calatia to the relief of Luceria, entered the valley unopposed, but found the exit blocked by the enemy; on marching back they saw that the entrance and the hills surrounding the plain were also occupied, and there was no way of escape. The plain which lies west of Caudium (Montesarchio) seems, despite the older views, to be the only possible site for such a disaster to an army of as many as 40,000 men; and there is no doubt that the Romans wished to leave it by the defile on the east, through which later ran the Via Appia to Beneventum. The existence of three ancient bridges on the line of the modern road renders it impossible to suppose that its course can be essentially different from that of the ancient, though Hülsen makes the two diverge considerably after passing Montesarchio. There are, however, two possible entrances—one on the north by Moiano, and one on the west by Arpaia; the former seems to answer better to Livy's description (*via alia per cavam rupem*), while the latter is the shortest route, having been, later on, followed by the Via Appia, and bore the name Furculae Caudinae in the middle ages.

See C. Hülsen in Pauly-Wissowa, *Realencyclopädie*, iii. (1802).

(T. As.)

CAUDLE (through the O. Fr. *caudel*, from the Med. Lat. *caldellum*, a diminutive of *caldum*, a warm drink, from *calidus*, hot), a drink of warm gruel, mixed with spice and wine, formerly given to women in childbed.

CAUL (from O. Eng. *calle*, Fr. *cale*, a cap), a close-fitting woman's cap, especially one made of network worn in the 16th and 17th centuries; hence the membranous covering to the heart or brain, the *omentum*, or the similar covering to the intestines, and particularly, a portion of the *amnion*, which is sometimes found remaining round the head of a child after birth. To this, called in Scotland "sely how," holy or lucky hood, many superstitions have been attached; it was looked on as a sign of good luck, and when preserved, was kept as a protection against drowning.

CAULAINCOURT, ARMAND AUGUSTIN LOUIS, MARQUIS DE (1773-1827), French general and diplomatist, was born of a noble family. He early entered the army, did not emigrate in the revolution, but was deprived of his grade as captain in 1793 and served in the ranks. In 1795, through the protection of L. Hoche, he became captain again, was colonel in the Army of the Rhine in 1799-1800, and after the peace of Lunéville (1801) was sent to St Petersburg to negotiate an understanding between Russia and France. On his return he was named aide-de-camp of the First Consul. He was employed to seize some agents of the English government in Baden in 1804, which led to the accusation that he was concerned in the arrest of the due d'Enghien, an accusation against which he never ceased to protest. After the establishment of the empire he received various honours and the title of duke of Vicenza (1808). Napoleon sent him in 1807 as ambassador to St Petersburg, where Caulaincourt tried to maintain the alliance of Tilsit, and although Napoleon's ambition made the task a difficult one, Caulaincourt succeeded in it for some years. In 1811 he strongly advised Napoleon to renounce his proposed expedition to Russia. During the war he accompanied the emperor, and was one of those whom Napoleon took along with him when he suddenly abandoned his army in Poland to return to Paris (December 1812). During the last years of the empire, Caulaincourt was charged with all the diplomatic negotiations. He signed the armistice of Pleswitz, June 1813, represented France at the congress of Prague, in August 1813, at the congress of Chatillon, in February 1814, and concluded the 557treaty of Fontainebleau on the 10th of April 1814. During the first Restoration, Caulaincourt lived in obscure retirement. When Napoleon returned from Elba, he became minister of foreign affairs, and tried to persuade Europe of the emperor's peaceful intentions. After the second Restoration, Caulaincourt's name was on the list of those proscribed, but it was erased on the personal intervention of Alexander I. with Louis XVIII.

Caulaincourt's memoirs appeared under the title *Souvenirs du duc de Vicence* in 1837-1840. See A. Vandal, *Napoléon et Alexandre* (Paris, 1891-1895); Tatischeff, *Alexandre Ier et Napoleon* (Paris, 1892); H. Houssaye, 1814 (Paris, 1888), and 1815 (Paris, 1893).

CAULICULUS (from Lat. *caulis*, a stalk), in architecture, the Stalks (eight in number) with two leaves from which rise the helices or spiral scrolls of the Corinthian capital to support the abacus.

CAULON (Gr. καυλωνία), a town of the district of the Bruttii, Italy, on the east coast. Its exact site is uncertain (though the name has been given to a modern village), and depends on the identification of the river Sagras. It was the southernmost of the Achaean colonies, founded either by Croton or direct from Greece itself. In the 7th century it was allied with Croton and Sybaris, and its coins, which go back to 550 B.C., prove its importance. It took the side of Athens in the Peloponnesian War. In 388 B.C. it was destroyed by Dionysius, but soon afterwards restored. It was captured during the invasion of Pyrrhus by Campanian troops. Strabo speaks of it as deserted in his time. The erection of the lighthouse at Capo Stilo, on the site of one of the medieval guard towers of the coast, led to the discovery of a wall of Greek origin, and close by of a number of terra-cottas, belonging perhaps to a temple erected in honour of the deities of the sea. Other remains were found at Fontanelle, 2½ m. away, including the fragment of a capital of an archaic Greek temple (P. Orsi in *Notizie degli Scavi*, 1891, 61). These buildings may be connected with the Caulon or a village dependent on it.

(T. As.)

CAUSATION or CAUSALITY (Lat. *causa*, derived perhaps from the root *cav-*, as in *caveo*, and meaning something taken care of; corresponding to Gr. αἰτία), a philosophical term for the operation of causes and for the mental conception of cause as operative throughout the universe. The word "cause" is correlative to "effect." Thus when one thing B is regarded as taking place in consequence of the action of another thing A, then A is said to be the cause of B, and B the effect of A. The philosophical problems connected with causation are both metaphysical and psychological. The metaphysical problem is part of the whole theory of existence. If everything is to be regarded as causally related with simultaneous and prior things or actions, it follows logically that the investigation of existence must, by hypothesis, be a regress to infinity, *i.e.* that we cannot conceive a beginning to existence. This explanation has led to the postulate of a First Cause, the nature of which is variously explained. The empirical school sees no difficulty in assuming a single event; but such a theory seems to deny the validity of the original hypothesis. Theologians assert a divine origin in the form of a personal self-existent creator, while some metaphysical schools, preferring an impersonal First Cause, substitute the doctrine of the Absolute (*q.v.*). All the explanations are alike in this respect, that at a certain point they pass from the sphere of the senses, the physical world, to a metaphysical sphere in which the data and the intellectual operation of cognizing them are of a totally different quality. For example, the causal connexion between drunkenness and alcohol is not of the same observable character as that which is inferred between the infinite First Cause and the whole domain of sense-given phenomena.

A second metaphysical problem connected with causation arises when we consider the nature of necessity. It is generally assumed when two things are spoken of as cause and effect that their relation is a necessary one, or, in other words, that given the cause the effect must follow. The arguments connected with this problem belong to psychological discussions of causation. It is sufficient here to state that, in so far as causation is regarded as necessary connexion, it can form no part of a purely empirical theory of existence. The senses can say only that in all observed cases B has followed A, and this does not establish necessary connexion. The idea of causation is a purely intellectual (a priori) one.

The psychological problems connected with causation refer (1) to the origin of the conception in our minds; (2) to the validity of the conception. As regards the origin of the conception modern psychological analysis does not carry us beyond the doctrine of Locke contained in his chapter on "Power" (*Essay*, bk. ii. ch. 21), wherein he shows that the idea of power is got from the knowledge of our own activity. "Bodies by their causes," he says, "do not afford us so clear and distinct an idea of active power as we have from reflection on the operation of our minds." Putting Locke's doctrine into modern language, we may say that a man has the conception of cause primarily because he himself is a cause. The conception thus obtained we "project," that is, transfer to external objects, so far as we may find it useful to do so. Thus it is by a sort of analogy that we say that the sun is the "cause" of daylight. The rival theory to Locke's is that of Hume (*Treatise*, bk. i.), who derives the conception from the unaided operation of custom. When one object, A, has been noticed frequently to precede another object, B, an association between A and B is generated; and by virtue of this association, according to Hume, we say that A is the cause of B. The weakness of this account is that many invariable successions, such as day and night, do not make us regard the earlier members of the successions as causing the later; while in numberless cases we assert a causal connexion between two objects from a single experience of them.

We may proceed now to consider the validity of the conception of causation, which has been attacked from two sides. From the side of absolute idealism it is argued that the conception of cause, as involving a transition in time, cannot be ultimately valid, since the time-relation is not ultimately real. Upon this view (ably stated in Professor Bosanquet's *Logic*, bk. i. ch. 6) the more we know of causes and effects the less relevant becomes the time-relation and the nearer does the conception of cause and effect approach to another conception which is truly valid, the conception of ground and consequence. This means that, viewed from the standpoint of science, a draught of alcohol *causes* intoxication in no other sense than the triangularity of a triangle causes the interior angles to be equal to two right angles. This argument ceases to have cogency so soon as we deny its fundamental proposition that the time-relation is not ultimately real, but is irrelevant from the standpoint of science. This is a sheer assertion, contrary to all ordinary experience, which we have as much right to deny as the absolute idealists to affirm. It is only plausible to those who are committed to the Hegelian view of reality as consisting of a static system of universals, a view which has long been discredited in Germany, its native land, and is fast losing ground in England. Against the Hegelians we must maintain that the common distinction between "ground" and "cause" is perfectly justifiable. Whereas "ground" is an appropriate term for the relations within a static, simultaneous system, "cause" is appropriate to the relations within a dynamic, successive system.

From the other side the validity of causation has been attacked in the interests of the naturalism of the mechanical sciences. J.S. Mill argues that, scientifically, the cause of anything is the total assemblage of the conditions that precede its appearance, and that we have no right to give the name of cause to one of them exclusively of the others. The answer to this is that Mill fails to recognize that cause is a conception which we find useful in our dealings with nature, and that whatever conceptions we find useful we are justified in using. Among the conditions of an event there are always one or two that stand in specially close relation to it from our point of view; *e.g.* the draught of alcoholic liquor is more closely related to the man's drunkenness than is the attraction of the earth's gravity, though that also must co-operate in producing the effect. Such closely related conditions we find it convenient to single out by a term which expresses their analogy to the cause of causes, human volition.

558

These are the questions respecting causation which are matters of present controversy; there are in addition many other points which belong to the controversies of the past. Among the most important are Aristotle's classification of causes into material, formal, efficient and final, set forth in his *Physics* and elsewhere, and known as his doctrine of the Four Causes; Geulincx's Occasional Causes, meant as a solution of certain difficulties in the cosmology of Descartes; Leibnitz's law of Sufficient Reason; and Kant's explanation of cause and effect as an a priori category of the understanding, intended as an answer to

Hume's scepticism, but very much less effective than the line of explanation suggested by Locke.

The following is a list of the various technical terms connected with causation which have been distinguished by logicians and psychologists.

The four Aristotelian causes are: (1) *Material cause* (ὕλη) the material out of which a thing is made; the material cause of a house is the bricks and mortar of which it is composed. (2) *Formal cause* (εἶδος, λόγος, τὸ τί ἦν εἶναι), the general external appearance, shape, form of a thing; the formal cause of a triangle is its triangularity. (3) *Efficient cause* (ἀρχὴ τῆς κινήσεως), the alcohol which makes a man drunk, the pistol-bullet which kills. This is the cause as generally understood in modern usage. (4) *Final cause* (τέλος, τὸ οὖ ἕνεκα), the object for which an action is done or a thing produced; the final cause of a commercial man's enterprise is to make his livelihood (see TELEOLOGY). This last cause was rejected by Bacon, Descartes and Spinoza, and indeed in ordinary usage the cause of an action in relation to its effect is the desire for, and expectation of, that effect on the part of the agent, not the effect itself. The *Proximate cause* of a phenomenon is the immediate or superficial as opposed to the *Remote* or *Primary cause*. Plurality of Causes is the much criticized doctrine of J.S. Mill that a fact may be the uniform consequent of several different antecedents. *Causa essendi* means the cause whereby a change is what it is, as opposed to the *causa cognoscendi*, the cause of our knowledge of the event; the two causes evidently need not be the same. An object is called *causa immanens* when it produces its changes by its own activity; a *causa transiens* produces changes in some other object. *Causa sui* is a term applied to God by Spinoza to denote that he is dependent on nothing and has no need of any external thing for his existence. *Vera causa* is a term used by Newton in his *Principia*, where he says, "No more causes of natural things are to be admitted than such as are both true and sufficient to explain the phenomena of those things"; *verae causae* must be such as we have good inductive grounds to believe do exist in nature, and do perform a part in phenomena analogous to those we would render an account of.

CAUSEWAY, a path on a raised dam or mound across marshes or low-lying ground; the word is also used of old paved highways, such as the Roman military roads. "Causey" is still used dialectically in England for a paved or cobbled footpath. The word is properly "causey-way," from *causey*, a mound or dam, which is derived, through the Norman-French *caucie*(cf. modern *chaussée*), from the late Latin *via calciata*, a road stamped firm with the feet (*calcare*, to tread).

CAUSSES (from Lat. *calx* through local Fr. *caous*, meaning "lime"), the name given to the table-lands lying to the south of the central plateau of France and sloping westward from the Cévennes. They form parts of the departments of Lozère, Aveyron, Card, Hérault, Lot and Tarn-et-Garonne. They are of limestone formation, dry, sterile and treeless. These characteristics are most marked in the east of the region, where the Causse de Sauveterre, the Causse Méjan, the Causse Noir and the Larzac flank the Cévennes. Here the Causse Méjan, the most deserted and arid of all, reaches an altitude of nearly 4200 ft. Towards the west the lesser causses of Rouergue and Quercy attain respectively 2950 ft. and 1470 ft. Once an uninterrupted table-land, the causses are now isolated from one another by deep rifts through which run the Tarn, the Dourbie, the Jonte and other rivers. The summits are destitute of running water, since the rain as it falls either sinks through the permeable surface soil or runs into the fissures and chasms, some of great depth, which are peculiar to the region. The inhabitants (*Caussenards*) of the higher causses cultivate hollows in the ground which are protected from the violent winds, and the scanty herbage permits of the raising of sheep, from the milk of which Roquefort cheeses are made. In the west, where the rigours of the weather are less severe, agriculture is more easily carried on.

CAUSSIN DE PERCEVAL, ARMAND-PIERRE (1795-1871), French orientalist, was born in Paris on the 13th of January 1795. His father, Jean Jacques Antoine Caussin de Perceval (1759-1835), was professor of Arabic in the Collège de France. In 1814 he went to Constantinople as a student interpreter, and afterwards travelled in Asiatic Turkey, spending a year with the Maronites in the Lebanon, and finally becoming dragoman at Aleppo. Returning to Paris, he became professor of vulgar Arabic in the school of living Oriental languages in 1821, and also professor of Arabic in the College de France in 1833. In 1849 he was elected to the Academy of Inscriptions. He died at Paris during the siege on the 15th of January 1871.

Caussin de Perceval published (1828) a useful *Grammaire arabe vulgaire*, which passed through several editions (4th ed., 1858), and edited and enlarged Élie Bocthor's 1 *Dictionnaire français-arabe* (2 vols., 1828; 3rd ed., 1864); but his great reputation rests almost entirely on one book, the *Essai sur l'histoire des Arabes avant l'Islamisme, pendant l'époque de Mahomet* (3 vols., 1847-1849), in which the native traditions as to the early history of the Arabs, down to the death of Mahommed and the complete subjection of all the tribes to Islam, are brought together with wonderful industry and set forth with much learning and lucidity. One of the principal MS. sources used is the great *Kitáb al-Agháni* (Book of Songs) of Abu Faraj, which has since been published (20 vols., Boulak, 1868) in Egypt; but no publication of texts can deprive the *Essai*, which is now very rare, of its value as a trustworthy guide through a tangled mass of tradition.

CAUSTIC (Gr. καυστικός, burning), that which burns. In surgery, the term is given to substances used to destroy living tissues and so inhibit the action of organic poisons, as in bites, malignant disease and gangrenous processes. Such substances are silver nitrate (lunar caustic), the caustic alkalis (potassium and sodium hydrates), zinc chloride, an acid solution of mercuric nitrate, and pure carbolic acid. In mathematics, the "caustic surfaces" of a given surface are the envelopes of the normals to the surface, or the loci of its centres of principal curvature.

In optics, the term *caustic* is given to the envelope of luminous rays after reflection or refraction; in the first case the envelope is termed a catacaustic, in the second a diacaustic. Catacaustics are to be observed as bright curves when light is allowed to fall upon a polished riband of steel, such as a watch-spring, placed on a table, and by varying the form of the spring and moving the source of light, a variety of patterns may be obtained. The investigation of caustics, being based on the assumption of the rectilinear propagation of light, and the validity of the experimental laws of reflection and refraction, is essentially of a geometrical nature, and as such it attracted the attention of the mathematicians of the 17th and succeeding centuries, more notably John Bernoulli, G.F. de l'Hôpital, E.W. Tschirnhausen and Louis Carré.

The simplest case of a caustic curve is when the reflecting surface is a circle, and the luminous rays emanate from a point on the circumference. If in fig. 1 AQP be the reflecting circle having C as centre, P the luminous point, and PQ any *Caustics by reflection.* incident ray, and we join CQ it follows, by the law of the equality of the angles of incidence and reflection, that the reflected ray QR is such that the angles RQC and CQP are equal; to determine the caustic, it is necessary to determine the envelope of this line. This may be readily accomplished geometrically or analytically, and it will be found that the envelope is a cardioid (*q.v.*), *i.e.* an epicycloid in which the radii of the fixed and rolling circles are equal. When the rays are parallel, the reflecting surface 559 remaining circular, the question can be similarly treated, and it is found that the caustic is an epicycloid in which the radius of the fixed circle is twice that of the rolling circle (fig. 2). The geometrical method is also applicable when it is required to determine the caustic after any number of reflections at a spherical surface of rays, which are either parallel or diverge from a point on the circumference. In both cases the curves are epicycloids; in the first case the radii of the rolling and the fixed circles are $a(2n-1)/4n$ and $a/2n$, and in the second, $an/(2n+1)$ and $a/(2n+1)$, where a is the radius of the mirror and n the number of reflections.

The Cartesian equation to the caustic produced by reflection at a circle of rays diverging from any point was obtained by Joseph Louis Lagrange; it may be expressed in the form

$$\{ (4c^2 - a^2) (x^2 + y^2)) - 2a^2cx - a^2c^2 \}3 = 27a4c^2y^2 (x^2 + y^2 - c^2)^2,$$

where a is the radius of the reflecting circle, and c the distance of the luminous point from the centre of the circle. The polar form is $\{(u + p) \cos \tfrac{1}{2}\theta\}2/3 + \{(u - p) \sin \tfrac{1}{2}\theta\}2/3 = (2k)2/3$, where p and k are the reciprocals of c and a, and u the reciprocal of the radius vector of any point on the caustic. When c = a or = ∞ the curve reduces to the cardioid or the two cusped epicycloid previously discussed. Other forms are shown in figs. 3, 4, 5, 6. These curves were traced by the Rev. Hammet Holditch (*Quart. Jour. Math.* vol. i.).

Secondary caustics are orthotomic curves having the reflected or refracted rays as normals, and consequently the proper caustic curve, being the envelope of the normals, is their evolute. It is usually the case that the secondary caustic is easier to determine than the caustic, and hence, when determined, it affords a ready means for deducing the primary caustic. It may be shown by geometrical considerations that the secondary caustic is a curve similar to the first positive pedal of the reflecting curve, of twice the linear dimensions, with respect to the luminous point. For a circle, when the rays emanate from any point, the secondary caustic is a limaçon, and hence the primary caustic is the evolute of this curve.

FIG. 6.

The simplest instance of a caustic by refraction (or diacaustic) is when luminous rays issuing from a point are refracted at a straight line. It may be shown geometrically that the secondary caustic, if the second medium be less refractive than the first, is an **Caustics by refraction.** ellipse having the luminous point for a focus, and its centre at the foot of the perpendicular from the luminous point to the refracting line. The evolute of this ellipse is the caustic required. If the second medium be more highly refractive than the first, the secondary caustic is a hyperbola having the same focus and centre as before, and the caustic is the evolute of this curve. When the refracting curve is a circle and the rays emanate from any point, the locus of the secondary caustic is a Cartesian oval, and the evolute of this curve is the required diacaustic. These curves appear to have been first discussed by Gergonne. For the caustic by refraction of parallel rays at a circle reference should be made to the memoirs by Arthur Cayley.

REFERENCES.—Arthur Cayley's "Memoirs on Caustics" in the *Phil. Trans.* for 1857, vol. 147, and 1867, vol. 157, are especially to be consulted. Reference may also be made to R.S. Heath's *Geometrical Optics* and R.A. Herman's *Geometrical Optics*(1900).

1Élie Bocthor (1784-1821) was a French orientalist of Coptic origin. He was the author of a *Traité des conjugaisons* written in Arabic, and left his Dictionary in MS.

CAUTERETS, a watering-place of south-western France in the department of Hautes-Pyrénées, 20 m. S. by W. of Lourdes by rail. Pop. (1906) 1030. It lies in the beautiful valley of the Gave de Cauterets, and is well known for its copious thermal springs. They are chiefly characterized by the presence of sulphur and silicate of soda, and are used in the treatment of diseases of the respiratory organs, rheumatism, skin diseases and many other maladies. Their temperature varies between 75° and 137° F. The springs number twenty-four, and there are nine bathing establishments. Cauterets is a centre for excursions, the Monné (8935 ft.), the Cabaliros (7655 ft.), the Pic de Chabarrou (9550 ft.), the Vignemale (10,820 ft.), and other summits being in its neighbourhood.

CAUTIN, a province of southern Chile, bounded N. by Arauco, Malleco and Bio-Bio, E. by Argentina, S. by Valdivia, and W. by the Pacific. Its area is officially estimated at 5832 sq. m. Cautin lies within the temperate agricultural and forest region of the south, and produces wheat, cattle, lumber, tan-bark and fruit. The state central railway from Santiago to Puerto Montt crosses the province from north to south, and the Cautin, or Imperial, and Tolten rivers (the latter forming its southern boundary) cross from east to west, both affording excellent transportation facilities. The province once formed part of the territory occupied by the Araucanian Indians, and its present political existence dates from 1887. Its population (1905) was 96,139, of whom a large percentage were European immigrants, principally Germans. The capital is Temuco, on the Rio Cautin; pop. (1895) 7078. The principal towns besides Temuco are Lautaro (3139) and Nueva Imperial (2179), both of historic interest because they were fortified Spanish outposts in the long struggle with the Araucanians.

CAUTLEY, SIR PROBY THOMAS (1802-1871), English engineer and palaeontologist, was born in Suffolk in 1802. After some years' service in the Bengal artillery, which he joined in 1819, he was engaged on the reconstruction of the Doab canal, of which, after it was opened, he had charge for twelve years (1831-1843). In 1840 he reported on the proposed Ganges canal, for the irrigation of the country between the rivers Ganges, Hindan and Jumna, which was his most important work. This project was sanctioned in 1841, but the work was not begun till 1843, and even then Cautley found himself hampered in its execution by the opposition of Lord Ellenborough. From 1845 to 1848 he was absent in England owing to ill-health, and on his return to India he was appointed director of canals in the North-Western Provinces. After the Ganges canal was opened in 1854 he went back to England, where he was made K.C.B., and from 1858 to 1868 he occupied a seat on the council of India. He died at Sydenham, near London, on the 25th of January 1871. In 1860 he published a full account of the making of the Ganges canal, and he also contributed numerous memoirs, some written in collaboration with Dr Hugh Falconer, to the *Proceedings* of the Bengal Asiatic Society and the Geological Society of London on the geology and fossil remains of the Sivalik Hills.

CAUVERY, or KAVERI, a river of southern India. Rising in Coorg, high up amid the Western Ghats, in 12° 25′ N. lat. and 75° 34′ E. long., it flows with a general south-eastern direction across the plateau of Mysore, and finally pours itself into the Bay of Bengal through two principal mouths in Tanjore district. Its total length is 472 m., the estimated area of its basin 27,700 sq.m. The course of the river in Coorg is very tortuous. Its bed is generally rocky; its banks are high and covered with luxuriant vegetation. On entering Mysore it passes through a narrow gorge, but presently widens to an average breadth of 300 to 400 yds. Its bed continues rocky, so as to forbid all navigation; but its banks are here bordered with a rich strip of cultivation. In its course through Mysore the channel is interrupted by twelve anicuts or dams for the purpose of irrigation. From the most important of these, known as the Madadkatte, an artificial channel is led to a distance of 72 m., irrigating an area of 10,000 acres, and ultimately bringing a water-supply into the town of Mysore. In Mysore state the Cauvery forms the two islands of Seringapatam and Sivasamudram, which vie in sanctity with the island of Seringam lower down in Trichinopoly district. Around the island of Sivasamudram are the celebrated falls of the Cauvery, unrivalled for romantic beauty. The river here branches into two channels, each of which makes a descent of about 200 m. 560in a succession of rapids and broken cascades. After entering the Madras presidency, the Cauvery forms the boundary between the Coimbatore and Salem districts, until it strikes into Trichinopoly district. Sweeping past the historic rock of Trichinopoly, it breaks at the island of Seringam into two channels, which enclose between them the delta of Tanjore, the garden of southern India. The northern channel is called the Coleroon (Kolidam); the other preserves the name of Cauvery. On the seaward face of its delta are the open roadsteads of Negapatam and French Karikal. The only navigation on any portion of its course is carried on in boats of basket-work. It is in the delta that the real value of the river for irrigation becomes conspicuous. This is the largest delta system, and the most profitable of all the works in India. The most ancient irrigation work is a massive dam of unhewn stone, 1080 ft. long, and from 40 to 60 ft. broad, across the stream of the Cauvery proper, which is supposed to date back to the 4th century, is still in excellent repair, and has supplied a model to British engineers. The area of the ancient system was 669,000 acres, the modern about 1,000,000 acres. The chief modern work is the anicut across the Coleroon, 2250 ft. long, constructed by Sir Arthur Cotton between 1836 and 1838. The Cauvery Falls have been utilized for an electric installation, which supplies power to the Kolar gold-mines and light to the city of Mysore.

The Cauvery is known to devout Hindus as Dakshini Ganga, or the Ganges of the south, and the whole of its course is holy ground. According to the legend there was once born upon earth a girl named Vishnumaya or Lopamudra, the daughter of Brahma; but her divine father permitted her to be regarded as the child of a mortal, called Kavera-muni. In order to obtain beatitude for her adoptive father, she resolved to become a river whose waters should purify from all sin. Hence it is that even the holy Ganges resorts underground once in the year to the source of the Cauvery, to purge herself from the pollution contracted from the crowd of sinners who have bathed in her waters.

CAVA DEI TIRRENI, a town and episcopal see of Campania, Italy, in the province of Salerno, 6 m. N.W. by rail from the town of Salerno. Pop. (1901) town, 7611; commune, 23,415. It lies fairly high in a richly cultivated valley, surrounded by wooded hills, and is a favourite resort of foreigners in spring and autumn, and of the Neapolitans in summer. A mile to the south-west is the village of Corpo di Cava (1970 ft.), with the Benedictine abbey of La Trinità della Cava, founded in 1025 by St Alferius. The church and the greater part of the buildings were entirely modernized in 1796. The old Gothic cloisters are preserved. The church contains a fine organ and several ancient sarcophagi. The archives, now national property, include documents and MSS. of great value (*e.g.* the *Codex Legum Longobardorum* of 1004) and fine *incunabula*. The abbot is keeper, and also head of a boarding school.

See M. Morcaldi, *Codex Diplomaticus Cavensis* (Naples and Milan, 1873-1893).

CAVAEDIUM, in architecture, the Latin name for the central hall or court within a Roman house, of which five species are described by Vitruvius. (1) The *Tuscanicum* responds to the greater number apparently of those at Pompeii, in which the timbers of the roof are framed together, so as to leave an open space in the centre, known as the compluvium; it was through this opening that all the light was received, not only in the hall itself, but in the rooms round. The rain from the roof was collected in gutters round the compluvium, and discharged from thence into a tank or open basin in the floor called the impluvium. (2) In the *tetrastylon* additional support was required in consequence of the dimensions of the hall; this was given by columns placed at the four angles of the impluvium. (3) *Corinthian* is the term given to the species where additional columns were required. (4) In the *displuviatum* the roofs, instead of sloping down towards the compluvium, sloped outwards, the gutters being on the outer walls; there was still an opening in the roof, and an impluvium to catch the rain falling through. This species of roof, Vitruvius states, is constantly in want of repair, as the water does not easily run away, owing to the stoppage in the rain-water pipes. (5) The *testudinatum* was employed when the hall was small and another floor was built over it; no example of this type has been found at Pompeii, and only one of the cavaedium displuviatum.

CAVAGNARI, SIR PIERRE LOUIS NAPOLEON (1841-1879), British military administrator, the son of a French general by his marriage with an Irish lady, was born at Stenay, in the department of the Meuse, on the 4th of July 1841. He nevertheless obtained naturalization as an Englishman, and entered the military service of the East India Company. After passing through the college at Addiscombe, he served through the Oudh campaign against the mutineers in 1858 and 1859. In 1861 he was appointed an assistant commissioner in the Punjab, and in 1877 became deputy commissioner of Peshawar and took part in several expeditions against the hill tribes. In 1878 he was attached to the staff of the British mission to Kabul, which the Afghans refused to allow to proceed. In May 1879, after the death of the amir Shere Ali, Cavagnari negotiated and signed the treaty of Gandamak with his successor, Yakub Khan. By this the Afghans agreed to admit a British resident at Kabul, and the post was conferred on Cavagnari, who also received the Star of India and was made a K.C.B. He took up his residence in July, and for a time all seemed to go well, but on the 3rd of September Cavagnari and the other European members of the mission were massacred in a sudden rising of mutinous Afghan troops. (See AFGHANISTAN.)

CAVAIGNAC, JEAN BAPTISTE (1762-1829), French politician, was born at Gourdon (Lot). He was sent by his department as deputy to the Convention, where he associated himself with the party of the Mountain and voted for the death of Louis XVI. He was constantly employed on missions in the provinces, and distinguished himself by his rigorous repression of opponents of the revolution in the departments of Landes, Basses-Pyrénées and Gers. With his colleague Jacques Pinet (1754-1844) he established at Bayonne a revolutionary tribunal with authority in the neighbouring towns. Charges of cruelty were preferred against him by a local society before the Convention in 1795, but were dismissed. He had represented the Convention in the armies of Brest and of the Eastern Pyrenees in 1793, and in 1795 he was sent to the armies of the Moselle and the Rhine. He filled various minor administrative offices, and in 1806 became an official at Naples in Murat's government. During the Hundred Days he was prefect of the Somme. At the restoration he was proscribed as a regicide, and spent the last years of his life at Brussels, where he died on the 24th of March 1829. His second son was General Eugène Cavaignac (*q.v.*).

The eldest son, ELÉONORE LOUIS GODEFROI CAVAIGNAC (1801-1845), was, like his father, a republican of the *intransigeant* type. He was bitterly disappointed at the triumph of the monarchical principle after the revolution of July 1830, in which he had taken part. He took part in the Parisian risings of October 1830, 1832 and 1834. On the third occasion he was imprisoned, but escaped to England in 1835. When he returned to France in 1841 he worked on the staff of *La Réforme*, and carried on an energetic republican propaganda. In 1843 he became president of the Society of the Rights of Man, of which he had been one of the founders in 1832. He died on the 5th of May 1845. The recumbent statue (1847) of Godefroi Cavaignac on his tomb at Montmartre (Paris) is one of the masterpieces of the sculptor Francois Rude.

Jean Baptiste's brother, JACQUES-MARIE, VICOMTE CAVAIGNAC (1773-1855), French general, served with distinction in the army under the republic and successive governments. He commanded the cavalry of the XI. corps in the retreat from Moscow, and eventually became Vicomte Cavaignac and inspector-general of cavalry.

CAVAIGNAC, LOUIS EUGÈNE (1802-1857), French general, son of J.B. Cavaignac, was born at Paris on the 15th of October 1802. After going through the usual course of study for the military profession, he entered the army as an engineer officer in 1824, and served in the Morea in 1828, becoming captain in the following year. When the revolution of 1830 broke out 561he was stationed at Arras, and was the first officer of his regiment to declare for the new order of things. In 1831 he was removed from active duty in consequence of his declared republicanism, but in 1832 he was recalled to the service and sent to Algeria. This continued to be the main sphere of his activity for sixteen years, and he won especial distinction in his fifteen months' command of the exposed garrison of Tlemçen, a command for which he was selected by Marshal Clausel (1836-1837), and in the defence of Cherchel (1840). Almost every step of his promotion was gained on the field of battle, and in 1844 the duc d'Aumale himself asked for Cavaignac's promotion to the rank of *maréchal de camp*. This was made in the same year, and he held various district commands in Algeria up to 1848, when the provisional government appointed him governor-general of the province with the rank of general of division. The post of minister of war was also offered to Cavaignac, but he refused it owing to the unwillingness of the government to quarter troops in Paris, a measure which the general held to be necessary for the stability of the new régime. On his election to the National Assembly, however, Cavaignac returned to Paris. When he arrived on the 17th of May he found the capital in an extremely critical state. Several *émeutes* had already taken place, and by the 22nd of June 1848 a formidable insurrection had been organized. The only course now open to the National Assembly was to assert its authority by force. Cavaignac, first as minister of war and then as dictator, was called to the task of suppressing the revolt. It was no light task, as the national guard was untrustworthy, regular troops were not at hand in sufficient numbers, and the insurgents had abundant time to prepare themselves. Variously estimated at from 30,000 to 60,000 men, well armed and organized, they had entrenched themselves at every step behind formidable barricades, and were ready to avail themselves of every advantage that ferocity and despair could suggest to them. Cavaignac failed perhaps to appreciate the political exigencies of the moment; as a soldier he would not strike his blow until his plans were matured and his forces sufficiently prepared. When the troops at last advanced in three strong columns, every inch of ground was disputed, and the government troops were frequently repulsed, till, fresh regiments arriving, he forced his way to the Place de la Bastille and crushed the insurrection in its headquarters. The contest, which raged from the 23rd to the morning of the 26th of June, was without doubt the bloodiest and most resolute the streets of Paris have ever seen, and the general did not hesitate to inflict the severest punishment on the rebels.

Cavaignac was censured by some for having, by his delay, allowed the insurrection to gather head; but in the chamber he was declared by a unanimous vote to have deserved well of his country. After laying down his dictatorial powers, he continued to preside over the Executive Committee till the election of a regular president of the republic. It was expected that the suffrages of France would raise Cavaignac to that position. But the mass of the people, and especially the rural population, sick of revolution, and weary even of the moderate republicanism of Cavaignac, were anxious for a stable government. Against the five and a half million votes recorded for Louis Napoleon, Cavaignac received only a million and a half. Not without chagrin at his defeat, he withdrew into the ranks of the opposition. He continued to serve as a representative during the short remainder of the republic. At the *coup d'état* of the 2nd December 1851 he was arrested along with the other members of the opposition; but after a short imprisonment at Ham he was released, and, with his newly-married wife, lived in retirement till his death, which took place at Ourne (Sarthe) on the 28th of October 1857.

His son, JACQUES MARIE EUGÈNE GODEFROI CAVAIGNAC (1853-1905), French politician, was born in Paris on the 21st of May 1853. He made public profession of his republican principles as a schoolboy at the Lycée Charlemagne by refusing in 1867 to receive a prize at the Sorbonne from the hand of the prince imperial. He received the military medal for service in the Franco-Prussian War, and in 1872 entered the École Polytechnique. He served as a civil engineer in Angoulême until 1881, when he became master of requests in the council of state. In the next year he was elected deputy for the arrondissement of Saint-Calais (Sarthe) in the republican interest. In 1885-1886 he was under-secretary for war in the Henri Brisson ministry, and he served in the cabinet of Émile Loubet (1892) as minister of marine and of the colonies. He had exchanged his moderate republicanism for radical views before he became war minister in the cabinet of Léon Bourgeois (1895-1896). He was again minister of war in the Brisson sabinet in July 1898, when he read in the chamber a document which definitely incriminated Captain Alfred Dreyfus. On the 30th of August, however, he stated that this had been discovered to be a forgery by Colonel Henry, but he refused to concur with his colleagues in a revision of the Dreyfus prosecution, which was the logical outcome of his own exposure of the forgery. Resigning his portfolio, he continued to declare his conviction of Dreyfus's guilt, and joined the Nationalist group in the chamber, of which he became one of the leaders. He also was an energetic supporter of the Ligue de la Patrie

Française. In 1899 Cavaignac was an unsuccessful candidate for the presidency of the republic. He had announced his intention of retiring from political life when he died at his country-seat near Flée (Sarthe) on the 25th of September 1905. He wrote an important book on the *Formation de la Prusse contemporaine* (2 vols., 1891-1898), dealing with the events of 1806-1813.

CAVAILLON, a town of south-eastern France in the department of Vaucluse, 20 m. S.E. of Avignon by rail. Pop. (1906) town, 5760; commune, 9952. Cavaillon lies at the southern base of Mont St Jacques on the right bank of the Durance above its confluence with the Coulon. It has a hôtel de ville of the 18th century, a church of the 12th century, dedicated to St Véran, and the mutilated remains of a triumphal arch of the Roman period. The town is an important railway junction and the commercial centre of a rich and well-irrigated plain, which produces melons and other fruits, early vegetables (artichokes, tomatoes, celery, potatoes), and other products in profusion. Silk-worms are reared, and silk is an important article of trade. The preparation of preserved vegetables, fruits and other provisions, distilling, and the manufacture of straw hats and leather are carried on. Numerous minor relics of the Roman period have been found to the south of the present town, on the site of the ancient *Cabellio*, a place of some note in the territory of the Cavares. In medieval and modern history the town has for the most part followed the fortunes of the Comtat Venaissin, in which it was included. Till the time of the Revolution it was the see of a bishop, and had a large number of monastic establishments.

CAVALCANTI, GUIDO (c. 1250-1300), Italian poet and philosopher, was the son of a philosopher whom Dante, in the *Inferno*, condemns to torment among the Epicureans and Atheists; but he himself was a friend of the great poet. By marriage with Beatrice, daughter of Farinata Uberti, he became head of the Ghibellines; and when the people, weary of continual brawls, aroused themselves, and sought peace by banishing the leaders of the rival parties, he was sent to Sarzana, where he caught a fever, of which he died. Cavalcanti has left a number of love sonnets and canzoni, which were honoured by the praise of Dante. Some are simple and graceful, but many are spoiled by a mixture of metaphysics borrowed from Plato, Aristotle and the Christian Fathers. They are mostly in honour of a French lady, whom he calls Mandetta. His *Canzone d'Amore* was extremely popular, and was frequently published; and his complete poetical works are contained in Giunti's collection (Florence, 1527; Venice, 1531-1532). He also wrote in prose on philosophy and oratory.

See D.G. Rossetti, *Dante and his Circle* (1874).

CAVALIER, JEAN (1681-1740), the famous chief of the Camisards (*q.v.*), was born at Mas Roux, a small hamlet in the commune of Ribaute near Anduze (Gard), on the 28th of November 1681. His father, an illiterate peasant, had been compelled by persecution to become a Roman Catholic along 562with his family, but his mother brought him up secretly in the Protestant faith. In his boyhood he became a shepherd, and about his twentieth year he was apprenticed to a baker. Threatened with prosecution for his religious opinions he went to Geneva, where he passed the year 1701; he returned to the Cévennes on the eve of the rebellion of the Camisards, who by the murder of the Abbé du Chayla at Pont-de-Monvert on the night of the 24th of July 1702 raised the standard of revolt. Some months later he became their leader. He showed himself possessed of an extraordinary genius for war, and Marshal Villars paid him the high compliment of saying that he was as courageous in attack as he was prudent in retreat, and that by his extraordinary knowledge of the country he displayed in the management of his troops a skill as great as that of the ablest officers. Within a period of two years he was to hold in check Count Victor Maurice de Broglie and Marshal Montrevel, generals of Louis XIV., and to carry on one of the most terrible partisan wars in French history.

He organized the Camisard forces and maintained the most severe discipline. As an orator he derived his inspiration from the prophets of Israel, and raised the enthusiasm of his rude mountaineers to a pitch so high that they were ready to die with their young leader for the sake of liberty of conscience. Each battle increased the terror of his name. On

Christmas day 1702 he dared to hold a religious assembly at the very gates of Alais, and put to flight the local militia which came forth to attack him. At Vagnas, on the 10th of February 1703, he routed the royal troops, but, defeated in his turn, he was compelled to find safety in flight. But he reappeared, was again defeated at Tour de Bellot (April 30), and again recovered himself, recruits flocking to him to fill up the places of the slain. By a long series of successes he raised his reputation to the highest pitch, and gained the full confidence of the people. It was in vain that more rigorous measures were adopted against the Camisards. Cavalier boldly carried the war into the plain, made terrible reprisals, and threatened even Nîmes itself. On the 16th of April 1704 he encountered Marshal Montrevel himself at the bridge of Nages, with 1000 men against 5000, and, though defeated after a desperate conflict, he made a successful retreat with two-thirds of his men. It was at this moment that Marshal Villars, wishing to put an end to the terrible struggle, opened negotiations, and Cavalier was induced to attend a conference at Pont d'Avène near Alais on the 11th of May 1704, and on the 16th of May he made submission at Nîmes. These negotiations, with the proudest monarch in Europe, he carried on, not as a rebel, but as the leader of an army which had waged an honourable war. Louis XIV. gave him a commission as colonel, which Villars presented to him personally, and a pension of 1200 livres. At the same time he authorized the formation of a Camisard regiment for service in Spain under his command.

Before leaving the Cévennes for the last time he went to Alais and to Ribaute, followed by an immense concourse of people. But Cavalier had not been able to obtain liberty of conscience, and his Camisards almost to a man broke forth in wrath against him, reproaching him for what they described as his treacherous desertion. On the 21st of June 1704, with a hundred Camisards who were still faithful to him, he departed from Nîmes and came to Neu-Brisach (Alsace), where he was to be quartered. From Dijon he went on to Paris, where Louis XIV. gave him audience and heard his explanation of the revolt of the Cévennes. Returning to Dijon, fearing to be imprisoned in the fortress of Neu-Brisach, he escaped with his troop near Montbéliard and took refuge at Lausanne. But he was too much of a soldier to abandon the career of arms. He offered his services to the duke of Savoy, and with his Camisards made war in the Val d'Aosta. After the peace he crossed to England, where he formed a regiment of refugees which took part in the Spanish expedition under the earl of Peterborough and Sir Cloudesley Shovel in May 1705. At the battle of Almansa the Camisards found themselves opposed to a French regiment, and without firing the two bodies rushed one upon the other. Cavalier wrote later (July 10, 1707): "The only consolation that remains to me is that the regiment I had the honour to command never looked back, but sold its life dearly on the field of battle. I fought as long as a man stood beside me and until numbers overpowered me, losing also an immense quantity of blood from a dozen wounds which I received." Marshal Berwick never spoke of this tragic event without visible emotion.

On his return to England a small pension was given him and he settled at Dublin, where he published *Memoirs of the Wars of the Cévennes under Col. Cavalier*, written in French and translated into English with a dedication to Lord Carteret (1726). Though Cavalier received, no doubt, assistance in the publication of the Memoirs, it is none the less true that he provided the materials, and that his work is the most valuable source for the history of his life. He was made a general on the 27th of October 1735, and on the 25th of May 1738 was appointed lieutenant-governor of Jersey. Writing in the following year (August 26, 1739) he says: "I am overworked and weary; I am going to take the waters in England so as to be in a fit condition for the war against the Spaniards if they reject counsels of prudence." He was promoted to the rank of major-general on the 2nd of July 1739, and died in the following year. In the parochial register of St Luke's, Chelsea, there is an entry: "Burial A.D. 1740, May 18, Brigadier John Cavalier."

There is a story which represents him as the fortunate rival of Voltaire for the hand of Olympe, daughter of Madame Dunoyer, author of the *Lettres galantes*. During his stay in England he married the daughter of Captain de Ponthieu and Marguerite de la Rochefoucauld, refugees living at Portarlington. Malesherbes, the courageous defender of Louis XVI., bears the following eloquent testimony to this young hero of the Cévennes:—"I confess," he says, "that this warrior, who, without ever having served, found himself by the mere gift of nature a great general,—this Camisard who was bold to punish a crime in the presence of a fierce troop which maintained itself by little crimes—this coarse peasant who, when admitted at twenty years of age into the society of cultivated people, caught their manners and won their love and esteem, this man who, though accustomed to a stormy life, and having just cause to be proud of his success, had yet enough philosophy in him by nature to enjoy for thirty-five years a tranquil private life—appears to me to be one of the rarest characters to be found in history."

For a more detailed account see F. Puaux, *Vie de Jean Cavalier* (1868); David C.A. Agnew, *Protestant Exiles from France*, ii. 54-66 (Lond., 1871); Charvey, *Jean Cavalier: nouveaux documents inédits* (1884). Eugène Sue popularized the name of the Camisard chief in *Jean Cavalier ou les fanatiques des Cévennes* (1840).

(F. Px.)

CAVALIER, a horseman, particularly a horse-soldier or one of gentle birth trained in knightly exercises. The word is taken from one of the French words which derived ultimately from the Late Lat. *caba'larius*, a horseman, from Lat. *caballus*, properly a pack-horse, which gave the Fr. *cheval.* a *chevalier*. This last word is the regular French for "knight," and is chiefly used in English for a member of certain foreign military or other orders, particularly of the Legion of Honour. Cavalier in English was early applied in a contemptuous sense to an overbearing swashbuckler—a roisterer or swaggering gallant. In Shakespeare (2 *Henry IV*. v. iii. 62) Shallow calls Bardolph's companions "cavaleros." "Cavalier" is chiefly associated with the Royalists, the supporters of Charles I. in the struggle with the Parliament in the Great Rebellion. Here again it first appears as a term of reproach and contempt, applied by the opponents of the king. Charles in the *Answer to the Petition* (June 13, 1642) speaks of cavaliers as a "word by what mistake soever it seemes much in disfavour." Further quotations of the use of the word by the Parliamentary party are given in the *New English Dictionary*. It was soon adopted (as a title of honour) by the king's party, who in return applied Roundhead to their opponents, and at the Restoration the court party preserved the name, which survived till the rise of the term Tory (see WHIG AND TORY). The term "cavalier" has been adopted from the French as a term in fortification for a work of great command constructed in the 563interior of a fort, bastion or other defence, so as to fire over the main parapet without interfering with the fire of the latter. A greater volume of fire can thus be obtained, but the great height of the cavalier makes it an easy target for a besieger's guns.

CAVALIERE, EMILIO DEL, 16th-century Italian musical composer, was born in Rome about 1550 of a noble family. He held a post at the court of Ferdinand I. of Tuscany from 1588 to 1597, and during his residence at Florence was on terms of intimacy with J. Peri, O. Rinuccini, G. Caccini and the rest of the Bardi circle. In 1597 he returned to Rome, and became connected with the Congregation of the Oratory founded by St Philip Neri. Here in 1600 was performed Cavaliere's contribution to the musical reformation initiated by his circle of friends in Florence—*La Rappresentazione di Anima e di Corpo*, a sacred drama, which is regarded as the first example of what is now called oratorio. It is generally supposed that he was no longer living when the work was performed, but some authorities assign 1602 as the date of his death.

Cavaliere's style is more facile than that of Peri and Caccini, but he is inferior to them in depth of musical expression. He is, however, important as being the first to apply the new monodic style to sacred music, and as the founder of the Roman school of the 17th century which included Mazzocchi, Carissimi and Alessandro Scarlatti.

See also H. Goldschmidt, *Studien zur Geschichte der italienischen Oper im 17. Jahrhundert*, Band i.

CAVALLI, FRANCESCO (1599?-1676), Italian musical composer, was born at Crema in 1599 or 1600. His real name was Pier Francesco Caletti-Bruni, but he is better known by that of Cavalli, the name of his patron, a Venetian nobleman. He became a singer at St Mark's in Venice in 1617, second organist in 1639, first organist in 1665, and in 1668*maestro di cappella*. He is, however, chiefly important for his operas. He began to write for the stage in 1639 (*Le Nozze di Teti e di Peleo*), and soon established so great a reputation that he was summoned to Paris in 1660 to produce an opera (*Serse*) at the Louvre in honour of the marriage of Louis XIV. He visited Paris again in 1662, bringing out his *Ercole Amante*. His death occurred in Venice on the 14th of January 1676. Twenty-seven operas of Cavalli are still extant, most of them being preserved in the library of St Mark at Venice. Monteverde had found opera a musico-literary experiment, and left it a magnificent dramatic spectacle. Cavalli succeeded in making opera a popular entertainment. He reduced Monteverde's extravagant orchestra to more practical limits, introduced melodious arias into his music and popular types into his *libretti*. His operas have all the characteristic exaggerations and absurdities of the 17th century, but they have also a remarkably strong sense of dramatic effect as well as a great musical facility, and a grotesque humour which was characteristic of Italian grand opera down to the death of Alessandro Scarlatti.

CAVALLINI, PIETRO (c. 1259-1344), Italian painter, born in Rome, was an artist of the earliest epoch of the modern Roman school, and was taught painting and mosaic by Giotto while employed at Rome; it is believed that he assisted his master in the mosaic of the Navicella or ship of St Peter, in the porch of the church of that saint. He also studied under the Cosmati. Lanzi describes him as an adept in both arts, and mentions with approbation his grand fresco of a Crucifixion at Assisi, still in tolerable preservation; he was, moreover, versed in architecture and in sculpture. According to George Vertue, it is highly probable that Cavallini executed, in 1279, the mosaics and other ornaments of the tomb of Edward the Confessor in Westminster Abbey. He would thus be the "Petrus Civis Romanus" whose name is inscribed on the shrine; but a comparison of dates invalidates this surmise. He died in 1344, at the age of eighty-five, in the odour of sanctity, having in his later years been a man of eminent piety. He is said to have carved for the Basilica of San Paolo fuori le Mura, close to Rome, a crucifix which spoke in 1370 to a female saint. Some highly important works by Cavallini in the church of Santa Cecilia in Trastevere, Rome, have been recently discovered.

CAVALLO, TIBERIUS (1749-1809), Anglo-Italian electrician and natural philosopher, was born on the 30th of March 1749 at Naples, where his father was a physician. In 1771 he came to England with the intention of pursuing a mercantile career, but he soon turned his attention to scientific work. Although he made several ingenious improvements in scientific instruments, his mind was rather imitative and critical than creative. He published numerous works on different branches of physics, including *A Complete Treatise on Electricity* (1777),*Treatise on the Nature and Properties of Air and other permanently Elastic Fluids* (1781),*History and Practice of Aerostation* (1785), *Treatise on Magnetism* (1787), *Elements of Natural and Experimental Philosophy* (1803), *Theory and Practice of Medical Electricity*(1780), and *Medical Properties of Factitious Air* (1798). He died in London on the 21st of December 1809.

CAVALLOTTI, FELICE (1842-1898), Italian politician, poet and dramatic author, was born at Milan on the 6th of November 1842. In 1860 and 1866 he fought with the Garibaldian Corps, but first attained notoriety by his anti-monarchical lampoons in the*Gazzetta di Milano* and in the *Gazzettina Rosa* between 1866 and 1872. Elected to parliament as deputy for Corteolona in the latter year, he took the oath of allegiance after having publicly impugned its validity. Eloquence and turbulent, combativeness in and out of parliament secured for him the leadership of the extreme Left on the death of Bertani in 1886. During his twelve years' leadership his party increased in number from twenty to seventy, and at the time of his death his parliamentary influence was greater than ever before. Though ambitious and addicted to defamatory methods of personal attack which sometimes savoured of political blackmail, Cavallotti's eloquent advocacy of democratic reform, and apparent generosity of sentiment, secured for him a popularity surpassed by that of no contemporary save Crispi. Services rendered in the cholera epidemic of 1885, his numerous lawsuits and thirty-three duels, his bitter campaign against Crispi, and his championship of French interests, combined to enhance his notoriety and to increase his political influence. By skilful alliances with the marquis di Rudini he more than once obtained practical control of the Italian government, and exacted notable concessions to Radical demands. He was killed on the 6th of March 1898 in a duel with Count Macola, editor of the conservative *Gazetta di Venezia*, whom he had assailed with characteristic intemperance of language. By his death the house of Savoy lost a relentless foe, and the revolutionary elements in Italy a gifted, if not entirely trustworthy, leader.

(H. W. S.)

CAVALRY (Fr. *cavalerie*, Ger. *Kavallerie* or *Reiterei*, derived ultimately from late Lat.*caballus*, horse), a word which came into use in military literature about the middle of the 16th century as applied to mounted men of all kinds employed for combatant purposes, whether intended primarily for charging in masses, in small bodies, or for dismounted fighting. By degrees, as greater refinement of terminology has become desirable, the idea has been narrowed down until it includes only "horsemen trained to achieve the purpose of their commander by the combined action of man and horse," and this definition will be found to cover the whole field of cavalry activity, from the tasks entrusted to the cavalry "corps" of 10,000 sabres down to the missions devolving on isolated squadrons and even troops.

History—The evolution of the cavalry arm has never been uniform at any one time over the surface of the globe, but has always been locally modified by the conditions of each community and the stage of intellectual development *Early use of mounted warriors.* to which at any given moment each had attained. The first condition for the existence of the arm being the existence of the horse itself, its relative scarcity or the reverse and its adaptability to its environment in each particular district have always exercised a preponderating influence on the development of cavalry organization and tactics. The indigenous horses of Europe and Asia being very small, the first application of their capabilities for war purposes seems everywhere to have been as draught animals for chariots, the construction of which implies not only the 564existence of level surfaces, perhaps of actual roads, but a very considerable degree of mechanical skill in those who designed and employed them. The whole of the classical and Oriental mythologies, together with the earliest monuments of Egypt, Assyria and India, are convincing on this point. Nowhere can we find a trace either of description or delineation of animals physically capable of carrying on their backs the armed men of the period. All the earliest allusions to the use of the horse in war either point directly to the employment as a draught animal, or where not specific, as in the description of the war-horse in Job, they would apply equally well to one harnessed to a chariot as to one ridden under the saddle.

The first trace of change is to be found, according to Prof. Wm. Ridgeway (*Origin and Influence of the Thoroughbred Horse*, p. 243), in an Egyptian relief showing Nubians mounted on horses of an entirely different breed, taller and more powerful than any which had gone before them. These horses appear to have come from the vicinity of Dongola, and the strain still survives in the Sudan. The breed is traced into Arabia, where only second-rate horses had been reared hitherto. and thence to different parts of Europe, where eventually centres of cavalry activity developed. The first detailed evidence of the existence of organized bodies of mounted men is to be found in Xenophon, whose instructions for the breaking, training and command of a squadron remain almost as a model for modern practice. Their tactical employment, however, seems still to have been relatively insignificant, for the horses were still far too small and too few to deliver a charge with sufficient momentum to break the heavy armed and disciplined hoplites. The strain of ancient battle was of an entirely different order to that of modern fighting. In the absence of projectiles of sufficient range and power to sweep a whole area, the fighting was entirely between the front ranks of the opposing forces. When a front rank fighter fell, his place was immediately taken by his comrade in the rear, who took up the individual combat, excited by his comrade's fate but relatively fresh in mind and muscle. This process of feeding the fight from the rear could be protracted almost indefinitely. If then, as a consequence of a charge, a few mounted men did penetrate the ranks, they encountered such a crowd of well-protected and fresh swordsmen that they were soon pulled off their ponies and despatched. Now and again great leaders, Alexander, Hannibal and Scipio Africanus, for instance, succeeded in riding down their opponents, but in the main, and as against the Roman infantry in particular, mounted troops proved of very little service on the battlefield.

It was, however, otherwise in the sphere of strategy. There, information was of even greater importance, because harder to obtain, than it is nowadays, and the army which could push out its feelers to the greater distance, surround its enemy and intercept his communications, derived nearly the same advantages as it does at present. Hence both sides provided themselves with horsemen, and when these met, each in the performance of their several duties, charges of masses naturally ensued. This explains the value attaching in the old days to the possession of horse-flesh and the rapid spread of the relatively new Dongola or African strain over the then known world.

The primitive instinct of aboriginal man is to throw stones or other missiles for purposes of defence (apes will throw anything they can find, but they never use sticks); hence, as the Romans penetrated ever farther amongst the barbarian tribes, their horsemen in first line found ever-increasing need for protection against projectiles. But the greater the weight of armour carried, the greater the demands upon the endurance of the horse. Then, as the weight-carrying breed was expensive and, with the decay of the Roman Empire, corruption and peculation spread, a limit was soon placed on the multiplication of charging cavalry, and it became necessary to fall back on the indigenous pony, which could only carry a rider from place to place, not charge. Thus there was a gradual levelling down of the mounted arms, the heavy cavalry becoming too heavy to gallop and the light not good enough for united action. Against such opponents, the lighter and better mounted tribesmen of Asia found their task easy. They cut off the supplies of the marching infantry, filled up or destroyed the wells, &c., and thus demonstrated the strategic necessity of superior mobility.

With the decay of civilization discipline also disappeared, and, as discipline consists essentially in the spirit of self-sacrifice for the good of the community, its opposite, self-preservation, became the guiding principle. This in turn led to the increase of armour carried, and thence to the demand for heavier horses, and this demand working through several centuries led ultimately to the breeding of the great weight-carrying animals on whose existence that of medieval chivalry depended. These horses, however, being very costly and practically useless for general purposes, could only become the property of the wealthy, who were too independent to feel the need of combination, and preferred to live on the spoliation and taxation of the weak. This spoliation eventually impelled the weaker men to combine, and at first their combination took the form of the construction of fortified places, against which mounted men were powerless. On the other hand, expense put a limit to the area which fortifications could enclose, and this again limited the supplies for the garrison. Horsemen sweeping the country for miles around had no difficulty in feeding themselves, and the surrender of all beleaguered places through starvation was ultimately inevitable, unless food could be introduced from allied towns in the vicinity. It was of no use to introduce fighting men only into a place which primarily required food (cf. Lucknow, 1857) to protract its resistance. Hence some means had to be found to surround the supply-convoys with a physically impenetrable shield, and eighteen-foot pikes in the hands of powerful disciplined soldiers met the requirements. Against eight to ten ranks of such men the best cavalry in the world, relying only on their swords, were helpless, and for the time (towards the close of the 15th century) infantry remained masters of the field on the continent of Europe.

England meanwhile had developed on lines of her own. Thanks to her longbowmen and the military genius of her leaders, she might have retained indefinitely the command of the continent had it not been for the invention of gunpowder, which, though readily accepted by the English for sieges in France, proved the ultimate cause of their undoing. It was the French who developed the use of siege artillery most rapidly, and their cavalry were not slow to take the hint; unlike the longbow and the crossbow, the pistol could be used effectively from horseback, and presently the knights and their retainers, having the deepest purses, provided themselves with long pistols in addition to their lances and swords. These weapons sent a bullet through any armour which a foot-soldier could conveniently carry, or his commander afford, and if anything went wrong with their mechanism (which was complicated and uncertain) the speed of his horse soon carried the rider out of danger. A new form of attack against infantry, introduced by the French at Cerisoles, 1544, thus developed itself. A troop or squadron, formed in from twelve to sixteen ranks, trotted up to within pistol shot of the angle of the square to be attacked and halted; then each rank in succession cantered off man by man to the left, discharging his pistol at the square as he passed, and riding back to his place behind the column to reload. This could be prolonged indefinitely, and against such tactics the infantry were powerless. The stakes carried by English archers to check the direct charge of horsemen became useless, as did also *chevaux de frise*, though the latter (which originated in the 14th century) continued to be employed by the Austrians against the swiftly-charging Turks till the close of the 17th century. Thus it became necessary to devise some new impediment which, whilst remaining mobile, would also give cover and an advantage in the final hand-to-hand shock. The problem was solved in Bohemia, Poland and Moravia (Hussite wars, about 1420), where, distances being great and the country open, greater mobility and capacity in the convoys became essential. Great trains of wagons were placed in charge of an infantry escort, of which a part had become possessed of firearms, and these moved across country in as many as twelve parallel lines drilled to form *laagers*, as nowadays 565in South Africa. Again the cavalry proved helpless, and for nearly a century in central Europe the word "*Wagenburg*" (wagon-fortress) became synonymous with "army." Then an unfortunate inspiration came to the wagon-men. A large gun was relatively cheaper to manufacture, and more effective than a small one. To keep their assailants at a distance, they mounted wall-pieces of about one-inch bore on their wagons. For a moment the balance inclined in their favour, but the cavalry were quick to see their advantage in this new idea, and they immediately followed suit. They, too, mounted guns on wheels, and, as their mobility gave them choice of position, they were able to concentrate their fire against any side of the laager, and again ultimate surrender was the only way out of the defenders' dilemma.

The interesting problem thus raised was never finally solved, for the scene of action now shifted to western Europe, to the valley of the Po, and more particularly to the Netherlands, where fortresses were closer together and the clayey nature of the Rhine delta had already made paved roads necessary. Then, the *Wagenburg* being no longer needed for the short transits between one fortified town and another, the infantry reasserted themselves. Firearms having been much improved in the interval the spearmen (pikemen) had already (about 1515) learnt to protect themselves by musketeers trained to take advantage of cover and ground somewhat in the same fashion as the modern skirmisher. These musketeers kept light guns at a distance from their pikemen, but dared not venture far out, as their fire was altogether inadequate to stop a rush of horsemen; when the latter threatened to intervene, they had to run for safety to the squares of pikemen, whom they assisted in turn by keeping the cavalry beyond pistol range. Hence the horsemen had to fall back upon more powerful guns, and these, being slow and requiring more train, could be most economically protected by infantry (see also ARTILLERY).

Thus about the close of the 16th century western armies differentiated themselves out into the still existing three types—cavalry, artillery and infantry. Moreover, each type was subdivided, the cavalry becoming heavy, medium *17th-century progress.*and dragoons. At this period there was nothing to disturb the equilibrium of two contending forces except the characters of their respective leaders. The mercenary element had triumphed everywhere over the feudal levies. The moral qualities of all were on the same indifferent level, and battles in the open followed one recognized course. Neither army being able to outmarch the other, both drew up masses of pikes in parallel lines. The musketeers covered the deployment of the heavy guns on either side, the cavalry drew up on the wings and a strictly parallel fight ensued, for in the absence of a common cause for which men were willing to die, plunder was the ruling motive, and all control and discipline melted in the excitement of the contest.

It is to the growth of Protestantism that cavalry owes its next great forward leap. To sweep the battlefield, it was absolutely essential that men should be ready to subordinate selfish considerations to the triumph of their cause. The Roman Catholicism of the day gave many loopholes for the evasion of clear duty, but from these the reformed faith was free, and it is to the reawakened sense of duty that Gustavus Adolphus appealed. This alone rendered combination amongst his subordinate leaders possible, and on this power of combination all his victories depended. Other cavalry soldiers, once let loose in the charge, could never be trusted to return to the field, the prospective plunder of the enemy's baggage being too strong a temptation; but the king's men could be depended on, and once brought back in formed bodies, they rode over the enemy's skirmishers and captured his batteries. Then the equilibrium of force was destroyed, and all arms combined made short work of the opposing infantry alone (Breitenfeld, 1631). But the Swedish king perished with his work half done, and matters reverted to their former condition until the appearance of Cromwell, another great leader capable of animating his men with the spirit of devotion, again rendered the cavalry arm supreme. The essence of his success lay in this, that his men were ready everywhere and always to lay down their lives for their common cause. Whether scouting 70 m. to the front of their army, or fighting dismounted to delay the enemy at defiles or to storm fortified strongholds, or charging home on the battlefield, their will power, focused on, and in turn dependent on, the personality of their great leader, dominated all human instincts of fear, rapacity or selfishness. It is true that they had not to ride against the modern rifle, but it is equally true that there was no quick-firing artillery to carry terror through the enemy's army, and it was against masses of spearmen and musketeers, not then subjected to bursting shells or the lash of shrapnel and rifle bullets, that the final charges had always to be ridden home.

Each succeeding decade thereafter has seen a steady diminution in the ultimate power of resistance of the infantry, and a corresponding increase in the power of fire preparation at the disposal of the supreme leader; and the chances of cavalry have fluctuated with the genius of that leader in the employment of the means at his disposal, and the topographical conditions existing within each theatre of war. During the campaigns in Flanders, with its multiplicity of fortresses and clayey soil, cavalry rapidly degenerated into mounted infantry, throwing aside sword and lance-proof armour, and adopting long muskets and heavier ammunition. Presently they abandoned the charge at a gallop and reverted to an approach at the trot, and if (as at Blenheim) their influence proved decisive on the field of battle, this was because the conditions were common to both combatants, and the personal influence of "Corporal John," as his soldiers called Marlborough, ensured greater steadiness and better co-operation.

When Frederick II. became king of Prussia (1740), he found his cavalry almost at the nadir of efficiency; even his cuirassiers drilled principally on foot. "They can manoeuvre," on foot, "with the same precision as *Frederick II.; reform of the Prussian cavalry.* my grenadiers, but unfortunately they are equally slow." His enemies the Austrians, thanks to their wars against the Turks who always charged at a gallop, had maintained greater dash and mobility, and at Mollwitz the Prussians only escaped disaster by the astounding rapidity of their infantry fire. In disgust the king then wrote, "Die Cavallerie is nicht einmal werth dasz sie der Teufel weck holet," and he immediately set about their reform with his usual energy and thoroughness. Three years after Mollwitz, the result of his exertions was apparent in the greatly increased importance the arm acquired on the battlefield, and the charge of the Bayreuth dragoons at Hohenfriedberg (June 4, 1745), who with 1500 horses rode over and dispersed 20 Austrian battalions, bringing in 2500 prisoners and 67 colours, will always rank as one of the most brilliant feats in military history.1 The following years of peace (1745-1756) were devoted to the methodical preparation of the cavalry to meet the requirements that Frederick's methods of war would make upon them, and it is to this period that the student should devote special attention. From the very outbreak of the Seven Years' War (1756) this training asserted its influence, and Rossbach (1757) and Zorndorf (1758) are the principal examples of what cavalry handled in masses can effect. At Rossbach General v. Seydlitz, at the head of 38 squadrons, practically began and ended the destruction of the French army, and at Zorndorf he saved the day for the Prussians by a series of the most brilliant charges, which successively destroyed the Russian right wing and centre. These battles so conclusively demonstrated the superiority of the Prussian cavalry that their enemies completely altered their tactical procedure. They now utilized their enormous numerical superiority by working in two separate armies, each almost as strong as the whole Prussian force. When the latter moved against either, the one threatened immediately threw up heavy entrenchments, against which cavalry were, of course, ineffective, whilst the other pursued its march. When Frederick, having more or less beaten his immediate opponent, 566began to threaten the other army it entrenched likewise. Against these methods the Prussian army soon wore itself out, and though from time to time the cavalry locally distinguished itself, no further opportunities for great decisive blows presented themselves.

The increased demands made upon the mobility of the Prussian horsemen naturally resulted in the gradual rejection of everything which was not essential to their striking power. The long muskets and bayonets were laid aside, but the cuirass was retained for the mêlée, and by the close of the great struggle the various branches of the arm had differentiated themselves out into the types still adhered to, heavy cavalry, dragoons, hussars, whose equipment as regards essentials thenceforward hardly varied up to the latter years of the 19th century. The only striking difference lies in the entire rejection of the lance in the armament of the charging squadrons, and the reason is characteristic of the principles of the day. The Prussian cavalry had realized that success was decided, not primarily by actual collision, but by the moral effect of the appearance of an absolutely closed wall of horsemen approaching the adversary at full speed. If the necessary degree of cohesion was attained, the other side was morally beaten before collision took place, and either turned to flight, or met the shock with so little resolution that it was ridden over without difficulty. In the former case any weapon was good enough to kill a flying enemy; in the latter, in the mêlée which then ensued, the crush in the ranks of the victors was still so great that the lance was a hindrance rather than a help.

In the years succeeding the war the efficiency of the Prussian cavalry sank very rapidly, the initial cause being the death of Seydlitz at the early age of fifty-two. His personality had alone dominated the discontent, lethargy and hopelessness created by ruthless financial economies. When he was gone, as always in the absence of a great leader, men adapted their lives to the line of least resistance. In thirty years the wreck was complete, and within the splendid squadrons which had been accustomed to manoeuvre with perfect precision at the highest speed, there were (as F.A. von der Marwitz in his *Nachlass* clearly shows) not more than seven thoroughly trained men and horses to each, the remainder being trained for little longer and receiving less attention than is the case with modern 2nd line or auxiliary cavalry.

For the generation preceding the outbreak of the French Revolution, Frederick the Great's army, and especially his cavalry, had become the model for all Europe, but the mainspring of the excellence of his squadrons *Cavalry in the revolutionary wars.*was everywhere overlooked. Seydlitz had manoeuvred great masses of horsemen, therefore every one else must have great masses also; but no nation grasped the secret, viz. the unconditional obedience of the horse to its rider, on which his success had depended. Neither was it possible under the prevailing social conditions to secure the old stamp of horse, or the former attention to detail on the part of men and officers. In France, owing to the agricultural decay of the country, suitable remounts for charging cavalry were almost unobtainable, and as this particular branch of the army was almost exclusively commanded by the aristocracy it suffered most in the early days of the Revolution. The hussars, being chiefly recruited and officered by Alsatians and Germans from the Rhine provinces, retained their individuality and traditions much longer than the dragoons and cuirassiers, and, to the very close of the great wars, we find them always ready to charge at a gallop; but the unsteadiness and poor horsemanship of the other branches was so great that up to 1812, the year of their destruction, they always charged at a trot only, considering that the advantage of superior cohesion thus gained more than balanced the loss of momentum due to the slower pace.

Generally, the growth of the French cavalry service followed the universal law. The best big horses went to the heavy charging cavalry, viz. the cuirassiers, the best light horses to the hussars, and the dragoons received the remainder, for in principle they were only infantry placed on horseback for convenience of locomotion, and were not primarily intended for combined mounted action. Fortunately for them, their principal adversaries, the Austrians, had altogether failed to grasp the lesson of the Seven Years' War. Writing in 1780

Colonel Mack, a very capable officer, said, "Even in 1769, the cavalry could not ride, could not manage to control their horses. Not a single squadron could keep its dressing at a gallop, and before they had gone fifty yards at least ten out of forty horses in the first rank would break out to the front," and though the veteran field marshal Lacy issued new regulations, their spirit seems always to have escaped the executive officers. The British cavalry was almost worse off, for economy had reduced its squadrons to mere skeletons, and the traditional British style of horsemanship, radically different from that in vogue in France, made their training for combined action even more difficult than elsewhere. Hence the history of cavalry during the earlier campaigns of the Revolution is marked by no decisive triumphs, the results are always inadequate when judged by the magnitude of the forces employed, and only the brilliant exploit of the 15th Light Dragoons (now Hussars) at Villers en Couché (April 24, 1794) deserves to be cited as an instance of the extraordinary influence which even a few horsemen can exercise over a demoralized or untrained mob of infantry.

Up to the campaign of Poland (see NAPOLEONIC CAMPAIGNS) French victories were won chiefly by the brilliant infantry fighting, cavalry only intervening (as at Jena) to charge a beaten enemy and complete his destruction by pursuit. But after the terrible waste of life in the winter of 1806-7, and the appalling losses in battle, Napoleon introduced a new form of attack. The case-shot preparation of his artillery (see ARTILLERY) sowed confusion and terror in the enemy's ranks, and the opportunity was used by masses of cavalry. Henceforward this method dominated the Napoleonic tactics and strategy. The essential difference between this system and the Frederician lies in this, that with the artillery available in the former period it was not possible to say in advance at what point the intervention of cavalry would be necessary, hence the need for speed and precision of manoeuvre to ensure their arrival at the right time and place. Napoleon now selected beforehand the point he meant to overwhelm and could bring his cavalry masses within striking distance at leisure. Once placed, it was only necessary to induce them to run away in the required direction to overwhelm everything by sheer weight of men and horses. This method failed at Waterloo because the ground was too heavy, the slope of it against the charge, and the whole condition of the horses too low for the exertion demanded of them.

The British cavalry from 1793 to 1815 suffered from the same causes which at the beginning of the 20th century brought about its breakdown in the South African War. Oversea transport brought the horses to land in poor condition, and it was rarely possible to afford them sufficient time to recover and become accustomed to the change in forage, the conditions of the actual theatre of operations, &c., before they had to be led against the enemy—hence a heavy casualty roll and the introduction into the ranks of raw unbroken horses which interfered with the precision of manoeuvre of the remainder. Their losses (about 13% per annum) were small as compared with those of South Africa, but this is mainly accounted for by the fact that, operations being generally in the northern hemisphere, the change of climate was never so severe. Tactically, they suffered, like the Austrians and Prussians, from the absence of any conception of the Napoleonic strategy amongst their principal leaders. As it was not known where the great blow was to fall, they were distributed along the whole line, and thus became habituated to the idea of operating in relatively small bodies. This is the worst school for the cavalry soldier, because it is only when working in masses of forty to sixty squadrons that the cumulative consequences of small errors of detail become so apparent as to convince all ranks of the necessity of conforming accurately to established prescriptions. Nevertheless, they still retained the practice of charging at a gallop, and as a whole were by far the most efficient body of horsemen who survived at the close of the great wars.

In the reaction that then ensued all over Europe, cavalry 567practically ceased to exist. The financial and agricultural exhaustion of all countries, and of Prussia in particular, was so complete that money was nowhere to be found for the great**Later 19th century.** concentrations and manoeuvre practices which are more essential to the efficiency of the cavalry than to that of the other arms. Hence a whole generation of officers grew up in ignorance of the fundamental principles which govern the employment of their arm. It was not till 1848 that the Prussians began again to unite whole cavalry divisions for drill and manoeuvre, and the soldiers of the older generation had not yet passed away when the campaigns of 1866 and 1870 brought up again the realities of the battle-field. Meanwhile the introduction of long-range artillery and small arms had entirely destroyed the tactical relation of the three arms on which the Napoleonic tactics and strategy had been based, and the idea gained ground that the battle-field would no longer afford the same opportunities to cavalry as before. The experiences gained by the Americans in the Civil War helped to confirm this preconception. If in battles waged between infantries armed only with muzzle-loading rifles, cavalry could find no opportunity to repeat past exploits, it was argued that its chances could not fail to be still further reduced by the breech-loader. But this reasoning ignored the principal factors of former successes. The mounted men in America failed not as a consequence of the armament they encountered, but because the war brought out no Napoleon to create by his skill the opportunity for decisive cavalry action, and to mass his men beforehand in confident anticipation. The same reasoning applies to the European campaigns of 1866 and 1870, and the results obtained by the arm were so small, in proportion to the numbers of squadrons available and to their cost of maintenance as compared with the other arms, that a strong reaction set in everywhere against the existing institutions, and the re-creation of the dragoon, under the new name of mounted rifleman, was advocated in the hope of obtaining a cheap and efficient substitute for the cavalryman.

Later events in South Africa and in Manchuria again brought this question prominently to the front, but the essential difference between the old and new schools of thought has not been generally realized. The "mounted rifle" adherents base their arguments on the greatly increased efficiency of the rifle itself. The "cavalry" school, on the other hand, maintains that, the weapons themselves being everywhere substantially equal in efficiency, the advantage rests with the side which can create the most favourable conditions for their employment, and that, fundamentally, superior mobility will always confer upon its possessor the choice of the circumstances under which he will elect to engage. Where the two sides are nearly equally matched in mobility, neither side can afford the time to dismount, for the other will utilize that time to manoeuvre into a position which gives him a relative superiority for whichever form of attack he may elect to adopt, and this relative superiority will always more than suffice to eliminate any advantage in accuracy of fire that his opponent may have obtained by devoting his principal attention to training his men on the range instead of on the mounted manoeuvre ground.

Finally, the "cavalry" school reasons that in no single campaign since Napoleon's time have the conditions governing encounters been normal. Either the roadless and barren nature of the country has precluded of itself the rapid marching which forms the basis of all modern strategy, as in America, Turkey, South Africa and Manchuria, or the relative power of the infantry and artillery weapons, as in Bohemia (1866) and in France (1870), has rendered wholly impossible the creation of the great tactical opportunity characteristic of Napoleon's later method, for there then existed no means of overwhelming the enemy with a sufficient hail of projectiles to render the penetration of the cavalry feasible. The latest improvement in artillery, viz. the perfected shrapnel and the quick-firing guns, have, however, enormously facilitated the attainment of this primary fire superiority, and, moreover, it has simplified the procedure to such a degree that Napoleon is no longer needed to direct. The battles of the future will thus, in civilized countries, revert to the Napoleonic type, and the side which possesses the most highly trained and mobile force of cavalry will enjoy a greater relative superiority over its adversary than at any period since the days of Frederick.

The whole experience of the past thus goes to show that no nation in peace has ever yet succeeded in maintaining a highly trained cavalry sufficiently numerous to meet all the demands of a great war. Hence at the outbreak of hostilities there has always been a demand for some kind of supplementary force which can relieve the regular squadrons of those duties of observation and exploration which wear down the horses most rapidly and thus render the squadrons ineffective for their culminating duty on the battle-field. This demand has been met by the enrolment of men willing to fight and rendered mobile by mounts of an inferior description, and the greater the urgency the greater has been the tendency to give them arms which they can quickly learn to use. To make a man an expert swordsman or lancer has always taken years, but he can be taught to use a musket or rifle sufficiently for his immediate purpose in a very short time. Hence, to begin with, arms of this description have invariably been issued to him. But once these bodies have been formed, and they have come into collision with trained cavalry, the advantages of mobility, combined with the power of shock, have become so apparent to all, that insensibly the "dragoon" has developed into the cavalry soldier, the rate of this evolution being conditioned by the nature of the country in which the fighting took place.

This evolution is best seen in the American Civil War. The men of the mounted forces engaged had been trained to the use of the rifle from childhood, while the vast majority had never seen a sword, hence the formation of "mounted rifles"; and these "mounted rifles" developed precisely in accordance with the nature of their surroundings. In districts of virgin forests and marshland they remained "mounted rifles," in the open prairie country of the west they became cavalry pure and simple, though for want of time they never rivalled the precision of manoeuvre and endurance of modern Prussian or Austrian horse. In South Africa the same sequence was followed, and had the Boer War lasted longer it is certain that such Boer leaders as de Wet and de la Rey would have reverted to cavalry tactics of shock and cold steel at the earliest possible opportunity.

Therefore when we find, extending over a cycle of ages, the same causes producing the same effects, the natural conclusion is that the evolution of the cavalry arm is subject to a universal law which persists in spite of all changes of armament.

Employment of Cavalry.—It is a fundamental axiom of all military action that the officer commanding the cavalry of any force comprising the three arms of the service is in the strictest sense an executive officer under the officer commanding that particular force as a whole. The latter again is himself responsible to the political power he represents. When intricate political problems are at stake, it may be, and generally is, quite impracticable that any subordinate can share the secret knowledge of the power to which he owes his allegiance.

The essence of the value of the cavalry soldier's services lies in this, that the demand is never made upon him in its supremest form until the instinct of the real commander realizes that the time has come. Whether it be to cover a retreat, and by the loss of hundreds to save the lives of tens of thousands, or to complete a victory with commensurate results in the opposite direction, the obligation remains the same—to stake the last man and horse in the attainment of the immediate object in view, the defeat of the enemy. This at once places the leader of cavalry in face of his principal problem. It is a matter of experience that the broader the front on which he can deliver a charge, the greater the chances of success. However strong the bonds of discipline may be, the line is ultimately, and at a certain nervous tension, only a number of men on horses, acting and reacting on one another in various ways. When therefore, of two lines, moving to meet one another at speed, one sees itself overlapped to either hand, the men in the line thus overlapped invariably and inevitably tend to open outwards, so as at least to meet their enemy on an equal frontage. Hence 568 every cavalry commander tries to strike at the flank of his enemy, and the latter manoeuvres to meet him, and if both have equal mobility, local collision must ensue on an equal and parallel front. Therefore both strive to put every available man and horse in their first line, and if men and horses were invulnerable such a line would sweep over the ground like a scythe and nothing could withstand it. Since, however, bullets kill at a distance, and inequalities and unforeseen difficulties of the ground may throw hundreds of horses and riders, a working compromise has to be found to meet eventualities, and, other things being equal, victory inclines to the leader who best measures the risks and uncertainties of his undertaking, and keeps in hand a sufficient reserve to meet all chances.

Thus there has arisen a saying, which is sometimes regarded as axiomatic, that in cavalry encounters the last closed reserve always wins. The truth is really that he who has best judged the situation and the men on both sides finds himself in possession of the last reserve at the critical moment. The next point is, how to ensure the presence of this reserve, and what is the critical moment. The battle-field is the critical moment in each phase of every campaign—not the mere chance locality on which a combat takes place, but the decisive arena on which the strategic consequences of all pre-existing conditions of national cohesion, national organization and of civilization are focussed. It is indeed the judgment-seat of nature, on which the right of the race to survive in the struggle for existence is weighed and measured in the most impartial scales.

Before, however, the final decision of the battle-field can be attained, a whole series of subordinate decisions have to be fought out, success in each of which conditions the result of the next series of encounters. Every commanding officer of cavalry thus finds himself successively called on to win a victory locally at any cost, and the question of economy of force does not concern him at all. Hence the same fundamental rules apply to all cavalry combats, of whatever magnitude, and condition the whole of cavalry tactics. Broadly speaking, if two cavalries of approximately equal mobility manoeuvre against each other in open country, neither side can afford the loss of time that dismounting to fight on foot entails. Hence, assuming that at the outset of a campaign each side aims at securing a decisive success, both seek out an open plain and a mounted charge, sword in hand, for the decision. When the speed and skill of the combatants are approximately equal, collision ensues simultaneously along parallel fronts, and the threat of the overlapping line is the principal factor in the decision. The better the individual training of man and horse the less will be the chances of unsteadiness or local failures in execution, and the less the need of reserves; hence the force which feels itself the most perfect in the individual efficiency of both man and horse (on which therefore the whole ultimately depends) can afford to keep fewer men in reserve and can thus increase the width of its first line for the direct collision. Careful preparation in peace is therefore the first guarantee of success in action. This means that cavalry, unlike infantry, cannot be expanded by the absorption of reserve men and horses on the outbreak of hostilities, but must be maintained at war strength in peace, ready to take the field at a moment's notice, and this is actually the standard of readiness attained on the continent of Europe at the present day.

Further, uniformity of speed is the essential condition for the execution of closed charges, and this obviously cannot be assured if big men on little horses and small men on big horses are indiscriminately mixed up in the same units. Horses and men have therefore been sorted out everywhere into three categories, *light, medium* and *heavy,* and in periods when war was practically chronic, suitable duties have been allotted to each. It is clear, on purely mechanical grounds, that the greater the velocity of motion at the moment of collision the greater will be the chances of success, and this greater speed will be on the side of the bigger horses as a consequence of their longer stride. On the other hand, these horses, by reason of their greater weight, are used up much more rapidly than small ones. Hence, to ensure the greater speed at the moment of contact, it is necessary to save them as much as possible to keep them fresh for the shock only, and this has been the practice of all great cavalry leaders all over the world, and has only been departed from under special circumstances, as by the Germans in France in 1870, when their cavalry practically rode everywhere unopposed.

Collisions, however, must be expected by every body of troops large or small; hence each regiment—ultimately each squadron—endeavours to save its horses as far as this is compatible with the attainment of the special object in view, and this has led everywhere and always to a demand for some intermediate arm, less expensive to raise and maintain than cavalry proper, and able to cover the ground with sufficient rapidity and collect the information necessary to ensure the proper direction of the cavalry commands. Originally this intermediate force received the designation of dragoons; but since under pressure of circumstances during long periods of war these invariably improved themselves into cavalry and became permanent units in the army organization, fresh names have had to be invented for them, of which Mounted Infantry and Mounted Rifles are the latest, and every improvement in firearms has led to an increased demand for their services.

It is now relatively easy to trace out the considerations which should govern the employment of his cavalry by the officer commanding a force of the three arms. Assuming for purposes of illustration an army numerically weak in cavalry, what course will best ensure the presence of the greatest number of sabres at the decisive point, *i.e.* on the battle-field? To push out cavalry screens far to the front will be to court destruction, nor is the information they obtain of much real service unless the means to act upon it at once is at hand. This can only be supplied economically by the use of strong advanced guards of infantry, and such supplementary security and information as these may require will be best supplied by

155

mounted infantry, the sacrifice of whom will disturb least the fighting integrity of the whole army.

Imagine an army of 300,000 men advancing by five parallel roads on a front of 50 m., each column (60,000 men, 2 army corps) being covered by a strong advance guard, coming in contact with a similarly constituted army moving in an opposite direction. A series of engagements will ensue, in each of which the object of the local commander will be to paralyse his opponent's will-power by a most vigorous attack, so that his superior officer following him on the same road will be free to act as he chooses. The front of the two armies will now be defined by a line of combats localized each about a comparatively small area, and between them will be wide gaps which it will be the chief business of the directing minds on either side to close by other troops as soon as possible. Generally the call will be made upon the artillery for this purpose, since they can cover the required distances far more rapidly than infantry. Now, as artillery is powerless when limbered up and always very vulnerable on the flanks of the long lines, a strong cavalry escort will have to be assigned to them which, trotting forward to screen the march, will either come in contact with the enemy's cavalry advancing with a similar object, or themselves find an opportunity to catch the enemy's guns at a disadvantage. These are opportunities for the cavalry, and if necessary it must sacrifice itself to turn them to the best account. The whole course of the battle depends on success or failure in the early formation of great lines of guns, for ultimately the victor in the artillery duel finds himself in command of the necessary balance of guns which are needed to prepare the way for his final decisive infantry attack. If this latter succeeds, then any mounted men who can gallop and shoot will suffice for pursuit. If it fails, no cavalry, however gallant, has any hope of definitely restoring the combat, for against victorious infantry, cavalry, now as in the past, can but gain a little time. This time may indeed be worth the price at which it can be bought, but it will always be more economical to concentrate all efforts to prevent the emergency arising.

After the Franco-German War much was written about the possibility of vast cavalry encounters to be fought far in advance of the main armies, for the purpose of obtaining information, and ideas were freely mooted of wide-flung raids traversing 569the enemy's communications, breaking up his depots, reserve formations, &c. But riper consideration has relegated these suggestions to the background, for it is now evident that such expeditions involve the dissemination of force, not its concentration. Austria and France for example would scarcely throw their numerically inferior cavalry against the Germans, and nothing would suit them better than that the latter should hurl their squadrons against the frontier guards, advanced posts, and, generally, against unbeaten infantry; nor indeed would the Germans stultify their whole strategic teaching by weakening themselves for the decisive struggle. It follows therefore that cavalry reconnaissance duties will be strictly local and tactical, and that arrangements will be made for procuring strategical information by wireless telegraphy, balloons, motor cars, bicycles, &c., and that on the whole that nation will be best served in war which has provided in peace a nucleus of mounted infantry capable of rapid expansion to fill the gap which history shows always to have existed between the infantry and the cavalry. Such troops need not be organized in large bodies, for their mission is to act by "slimness," not by violence. They must be the old "verlorene Haufe" (*anglice*, "forlorn hope") of former days, men whose individual bravery and decision is of the highest order. But they can never become a "decision-compelling arm," though by their devotion they may well hope to obtain the grand opportunity for their cavalry, and share with them in harvesting the fruits of victory.

The great cavalry encounters of forty to sixty squadrons on either side, which it has been shown must arise from the necessity of screening or preventing the formation of the all-important artillery lines, will take their form mainly from the topographical conditions of the district, and since on a front of 60 to 100 m. these may vary indefinitely, cavalry must be trained, as indeed it always has been, to fight either on foot or on horseback as occasion requires. In either case, thoroughness of preparation in horsemanship (which, be it observed, includes horsemastership) is the first essential, for in the end victory will rest with the side which can put in the right place with the greatest rapidity the greatest number of sabres or rifles. In the case of rifles there is a greater margin of time available and an initial failure is not irremediable, but the underlying principle is the same in either case; and since it is impossible to foretell exactly the conditions of the collision, all alike, according to the class to which they belong, must be brought up to the highest standard, for this alone guarantees the smooth and rhythmical motion required for covering long distances with the least expenditure of physical and nervous strength on the part both of horse and rider. As a consequence of successes gained in these preliminary encounters, opportunities will subsequently arise for the balance of fresh or rallied squadrons in hand to ride home upon masses of infantry disorganized and demoralized by the combined fire of infantry and artillery, and such opportunities are likely to be much more numerous at the outbreak of future wars than they have been in the past, because the enormous gain in range and rapidity of fire enables a far greater weight of metal to be concentrated on any chosen area within a given time. It cannot be too often reiterated that cavalry never has ridden over unshaken infantry of average quality by reason of its momentum alone, but that every successful cavalry charge has always owed its issue to a previously acquired moral superiority which has prevented the infantry from making adequate use of their means of defence. Nor will such charges entail greater losses than in the past, for, great though the increase of range of modern infantry weapons has been, the speed and endurance of cavalry has increased in a yet higher ratio; whereas in Napoleon's days, with an extreme range for musketry of 1000 yds., cavalry were expected only to trot 800 yds. and gallop for 200, nowadays with an extreme infantry range of under 4000 yds., the cavalry are trained to trot for 8000 yds. and gallop for 2000.

Neither the experiences in South Africa nor those in Manchuria seriously influenced the views of the leading cavalry experts as above outlined, for the conditions of both cases were entirely abnormal. No nation in western Europe can afford to mount the whole of its able-bodied manhood, nor, with the restricted area of its possessions, could repeat the Boer tactics with useful effect; in Manchuria, the theatre of operation was so far roadless, and the motives of both combatants so distinct from any conceivable as a basis for European strategy, that time was always available to construct entrenchments and obstacles physically insuperable to mounted arms. In western Europe, with its extreme development of communications, such tactics are impracticable, and under the system of compulsory service which is in force in all nations, an early decision must be sought at any cost. This motive imposes a rapid-marching campaign in the Napoleonic style, and in such warfare there is neither time nor energy available for the erection of extemporised fortresses. Victory must therefore fall to the side that can develop the greatest fire power in the shortest time. The greatest factor of fire power is the long artillery lines, and as cavalry is the one arm which by its mobility can hamper or prevent the formation of such lines, on its success in this task all else must depend. Hence both sides will concentrate every available horse and man for this special purpose, and on the issue of the collisions this mutual concentration must entail will hang the fate of the battle, and ultimately of the nation. But the cavalry which will succeed in this task will be the one in which the spirit of duty burns brightest, and the oath of allegiance, renewed daily on the cross of the sword, is held in the highest esteem.

Organization.—The existing organization of cavalry throughout the civilized world is an instance of the "survival of the fittest" in an extreme form. The execution of the many manoeuvres with the speed and precision which condition success is only possible by a force in which, as Frederick the Great said, "every horse and trooper has been finished with the same care that a watchmaker bestows upon each wheel of the watch mechanism." Uniformity of excellence is in fact the keystone of success, and this is only attainable where the mass is subdivided into groups, each of which requires superintendence enough to absorb the whole energy of an average commander. Thus it has been found by ages of experiment that an average officer, with the assistance of certain subordinates to whom he delegates as much or as little responsibility as he pleases, finds his time fully occupied by the care of about one hundred and fifty men and horses, each individual of which he must understand intimately, in character, physical strength and temper, for horse and man must be matched with the utmost care and judgment if the best that each is capable of is to be attained. The fundamental secret of the exceptional efficiency attained by the Prussian cavalry lies in the fact that they were the first to realize what the above implies. After the close of the Napoleonic Wars they made their squadron commanders responsible, not only for the training of the combatants of their unit, but also for the breaking in of remounts and the elementary teaching of recruits as well, and in this manner they obtained an intimate knowledge of their material which is almost unattainable by British officers owing to the conditions entailed by foreign service and frequent changes of garrisons.

Further, to obtain the maximum celerity of manoeuvre with the minimum exertion of the horses, the squadron requires to be subdivided into smaller units, generally known as *troops*, and experience has shown that with 128 sabres in the ranks (the average strength on parade, after deducting sick and young horses, and the N.C. officers required as troop guides, &c.) four troops best satisfy all conditions; as, with this number, the squadron will, under all circumstances of ground and surroundings, make any change of formation in less time and with greater accuracy than with any other number of subdivisions. The size of the unit next above the squadron, the *regiment*, is again fixed by the number of subordinates that an average commander can control, and the universal experience of all arms has settled this as not less than four and not more than eight. Experiments with eight and even ten squadrons have been tried both in Austria and Prussia, but only exceptional men have succeeded in controlling such large bodies effectively, and in the end the normal has been fixed at four or five squadrons in quarters, and three or four in the field. Of these, the larger number 570 is undoubtedly preferable, for, with the work of the quartermaster and the adjutant to supervise, in addition, the regimental commander is economically applied to the best advantage. The essential point, however, is that the officer commanding the regiment does not interfere in details, but commands his four squadron commanders, his quartermaster, and his adjutant, and holds them absolutely responsible for results.

There is no unity of practice in the constitution of larger units. Brigades vary according to circumstances from two regiments to four, and the composition of divisions fluctuates similarly. The custom in the German cavalry has been to form brigades of two regiments and divisions of three brigades, but this practice arose primarily from the system of recruiting and has no tactical advantage. The territory assigned to each army corps provides men and horses for two regiments of cuirassiers or lancers (classed as heavy in Germany), two of dragoons, and two of hussars, and since it is clearly essential to ensure uniformity of speed and endurance within those units most likely to have to work together, it was impossible to mix the different classes. But the views now current as to the tactical employment of cavalry contemplate the employment not only of divisions but of whole cavalry corps, forty to sixty squadrons strong, and these may be called on to fulfil the most various missions. The farthest and swiftest reconnaissances are the province of light cavalry, *i.e.* hussars, the most obstinate attack and defence of localities the task of dragoons, and the decisive charges on the battle-field essentially the duty of the heavy cavalry. It seems probable then that the brigade will become the highest unit the composition of which is fixed in peace, and that divisions and corps will be put together by brigades of uniform composition, and assigned to the several sections of the theatre of war in which each is likely to find the most suitable field for its special character. This was the case in the Frederician and Napoleonic epochs, when efficiency and experience in the field far outweighed considerations of administration and convenience in quarters.

Hitherto, horse artillery in Europe has always formed an integral portion of the divisional organization, but the system has never worked well, and in view of the technical evolution of artillery material is no longer considered desirable. As it is always possible to assign one or more batteries to any particular brigade whose line of march will bring it across villages, defiles, &c. (where the support of its fire will be essential), and on the battle-field itself responsibility for the guns is likely to prove more of a hindrance than a help to the cavalry commander, it is probable that horse artillery will revert to the inspection of its own technical officers, and that the sole tie which will be retained between it and the cavalry will be in the batteries being informed as to the cavalry units they are likely to serve with in war, so that the officers may make themselves acquainted with the idiosyncrasies of their future commanders. The same course will be pursued with the engineers and technical troops required for the cavalry, but it seems probable that, in accordance with a suggestion made by Moltke after the 1866 campaign, the supply columns for one or more cavalry corps will be held ready in peace, and specially organized to attain the highest possible mobility which modern technical progress can ensure.

The general causes which have led to the differentiation of cavalry into the three types—hussars, dragoons and heavy—have already been dealt with. Obviously big men on little horses cannot manoeuvre side by side with light men on big horses. Also, since uniformity of excellence within the unit is the prime condition of efficiency, and the greatest personal dexterity is required for the management of sword or lance on horseback, a further sorting out became necessary, and the best light weights were put on the best light horses and called hussars, the best heavy weights on the best heavy horses and called lancers, the average of either type becoming dragoons and cuirassiers. In England, the lance not being indigenous and the conditions of foreign service making adherence to a logical system impossible, lancers are medium cavalry, but the difference of weights carried and type of horses is too small to render these distinctions of practical moment. In Germany, where every suitable horse finds its place in the ranks and men have no right of individual selection, the distinctions are still maintained, and there is a very marked difference between the weights carried and the types of men and horses in each branch, though the dead weight which it is still considered necessary to carry in cavalries likely to manoeuvre in large masses hardly varies with the weight of the man or size of the horse.

Where small units only are required to march and scout, the kit can be reduced to a minimum, everything superfluous for the moment being carried on hired transport, as in South Africa. But when 10,000 horsemen have to move by a single road all transport must be left miles to the rear, and greater mobility for the whole is attained by carrying upon the horse itself the essentials for a period of some weeks. Still, even allowing for this, it is impossible to account for the extraordinary load that is still considered necessary. In India, the British lancer, averaging 11 st. per man, could turn out in marching order at 17 st. 8 ℔

(less forage nets). In Germany, the hussar, averaging 10 st. 6 ℔, rode at 18 st., also without forage, and the cuirassier at 21 st. to 22 st. Cavalry equipment is, in fact, far too heavy, for in the interests of the budgets of the departments which supply saddlery, harness, &c., everything is made so as to last for many years. Cavalry saddles fifty years old frequently remain in good condition, but the losses in horse-flesh this excessive solidity entails are ignored. The remount accounts are kept separately, and few realize that in war it is cheaper to replace a horse than a saddle. In any case, the armament alone of the cavalry soldier makes great demands on the horses. His sword and scabbard weigh about 4 ℔, carbine or rifle 7 ℔ to 9 ℔, 120 rounds of ammunition with pouches and belts about 12 ℔, lance about 5 ℔, and two days' forage and hay at the lowest 40 ℔, or a gross total of 70 ℔ or 5 st., which with 11 st. for the man brings the total to 16 st.; add to this the lightest possible saddle, bridle, cloak and blanket, and 17 st. 8 ℔ is approximately the irreducible minimum. It may be imagined what care and management of the horses is required to enable them under such loads to manoeuvre in masses at a trot, and gallop for distances of 5 m. and upwards without a moment for dismounting.

Reconnaissance and Scouting.—After 1870 public opinion, misled by the performances of the "ubiquitous Uhlan" and disappointed by the absence of great cavalry charges on the field of battle, came somewhat hastily to the conclusion that the day of "shock tactics" was past and the future of cavalry lay in acting as the eyes and ears of the following armies. But, as often happens, the fact was overlooked that the German cavalry screen was entirely unopposed in its reconnoitring expeditions, and it was not till long afterwards that it became apparent how very little these far-flung reconnaissances had contributed to the total success.

It has been calculated by German cavalry experts that not 1% of the reports sent in by the scouts during the advance from the Saar to the Meuse, August 1870, were of appreciable importance to the headquarters, and that before the orders based upon this evidence reached the front, events frequently anticipated them. Generally the conviction has asserted itself, that it is impossible to train the short-service soldiers of civilized nations sufficiently to render their reports worth the trouble of collating, and if a few cases of natural aptitude do exist nothing can ensure that these particular men should be sufficiently well mounted to transmit their information with sufficient celerity to be of importance. It is of little value to a commander to know that the enemy was at a given spot forty-eight hours previously, unless the sender of the report has a sufficient force at his disposal to compel the enemy to remain there; in other words, to attack and hold him. Cavalry and horse artillery alone, however, cannot economically exert this holding power, for, whatever their effect against worn-out men at the close of a great battle, against fresh infantry they are relatively powerless. Hence, it is probable that we shall see a revival of the strategic advanced guard of all arms, as in the Napoleonic days, which will not only reconnoitre, but fix the enemy until the army itself can execute the manoeuvre designed to effect his destruction. The general situation of the 571 enemy's masses will, in western Europe, always be sufficiently fixed by the trend of his railway communications, checked by reports of spies, newspapers, &c., for, with neutral frontiers everywhere within a few hours' ride for a motor cyclist, anything approaching the secrecy of the Japanese in Manchuria is quite unattainable, and, once the great masses begin to move, the only "shadowing" which holds out any hope of usefulness is that undertaken by very small selected parties of officers, perfectly mounted, daring riders, and accustomed to cover distances of 100 m. and upwards. These will be supported by motor cars and advanced feelers from the field telegraphs, though probably the motor car would carry the eye-witness to his destination in less time than it would take to draft and signal a complete report.

PLATE I.

SIXTEENTH-CENTURY CAVALRY.
(Walthausen's *Art militaire de la cavalerie*, circa 1600.)

PLATE II.

BATTLE OF STAFFARDA, 1690. (*From a contemporary engraving.*)

ACTION ON THE BULGANAK, 1854. (*From a lithograph by W. Simpson.*)

GERMAN GUARD DRAGOONS. (*Photo, Gebruder Haeckel.*)

Tactical scouting, now as always, is invaluable for securing the safety of the marching and sleeping troops, and brigade, divisional and corps commanders will remain dependent upon their own squadrons for the solution of the immediate tactical problem before them; but, since both sides will employ mounted men to screen their operations, intelligence will generally only be won by fighting, and the side which can locally develop a marked fire superiority will be the more likely to obtain the information it requires. In this direction the introduction of the motor car and of cyclists is likely to exercise a most important influence, but, whatever may be the conveyance, it must be looked upon as a means of advance only, never of retreat. The troops thus conveyed must be used to seize villages or defiles about which the cavalry and guns can manoeuvre.

Formations and Drill.—Cavalry, when mounted, act exclusively by "shock" or more precisely by "the threat of their shock," for the immediate result of collision is actually decided some instants before this collision takes place. Experience has shown that the best guarantee for success in this shock is afforded by a two-deep line, the men riding knee to knee within each squadron at least. Perfect cavalry can charge in larger bodies without intervals between the squadrons, but, ordinarily, intervals of about 10 yds. between adjacent squadrons are kept to localize any partial unsteadiness due to difficulties of ground, casualties, &c. The obvious drawbacks of a two-deep line are that it halves the possible extent of front, and that if a front-rank horse falls the rear-rank horse generally tumbles over it also. To minimize the latter evil, the charge in two successive lines, 150 to 200 yds. apart, has often been advocated, but this has never stood the test of serious cavalry fighting; first, because when squadrons are galloping fast and always striving to keep the touch to the centre, if a horse falls the adjacent horses close in with such force that their sidelong collision may throw down more and always creates violent oscillation; and secondly, because owing to the dust raised by the first rank the following one can never maintain its true direction. It is primarily to avoid the danger and difficulty arising from the dust that the ranks in manoeuvre are closed to within one horse's length, as, when moving at speed, the rear rank is past before the dust has time to rise.

Of all formations, the line is the most difficult to handle, and, particularly, to conceal—hence various formations in column are necessary for the preliminary manoeuvres requisite to place the squadrons in position for the final deployment previous to the charge. Many forms of these columns have been tried, but, setting aside the columns intended exclusively for marching along roads, of which "sections" (four men abreast) is most usual in England, only these survive:—

Squadron column.
Double   column   of
squadrons.
Half column.

In *squadron column*, the troops of the squadron formed are in line one behind the other at a distance equal to the front of the troop in line. The ideal squadron consists of 128 men formed in two ranks giving 64 files, and divided into four troops of 16 files—a larger number of troops makes the drill too complicated, a smaller number makes each troop slow and unhandy. When the squadron is weak, therefore, the troop should still be maintained as near 16 files as possible, the number of troops being if necessary reduced. Thus with only 32 files, two troops of 16 files would be better than four of only 8 files.

All other formations of the regiment or brigade are fundamentally derived from the squadron column, only varying with the order in which the squadrons are grouped, and the intervals which separate them. Thus the regiment may move in *line of squadron columns* at close interval, *i.e.* 11 paces apart or in *double column* as in the diagram. To form *line* for the charge, the squadrons open out, still in column, at full interval, *i.e.* the width they occupy when in line; and then on the command "Line to the front," each troop moves up to its place in line as shown in the diagram. When in line a large body of cavalry can no longer vary its direction without sacrificing its appearance of order, and as above pointed out, it is this appearance of order which really decides the result of the charge before the actual collision. Since, however, the enemy's movements may compel a change, an intermediate formation is provided, known as the "half column." When this formation is ordered, the troops within each squadron wheel half right or left, and each squadron is then able to form into column or line to the front as circumstances demand, or the whole line can be formed into column of troops by continuing the wheel and in this formation gallop out into a fresh direction, reforming line by a simple wheel in the shortest possible time.

BIBLIOGRAPHY.—G.H. Elliot, *Cavalry Literature* (1893); v. Bismarck, *Uses and Application of Cavalry in War* (1818, English translation by Lieut.-Col. Beamish, 1855); G.T. Denison, *A History of Cavalry* (1877); Prince Kraft zu Hohenlohe-Ingelfingen,*Letters on Cavalry* and *Conversations on Cavalry* (English translations, 1880 and 1892); Colonel Mitchell, *Considerations on Tactics* (1854) and *Thoughts on Tactics and Organization* (1838); E. Nolan, *Cavalry, its History and Tactics* (1855); Roemer,*Cavalry, its History, Management and Uses* (New York, 1863); Maitland, *Notes on Cavalry* (1878); F.N. Maude, *Cavalry versus Infantry and Cavalry, its Past and Future*; C. von Schmidt, *Instructions for the Training, Employment and Leading of Cavalry*(English translation, 1881); V. Verdy du Vernois, *The Cavalry Division* (1873); Maj.-Gen. Walker, *The Organization and Tactics of the Cavalry Division* (1876); C.W. Bowdler Bell, *Notes on the German Cavalry Regulations of 1886*; F. de Brack, *Light Cavalry Outposts* (English translation); Dwyer, *Seats and Saddles* (1869); J. Jacob,*Views and Opinions* (1857); F. Hoenig, *Die Kavallerie als Schlachtenkörper* (1884); Sir Evelyn Wood, *Achievements of Cavalry* (1893); H.T. Siborne, *Waterloo Letters*; Desbrière and Sautai, *La Cavalerie de 1740 à 1789* (1806); Warnery, *Remarques sur la cavalerie* (1781); v. Canitz, *Histoire des exploits et des vicissitudes de la cavalerie prussienne dans les campagnes de Frédéric II* (1849); Cherfils, *Cavalerie en campagne*(1888), 572.*Service de sûreté stratégique de la cavalerie* (1874); Bonie, *Tactique française, cavalerie en campagne, cavalerie au combat* (1887-1888); Foucart, *Campagne de Pologne, opérations de la cavalerie, nov. 1806-jan. 1807* (1882), *La Cavalerie pendant la campagne de Prusse* (1880); De Galliffet, *Projet d'instruction sur l'emploi de la cavalerie en liaison avec les autres armes* (1880), *Rapport sur les grandes manoeuvres de cavalerie de 1879*; Kaehler, *Die preussische Reiterei 1806-1876* (French translation,*La Cavalerie prussienne de 1806 à 1876*); *Cavalry Studies* (translated from the French of Bonie and the German of Kaehler, with a paper on U.S. cavalry in the Civil War); v. Bernhardi, *Cavalry in Future Wars* (English translation, 1906); P.S., *Cavalry in the Wars of the Future* (translated from the French by T. Formby, 1905); D. Haig, *Cavalry Studies* (1907); v. Pelet Narbonne, *Die Kavalleriedienst* (1901). *Cavalry on Service*(English translation, 1906); *Erziehung und Führung von Kavallerie*. The principal cavalry periodicals are the *Revue de cavalerie*, the *Kavalleristische Monatshefte*(Austrian), the *Cavalry Journal* (British), and the *Journal of the U.S. Cavalry Association*.

(F. N. M.)

1The loss of the regiment was twenty-eight killed and sixty-six wounded.

CAVAN, a county in the province of Ulster, Ireland, bounded N. by Fermanagh and Monaghan, E. by Monaghan and Meath, S. by Meath, Westmeath and Longford, and W. by Longford and Leitrim. The area is 477,399 acres, or about 746 sq. m. The surface of the county is uneven, consisting of hill and dale, without any great extent of level ground, but only in its northern extremity attaining a mountainous elevation. The barony of Tullyhaw, bordering on Fermanagh, a wild dreary mountain district, known as the kingdom of Glan or Glengavlin, contains the highest land in the county, reaching 2188 ft. in Cuilcagh, the place of inauguration for the Maguires, chieftains of Fermanagh, held in veneration by the peasantry, in connexion with legends and ancient superstitions. The remainder of the county is not deficient in wood, and contains numerous lakes, generally of small dimensions, but of much beauty, especially Lough Oughter, with its many inlets and islands formed by the Erne river, between the towns of Cavan and Killashandra. The county also shares with other counties the waters of Lough Gowna and Lough Sheelin, in which, as elsewhere in the county, the fishing is good. The chief river in the county is the Erne, which originates in Lough Scrabby, one of the minor sheets of water communicating with Lough Gowna on the borders of Longford. The river takes a northerly direction by Killashandra and Belturbet, being enlarged during its course by the Annalee and other smaller streams, and finally enters Lough Erne near the northern limit of the county. The other waters, consisting of numerous lakes and their connecting streams, are mostly tributary to the Erne. A copious spring called the Shannon Pot, at the foot of the Cuilcagh Mountain, in the barony of Tullyhaw, is regarded as the source of the river Shannon. The Blackwater, a tributary of the Boyne, also rises in this county, near Bailieborough. Several mineral springs exist in this county, the chief of which is near the once frequented village of Swanlinbar. In the neighbourhood of Belturbet, near the small lake of Annagh, is a carbonated chalybeate spring. There are several other springs of less importance; and the small Lough Leighs, or Lough-an-Leighaghs, which signifies the healing lake, on the summit of a mountain between Bailieborough and Kingscourt, is celebrated for its antiscorbutic properties. The level of this lake never varies. It has no visible supply nor vent for its discharge; nor is it ever frozen during the severest winters.

Geology.—This elongated county includes on the north-west some of the highland of Millstone Grit and Coal-Measures that rises above Lough Allen. The beds below these are referred to the English Yoredale series, and include some flaggy sandstones. It is on this series that the Shannon rises, under the high outlier of grit on Cuilcagh. The Carboniferous Limestone then stretches down to Cavan town, a bold outlier of the higher strata being left above Ballyconnell. The river Erne forms, in the limestone area, a characteristic series of expansions and loops, with islands between them, known as Lough Oughter. At this point we pass on to the axis of underlying Silurian strata that runs from Longford to Donaghadee in Co. Down, and the country becomes hilly and irregular, culminating about Cross Keys on the old Dublin coach-road. A patch of granite, indicating doubtless a core like that exposed at Newry, is seen in a hollow at Crossdoney. On the south side of this axis of older rocks, we reach Carboniferous shale and limestone at Lough Sheelin, and here enter on the great central plain. The extreme south-east of the county includes part of the Triassic outlier of Kingscourt. The coal-seams and concretions of clay-ironstone in the north-west area resemble those mentioned under the head of Co. Roscommon. Anthracite, probably of inorganic origin, has been mined without permanent success in the Silurian beds near Kilnaleck, and is traceable freely, associated with veins of quartz and haematite, at Ballyjamesduff a little farther east.

Climate and Industries.—The climate suffers from the dampness arising from the numerous lakes and the nature of the soil, and from the boisterous winds which frequently prevail, more especially in the higher districts. The soil is generally a stiff clay, cold and watery, but capable of much improvement by drainage, for which its undulating surface affords facilities. Only about one-sixteenth of the total area is quite barren. Agriculture makes little progress; the extent of the farms being generally small. Oats and potatoes are the principal crops. Flax, once of some importance, is almost neglected. In the mountainous parts, however, where the land is chiefly under grazing, the farms are larger, and in stock-raising the county is progressing.

Cavan is not a manufacturing county. The bleaching of linen and the distillation of whisky are both carried on to a small extent, but the people are chiefly employed in agricultural pursuits and in the sale of home produce. The soil in those districts not well adapted for tillage is peculiarly favourable for trees. The woods were formerly very considerable, and the timber found in the bogs is of large dimensions; but plantations are now chiefly found in demesnes, where they are extensive.

The county is not well served by railways. The Great Northern from Clones to Cavan, and the Midland Great Western from Mullingar in Westmeath to Cavan, form a through line from north to south. The Great Northern has branches to Belturbet from Ballyhaise, and to Cootehill from Ballybay; the Midland Great Western has a branch to Killashandra, and from Navan in Meath to Kingscourt, just within Cavan. The Cavan & Leitrim railway starts from Belturbet and soon leaves the county to the west.

Population and Administration.—The population (111,917 in 1891; 97,541 in 1901), of which about 80% are Roman Catholics, shows a decrease among the most serious of the Irish counties, and emigration returns are among the heaviest. The population is almost wholly rural, the only towns being the small ones of Cavan (pop. 2822, the county town), Cootehill (1509), Belturbet (1587) and Bailieborough (1004). The county is divided into eight baronies, and contains thirty-two parishes and parts of parishes. It is almost entirely within the Protestant and Roman Catholic dioceses of Kilmore. The assizes are held at Cavan, and quarter sessions are held at Cavan, Bailieborough, Cootehill and Ballyconnell. Before the Union the county returned six members to the Irish parliament, two for the county at large, and two for each of the boroughs of Cavan and Belturbet; but since that period it has been represented in the imperial parliament by two members only, for the east and west divisions.

History and Antiquities.—At the period of the English settlement, and for some centuries afterwards, this district was known as the Brenny, being divided between the families of O'Rourke and O'Reilly; and its inhabitants, protected by the nature of the country, long maintained their independence. In 1579 Cavan was made shire ground as part of Connaught, and in 1584 it was formed into a county of Ulster by Sir John Perrott, and subdivided into seven baronies, two of which were assigned to Sir John O'Reilly and three to other members of the family; while the two remaining, possessed by the septs of Mackernon and Magauran, and situated in the mountains bordering on O'Rourke's country, were left subject to their ancient tenures and the exactions of their Irish lord. The county subsequently came within the scheme for the plantation of Ulster under James I. The population is less mixed in race than in most parts of Ulster, being generally of Celtic extraction. Some few remains of antiquity remain in the shape of cairns, raths and the ruins of small castles, such as Cloughoughter Castle on an island (an ancient crannog) of Lough Oughter. Three miles from the town of Cavan is Kilmore, with its cathedral, a plain erection containing a Romanesque doorway brought from the abbey of Trinity Island, Lough Oughter. The bishopric dates 573from about 1450. A portion of a round tower is seen in the churchyard of the parish of Drumlane at Belturbet.

CAVAN, a market-town and the county town of Co. Cavan, Ireland, near the centre of the county, in the west parliamentary division, 85½ m. N.W. of Dublin by the Midland Great Western railway, and the terminus of a branch of the Great Northern railway from Clones. Pop. of urban district (1901), 2822. It is on one of the tributary streams of the Annalee river, in a broad valley surrounded on every side by elevated ground, with picturesque environs, notably the demesnes of Farnham and of Kilmore, which belongs to the bishops of that diocese. Cavan has no buildings of antiquarian interest, but the principal county institutions are here, and the most conspicuous building is the grammar school, founded by Charles I. It was rebuilt in 1819 on an eminence overlooking one of the main entrances into the town, and is capable of accommodating 100 resident pupils. The college of St Patrick is near the town. Cavan has some linen trade, and a considerable retail business is transacted in the town. A monastery of Dominican friars, founded by O'Reilly, chieftain of the Brenny, formerly existed here, and became the burial-place of the celebrated Irish general, Owen O'Neill, who died as is supposed by poison, in 1649, at Cloughoughter. There was also the castle of the O'Reillys, but this and all other antiquities of the town were swept away during the violent and continuous feuds to which the country was subjected. In 1690 the chief portion of the town was burned by the Enniskilleners under General Wolseley, when they routed a body of James II.'s troops under the duke of Berwick.

CAVANILLES, ANTONIO JOSÉ (1745-1804), Spanish botanist, was born at Valencia on the 16th of January 1745. He was educated at the university of that town, and in 1777 went to Paris, where he resided twelve years, engaged in the study of botany. In 1801 he became director of the botanic gardens at Madrid, where he died on the 4th of May 1804. In 1785-1786 he published *Monadelphiae Classis Dissertationes X.*, and in 1791 he began to issue *Icones et descriptiones plantarum Hispaniae.*

His nephew, ANTONIO CAVANILLES (1805-1864), was a distinguished advocate, and the author of a history of Spain, published at Madrid in 1860-1864.

CAVATINA (Ital. diminutive of *cavata*, the producing of tone from an instrument, plural*cavatine*), originally a short song of simple character, without a second strain or any repetition of the air. It is now frequently applied to a simple melodious air, as distinguished from a brilliant aria, recitative, &c., and often forms part of a large movement or *scena* in oratorio or opera.

CAVE, EDWARD (1691-1754), English printer, was born at Newton, Warwickshire, on the 27th of February 1691. His father, Joseph Cave, was of good family, but the entail of the family estate being cut off, he was reduced to becoming a cobbler at Rugby. Edward Cave entered the grammar school of that town, but was expelled for robbing the master's hen-roost. After many vicissitudes he became apprentice to a London printer, and after two years was sent to Norwich to conduct a printing house and publish a weekly paper. While still a printer he obtained a place in the post office, and was promoted to be clerk of the franks. He was at this time engaged in supplying London newsletters to various country papers; and his enemies, who had twice summoned him before the House of Commons for breach of privilege, now accused him of opening letters to obtain his news, and he was dismissed the service. With the capital which he had saved, he set up a small printing office at St John's Gate, Clerkenwell, which he carried on under the name of R. Newton. He had long formed a scheme of a magazine "to contain the essays and intelligence which appeared in the two hundred half-sheets which the London press then threw off monthly," and had tried in vain to persuade some publisher to take it up. In 1731 he himself put it into execution, and began the *Gentleman's Magazine* (see PERIODICALS), of which he was the editor, under the pseudonym "Sylvanus Urban, Gent." The magazine had a large circulation and brought a fortune to the projector. In 1732 he began to issue reports of the debates in both Houses of Parliament. He commissioned friends to note the speeches, which he published with the initial and final letters of personal names. In 1738 Cave was censured by parliament for printing the king's answer to an address before it had been announced by the speaker. From that time he called his reports the debates of a "parliament in the empire of Lilliput" (seeREPORTING). To piece together and write out the speeches for this publication was Samuel Johnson's first literary employment. In 1747 Cave was reprimanded for publishing an account of the trial of Lord Lovat, and the reports were discontinued till 1752. He died on the 10th of January 1754. Cave published Dr Johnson's *Rambler*, and his *Irene*, *London* and*Life of Savage*, and was the subject of a short biography by him.

CAVE, WILLIAM (1637-1713), English divine, was born at Pickwell in Leicestershire. He was educated at St John's College, Cambridge, and successively held the livings of Islington (1662), of All-Hallows the Great, Thames Street, London (1679), and of Isleworth in Middlesex (1690). Dr Cave was chaplain to Charles II., and in 1684 became a canon of Windsor. The two works on which his reputation principally rests are the *Apostolici*, or History of Apostles and Fathers in the first three centuries of the Church (1677), and*Scriptorum Ecclesiasticorum Historia Literaria* (1688). The best edition of the latter is the Clarendon Press, 1740-1743, which contains additions by the author and others. In both works he was drawn into controversy with Jean le Clerc, who was then writing his*Bibliothèque universelle*, and who accused him of partiality. He wrote several other works of the same nature which exhibit scholarly research and lucid arrangement. He is said to have been a good talker and an eloquent preacher. His death occurred at Windsor on the 4th of July 1713.

CAVE (Lat. *cavea*, from *cavus*, hollow), a hollow extending beneath the surface of the earth. The word "cavern" (Lat. *caverna*) is practically a synonym, though a distinction is sometimes drawn between sea caves and inland caverns, but the term "cave" is used here as a general description. Caves have excited the awe and wonder of mankind in all ages, and have been the centres round which have clustered many legends and superstitions. They were the abode of the sibyls and the nymphs in Roman mythology, and in Greece they were the temples of Zeus, Pan Dionysus, Pluto and the Moon, as well as the places where the oracles were delivered at Delphi, Corinth and Mount Cithaeron. In Persia they were connected with the obscure worship of Mithras. Their names frequently are survivals of the superstitious ideas of antiquity, as, for example, the Fairy, Dragon's, or Devil's Caves of France and Germany. Long after the Fairies and Little Men had forsaken the forests and glens of Germany, they dwelt in their palaces deep in the Harz Mountains, in the Dwarfholes, &c., whence they came from time to time into the upper air.

The Seven Sleepers of Ephesus slept their long sleep in a cave. The hills of Granada are still believed by the Moorish children to contain the great Boabdil and his sleeping host, who will awake, when an adventurous mortal invades their repose, to restore the glory of the Moors in Spain.

Caves have been used in all ages by mankind for habitation, refuge and burial. In the Old Testament we read that when Lot went up out of Zoar he dwelt in a cave with his two daughters. The five kings of the Canaanites took refuge from Joshua, and David from Saul, in the caves of Palestine, just as the Aquitani fled from Caesar to those of Auvergne, and the Arabs of Algeria to those of Dahra, where they were suffocated by Marshal Pelissier in 1845. In Central Africa David Livingstone discovered vast caves in which whole tribes found security with their cattle and household stuff.

The cave of Machpelah may be quoted as an example of their use as sepulchres, and the rock-hewn tombs of Palestine and of Egypt and the Catacombs of Rome probably owe their existence to the ancient practice of burial in natural hollows in the rock. We might therefore expect to find in them most important evidence as to the ancient history of mankind, which would reach long beyond written record; and since they have always 574been used by wild beasts as lairs we might reasonably believe also that their exploration would throw light upon the animals which have in many cases disappeared from the countries which they formerly inhabited. The labours of Buckland, Pengelly, Falconer, Lartet and Christy, and Boyd Dawkins have added an entirely new chapter to the history of man in Europe, as well as established the changes that have taken place in the European fauna. The physical history of caves will be taken first, and we shall then pass on to the discoveries relating to man and the lower animals which have been made in them of late years.

Physical History.—The most obvious agent in hollowing out caves is the sea. The set of the currents, the force of the breakers, the grinding of the shingle inevitably discover the weak places in the cliff, and leave caves as one of the results of their work, modified in each case by the local conditions of the rock. Those formed in this manner are easily recognized from their floors being rarely much out of the horizontal; their entrances are all in the same plane, or in a succession of horizontal and parallel planes, if the land has been elevated at successive times. From their inaccessible position they have been rarely occupied by man. Among them Fingal's Cave, on the island of Staffa, off the south-west coast of Scotland, hollowed out of columnar basalt, is perhaps the most remarkable in Europe. In volcanic regions also there are caves formed by the passage of lava to the surface of the ground, or by the expansion of steam and gases in the lava while it was in a molten state. They have been observed in the regions round Vesuvius and Etna, in Iceland and Teneriffe. We may take as an example the Grotto del Cane ("cave of the dog"), near Pozzuoli, a few miles to the south-west of Naples, remarkable for the flow of carbonic acid from crevices in the floor, which fills the lower part of the cave and suffocates any small animal, such as a dog, immersed long enough in it.

The most important class of caves, however, and that which immediately demands our notice, is that composed of those which have been cut out of calcareous rocks by the action of carbonic acid in the rain-water, combined with the mechanical friction of the sand and stones set in motion by the streams which have, at one time or another, flowed through them. They occur at various levels, and are to be met with wherever the strata are sufficiently compact to support a roof. Those of Brixham and Torquay and of the Eifel are in the Devonian limestone; those of Wales, Somerset, the Pennine chain, Ireland, the central and northern counties of Belgium, Saxony, and Westphalia, of Maine and Anjou, of Virginia and Kentucky, are in that of the Carboniferous age. The cave of Kirkdale in Yorkshire, and most of those in Franconia and Bavaria, penetrate Jurassic limestones. The Neocomian and

Cretaceous limestones contain most of the caverns of France, rendered famous by the discovery of the remains of the cave-men along with the animals which they hunted; as well as those of the Pyrenees, the Alps, Sicily, Greece, Dalmatia, Carniola and Palestine. The cave of Lunelviel near Montpellier is the most important of those which have been hollowed in limestones of the Tertiary age. They are also met with in rocks composed of gypsum; in Thuringia, for example, they occur in the saliferous and gypseous strata of the Zechstein, and in the gypseous Tertiary rocks of the neighbourhood of Paris, as, for example, at Montmorency.

Caves formed by the action of carbonic acid and the action of water are distinguished from others by the following characters. They open on the abrupt sides of valleys and ravines at various levels, and are arranged round the main axes of erosion, just as the branches are arranged round the trunk of a tree. In a great many cases the relation of the valley to the ravine, and of the ravine to the cave, is so intimate that it is impossible to deny that all three have been produced by the same causes. The caves themselves ramify in the same irregular fashion as the valleys, and are to be viewed merely as the capillaries in the general valley system through which the rain passes to join the main channels. Sometimes, as in the famous caves of Adelsberg, Kentucky, Wookey Hole in Somersetshire, the Peak in Derbyshire, and in many in the Jura, they are still the passages of subterranean streams; but very frequently the drainage has found an outlet at a lower level, and the ancient watercourses have been deserted. These in every case present unmistakable proof that they have been traversed by water in the sand, gravel and clay which they contain, as well as in the worn surfaces of the sides and bottom. In all districts where there are caves there are funnel-shaped depressions of various sizes called pot-holes or swallow-holes, or bêtoires, "chaldrons du diable," "marmites des géants," or "katavothra," in which the rain is collected before it disappears into the subterranean passages. They are to be seen in all stages, some being mere hollows which only contain water after excessive rain, while others are profound vertical shafts into which the water is continually falling. Gaping Ghyl, 330 ft., and Helln Pot in Yorkshire, 300 ft. deep, are examples of the latter class. The *cirques* described by M. Desnoyers belong to the same class as the swallow-holes.

The history of swallow-holes, caves, ravines and valleys in calcareous strata may be summed up as follows:—The calcareous rocks are invariably traversed by joints or lines of shrinkage, which are lines of weakness by which the direction of the drainage is determined; and they are composed to a large extent of carbonate of lime, which is readily exchanged into soluble bicarbonate by the addition of carbonic acid. The rain in its passage through the air takes up carbonic acid, and it is still further charged with it in percolating through the surface soil in which there is decomposing vegetable matter. As the raindrops converge towards some one point, determined by some local accident on the surface, and always in a line of joint, the carbonic acid attacks the carbonate of lime with which it comes into contact, and thus a funnel is gradually formed ending in the vertical joint below. Both funnel and vertical joint below are being continually enlarged by this process. This chemical action goes on until the free carbonic acid is used up. The subterranean passages are enlarged in this manner, and what was originally an insignificant network of fissures is developed into a series of halls, sometimes as much as from 80 to 100 ft. high. These results are considerably furthered by the mechanical friction of the pebbles and sand hurried along by the current, and by falls of rock from the roof produced by the removal of the underlying strata. In many cases the results of this action have produced a regular subterranean river system. The thick limestones of Kentucky, for example, are traversed by subterranean waters which collect in large rivers, and ultimately appear at the surface in full power. The river Axe, near Wells, the stream flowing out of the Peak Cavern at Castleton, Derbyshire, that at Adelsberg in Carniola, flow out of caverns in full volume. The river Styx and the waters of Acheron disappear in a series of caverns which were supposed to lead down to the infernal regions.

If the direction of the drainage in the rock has been altered, either by elevations such as those with which the geologist is familiar, or by the opening out of new passages at a lower level, these watercourses become dry, and present us with the caves which have afforded shelter to man and the wild animals from the remotest ages, sometimes high up on the side of a ravine, at other times close to the level of the stream at the bottom.

Caves, as a general rule, are as little effected by disturbances of the rock as the ravines and valleys, which have been formed, in the main, irrespective of the lines of fault or dislocation.

We must now examine what happens to the bicarbonate of lime which has been formed by the action of the acid on the limestone. If a current of air play upon the surface of the water, the carbonic acid, which floats up the lime, so to speak, is given off and the insoluble carbonate is deposited, and as a result of this action we have the elaborate and fantastic stony incrustations termed stalactites and stalagmites. The water percolating through the rock covers the sides of the cavern with a stalactitic drapery, and if a line of drops persistently falls from the same point to the floor, the calcareous deposit gradually descends from the roof, forming in some cases stony tassels, and in others long columns which are ultimately united to the calcareous boss formed by the plash of the water on the floor. The surface also of the pools is sometimes covered over with an ice-like sheet of stalagmite, which shoots from the sides, and sometimes forms a 575solid and firm floor when the water on which it was supported has disappeared. Sometimes the drops form a little calcareous basin, beautifully polished inside, which contains small pearl-like particles of carbonate of lime, polished by friction one against the other. The most beautiful stalactitic caves in Great Britain are those of Cheddar in Somerset, Caldy Island and Poole's Cavern at Buxton. A portion only of the carbonate of lime is thus deposited in the hollows of the rock from which it was taken; the rest is carried into the open air by the streams, in part deposited on the sides and bottom, forming tufa and the so-called petrifications, and partly being conveyed down to the sea to be ultimately secreted in the tissues of the Mollusca, Echinodermata and Foraminifera. Through these it is again collected in a solid form, and in the long course of ages it is again lifted up above the level of the water as limestone rock, and again undergoes the same series of changes. Thus the cycle of carbonate of lime is a neverending one from the land to the ocean, from the ocean to the land, and so it has been ever since the first stratum of limestone was formed out of the remains of the animals and plants of the sea. The rate of the accumulation of stalagmite in caverns is necessarily variable, since it is determined by the presence of varying currents of air. In the Ingleborough cavern a stalagmite, measured in 1839 and in 1873, is growing at the rate of .2946 in. per annum. It is obvious, therefore, that the vast antiquity of deposits containing remains of man underneath layers of stalagmite cannot be inferred from a thickness of a few inches or even of a few feet.

The intimate relation which exists between caves and ravines renders it extremely probable that many of the latter have been originally subterranean watercourses, which have been unroofed by the degradation of the rock. In all limestone districts ravines are to be found continued in the same direction as the caves, and the process of atmospheric erosion may be seen in the fallen blocks of stone which generally are to be met with at the mouths of the caverns. In illustration of this the valley and caves of Weathercote, in Yorkshire, may be quoted, or the source of the Axe at Wookey; and the ravine formed in this way has very frequently been widened out into a valley by the action of subaerial waste, or by the grinding of glaciers through it during the glacial stage of the Pleistocene period.

For further details as to the physical history of caverns we must refer the reader to the works quoted at the end of this article, by E.A. Martel, the intrepid explorer of most of the large European caves, including those of Great Britain and Ireland. The history of the *Glacières* or Ice-caves will be found in Browne's *Ice Caves in France and Switzerland*.

Classification.—The caves which have offered shelter to the *mammalia* are classified according to their contents, and are of various ages, ranging from the Pliocene to the present day. (1) Those containing the Pliocene *mammalia* belong to that age. (2) Those with the remains of the mammoth, woolly rhinoceros and other extinct species, or with paleolithic man (see ARCHAEOLOGY), are termed Pleistocene. These are sometimes called Quaternary, under the mistaken idea that they belong to an age succeeding the Tertiary period. (3) Those which contain the remains of the domestic animals in association with the remains of man either in the Neolithic, Bronze or Iron stages of civilization are termed Prehistoric. (4) The fourth group consists of those which can be brought into relation with the historic period, and are therefore termed Historic.

The Pliocene Caves.—It is a singular fact, only to be explained by the vast denudation of the earth's surface since the Pliocene Age, that only one cave referable to that age has as yet been discovered, that at Doveholes near Buxton, Derbyshire, described by Boyd Dawkins in 1903 (*Quart. Journ. Geol. Soc.*). The cave consists of a large horizontal chamber and a small passage, connected with a swallow-hole close by, and exposed in the working face of a quarry in 1901, at a depth of about 40 ft. from the surface. The locality is in the limestone plateau, 1158 ft. high, which forms the divide between the waters flowing into the Mersey on the west and the Humber on the east. Both swallow-hole and cave were completely blocked up with débris, and the latter was filled with red and yellow clay, horizontally stratified and containing pebbles of sandstone from the neighbouring ridge of Axe Edge, and bones and teeth of fossil mammals, some waterworn and others without traces of transport by water. All the mammals belong to well-known species found in the Pliocene strata of East Anglia, and in Auvergne and Italy. Among them were the sabre-toothed lion (*Machairodus crenatidens*), the hyena of Auvergne, the mastodon, and the southern elephant (*E. meridionalis*), and rhinoceros (*R. Etruscus*), and Steno's horse. Most of the bones had evidently been gnawed by hyenas and accumulated in one of their dens, and had afterwards been carried by water into the chambers deep down in the rock, where they were found. Since that time the general level of the district has been lowered by denudation to an extent of more than 230 ft., and all the hyena dens destroyed with the Pliocene surface not only in this district but generally over the world. In this case a covering of limestone some 270 ft. thick, including the depth from the present surface, protected the remains from the denuding forces.

The Pleistocene Caves.—The search after *ebur fossile* or unicorns' horn, or in other words the fossil bones which ranked high in the *materia medica* of the 16th and 17th centuries, led to the discovery of the ossiferous caverns of the Harz Mountains, and of Hungary and Franconia. The famous cave of Gailenreuth in the last of these districts was explored by Goldfuss in 1810. The bones of the hyena, lion, wolf, fox and stag, which it contained, were identified by Baron Cuvier, and some of the skulls have been proved by Busk to belong to the grizzly bear. They were associated with the bones of the reindeer, horse and bison, as well as with those of the great cave bear. These discoveries were of very great interest, because they established the fact that the above animals had lived in Germany in ancient times. The first bone cave systematically explored in England was one at Oreston near Plymouth in 1816, which proved that an extinct species of rhinoceros (*R. leptorhinus*) lived in that district. Four years later the famous hyena den at Kirkdale in Yorkshire was explored by Buckland. He brought forward proof that it had been inhabited by hyenas, and that the broken and gnawed bones of the mammoth, rhinoceros, stag, bison and horse belonged to animals which had been dragged in for food. He pointed out that all these animals had lived in Yorkshire in ancient times, and that it was impossible for the carcases of the rhinoceros, hyena and mammoth to have been floated from tropical regions into the places where he found their bones. He subsequently investigated bone caves in Derbyshire, South Wales and Somerset, as well as in Germany, and published his *Reliquiae Diluvianae* in 1822, a work which laid the foundations of the new science of cavehunting in this country. The well-known cave of Kent's Hole near Torquay furnished McEnery, between the years 1825 and 1841, with the first flint implements discovered in intimate association with the bones of extinct animals. He recognized the fact that they proved the existence of man in Devonshire while those animals were alive, but the idea was too novel to be accepted by his contemporaries. His discoveries have since been verified by the subsequent investigations carried on by Godwin Austen, and ultimately by the committee of the British Association, which worked for several years under the guidance of Pengelly. There are four distinct strata in the cave. 1st, The surface is composed of dark earth, and contains medieval remains, Roman pottery and articles which prove that it was in use during the Iron, Bronze and Neolithic Ages. 2nd, Below this is a stalagmite floor, varying in thickness from 1 to 3 ft., and covering (3rd) the red earth, which contained bones of the hyena, lion, mammoth, rhinoceros and other animals, in association with flint implements and an engraved antler, which proved man to have been an inhabitant of the cavern during the time of its deposition. 4th, Filling the bottom of the cave is a hard breccia, with the remains of bears and flint implements, in the main ruder than those found above; in some places it was no less than 12 ft. thick. The most remarkable animal found in Kent's Hole is the sabre-toothed carnivore, *Machairodus latidens* of Owen. While the value of McEnery's discoveries was in dispute the 576exploration of the cave of Brixham near Torquay in 1858 proved that man was coeval with the extinct mammalia, and in the following year additional proof was offered by the implements that were found in Wookey Hole. Similar remains have been met with in the caves explored since that time in Wales, and in England as far north as Derbyshire (Creswell), proving that palaeolithic man hunted the mammoth and rhinoceros and other extinct animals over the whole of southern and middle England.

The discoveries in Kent's Hole and in the Creswell caves prove further that palaeolithic man was in two stages of civilization—the ruder or riverdrift man, with implements of the type found in the river gravels (see ARCHAEOLOGY; and PALAEOLITHIC) being the older; and the more highly advanced, or the cave-man, mainly characterized by the better implements, and a singular facility in depicting animal life (as shown by the figure of a horse incised on the fragment of a bone found in the Creswell caves), being the newer. We may also conclude from the absence of palaeolithic implements from the glaciated regions in which most of these caves occur, that both riverdrift and cave-men dwelt in middle and northern Britain in the pre-glacial age, their remains being protected in the caverns from the denuding forces that removed all traces of their existence from the surface of the ground in glacial and post-glacial times. The riverdrift man is, however, proved to be post-glacial in southern and eastern England, by the occurrence of his implements in the river gravels of that age. Both these peoples inhabited southern England and the continent before and after the glacial period. The riverdrift man, whose implements occur in river deposits in middle and southern Europe, in Africa, Palestine and Hindustan, is everywhere in the same age of primitive barbarism, and has not as yet been identified with any living race. The cave-men are in a higher and more advanced stage, and led a life in Europe identical with that of the Eskimos in the Arctic regions.

The Pleistocene Caves of the European Continent.—The researches of Mortillet have proved that the same two groups of cave-dwellers occur in the caves of France, the older being represented by the Chelléen and Moustérien sections, and the newer by that of Solutré and La Madelaine. To the former belong the human remains found in the caverns of Spy and Neanderthal, which prove that the riverdrift man had "the most brutal of all known human skulls." To the latter we must assign all the caves and rock-shelters of Périgord, with the better implements, explored by Lartet and Christy in 1863-1864 in the valleys of the Vézère and Dordogne. These offer as vivid a picture of the life of the cave-men as that revealed of Italian manners in the 1st century by the buried cities of Herculaneum and Pompeii. The old floors of human occupation consist of broken bones of animals killed in the chase, mingled with rude implements and weapons of bone and unpolished stone, and with charcoal and burnt stones, which indicate the position of the hearths. Flakes without number, awls, lance-heads, hammers and saws made of flint rest *pêle-mêle* with bone needles, sculptured reindeer antlers, arrowheads and harpoons, and bones of the reindeer, bison, horse, ibex, Saiga antelope and musk sheep. These singular accumulations of débris mark the places where the ancient hunters lived, and are merely the refuse cast aside. The reindeer formed by far the greater portion of the food, and must have lived in enormous herds at that time in the centre of France. From this, as well as from the presence of the most arctic of the herbivores, the musk sheep, we may infer the severe climate of that portion of France at that time. Besides these animals the cave bear and lion have been met with in one, and the mammoth in five localities, and their remains bear marks of cutting or scraping which showed they fell a prey to the hunters. The most remarkable remains left behind in these refuse heaps are the sculptured reindeer antlers and figures engraved on fragments of schist and on ivory. A well-defined outline of an ox stands out boldly from one piece of antler; a second represents a reindeer kneeling down in an easy attitude with his head thrown up in the air so that the antlers rest on the shoulders, and the back forms an even surface for a handle, which is too small to be grasped by an ordinary European hand; in a third a man stands close to a horse's head, and on the other side of the same cylinder are two heads of bisons drawn with sufficient clearness to ensure recognition by any one who has seen that animal. On a fourth the natural curvature of one of the tines has been taken advantage of by the artist to engrave the head and the characteristic recurved horns of the ibex; and on a fifth horses are represented with large heads, upright dishevelled manes and shaggy ungroomed tails. The most striking figure is that of the mammoth engraved on a fragment of its own tusk; the peculiar spiral curvature of the tusk and the long mane, which are now not to be found in any living elephant, prove that the original was familiar to the eye of the artist. These drawings probably employed the idle hours of the hunter, and hand down to us the scenes which he witnessed in the chase. They are full of artistic feeling and are evidently drawn from life. The mammoth is engraved in its own ivory, and the reindeer and the stag on their respective antlers. Further researches have revealed the fact that in Auvergne and in the Pyrenees the cave-men ornamented some of their caves with incised figures and polychrome frescoes of the wild animals. Rivière has discovered on the walls of the grotto of La Mouthe (Dordogne) three large hunting scenes, one with bisons and horses, a second representing a primitive hut, a bison, reindeer, ibex and mammoth, and a third with a mammoth, hinds and horses. In the Pyrenees similar frescoes have been described by Cartailhac and Breuil. They are on the walls of the cavern and roof of Altamira, and on the walls of Marsoulas. The outlines have been engraved first, and afterwards filled in with colour in brown and red ochre and black oxide of manganese.

The cave-men ranged over middle Europe as far south as the Pyrenees and the Alps, and inhabited the caverns of Belgium and Germany, Hungary and Switzerland. Their remains have not as yet been met with in southern Europe. They lived by hunting and fishing, they were fire users, and lit up the darkness of their caves with stone lamps filled with fat (Altamira). They were clad in skins sewn together with sinews of reindeer or strips of intestines. They used huts as well as caves for habitation. They had a marvellous facility for drawing animal figures. They possessed no domestic animals, nor were they acquainted with spinning or with the potter's art. We have no evidence that they buried their dead—the interments, such as those of Aurignac, Les Eyzies and Mentone, most probably belonging to a later age.

If these remains be compared with those of existing races, it will be found that the cave-men were in the same hunter stage of civilization as the Eskimos, and that they are unlike any other races of hunters. If they were not allied to the Eskimos by blood, there can be no doubt that they handed down to the latter their art and their manner of life. The bone needles, and many of the harpoons, as well as the flint spearheads, arrowheads and scrapers, are of precisely the same form as those now in use amongst the Eskimos. The artistic designs from the caves of France, Belgium and Switzerland, are identical in plan and workmanship with those of the Eskimos, with this difference only, that the hunting scenes familiar to the Palaeolithic cave-dwellers were not the same as those familiar to the inhabitants of the shores of the Arctic Ocean. Each represented the animals which he knew, and the whale, walrus and seal were unknown to the inland dwellers of Aquitaine, just as the mammoth, bison and wild horse are unknown to the Eskimos. The reindeer, which they both knew, is represented in the same way by both. The practice of accumulating large quantities of the bones of animals round their dwelling-places, and the habit of splitting the bones for the sake of the marrow, are the same in both. The hides were prepared with the same sort of instruments, and the needles with which they were sewn together are of the same pattern. The stone lamps were used by both. In both there was the same disregard of sepulture. All these facts can hardly be mere coincidences caused by both peoples leading a savage life under similar conditions. The conclusion, therefore, seems inevitable that, so far as we have any evidence of the race to which the cave-dwellers belong, that evidence points only in the direction of the Eskimos. It is to a considerable extent confirmed by a consideration of the animals found in the caves. The reindeer and musk sheep afford food to the Eskimos now in the Arctic Circle, just as they afforded it to the cave-men in Europe; and both these animals have been traced by their remains from the Pyrenees to the north-east through Europe and Asia as far as the very regions in which they now live. The mammoth and bison also have been tracked by their remains in the frozen river gravels and morasses through Siberia as far as the American side of Bering Strait. Palaeolithic man appeared in Europe with the arctic mammalia, lived in Europe with them, and in all human probability retreated to the north-east along with them.

There are refuse heaps in north-eastern Siberia containing the remains of the mammoth and woolly rhinoceros as well as the reindeer and musk sheep, which may be referred with equal justice to the cave-men or to the Eskimos.

Ancient Geography of Europe.—The remains of man and the animals described in the preceding paragraphs have been introduced into the caves either by man or the wild beasts, or by streams of water, which may or may not now occupy their ancient courses; and the fact that the same species are to be met with in the caves of France, Switzerland and Britain implies that our island formed part of the continent, and that there were no physical barriers to prevent their migration from the Alps as far to the north-west as Ireland.

The same conclusion may be gathered from the exploration of caves in the south of Europe, which has resulted in the discovery of African species, in Gibraltar, Sicily and Malta. In the first of these the spotted hyena, the serval and Kaffre cat lie side by side with the horse, grizzly bear and slender rhinoceros (R. *leptorhinus*)—see Falconer's*Palaeontographical Memoirs.* To these African animals inhabiting the Iberian peninsula in the Pleistocene age, Lartet has added the African elephant and striped hyena, found in a stratum of gravel near Madrid, along with flint implements. The hippopotamus, spotted hyena and African elephant occur in the caves of Sicily, and imply that in ancient times there was a continuity of land between that spot and Africa, just as the presence of the *Elephas antiquus* proves the non-existence of the Straits of Messina during a portion, to say the least, of the Pleistocene age. A small species of hippopotamus (*H. Pentlandi*) occurs in incredible abundance in the Sicilian caves. It has also been found in those of Malta along with an extinct pigmy elephant species (*E. Melitensis*). It has also been discovered in Candia and in the Peloponnese. For these animals to have found their way to these regions, a continuity of land is necessary. The view advanced by Dr Falconer and Admiral Spratt, that Europe was formerly connected with Africa by a bridge of land extending southwards from Sicily, is fully borne out by these considerations. The present physical geography of the Mediterranean has been produced by a depression of land to the amount of about 400 fathoms, by which the Sicilo-African and Ibero-African barriers have been submerged, and Crete and Malta separated from the South-European continent. It is extremely probable that this submergence took place at the same time that the adjoining sea-bottom was elevated to about the same amount so as to constitute that region now known as the Sahara.

Pleistocene Caves of the Americas and Australia.—The Pleistocene caverns of the Euro-Asiatic continent contain the progenitors of the animals now alive in some parts of the Old World, the extinct forms being closely allied to those now living in the same geographical provinces. Those of Brazil and of Pennsylvania present us with animals whose nearest analogues are to be found in North and South America, such as sloths, armadillos and agoutis. Those, again, of Australia present us with marsupials (*metatheria*) only, allied to, or identical with, those of that most ancient continent. The extinct forms in each case are mainly those of the larger animals, which, from their large size, and low fecundity, would be specially liable to be beaten in the battle for life by their smaller and more fertile contemporaries, and less likely to survive those changes in their environment which have undoubtedly taken place in the long lapse of ages. It is, therefore, certain that the mammalian life in the Old, New and Australian worlds, was as well marked out into geographical provinces in the Pleistocene age as at the present time, and that it has been continuous in these areas from that remote time to the present day.

Prehistoric Caves of Neolithic Age in Europe.—The prehistoric caves are distinguished from Pleistocene by their containing the remains of domestic animals, and by the wild animals to which they have afforded shelter belonging to living species. They are divisible into three groups according to the traces of man which occur in them—into the Neolithic, Bronze and Iron Ages.

The Neolithic caves are widely spread throughout Europe, and have been used as the habitations and tombs of the early races who invaded Europe from the East with their flocks and herds. The first of these systematically explored was at Perthi Chwareu, near the village of Llandegla, Denbighshire, in 1869. In the following years five others were discovered close by, as well as a second group in the neighbourhood of Cefn on the banks of the Elwy. They contained polished celts, flint flakes, rude pottery and human skeletons, along with the broken bones of the pig, dog, horse, Celtic shorthorn and goat. The remains of the wild animals belong to the wolf, fox, badger, bear, wild boar, stag, roe, hare and rabbit. Most of the bones were broken or cut, and the whole group was obviously an accumulation which resulted from these caves having been used as dwellings. They had subsequently been used for burial. The human skeletons in them were of all ages, from infancy to old age; and the interments had been successive until each became filled. The bodies were buried in the contracted posture which is so characteristic of Neolithic interments generally. The men to whom these skeletons belonged were a short race, the tallest being about 5 ft. 6 in., and the shortest 4 ft. 10 in.; their skulls are orthognathic, or not presenting jaws advancing beyond a vertical line dropped from the forehead, in shape long or oval, and of fair average capacity. The face was oval, and the cheek bones were not prominent. Some of the individuals were characterized by a peculiar flattening of the shinbone (platycnemism), which probably stood in relation to the free action of the foot that was not hampered by the use of a rigid sole or sandal. This, however, cannot be looked upon as a race character, or as a tendency towards a simian type of leg. These Neolithic cave-dwellers have been proved to be identical in physique with the builders of the cairns and tumuli which lie scattered over the face of Great Britain and Ireland. (See Thurnam, *Crania Britannica*.) They have also been met with abundantly in France. In the Caverne de l'Homme Mort, for example, in the department of Lozère, explored in 1871, the association of remains was of precisely the same nature as those mentioned above, and the human skeletons were of the same small type. The same class of remains has also been discovered in Gibraltar, in the caves of Windmill Hill, and some others. The human remains examined by Busk are of precisely the same type as those of Denbighshire. In the work of Don Manuel Gongora J. Martinez (*Antiguedades prehistoricas de Andalusia*, 1868), several interments are described in the cave of Murcielagos, which penetrates the limestone out of which the grand scenery of the southern Sierra Nevada has been to a great extent carved. In one place a group of three skeletons was met with, one of which was adorned with a plain coronet of gold, and clad in a tunic made of esparto grass finely plaited, so as to form a pattern like that on some of the gold ornaments in Etruscan tombs. In a second spot farther within, twelve skeletons formed a semicircle round one covered with a tunic of skin, and wearing a necklace of esparto grass, ear-rings of black stone, and ornaments of shell and wild boar tusk. There were other articles of plaited esparto grass, such as baskets and sandals. There were also flint flakes, polished-stone axes, implements of bone and wood, together with pottery of the same type as that from Gibraltar. The same class of remains was discovered in the Woman's Cave, near Alhama de Granada. From the physical identity of the human remains in all these cases it maybe inferred that in the Neolithic Age a long-headed, 578small race inhabited the Iberian peninsula, extending through France, as far north as Britain, and to the north-west as far as Ireland—a race considered by Professor Busk "to be at the present day represented by at any rate a part of the population now inhabiting the Basque provinces." This identification of the ancient Neolithic cave-dwellers with the modern Basque-speaking inhabitant of the western Pyrenees is corroborated by the elaborate researches of Broca, Virchow and Thurnam on modern Basque skulls. It may, therefore, be concluded that in the Neolithic Age an Iberian population occupied the whole of the area mentioned above, inhabiting caves and burying their dead in caves and chambered tombs, and possessed of the same habits of life. The remains of the same small, oval-featured, long-headed race have been found in Belgium in the cave of Chauvaux, and they have been described by Sergi in southern Europe under the name of the Mediterranean race.

There is no evidence that any other race except the Iberic buried their dead in the caves of Britain in the Neolithic Age. In Belgium, however, the exploration of the cave of Sclaigneaux by Soreil proves that broad-headed men of the type defined by Huxley and Thurnam as brachycephalic, and characterized by high cheek-bones, projecting muscles and large stature, the average height being 5 ft. 8.4 in. (Thurnam), inhabited and buried their dead in the caves of that region. In France they occur in the sepulchral cave of Orrouy (Oise) in association with those of the Iberic type. They have also been met with in Gibraltar. This type is undistinguishable from the Celtic (Goidelic) or Gaulish, found so abundantly in the chambered tombs of the Neolithic Age in France. Both these ancient races are represented at the present day by the Basques and Aquitanians of France and Spain, and by the Celts or Gauls of France, Britain and the Mediterranean border of Spain, their relative antiquity being proved by an appeal to their history and geographical distribution. For just as the earliest records show that the Iberic power extended as far north as the Loire, and as far east as the Rhone, so we have proof of the gradual retrocession of the Iberic frontier southwards, under the attacks of the successive Celtic hordes, until ultimately we find the latter in possession of a considerable part of southern Spain, forming by their union with the conquered the powerful nation of Celt-Iberi. The Iberians were in possession of the continent before they were dispossessed by the Goidels, and at a later time by the Brythons. They are recognized by Tacitus in Britain in the Silures of Wales; and they are still to be seen in the small, dark, lithe inhabitants of North Wales. The discovery of the characteristic skulls of both these races in the same family vault in the cave of Gop near Prestatyn, Flintshire, proves that the two races were mingled together in Britain as far back as the Bronze Age.

From the present distribution of this non-Aryan race it is obvious that they were gradually pushed back westward by the advance of tribes coming from the East, and following those routes which were subsequently taken by the Low and High Germans.

The exploration of the Grotta dei Colombi, in the island of Palmaria, overlooking the Gulf of Spezzia, in 1873, proves that the stories scattered through the classical writers, that the caves on the Mediterranean shores were inhabited by cannibals, are not altogether without foundation. In it broken and cut bones of children and young adults were found along with those of the goat, hog, fox, wolf, wild-cat, flint flakes, bone implements and shells perforated for suspension.

Prehistoric Caves of Bronze and Iron Ages.—The extreme rarity of articles of bronze in the European caves implies that they were rarely used by the Bronze folk for habitation or burial. Bronze weapons mingled with gold ornaments have, however, been discovered in the Heatheryburn cave near Stanhope, Durham, as well as in those of Kirkhead in Cartmell, in Thor's cave in Staffordshire, and the Cat Hole in Gower in Glamorganshire. In the Iberian peninsula the cave of Cesareda, explored by Signor Delgado, in the valley of the Tagus, contained bronze articles, associated with broken and cut human bones, as well as those of domestic animals, rendering it probable that cannibalism was practised in early times in that region. Busk believes, however, that the facts are insufficient to support the charge of cannibalism against the ancient Portuguese.

Caves containing articles of iron, and therefore belonging to that division of the prehistoric age, are so unimportant that they do not deserve notice in this place. As man increased in civilization he preferred to live in houses of his own building, and he no longer buried his dead in the natural sepulchres provided for him in the rock.

Prehistoric caves have been rarely explored in extra-European areas. Among those which abound in Palestine, one in Mount Lebanon, examined by Canon Tristram, contained flint implements along with charcoal and broken bones and teeth, some of which may be referred to a small ox, undistinguishable from the small short-horn, *Bos longifrons*. In North America the remains found by F.W. Putnam in the caves of Kentucky, consisting of moccasins, rudely-plaited cloth, and other articles, may be referred to the same division.

Historic Caves in Britain.—The historic caves have only attracted notice in fairly recent years, and in Britain alone, principally through the labours of the Settle Cave Committee from the year 1869 to the present day. To them is due the exploration of the Victoria cave, which had been discovered and partially investigated as early as the year 1838. It consists of three large ill-defined chambers opening on the face of the cliff, 1450 ft. above the sea, and filled with debris very nearly up to the roof. It presented three distinct eras of occupation— one by hyenas, which dragged into it rhinoceroses, bisons, mammoths, horses, reindeer and bears. This was defined from the next occupation, which is probably of the Neolithic Age, by a layer of grey clay, on the surface of which rested a bone harpoon and a few flint flakes and bones. Then after an interval of débris at the entrance was a layer of charcoal, broken bones, fragments of old hearths, and numerous instruments of savage life associated with broken pottery, Roman coins, and the rude British imitations of them, various articles of iron, and elaborate personal ornaments, which implied a considerable development of the arts. The evidence of the coins stamps the date of the occupation of the cave to be between the first half of the 5th century and the English conquest. Some of the brooches present a peculiar flamboyant and spiral pattern in relief, of the same character as the art of some of the illuminated manuscripts, as for example one of the Anglo-Saxon gospels at Stockholm, and of the gospels of St Columban in Trinity College, Dublin. It is mostly allied to that work which is termed by Franks late Celtic. From its localization in Britain and Ireland, it seems to be probable that it is of Celtic derivation; and if this view be accepted, there is nothing at all extraordinary in its being recognized in the illuminated Irish gospels. Ireland, in the 6th and 7th centuries, was the great centre of art, civilization and literature; and it is only reasonable to suppose that there would be intercourse between the Irish Christians and those of the west of Britain, during the time that the Romano-Celts, or Brit-Welsh, were being slowly pushed westwards by the heathen English invader. Proof of such an intercourse we find in the brief notice of the *Annales Cambriae*, in which Gildas, the Brit-Welsh historian, is stated to have sailed over to Ireland in the year A.D. 565. It is by no means improbable that about this time there was a Brit-Welsh migration into Ireland, as well as into Brittany. Objects with these designs found in Germany are probably directly or indirectly due to the Irish missionaries, who spread Christianity through those regions. The early Christian art in Ireland grew out of the late Celtic, and is to a great extent free from the influence of Rome, which is stamped on the Brit-Welsh art of the same age in this country.

Several other ornaments with enamel deserve especial notice. The enamel, composed of red, blue and yellow, has been inserted into the hollows in the bronze, and then heated so as to form a close union with it. They are of the same design as those which have been met with in late Roman tumuli in this country, and in places which are mainly in the north. They all belong to a class named late Celtic by Franks, and are considered by him to be of British manufacture. This view is supported by the only 579reference to the art of enamelling furnished by the classical writers. Philostratus, a Greek sophist in the court of Julia Domna, the wife of the emperor Severus, writes, "It is said that the barbarians living in the ocean pour these colours (those of horse-trappings) on heated bronze, and that these adhere, grow as hard as stone, and preserve the designs that are made in them." It is worthy of remark that, since the emperor Severus built the wall which bears his name, marched in person against the Caledonians, and died at York, the account of the enamels may have reached Philostratus from the very district in which the Victoria Cave is situated.

Associated with these were bronze ornaments inlaid with silver, and miscellaneous iron articles, among which was a Roman key. Remains of this kind have been met with in the Albert and Kelko caves in the neighbourhood, in that of Dowkerbottom near Arncliffe, in that of Kirkhead on the northern shore of Morecambe Bay, in Poole's Cavern near Buxton, and in Thor's Cave near Ashbourne, and over a wide area ranging from Yorkshire and the Lake district southwards into Somerset and Devon.

List of Principal Animals and Objects found in Brit-Welsh Strata in Caves.

Animals.	Victoria.	Kelko.	Dowker-bottom.	Kirk-head.	Poole's-Cavern.	Thor's-Cave.	
DOMESTIC—							
Canis familiaris. Dog	×		×		×	?	
Sus scrofa. Pig	×		×		×	?	
Equus caballus. Horse	×		×		×	?	
Bos longifrons. Celtic short-horn	×		×		×	?	
Capra hircus. Goat	×		×		×	?	
WILD—							
Canis vulpes. Fox	×		×		×	?	
Meles taxus. Badger	×		×		·	×	

Cervus elaphus. Stag	×	×	×	?
Cervus capreolus. Roe	×	×	·	?
Roman coins, or imitations	×	×	×	×
Enamelled ornaments, in bronze	×	×	·	
Bronze ornaments, inlaid with silver	×	×	×	·
Iron articles	×	×	×	×
Samian ware	×	×	×	×
Black ware	×	×	×	×
Bone spoon fibulae	×	×	·	·
Bone combs	×	×	·	×

It is obvious in all these cases that men accustomed to luxury and refinement were compelled, by the pressure of some great calamity, to flee for refuge to caves with whatever they could transport thither of their property. The number of spindle-whorls and personal ornaments imply that they were accompanied by their families. We may also infer that they were cut off from the civilization to which they had been accustomed, because in some cases they extemporized spindle-whorls out of fragments of Samian ware, instead of using those which were expressly manufactured for the purpose. Why the caves were inhabited is satisfactorily explained by an appeal to contemporary history. In the pages of Gildas, in the *Anglo-Saxon Chronicle*, and in the *Annales Cambriae*, we have a graphic picture of that long war of invasion by which the inhabitants of the old Roman province of Britannia were driven back by the Jutes, Angles and Saxons, who crossed over with their families and household stuff. Slowly, and in the chances of a war which extended through three centuries, they were gradually pushed back into Cumberland, Wales and West Somerset, Devon and Cornwall. While this war was going on the coinage became debased and Roman coins afforded the patterns for the small bronze minimi, which are to be met with equally in these caves and in the ruins of Roman cities. As the tide of war rolled to the west, the English tongue and, until towards the close of the struggle, the worship of Thor and Odin supplanted the British tongue and the Christian faith, and a rude barbarism replaced what was left of the Roman civilization in the island. It is to this period that relics of this kind in the caves must be assigned. They are traces of the anarchy of those times, and complete the picture of the desolation of Britain, revealed by the ashes of the cities and villas that were burnt by the invader. They prove that the vivid account given by Gildas of the straits to which his countrymen were reduced was literally true.

The shrines of Zeus in the Idaean and Dictaean caves have been explored by Halbher and Orsi (*Antichità dell' antro de Zeus Ideo*) and by Arthur Evans and Hogarth (*Journal of Hellenic Studies*). These discoveries prove that the cult of Zeus began among the Mycenaean peoples some 2000 years B.C. according to Evans, and was practised far down into the later Greek times. They show that the Greeks are indebted to the Mycenaean peoples not only for their art, but for the chief of their divinities.

AUTHORITIES.—1. Britain: Boyd Dawkins, *Cave-hunting* (1874); *Early Man* (1880); Mattel, *Irlande et cavernes anglaises* (1897); Buckland, *Reliquiae Diluvianae* (1821); *Brit. Assoc. Reports* (1860-1875); *Journ. Anthrop. Inst.* (1870-1876); *Quart. Geol. Journ.* (1860-1875); Pengelly, *Trans. Devonshire Association.* 2. The European Continent: Martel, *Les Abîmes* (1894);

Cartailhac and Breuil, *L'Anthropologie*, xv., xvi.; Lartet and Christy, *Reliquiae Aquitanicae; Internat. Congress of Prehistoric Archaeology*; Marcel de Serres, *Les Ossemens fossiles de Lunel Viel*; Dupont, *L'Homme pendant les âges de la pierre dans les environs de Dinant-sur-Meuse*; Schmerling,*Recherches sur les ossemens fossiles découverts dans les cavernes de Liége*; Merk,*Excavations at Kesserloch*, transl. J.E. Lee (1876). For the chief American caves, seeLURAY CAVERN, MAMMOTH CAVE, WYANDOTTE CAVE, COLOSSAL CAVERN, JACOB'S CAVERN.

(W. B. D.)

CAVEA, the Latin name given to the subterranean cells in which the wild beasts were confined prior to the combats in the Roman arena. The term is sometimes applied to the amphitheatre (*q.v.*) itself.

CAVEAT (Latin for "let him beware," from *cavere*), in law, a notice given by the party interested (caveator) to the proper officer of a court of justice to prevent the taking of a certain step without warning. It is entered in connexion with dealings in land registered in the land registry, with the grant of marriage licences, to prevent the issuing of a lunacy commission, to stay the probate of a will, letters of administration, &c. Caveat is also a term used in United States patent law (see PATENTS).

Caveat emptor ("let the buyer beware") is a maxim which implies that the responsibility for making a bad bargain over a purchase rests on the purchaser. In an ordinary contract for the sale of goods, there is no implied warranty or condition as to the quality or fitness for any particular purpose of the goods supplied, with certain exceptions, and, therefore, the buyer takes at his own risk. The maxim does not apply (a) where the buyer, expressly or by implication, makes known to the seller the particular purpose for which the goods are required, so as to show that the buyer relies on the seller's skill or judgment, and that the goods are of a description which it is in the course of the seller's business to supply; (b) where goods are bought by description from a seller who deals in goods of that description, for there is an implied condition that the goods are of merchantable quality, though if the buyer has actually examined the goods, there is no implied condition as regards defects which the examination ought to have revealed; (c) where the usage of trade annexes an implied warranty or condition to the goods as to their quality or fitness for a particular purpose. The maxim of *caveat emptor* is said to owe its origin to the fact that in early times sales of goods took place principally in market overt. (See further SALE OF GOODS.)

CAVEDONE, JACOPO (1577-1660), Italian painter, born at Sassuolo in the Modenese, was educated in the school of the Caracci, and under them painted in the churches of Bologna. His principal works are the "Adoration of the Magi," the "Four Doctors," and the "Last Supper"; and more especially the "Virgin and Child in Glory," with San Petronio and other saints, painted in 1614, and now in the Bolognese Academy. Cavedone became an assistant to Guido Reni in Rome; his art was generally of a subdued undemonstrative character, with rich Titianesque colouring. In his declining years his energies broke down after his wife had been accused of witchcraft, and after the death of a cherished son. He died in extreme poverty, in a stable at Bologna.

CAVENDISH, GEORGE (1500-1562?), English writer, the biographer of Cardinal Wolsey, was the elder son of Thomas 580Cavendish, clerk of the pipe in the exchequer, and his wife, Alice Smith of Padbrook Hall. He was probably born at his father's manor of Cavendish, in Suffolk. Later the family resided in London, in the parish of St Alban's, Wood Street, where Thomas Cavendish died in 1524. Shortly after this event George married Margery Kemp, of Spains Hall, an heiress, and the niece of Sir Thomas More. About 1527 he entered the service of Cardinal Wolsey as gentleman-usher, and for the next three years he was divided from his wife, children and estates, in the closest personal attendance on the great man. Cavendish was wholly devoted to Wolsey's interests, and also he saw in this appointment an opportunity to gratify his master-passion, a craving "to see and be acquainted with strangers, in especial with men in honour and authority." He was faithful to his master in disgrace, and showed the courage of the "loyal servitor." It is plain that he enjoyed Wolsey's closest confidence to the end, for after the cardinal's death George Cavendish was called before the privy council and closely examined as to Wolsey's latest acts and words. He gave his evidence so clearly and with so much natural dignity, that he won the applause of the hostile council, and the praise of being "a just and diligent servant." He was not allowed to suffer in pocket by his fidelity to his master, but retired, as it would seem, a wealthy man to his estate of Glemsford, in West Suffolk, in 1530. He was only thirty years of age, but his appetite for being acquainted with strange acts and persons was apparently sated, for we do not hear of his engaging in any more adventures. It is not to be doubted that Cavendish had taken down notes of Wolsey's conversation and movements, for many years passed before his biography was composed. At length, in 1557, he wrote it out in its final form. It was not, however, possible to publish it in the author's lifetime, but it was widely circulated in MS. Evidently one of these MSS. fell into Shakespeare's hands, for that poet made use of it in his *King Henry VIII.*, although it is excessive to say, as Singer has done, that Shakespeare "merely put Cavendish's language into verse." The book was first printed in 1641, in a garbled text, and under the title of *The Negotiations of Thomas Wolsey*. The genuine text, from contemporary MSS., was given to the world in 1810, and more fully in 1815. Until that time it was believed that the book was the composition of George Cavendish's younger brother William, the founder of Chatsworth, who also was attached to Wolsey. Joseph Hunter proved this to be impossible, and definitely asserted the claim of George. The latter is believed to have died at Glemsford in or about 1562. The intrinsic value of Cavendish's *Life of Cardinal Wolsey* has long been perceived, for it is the sole authentic record of a multitude of events highly important in a particularly interesting section of the history of England. Its importance as a product of biographical literature was first emphasized by Bishop Creighton, who insisted over and over again on the claim of Cavendish to be recognized as the earliest of the great English biographers and an individual writer of particular charm and originality. He writes with simplicity and with a certain vivid picturesqueness, rarely yielding to the rhetorical impulses which governed the ordinary prose of his age.

(E. G.)

CAVENDISH, HENRY (1731-1810), English chemist and physicist, elder son of Lord Charles Cavendish, brother of the 3rd duke of Devonshire, and Lady Anne Grey, daughter of the duke of Kent, was born at Nice in October 1731. He was sent to school at Hackney in 1742, and in 1749 entered Peterhouse, Cambridge, which he left in 1753, without taking a degree. Until he was about forty he seems to have enjoyed a very moderate allowance from his father, but in the latter part of his life he was left a fortune which made him one of the richest men of his time. He lived principally at Clapham Common, but he had also a town-house in Bloomsbury, while his library was in a house in Dean Street, Soho; and there he used to attend on appointed days to lend the books to men who were properly vouched for. So methodical was he that he never took down a volume for his own use without entering it in the loan-book. He was a regular attendant at the meetings of the Royal Society, of which he became a fellow in 1760, and he dined every Thursday with the club composed of its members. Otherwise he had little intercourse with society; indeed, his chief object in life seems to have been to avoid the attention of his fellows. With his relatives he had little intercourse, and even Lord George Cavendish, whom he made his principal heir, he saw only for a few minutes once a year. His dinner was ordered daily by a note placed on the hall-table, and his women servants were instructed to keep out of his sight on pain of dismissal. In person he was tall and rather thin; his dress was old-fashioned and singularly uniform, and was inclined to be shabby about the times when the precisely arranged visits of his tailor were due. He had a slight hesitation in his speech, and his air of timidity and reserve was almost ludicrous. He was never married. He died at Clapham on the 24th of February 1810, leaving funded property worth £700,000, and a landed estate of £8000 a year, together with canal and other property, and £50,000 at his bankers.

Cavendish's scientific work is distinguished for the wideness of its range and for its extraordinary exactness and accuracy. The papers he himself published form an incomplete record of his researches, for many of the results he obtained only became generally known years after his death; yet in spite of the absence of anything approaching self-advertisement he acquired a very high reputation within his own country and abroad, recognized by the Institute of France in 1803 when it chose him as one of its eight foreign associates. Arsenic formed the subject of his first recorded investigation, on which he was engaged at least as early as 1764, and in 1766 he began those communications to the Royal Society on the chemistry of gases, which are among his chief titles to fame. The first (*Phil. Trans.*, 1766) consists of "Three papers containing experiments on Factitious Airs," dealing mostly with "inflammable air" (hydrogen), which he was the first to recognize as a distinct substance, and "fixed air" (carbon dioxide). He determined the specific gravity of these gases with reference to common air, investigated the extent to which they are absorbed by various liquids, and noted that common air containing one part in nine by volume of fixed air is no longer able to support combustion, and that the air produced by fermentation and putrefaction has properties identical with those of fixed air obtained from marble. In the following year he published a paper on the analysis of one of the London pump-waters (from Rathbone Place, Oxford Street), which is closely connected with the memoirs just mentioned, since it shows that the calcareous matter in that water is held in solution by the "fixed air" present and can be precipitated by lime. Electrical studies seem next to have engaged his attention, and in 1771 and 1772 he read to the Royal Society his "Attempt to explain some of the principal phenomena of electricity by an elastic fluid," which was followed in 1775 by an "Attempt to imitate the effects of the Torpedo (a fish allied to the ray)" (*Phil. Trans.*, 1776). But these two memoirs contain only a part of the electrical researches he carried out between 1771 and 1781, and many more were found after his death in a number of sealed packets of papers. The contents of these for a long time remained unknown, but ultimately by permission of the duke of Devonshire, to whom they belonged, they were edited by James Clerk Maxwell and published in 1879 by the Cambridge University Press as the *Electrical Researches of the Hon. Henry Cavendish*. About 1777 or 1778 he resumed his pneumatic inquiries, though he published nothing on the subject till 1783. In that year he described a new eudiometer to the Royal Society and detailed observations he had made to determine whether or not the atmosphere is constant in composition; after testing the air on nearly 60 different days in 1781 he could find in the proportion of oxygen no difference of which he could be sure, nor could he detect any sensible variation at different places. Two papers on "Experiments with Airs," printed in the *Phil. Trans.* for 1784 and 1785, contain his great discoveries of the compound nature of water and the composition of nitric acid. Starting from an experiment, narrated by Priestley, in which John Warltire fired a mixture of common air and hydrogen by electricity, with the result that there was a diminution of volume and a deposition of moisture,581Cavendish burnt about two parts of hydrogen with five of common air, and noticed that almost all the hydrogen and about one-fifth of the common air lost their elasticity and were condensed into a dew which lined the inside of the vessel employed. This dew he judged to be pure water. In another experiment he fired, by the electric spark, a mixture of hydrogen and oxygen (dephlogisticated air), and found that the resulting water contained nitric acid, which he argued must be due to the nitrogen present as an impurity in the oxygen ("phlogisticated air with which it [the dephlogisticated air] is debased"). In the 1785 paper he proved the correctness of this supposition by showing that when electric sparks are passed through common air there is a shrinkage of volume owing to the nitrogen uniting with the oxygen to form nitric acid. Further, remarking that little was known of the phlogisticated part of our atmosphere, and thinking it might fairly be doubted "whether there are not in reality many different substances confounded together by us under the name of phlogisticated air," he made an experiment to determine whether the whole of a given portion of nitrogen (phlogisticated air) of the atmosphere could be reduced to nitric acid. He found that a small fraction, not more than 1/120 th part, resisted the change, and in this residue he doubtless had a sample of the inert gas argon which was only recognized as a distinct entity more than a hundred years later. His last chemical paper, published in 1788, on the "Conversion of a mixture of dephlogisticated and phlogisticated air into nitrous acid by the electric spark," describes measures he took to authenticate the truth of the experiment described in the 1785 paper, which had "since been tried by persons of distinguished ability in such pursuits without success." It may be noted here that, while Cavendish adhered to the phlogistic doctrine, he did not hold it with anything like the tenacity that characterized Priestley; thus, in his 1784 paper on "Experiments on Air," he remarks that not only the experiments he is describing, but also "most other phenomena of nature seem explicable as well, or nearly as well," upon the Lavoisierian view as upon the commonly believed principle of phlogiston, and he goes on to give an explanation in terms of the antiphlogistic hypothesis.

Early in his career Cavendish took up the study of heat, and had he promptly published his results he might have anticipated Joseph Black as the discoverer of latent heat and of specific heat. But he made no reference to his work till 1783, when he presented to the Royal Society some "Observations on Mr Hutchins's experiments for determining the degree of cold at which quicksilver freezes." This paper, with others published in 1786 and 1788, is concerned with the phenomena attending the freezing of various substances, and is noteworthy because in it he expresses doubt of the supposition that "the heat of bodies is owing to their containing more or less of a substance called the matter of heat," and inclines to Newton's opinion that it "consists in the internal motion of the particles of bodies." His "Account of the Meteorological Apparatus used at the Royal Society's House" (*Phil. Trans.*, 1776) contains remarks on the precautions necessary in making and using thermometers, a subject which is continued in the following year in a report signed by him and six others.

Cavendish's last great achievement was his famous series of experiments to determine the density of the earth (*Phil. Trans.*, 1798). The apparatus he employed was devised by the Rev. John Michell, though he had the most important parts reconstructed to his own designs; it depended on measuring the attraction exercised on a horizontal bar, suspended by a vertical wire and bearing a small lead ball at each end, by two large masses of lead. (SeeGRAVITATION.) The figure he gives for the specific gravity of the earth is 5.48, water being 1, but in fact the mean of the 29 results he records works out at 5.448. Other publications of his later years dealt with the height of an aurora seen in 1784 (*Phil. Trans.*, 1790), the civil year of the Hindus (*Id.*, 1792), and an improved method of graduating astronomical instruments (*Id.*, 1809). Cavendish also had a taste for geology, and made several tours in England for the purpose of gratifying it.

A life by George Wilson (1818-1859), printed for the Cavendish Society in 1851, contains an account of his writings, both published and unpublished, together with a critical inquiry into the claims of all the alleged discoverers of the composition of water. Some of his instruments are preserved in the Royal Institution, London, and his name is commemorated in the Cavendish Physical Laboratory at Cambridge, which was built by his kinsman the 7th duke of Devonshire.

CAVENDISH [CANDISH], **THOMAS** (1555?-1592), the third circumnavigator of the globe, was born at Trimley St Martin, Suffolk. On quitting Corpus Christi College, Cambridge (without a degree), he almost ruined himself by his extravagance as a courtier. To repair his fortune he turned to maritime and colonial enterprise, and in 1585 accompanied Sir Richard Grenville to America. Soon returning to England, he undertook an elaborate imitation of Drake's great voyage. On the 21st of July 1586, he sailed from Plymouth with 123 men in three vessels, only one of which (the "Desire," of 140 tons) came home. By way of Sierra Leone, the Cape Verde Islands and C. Frio in Brazil, he coasted down to Patagonia (where he discovered "Port Desire," his only important contribution to knowledge), and passing through Magellan's Straits, fell upon the Spanish settlements and shipping on the west coast of South and Central America and of Mexico. Among his prizes were nineteen vessels of worth, and especially the treasure-galleon, the "Great St Anne," which he captured off Cape St Lucas, the southern extremity of California (November 14, 1587). After this success he struck across the Pacific for home; touched at the Ladrones, Philippines, Moluccas and Java; rounded the Cape of Good Hope; and arrived again at Plymouth (September 9-10, 1588), having circumnavigated the globe in two years and fifty days. It is said that his sailors were clothed in silk, his sails were damask, and his top-mast covered with cloth of gold. Yet by 1591 he was again in difficulties, and planned a fresh American and Pacific venture. John Davis (*q.v.*) accompanied him, but the voyage (undertaken with five vessels) was an utter failure, much of the fault lying with Cavendish himself, who falsely accused Davis, with his last breath, of deserting him (May 20, 1592). He died and was buried at sea, on the way home, in the summer of 1592.

See Hakluyt's *Principal Navigations*, (a) edition of 1589, p. 809 (N.H.'s narrative of the voyage of 1586-1588); (b) edition of 1599-1600, vol. iii. pp. 803-825 (Francis Pretty's narrative of the same); (c) edition of 1599-1600, vol. iii. pp. 251-253 (on the venture of 1585); (d) edition of 1599-1600, vol. iii. pp. 845-852 (John Lane's narrative of the last voyage, of 1591-1592); also *Stationers' Registers* (Arber), vol. ii. pp. 505-509; the Molyneux Globe of 1592, in the library of the Middle Temple, London, and the Ballads in *Biog. Brit.*, vol. i. p. 1196.

CAVENDISH, SIR WILLIAM (c. 1505-1557), founder of the English noble house of Cavendish, was the younger brother of George Cavendish (*q.v.*). His father, Thomas, was a descendant of Sir John Cavendish, the judge, who in 1381 was murdered by Jack Straw's insurgent peasants at Bury St Edmunds. Of William's education nothing seems known, but in 1530 he was appointed one of the commissioners for visiting monasteries; he worked directly under Thomas Cromwell, whom he calls "master" and to whom many of his extant letters are addressed. In 1541 he was auditor of the court of augmentations, in 1546 treasurer of the king's chamber, and was knighted and sworn of the privy council. Under Edward VI. and Mary he continued in favour at court; during the latter's reign he partially conformed, but on the occasion of the war with France he with other Derbyshire gentlemen refused the loan of £100 demanded by the queen. He died in 1557. Cavendish acquired large properties from the spoils of the monasteries, but in accordance with the wish of his third wife Elizabeth he sold them to purchase land in Derbyshire. This wife was the celebrated "building Bess of Hardwick," daughter of John Hardwicke, of Hardwicke, Derbyshire; she completed the original building of Chatsworth House,—begun in 1553 by her husband,—of which nothing now remains. Her fourth husband was George Talbot, 6th earl of Shrewsbury. By her Cavendish had six children; an elder son who died without issue; William, who in 1618 was created earl of Devonshire; Charles, whose son William became 1st duke of Newcastle; 582Frances, who married Sir Henry Pierpont, was the ancestress of the dukes of Kingston; Elizabeth, who married Charles Stuart, earl of Lennox, and was the mother of Arabella Stuart; and Mary, who married Gilbert Talbot, 7th earl of Shrewsbury.

CAVETTO (Ital. diminutive of *cavo*, hollow), in architecture, the term given to a hollow concave moulding sometimes employed in the place of the cymatium of a cornice, as in that of the Doric order of the theatre of Marcellus. It forms the crowning feature of the Egyptian temples, and took the place of the cymatium in many of the Etruscan temples.

CAVIARE, or CAVIAR, the roe of various species of *Acipenser* or sturgeon (*q.v.*), prepared, in several qualities, as an article of food. The word is common to most European languages and supposed to be of Turk or Tatar origin, but the Turk word *khavyah* is probably derived from the Ital. *caviale*; the word does not appear in Russian. The best caviare, which can only be made in winter and is difficult to preserve, is the loosely granulated, almost liquid, kind, known in Russia as *ikra*. It is prepared by beating the ovaries and straining through a sieve to clear the eggs of the membranes, fibres and fatty matter; it is then salted with from 4-6% of salt. The difficulty of preparation and of transport has made it a table delicacy in western Europe, where it has been known since the 16th century, as is evidenced by Hamlet's "His play ... pleased not the million, 'twas caviare to the general." It is eaten either as an *hors d'oeuvre*, particularly in Russia and northern Europe with kummel or other liqueurs, or as a savoury, or as a flavouring to other dishes. The coarser quality, in Russia known as *pájusnaya* (from *pajus*, the adherent skin of the ovaries), is more strongly salted in brine and is pressed into a more solid form than the *ikra*; it is then packed in small barrels or hermetically-sealed tins. This forms a staple article of food in Russia and eastern Europe. Though the best forms of caviare are still made in Russia, and the greater quantity of the coarser kinds are exported from Astrakhan, the centre of the trade, larger amounts are made each year for export in America and also in Germany, Norway and Sweden. The roe of tunny and mullet, pickled in brine and vinegar, is used, under the name of "Botargo," along the Mediterranean littoral and in the Levant.

CAVITE, a fortified seaport, the capital of the province of Cavite, Luzon, Philippine Islands, and the seat of the principal Asiatic naval station of the United States, on a forked tongue of land in Manila Bay, 8 m. S. of the city of Manila. Pop. (1903) 4494; with the barrios of San Roque and Caridad (on the main peninsula), which are under the municipal government of Cavite (15,630). Cavite is the terminus of a railway which follows the shore of the bay from Manila. The northern part of the town, Sangley Point (one of the two forks of the main peninsula), is the principal coaling station of the U.S. fleet in Asiatic waters. The naval station proper and the old town of Cavite are on the south fork of the peninsula. Cavite's buildings are mostly of stone, with upper storeys of wood; its streets are narrow and crooked. It has five churches (one of these is an independent Filipino church), and is the seat of a provincial high school. Cavite has long been the principal naval base of the Philippine Islands, and one of the four Spanish penitentiaries in the Islands was here. During the 19th century Cavite was the centre of political disturbances in the Philippines; in 1896 on the parade ground thirteen political prisoners were executed, and to their memory a monument was erected in 1906 at the head of the isthmus connecting with the main peninsula. The town was nearly destroyed by an earthquake in 1880. It was taken from the Spanish by an American squadron under Commodore George Dewey in May 1898.

CAVOUR, CAMILLO BENSO, COUNT (1810-1861), Italian statesman, was born at Turin on the 1st of August 1810. The Bensos, who belonged to the old Piedmontese feudal aristocracy, were a very ancient house, said to be descended from a Saxon warrior who settled at Santena in the 12th century and married a Piedmontese heiress; Camillo's father, the marquis Michele, married a noble Genevese lady, and both he and his wife held offices in the household of Prince Borghese, the governor of Piedmont under Napoleon, and husband of the latter's sister, Pauline Bonaparte. Being a younger son (his brother Gustavo was the eldest) Cavour was destined for the army, and when ten years old he entered the military academy at Turin. On leaving the college at the age of sixteen he was first of his class, and received a commission in the engineers. He spent the next five years in the army, residing at Ventimiglia, Genoa, and various Alpine fortresses to superintend defence works; but he spent his leisure hours in study, especially of the English language. He soon developed strongly marked Liberal tendencies and an uncompromising dislike for absolutism and clericalism, which, as he had not acquired the art of reticence, made him a suspect in the eyes of the police and of the reactionaries; at the same time he does not seem to have joined any secret society, for he was too loyal to conspire against the king whose uniform he wore, and he did not believe that the time was yet ripe for a revolution. But after the accession to the throne of Charles Albert, whom he always distrusted, he felt that his position in the army was intolerable, and resigned his commission (1831). From that moment we find him in the ranks of the opponents of the government, although his was always a loyal and straightforward opposition which held aloof from conspiracies. During the next few years he devoted himself to the study of political and social problems, to foreign travel, and to acquiring a thorough knowledge of practical agriculture. Cavour's political ideas were greatly influenced by the July revolution of 1830 in France, which proved that an historic monarchy was not incompatible with Liberal principles, and he became more than ever convinced of the benefits of a constitutional monarchy as opposed both to despotism and to republicanism. But he was not affected by the doctrinaire Liberalism of the time, and his views were strengthened by his studies of the British constitution, of which he was a great admirer; he was even nicknamed "Milord Camillo." He frequently visited Paris and London, where he plunged into the political and social questions of the day, and contributed among other essays two admirable and prophetic articles, one on the Irish question, in which he strongly defended the Union, and another on the Corn Laws. He applied his knowledge of agriculture to the management of his father's estate at Leri, which he greatly improved, he founded the Piedmontese Agricultural Society, and took the lead in promoting the introduction of steam navigation, railways and factories into the country.

Thus his mind gradually evolved, and he began to dream dreams of a united Italy free of foreign influence, but owing to the reactionary policy of the Piedmontese government he was unable to take any active part in politics. In 1847, however, the psychological moment seemed to have arrived, for the new pope, Pius IX., showed marked Liberal tendencies and seemed ready to lead all the forces of Italian patriotism against the Austrian domination. The hopes of the Italian Liberals rose high and the so-called neo-Guelph party, represented by such men as Vincenzo Gioberti and Cesare Balbo, believed that an Italian confederation might be formed under the presidency of the pope. Cavour, although he realized that a really Liberal pope was an impossibility, saw the importance of the movement and the necessity of profiting by it. Together with Balbo, P. di Santa Rosa, and M. Castelli, he founded a newspaper at Turin called *Il Risorgimento*, which advocated the ideas of constitutional reform in Piedmont, with a view to preparing that country for an important role in the upheaval which seemed imminent In January 1848 the revolution first broke out in Sicily. Cavour, in a speech before a delegation of journalists, declared that the king must take a decided line and grant his people a constitution. Strong pressure was brought to bear on Charles Albert, and after much hesitation he was induced to grant a charter of liberties (February 8, 1848). Cesare Balbo was called upon to form the first constitutional ministry; but Cavour was not offered a seat in it, being suspected by Liberals and Conservatives alike. He continued his journalistic activity, and his articles in the *Risorgimento* came to exercise great influence both on the king and on public opinion. When the news of the revolt of the Milanese against the Austrians, known as the Five Days, reached Turin on the 19th of March, Cavour felt that the time for Piedmont to act with energy had come, and advocated war against Austria. "After deliberately weighing each word," he wrote, "we are bound in conscience to declare that only one path is open to the nation, the government, and the king: war, immediate war!" Piedmont was the only part of Italy enjoying a government at once national and independent, and if it did not hasten to the assistance of the Milanese in their desperate struggle, if possible before the Austrians were expelled, the monarchy could not survive. The situation was most critical, and even the British government was not friendly to Piedmont; but Cavour was prepared to face any danger rather than see his country inactive. In an article in the *Risorgimento* he declared that, while he never believed that material help was to be expected from England, he was convinced that she would not actively help Austria to crush the revolution, but that if she did "she would have against her a coalition not of princes, but of peoples." Cavour's article made such an impression that it put an end to the king's vacillations, and a few days after its appearance war was declared (March 25).

For a few months patriotic and revolutionary enthusiasm carried all before it. In Hungary, in Germany, in Paris, in Vienna itself the revolution was triumphant; constitutions were granted, dynasties tottered and fell, and provisional governments were set up. In all parts of Italy, too, revolts broke out against the established order. But the Piedmontese army, although the troops behaved with gallantry, was no match for Austria's veteran legions, and except in a few minor engagements, in one of which Cavour's nephew Gustavo was killed, it was generally unsuccessful, and an armistice was concluded in the summer. In the meanwhile the elections were being held in Piedmont. Cavour himself was not returned until the supplementary elections in June, and he took his seat in parliament on the right as a Conservative. His parliamentary career was not at first very successful; he was not a ready speaker; his habit of talking French made Italian difficult for him, and, although French was at that time allowed in the chamber, he preferred to speak Italian. But he gradually developed a strong argumentative power, his speeches became models of concise reasoning, and he rose at times to the highest level of an eloquence which was never rhetorical. After the dissolution in January 1849, Cavour was not re-elected. The new parliament had to discuss, in the first instance, the all-important question of whether the campaign should be continued now that the armistice was about to expire. The king decided on a last desperate throw, and recommenced hostilities. On the 23rd of March the Piedmontese were totally defeated at Novara, a disaster which was followed immediately by the abdication of Charles Albert in favour of his son Victor Emmanuel II.

Although the new king was obliged to conclude peace with Austria and the Italian revolution was crushed, Cavour nevertheless did not despair; he believed that so long as the constitution was maintained in Piedmont, the Italian cause was safe. There were fresh elections in July, and this time Cavour was returned. He was still in the difficult position of a moderate Liberal at a time when there seemed to be room for none but reactionaries and conspirators, but by his consummate ability he convinced men that his attitude was the right one, and he made it triumph. His speech on the 7th of March 1850, in which he said that, "Piedmont, gathering to itself all the living forces of Italy, would be soon in a position to lead our mother-country to the high destinies to which she is called," made a deep impression, for it struck the first note of encouragement after the dark days of the preceding year. He supported the ministry of which Massimo d' Azeglio was president in its work of reform and restoration, and in October of the same year, on the death of Santa Rosa, he himself was appointed minister of agriculture, industry and commerce. In 1851 he also assumed the portfolio of finance, and devoted himself to the task of reorganizing the Piedmontese finances. By far the ablest man in the cabinet, he soon came to dominate it, and, in his anxiety to dominate the chamber as well, he negotiated the union of the Right Centre with the Left Centre (a manoeuvre known as the *connubio*), and promoted the election of Urbano Rattazzi to the presidency of the chamber. This, which he accomplished without d' Azeglio's knowledge, led to a split between that statesman and Cavour, and to the latter's resignation. Cavour has been blamed for not informing his colleagues of the compact, but for public reasons it was not desirable that the *connubio* should be discussed before it was consummated. D' Azeglio indeed bore no malice, and remained Cavour's friend. Cavour made use of his freedom to visit England and France again, in order to sound public opinion on the Italian question. In London he found the leaders of both parties friendly, and Lord Palmerston told him that if the constitutional experiment in Piedmont succeeded the Italian despots were doomed. At this time Sir James Hudson was appointed British minister at Turin, where he became the intimate friend of Cavour and gave him valuable assistance. In Paris, Cavour had a long interview with Prince Louis Napoleon, then president of the republic, and he already foresaw the great part which that ruler was destined to play in Italian affairs. He also met several Italian exiles in France.

On Cavour's return he found the country in the throes of a new cabinet crisis, in consequence of which, on d' Azeglio's recommendation, he was invited to form a ministry. By the 4th of November he was prime minister, a position which he held with two short interruptions until his death. He devoted the first years of his premiership to developing the economic resources of the country; but in preparing it for greater destinies, he had to meet the heavy expenditure by increased taxation, and some of his measures made him the object of hostile demonstrations, although he soon outlived his unpopularity. Cavour's first international difficulty was with Austria; after the abortive rising at Milan in February 1853, the Austrian government, in addition to other measures of repression, confiscated the estates of those Lombards who had become naturalized Piedmontese, although they had nothing to do with the outbreak. Cavour took a strong line on this question, and on Austria's refusal to withdraw the obnoxious decree, he recalled the Piedmontese minister from Vienna, thus by his very audacity winning the sympathy of the Western powers.

Then followed the Crimean War, in which Cavour first showed his extraoidinary political insight and diplomatic genius. The first suggestion of Piedmontese co-operation is usually believed to have come from England, who desired the Italian contingent, not only as material assistance, but also in order to reduce the overwhelming French preponderance. From the Piedmontese point of view there were several reasons why Cavour should desire his country to participate in the campaign. Firstly, it was advisable to use every opportunity of making the Italian question an international one; secondly, by joining the alliance Piedmont would place the Western powers under an obligation; thirdly, Cavour, like Balbo, believed that the Italian question was bound up with the Eastern problem, and as Austria was demanding the permission of the powers to occupy Alessandria, as a guarantee that Piedmont would not profit by the war in the East to create trouble in Italy, Piedmontese participation would in itself prove the best guarantee; and finally, as he always looked to Italy and not merely to Piedmont, he felt that, having proved to Europe that Italians could combine order with liberty, it remained to show that they were capable of fighting as well. But there were serious difficulties in the way. Had Austria joined the allies, as at one time seemed probable, Sardinia's position fighting by her side would have been an impossible one. On the other hand, Piedmont could not demand definite promises of future aid from the Western powers as some politicians desired, because these would never have been given, lest Austria should be offended and driven into the arms of Russia. Then, both the extreme Conservatives and the extreme Radicals were opposed to expenditure on foreign adventures for which they could see no use. In all these difficulties, however, Cavour was loyally supported by the king, who saw the advantages of Piedmontese participation, even if unattended by definite promises. General Dabormida, the minister of foreign affairs, disapproved of this policy and resigned. The vacant portfolio was offered to d'Azeglio, who refused it; whereupon Cavour assumed it himself. On the same 584day (January 10, 1855) the treaty with France and England was signed, and shortly afterwards 15,000 Piedmontese troops under General La Marmora were despatched to the Crimea.

Events at first seemed to justify the fears of Cavour's opponents. Cholera attacked the Piedmontese soldiers, who for a long time had no occasion to distinguish themselves in action; public opinion became despondent and began to blame Cavour, and even he himself lost heart. Then came the news of the battle of the Tchernaya, fought and won by the Italians, which turned sadness and doubt into jubilation. Joy was felt throughout Italy, especially at Milan, where the victory was the first sign of daylight amid the gloom caused by the return of the Austrians. Everyone realized that the Piedmontese contingent was fighting Italy's battles. But to Cavour the announcement that Russia had accepted Austrian mediation (January 16, 1856) was a great disappointment. He had always hoped that if the war continued Austria would be forced to side with Russia in return for the aid given by the emperor Nicholas in suppressing the Hungarian revolt in 1849, and the Western powers would then have an opportunity of helping the Italian cause. He sent a memorandum, at Napoleon's request, to Count Walewski, the French minister of foreign affairs, setting forth a kind of minimum programme of Piedmont's claims. On the summoning of the congress of Paris at the conclusion of the war, Cavour first proposed that d'Azeglio should represent Piedmont, and on the latter's refusal decided to go himself. After much discussion, and in spite of the opposition of Austria, who as mediator occupied a predominant position, behaving "as though she had taken Sevastopol," Cavour obtained that Piedmont should be treated as one of the great powers. Although he did not expect that the congress would liberate Italy, yet by his marvellous diplomatic skill, far superior to that of his colleagues, he first succeeded in isolating Austria, secondly in indirectly compromising Napoleon in the Italian question, and thirdly in getting the wretched conditions of Italy discussed by the representatives of the great powers, who declared that some remedy to that state of things was necessary, not in the interests of Italy alone, but of all Europe. A scheme of reform proposed by Count Walewski gave Cavour the opportunity to plead the Italian cause, and from that moment it was manifest to all that the liberation of Italy was personified in him, the statesman who came to hold all the strings of European politics in his hands.

Cavour's chief measure of internal reform during this period was a bill for suppressing all monastic orders unconnected with education, preaching or charity; this aroused strong opposition from the extremists of both parties and also from the king, and led to the minister's resignation. But he was soon recalled, for the country could not do without him, and the bill was passed (May 29, 1855).

Cavour now saw that war with Austria was merely a question of time, and he began to establish connexions with the revolutionists of all parts of Italy, largely by means of La Farina; but it was necessary that this policy should not be advertised to Europe, and he strongly discountenanced Mazzini's abortive revolutionary attempts. He continued to strengthen Piedmont's military resources, and the army soon grew too large for the country and was obviously destined for more than merely defensive purposes. But he well knew that although Piedmont must be made as efficient as possible from the military point of view, it could not defeat Austria single-handed. He would have preferred an alliance with Great Britain, who would never demand territorial compensation; but although British sympathies were wholly Italian, the government was desperately anxious to avoid war. From Napoleon more was to be hoped, for the emperor still preserved some of his revolutionary instincts, while the insecurity of his situation at home made him eager to gain popularity by winning military glory abroad; but he still hesitated, and Cavour devoted the whole of his ability to overcoming his doubts. In the midst of these negotiations came Orsini's attempt on Napoleon's life (January 14, 1858), which threatened to alienate his Italian sympathies and cause serious embarrassments to Piedmont. But after some remonstrances to Piedmont for not acting with sufficient energy against the revolutionists, the incident was settled: and Napoleon was, in fact, afraid that if he did not help the Italian cause more such attempts would be made. A month after the Orsini outrage he laid before Cavour a proposal for a Franco-Piedmontese alliance and the marriage of Prince Jerome Bonaparte with Princess Clothilde, the daughter of Victor Emmanuel.

An "accidental" meeting between Napoleon and Cavour was arranged and took place at Plombières in July, and although no one knew what passed, the news of it fell like a bombshell on the diplomatic world. No definite treaty was signed, but the basis of an agreement was laid, whereby France and Piedmont were to declare war against Austria with the object of expelling her from Italy, and a north Italian state was to be formed; in exchange for this help France was to receive Savoy and possibly Nice. But the emperor still hesitated, and refused to decide on war unless Austria attacked Piedmont; the British government, too, in its anxiety to preserve peace, was not very friendly to the Italian cause. Cavour saw that the only way to overcome all these obstacles was to force Austria's hand. Then there was the danger lest an Italy freed by French arms should be overwhelmed under French predominance; for this reason Cavour was determined to secure the co-operation of volunteers from other parts of Italy, and that the war should be accompanied by a series of risings against Austria and the local despots. It was also necessary that the risings should break out in the various provinces *before* the Piedmontese and French troops arrived, so that the latter should not appear as invaders and conquerors, but merely as liberators.

The moment war was seen to be imminent, parties of Italians of all classes, especially Lombards, poured into Piedmont to enlist in the army. Cavour also had a secret interview with Garibaldi, with whom he arranged to organize volunteer corps so that the army should be not merely that of Piedmont, but of all Italy. Every day the situation grew more critical, and on the 10th of January 1859 the king in his speech from the throne pronounced the memorable words "that he could not remain deaf to the cry of pain (*il grido di dolore*) that reached him from all parts of Italy"—words which, although actually suggested by Napoleon, rang like a trumpet-call throughout the land. In the meanwhile the marriage negotiations were concluded, and during the emperor's visit to Turin a military convention was signed between the two states, and Savoy and Nice were promised to France as a reward for the expulsion of the Austrians from Italy. But the British government was still unfavourable, and Napoleon, ever hesitating, again sought an excuse for backing out of his engagements; he jumped at the Russian proposal to settle the Italian question by means of his own favourite expedient, a congress. To this Austria agreed on condition that Piedmont should disarm and should be excluded from the congress; England supported the scheme, but desired that all the Italian states should be represented. Cavour was in despair at the turn events were taking, and appealed to Napoleon, actually threatening to emigrate to America and publish all his correspondence with the emperor if the latter did not keep his engagements. He decided at last most reluctantly to accept the English proposal, lest Piedmont should be abandoned by all, but clung to the hope that Austria would reject it. On the 19th of April the Austrian emperor, on the advice of the military party, did reject it; and on the 23rd, to Cavour's inexpressible joy, Austria sent an ultimatum demanding the disarmament of Piedmont. Cavour replied that his government had agreed to the congress proposed by the powers and that it had nothing more to say. On quitting the chamber that day he said to a friend: "I am leaving the last sitting of the last Piedmontese parliament"— the next would represent united Italy. France now allied herself definitely with Piedmont, and England, delighted at Cavour's acquiescence to her own proposal and enraged by Austria's ultimatum, became wholly friendly to the Italian cause. A few days later Austria declared war.

585

As La Marmora now took the chief command of the army, Cavour added the ministry of war to the others he already held. His activity at this time was astounding, for he was virtually dictator and controlled single-handed nearly all the chief offices of the state. The French troops entered Piedmont, where they were received with enthusiasm, and the allies marched into Lombardy; the victory of Magenta, which opened the gates of Milan to them, was shortly followed by that of Solferino. The people rose in arms at Parma, Modena, Florence and Bologna, which had been occupied by Austria for the pope since 1849; the local princes were expelled and provisional governments set up. Cavour sent special commissioners to take charge of the various provinces in Victor Emmanuel's name. But these events, together with Prussia's menacing attitude, began to alarm Napoleon, who, although he wished to destroy Austrian influence in Italy, was afraid of a large and powerful Italian state. Consequently, after Solferino, he concluded an armistice with Austria at Villafranca on the 8th of July, without previously informing Cavour. When Cavour heard of it he was thunderstruck; he immediately interviewed the king at Monzambano, and in violent, almost disrespectful language implored him not to make peace until Venice was free. But Victor Emmanuel saw that nothing was to be gained by a refusal, and much against his own inclination, signed the peace preliminaries at Villafranca, adding the phrase, "pour ce qui me concerne," which meant that he was not responsible for what the people of other parts of Italy might do (July 12). Lombardy was to be ceded to Piedmont, Venetia to remain Austrian, the deposed princes to be reinstated, and the pope made president of an Italian confederation.

The cabinet resigned the next day, but remained in office provisionally, and Cavour privately advised the revolutionists of central Italy to resist the return of the princes, by force if necessary: "for we must now become conspirators ourselves," he said. His policy was thus continued after he left office, and Palmerston, who had meanwhile succeeded Malmesbury as foreign minister, informed France and Austria that Great Britain would never tolerate their armed intervention in favour of the central Italian despots. The new Piedmontese ministry, of which La Marmora was the president, but Rattazzi the leading spirit, hesitated between annexing central Italy and agreeing to the terms of peace, but on the 10th of November peace was signed at Zürich. Napoleon proposed a new congress, which never met, and on the fall of the Rattazzi-La Marmora cabinet the king, in spite of the quarrel at Monzambano, asked Cavour to take office again. By January he was once more premier, as well as minister for foreign affairs and of the interior. His first act was to invite the people of Italy to declare their own wishes with regard to annexation to Piedmont; but Napoleon still refused to consent to the union of Tuscany with Piedmont, for he contemplated placing one of his own relatives on the throne of the grand-duchy. Cavour now saw that Napoleon might be ready to deal, and, although the bargain of the preceding year had not been exactly fulfilled, as the Austrians were still in Venice, he again brought forward the question of Nice and Savoy. To Cavour no less than to the king the loss of these two provinces was a cruel wrench, but it was a choice between them and central Italy. The plebiscites in the latter region had unanimously declared in favour of union with Piedmont, and Napoleon became more pressing, going so far as to threaten that unless the cession were made, the French troops would leave Lombardy at the mercy of Austria and occupy Bologna and Florence. On the 24th of March the treaty was signed and the emperor's opposition to the annexation of central Italy withdrawn. On the 2nd of April the parliament representing Piedmont, the duchies of Parma and Modena, Tuscany and Romagna, met, and Cavour had the difficult and ungrateful task of explaining the cession of Nice and Savoy. In spite of some opposition, the agreement was ratified by a large majority.

The situation in the kingdom of Naples was now becoming critical, but there seemed as yet little chance of union with upper Italy, for the Bourbon government was a more or less regular one, and, although risings had broken out, there was no general revolution. Cavour therefore had to follow a somewhat double-faced policy, on the one hand negotiating with the Bourbon king (Francis II.), suggesting a division of Italy between him and Victor Emmanuel, and on the other secretly backing up the revolutionary agitation. Having now learnt that Garibaldi was planning an expedition to Sicily with his volunteers, he decided, after some hesitation, not to oppose its departure; on the 5th of May it sailed from Quarto near Genoa, and Cavour was only deterred from declaring war on Naples by the fear of foreign complications. Garibaldi with his immortal Thousand landed at Marsala, and the whole rotten fabric of the Bourbon government collapsed. At Palermo they were welcomed by the Piedmontese admiral Persano, and soon the whole island was occupied and Garibaldi proclaimed dictator. The general now proposed to cross over to the mainland, and this placed Cavour in a serious dilemma; Russia and Austria protested against the expedition, France and Prussia were unfriendly, Great Britain alone remained warmly pro-Italian. He still hoped for a revolution in Naples, so that King Victor's authority might be established before Garibaldi's arrival, but this proved impossible. When Garibaldi crossed the straits of Messina the Neapolitan government fell, and he entered Naples in triumph. But there was still danger that he might be subsequently defeated, for the Neapolitan army was still a force in being, and Cavour feared, moreover, that, although Garibaldi himself had always loyally acted in the king of Italy's name, the red republicans around him might lead him to commit some imprudence and plunge the country into anarchy. The cession of Nice, Garibaldi's birthplace, had made an impassable gulf between the two men, and neither quite trusted the other. Cavour also feared that Garibaldi might invade the papal states, which would have led to further international complications. In any case, Rome must not be touched for the present, since Napoleon was pledged to protect the pope; but as the latter had made large armaments, and his forces, consisting largely of brigands and foreigners under the French general Lamoricière, were in a menacing attitude on the frontier, Cavour decided on the momentous step of annexing the papal states with the exception of the Roman province. The Italian army crossed the frontier from Romagna on the 11th of September, whereupon every power, except Great Britain and Sweden, withdrew its minister from Turin. But the troops advanced and were everywhere received with open arms by the people; Ancona was taken, Lamoricière was defeated and captured at the battle of Castelfidardo, and on the 20th King Victor marched into the Neapolitan kingdom. On the 1st of October Garibaldi defeated the Neapolitan troops on the Volturno, and Gaeta alone, where King Francis of Naples had retired, still held out.

New difficulties with Garibaldi arose, for he would not resign his dictatorship of the southern provinces, and wished to march on Rome. Cavour had to use all his tact to restrain him and at the same time not to appear ungrateful. He refused to act despotically, but summoned parliament to vote on the annexation, which it did on the 11th. Two days later Garibaldi magnanimously gave in to the nation's will and handed his conquests over to King Victor as a free gift. Gaeta was invested, and after a siege prolonged through the action of Napoleon, who for some reason unknown kept his fleet before the town, preventing any attack by sea until England induced him to withdraw it, the garrison surrendered on the 13th of February, and King Francis retired to Rome. Parliament was dissolved once more; the new chamber showed an overwhelming majority in favour of Cavour, and Victor Emmanuel was proclaimed king of Italy.

The last question with which Cavour had to deal was that of Rome. For some years past the pope had only been able to maintain his authority by the help of foreign troops, and Cavour saw that as long as this state of things lasted there could be no united Italy. In October he declared in parliament that Rome must be the capital of Italy, for no other city was recognized as such by the whole country, and in January 1861 a resolution to that effect was passed. But owing to Napoleon's attitude he had to proceed warily, and made no attempt for the present to 586carry out the nation's wishes. At the same time he was anxious that the church should preserve the fullest liberty, and he believed in the principle of "a free church in a free state." His great dream, save for Rome and Venice, was now realized, and Italy was free and united. But the wear and tear of these last years had been almost unbearable, and at last began to tell; the negotiations with Garibaldi were particularly trying, for while the great statesman wished to treat the hero and his volunteers generously, far more so than seemed wise to the Conservatives and the strictly military party, he did not wish the Italian cause to be endangered by their imprudences, and could not permit all the Garibaldian officers to be received into the regular army with the same grades they held in the volunteer forces. This question, together with that of Nice, led to a painful scene in the chamber between the two men, although they were formally reconciled a few days later. For some time past Cavour had been unwell and irritable, and the scene with Garibaldi undoubtedly hastened his end. A fever set in, and after a short illness he passed away on the 6th of June 1861. He was buried at his ancestral castle of Santena.

The death of Cavour was a terrible loss to Italy; there remained many problems to be solved in which his genius and personality were urgently needed. But the great work had been carried to such a point that lesser men might now complete the structure. He is undoubtedly the greatest figure of the *Risorgimento*, and although other men and other forces co-operated in the movement, it was Cavour who organized it and skilfully conducted the negotiations which overcame all, apparently insuperable, obstacles. "That which in Alfieri and Gioberti was lacking," wrote T. Artom, his private secretary, "a deep and lively sense of reality, Cavour possessed to a supreme degree. He was not a *littérateur*, he was never a political dreamer. His views broadened progressively; at each stage he discovered a new horizon, and he followed his path without ever seeking anything save what was real and possible." He was gifted with pronounced political genius and with an astounding power of foresight. In his ideas he was always a moderate Liberal, and although he disapproved of republicanism, he was an ardent constitutionalist, ever refusing to resort to arbitrary methods, for he felt that, the Italian character being what it is, Italian unity could not last if unsupported by popular feeling. In meeting opposition he could not, like Bismarck, rely on a great military power, for the Piedmontese army was a small one; Austria must first be isolated and then an alliance had to be obtained with some other power. Some of his acts, especially his policy towards the Neapolitan kingdom, have been criticized as politically immoral; but apart from the fact that few revolutions—and Cavour, after all, was a revolutionist—can be conducted without attacking vested rights, it is hard to see that any policy which led to the destruction of a government, rightly described as the "negation of God on earth," could be deemed immoral. He has been accused of changing his views, but what statesman has not? Moreover, in the extremely complicated and difficult diplomatic situations which he had to face, what was impossible or dangerous one day became possible and desirable the next. This was particularly the case with the Neapolitan question. Cavour's one absorbing passion was the liberation and regeneration of Italy, and to this he devoted his whole life and talent.

BIBLIOGRAPHY.—G. Buzziconi, *Bibliografia Cavouriana* (Turin, 1898); Countess Evelyn Martinengo Cesaresco, *Cavour* (London, 1898), an excellent and handy little monograph which brings out the chief points of Cavour's life in the right light; G. Massari, *Il Conte di Cavour* (Turin, 1873); W. de la Rive, *Le Comte de Cavour* (Paris, 1862), interesting and valuable as the work of a contemporary and intimate friend of Cavour; L. Chiala, *Lettere edite ed inedite del Conte di Cavour* (7 vols., Turin, 1883-1887); D. Zanichelli, *Gli Scritti del Conte di Cavour* (Bologna, 1892), and *Cavour* (Florence, 1905); H. von Treitschke, "Cavour," in his *Historische und politische Aufsatze* (Leipzig, 1871); E. Dicey, *A Memoir of Cavour* (London, 1861); Conte C. di Cavour, *Discorsi parlamentari* (8 vols., Turin, 1863-1872), *Opere politico-economiche* (Cuneo, 1855); F.X. Krauss, *Cavour* (Mainz, 1902); E. Artom, *L'Opere politica del Senatore T. Artom nel Risorgimento Italiano* (Bologna, 1906), a biography of Cavour's devoted private secretary, containing new material.

(L. V.*)

CAVOUR (anc. *Caburrum* or *Forum Vibii*), a town of Piedmont, Italy, in the province of Turin, 32 m. S.W. by rail and steam tram (via Pinerolo from the town of Turin). Pop. (1901) town, 2091; commune, 6843. It lies on the north side of a huge isolated mass of granite (the Rocca di Cavour) which rises from the plain. On the summit was the Roman village, which belonged to the province of the Alpes Cottiae. There are some ruins of medieval fortifications. The town gave its name to the Benso family of Chieri, who were raised to the marquisate in 1771, and of which the statesman Cavour was a member.

For the ancient name see Th. Mommsen in *Corp. Inscrip. Lat.* v. (Berlin, 1877), p. 825.

CAVY, a name commonly applied to several South American rodent animals included in the family *Caviidae* (see RODENTIA), but perhaps properly applicable only to those belonging to the typical genus *Cavia*, of which the most familiar representative is the domesticated guinea-pig. Cavies in general, the more typical representatives of the *Caviidae*, are rodents with hoof-like nails, four front and three hind toes, imperfect collar-bones, and the cheek-teeth divided by folds of enamel into transverse plates. The tail is short or rudimentary, the incisors are short, and the outer surface of the lower jaw is marked by a distinct ridge.

True cavies, or couies (*Cavia*), are best known by the guinea-pig, a domesticated and parti-coloured race derived from one of the wild species, all of which are uniformly coloured. They are comparatively small and stoutly built animals, with short, rounded ears and no tail. In habits they are partly diurnal; and live either in burrows among the crevices of rocks, beneath the leaves of aquatic plants in marshy districts, or underneath the floors of outbuildings. Their cries are faint squeaks and grunts. They feed upon nearly all vegetable substances, but drink little. Generally they associate in small societies, and seldom wander far from home. Although the guinea-pig is a fertile breeder, the wild species only produce one or two young at a birth, and this but once in a year. The young come into the world in a highly developed condition, being able to feed themselves the day following their birth. Cavies are widely distributed in South America, and are represented by several species. Among them may be mentioned the aperea or restless cavy (*C. porcellus* or *C. aperea*) of Brazil; the Bolivian *C. boliviensis*, found at great elevations in the Andes; the Brazilian rock-cavy (*C. rupestris*), characterized by its short blunt claws; and the Peruvian *C. cutleri*. The latter was tamed by the Incas, and is the ancestor of the guinea-pig. As to the origin of that name, some writers consider it a corruption of Guiana-pig, but it is more probable that the word "Guinea" merely signifies foreign. The guinea-pig is a singularly inoffensive and defenceless creature, of a restless disposition, and wanting in that intelligence which usually characterizes domestic pets, although said to show some discrimination. It is of no particular service to man, neither its flesh nor its fur being generally put to use, while the statement that its presence is sufficient to drive off rats and mice appears to be without foundation. It is exceedingly prolific, beginning to breed at the age of two months; the number of young varying, according to the age of the parent, from four to twelve. It has been calculated that a single pair of guinea-pigs may prove the parent stock of a thousand individuals in a single year.

A very different animal is the Patagonian cavy, or mara (*Dolichotis patachonica*), the typical representative of a genus characterized by long limbs, comparatively large ears, and a short tail. The animal is about the size of a hare, to which it approximates in form and habits. It is most abundant in the open districts of Patagonia, but also ranges on to the Argentina Pampas, where it is now scarce. Although occasionally seen in large flocks, the mara is more commonly found in small parties or in pairs, the parties commonly moving in single file. It has a peculiar kind of hopping gait; and is mainly diurnal, in accordance with which habit its eyes are protected by lashes. It lives in a burrow, generally excavated by itself; but when pursued, seeks safety in flight, rather than by a retreat to its hole. From two to five young are produced twice a year. A 587much smaller species, *D. salinicola*, without the characteristic black band above the tail, inhabits the salt-plains of Argentina. Maras have been introduced into several British parks. Fossil species of *Dolichotis* occur in the caverns of Brazil, and also in the superficial deposits of Argentina.

(R. L.*)

CAWDOR, a village and parish of Nairnshire, Scotland. Pop. of parish (1901) 925. The village is situated 5 m. S.S.W. of Nairn and 3 m. from Gollanfield Junction on the Highland railway. The castle was the scene, according to the tradition which Shakespeare has perpetuated, of the murder of King Duncan by Macbeth, thane of Cawdor (or Calder), in 1040. Since the oldest part of the structure dates from 1454, however, and seemingly had no predecessor, the tradition has no foundation in fact. The building stands on the rocky bank of Cawdor Burn, a right-hand tributary of the Nairn. The massive keep with small turrets is the original portion of the castle, and to it were added, in the 17th century, the modern buildings forming two sides of a square.

Kilravock (pronounced *Kilrawk*) Castle, 1½ m. W. of Cawdor, occupies a commanding site on the left bank of the Nairn. Its keep dates from 1460, and the later buildings belong to the 17th century. It has been continuously tenanted by the Roses, one of the most remarkable families in Scotland. They came over with William the Conqueror and settled at Kilravock in 1293, since which date son has succeeded father without the interposition of a collateral heir, an instance of direct descent unique in Scottish history. Moreover, nearly every Rose has borne the Christian name of Hugh, and only one attained to a higher social rank than that of laird. Queen Mary was received at the castle in 1562, and Prince Charles Edward was entertained four days before the battle of Culloden. The gardens are remarkable for their beauty.

CAWNPORE, or KANPUR, a city and district of British India in the Allahabad division of the United Provinces. The city is situated on the south bank of the Ganges, 40 m. south-west of Lucknow, and formed from early times a frontier outpost of the people of Oudh and Bengal against their northern neighbours. Clive selected it, on account of its commanding position, as the cantonment for the brigade of troops lent him by the nawab of Oudh. In 1801, when the Ceded Provinces were acquired by the East India Company, it became the chief British frontier station. But by the time of the Mutiny the frontier had left it behind, and it was denuded of troops. Now it is chiefly known as the junction of four railways, the East Indian, Oudh & Rohilkand, Rajputana and Indian Midland, and as a great emporium for harness, shoes and other leather-work. In 1901 the population was 197,170, showing an increase of 4% in the decade. In 1903 the city was devastated by an epidemic of plague.

The name of Cawnpore is indelibly connected with the blackest episode in the history of the Indian Mutiny—the massacre here in July 1857 of hundreds of women and children by the Nana Sahib. The full details of the siege and massacre will be found under INDIAN MUTINY, and here it will suffice to refer to the local memorials of that evil time. The entrenchment, where General Sir H.M. Wheeler with his small band of soldiers and the European and Eurasian residents were exposed for 21 days to the fire of the mutineers, is merely a bare field, containing the well where many women and children were shot while getting water. This well is now surrounded by an enclosure with an inscription upon its cross. About three-quarters of a mile away, on the banks of the river Ganges, is the Massacre Ghat. A grassy road between banks 10 to 12 ft. high leads down to the river, and it was among the trees on these banks that the murderers concealed themselves who shot down the little garrison as soon as they were embarked in the boats which were to take them to safety. On the river bank is a temple to Siva, of hexagonal shape, old and going to ruin. Steps lead from this temple to an enclosed flight of stairs, which in the cold season descend to the water, but in the rains are covered almost to the top. This is the ghat where some 600 helpless people were slain, in spite of a promise of safe-conduct from the Nana. The remaining 200 victims, who had escaped the bullets of the siege and survived the butchery of the river bank, were massacred afterwards and cast down the famous well of Cawnpore, which is now marked by a memorial and surrounded by gardens. The memorial is crowned by the figure of an angel in white marble, and on the wall of the well itself is the following inscription:—

Sacred to the perpetual Memory of a great company of
Christian people, chiefly Women and Children, who near
this
spot were cruelly murdered by the followers of the rebel
Nana Dhundu Pant, of Bithur, and cast, the dying with
the
dead, into the well below, on the xvth day of July,
MDCCCLVII.

The DISTRICT OF CAWNPORE is situated between the Ganges and Jumna rivers, and is a portion of the well-watered and fertile tract known as the Doab, the total area being 2384 sq. m. The general inclination of the country is from north to south. Besides the two great rivers, the principal streams are the Arand or Rhind, the Kavan or Singar, the Isan and the Pandu. The district is watered by four branches of the Ganges canal, and traversed by two lines of railway. It used to be a great centre of the indigo industry, which has now declined. The population in 1901 was 1,258,868, showing an increase of 4% during the decade.

CAXTON, WILLIAM (c. 1422-1491), the first English printer, was born somewhere in the Weald of Kent, perhaps at Tenterden. The name, which was apparently pronounced Cauxton, is identical with Causton, the name of a manor in the parish of Hadlow, and was a fairly common surname in the 15th century. The date of Caxton's birth was arbitrarily fixed in 1748 by Oldys as 1412. Blades, however, inferred that in 1438, when he was apprenticed to Robert Large, he would not have been more than sixteen years of age. This would place his birth in 1422-1423. Robert Large was a rich silk mercer who became sheriff in 1430 and lord mayor of London in 1439, and the fact of Caxton's apprenticeship to him argues that Caxton's own parents were in a good position. Large died in 1441, leaving a small bequest to Caxton, and his executors would be bound to place the young man where he could finish his term. He was probably sent direct to Bruges, then the central foreign market of the Anglo-Flemish trade, for he presently entered business there on his own account. In 1450 his name appears in the Bruges records as standing joint surety for the sum of £100; and in 1463 he was acting governor of the company of Merchant Adventurers in the Low Countries. This association, sometimes known as the "English Nation," was dominated by the Mercers' Company, to the livery of which Caxton had been formally admitted in London in 1453. The first governor, appointed in terms of a charter granted by Edward IV. in 1462, was W. Obray, but Caxton's position is definitely asserted in 1464. In that year he was appointed, together with Sir Richard Whitehill, to negotiate with Philip, duke of Burgundy, the renewal of a treaty concerning the wool trade, which was about to expire. These attempts failed, but he was again employed, with two other members of the Mercers' Company, in a similar but successful mission in October 1468 to the new duke, Charles the Bold, who earlier in the year had married Princess Margaret of York, sister of Edward IV. The last mention of Caxton in the capacity of governor of the "English Nation" is on the 13th of August 1469, and it was probably about that time that he entered the household of the duchess Margaret, possibly in the position of commercial adviser. In his diplomatic mission in 1468 he had been associated with Lord Scales, afterwards Earl Rivers and one of his chief patrons, and at the Burgundian court he must have come in touch with Edward IV. during his brief exile in 1470.

He had begun his translation of the popular medieval romance of Troy, *The Recuyell of the Historyes of Troye*, from the French of Raoul le Fèvre, early in 1469; and, after laying it aside for some time, he resumed it at the wish of the duchess Margaret, to whom the MS. was presented in September 1471. During his thirty-three years' residence in Bruges Caxton would have access to the rich libraries of the duke of Burgundy and other nobles, and about this time he learned the art of printing. His disciple, Wynkyn de Worde, says that he was taught at Cologne, probably during a visit there in 1471, recorded in the preface to 588the*Recuyell*; Blades suggests that he learnt from Colard Mansion, but there is no evidence that Mansion set up his press at Bruges before 1474. He ceased to be a member of the gild of St John (a gild of illuminators) in 1473, and the first dated book he is known to have printed is dated 1476. Mansion and Caxton were partners or associates at Bruges, where Caxton printed his *Recuyell* in 1474 or 1475. His second book, *The Game and Playe of Chesse*, from the *Liber de ludo scacchorum* of Jacobus de Cessolis through the French of Jehan de Vignay, was finished in 1474, and printed soon after; the last book printed by Mansion and Caxton at Bruges was the *Quatre derrenieres choses*, an anonymous treatise usually known as *De quattuor novissimis*. Other books in the same type were printed by Mansion at Bruges after Caxton's departure.

By September 1476 Caxton had established himself in the almonry at Westminster at the sign of the Red Pale. Robert Copland the printer, who was afterwards one of Caxton's assistants, states that Caxton began by printing small pamphlets. The first dated book printed in England was Lord Rivers's translation (revised by Caxton) of *The Dictes or sayengis of the philosophres* (1477). From this time until his death in 1401 Caxton was busy writing and printing. His services to English literature, apart from his work as a printer (see TYPOGRAPHY), are very considerable. His most important original work is an eighth book added to the *Polychronicon* (vol. viii. in the Rolls Series edition) of Ralph Higden. Caxton revised and printed John of Trevisa's work, and brought down the narrative himself from 1358 to 1460, using as his authorities *Fasciculus temporum*, a popular work in the 15th century, and an unknown *Aureus de universo*. In the year before his death he complained in the preface to his *Eneydos* of the changing state of the English language, a condition of things which he did as much as any man to remedy. He printed Chaucer's *Canterbury Tales* (1478? and 1483), *Troilus and Creseide* (1483?), the *House of Fame* (1483?), and the translation of Boethius (1478?); Gower's *Confessio Amantis* (1483), and many poems of Lydgate. His press was, however, not worked for purely literary ends, but was a commercial speculation. For the many service-books which he printed there was no doubt a sure sale, and he met the taste of the upper classes by the tales of chivalry which issued regularly from his press. He printed Malory's *Morte d'Arthur*, and himself translated from the French the *Boke of Histories of Jason* (1477?), *The Historye of Reynart the Foxe* (from the Dutch, 1481 and 1489?), *Godfrey of Boloyne* or *The Siege and Conqueste of Jherusalem* (1481), *The Lyf of Charles the Grete* (1485), *The Knyght Parys and the Fayr Vyenne* (1485), *Blanchardyn and Eglantine* (1489?), *The Foure Sonnes of Aymon* (1489?); also the *Morale Proverbs* (1478), and the *Fayttes of Armes and of Chyualrye* (1489) of Christine de Pisan. The most ambitious production of his press was perhaps his version of the *Golden Legend*, the translation of which he finished in November 1483. It is based on the lives of the saints as given in the 13th century *Legenda aurea* of Jacobus de Voragine, but Caxton chiefly used existing French and English versions for his compilation. The book is illustrated by seventy woodcuts, and Caxton says he was only encouraged to persevere in his laborious and expensive task by the liberality of William, earl of Arundel. The idleness which he so often deprecates in his prefaces was no vice of his, for in addition to his voluminous translations his output as a printer was over 18,000 pages, and he published ninety-six separate works or editions of works, with apparently little skilled assistance, though later printers, Wynkyn de Worde, Robert Copland and possibly Richard Pynson, were trained under him.

The different founts of type used by Caxton are illustrated by Blades and Duff, and there is an excellent selection of Caxtons in the British Museum, in the University library at Cambridge, besides those in private hands. A record price for a Caxton was reached in 1902 when Mr Bernard Quaritch paid £2225 for *The Royal Book* (1487?), a translation of the popular *Somme des vices et des vertus*. His books have no title-pages, and from 1487 onwards are usually adorned with a curious device, consisting of the letters W.C. separated by a trade mark, with an elaborate border above and below. The flourishes on the trade mark have been fancifully interpreted as S.C. for Sancta Colonia, implying that Caxton learnt his art at Cologne, and the whole mark has been read as 74, for 1474, the date of his first printed book. This device was first used in an edition of the Sarum missal, printed for Caxton by George Maynial in Paris, and was subsequently adopted with small alterations by his successor at the Westminster press, Wynkyn de Worde. The first of his books containing woodcut illustrations was his *Myrrour of the World* (1481), translated from Vincent de Beauvais, which has diagrams and pictures for the assistance of young students. He had used a woodcut initial letter in his broadside *Indulgence* printed in 1480.

No record of Caxton's marriage or of the birth of his children has been found, but Gerard Croppe was separated from his wife Elizabeth, daughter of William Caxton, before 1496, when Croppe made certain claims in connexion with his father-in-law's will.

AUTHORITIES.—Earlier biographies of Caxton were superseded by the work of William Blades, whose *Life and Typography of William Caxton* (2 vols., 1861-1863) remains the standard authority. It contains a bibliography of each of the works issued from Caxton's press. For later discoveries see George Bullen's *Catalogue* of the Caxton celebration loan collection exhibited in 1877; articles by E.J.L. Scott in the *Athenaeum* (Feb. 10, 1900; May 21 and June 8, 1892); articles in *Notes and Queries* (April 21, 1900; Feb. 24, 1906), and the publications of the Caxton Club, Chicago, notably *William*

Caxton, by E. Gordon Duff (1905). See also *Census of Caxtons*, by Seymour de Ricci, No. xv. of the illustrated monographs of the Bibliographical Society, 1909. Many of Caxton's translations are available in modern reprints; the *Golden Legend*, the *Recuyell* and *Godeffroy of Boloyne*, were printed by William Morris at the Kelmscott Press in 1892-1893; the *Boke of Curtesye* (1868), the *Lyf of Charles the Crete*(1880), Alain Chartier's *Curial* (1888), *Foure Sonnes of Aymon* (1884), *Eneydos*(1890), *Blanchardyn and Eglantine* (1890), and others, by the Early English Text Society. For modern editions of *Reynart* see REYNARD THE FOX. No authentic portrait of Caxton is known, but a MS. at Magdalene College, Cambridge, of the last six books of the *Metamorphoses of Ovid*, translated by Caxton, is probably in his handwriting.

CAYENNE, a seaport and the capital of French Guiana, on the N.W. extremity of the island of Cayenne, and near the mouth of the river of that name, in 4° 56′ 28″ N., and 52° 20′ 36″ W. Pop. about 12,600. The town forms an almost perfect square, and has clean and well-macadamized streets. The houses, mostly of two storeys, are of wood, strengthened on the first and ground floors by brickwork. In the old town, which contains the government-house and Jesuits' College, the streets are not so regularly and well built as in the new. The Place d'Armes, a fine quadrangular space, lies between them. To the right of the governor's house is Mount Cépéron, on which stand Fort St Michel, the marine barracks, the signal station and the lighthouse. Here, too, are the capacious reservoirs for the water-supply of the town, the source of which is a lake to the south of the island. The harbour is shallow at its entrance, and craft drawing more than 14 ft. are obliged to anchor 6 m. from the town. There is no dock for the repair of vessels; but there are two quays at the town. The principal exports of Cayenne are gold, cocoa, phosphates, hides, woods and spices. The imports are French wines, spirits and liqueurs; silk and cotton stuffs, tobacco, hardware, glass, earthenware, clothing, preserved meat, fish, and vegetables, maize, flour, hay, bran, oils and cattle. There is a regular mail service between Cayenne and Martinique once a month. Cayenne is the seat of the government of French Guiana, and was formerly a penal settlement for political offenders. Food as well as clothing is exorbitantly dear, the only cheap articles of consumption being bread and French wines. The temperature of Cayenne is between 76° and 88° Fahr. throughout the year; but the heat is tempered by easterly winds. Between December and March a north wind blows, unfavourable to weak constitutions. Yellow and other fevers often attack the 589inhabitants of the town, but the climate, though moist, is as a whole healthy. (See GUIANA.)

CAYENNE PEPPER (GUINEA PEPPER, SPANISH PEPPER, CHILLY), a preparation from the dried fruit of various species of *Capsicum*, a genus of the natural order Solanaceae. The true peppers are members of a totally distinct order, Piperaceae. The fruits of plants of the genus*Capsicum* have all a strong, pungent flavour. The capsicums bear a greenish-white flower, with a star-shaped corolla and five anthers standing up in the centre of the flower like a tube, through which projects the slender style. The pod-like fruit consists of an envelope at first fleshy and afterwards leathery, within which are the spongy pulp and several seeds. The plants are herbaceous or shrubby; the leaves are entire, and alternate, or in pairs near one another; the flowers are solitary and do not arise in the leaf-axils. There are about thirty species, natives of Central and South America. They are now grown in various parts of the world, both for the sake of the fruit and for ornament. In England the annual sorts are sown from March to the middle of April under a frame. They can be planted out when 2 or 3 in. high, and in June may be transferred to a light rich soil in the open garden. They flower in July or August, and produce pods from August till the end of September. The perennial and shrubby kinds may be wintered in a conservatory. Several species or varieties are used to make cayenne pepper. The annual or common capsicum (*C. annuum*), the Guinea pepper plant, was brought to Europe by the Spaniards, and was grown in England in 1548. It is indigenous to South America, but is now cultivated in India, Hungary, Italy, Spain and Turkey, with the other species of capsicum. It is a hardy herbaceous plant, which attains a height of 2 or 3 ft. There are numerous cultivated forms, differing in the shape and colour of the pod, which varies from more or less roundish to narrow-conical, with a smooth or wrinkled coat, and white, yellow, red or black in colour. The principal source of cayenne pepper is *C. frutescens*, the spur or goat pepper, a dwarf shrub, a native of South America, but commonly cultivated in the East Indies. It produces a small, narrow, bright red pod, having very pungent properties. *C. tetragonum*, or bonnet pepper, is a species much esteemed in Jamaica; it bears very fleshy fruits. Other well-known kinds of capsicum are the cherry pepper (*C. cerasiforme*), with small berries; bell pepper (*C. grossum*), which has thick and pulpy fruit, well adapted for pickling; and berry or bird pepper (*C. baccatum*). The last mentioned has been grown in England since 1731; its fruit is globular, and about the size of a cherry. The West Indian stomachic *man-dram* is prepared by mashing a few pods of bird pepper and mixing them with sliced cucumber and shallots, to which have been added a little lime-juice and Madeira wine. Chillies, the dried ripe or unripe fruit of capsicums, especially *C. annuum* and *C. frutescens*, are used to make chilly-vinegar, as well as for pickles. Cayenne pepper is manufactured from the ripe fruits, which are dried, ground, mixed with wheat flour, and made into cakes with yeast; the cakes are baked till hard like biscuit, and then ground and sifted. The pepper is sometimes prepared by simply drying the pods and pounding them fine in a mortar. Cayenne pepper is occasionally adulterated with red lead, vermilion, ochre, salt, ground-rice and turmeric. The taste of the pepper is impaired by exposure to damp and the heat of the sun. Chillies have been in use from time immemorial; they are eaten in great quantity by the people of Guiana and other warm countries, and in Europe are largely consumed both as a spice and as medicine.

The dried ripe fruit of *Capsicum frutescens* from Zanzibar, known as pod pepper and Guinea pepper, is official in the British Pharmacopoeia under the name *Capsici Fructus*. The fruit has a characteristic, pungent odour and an intensely bitter taste. The chief constituents are a crystallizable resin, capsaicin, a volatile alkaloid, capsicine and a volatile oil. The dose is ½-1 grain. The British Pharmacopoeia contains two preparations of capsicum, a tincture (dose 5-15 minims) and an ointment. Externally the drug has the usual action of a volatile oil, being a very powerful counter-irritant. It does not, however, cause pustulation. Its internal action is also that of its class, but its marked contact properties make it specially useful in gastriatony and flatulence, and sometimes in hysteria.

CAYEY, an inland district and mountain town of the department of Guayama, Porto Rico, celebrated for its cool, invigorating climate and the beauty of its scenery. Pop. (1899) of the town, 3763; of the district, 14,442. The town is surrounded by mountain summits, the highest of which, El Torito, rises to an elevation of 2362 ft. above sea-level. It was made a military post by the Spaniards and used as an acclimatizing station. The old Spanish barracks have been enlarged and improved by the American military authorities and, under the name of "Henry Barracks," are used for the same purpose. The town is a popular summer resort for residents of the coast cities. The surrounding country is wooded and very fertile, being especially noted for its coffee and tobacco. The town has large cigar factories. Cayey is connected with Guayama by an excellent military road.

CAYLEY, ARTHUR (1821-1895), English mathematician, was born at Richmond, in Surrey, on the 16th of August 1821, the second son of Henry Cayley, a Russian merchant, and Maria Antonia Doughty. His father, Henry Cayley, retired from business in 1829 and settled in Blackheath, where Arthur was sent to a private school kept by the Rev. G.B.F. Potticary; at the age of fourteen he was transferred to King's College school, London. He soon showed that he was a boy of great capacity, and in particular that he was possessed of remarkable mathematical ability. On the advice of the school authorities he was entered at Trinity College, Cambridge, as a pensioner. He was there coached by William Hopkins of Peterhouse, was admitted a scholar of the college in May 1840, and graduated as senior wrangler in 1842, and obtained the first Smith's Prize at the next examination. In 1842, also, he was elected a fellow of Trinity, and became a major fellow in 1845, the year in which he proceeded to the M.A. degree. He was assistant tutor of Trinity for three years. In 1846, having decided to adopt the law as a profession, he left Cambridge, entered at Lincoln's Inn, and became a pupil of the conveyancer Mr Christie. He was called to the bar in 1849, and remained at the bar fourteen years, till 1863, when he was elected to the new Sadlerian chair of pure mathematics in the university of Cambridge. He settled at Cambridge in the same year, and married Susan, daughter of Robert Moline of Greenwich. He continued to reside in Cambridge and to hold the professorship till his death, which occurred on the 26th of January 1895. From the time he went first to Cambridge till his death he was constantly engaged in mathematical investigation. The number of his papers and memoirs, some of them of considerable length, exceeds 800; they were published, at the time they were composed, in various scientific journals in Europe and America, and are now embodied, through the enterprise of the syndics of the Cambridge University Press, in thirteen large quarto volumes. These form an enduring monument to his fame. He wrote upon nearly every subject of pure mathematics, and also upon theoretical dynamics and spherical and physical astronomy. He was quite as much a geometrician as he was an analyst. Among his most remarkable works may be mentioned his ten memoirs on quantics, commenced in 1854 and completed in 1878; his creation of the theory of matrices; his researches on the theory of groups; his memoir on abstract geometry, a subject which he created; his introduction into geometry of the "absolute"; his researches on the higher singularities of curves and surfaces; the classification of cubic curves; additions to the theories of rational transformation and correspondence; the theory of the twenty-seven lines that lie on a cubic surface; the theory of elliptic functions; the attraction of ellipsoids; the British Association Reports, 1857 and 1862, on recent progress in general and special theoretical dynamics, and on the secular acceleration of the moon's mean motion. He is justly regarded as one of the greatest of mathematicians. Competent judges have compared him to Leonhard Euler for his range, analytical power and introduction of new and fertile theories. He was the recipient of nearly every academic distinction that can be conferred upon an eminent man 590of science. Amongst others may be noted honorary degrees by the universities of Oxford, Dublin, Edinburgh, Göttingen, Heidelberg, Leiden and Bologna. He was fellow or foreign corresponding member of the French Institute, the academies of Berlin, Göttingen, St Petersburg, Milan, Rome, Leiden, Upsala and Hungary; and he was nominated an officer of the Legion of Honour by President Carnot. At various times he was president of the Cambridge Philosophical Society, of the London Mathematical Society and of the Royal Astronomical Society. He was elected a fellow of the Royal Society in 1852, and received from that body a Royal medal in 1859 and the Copley medal in 1882. He also received the De Morgan medal from the London Mathematical Society, and the Huygens medal from Leiden. His nature was noble and generous, and the universal appreciation of this fact gave him great influence in his university. His portrait, by Lowes Dickinson, was placed in the hall of Trinity College in 1874, and his bust, by Henry Wiles, in the library of the same college in 1888.

(P. A. M.)

CAYLUS, ANNE CLAUDE PHILIPPE DE TUBIÈRES DE GRIMOARD DE PESTELS DE LÉVIS, COMTE DE, Marquis d'Esternay, baron de Bransac (1692-1765), French archaeologist and man of letters, was born at Paris on the 31st of October 1692. He was the eldest son of Lieutenant-General Count de Caylus. His mother, Marthe Marguerite le Valois de Vilette de Murçay, comtesse de Caylus (1673-1729), was a cousin of Mme de Maintenon, who brought her up like her own daughter. She wrote valuable memoirs of the court of Louis XIV. entitled *Souvenirs*; these were edited by Voltaire (1770), and by many later editors, notably Renouard (1806), Ch. Asselineau (1860), M. de Lescure (1874), M.E. Raunié (1881), J. Soury (1883). While a young man Caylus distinguished himself in the campaigns of the French army, from 1709 to 1714. After the peace of Rastadt he spent some time in travelling in Italy, Greece, the East, England and Germany, and devoted much attention to the study and collection of antiquities. He became an active member of the Academy of Painting and Sculpture and of the Academy of Inscriptions. Among his antiquarian works are *Recueil d'antiquités égyptiennes, étrusques, grecques, romaines, et gauloises* (6 vols., Paris, 1752-1755), *Numismata Aurea Imperatorum Romanorum*, and a *Mémoire* (1755) on the method of encaustic painting with wax mentioned by Pliny, which he claimed to have rediscovered. Diderot, who was no friend to Caylus, maintained that the proper method had been found by J.J. Bachelier. Caylus was an admirable engraver, and copied many of the

paintings of the great masters. He caused engravings to be made, at his own expense, of Bartoli's copies from ancient pictures and published *Nouveaux sujets de peinture et de sculpture* (1755) and *Tableaux tirés de l'Iliade, de l'Odysse, et de l'Enéide*(1757). He encouraged artists whose reputations were still in the making, but his patronage was somewhat capricious. Diderot expressed this fact in an epigram in his *Salon* of 1765: "La mort nous a délivrés du plus cruel des amateurs." Caylus had quite another side to his character. He had a thorough acquaintance with the gayest and most disreputable sides of Parisian life, and left a number of more or less witty stories dealing with it. These were collected (Amsterdam, 1787) as his *Oeuvres badines complètes*. The best of them is the*Histoire de M. Guillaume, cocher* (c. 1730).

The *Souvenirs du comte de Caylus*, published in 1805, is of very doubtful authenticity. See also A. and J. de Goncourt, *Portraits intimes du XVIIIe siècle*; Ch. Nisard's edition of the *Correspondance du comte de Caylus avec le père Paciaudi*(1877); and a notice by O. Uzanne prefixed to a volume of his *Facéties* (1879).

CAYMAN ISLANDS, a group of three low-lying islands in the West Indies. They consist of Grand Cayman, Little Cayman and Cayman Brac, and are situated between 79° 44' and 80° 26' W. and 19° 44' and 19° 46' N., forming a dependency of Jamaica, which lies 178 m. E.S.E. Grand Cayman, a rock-bound island protected by coral reefs, is 17 m. long and varies from 4 m. to 7 m. in breadth. It has two towns, Georgetown and Boddentown. Little Cayman and Cayman Brac are both about 70 m. E.N.E. of Grand Cayman. Excepting near the rocky coast, the islands are fruitful, mahogany and other valuable timbers with some dyewood are grown, and large quantities of coco-nuts are produced by the two smaller islands. Phosphate deposits of considerable value are worked, but the principal occupation of the inhabitants is catching turtles for export to Jamaica. The people are excellent shipwrights and do a considerable trade in schooners built of native wood. The islands are governed by a commissioner, and the laws passed by the local legislative assembly are subject to the assent of the governor of Jamaica. The population of the group is about 5000. The islands were discovered by Columbus, who named them Tortugas from the turtles with which the surrounding sea abounds. They were never occupied by the Spaniards and were colonized from Jamaica by the British.

CAZALÈS, JACQUES ANTOINE MARIE DE (1758-1805), French orator and politician, was born at Grenade in Languedoc, of a family of the lower nobility. Before 1789 he was a cavalry officer, but in that year was returned as deputy to the states general. In the Constituent Assembly he belonged to the section of moderate royalists who sought to set up a constitution on the English model, and his speeches in favour of retaining the right of war and peace in the king's hands and on the organization of the judiciary gained the applause even of his opponents. Apart from his eloquence, which gave him a place among the finest orators of the Assembly, Cazalès is mainly remembered for a duel fought with Barnave. After the insurrection of the 10th of August 1792, which led to the downfall of royalty, Cazalès emigrated. He fought in the army of the *émigrés* against revolutionary France, lived in Switzerland and in England, and did not return to France until 1803. He died on the 24th of November 1805. His son, Edmond de Cazalès, wrote philosophical and religious studies.

See *Discours de Cazalès*, edited by Chare (Paris, 1821), with an introduction; F.A. Aulard, *Les Orateurs de la Constituante* (2nd ed., Paris, 1905.)

CAZALIS, HENRI (1840-1909), French poet and man of letters, was born at Cormeilles-en-Parisis (Seine-et-Oise) in 1840. He wrote under the pseudonyms of Jean Caselli and Jean Lahor. His works include: *Chants populaires de l'Italie* (1865); *Vita tristis,Rêveries fantastiques, Romances sans musique* (1865); *Le Livre du néant* (1872); *Henry Regnault, sa vie et son oeuvre* (1872); *L'Illusion* (1875-1893); *Melancholia* (1878); *Cantique des cantiques* (1885); *Les Quatrains d'Al-Gazali* (1895); *William Morris* (1897). The author of the *Livre du néant* has a predilection for gloomy subjects and especially for pictures of death. His oriental habits of thought earned for him the title of the "Hindou du Parnasse contemporain." He died in July 1909.

197

See a notice by P. Bourget in *Anthologie des poètes fr. du XIXe siècle* (1887-1888); J. Lemaître, *Les Contemporains* (1889); E. Faguet in the *Revue bleue* (October 1893).

CAZEMBE, the hereditary name of an African chief, whose territory was situated south of Lake Mweru and north of Bangweulu, between 9° and 11°S. In the end of the 18th century the authority of the Cazembe was recognized over a very extensive district. The kingdom, known also as the Cazembe, continued to exist, though with gradually diminishing power and extent, until the last quarter of the 19th century, when the Cazembe sank to the rank of a petty chief. The country is now divided between Great Britain and Belgian Congo. The British half, lying east of the Luapula, forms part of Rhodesia, and the chief town in it is called Kazembe. The native state, ruled by a negro race who overcame the aboriginals, had attained a certain degree of civilization. Agriculture was diligently followed, and cotton cloth, earthenware and iron goods manufactured. The country contains rich deposits of copper, and copper ore was one of the principal articles of export. The Cazembe had despotic power and used it in barbarous fashion. He had hundreds of wives, and his chiefs imitated his example according to their means. On his accession every new Cazembe chose a new site for his residence. In 1796 the Cazembe was visited by Manoel Caetano Pereira, a Portuguese merchant; and in 1798 a more important journey to the same region was undertaken by Dr Francisco José Maria de Lacerda. He died in that country on 591 the 18th of October that year, but left behind him a valuable journal. In 1802 two native traders or *pombeiros*, Pedro João Baptista and Amaro José, were sent by the Portuguese on a visit to the Cazembe; and in 1831 a more extensive mission was despatched by the Portuguese governor of Sena. It consisted of Major José Monteiro and Antonio Gamitto, with an escort of 20 soldiers and 120 negro slaves as porters; but its reception by the Cazembe was not altogether satisfactory. In 1868 David Livingstone visited the Cazembe, whose capital at that time numbered no more than 1000 souls. Since 1894, when the country was divided between Britain and the Congo State, it has been thoroughly explored. An important copper mining industry is carried on in the Congo division of the territory.

See *The Lands of the Cazembe*, published by the Royal Geographical Society in 1873, containing translations of Lacerda and Baptista's journals, and a résumé of Gamitto's *O Muata Cazembe* (Lisbon, 1854); also Livingstone's *Last Journals* (London, 1874).

CAZIN, JEAN CHARLES (1840-1901), French landscape-painter, son of a well-known doctor, F.J. Cazin (1788-1864), was born at Samer, Pas-de-Calais. After studying in France, he went to England, where he was strongly influenced by the pre-Raphaelite movement. His chief earlier pictures have a religious interest, shown in such examples as "The Flight into Egypt" (1877), or "Hagar and Ishmael" (1880, Luxembourg); and afterwards his combination of luminous landscape with figure-subjects ("Souvenir de fête," 1881; "Journée faite," 1888) gave him a wide repute, and made him the leader of a new school of idealistic subject-painting in France. He was made an officer of the Legion of Honour in 1889. His charming and poetical treatment of landscape is the feature in his painting which in later years has given them an increasing value among connoisseurs. His wife, Marie Cazin, who was his pupil and exhibited her first picture at the Salon in 1876, the same year in which Cazin himself made his début there, was also a well-known artist and sculptor.

CAZOTTE, JACQUES (1719-1792), French author, was born at Dijon, on the 17th of October 1719. He was educated by the Jesuits, and at twenty-seven he obtained a public office at Martinique, but it was not till his return to Paris in 1760 with the rank of commissioner-general that he made a public appearance as an author. His first attempts, a mock romance, and a coarse song, gained so much popularity, both in the Court and among the people, that he was encouraged to essay something more ambitious. He accordingly produced his romance, *Les Prouesses inimitables d'Ollivier, marquis d'Édesse*. He also wrote a number of fantastic oriental tales, such as his *Mille et une fadaises, Contes à dormir debout* (1742). His first success was with a "poem" in twelve cantos, and in prose intermixed with verse, entitled *Ollivier* (2 vols., 1762), followed in 1771 by another romance, the *Lord Impromptu*. But the most popular of his works was the *Diable amoureux* (1772), a fantastic tale in which the hero raises the devil. The value of the story lies in the picturesque setting, and the skill with which its details are carried out. Cazotte possessed extreme facility and is said to have turned off a seventh canto of Voltaire's *Guerre civile de Genève* in a single night. About 1775 Cazotte embraced the views of the Illuminati, declaring himself possessed of the power of prophecy. It was upon this fact that La Harpe based his famous *jeu d'esprit*, in which he represents Cazotte as prophesying the most minute events of the Revolution. On the discovery of some of his letters in August 1792, Cazotte was arrested; and though he escaped for a time through the love and courage of his daughter, he was executed on the 25th of the following month.

The only complete edition is the *Œuvres badines et morales, historiques et philosophiques de Jacques Cazotte* (4 vols., 1816-1817), though more than one collection appeared during his lifetime. An édition de luxe of the *Diable amoureux* was edited (1878) by A.J. Pons, and a selection of Cazotte's *Contes*, edited (1880) by Octave Uzanne, is included in the series of *Petits Conteurs du XVIIIe siècle*. The best notice of Cazotte is in the *Illuminés* (1852) of Gérard de Nerval.

CEANOTHUS, in botany, a genus of the natural order Rhamnaceae, containing about forty species of shrubs or small trees, natives of North America. They are very attractive from their dense panicles of white or blue flowers, and several species are known as garden plants. The leaves of one of these, *C. americanus*, New Jersey tea, or red-root, are used instead of the true tea; the root, which contains a red colouring matter, has long been employed by the Indians as a febrifuge.

CEARÁ, a northern maritime state of Brazil, bounded N. by the Atlantic, E. by the Atlantic and the states of Rio Grande do Norte and Parahyba, S. by Pernambuco, and W. by Piauhy; and having an area of 40,253 sq. m. It lies partly upon the north-east slope of the great Brazilian plateau, and partly upon the sandy coastal plain. Its surface is a succession of great terraces, facing north and north-east, formed by the denudation of the ancient sandstone plateau which once covered this part of the continent; the terraces are seamed by watercourses, and their valleys are broken by hills and ranges of highlands. The latter are usually described as mountain ranges, but they are, in fact, only the remains of the ancient plateau, capped with horizontal strata of sandstone, and having a remarkably uniform altitude of 2000 to 2400 ft. The flat top of such a range is called a *chapada* or *taboleira*, and its width in places is from 32 to 56 m. The boundary line with Piauhy follows one of these ranges, the Serra de Ibiapaba, which unites with another range on the southern boundary of the state, known as the Serra do Araripe. Another range, or escarpment, crosses the state from east to west, but is broken into two principal divisions, each having several local names. These ranges are not continuous, the breaking down of the ancient plateau having been irregular and uneven. The higher ranges intercept considerable moisture from the prevailing trade winds, and their flanks and valleys are covered with forest, but the plateaus are either thinly wooded or open campo. These upland forests are of a scrubby character and are called *catingas*.

The sandy, coastal plain, with a width of 12 to 18 m., is nearly bare of vegetation. The rivers of the state are small and, with one or two exceptions, become completely dry in the dry season. The largest is the Jaguaribe, which flows entirely across the state in a north-east direction with an estimated length of 210 to 465 m. The year is divided into a rainy and dry season, the rains beginning in January to March and lasting until June. The dry season, July to December, is sometimes broken by slight showers in September and October, but these are of very slight importance. The soil is thin and porous and does not retain moisture, consequently the long, dry season turns the country into a barren desert, relieved only by vegetation along the river courses and mountain ranges, and by the hardy, widely-distributed carnahuba palm (*Copernicia cerifera*), which in places forms groves of considerable extent. Sometimes the rains fail altogether, and then a drought (*sêcca*) ensues, causing famine and pestilence throughout the entire region. The most destructive droughts recorded are those of 1711, 1723, 1777-1778, 1790, 1825, 1844-1845, and 1877-1878, the last-mentioned destroying nearly all the live-stock in the state, and causing the death through starvation and pestilence of nearly half-a-million people, or over half the population. The climate, which is generally described as healthful, is hot and humid on the coast, tempered by the cool trade winds; but in the more elevated regions it is very hot and dry, although the nights are cool. The sandy zone along the coast is nearly barren, but behind this is a more elevated region with broken surfaces and sandy soil which is amenable to cultivation and produces fruit and most tropical products when conditions are favourable.

The higher plateau is devoted almost exclusively to cattle-raising, once the principal industry of the state, though recurring sêccas have been an insuperable obstacle to its profitable development. There is still a considerable export of cattle, hides and skins, but no effort is made to develop the production of jerked beef on a large scale. Horses are raised to a limited extent; also goats, sheep and swine. The principal agricultural products are cotton, coffee, sugar, mandioca and tropical fruits. The production of cotton has increased largely since the development of cotton manufactures in Brazil. The natural vegetable productions are important, and include *maniçoba* or Ceará rubber, carnahuba wax and fibre, cajú wine and ipecacuanha.

592

There are two lines of railway running inland from the coast: the Baturité line from Fortaleza to Senador Pompeu, 179 m., and the Sobral line from Camocim (a small port) to Ipú, 134 m. These railways were built by the national government after the drought of 1877-1878 to give work to the starving refugees, and are now operated under leases. Great dams were also begun for irrigation purposes.

The misfortunes and poverty of the people have hindered their material development to a large extent, but another obstacle is to be found in their racial and social composition. Only a very small percentage of the population which numbered 805,687 in 1890, and 849,127 in 1900, is of pure European origin, the great majority being of the coloured races and their mixtures with the whites. The number of landed proprietors, professional men, merchants, &c., is comparatively small (about one-sixth), and a part of these are of mixed blood; the remaining five-sixths own no property, pay no taxes, and derive no benefits from the social and political institutions about them beyond the protection of the proprietors upon whose estates they live, the nominal protection of the state, and an occasional day's wage. Education has made no impression upon such people, and is confined almost exclusively to the upper classes, from which some of the most prominent men in Brazilian politics and literature have come. The state of Ceará has formed a bishopric of the Roman Catholic Church since 1853, the bishop having his residence at Fortaleza. The state is represented in the national congress by three senators and ten deputies. Its local government is vested in a president and legislative assembly of one chamber elected for a period of four years. Three vice-presidents are elected at the same time who succeed to the presidency in case of a vacancy according to the number of votes received. The judicial organization consists of the tribunal da Relaçáo at the state capital and subordinate courts in the *comarcas* and *termos*. The judges of the higher courts are appointed for life. The capital of the state is Fortaleza, sometimes called Ceará, which is also the principal commercial centre and shipping port. The principal towns are Aracaty, Baturité, Acarahú, Crato, Maranguape and Sobral.

The territory of Ceará includes three of the *capitanias* originally granted by the Portuguese crown in 1534. The first attempts to settle the territory failed, and the earliest Portuguese settlement was made near the mouth of the Rio Camocim in 1604. The French were already established on the coast, with their headquarters at Saint Louis, now Maranhão. Ceará was occupied by the Dutch from 1637 to 1654, and became a dependency of Pernambuco in 1680; this relationship lasted until 1799, when the *capitania* of Ceará was made independent. The *capitania* became a province in 1822 under Dom Pedro I. A revolution followed in 1824, the president of the province was deposed fifteen days after his arrival, and a republic was proclaimed. Internal dissensions immediately broke out, the new president was assassinated, and after a brief reign of terror the province resumed its allegiance to the empire. Ceará was one of the first provinces of Brazil to abolish slavery.

200

See Rodolpho Theophilo, *Historia da Secca do Ceará, 1877 a 1880* (Fortaleza, 1883); Professor and Mrs Louis Agassiz, *A Journey in Brazil* (Boston, 1869); George Gardiner, *Travels in the Interior of Brazil* (London, 1846); C.F. Hartt, *Geology and Physical Geography of Brazil* (Boston, 1870); and H.H. Smith, *Brazil: the Amazon and the Coast* (New York, 1879).

CEAWLIN (d. 593), king of the West Saxons, first mentioned in the *Anglo-Saxon Chronicle* under the date 556 as fighting with his father Cynric against the Britons at the battle of Beranbyrig or Barbury Hill. Becoming king in 560, he began a career of conquest. Silchester was taken, and moving eastwards Ceawlin and his brother Cutha defeated the forces of Æthelberht, king of Kent, at the battle of Wibbandun in 568. In 577 he led the West Saxons from Winchester towards the Severn valley; gained an important victory over some British kings at Deorham, and added the district round Gloucester, Bath and Cirencester to his kingdom. A further advance was begun in 583. Uriconium, a town near the Wrekin, and Pengwyrn, the modern Shrewsbury, were destroyed; but soon Ceawlin was defeated by the Britons at Fethanleag or Faddiley, near Nantwich, and his progress was effectually checked. Intestine strife among the West Saxons followed. In 591 Ceawlin lost the western part of his kingdom, and in 592 Was defeated by his nephew, Ceolric, at Wanborough, and driven from Wessex. He was killed in 593, possibly in an attempt to regain his kingdom. Ceawlin is included in the *Chronicle* among the Bretwaldas.

See *Two of the Saxon Chronicles*, ed. by C. Plummer (Oxford, 1892); *Dictionary of National Biography*, vol. ix (London, 1887); E. Guest, *Origines Celticae*, vol. ii. (London, 1883).

CEBES, the name of two Greek philosophers, (1) CEBES OF CYZICUS, mentioned in Athenaeus (iv. 156 D), seems to have been a Stoic, who lived during the reign of Marcus Aurelius. Some would attribute to him the *Tabula Cebetis* (see below), but as that work was well known in the time of Lucian, it is probably to be placed earlier. (2) CEBES OF THEBES, a disciple of Socrates and Philolaus. He is one of the speakers in the *Phaedo* of Plato, in which he is represented as an earnest seeker after virtue and truth, keen in argument and cautious in decision. Three dialogues, the Έβδόμη, the Φρύνιχος and the Πίναξ or *Tabula*, are attributed to him by Suidas and Diogenes Laërtius. The two former are lost, and most scholars deny the authenticity of the *Tabula* on the ground of material and verbal anachronisms. They attribute it either to Cebes of Cyzicus (above) or to an anonymous author, of the 1st century A.D., who assumed the character of Cebes of Thebes. The work professes to be an interpretation of an allegorical picture in the temple of Cronus at Athens or Thebes. The author develops the Platonic theory of pre-existence, and shows that true education consists not in mere erudition, but rather in the formation of character.

The *Tabula* has been widely translated both into European languages and into Arabic (the latter version published with the Greek text and Latin translation by Salmasius in 1640). It is usually printed together with Epictetus. Separate editions by C.S. Jerram (with introduction and notes, 1878), C. Prächter (1893), and many others. See Zeller's *History of Greek Philosophy*; F. Klopfer, *De Cebetis Tabula* (1818-1822); C. Prächter, *Cebetis Tabula quanam aetate conscripta esse videatur* (1885).

CEBÚ, a city and municipality, port of entry, and the capital of the province of Cebú, island of Cebú, Philippine Islands, on the E. coast, a little N. of the centre. Pop. (1903) of the city proper, 18,330; of the municipality, 31,079; in the same year, after the census enumeration, the neighbouring municipalities of Mabolo (pop. 1903, 8454) and El Pardo (pop. 6461) were added to the municipality of Cebú. The surrounding country, which is level and fertile, is traversed by several good carriage roads. The port, formed by the north-west shore of the island of Mactán, is well protected from violent winds, and in front of it stands a picturesque Spanish fort. The streets are wide and regularly laid out. The government buildings are fairly good, and the church buildings very fine. Cebú is an episcopal see, and the palace of the bishop, although small, is widely known for its interior decorations. The Augustinian church is famous for its so-called miraculous image of Santo Niño. The Recoleto monastery and the seminary of San Carlos are worthy of mention. The cathedral was finished toward the end of the eighteenth century. The San José hospital here was founded by one of the religious orders. There was a leper hospital in the outskirts of the city until 1906, when a leper colony was established on the island of Culión. Commercially, Cebú is the second city of the Philippines. Hemp, tobacco, sugar and copra are the most important exports. In addition to the trade with foreign ports, an important domestic commerce is carried on with Manila, Bohol, Negros and northern Mindanao. Salt, pottery and fabrics of silk, sinamay, hemp and cotton are manufactured, and sugar sacks are woven in considerable quantity. The island of Cebú is known for its excellent mangoes and for the rare cornucopia-shaped sponges, called Venus's flower basket (*Euplectella aspergillum*), found here. Historically Cebú is famous as the scene of Magellan's landing in 1521. A cross, said to be the one first erected by him, is still preserved in the cathedral. The great explorer lost his life in the neighbouring island of Mactán; a monument marks the place where he was 593killed. The first Spanish settlement in the Philippines was established at Cebú in 1565, and from that year to 1571 it was the capital of the colony. The city is unincorporated. The language is Cebú-Visayan.

CECCO D'ASCOLI (1257-1327), the popular name of FRANCESCO DEGLI STABILI, a famous Italian encyclopaedist and poet—Cecco being the diminutive of Francesco, and Ascoli, in the marshes of Ancona, the place of the philosopher's birth. He devoted himself to the study of mathematics and astrology, and in 1322 was made professor of the latter science at the university of Bologna. It is alleged that he entered the service of Pope John XXII. at Avignon, and that he cultivated the acquaintance of Dante only to quarrel with the great poet afterwards; but of this there is no evidence. It is certain, however, that, having published a commentary on the sphere of John de Sacrobosco, in which he propounded audacious theories concerning the employment and agency of demons, he got into difficulties with the clerical party, and was condemned in 1324 to certain fasts and prayers, and to the payment of a fine of seventy crowns. To elude this sentence he betook himself to Florence, where he was attached to the household of Carlo di Calabria. But his free-thinking and plain speaking had got him many enemies; he had attacked the *Commedia* of Dante, and the *Canzone d'Amore* of Guido Cavalcanti; and his fate was sealed. Dino di Garbo, the physician, was indefatigable in pursuit of him; and the old accusation of impiety being renewed, Cecco was again tried and sentenced, this time to the stake. He was burned at Florence the day after sentence, in the seventieth year of his age.

Cecco d'Ascoli left many works in manuscript, most of which have never been given to the world. The book by which he achieved his renown and which led to his death was theAcerba (from *acervus*), an encyclopaedic poem, of which in 1546, the date of the last reprint, more than twenty editions had been issued. It is unfinished, and consists of four books insesta rima. The first book treats of astronomy and meteorology; the second of stellar influences, of physiognomy, and of the vices and virtues; the third of minerals and of the love of animals; while the fourth propounds and solves a number of moral and physical problems. Of a fifth book, on theology, the initial chapter alone was completed. A man of immense erudition and of great and varied abilities, Cecco, whose knowledge was based on experiment and observation (a fact that of itself is enough to distinguish him from the crowd of savants of that age), had outstripped his contemporaries in many things. He knew of metallic aerolites and shooting stars; the mystery of the dew was plain to him; fossil plants were accounted for by him through terrene revolutions which had resulted in the formation of mountains; he is even said to have divined the circulation of the blood. Altogether a remarkable man, he may be described as one of the many Cassandras of the middle ages—one of the many prophets who spoke of coming light, and were listened to but to have their words cast back at them in accusations of impiety and sentences of death.

The least faulty of the many editions of the *Acerba* is that of Venice, dated 1510. The earliest known, which has become excessively rare, is that of Brescia, which has no date, but is ascribed to 1473 or thereabouts.

CECIL, the name of a famous English family. This house, whose two branches hold each a marquessate, had a great statesman and administrator to establish and enrich it. The first Lord Burghley's many inquiries concerning the origin of his family created for it more than one splendid and improbable genealogy, although his grandfather is the first ascertained ancestor. In the latter half of the 15th century a family of yeomen or small gentry with the surname of Seyceld, whose descendants were accepted by Lord Burghley as his kinsmen, lived on their lands at Allt yr Ynys in Walterstone, a Herefordshire parish on the Welsh marches. Of the will of Richard ap Philip Seyceld of Allt yr Ynys, made in 1508, one David ap Richard Seyceld, apparently his younger son, was overseer. This David seems identical with David Cyssell, Scisseld or Cecill, a yeoman admitted in 1494 to the freedom of Stamford in Lincolnshire. He may well have been one of those men from the Welsh border who fought at Bosworth, for at the funeral of Henry VII. he appears as a yeoman of the guard and is given a livery of black cloth. At Stamford he prospered, being three times mayor and three times member of parliament for the borough, and he served as sheriff of Northamptonshire in 1532-1533. Remaining in the service of Henry VIII. he was advanced to be yeoman of the chamber and sergeant-at-arms, being rewarded with several profitable leases and offices. His first wife was the daughter of a Stamford alderman, and his second the already twice widowed heir of a Lincolnshire squire. By the first marriage David Cecil left at his death in 1536 a son and heir, Richard Cecil, who enjoyed a place at court as yeoman of the king's wardrobe under Henry VIII. and Edward VI. A gentleman of the privy chamber and sometime sheriff of Rutland, Richard Cecil had his share at the distribution of abbey lands, St Michael's priory in Stamford being among the grants made to him. William Cecil, only son of Richard, was born, by his own account, in 1520, at Bourne in Lincolnshire. He advanced himself first in the service of the protector Somerset, after whose fall, his great abilities being necessary to the council, he was made a secretary of state and sworn of the privy council. In 1571 he was created Lord Burghley, and from 1572, when he was given the Garter, he was lord high treasurer and principal minister to Queen Elizabeth. By his first wife, Mary Cheke, sister of the scholar Sir John Cheke, tutor to Edward VI., he was father to Thomas, first earl of Exeter. By a second wife, Mildred Cooke, the most learned lady of her time, he had an only surviving son, Robert Cecil, ancestor of the house of Salisbury.

Created earl of Exeter by James I., the second Lord Burghley was more soldier than statesman, and from his death to the present day the elder line of the Cecils has taken small part in public affairs. William Cecil, 2nd earl of Exeter, took as his first wife the Lady Roos, daughter and heir of the 3rd earl of Rutland of the Manners family. The son of this marriage inherited the barony of Roos as heir general, and died as a Roman Catholic at Naples in 1618 leaving no issue. A third son of the 1st earl was Edward Cecil, a somewhat incompetent military commander, created in 1625 Lord Cecil of Putney and Viscount Wimbledon, titles that died with him in 1638, although he was thrice married. In 1801 a marquessate was given to the 10th earl of Exeter, the story of whose marriage with Sarah Hoggins, daughter of a Shropshire husbandman, has been refined by Tennyson into the romance of "The Lord of Burleigh." This elder line is still seated at Burghley, the great mansion built by their ancestor, the first lord.

The younger or Hatfield line was founded by Robert Cecil, the only surviving son of the great Burghley's second marriage. As a secretary of state he followed in his father's steps, and on the death of Elizabeth he may be said to have secured the accession of King James, who created him Lord Cecil of Essendine (1603), Viscount Cranborne (1604), and earl of Salisbury (1605). Forced by the king to exchange his house of Theobalds for Hatfield, he died in 1612, worn out with incessant labour, before he could inhabit the house which he built upon his new Hertfordshire estate. Of Burghley and his son Salisbury, "great ministers of state in the eyes of Christendom," Clarendon writes that "their wisdom and virtues died with them." The 2nd earl of Salisbury, "a man of no words, except in hunting and hawking," was at first remarked for his obsequiousness to the court party, but taking no part in the Civil War came at last to sit in the Protector's parliament. After the Restoration, Pepys saw him, old and discredited, at Hatfield, and notes him as "my simple Lord Salisbury." The 7th earl was created marquess of Salisbury in 1789.

Hatfield House, a great Jacobean mansion which has suffered much from restoration and rebuilding, contains in its library the famous series of state papers which passed through the hands of Burghley and his son Salisbury, invaluable sources for the history of their period.

(O. BA.)

CECILIA, SAINT, in the Catholic Church the patron saint of music and of the blind. Her festival falls on the 22nd of November. It was long supposed that she was a noble lady of Rome 594who, with her husband and other friends whom she had converted, sufferedmartyrdom, c. 230, under the emperor Alexander Severus. The researches of de Rossi, however (*Rom. sott.* ii. 147), go to confirm the statement of Fortunatus, bishop of Poitiers (d. 600), that she perished in Sicily under Marcus Aurelius between 176 and 180. A church in her honour existed in Rome from about the 4th century, and was rebuilt with much splendour by Pope Paschal I. about the year 820, and again by Cardinal Sfondrati in 1599. It is situated in the Trastevere near the Ripa Grande quay, where in earlier days the Ghetto was located, and gives a "title" to a cardinal priest. Cecilia, whose musical fame rests on a passing notice in her legend that she praised God by instrumental as well as vocal music, has inspired many a masterpiece in art, including the Raphael at Bologna, the Rubens in Berlin, the Domenichino in Paris, and in literature, where she is commemorated especially by Chaucer's "Seconde Nonnes Tale," and by Dryden's famous ode, set to music by Handel in 1736, and later by Sir Hubert Parry (1889).

Another St Cecilia, who suffered in Africa in the persecution of Diocletian (303-304), is commemorated on the 11th of February.

See U. Chevalier, *Répertoire des sources historiques* (1905), i. 826 f.

CECROPIA, in botany, a genus of trees (natural order Moraceae), native of tropical America. They are of very rapid growth, affording a light wood used for making floats. *C. peltata* is the trumpet tree, so-called from the use made of its hollow stems by the Uaupé Indians as a musical instrument. It is a tree reaching about 50 ft. in height with a large spreading head, and deeply lobed leaves 12 in. or more in diameter. The hollows of the stem and branches are inhabited by ants, which in return for the shelter thus afforded, and food in the form of succulent growths on the base of the leaf-stalks, repel the attacks of leaf-cutting ants which would otherwise strip the tree of its leaves. This is an instance of "myrmecophily," *i.e.* a living together for mutual benefit of the ants and the plant.

CECROPS (Κέκροψ), traditionally the first king of Attica, and the founder of its political life (Pausanias ix. 33). He was said to have divided the inhabitants into twelve communities, to have instituted the laws of marriage and property, and a new form of worship. The introduction of bloodless sacrifice, the burial of the dead, and the invention of writing were also attributed to him. He is said to have acted as umpire during the dispute of Poseidon and Athena for the possession of Attica. He decided in favour of the goddess, who planted the first olive tree, which he adjudged to be more useful than the horse (or water) which Poseidon caused to spring forth from the Acropolis rock with a blow of his trident (Herodotus viii. 55; Apollodorus iii. 14). As one of the autochthones of Attica, Cecrops is represented as human in the upper part of his body, while the lower part is shaped like a dragon (hence he is sometimes called διφυής or *geminus*, Diod. Sic. i. 28; Ovid, *Metam.* ii. 555). Miss J. E. Harrison (in *Classical Review*, January 1895) endeavours to show that Cecrops is the husband of Athene, identical with the snake-like Zeus Soter or Sosipolis, and the father of Erechtheus-Erichthonius.

CEDAR (Lat. *cedrus*, Gr. κέδρος), a name applied to several members of the natural order Coniferae. The word has been derived from the Arabic *Kedr*, worth or value, or from*Kedrat*, strong, and has been supposed by some to have taken its origin from the brook Kedron, in Judaea.

Cedrus Libani, the far-famed Cedar of Lebanon, is a tree which, on account of its beauty, stateliness and strength, has always been a favourite with poets and painters, and which, in the figurative language of prophecy, is frequently employed in the Scriptures as a symbol of power, prosperity and longevity. It grows to a vertical height of from 50 to 80 ft.—"exalted above all trees of the field"—and at an elevation of about 6000 ft. above sea-level. In the young tree, the bole is straight and upright, and one or two leading branches rise above the rest. As the tree increases in size, however, the upper branches become mingled together, and the tree is then clump-headed. Numerous lateral ramifying branches spread out from the main trunk in a horizontal direction, tier upon tier, covering a compass of ground the diameter of which is often greater than the height of the tree. William Gilpin, in his *Forest Scenery*, describes a cedar which, at an age of about 118 years, had attained to a height of 53 ft. and had a horizontal expanse of 96 ft. The branchlets of the cedar take the same direction as the branches, and the foliage is very dense. The tree, as with the rest of the fir-tribe, except the larch, is evergreen; new leaves are developed every spring, but their fall is gradual. In shape the leaves are straight, tapering, cylindrical and pointed; they are about 1 in. long and of a dark green colour, and grow in alternate tufts of about thirty in number. The male and female flowers grow on the same tree, but are separate. The cones, which are on the upper side of the branches, are flattened at the ends and are 4 to 5 in. in length and 2 in. wide; they take two years to come to perfection and while growing exude much resin. The scales are close pressed to one another and are reddish in colour. The seeds are provided with a long membranous wing. The root of the tree is very strong and ramifying. The cedar flourishes best on sandy, loamy soils. It still grows on Lebanon, though for several centuries it was believed to be restricted to a small grove in the Kadisha valley at 6000 ft. elevation, about 15 m. from Beyrout. The number of trees in this grove has been gradually diminishing, and as no young trees or seedlings occur, the grove will probably become extinct in course of time. Cedars are now known to occur in great numbers on Mt. Lebanon, chiefly on the western slopes, not forming a continuous forest, but in groves, some of which contain several thousands of trees. There are also large forests on the higher slopes of the Taurus and Anti-Taurus mountains. Lamartine tells us that the Arabs regard the trees as endowed with the principles of continual existence, and with reasoning and prescient powers, which enable them to prepare for the changes of the seasons.

The wood of the cedar of Lebanon is fragrant, though not so strongly scented as that of the juniper or red-cedar of America. The wood is generally reddish-brown, light and of a coarse grain and spongy texture, easy to work, but liable to shrink and warp. Mountain-grown wood is harder, stronger, less liable to warp and more durable.

The cedar of Lebanon is cultivated in Europe for ornament only. It can be grown in parks and gardens, and thrives well; but the young plants are unable to bear great variations of temperature. The cedar is not mentioned in Evelyn's *Silva* (1664), but it must have been introduced shortly afterwards. The famous Enfield cedar was planted by Dr Robert Uvedale, (1642-1722), a noted schoolmaster and horticulturist, between 1662-1670, and an old cedar at Bretby Park in Derbyshire is known to have been planted in 1676. Some very old cedars exist also at Syon House, Woburn Abbey, Warwick Castle and elsewhere, which presumably date from the 17th century. The first cedars in Scotland were planted at Hopetoun House in 1740; and the first one said to have been introduced into France was brought from England by Bernard de Jussieu in 1734, and placed in the Jardin des Plantes. Cedar-wood is earliest noticed in Leviticus xiv. 4, 6, where it is prescribed among the materials to be used for the cleansing of leprosy; but the wood there spoken of was probably that of the juniper. The term *Eres* (cedar) of Scripture does not apply strictly to one kind of plant, but was used indefinitely in ancient times, as is the word cedar at present. The term *arzis* applied by the Arabs to the cedar of Lebanon, to the common pine-tree, and to the juniper; and certainly the "cedars" for masts, mentioned in Ezek. xxvii. 5, must have been pine-trees. It seems very probable that the fourscore thousand hewers employed by Solomon for cutting timber did not confine their operations simply to what would now be termed cedars and fir-trees. Dr John Lindley considered that some of the cedar-trees sent by Hiram, king of Tyre, to Jerusalem might have been procured from Mount Atlas, and have been identical with *Callitris quadrivalvis*, or arar-tree, the wood of which is hard and durable, and was much in request in former times for the building of temples. The timber-work of the roof of Cordova cathedral, built eleven centuries ago, is composed of it. In the time of 595Vitruvius "cedars" were growing in Crete, Africa and Syria. Pliny says that their wood was everlasting, and therefore images of the gods were made of it; he makes mention also of the oil of cedar, or *cedrium*, distilled from the wood, and used by the ancients for preserving their books from moths and damp; papyri anointed or rubbed with cedrium were on this account called *ced ati libri*. Drawers of cedar or chips of the wood are now employed to protect furs and woollen stuffs from injury by moths. Cedar-wood, however, is said to be injurious to natural history objects, and to instruments placed in cabinets made of it, as the resinous matter of the wood becomes deposited upon them. *Cedria*, or cedar resin, is a substance similar to mastic, that flows from incisions in the tree; and cedar manna is a sweet exudation from its branches.

The genus *Cedrus* contains two other species closely allied to *C. Libani*—*Cedrus Deodara*, the deodar, or "god tree" of the Himalayas, and *Cedrus atlantica*, of the Atlas range, North Africa. The deodar forms forests on the mountains of Afghanistan, North Beluchistan and the north-west Himalayas, flourishing in all the higher mountains from Nepal up to Kashmir, at an elevation of from 5500 to 12,000 ft.; on the peaks to the northern side of the Boorung Pass it grows to a height of 60 to 70 ft. before branching. The wood is close-grained, long-fibred, perfumed and highly resinous, and resists the action of water. The foliage is of a paler green, the leaves are slender and longer, and the twigs are thinner than those of *C. Libani*. The tree is employed for a variety of useful purposes, especially in building. It is now much cultivated in England as an ornamental plant. *C. atlantica*, the Atlas cedar, has shorter and denser leaves than *C. Libani*; the leaves are glaucous, sometimes of a silvery whiteness, and the cones smaller than in the other two forms; its wood also is hard, and more rapid in growth than is that of the ordinary cedar. It is found at an altitude above the sea of from 4000 to 6000 ft.

The name cedar is applied to a variety of trees, including species of several genera of Conifers, *Juniperus*, *Thuja*, *Libocedrus* and *Cupressus*. *Thuja gigantea* of western North America is known in the United States as White (or Yellow) cedar, and the same name is applied to *Cupressus Lawsoniana*, the Port Orford or Oregon cedar, a native of the north-west States, and one of the most valuable juniper trees of North America. The Bermuda cedar (*Juniperus bermudiana*) and the red or American cedar (*J. virginiana*) are both much used in joinery and in the manufacture of pencils; though other woods are now superseding them for pencil-making. The Japanese cedar (*Cryptomeria japonica*) is a kind of cypress, the wood of which is very durable. Another species of cypress (*Cupressus thyoides*, also known as *Chamaecyparis thyoides* or *sphaeroidea*), found in swamps in the south of Ohio and Massachusetts, is known as the American white cedar. It has small leaves and fibrous bark, the wood is light, soft and easily-worked, and very durable in contact with the soil, and is much used for boat-building and for making fences and coopers' staves. The Spanish cedar is a name applied to *Juniperus thurifera*, a native of the western Mediterranean region, and also to another species, *J. Oxycedrus*, a common plant in the Mediterranean region, forming a shrub or low tree with spreading branches and short, stiff, prickly leaves. The latter was much used by the Greeks for making images; and its empyreumatic oil, Huile de Cade, is used medicinally for skin-diseases. A species of cypress, *Cupressus lusitanica*, which has been naturalized in the neighbourhood of Cintra is known as the cedar of Goa. The genus *Widdringtonia* of tropical and South Africa is also known locally as cedar. *W. juniperoides* is the characteristic tree of the Cederberg range in Cape Colony, while *W. Whytei*, recently discovered in Nyasaland and Rhodesia (the Mlanje cedar) is a fine tree reaching 150 ft. in height, and yielding an ornamental light yellow-brown wood, suitable for building. The order Cedrelaceae (which is entirely distinct from the Conifers) includes, along with the mahoganies and other valuable timber-trees, the Jamaica and the Australian red cedars, *Cedrela odorata*, and *C. Toona* respectively. The cedar-wood of Guiana, used for making canoes, is a species of the natural order Burseraceae, *Icica altissima*. It is a large tree, reaching 100 ft. in height, the wood is easily worked, fragrant and durable.

See Gordon's *Pinetum*; Loiseleur-Deslongchamps, *Histoire du cèdre du Liban* (Paris, 1838); Loudon, *Arboretum Britannicum*, vol. iv. pp. 2404-2432 (London, 1839); Marquis de Chambray, *Traité pratique des arbres résineux conifères* (Paris, 1845); J.D. Hooker, *Nat. Hist. Review* (January, 1862), pp. 11-18; Brandis, *Forest Flora of North-west and Central India*, pp. 516-525 (London, 1874); Veitch, *Manual of Coniferae* (2nd ed., London, 1900).

CEDAR CREEK, a small branch of the North Fork of the Shenandoah river, Virginia, U.S.A. It is known in American history as the scene of a memorable battle, which took place on the 19th of October 1864, between the Union army under Major-General P.H. Sheridan and the Confederates under Lieut.-General J.A. Early. (See SHENANDOAH VALLEY CAMPAIGNS.)

CEDAR FALLS, a city of Black Hawk county, Iowa, U.S.A., on the Cedar river, about 100 m. W. of Dubuque. Pop. (1890) 3459; (1900) 5319; (1905, state census) 5329 (872 being foreign-born); (1910) 5012. It is served by the Chicago, Rock Island & Pacific, the Illinois Central, the Chicago Great Western, and the Waterloo, Cedar Falls & Northern railways. Its manufactures include flour, ground feed, other cereal preparations, hardware specialties, canned vegetables (especially Indian corn), and planing-mill products. It is the seat of the state normal school (1876), and has a public library. The settlement of the place, the oldest in the county, was begun in 1847; it was laid out as a town in 1851, incorporated as a village in 1857, chartered as a city in 1865, and for a short time in 1853 was the county-seat.

CEDAR RAPIDS, a city of Linn county, Iowa, U.S.A., on the Cedar river, in the east central part of the state. Pop. (1890) 18,020; (1900) 25,656, of whom 4478 were foreign-born, an unusually large and influential part being Bohemians; (1910 census) 32,811. It is served by the Chicago, Milwaukee & Saint Paul, the Chicago & North-Western, the Chicago, Rock Island & Pacific (which has repair shops here), and the Illinois Central railways, and by interurban electric lines. The city has an air of substantial prosperity; its principal streets are from 80 ft. to 120 ft. wide, paved with brick and asphalt, and well shaded. Prominent among its buildings are the federal building, the auditorium, the public library and the Masonic library, which contains one of the best collections of Masonic literature in the world. The city has two well-equipped hospitals, a home for aged women, a home for the friendless, and four parks. The grounds of the Cedar Rapids country club comprise 180 acres. Cedar Rapids is in a rich agricultural country. The name of the city was suggested from the rapids in the river, which afford abundant water power and have enabled the city to take first rank in Iowa (1905) as a manufacturing centre. From 1900 to 1905 there was an increase in the value of its manufactured products from $11,135,435 to $16,279,706, or 46.2%. More than one-fourth of the value of its manufactures is in Quaker Oats and other food preparations; among those of less importance are lumber and planing-mill products, foundry and machine-shop products, furniture, patent medicines, pumps, carriages and waggons, packed meats and agricultural implements. Cedar Rapids has also a large grain trade and a large jobbing business, especially in dry goods, millinery, groceries, paper and drugs. At Cedar Rapids are Coe College (co-educational; Presbyterian), which grew out of the Cedar Rapids Collegiate Institute (1851), was named in honour of Daniel Coe, a benefactor, and was chartered under its present name and opened in 1881; the Interstate Correspondence schools, and the Cedar Rapids business college. The first settlers came in 1838; but the city's early growth was slow, and it was not incorporated until 1856. It has been governed by commission since 1908.

CEFALU (anc. *Cephaloedium*), a seaport and episcopal see of the province of Palermo, Sicily, 42 m. E. of Palermo by rail. Pop. (1901) 13,273. The ancient town (of Sicel origin, probably, despite its Greek name) takes its name from the headland (κεφαλή, head) upon which it stood (1233 ft.); its fortifications extended to the shore, on the side where the modern town now is, in the form of two long walls protecting the port. There are remains of a wall of massive rectangular blocks of stone at the 596modern Porta Garibaldi on the south. It does not appear in history before 396 B.C., and seems to have owed its importance mainly to its naturally strong position. The only ancient remains on the mountain are those of a small building in good polygonal work (a style of construction very rare in Sicily), consisting of a passage on each side of which a chamber opens. The doorways are of finely-cut stone, and of Greek type, and the date, though uncertain, cannot, from the careful jointing of the blocks, be very early. On the summit of the promontory are extensive remains of a Saracenic castle. The new town was founded at the foot of the mountain, by the shore, by Roger II. in 1131, and the cathedral was begun in the same year. The exterior is well preserved, and is largely decorated with interlacing pointed arches; the windows also are pointed. On each side of the façade is a massive tower of four storeys. The round-headed Norman portal is worthy of note. The interior was restored in 1559, though the pointed arches of the nave, borne by ancient granite columns, are still visible: and the only mosaics preserved are those of the apse and the last bay of the choir: they are remarkably fine specimens of the art of the period (1148) and, though restored in 1859-1862, have suffered much less than those at Palermo and Monreale from the process. The figure of the Saviour is especially fine. The groined vaulting of the roof is visible in the choir and the right transept, while the rest of the church has a wooden roof. Fine cloisters, coeval with the cathedral, adjoin it. (See G. Hubbard in *Journal of the R.I.B.A.* xv. 333 sqq., 1908.) The harbour is comparatively small.

(T. AS.)

CEHEGÍN, a town of south-eastern Spain, in the province of Murcia, on the right bank of the river Caravaca, a small tributary of the Segura. Pop. (1900) 11,601. Cehegín has a thriving trade in farm produce, especially wine, olive oil and hemp; and various kinds of marble are obtained from quarries near the town. Some of the older houses, however, as well as the parish church and the convent of San Francisco, which still has well-defined Roman inscriptions on its walls, are built of stone from the ruins of *Begastri*, a Roman colony which stood on a small adjacent hill known as the Cabecico de Roenas. The name *Cehegín* is sometimes connected by Spanish antiquaries with that of the *Zenaga*, *Senhaja* or *Senajeh*, a North African tribe, which invaded Spain in the 11th century.

CEILING (from a verb "to ceil," *i.e.* to line or cover; of disputed etymology, but apparently connected with Fr. *ciel*, Lat. *caelum*, sky), in architecture, the upper covering of a church, hall or room. Ceilings are now usually formed of plaster, but in former times they were commonly either boarded (of which St Albans cathedral is perhaps the earliest example), or showed the beams and joists, which in England were moulded and carved, and in France and Italy were richly painted and gilded. Sometimes the ceilings were horizontal, sometimes canted on two sides, and sometimes they take the form of a barrel-vault. Ribs are sometimes planted on the boarding to divide up the surface, and their intersections are enriched with bosses. About the middle of the 16th century the ceilings were formed in plaster with projecting ribs, interlaced ornament and pendants, and the characteristics of the Elizabethan style. At Bramall Hall, Broughton Castle, Hatfield, Knowle, Sizergh and Levens in Westmorland, and Dorfold in Cheshire, are numerous examples, some with pendants. In Italy, at the same period, the plaster ceilings were based on the forms taken by vaulting; they were of infinite variety and were richly decorated with sunk panels containing the Roman conventional foliage. Raphael, about 1520, reproduced in the Vatican some of the stucco-duro ornament which he had studied in the Golden House of Nero, excavated under his directions. Later, about the middle of the 16th century, great coves were formed round the room, which were decorated with cartouches and figures in relief, garlands and swags. The great halls of the Ducal Palace at Venice and the galleries of the Pitti Palace at Florence were ceiled in this way. These coved ceilings were introduced into England in the middle of the 17th century. In Holyrood Palace at Edinburgh there is a fine ceiling of 1671, with figures (probably executed by Italian craftsmen) and floral wreaths.

At Coleshill, Berkshire, a ceiling by Inigo Jones (1650) shows a type which became more or less universal for a century, viz. deeply sunk panels with modillions round, and bands enriched with foliage, fruit, &c., in bold relief. Wren, Nicholas Hawksmoor, James Gibbs, John Webb and other architects continued on the same lines, and in 1760 Robert Adam introduced his type of ceiling, sometimes horizontal, and sometimes segmental, in which panels are suggested only, with slight projecting lines and rings of leaves, swags and arabesque work, which, like Raphael's, was found on the ceilings of the Roman tombs and baths in Rome and Pompeii. George Richardson followed with similar work, and Sir W. Chambers, in the rooms originally occupied by the Royal Academy and the learned societies in Somerset House, designed many admirable ceilings. The moulds of all the ornamental devices of Robert Adam are preserved and are still utilized for many modern ceilings.

(R. P. S.)

CEILLIER, REMY (1688-1761), Benedictine monk of the Lorraine congregation of St Vannes. He was the compiler of an immense Patrology, *Histoire générale des auteurs sacrés et ecclésiastiques* (23 vols., Paris, 1720-1763), being a history and analysis of the writings of all the ecclesiastical writers of the first thirteen centuries. He put infinite trouble and time into the work, and many portions of it are exceedingly well done. A later and improved edition was produced in Paris, 1858, in 14 vols. Ceillier's other work, *Apologie de la morale des pères de l'église* (Paris, 1718), also won some celebrity.

CELAENAE, an ancient city of Phrygia, situated on the great trade route to the East. Its acropolis long held out against Alexander in 333 and surrendered to him at last by arrangement. His successor, Eumenes, made it for some time his headquarters, as did Antigonus until 301. From Lysimachus it passed to Seleucus, whose son Antiochus, seeing its geographical importance, refounded it on a more open site as Apamea (*q.v.*). West of the acropolis were the palace of Xerxes and the Agora, in or near which is the cavern whence the Marsyas, one of the sources of the Maeander, issues. According to Xenophon, Cyrus had a palace and large park full of wild animals at Celaenae.

See G. Weber, *Dineir-Celènes* (1892).

CELANDINE, *Chelidonium majus,* a member of the poppy family, an erect branched herb from 1 to 2 ft. high with a yellow juice, much divided leaves, and yellow flowers nearly an inch across, succeeded by a narrow thin pod opening by a pair of thin valves, separating upwards. The plant grows in waste places and hedgerows, and is probably an escape from cultivation. The lesser celandine is a species of *Ranunculus* (*R. Ficaria*), a small low-growing herb with smooth heart-shaped leaves and bright yellow flowers about an inch across, borne each on a stout stalk springing from a leaf-axil. It flowers in early spring, in pastures and waste-places.

CELANO, a town of the Abruzzi, Italy, in the province of Aquila, 73 m. E. of Rome by rail. Pop. (1901) 9725. It is finely situated on a hill above the Lago Fucino, and is dominated by a square castle, with round towers at the angles, erected in its present form in 1450. It contains three churches with 13th century façades in the style of those of Aquila. The origin of the town goes back to Lombard times. A count of Celano is first mentioned in 1178. It was the birthplace of Thomas of Celano, the author of the *Dies Irae*.

CELEBES,1 one of the four Great Sunda Islands in the Dutch East Indies. Its general outline is extremely irregular, and has been compared to that of a starfish with the rays torn off from one side, corresponding to the west side of the island. It consists of four great peninsulas, extending from a comparatively small nucleus towards the north-east, east, south-east and south, and separated by the three large gulfs of Tomini or Gorontalo, Tolo or Tomaiki, and Boni. Of these gulfs the first is by far the largest, the other two having much wider entrances and not extending so far inwards. Most important among the smaller inlets are the bays of Amurang, Kwandang and Tontoli on the 597north coast, Palos and Pare-Pare on the west, and Kendari or Vosmaer on the east. Of the numerous considerable islands which lie north-east, east and south of Celebes (those off the west coast are few and small), the chief are prolongations of the four great peninsulas—the Sangir and Talaut islands off the north-east, the Banggai and Sula off the east, Wuna and Buton off the south-east, and Saleyer off the south. Including the adjacent islands, the area of Celebes is estimated at 77,855 sq. m. and the population at 2,000,000; without them the area is 69,255 sq. m. and the population 1,250,000.

The scenery in Celebes is most varied and picturesque. "Nowhere in the archipelago," wrote A. R. Wallace, "have I seen such gorges, chasms and precipices as abound in the district of Maros" (in the southern peninsula); "in many parts there are vertical or even overhanging precipices five or six hundred feet high, yet completely clothed with a tapestry of vegetation." Much of the country, especially round the Gulf of Tolo, is covered with primeval forests and thickets, traversed by scarcely perceptible paths, or broken with a few clearings and villages. A considerable part of the island has been little explored, but the general character seems to be mountainous. Well-defined ranges prolong themselves through each of the peninsulas, rising in many places to a considerable elevation. Naturally there are no great river-basins or extensive plains, but one of the features of the island is the frequent occurrence, not only along the coasts, but at various heights inland, of beautiful stretches of level ground often covered with the richest pastures. Minahassa, the north-eastern extremity, consists of a plateau divided into sections by volcanoes (Klabat, 6620 ft., being the highest). Sulphur springs occur here. In the west of the northern peninsula the interior consists in part of plateaus of considerable extent enclosed by the coast ranges. Near Lake Posso, in the centre of the island, the mountains are higher; the Tampiko massif has a height of nearly 5000 ft., the chains south and west of the lake have a general altitude of about 5450 ft., with peaks still loftier. In the southern peninsula two chains stretch parallel with the west and east coasts; the former is the higher, with a general altitude of 3200 ft. In the south it joins the Peak of Bonthain, or Lompo-battang, a great volcanic mass 10,088 ft. high. In the east central part of the island the mountain Koruve exceeds 10,000 ft., and is supposed to be the highest in the island. An alluvial coast plain, 7 to 9 m. wide, stretches along the foot of the western chain, and between the two chains is the basin of the Walannaë river, draining northward into Lake Tempe. Little is known of the orography of the eastern peninsula. At the base of the south-eastern there is another large lake, Tovieti. In this peninsula there are parallel ranges on the east and west flanks. The trench between them is partly occupied by the vast swamp of Lake Opa.

The rivers of the narrow mountainous peninsulas form many rapids and cataracts; as the Tondano, draining the lake of the same name to the north-west coast of Minahassa at Menado; the Rano-i-Apo, flowing over the plateau of Mongondo to the Gulf of Amurang; the Poigar, issuing from a little-known lake of that plateau; the Lombagin, traversing narrow cañons; and the river of Boni, which has its outfall in the plain of Gorontalo, near the mouth of the Bolango or Tapa, the latter connected by a canal with the Lake of Limbotto. All these rivers are navigable by praus or rafts for only a few miles above the mouth. In central Celebes, the Kodina flows into Lake Posso, and the Kalaëna discharges to the Gulf of Boni; the Posso, navigable by *blottos* (canoes formed of hollowed tree-trunks), is the only river flowing from the lake to the Gulf of Tomini. The rivers of the southern peninsula, owing to the relief of the surface, are navigable to a somewhat greater extent. The Walannaë flows into Lake Tempe, and, continued by the Jenrana (Tienrana), which discharges into the Gulf of Boni, is navigable for small boats; the Sadang, with many affluents, flows to the west coast, and is navigable by *sanpans*. The Jenemaja is a broad river, navigable far from the mouth. The coasts of Celebes are often fertile and well populated; but, as shown by the marine charts, many sand, mud and stone banks lie near the shore, and consequently there are few accessible or natural ports or good roadsteads.

Geology.—The geological observations on Celebes are too scattered to reveal its structure. The greater part of the island seems to be formed of gneiss and other crystalline rocks. These are overlaid by conglomerates, limestones and clay slates of very doubtful age, the most interesting being a radiolarian clay which occurs on the south side of the Matinang Mountains, at the north end of Lake Posso, &c.; it may correspond with the radiolarian cherts of Borneo. Tertiary beds are found, especially near the coast. The Eocene includes a series of sandstones and marls with lignite, and these are overlaid by nummulite limestones. The Miocene contains an *Orbitoides*limestone. Intrusive and volcanic rocks of great variety and of various ages occur. Peridotite and gabbro form much of the eastern peninsula (Banggai). Leucite and nepheline rocks have been found in various parts of the island, especially in the south-west. In Minahassa, at the northern extremity, there is a large area of tuffs and agglomerates consisting chiefly of augite andesite, and in this area there are many recent volcanic cones. Eruptions still take place at intervals, but the volcanoes for the most part seem to have reached the solfataric stage.

Climate.—The climate of the island, everywhere accessible to the influence of the sea, is maritime-tropical, the temperature ranging generally between 77° and 80° F., the extremes being about 90° and 70° F., only on the higher mountains falling during the night to 54° or 55° F. The rainfall in the northern peninsula (north of the equator) differs from that of the southern; the former has rains (not caused by the monsoon), and of smaller amount, 102 in. annually; the latter has a greater rainfall, 157 in., brought by the north-western monsoon, and of which the west coast receives a much larger share than the east.

Fauna and Flora.—In spite of its situation in the centre of the archipelago, Celebes possesses a fauna of a very distinctive kind. The number of species is small, but in many cases they are peculiar to the island. Of land birds, for example, about 160 species are known, and of these not less than about 90 are peculiar, the majority of the remainder being Asiatic in distinction from Australian. Mammals are few in species, but remarkable, especially *Macacus niger*, an ape found nowhere else but in Bachian; *Anoa depressicornis*, a small ox-like quadruped which inhabits the mountainous districts; and the babirusa or pig-deer of the Malays. Some of the animals are probably descendants of specimens introduced by man; others are allied in species, but not identical, with mammals of Java and Borneo; others again, including the three just mentioned, are wholly or practically confined to Celebes. There are no large beasts of prey, and neither the elephant, the rhinoceros nor the tapir is represented. Wild-buffaloes, swine and goats are pretty common; and most of the usual domestic animals are kept. The horses are in high repute in the archipelago; formerly about 700 were yearly exported to Java, but the supply has considerably diminished.

The same peculiarity of species holds in regard to the insects of the Celebes (so far as they are known) as to the mammals and birds. Out of 118 species of butterflies, belonging to four important classes, no fewer than 86 are peculiar; while among the rose-chafers or *Cetoniinae* the same is the case in 19 out of 30. Equally remarkable with this presence of peculiar species is the absence of many kinds that are common in the rest of the archipelago; and these facts have been considered to indicate connexion with a larger land-mass at a very distant geological epoch, and the subsequent continuous isolation of Celebes. This view, however, has been controverted. It is held that in the Miocene and Pliocene periods there were land connexions with the Philippines, Java and the Moluccas, and through the last with Australasian lands to the east and south-east. Migration of species took place along these lines in both directions. Those immigrants which remained in what is now Celebes may have developed new species. Moreover, while Celebes has species which are peculiar to itself and one other of the islands just mentioned, it has none which it shares exclusively with Borneo, and thus the importance of the Macassar Strait as a biological division is indicated.

Vegetation is extremely rich; but there are fewer large trees than in the other islands of the archipelago. Of plants that 598furnish food for man the most important are rice, maize and millet, coffee, the coco-nut tree, sago-palm, the obi or native potato, the bread-fruit and the tamarind; with lemons, oranges, mangosteens, wild-plums, Spanish pepper, beans, melons and sugar-cane. The shaddock is to be found only in the lower plains. Indigo, cotton and tobacco are grown; the bamboo and the ratan-palm are common in the woods; and among the larger trees are sandal-wood, ebony, sapan and teak. The palm, *Arenga saccharifera*, furnishes *gemuti* fibres for ropes; its juice is manufactured into sugar and a beverage called sagueir; and intoxicating drinks are prepared from several other palms.

Products.—As in natural vegetation and fauna, so in cultivated products, Celebes, apart from its peculiarities, presents the transitional link between the Asiatic and the Australian regions of the Malayan province. For example, rice is produced here in smaller quantity and of inferior quality to that in the western part of the archipelago, but superior to that in the eastern section, where sago and sorghum form the staple articles of food. The products of the forests supply about half the total exports. The fisheries include trepang, turtle and pearl oysters. Gold is worked under European direction in the district of Gorontalo, but with only partial success; the search for coal in the southern peninsula has yielded no satisfactory results; tin, iron and copper, found in the eastern peninsula and elsewhere, are utilized only for native industries.

Natives.—The native population of the island is all of Malayan stock. The three most important peoples are the Bugis (*q.v.*) the Macassars and the Mandars. The medley of other

Malayan tribes, of a more or less savage type, living in the island, are known under the collective name of Alfuros (*q.v.*). The Macassars are well-built and muscular, and have in general a dark-brown complexion, a broad and expressive face, black and sparkling eyes, a high forehead, a flattish nose, a large mouth and long black soft hair. The women are sprightly, clever and amiable. The men are brave and not treacherous, but ambitious, jealous and extremely revengeful. Drunkenness is rare, but they are passionate, and running amuck is frequent among them. In all sorts of bodily exercises, as swinging, wrestling, dancing, riding and hunting, they take great pleasure. Though they call themselves Mahommedans, their religion is largely mingled with pagan superstitions; they worship animals, and a certain divinity called Karaeng Lové, who has power over their fortune and health. Except where Dutch influence has made itself felt, little attention has been paid by the native races to agriculture; and their manufacturing industries are few and limited. The weaving of cotton cloth is principally carried on by women; and the process, at least for the finer description, is tedious in the extreme. The houses are built of wood and bamboo; and as the use of diagonal struts is not practised, the walls soon lean over from the force of the winds. The Macassar language, which belongs to the Malayo-Javanese group, is spoken in many parts of the southern peninsula; but it has a much smaller area than the Buginese, which is the language of Boni. It is deficient in generalizations; thus, for example, it has words for the idea of carrying in the hand, carrying on the head, carrying on the shoulder, and so on, but has no word for carrying simply. It has adopted a certain number of vocables from Sanskrit, Malay, Javanese and Portuguese, but on the whole is remarkably pure, and has undergone comparatively few recent changes. It is written in a peculiar character, which has displaced, and probably been corrupted from, an old form employed as late as the 17th century. Neither bears any trace of derivation from the Sanskrit alphabet. The priests affect the use of the Arabic letters. The literature is poor, and consists largely of romantic stories from the Malay, and religious treatises from the Arabic. Of the few original pieces the most important are the early histories of Goa, Tello and some other states of Celebes, and the *Rapang*, or collection of the decrees and maxims of the old princes and sages. The more modern productions are letters, laws and poems, many of the last of considerable beauty.

Divisions, Towns, Population.—Celebes is divided by the Dutch, for administrative purposes, into the government of Celebes with dependencies (south-eastern and southern peninsulas and all west coast), and the residency of Menado (north-eastern peninsula and coast of Gulf of Tomini). The eastern peninsula and coast of the Gulf of Tolo belong politically to the residency of Ternate (*q.v.*). The following table shows approximately the distribution and composition of the population:—

	Europeans.	Chinese.	Arabs.	Other Oriental Foreigners.	Natives.	Total.
Government of Celebes and Dependencies	1,414	3,738	54	54	4,09,739	4,15,499
Residency of Menado—						
Minahassa	836	3,574	86	16	430,941	36,406
Gorontalo	115	505	33	.		

The *Government of Celebes and Dependencies* is subdivided into the government territory, the vassal states (Boni, *q.v.*, and Ternate), and the federal countries. The density of population for the whole government is estimated as 3.7 or 4 per sq. m., varying from 2.2 in the vassal and federated states to 14.7 to 18.4 for Macassar and the districts directly governed by the Dutch. The density of population in districts outside the influence of

European government sinks to 1 and less per sq. m. As in the case of Minahassa, the difference must be explained by physical and moral conditions. Two-thirds of the natives live by agriculture, and one-third by trade, navigation, shipbuilding and other industries. In agreement with these principal occupations, the centres of population are found in southern Celebes, on the coast (not in the interior plains or on the lake, as in Menado). Palos (3000), with good port; Pare-Pare, connected by road with Lake Tempe; and Macassar (17,925), the seat of the governor and the centre of trade for the eastern part of the archipelago. On the south coast must also be named Bonthain (4000); on the east coast, Balong-Nipa; and Buton and Saleyer, seats of administration and ports of call on the island groups of the same names.

The *Residency of Menado* comprises three districts: Minahassa, the little states along the north coast west of Minahassa, and Gorontalo, including the other states of the northern peninsula lying along the Gulf of Tomini. The density of population being calculated at about 2.7 to 3 per sq. m. for Celebes, is 16.2 for Minahassa, but only 1.5 to 2 for the Residency of Menado. Centres of population in Menado are Amurang (3000), the seat of a Dutch controller, and a calling place for the steamers of the Indian Packet Company; Menado (10,000), the chief town of the residency, the principal station of the Dutch missionaries, with a fair amount of trade, but an unsafe roadstead; Tondano (12,000), near the lake and river of the same name, at an altitude of nearly 2000 ft., and one of the chief centres; Gorontalo, one of the most important towns of Celebes, carrying on direct trade with Singapore and Europe. All the other coast places have some importance as chief villages of the little states and as ports of call for the vessels of the steam packet company, but have only from 500 to 1000 inhabitants.

History.—Celebes was first discovered by the Portuguese in the early part of the 16th century, the exact date assigned by some authorities being 1512. The name is not used by the natives, and is apparently of foreign origin, but has been variously derived, *e.g.* from the mountain of Klabat or Kalabat, or from *Seli Besi*, an iron kris carried by the natives, of whom those who were first asked for the name of the island were conceived, according to this theory, to have misunderstood their questioners. At the time of the Portuguese discovery, the Macassars were the most powerful people in the island, having successfully defended themselves against the king of the Moluccas and the sultan of Ternate. In 1609 the British attempted to gain a footing. At what time the Dutch first arrived is not certainly known, but it was probably in the end of the 16th or beginning of the 17th century, since in 1607 they formed a connexion with Macassar. In 1611 the Dutch East Indian Company obtained the monopoly of trade on the island of Buton; and in 1618 an insurrection in Macassar gave them an opportunity of obtaining a definite establishment there. In 1660 the kingdom was subjugated, but in 1666 the war broke out anew. It was brought to an end in the following year, and the treaty of Bonga or Banga was signed, by which the Dutch were recognized as protectors. 599In 1683 the north-eastern part of the island was conquered by Robert Paddenburg and placed under the command of the governor of the Moluccas. In 1703 a fort was erected at Menado. The kingdom of Boni was successfully attacked in 1824, and in August of that year the Bonga treaty was renewed in a greatly modified form. Since then the principal military event is the Boni insurrection which was quelled in 1859, but this was far from pacifying the country permanently. A series of revolts of various chiefs in 1905-6 was not arrested without considerable fighting, but after this the whole island was brought under Dutch authority, even where native rule survived.

BIBLIOGRAPHY.—In P.J. Veth's *Woordenboek van Nederlandsch Indie* there will be found an extensive bibliography of Celebes drawn up by H.C. Millies. For additional bibliography and data for the island and its population, see C.M. Kan, "Celebes," in the*Encyclopaedie van Nederlandsch Indie*, ed. by P.A. van der Lith and A.H. Spaan (The Hague, 1895), &c., vol. i. p. 314. See P. and F. Sarasin (who have carried out extensive explorations in the island), "Berichte aus Celebes," *Zeitschr. der Ges. f. Erdk.* xxix. 351;*Entwurf einer geographisch-geologischen Beschreibung der Insel Celebes* (Wiesbaden, 1901); *Reisen in Celebes, 1893-1896, 1902-1903* (Wiesbaden, 1905); *Versuch einer Anthropologie der Insel Celebes* (Wiesbaden, 1906); C. van der Hart, *Reize rondon het Eiland Celebes* (The Hague, 1853); Capt. R. Mundy, *Narrative of Events in Borneo and Celebes* (London, 1848); P.J. Veth, *Een Nederlandsch reiziger op Zuid Celebes*(Amsterdam, 1875); J.G.F. Riedel, *Het landschap Boeool, Noord Selebes* (1872); and "Die

Landschaften Holontalo, Limoeto," &c., in *Zeitschr. fur Ethnologie* (1871); H. Bücking, "Beiträge zur Geologie von Celebes," *Samml. geol. Reichsmus. Leiden*, vol. vii. pp. 29-205 (1902), pp. 221-224 (1904); and various articles in *Tijdschrift v.h. Aardrijkskundig Genootschap* and *Tijdsch. v.h. Batavian. Gen.*

1The second syllable is accented.

CELERY (*Apium graveolens*), a biennial plant belonging to the natural order Umbelliferae, which, in its wild state, occurs in England by the sides of ditches and in marshy places, especially near the sea, producing a furrowed stalk and compound leaves with wedge-shaped leaflets, the whole plant having a coarse, rank taste and a peculiar smell. It is also widely distributed in the north temperate region of the Old World. By cultivation and blanching the stalks lose their acrid qualities and assume the mild sweetish aromatic taste peculiar to celery as a salad plant. The plants are raised from seed, sown either in a hot bed or in the open garden, according to the season of the year, and after one or two thinnings out and transplantings, they are, on attaining a height of 6 or 8 in., planted out in deep trenches for convenience of blanching, which is effected by earthing up and so excluding the stems from the influence of light. A large number of varieties are cultivated by gardeners, which are ranged under two classes, white and red,—the white varieties being generally the best flavoured and most crisp and tender. As a salad plant, celery, especially if at all "stringy," is difficult of digestion. Both blanched and green it is stewed and used in soups, the seeds also being used as a flavouring ingredient. In the south of Europe celery is seldom blanched, but is much used in its natural condition.

Celeriac, or turnip-rooted celery (*Apium graveolens* var. *rapaceum*), is a variety cultivated more on account of its roots than for the stalks, although both are edible and are used for salads and in soups. It is chiefly grown in the north of Europe. As the tops are not required, trenching is unnecessary, otherwise the cultivation is the same as for celery.

CÉLESTE, MADAME (1815-1882), French dancer and actress, was born in Paris on the 16th of August 1815. As a little girl she was a pupil in the ballet class at the Opéra. When fifteen, she had an offer from the United States, and made her début at the Bowery theatre, New York. Returning to England, she appeared at Liverpool as Fenella in *Masaniello*, and also in London (1831). In 1834 she aroused such enthusiasm in America that her admirers carried her on their shoulders and took the horses out of her carriage in order to pull it themselves. It is even said that President Jackson introduced her to his cabinet as an adopted citizen of the Union. Having made a large fortune, she returned to England in 1837. She now gave up dancing, and appeared as an actress, first at Drury Lane and then at the Haymarket. In 1844 she joined Benjamin Webster in the management of the Adelphi, and afterwards took the sole management of the Lyceum till 1861. She made a third visit to the United States from 1865 to 1868, and retired in 1870. Her favourite part was Miami in Buckstone's *Green Bushes*. She died in Paris on the 12th of February 1882.

CELESTINA, LA, the popular alternative title attached from 1519 (or earlier) to the anonymous *Comedia de Caliste y Melibea*, a Spanish novel in dialogue which was celebrated throughout Europe during the 16th century. In the two earliest known editions (Burgos, 1499, and Seville, 1501) the *Comedia* consists of sixteen acts; the reprints issued after 1501 are entitled *Tragicomedia de Calisto y Melibea*, and contain twenty-one acts. Three of these reprints include a twenty-second act which is admittedly spurious, and the authenticity of Acts XVII.-XXI. is disputed. The authorship of the *Celestina* and the date of its composition are doubtful. An anonymous prefatory letter in the editions subsequent to 1501 attributes the book to Juan de Mena or Rodrigo Cota, but this ascription is universally rejected. The prevailing opinion is that the author of the twenty-one acts was Fernando de Rojas, apparently a Spanish Jew resident at the Puebla de Montalban in the province of Toledo; R. Foulché-Delbose, however, maintains that the original sixteen acts are by an unknown writer who had no part in the five supplementary acts. Some scholars give 1483 as the date of composition; others hold that the book was written in 1497. These questions are still unsettled. Though profoundly original in treatment, the *Celestina* has points of analogy with the work of earlier writers, such as Juan Ruiz (*q.v.*), the archpriest of Hita; his rapid sketches of Trota-conventas, Melón and Endrina no doubt suggested the finished portraits of Celestina, Calisto and Melibea, and the closing scene in the *Celestina* recalls the suicide in Diego Fernandez de San Pedro's *Cárcel de Amor*. Allowing for these and other debts of the same kind, it cannot be denied that the *Celestina* excels all earlier Spanish works in tragic force, in impressive conception, and in the realistic rendering of characters drawn from all classes of society. It passed through innumerable editions in Spain, and was the first Spanish book to find acceptance throughout western Europe. At least twenty works by well-known Spanish authors are derived from it; it was adapted for the English stage as early as 1525-1530, and was translated into Italian (1505), French (1527) and other European languages. A Latin version by Caspar Barth was issued under the title of *Pornoboscodidascalus latinus*(1624) with all the critical apparatus of a recognized classic. James Mabbe's English rendering (1631) is one of the best translations ever published. The original edition of 1499 has been reprinted by R. Foulché-Delbose in the *Bibliotheca Hispanica* (1902), vol. xii.

BIBLIOGRAPHY.—R. Foulché-Delbose, "Observations sur la Célestine" in the *Revue hispanique* (Paris, 1900), vol. vii. pp. 28-80 and (Paris. 1902) vol. ix. pp. 171-199; K. Haebler, "Bemerkungen zur Celestina" in the *Revue hispanique* (Paris, 1902), vol. ix. pp. 139-170; and M. Menéndez y Pelayo's introduction to the *Celestina* (Vigo, 1899-1900)

(J. F.-K.)

CELESTINE (CAELESTINUS), the name of five popes.

CELESTINE I., pope from 422 to 432. At his accession the dissensions caused by the faction of Eulalius (see BONIFACE I.) had not yet abated. He, however, triumphed over them, and his episcopate was peaceful. When the doctrines of Nestorius were denounced to him, he instructed Cyril, bishop of Alexandria, to follow up the matter. The emperor Theodosius II. convoked an ecumenical council at Ephesus, to which Celestine sent his legates. He had some difficulties with the bishops in Africa on the question of appeals to Rome, and with the bishops of Provence with regard to the doctrines of St Augustine. To expedite the extirpation of Pelagianism, he sent to Britain a deacon called Palladius, at whose instigation St Germanus of Auxerre crossed the English Channel, as delegate of the pope and bishops of Gaul, to inculcate orthodox principles upon the clergy of Britain. He also commissioned Palladius to preach the gospel in Ireland which was beginning to rally to Christianity. Celestine was the first pope who is known to have taken a direct interest in the churches of Britain and Ireland.

(L. D.*)

CELESTINE II., pope in 1143-1144. Guido of Città di Castello (Tiferno), born of noble Tuscan family, able and learned, studied 600under Abelard and became a cardinal priest. Elected the successor of Innocent II. on the 26th of September 1143, he died on the 8th of March following. He removed the interdict which Innocent had employed against Louis VII. of France. At the time of his death he was on the verge of a controversy with Roger of Sicily.

See A. Certini, *Vita* (Foligno, 1716); M. Bouquet, *Recueil des historiens des Gaules*(Paris, 1738 ff.), tome 15, 408-411; Migne, *Patrologiae cursus completus*, 179, 765-820; P. Jaffé, *Regesta Pontificum Romanorum*, 2nd ed. vol. ii. (Lipsiae, 1888), 1 ff.; Wetzer und Welte, *Kirchenlexikon*, 2nd ed. vol. iii. (Freiburg, 1884), 578 ff.; Herzog-Hauck, *Realencyklopadie*, 3rd ed. vol. iv. (Leipzig, 1898), 201.

CELESTINE III. (Giacinto Bobo), pope from 1191 to 1198, was cardinal deacon of Santa Maria in Cosmedin as early as 1144, and had reached the age of eighty-five when chosen on the 30th of March 1191 to succeed Clement III. The first pope of the house of the Orsini, his policy was marked by mildness and indecision. Henry VI. of Germany at once forced the pontiff to crown him emperor, and three or four years later took possession of the Norman kingdom of Sicily; he refused tribute and the oath of allegiance, and even appointed bishops subject to his own jurisdiction; moreover, he gave his brother in fief the estates which had belonged to the countess Matilda of Tuscany. Celestine did not dare so much as to threaten him with excommunication. It was Celestine's purpose to lay England under the interdict; but Prince John and the barons still refused to recognize the papal legate, the bishop of Ely. Richard I. had been set free before the dilatory pope put Leopold of Austria under the ban. In his last sickness Celestine wished to resign his office, but the cardinals protested. Death released him from his perplexities on the 8th of January 1198.

See "Epistolae Coelestini III. Papae," in M. Bouquet, *Receuil des historiens des Gaules et de la France*, tome 19 (Paris, 1738 ff.); J.P. Migne, *Patrologiae cursus completus*, tome 206 (Paris, 1855), 867 ff.; further sources in *Neues Archiv für die ältere deutsche Geschichtskunde*, 2. 218; 11. 398 f.; 12.411-414; P. Jaffé, *Regesta Pontificum Romanorum*, vol. ii. (2nd ed.. Leipzig, 1888), 577 ff.

(W. W. R.*)

CELESTINE IV. (Godfrey Castiglione), pope in 1241, son of a sister of Urban III. (1185-1187), was archpriest and chancellor at Milan. After Urban's death he entered the Cistercian monastery at Hautecombe in Savoy. In 1227 Gregory IX. created him cardinal priest of St Mark's, and in 1233 made him cardinal bishop of Sabina. Elected to succeed Gregory on the 25th of October 1241, he died on the 10th of November, before consecration, and was buried in St Peter's.

See A. Potthast, *Regesta Pontificum Romanorum*, vol. i. (Berlin, 1874), 940 f.

CELESTINE V. (St Peter Celestine), pope in 1294, was born of poor parents at Isernia about 1215, and early entered the Benedictine order. Living as a hermit on Monte Morrone near Sulmone in the Abruzzi, he attracted other ascetics about him and organized them into a congregation of the Benedictines which was later called the Celestines (*q.v.*). The assistance of a vicar enabled him to escape from the growing administrative cares and devote himself solely to asceticism, apparently the only field of human activity in which he excelled. His *Opuscula*, published by Telera at Naples in 1640, are probably not genuine; he was *indoctus libris*. A fight between the Colonna and the Orsini, as well as hopeless dissensions among the cardinals, prevented a papal election for two years and three months after the death of Nicholas IV. Charles II. of Naples, needing a pope in order that he might regain Sicily, brought about a conclave. As the election of any cardinal seemed impossible, on the 5th of July 1294 the Sacred College united on Pietro di Morrone; the cardinals expected to rule in the name of the celebrated but incapable ascetic. Apocalyptic notions then current doubtless aided his election, for Joachim of Floris and his school looked to monasticism to furnish deliverance to the church and to the world. Multitudes came to Celestine's coronation at Aquila, and he began his reign the idol of visionaries, of extremists and of the populace. But the pope was in the power of Charles II. of Naples, and became his tool against Aragon. The king's son Louis, a layman of twenty-one, was made archbishop of Lyons. The cardinals, scarcely consulted at all, were discontented. The pope, who wanted more time for his devotions, offered to leave three cardinals in charge of affairs; but his proposition was rejected. He then wished to abdicate, and at length Benedetto Gaetano, destined to succeed him as Boniface VIII., removed all scruples against this unheard-of procedure by finding a precedent in the case of Clement I. Celestine abdicated on the 13th of December 1294. There is no sufficient ground for finding an allusion to this act in the noted line of Dante, "Che fece per viltate il gran rifiuto" ("who made from cowardice the great refusal," *Inferno*, 3, 60). Boniface at length put him in prison for safe keeping; he died in a monastic cell in the castle of Fumone near Anagni on the 19th of May 1296. He was canonized by Clement V. in 1313.

See Wetzer und Welte and Herzog-Hauck (with excellent bibliography) as above; Jean Aurélien, Supérieur de la Congrégation des Célestins, *La Vie admirable de ... Saint Pierre Célestin* (Bar-le-Duc, 1873); H. Finke, *Aus den Tagen Bonifaz VIII.* (Münster, 1902), pp. 24-43.

(W. W. R.*)

CELESTINE, or CELESTITE, a name applied to native strontium sulphate ($SrSO_4$), having been suggested by the celestial blue colour which it occasionally presents. This colour has been referred to a trace of iron phosphate, but in some cases such an explanation appears doubtful. The mineral is usually colourless, or has only a delicate shade of blue. Celestine crystallizes in the orthorhombic system, being isomorphous with barytes (*q.v.*). The angle between the prism faces is 76° 17′. The cleavage is perfect parallel to the basal pinacoid, and less marked parallel to the prism. Although celestine much resembles barytes in its physical properties, having for example the same degree of hardness (3), it is less dense, its specific gravity being 3.9. Celestine is a less abundant mineral than barytes. It is, however, much more soluble, and occurs frequently in mineral waters. W.W. Stoddart showed that many plants growing on Keuper marls containing celestine near Bristol appropriated the strontium salt, and the metal could be detected spectroscopically in their ashes.

Celestine occurs in the Triassic rocks of Britain, especially in veins and geodes in the Keuper marl in the neighbourhood of Bristol. At Wickwar and Yate in Gloucestershire it is worked for industrial purposes. Colourless crystals, of great beauty, occur in association with calcite and native sulphur in the sulphur deposits of Sicily, as at Girgenti. Fine blue crystals are yielded by the copper mines of Herrengrund, in Hungary; a dark blue fibrous form is known from Jena; and small crystals occur in flint at Meudon near Paris. Very large tabular crystals are found in limestone on Strontian Island in Lake Erie; and a blue fibrous variety from near Frankstown, Blair Co., Penn., is notable as having been the original celestine on which the species was founded by A.G. Werner in 1798.

Celestine is much used for the preparation of strontium hydrate, which is employed in refining beetroot sugar in Germany. The mineral is used also as a source of various salts of strontium such as the nitrate, which finds application in pyrotechny for the production of red fire.

(F. W. R.*)

CELESTINES, a religious order founded about 1260 by Peter of Morrone, afterwards Pope Celestine V. (1294). It was an attempt to unite the eremitical and cenobitical modes of life. Peter's first disciples lived as hermits on Mount Majella in the Abruzzi. The Benedictine rule was taken as the basis of the life, but was supplemented by regulations notably increasing the austerities practised. The form of government was borrowed largely from those prevailing in the mendicant orders. Indeed, though the Celestines are reckoned as a branch of the Benedictines, there is little in common between them. For all that, St Celestine, during his brief tenure of the papacy, tried to spread his ideas among the Benedictines, and induced the monks of Monte Cassino to adopt his idea of the monastic life instead of St Benedict's; for this purpose fifty Celestine monks were introduced into Monte Cassino, but on Celestine's abdication of the papacy the project fortunately was at once abandoned. During the founder's lifetime the order spread rapidly, and eventually 601 there were about 150 monasteries in Italy, and others in France, Bohemia and the Netherlands. The French houses, twenty-one in number, formed a separate congregation, the head-house being in Paris. The French Revolution and those of the 19th century destroyed their houses, and the Celestine order seems no longer to exist.

Peter of Morrone was in close contact with the Franciscan Spirituals of the extreme type (see FRANCISCANS), and he endeavoured to form an amalgamation between them and his hermits, under the title "Poor Hermits of Celestine." On his abdication the amalgamation was dissolved, and the Franciscan element fled to the East and was finally suppressed by Boniface VIII. and compelled to re-enter the Franciscan order. The habit of the Celestines was black.

See Helyot, *Histoire des ordres religieux* (1792), vi. c. 23; Max Heimbucher, *Orden und Kongregationen* (1896), i. § 22, p. 134; the art. "Cölestiner" in Wetzer und Welte,*Kirchenlexicon* (ed. 2), and Herzog-Hauck, *Realencyklopädie* (ed. 3).

(E. C. B.)

CELIBACY (Lat. *caelibatus*, from *caelebs*, unmarried), the state of being unmarried, a term now commonly used in the sense of complete abstinence from marriage; it originally included the state of widowhood also, and any one was strictly a *caelebs* who had no existing spouse. Physicians and physiologists have frequently discussed celibacy from their professional point of view; but it will be sufficient to note here the results of statistical inquiries. It has been established by the calculations of actuaries that married persons—

women in a considerable, but men in a much greater degree——have at all periods of life a greater probability of living than the single. From the point of view of public utility, the state has sometimes attempted to discourage celibacy. The best-known enactment of this kind is that of the emperor Augustus, best known as *Lex Julia et Papia Poppaea*. This disabled*caelibes* from receiving an inheritance unless the testator were related to them within the sixth degree; it limited the amount which a wife could take by a husband's will, or the husband by the wife's, unless they had children; and preference was given to candidates for office in proportion to the number of their children.1 Ecclesiastical legislators, on the other hand, have frequently favoured the unmarried state; and celibacy, partial or complete, has been more or less stringently enforced upon the ministers of different religions; many instances are quoted by H.C. Lea. The best known, of course, are the Roman Vestals; though here even the great honours and privileges accorded to these maidens were often insufficient to keep the ranks filled. In the East, however, this and other forms of asceticism have always flourished more freely; and the Buddhist monastic system is not only far older than that of Christendom, but also proportionately more extensive.2 In early Judaism, chastity was indeed enjoined upon the priests at certain solemn seasons; but there was no attempt to enforce celibacy upon the sacerdotal caste. On the contrary, all priests were the sons of priests, and the case of Elizabeth shows that here, as throughout the Jewish people, barrenness was considered a disgrace. But Alexander's conquests brought the Jews into contact with Hindu and Greek mysticism; and this probably explains the growth of the ascetic Essenes some two centuries before the Christian era. The adherents of this sect, unlike the Pharisees and Sadducees, were never denounced by Christ, who seems on the contrary to have had real sympathy with the voluntary celibacy of an exceptional few (Matt. xix. 12). St Paul's utterances on this subject, though they go somewhat further, amount only to the assertion that a struggling missionary body will find more freedom in its work in the absence of wives and children. At the same time, St Paul claimed emphatically for himself and the other apostles the right of leading about a wife; and he names among the qualifications for a bishop, an elder and a deacon, that he should be "the husband of one wife." Indeed it was freely admitted by the most learned men of the middle ages and Renaissance that celibacy had been no rule of the apostolic church; and, though writers of ability have attempted to maintain the contrary even in modern times, their contentions are unhesitatingly rejected by the latest Roman Catholic authority.3

The gradual growth of clerical celibacy, first as a custom and then as a rule of discipline, can be traced clearly enough even through the scanty records of the first few centuries. The most ascetic Christians began to question the legality of second marriages on the part of either sex, as even paganism had often reprobated second marriages of women. Though these extremists were presently branded as heretics for their eccentric ultra-ascetic tenets (Montanists, Cathari), yet as early as Tertullian's time (c. A.D. 220) the right of second marriages was theoretically denied to the priesthood. This was logically followed by a revival of the old Levitical rule which required that priests should marry none but virgins (Lev. xxi. 7, 13). Both these rules, however, proved difficult of enforcement and seem to have rested only on a vague basis of public opinion; twice-married men (*digami*) were admitted to the priesthood by Pope Calixtus I. (219-222), and even as late as the beginning of the 5th century we find husbands of widows consecrated to the episcopate. The so-called Apostolical Constitutions and Canons, the latter of which were compiled in the 4th century, give us the first clear and fairly general rules on the subject. Here we find "bishops and priests allowed to retain the wives whom they may have had before ordination, but not to marry in orders; the lower grades, deacons, subdeacons, &c., allowed to marry after entering the church; but all were to be husbands of but one wife, who must be neither a widow, a divorced woman nor a concubine" (Lea i. 28). Many causes, however, were already at work to carry public feeling beyond this stage. Quite apart from the few enthusiasts who would have given a literal interpretation to the text in Matt. xix. 12, vows of virginity became more and more frequent as the virtue itself was lauded by ecclesiastical writers in language of increasing fervour. These vows were at first purely voluntary and temporary; but public opinion naturally grew less and less tolerant of those who, having once formed and published so solemn a resolution, broke it afterwards. Again not only was the church doctrine itself more or less consciously influenced by the Manichaean tenet of the diabolical origin of all matter, including the human body, but churchmen were also naturally tempted to compete in asceticism with the many heretics who held this tenet, and whose abstinence brought them so much popular consideration. Moreover, in proportion as the clergy, no longer mere ringleaders of a despised and persecuted sect, became beneficiaries and administrators of rich endowments—and this at a time when the external safeguards against embezzlement were comparatively weak—a strong feeling grew up among the laity that church revenues should not go to support the priest's family.4 Lastly, such partial attempts as we have already described to enforce upon the clergy a special rule of continence, by their very failure, suggested more heroic measures. Therefore, side by side with the evidence for difficult enforcement of the old rules, we find an equally constant series of new and more stringent enactments.

The first church council which definitely forbade marriage to the higher clergy was the local Spanish synod of Elvira (A.D. 305). A similar interpretation has sometimes been claimed for the third canon of that general council of Nicaea to which we 602owe the Nicene creed (325), but this is now abandoned by the best authorities on all sides. There can be no doubt, however, that the 4th century opened a wide breach in this respect between the Eastern and Western churches. The modern Greek custom is "(a) that most candidates for Holy Orders are dismissed from the episcopal seminaries shortly before being ordained deacons, in order that they may marry (their partners being in fact mostly daughters of clergymen), and after their marriage, return to the seminaries in order to take the higher orders; (b) that, as priests, they still continue the marriages thus contracted, but may not remarry on the death of their wife; and (c) that the Greek bishops, who may not continue their married life, are commonly not chosen out of the ranks of the married secular clergy, but from among the monks."5 The Eastern Church, therefore, still adheres fairly closely to the rules laid down by the Apostolical Canons in the 4th century. In the West, however, a decisive forward step was taken by Popes Damasus and Siricius during the last quarter of that century. The famous decretal of Siricius (385) not only enjoined strict celibacy on bishops, priests and deacons, but insisted on the instant separation of those who had already married, and prescribed the punishment of expulsion for disobedience (Siric. *Ep.* i. c. 7; Migne, *P.L.* xiii. col. 1138). Although we find Siricius a year later writing to the African Church on this same subject in tones rather of persuasion than of command, yet the beginning of compulsory sacerdotal celibacy in the Western Church may be conveniently dated from his decretal of A.D. 385. Leo the Great (d. 461) and Gregory the Great (d. 604) further extended the rule of celibacy to subdeacons.

For the next three or four centuries there is little to note but the continual evidence of open or secret resistance to these decrees, and the parallel frequency and stringency of ecclesiastical legislation, which by its very monotony bears witness to its own want of success. At least seven episcopal constitutions of the 8th and 9th centuries forbade the priest to have even his mother or his sister in the house.6 Nor did the only difficulty lie in such secret breaches of the law; in many districts the priesthood tended to become a mere hereditary caste, to the disadvantage of church and state alike. In northern and southern Italy public clerical marriages were extremely frequent, whether with or without regular forms.7The see of Rouen was held for more than a century (942-1054) by three successive bishops who were family men and two of whom were openly married.8 In England St Swithun (d. 862) was married, though very likely by special papal dispensation; and the married clergy were apparently predominant in Alfred's time. In spite of Dunstan's reforms at the end of the 10th century, the Norman Lanfranc found so many wedded priests that he dared not decree their separation; and when his successor St Anselm attempted to go further, this seemed a perilous novelty even to so distinguished an ecclesiastic as Henry of Huntingdon, who wrote: "About Michaelmas of this same year (1102) Archbishop Anselm held a council in London, wherein he forbade wives to the English priesthood, heretofore not forbidden; which seemed to some a matter of great purity, but to others a perilous thing, lest the clergy, in striving after a purity too great for human strength, should fall into horrible impurity, to the extreme dishonour of the Christian name" (lib. vii.; Migne, *P.L.* cxcv. col.

944). Yet this was at a time when the decisive and continued action of two great popes ought to have left no possible doubt as to the law of the church.

The growing tendency of the clergy to look upon their endowments as hereditary fiefs, their consequent worldliness and (it must be added) their vices, aroused the indignation of two very remarkable men in the latter half of the 11th century. St Pietro Damiani (988-1072) was a scholar, hermit and reformer, who did more perhaps than any one else to combat the open marriages of the clergy. He complained that exhortation was wasted even on the bishops, "because they despair of attaining to the pinnacle of chastity, and have no fear of condemnation in open synod for the vice of lechery.... If this evil were secret [he adds], it might perhaps be borne."9 His *Liber Gomorrhianus*, addressed to and approved by St Leo IX., is sufficient in itself to explain the vehemence of his crusade, though it emphasizes even more strongly the impolicy of proceeding more severely against the open marriages of the clergy than against concubinage and other less public vices.10 Damiani found a powerful ally in the equally ascetic but far more imperious and statesmanlike Hildebrand, afterwards Pope Gregory VII. Under the influence of these two men, five successive popes between 1045 and 1073 attempted a radical reform; and when, in this latter year, Hildebrand himself became pope, he took measures so stringent that he has sometimes been erroneously represented not merely as the most uncompromising champion, but actually as the author of the strict rule of celibacy for all clerics in sacred orders. His mind, strongly imbued with the theocratic ideal, saw more clearly than any other the enormous increase of influence which would accrue to a strictly celibate body of clergy, separated by their very ordination from the strongest earthly ties; and no statesman has ever pursued with greater energy and resolution a plan once formulated. In order to break down the desperate, and in many places organized, resistance of the clergy, he did not shrink from the perilous course, so contrary to his general policy, of subjecting them to the judgment of the laity. Not only were concubinary priests—a term which was now made to include also those who had openly married—forbidden to serve at the altar and threatened with actual deposition in cases of contumacy, but the laity were warned against attending mass said by "any priest certainly known to keep a concubine or *subintroducta*."11

But these heroic measures soon caused serious embarrassment. If the laity were to stand aloof from all incontinent priests, while (as the most orthodox churchmen constantly complained) many priests were still incontinent, then this could only result in estranging large bodies of the laity from the sacraments of the church. It became necessary, therefore, to soften a policy which to the lay mind might imply that the virtue of a sacrament was weakened by the vices of its ministers; and, whereas Peter Lombard (d. 1160) concludes that no excommunicated priest can effect transubstantiation, St Thomas Aquinas (d. 1274) agrees with all the later Schoolmen in granting him that power, though to the peril of his own soul.12For, by the last quarter of the 13th century, the struggle had entered upon a new phase. The severest measures had been tried, especially against the priests' unhappy partners. As early as the council of Augsburg (952) these were condemned to be scourged, while Leo II. and Urban II., at the councils of Rome and Amalfi (1051, 1089), 603adjudged them to actual slavery.13 Such enactments naturally defeated their own purpose. More was done by the gentler missionary zeal of the Franciscans and Dominicans in the early 13th century; but St Thomas Aquinas had seen half a century of that reform and had recognized its limitations; he therefore attenuated as much as possible the decree of Nicholas II. His contemporary St Bonaventura complained publicly that he himself and his fellow-friars were often compelled to hold their tongues about the evil clergy; partly because, even if one were expelled, another equally worthless would probably take his place, but "perhaps principally lest, if the people altogether lost faith in the clergy, heretics should arise and draw the people to themselves as sheep that have no shepherd, and make heretics of them, boasting that, as it were by our own testimony, the clergy were so vile that none need obey them or care for their teaching."14 In other passages of his works St Bonaventura tells us plainly how little had as yet been gained by suppressing clerical marriages; and the evidence of orthodox and distinguished churchmen for the next three centuries is equally decisive. Alvarez Pelayo, a Spanish bishop and papal penitentiary, wrote in 1322 "The clergy sin commonly in these following ways ... fourthly, in that they live very incontinently, and would that they had never promised continence; especially in Spain and southern Italy, in which provinces the sons of the laity are scarcely more numerous than those of the clergy." Cardinal Pierre d'Ailly pleaded before the council of Constance in 1415 for the reform of "that most scandalous custom, or rather abuse, whereby many [clergy] fear not to keep concubines in public."15

Meanwhile, as has been said above, the custom of open marriage among clergy in holy orders (priests, deacons and subdeacons) was gradually stamped out. A series of synods, from the early 12th century onwards, declared such marriages to be not only unlawful, but null and void in themselves. Yet the custom lingered sporadically in Germany and England until the last few years of the 13th century, though it seems to have died out earlier in France and Italy. There was also a short-lived attempt to declare that even a clerk in lower orders should lose his clerical privileges on his marriage; but Boniface VIII. in 1300 definitely permitted such marriages under the already-quoted conditions of the Apostolic Canons; in these cases, however, a bishop's licence was required to enable the cleric to officiate in church, and the episcopal registers show that the diocesans frequently insisted on the celibacy of parish-clerks. As the middle ages drew to a close, earnest churchmen were compelled to ask themselves whether it would not be better to let the priests marry than to continue a system under which concubinage was even licensed in some districts.16 Serious proposals were made to reintroduce clerical marriage at the great reforming councils of Constance (1415) and Basel (1432); but the overwhelming majority of orthodox churchmen were unwilling to abandon a rule for which the saints had fought during so many centuries, and to which many of them probably attributed an apostolic origin.17 This conservative attitude was inevitably strengthened by the attacks first of Lollard and then, of Lutheran heretics; and Sir Thomas More was driven to declare, in answer to Tyndale, that the marriage of priests, being essentially null and void, "defileth the priest more than double or treble whoredom." It is well known that this became one of the most violently disputed questions at the Reformation, and that for eight years it was felony in England to defend sacerdotal marriage as permissible by the law of God (Statute of the Six Articles, 31 Hen. VIII. c. 14). The diversity of practice on this point drew one of the sharpest lines between reformers and orthodox, until the disorders introduced by these religious wars tempted the latter to imitate in considerable numbers the licence of their rivals.18 This moved the emperor Charles V. to obtain from Paul III. dispensations for married priests in his dominions; and his successor Ferdinand, with the equally Catholic sovereigns of France, Bavaria and Poland, pleaded strongly at the council of Trent (1545) for permissive marriage. The council, after some hesitation, took the contrary course, and in the 9th canon of its 24th session it erected sacerdotal celibacy practically, if not formally, into an article of faith. In spite of this, the emperor Joseph II. reopened the question in 1783. In France the revolutionary constitution of 1791 abolished all restrictions on marriage, and during the Terror celibacy often exposed a priest to suspicion as an enemy to the Republic; but the better part of the clergy steadily resisted this innovation, and it is estimated that only about 2% were married. The Old Catholics adopted the principle of sacerdotal marriage in 1875.

The working of the system in modern times is perhaps too controversial a question to be discussed here; but one or two points may be noted on which all fairly well informed writers would probably agree. It can scarcely be denied that the Roman Catholic clergy have always owed much of their influence to their celibacy, and that in many cases this influence has been most justly earned by the celibate's devotion to an unworldly ideal. Again, the most adverse critics would admit that much was done by the counter-Reformation, and that modern ecclesiastical discipline on this point is considerably superior to that of the middle ages; while, on the other hand, many authorities of undoubted orthodoxy are ready to confess that it is not free from serious risks even in these days of easy publicity and stringent civil discipline.19 Lastly, statistical research has shown that the children of the married British clergy have been distinguished far beyond their mere numerical proportion.20

AUTHORITIES.—Henry Charles Lea, *History of Sacerdotal Celibacy* (3rd ed., 1907, 2 vols), is by far the fullest and best work on this subject, though a good deal of important matter omitted by Dr Lea may be found in *Die Einführung der erzwungenen Ehelosigkeit* by the brothers Johann Anton and Augustin Theiner, which was put on the Roman *Index*, though Augustin afterwards became archivist at the Vatican (Altenburg, 1828, 2 vols.). The history of monastic celibacy has not yet been fully treated anywhere; the most important evidence of the episcopal registers is either still in MS. or has been published only in comparatively recent years. The most learned work on clerical celibacy from the strictly conservative point of view is that of Francesco Antonio Zaccaria, *Storia Polemica del celibato sacro* (Rome, 1774); but many of his most important 604conclusions are set aside by the abbé E. Vacandard in his contribution to the *Dictionnaire de théologie catholique* (vol. ii. art. "Célibat ecclésiastique").

(G. G. CO.)

1W. Smith, *Dict. of Greek and Roman Antiquities* (3rd ed.), vol. ii. p. 44.

2"In the 14th century, the city of Ilchi, in Chinese Tartary, possessed 14 monasteries, averaging 3000 devotees in each; while in Tibet, at the present time, there are in the vicinity of Lhassa 12 great monasteries, containing a population of 18,500 lamas. In Ladak the proportion of lamas to the laity is as 1 to 13, in Spiti 1 to 7, and in Burmah 1 to 30" (Lea i. 103).

31 Cor. vii. 25 sq., ix. 5; 1 Tim. iii. 2, 11, 12; Titus i. 6; E. Vacandard in *Dict. de Théol. Cath.*, *s.v.* "Célibat."

4This was a natural argument for the defenders of clerical celibacy even in far later times. St Bonaventura (d. 1274) puts this very strongly: "For if archbishops and bishops now had children, they would rob and plunder all the goods of the Church so that little or nothing would be left for the poor. For since they now heap up wealth and enrich nephews removed from them by almost incalculable degrees of affinity, what would they do if they had legitimate children?... Therefore the Holy Ghost in His providence hath removed this stumbling-block," &c. &c. (*In Sent.* lib. iv. dist. xxxvii art. i. quaest. 3).

5Hefele, *Beitrage zur Kirchengesch. u.s.w.* i. 139.

6See the quotations in Lea i. 156. These prohibitions were renewed in the 13th and 14th centuries (ibid. i. 410).

7Ratherius, *Itinerarium*, c. 5 (Migne, *P.L.* cxxxvi. col. 585). Gulielmus Apulus writes of southern Italy in 1059: "In these parts priests, deacons and the whole clergy were publicly married" (*De Normann.* lib. ii.).

8Dom Pommeraye, *S. Rotomag. Eccl. Concilia*, pp. 56, 65; cf. similar instances on p. 315 of Dr A. Dresdner's *Kultur-und Sittengeschichte d. italienischen Geistlichkeit im 10. und 11. Jhdt.* (Breslau, 1890).

9*Opusc.* xvii. praef. The saint's evidence is carefully weighed by Dresdner (l.c.), especially on pp. 309 ff. and 321 ff.

10Even Pope Innocent III. was compelled to decide that priests who had kept two or more concubines, successively or simultaneously, did not thereby incur the disabilities which attended digamists; or, in other words, that a layman who had contracted two lawful marriages and then proceeded to ordination on the death of his second wife, could be absolved only by the pope; whereas the concubinary priest, "as a man branded with simple fornication," might receive a valid dispensation from his own bishop (Letter to archbishop of Lund in 1212. *Regest.* lib. xvi. ep. 118; Migne, *P.L.* ccxvi. col. 914). As the great canonist Gratian remarked on a similar decretal of Pope Pelagius, "Here is a case where lechery has more rights at law than has chastity" (*Decret.* p. i. dist. xxxiv. c. vii. note a).

11The actual originator of this policy was Nicholas II., probably at Hildebrand's suggestion; but the decree remained practically a dead letter until Gregory's accession.

12Peter Lombard, *Sentent.* lib. iv. dist. 13; Aquinas, *Summa Theol.* pars iii. Q. lxxxiii. art. 7, 9.

13Labbe-Mansi, *Concilia*, vol. xix. col. 796 and xx. col. 724. Dr Lea is probably right in suggesting that it was a confused recollection of these decrees which prompted one of Cranmer's judges to assure him that "his children were bondmen to the see of Canterbury." Strype, *Memorials of Cranmer*, bk iii. c. 28 (ed. 1812, vol. i. p. 601).

14Bonaventura, *Libell. Apologet.* quaest. i.; cf. his parallel treatise *Quare Fratres Minores praedicent.* The first visitation of his friend Odo Rigaldi, archbishop of Rouen, shows that about 15% of the parish clergy in that diocese were notoriously incontinent (*Regestrum Visitationum*, ed. Bonnin, Rouen, 1852, pp. 17 ff.). Vacandard (loc. cit. p. 2087) appeals rather misleadingly to this record as proving the progress made during the half-century before

Odo's time. It is probable that there were many more offenders than these 15% known to the archbishop.

15Alvarus Pelagius, *De Planctu Ecclesiae*, ed. 1517, f. 131a, col. 2; cf. f. 102b, col. 2; Hermann von der Hardt, *Constantiensis Concilii*, &c. vol. i. pars. viii. col. 428.

16This more or less regular sale of licences by bishops and archdeacons flourished from the days of Gregory VII. to the 16th century; see index to Lea, *s.v.* "Licences." Dr Lea has, however, omitted the most striking authority of all. Gascoigne, the most distinguished Oxford chancellor of his day, writing about 1450 of John de la Bere, then bishop of St David's, says that he had refused to separate the clergy of his diocese from their concubines, giving publicly as his reason, "for then I your bishop should lose the 400 marks which I receive yearly in my diocese for the priests' lemans" (Gascoigne, *Lib. Ver.* ed. Rogers, p. 36). Even Sir Thomas More, in his polemic against the Reformers, admitted that this concubinage was too often tolerated in Wales (*English Works*, ed. 1557, p. 231, cf. 619).

17One of Dr Lea's few serious mistakes is his acceptance of the spurious pamphlet in favour of priestly marriage which was attributed in the 11th century to St Ulrich of Augsburg (i. 171).

18Janssen, *Gesch. d. deutschen Volkes*, 13th ed., vol. viii. pp. 423, 4, 9; 434; Lea ii. 195, 204. ff.

19Lea (ii. 339. ff.) gives a long series of quotations to this effect from church synods and orthodox disciplinary writers of modern times.

20Havelock Ellis, *A Study of British Genius* (London, 1904, p. 80), "Even if we compare the church with the other professions with which it is most usually classed, we find that the eminent children of the clergy considerably outnumber those of lawyers, doctors and army officers put together." Mr Ellis points put, however, that "the clerical profession ... also produces more idiots than any other class."

CELL (from Lat. *cella*, probably from an Indo-European *kal*—seen in Lat. *celare*, to hide; another suggestion connects the word with Lat. *cera*, wax, taking the original meaning to refer to the honeycomb), in its earliest application a small detached room in a building, particularly a small monastic house (see ABBEY), generally in the country, belonging to large conventual buildings, and intended for change of air for the monks, as well as places to reside in to look after the lands, vassals, &c. Thus Tynemouth was a cell to St Albans; Ashwell, Herts, to Westminster Abbey. The term was also used of the small sleeping apartments of the monks, or a small apartment used by the anchorite or hermit. This use still survives in the application to the small separate chambers in a prison (*q.v.*) in which prisoners are confined. The word is applied to various small compartments which build up a compound structure such as a honeycomb, to the minute compartments in a tissue, &c. More particularly the word is used, in electrical science, of the single constituent compartments of a voltaic battery (*q.v.*), and in biology of the living units of protoplasm of which plants and animals are composed (see CYTOLOGY).

CELLA, in architecture, the Latin name for the sanctuary of a Roman temple, corresponding with the naos of the Greek temple. In the Etruscan temples, according to Vitruvius, there were three cellas, side by side; and in the temple of Venus built by Hadrian at Rome there were two cellas, both enclosed, however, in a single peristyle.

CELLARET (*i.e.* little cellar), strictly that portion of a sideboard which is used for holding bottles and decanters, so called from a cellar (which in general may be any underground unlighted apartment) being commonly used for keeping wine. Sometimes it is a drawer, divided into compartments lined with zinc, and sometimes a cupboard, but still an integral part of the sideboard. In the latter part of the 18th century, when the sideboard was in process of evolution from a side-table with drawers into the large and important piece of furniture which it eventually became, the cellaret was a detached receptacle. It was most commonly of mahogany or rosewood, many-sided or even octagonal, and occasionally oval, bound with broad bands of brass and lined with zinc partitions to hold the ice for cooling wine. Sometimes a tap was fixed in the lower part for drawing off the water from the melted ice. Cellarets were usually placed under the sideboard, and were, as a rule, handsome and well-proportioned; but as the artistic impulse which created the great 18th-century English school of furniture died away, their form grew debased, and under the influence of the English Empire fashion, which drew its inspiration from a bastard classicism, they assumed the shape of sarcophagi incongruously mounted with lions' heads and claw-feet. Hepplewhite called them "gardes du vin"; they are now nearly always known as "wine-coolers."

CELLE, a town of Germany, in the Prussian province of Hanover, on the left bank of the navigable Aller, near its junction with the Fuse and the Lachte, 23 m. N.E. of Hanover, on the main Lehrte-Hamburg railway. Pop. (1905) 21,400. The town has a Roman Catholic and five Protestant churches, among the latter the town-church with the burial vault of the dukes of Lüneburg-Celle. Here rest the remains of Sophia Dorothea, wife of the elector George of Hanover, afterwards George I. of England, and those of Caroline Matilda, the divorced wife of Christian VII. of Denmark and sister of George III. of England, who resided here from 1772 until her death in 1775. The most interesting building in Celle is the former ducal palace, begun in 1485 in Late Gothic style, but with extensive Renaissance additions of the close of the 17th century. The building of the court of appeal (*Oberlandesgericht*), with a valuable library of 60,000 volumes and many MSS., including a priceless copy of the *Sachsenspiegel*, the museum and the hall of the estates (*Landschaftshaus*) are also worthy of notice. There are manufactures of woollen yarn, tobacco, biscuits, umbrellas and printers' ink, and a lively trade is carried on in wax, honey, wool and timber. Celle is the seat of the court of appeal from the superior courts of Aurich, Detmold, Göttingen, Hanover, Hildesheim, Lüneburg, Osnabrück, Stade and Verden. Founded in 1292, the town was the residence of the dukes of Lüneburg-Celle, a cadet branch of the ducal house of Brunswick, from the 14th century until 1705.

See Dehning, *Geschichte der Stadt Celle* (Celle, 1891).

CELLIER, ALFRED (1844-1891), English musical composer, was born at Hackney on the 1st of December 1844. From 1855 to 1860 he was a chorister at the Chapel Royal, St James's, under the Rev. Thomas Helmore, where Arthur Sullivan was one of his youthful colleagues. His first appointment was that of organist at All Saints' church, Blackheath (1862). In 1866 he succeeded Dr Chipp as director of the Ulster Hall concerts, Belfast, at the same time acting as conductor of the Belfast Philharmonic Society. In 1868 he returned to London as organist of St Alban's, Holborn. From 1871 to 1875 he was conductor at the Prince's theatre, Manchester; and from 1877 to 1879 at various London theatres. During this period he composed many comic operas and operettas, of which the most successful was *The Sultan of Mocha*, which was produced at Manchester in 1874, in London at the St James's theatre in 1876, and revived at the Strand theatre in 1887. In 1880 Cellier visited America, producing a musical version of Longfellow's *Masque of Pandora* at Boston (1881). In 1883 his setting of Gray's *Elegy* in the form of a cantata was produced at the Leeds Festival. In 1886 he won the great success of his life in *Dorothy*, a comic opera written to a libretto by B.C. Stephenson, which was produced at the Gaiety theatre on the 25th of September 1886, and, transferred first to the Prince of Wales theatre and subsequently to the Lyric theatre, ran until April 1889. *Doris* (1889), and *The Mountebanks*, which was produced in January 1892, a few days after the composer's death, were less successful. Cellier owed much to the influence of Sir Arthur Sullivan. He had little of the latter's humour and vivacity, but he was a fertile melodist, and his writing was invariably distinguished by elegance and refinement. He died in London on the 28th of December 1891.

CELLINI, BENVENUTO (1500-1571), Italian artist, metal worker and sculptor, was born in Florence, where his family, originally landowners in the Val d'Ambra, had for three generations been settled. His father, Giovanni Cellini, was a musician and artificer of musical instruments; he married Maria Lisabetta Granacci, and eighteen years elapsed before they had any progeny. Benvenuto (meaning "Welcome") was the third child. The father destined him for the same profession as himself, and endeavoured to thwart his inclination for design and metal work. When he had reached the age of fifteen his youthful predilection had become too strong to be resisted, and his father reluctantly gave consent to his being apprenticed to a goldsmith, Antonio di Sandro, named Marcone. He had already attracted some notice in his native place, when, being implicated in a fray with some of his companions, he was banished for six months to Siena, where he worked for Francesco Castoro, a goldsmith; from thence he removed to Bologna, where he became a more accomplished flute-player and made progress in the goldsmith's art. After visiting Pisa, and after twice resettling for a while in Florence (where he was visited by the sculptor Torrigiano, who unsuccessfully suggested his accompanying him to England), he decamped to Rome, aged nineteen. His first attempt at his craft here was a silver casket, followed by some silver candlesticks, and later by a vase for the bishop of Salamanca, which introduced him to the favourable notice of Pope Clement VII.; likewise at a later date one of his celebrated works, the gold medallion of "Leda and the Swan,"—the head and torso of Leda cut in hard stone—executed for Gonfaloniere Gabbriello Cesarino, which is now in the Vienna museum; he also reverted to music, practised flute-playing, and was appointed one of the pope's court-musicians. In the attack upon Rome by the constable de Bourbon, which occurred immediately after, in 1527, the bravery and address of Cellini proved of signal service 605to the pontiff; if we may believe his own accounts, his was the very hand which shot the Bourbon dead, and he afterwards killed Philibert, prince of Orange. His exploits paved the way for a reconciliation with the Florentine magistrates, and his return shortly after to his native place. Here he assiduously devoted himself to the execution of medals, the most famous of which (executed a short while later) are "Hercules and the Nemean Lion," in gold repoussé work, and "Atlas supporting the Sphere," in chased gold, the latter eventually falling into the possession of Francis I. From Florence he went to the court of the duke of Mantua, and thence again to Florence and to Rome, where he was employed not only in the working of jewelry, but also in the execution of dies for private medals and for the papal mint. Here in 1529 he avenged a brother's death by slaying the slayer; and shortly afterwards had to flee to Naples to shelter himself from the consequences of an affray with a notary, Ser Benedetto, whom he wounded. Through the influence of several of the cardinals he obtained a pardon; and on the elevation of Paul III. to the pontifical throne he was reinstated in his former position of favour, notwithstanding a fresh homicide of a goldsmith which he had committed more by accident than of malice prepense in the interregnum. Once more the plots of Pierluigi Farnese, a natural son of Paul III., led to his retreat from Rome to Florence and Venice, and once more he was restored with greater honour than before. On returning from a visit to the court of Francis I., being now aged thirty-seven, he was imprisoned on a charge (apparently false) of having embezzled during the war the gems of the pontifical tiara; he remained some while confined in the castle of Sant' Angelo, escaped, was recaptured, and treated with great severity, and was in daily expectation of death on the scaffold. At last, however, he was released at the intercession of Pierluigi's wife, and more especially of the Cardinal d' Este of Ferrara, to whom he presented a splendid cup. For a while after this he worked at the court of Francis I. at Fontainebleau and in Paris; but he considered the duchesse d'Étampes to be set against him, and the intrigues of the king's favourites, whom he would not stoop to conciliate and could not venture to silence by the sword, as he had silenced his enemies in Rome, led him, after about five years of laborious and sumptuous work, and of continually-recurring jealousies and violences, to retire in 1545 in disgust to Florence, where he employed his time in works of art, and exasperated his temper in rivalries with the uneasy-natured sculptor Baccio Bandinelli. The first collision between the two had occurred several years before when Pope Clement VII. commissioned Cellini to mint his coinage. Now, in an altercation before Duke Cosimo, Bandinelli insultingly stigmatized Benvenuto as guilty of gross immorality; in his autobiography Cellini rather repels than denies the charge, but he certainly repels it with demonstrative and grotesque vivacity. Two somewhat similar charges had been made ere this: one in Paris, which he braved out in court—the other, in Florence, was a mere private quarrel, and perhaps undeserving of attention. During the war with Siena Cellini was appointed to strengthen the defences of his native city, and, though rather shabbily treated by his ducal patrons, he continued to gain the admiration of his fellow-citizens by the magnificent works which he produced. He died in Florence in 1571, unmarried, and leaving no posterity, and was buried with great pomp in the church of the Annunziata. He had supported in Florence a widowed sister and her six daughters.

Besides the works in gold and silver which have been adverted to, Cellini executed several pieces of sculpture on a grander scale. The most distinguished of these is the bronze group of "Perseus holding the head of Medusa," a work (first suggested by Duke Cosimo de' Medici) now in the Loggia dei Lanzi at Florence, full of the fire of genius and the grandeur of a terrible beauty, one of the most typical and unforgettable monuments of the Italian Renaissance. The casting of this great work gave Cellini the utmost trouble and anxiety; and its completion was hailed with rapturous homage from all parts of Italy. The original relief from the foot of the pedestal—Perseus and Andromeda—is in the Bargello, and replaced by a cast.

Not less characteristic of its splendidly gifted and barbarically untameable author are the autobiographical memoirs which he composed, beginning them in Florence in 1558,—a production of the utmost energy, directness and racy animation, setting forth one of the most singular careers in all the annals of fine art. His amours and hatreds, his passions and delights, his love of the sumptuous and the exquisite in art, his self-applause and self-assertion, running now and again into extravagances which it is impossible to credit, and difficult to set down as strictly conscious falsehoods, make this one of the most singular and fascinating books in existence. Here we read, not only of the strange and varied adventures of which we have presented a hasty sketch, but of the devout complacency with which Cellini could contemplate a satisfactorily achieved homicide; of the legion of devils which he and a conjuror evoked in the Colosseum, after one of his not innumerous mistresses had been spirited away from him by her mother; of the marvellous halo of light which he found surrounding his head at dawn and twilight after his Roman imprisonment, and his supernatural visions and angelic protection during that adversity; and of his being poisoned on two several occasions. If he is unmeasured in abusing some people, he is also unlimited in praising others. The autobiography has been translated into English by Thomas Roscoe, by J.A. Symonds, and by A. Macdonald. Cellini also wrote treatises on the goldsmith's art, on sculpture, and on design (translated by C.R. Ashbee, 1899).

Among his works of art not already mentioned, many of which have perished, were a colossal Mars for a fountain at Fontainebleau and the bronzes of the doorway, coins for the Papal and Florentine states, a Jupiter in silver of life size, and a bronze bust of Bindo Altoviti. The works of decorative art are, speaking broadly, rather florid than chastened in style.

In addition to the bronze statue of Perseus and the medallions already referred to, the works of art in existence to-day executed by him are the celebrated salt-cellar made for Francis I. at Vienna; a medallion of Clement VII. in commemoration of the peace between the Christian princes, 1530, with a bust of the pope on the reverse and a figure of Peace setting fire to a heap of arms in front of the temple of Janus, signed with the artist's name; a medal of Francis I. with his portrait, also signed; and a medal of Cardinal Pietro Bembo. Cellini, while employed at the papal mint at Rome during the papacy of Clement VII. and later of Paul III., executed the dies of several coins and medals, some of which still survive at this now defunct mint. He was also in the service of Alessandro de' Medici, first duke of Florence, for whom he executed in 1535 a forty-soldi piece with a bust of the duke on one side and standing figures of the saints Cosmo and Damian on the other. Some connoisseurs attribute to his hand several plaques, "Jupiter crushing the Giants," "Fight between Perseus and Phinaeus," a Dog, &c.

The important works which have perished include the uncompleted chalice intended for Clement VII.; a gold cover for a prayer-book as a gift from Pope Paul III. to Charles V.,—both described at length in his autobiography; large silver statues of Jupiter, Vulcan and Mars, wrought for Francis I. during his sojourn in Paris; a bust of Julius Caesar; and a silver cup for the cardinal of Ferrara. The magnificent gold "button," or morse, made by Cellini for the cope of Clement VII., the competition for which is so graphically described in his autobiography, appears to have been sacrificed by Pius VI., with many other priceless specimens of the goldsmith's art, in furnishing the indemnity of 30,000,000 francs demanded by Napoleon at the conclusion of the campaign against the States of the Church in 1797. According to the terms of the treaty, the pope was permitted to pay a third of that sum in plate and jewels. Fortunately there are in the print room of the British Museum three water-colour drawings of this splendid morse by F. Bertoli, done at the instance of an Englishman named Talman in the first half of the 18th century. The obverse and reverse, as well as the rim, are drawn full size, and moreover the morse with the precious stones set therein, including a diamond then considered the second largest in the world, is fully described.

606
BIBLIOGRAPHY.—The autobiography already named is the foundation of most of the works written concerning Cellini's life. See also *Cellini, His Times and Contemporaries*, by "the Author of the Life of Sir Kenelm Digby" (1899); L. Dimier, *Cellini à la cour de France* (1898); Eugène Plon, *Cellini, orfèvre, médailleur, &c.* (1883); Bolzenthal,*Skizzen zur Kunstgeschichte der modernen Medaillen-Arbeit 1429-1840* (Berlin, 1840); A. Armand, *Les Médailleurs italiens des XVe et XVIe siècles* (3 vols., Paris, 1883-1887); Dr Francesco Tassi, *Vita di Benvenuto Cellini* (Firenze, 1829), *Vita di Benvenuto Cellini scritta da lui medisimo* (1832); E. Babelon, *La Gravure en pierres fines* (Paris, 1894); A. Heiss, *Les Médailleurs florentins* (Paris, 1887); J. Friedländer, *Die italienischen Schaumünzen des fünfzehnten Jahrhunderts* (Berlin, 1880-1882); N. Rondot, *Les Médailleurs lyonnais* (Mâcon, 1897); Dr Julius Cahn, *Medaillen und Plaketten der Sammlung W.P. Metzler* (Frankfort-on-Main, 1898); Molinier, *Les Plaquettes*; I.B. Supino, *Il Medagliere Mediceo nel R. Museo Nazionale di Firenze* (Florence, 1899);*L'Arte di Benvenuto Cellini* (Florence, 1901); C. von Fabriczy, *Medaillen der italienischen Renaissance* (Leipzig); L. Forrer, *Biographical Dictionary of Medallists, &c.* (London, 1904), &c.

(W. M. R.; E. A. J.)

CELLULOSE, the name given to both an individual—cellulose proper, in the restricted sense of a chemical individual—and to a group of substances, the celluloses or cellulose group, which constitute in infinitely varied forms the containing envelope of the plant cell. They are complex carbohydrates, or "saccharo-colloids" (Tollens), and are resolved by ultimate hydrolysis into monoses. The typical cellulose is represented by the empirical formula $C_6H_{10}O_5$, identical with that of starch, with which it has many chemical analogies as well as physiological correlations. The representative "cellulose" is the main constituent of the cotton fibre substance, and is obtainable by treating the raw fibre with boiling dilute alkalis, followed by chlorine gas or bromine water, or simply by alkaline oxidants. The cellulose thus purified is further treated with dilute acids, and then exhaustively with alcohol and ether. Chemical filter-paper (Swedish) is practically pure cellulose, the final purification consisting in exhaustive treatment with hydrofluoric acid to remove silicious inorganic residues. The "cellulose" group, however, comprises a series of substances which, while presenting the characters generally similar to those of cotton cellulose, also exhibit marked divergences. The resemblances are maintained in their synthetical reactions; but reactions involving the decomposition of the complex show many variations. For example, cotton cellulose is difficultly hydrolysed; other celluloses are more or less readily split up by dilute acids, the extreme members readily yielding sugars: the hexoses—dextrose, mannose and galactose; and the pentoses—xylose and arabinose; these less resistant cell-wall constituents are termed hemi-celluloses.

The celluloses proper are essentially non-nitrogenous, though originating in the cell protoplasm. The cell-walls of the lower cryptogams, similarly purified, retain a notable proportion—2.0-4.0%—of constitutional nitrogen. When hydrolysed these fungoid celluloses yield, in addition to monoses, glucosamine and acetic acid. The celluloses of the phanerogams are generally associated, in a degree ranging from physical mixture to chemical union, with other complicated substances, constituting the "compound celluloses." The nature of the associated groups affords a convenient classification into pecto-celluloses, ligno-celluloses and cuto-celluloses. *Pecto-celluloses* are so named because the associated substances—carbohydrates, together with their oxidation products, *i.e.* containing either two carbonyls (CO) in the unit group or carboxyl (CO·OH) groups in a complex—are readily hydrolysed by weak acids to the gelatinous "pectic acids" or their salts. *Ligno-celluloses* are the substances of lignified tissue, the non-cellulose constituents of which are characterized by the presence of benzenoid and furfuroid groups; and although essentially complex, they may be regarded as homogeneous, and are conveniently grouped under the name *lignone*. The lignone complex reacts, by its unsaturated groups, with the halogens. It is a complex containing but little hydroxyl; and is of relatively high carbon percentage (55.0-57.0%).*Cuto-celluloses* predominate in the protective coatings of plant organs, and are characterized by constituent groups, the decomposition products of which are compounds of the fatty series, and also wax alcohols, acids, cholesterols, &c.

The typical pecto-cellulose is the flax fibre, *i.e.* the bast fibre of the flax plant (*Linum usitatissimum*), as it occurs in the plant, or as the commercial textile fibre in its raw state. Rhea, or ramie, is another leading textile fibre in which the cellulose occurs associated with alkali-soluble colloidal carbohydrates. Pecto-celluloses are found in the stems of the Gramineae (cereal straws, esparto), and in the fibro-vascular bundles of monocotyledons used as textile and rope-making fibres. They are the chief constituents of the fleshy parenchyma of fruits, tubers, rhizomes. Ligno-celluloses find their chemical representative in the jute fibre. They constitute the woods, and are therefore of the widest distribution and the highest industrial utility. It is important to note that a complex having all the chemical characteristics of a ligno-cellulose occurs in a soluble colloidal form in the juice of the white currant. The formation of ligno-cellulose is the chemical equivalent of the morphological change of the plant cell known as "lignification." The topical cuto-celluloses are the epidermal tissues of all growing plants or organs, which are easily detached from the underlying tissues which it is their function to protect. To subserve this function, they are extremely resistant to the attack of reagents. The associated groups are mostly of the normal saturated series, and of very high molecular weight.

Cellulose and Botanical Science.—The elaboration of cellulose, *i.e.* of the cell walls, and its morphological and physiological aspects are discussed in the articles PLANTS: *Physiology, Anatomy*: and CYTOLOGY; while in the article COAL the part played by cellulose in the formation of these deposits receives treatment: here we may deal with its general relation to agriculture. In the analysis of fodder plants and other vegetable produce, the residue obtained after successive acid and alkaline hydrolysis is the "crude fibre" of the agricultural chemist, and is generally taken as a measure of the actual cellulose contents of the raw material. We give in tabular form the average percentage of crude fibre in typical food-stuffs and agricultural produce:—

SEEDS

Seeds of Cereals.	Per cent of Fibre.	Legumin ous and Oil Seeds.	Per cent of Fibre.
Wheat	2.8	Rape	6.4
Barley	6.3	Cotton	7.5
Oats	9.0	Beans	10.0
Maize	5.2	Peas	10.0
Rye	8.0	Lentils	10.0
Rice	2.5	Vetches	7.2

FODDER CROPS

Stems and Foliage of Root Crops.	Per cent of Fibre.	Fodder Crops.	Per cent of Fibre.*	Cereal Straws.	Per cent of Fibre.
White Turnip	3.9	Grasses	32.0	Oats	60.68

Swedish Turnip	4.2	Meadow Hay	25.8	Wheat	75.77
Carrot	3.1	Clover & Trefoil	23.5	Barley	71.74
Mangel	2.6	Vetches	25.9		
Parsnip	2.6	Lucerne	26.7		
		Sainfoin	28.7		

* This percentage is calculated on airdry-produce containing 15% of water.

	Leguminous.	Oil Seeds.	Stems and Foliage of Root Crops.	Fodder Crops.	Cereal Straws.
Average % of water	14	7	87	70-80	15

607

The above figures have a purely empirical value, since they represent a complicated mixture of various residues derived from the celluloses and compound celluloses. This mixture may be further resolved, and by special quantitative methods the proportions of actual cellulose, ligno-cellulose and cuto-celluloses estimated (J. König, *Ber.*, 1906, 39, p. 3564). The figures are taken as an inverse measure of digestibility; at the same time it has been established that this group of relatively indigestible food constituents are more or less digestible and assimilable as flesh and fat producers. The percentage or coefficient of digestibility of the celluloses of the more important food-stuffs—green fodder, hay, straw and grains—varies from 20 to 75%. It has also been established that their physiological efficiency is, under certain conditions, quite equal to that of starch.

It must also be borne in mind that the indigestible food residues, as finally voided by the animal, have played an important mechanical part as an aid to digestion of those constituents more readily attacked in the digestive tract of animals. They are further an important factor of the agricultural cycle. Returned to the soil as "farm-yard manure," mixed with other cellulosic matter which has served as litter, they add "fibre" to the soil and, as a mechanical diluent of the mineral soil components, maintain this in a more open condition, penetrable by the atmospheric gases, and promoting distribution of moisture. Further by breaking down, with production of "humus," a complex of colloidal "unsaturated" bodies of acid function, they fulfil important chemical functions by interaction with the mineral soil constituents.

Chemistry of Cellulose.—Purified cotton cellulose, which is the definitive prototype of the cellulose group or series, is a complex of monoses or their "residues." It is resolved by solution in sulphuric acid and subsequent hydrolysis of the esters thus produced into dextrose. This fundamental fact with its elementary composition, most simply expressed by the formula $C_6H_{10}O_5$, has caused it to be regarded as a polyanhydride of dextrose. Forming, as it does, simple esters in the ratio of the reacting hydroxyls $3OH$: $C_6H_{10}O_5$, and taking into account its direct converson into ω-brom-methyl furfural (Fenton) a constitutional formula has been proposed by A.G. Green (*Zeit. Farb. Textil Chem.* 3, pp. 97 and 309 (1904)), which is a useful generalization of its reactions, and its ultimate relations to the simpler carbohydrates, viz.,   Green considers, moreover, that a group thus formulated may consistently represent the actual dimensions of the reacting unit, but that unit of larger dimensions, if postulated, is easily derived from the above by oxygen linkings.

From another point of view the unit group has been formulated as the main linking of such units in the complex taking place as between their respective CO and CH2 groups in the alternative enolic form CH—C(OH). This view gives expression to the genetic relations of the celluloses to the ligno-celluloses, to the tendency to carbon condensation as in the formation of coals, and pseudo-carbons, to the relative resistance of cellulose to hydrolysis, and its other points of differentiation from starch, and more particularly to the ketonic character of its carbonyl (CO) groups, which is also more in harmony with the experimental facts established by Fenton as to the production of methyl furfural.

The probability, however, is that no simple molecular formula adequately represents the constitution of cellulose as it actually exists or indeed reacts. On the other hand, it has been suggested that cellulose is to be regarded as representing a condition of matter analogous to that of a saline electrolyte in solution, *i.e.* as a complex of molecular aggregates, and of residues (of monose groups) having distinct and opposite polarities; such a complex is essentially labile and its configuration will change progressively under reaction. The exposition of this view is the subject of a publication by Cross and Bevan (*Researches on Cellulose*, ii. 1906). The main purpose is to give full effect to the colloidal characteristics of cellulose and its derivatives, with reference to the modern theory of the colloidal state as involving a particular internal equilibrium of amphoteric electrolytes.

The typical cellulose is a white fibrous substance familiar to us in the various forms of bleached cotton. Other fibrous celluloses are equally characteristic as to form and appearance, *e.g.* bleached flax, hemp, ramie. It is hygroscopic, absorbing 6 to 7% its weight of moisture from the air. When dry, it is an electrical insulator, and has a specific inductive capacity of about 7: when wetted it is a conductor, and manifests electrolytic phenomena.[1] It is insoluble in water and in the ordinary solvents; it dissolves, however, in a 40-50% solution of zinc chloride, and in ammoniacal solutions of copper oxide (3% CuO, 15% NH3): from these solutions it is obtained as a highly hydrated, gelatinous precipitate, from the former by dilution or addition of alcohol, from the latter by acidification; these solutions have important industrial application. Projected or drawn into a precipitating solution they may be solidified continuously to threads of various, but controlled dimensions: the regenerated cellulose, now amorphous, in its finer dimensions is known as artificial silk or lustra-cellulose. These forms of cellulose retain the general characters of the original fibrous and "natural" celluloses. In composition they differ somewhat by combination with water (of hydration), which they retain in the air-dry condition. They also further combine with an increased proportion of atmospheric moisture, viz. up to 10-11% of their weight.

Derivatives.—Important derivatives are the esters or ethereal salts of both inorganic and organic acids, cellulose behaving as an alcohol, the highest esters indicating that it reacts as a trihydric alcohol of the formula n[C6H7O2(OH)3]. The nitrates result by the action of concentrated nitric acid, either alone or in the presence of sulphuric acid: the normal dinitrate represents a definite stage in the series of nitrates, and the ester at this point manifests the important property of solubility in various alcoholic solvents, notably ether-alcohol. Such nitrates are the basis of collodion, of artificial silk by the processes of Chardonnet and Lehner, and of celluloid or xylonite. Higher nitrates are also obtainable up to the limit of the trinitrate, which is insoluble in ether or alcohol, but is soluble in nitroglycerin, nitrobenzene and other solvents. These higher nitrates are the basis of the most important modern explosives.

Cellulose reacts directly with acetic anhydride to form low esters; in the presence of sulphuric acid the reaction proceeds to higher limits; the triacetate is soluble in chloroform. The acid sulphuric ester, C6H8O3(SO4H)2, is obtained by the action of sulphuric acid, but its relation to the original cellulose is doubtful. The monobenzoate and dibenzoate are formed by benzoyl chloride reacting on alkali-cellulose (see below). Cellulose xanthates are obtained from carbon bisulphide and alkali-cellulose; these are water soluble derivatives and the basis of "viscose," and of important industries. Mixed esters—aceto-sulphate, aceto-benzoate, nitrobenzoyl nitrates, aceto-nitro-sulphates—have also been investigated.

Cellulose (cotton), when treated with a 15-20% caustic soda solution, gives the compound C6H10O5·H2O·2NaOH, alkali-cellulose, the original riband-like form with reticulated walls of the cellulose being transformed into a smooth-walled cylinder. The structural changes in the ultimate fibre determine very considerable changes in the dimensions of fabrics so treated. The reactions and structural changes were investigated by J. Mercer, and are known generally as "mercerization." In recent years a very large industry in "mercerized" fabrics (cotton) has resulted from the observation that if the shrinkages of the yarns and fabrics be antagonized by mechanical means, a very high lustre is developed.

Similar, but less definite compounds, are formed with the oxides of lead, manganese, barium, iron, aluminium and chromium. These derivatives, which also find industrial applications in the dyeing and printing of fabrics, differ but little in 608appearance from the original cellulose, and are without influence on its essential characteristics.

Decompositions.—Hydrolysis:—By solution in sulphuric acid followed by dilution and boiling the diluted solution cellulose hydrolyses to fermentable sugars; this reaction is utilized industrially in the manufacture of glucose from rags. Hydrochloric acid produces a friable mass of "hydrocellulose," probably $C12H22O11$, insoluble in water, but readily attacked by alkalis, with the production of soluble derivatives; some dextrose is formed in the original reaction. Hydrobromic acid in ethereal solution gives furfurane derivatives. Cold dilute acids have no perceptible action on cellulose. The actions of such acids are an important auxiliary to bleaching, dyeing and printing processes, but they require careful limitation in respect of concentration and temperature. Cellulose is extremely resistant to the action of dilute alkalis: a 1-2% solution of sodium hydrate having little action at temperatures up to 150° hence the use of caustic soda, soda ash and sodium silicate in bleaching processes, *i.e.* for the elimination of the non-cellulose components of the raw fibres. Oxidation in acid solutions gives compounds classed as "oxycelluloses," insoluble in water, but more or less soluble in alkalis; continued oxidation gives formic, acetic and carbonic acids. Oxidation in alkaline solution is more easily controlled and limited; solutions of bleaching powder, or more generally of alkaline hydrochlorites, receive industrial application in oxidizing the coloured impurities of the fibre, or residues left after more or less severe alkali treatments, leaving the cellulose practically unaffected. This, however, is obviously a question of conditions: this group of oxidants also oxidize to oxycellulose, and under more severe conditions to acid products, *e.g.* oxalic and carbonic acids. Certain bacteria also induce decompositions which are resolutions into ultimate products of the lowest molecular dimensions, as hydrogen, carbon dioxide, methane, acetic acid and butyric acid (Omeliansky) (*Handb. Techn. Mykologie* [F. Lafar] pp. 245-268), but generally the cellulose complex is extremely resistant to the organic ferments. Cellulose burns with a luminous flame to carbon dioxide and water; dry distillation gives a complicated mixture of gaseous and liquid products and a residue of charcoal or pseudo-carbon. Chromic acid in sulphuric acid solutions effects a complete oxidation, *i.e.* combustion to water and carbonic acid.

Ligno-celluloses.—These compounds have many of the characteristics of the cellulose esters; they are in effect ethereal compounds of cellulose and the quinonoid lignone complex, and the combination resists hydrolysis by weak alkalis or acids. The cellulose varies in amount from 80 to 50%, and the lignone varies inversely as the degree of lignification, that is, from the lignified bast fibre of annuals, of which jute is a type, to the dense tissues of the perennial dicotyledonous woods, typified by the beech. The empirical formula of the lignone complex varies from $C19H22O9$ (jute) to $C26H30O10$ (pine wood). In certain reactions the non-cellulose or lignone constituents are selectively converted into soluble derivatives, and may be separated as such from the cellulose which is left; for example, chlorination gives products soluble in sodium sulphite solution, by the combination of unsaturated groups of the lignone with the halogen, while digestion with bisulphite solutions at elevated temperatures (140°-160°) gives soluble sulphonated derivatives. This last reaction is employed industrially in the preparation of cellulose for paper-making from coniferous woods. These reactions are "quantitative" since they depend upon well-defined constitutional features of the lignone complex, and the resolution of the ligno-cellulose takes place with no further change in the lignone than the synthetical combination with the substituting groups. The constituent groups of the lignone specifically reacting are of benzenoid type of the probable form deduced from the similarity of the chlorinated derivatives to mairogallol, the product of the action of chlorine on pyrogallol in acetic acid solution (A. Hantzsch, *Ber.* 20, p. 2033). The complex contains methoxy $(OCH3)$ groups. There is also present a residue which is readily broken down by oxidizing agents, and indeed by simple hydrolysis, to acetic acid. Another important group of actual constituents are pentosanes—partially isolated as "wood gum" by solution in alkalis—and furfural derivatives

231

(hydroxy furfurals) derived from these. The actual constitutional relationships of these main groups, as well as the localization of the methoxy groups, are still problematical.

Certain colour reactions are characteristic, though they are in some cases reactions of certain constituents invariably present in the natural forms of the ligno-cellulose; which may be removed without affecting the essential character of the lignone complex. Aniline salts generally give a yellow coloration, dimethyl-para-phenylenediamine gives a deep red coloration, phloroglucin in hydrochloric acid gives a crimson coloration. Reactions more definitely characteristic of the lignone are:—ferric ferrocyanide, which is taken up and transformed into Prussian blue throughout the fibre, without affecting its structure, although there may be as much as a 50% gain in weight; iodine in potassium iodide solution gives a deep brown colour due to absorption of the halogen, a reaction which admits of quantitative application, *i.e.* as a measure of the proportion of ligno-cellulose in a fibrous mixture; nitric acid gives a deep orange yellow coloration; digested with the dilute acid (5-10% HNO3) at 50° the ligno-celluloses are entirely resolved, the lignone complex being attacked and dissolved in the form of nitroso-ketonic acids, which, on continued heating, are finally resolved to oxalic, acetic, formic and carbonic acids.

Derivatives of Ligno-cellulose.—By reaction with chlorine jute yields the derivative C19H18Cl4O9, soluble in alcohol, and in acetic acid; this derivative has the reactions of a quinone chloride. By reaction with sodium sulphite it is converted into a hydroquinone sulphonate of deep purple colour. The reaction of the ligno-celluloses (pine wood) with the bisulphites yields the soluble derivatives of the general formula C26H29O9SO3H (containing two OCH3 groups). Jute reacts with nitric acid in presence of sulphuric acid to form nitrates; and with acetic anhydride to form low acetates. It reacts with alkaline hydrates with structural changes similar to those obtained with cotton; and by the further action of benzoyl chloride and of carbon bisulphide upon the resulting compounds there result the corresponding benzoates and xanthates respectively. But these synthetical derivatives are mixtures of cellulose and lignone derivatives, and so far of merely theoretical interest.

Decompositions of Ligno-cellulose.—In addition to the specific resolutions above described which depend upon the distinctive chemical characters of the cellulose and lignone respectively, the following may be noted: to simple hydrolytic agents the two groups are equally resistant, therefore by boiling with dilute acids or alkalis the groups are attacked *pari passu*. Weak oxidants may also be used as bleaching agents to remove coloured by-products without seriously attacking the ligno-cellulose, which is obtained in its bleached form. Nitric acid of all strengths effects complete resolution. Chromic acid in dilute solutions combines with the lignone complex, but in presence of hydrolysing acids total oxidation of the lignone is determined. The principal products are oxalic, carbonic, formic and acetic acids. This reaction is an index of constitution. Generally, the lignone is attacked under many conditions and by many reagents which are without action upon cellulose, by virtue of its unsaturated constitution, and its acid and aldehydic residues.

Cuto-cellulose.—A typical cuto-cellulose is the cuticle (peel) of the apple which, when purified by repeated hydrolytic treatment and finally by alcohol and ether, gives a product of the composition C = 75.66%, H = 11.37%, O = 14.97%. Hydrolysis by strong alkalis gives stearo-cutic acid, C28H48O4, and oleo-cutic acid, C14H20O4 (Frémy). Cork is a complex mixture containing various compound celluloses: extraction with alcohol removes certain fatty alcohols and acids, and aromatic derivatives related to tannic acid; the residue is probably a mixture of cellulose, ligno-cellulose, cerin, C20H32O and suberin; the latter yields 609stearic acid, C18H36O2 and the acid C22H42O3. The cuto-celluloses have been only superficially investigated, and, with the exception of cork, are of but little direct industrial importance.

Industrial Uses of Cellulose.—The applications of cellulose to the necessities of human life, infinitely varied in kind as they are colossal in magnitude, depend upon two groups of qualities or properties, (1) structural, (2) chemical. The manufactures of vegetable textiles and of paper are based upon the fibrous forms of the naturally occurring celluloses, together with such structural qualities as are expressed in the terms strength, elasticity, specific gravity. As regards chemical properties, those which come into play are chiefly the negative quality of resistance to chemical change; this is obviously a primary factor of value in enabling fabrics to withstand wear and tear, contact with atmospheric oxygen and water, and such chemical treatments as laundrying; positive chemical properties are brought into play in the auxiliary processes of dyeing, printing, and the treatment and preparation in connexion with these. Staple textiles of this group are cotton, flax, hemp and jute; other fibres are used in rope-making and brush-making industries. These subjects are treated in special articles under their own headings and in the article FIBRES. The course of industrial development in the 19th century has been one of enormous expansion in use and considerable refinement in methods of preparation and manufacture. Efforts to introduce new forms of cellulose have had little result. Rhea or ramie has been a favourite subject of investigation; the industry has been introduced into England, and doubtless its development is only a question of time, as on the continent of Europe the production of rhea yarns is well established, though it is still only a relatively small trade—probably two or three tons a day total production. The paper trade has required to seek new sources of cellulose, in consequence of the enormous expansion of the uses of paper. Important phases of development were: (1) in the period of 1860 to 1870, the introduction of esparto, which has risen to a consumption of 250,000 tons a year in the United Kingdom, at which figure it remains fairly steady; (2) the decade 1870 to 1880, which saw the development of the manufacture of cellulose from coniferous woods, and this industry now furnishes a staple of world-wide consumption, though the industry is necessarily localized in countries where the coniferous woods are available in large quantities. As a development of the paper industry we must mention the manufacture of paper textiles, based upon the production of pulp yarns. Paper pulps are worked into flat strips, which are then rolled into cylindrical form, and by a final twisting process a yarn is produced sufficiently strong to be employed in weaving.

What we may call the special cellulose industries depend upon specific chemical properties of cellulose, partly intrinsic, partly belonging to the derivatives such as the esters. Thus the cellulose nitrates are the bases of our modern high explosives, as well as those now used for military purposes. Their use has been steadily developed and perfected since the middle of the 19th century. The industries in celluloid, xylonite, &c., also depend upon the nitric esters of cellulose, and the plastic state which they assume when treated with solvent liquids, such as alcohol, amyl acetate, camphor and other auxiliaries, in which state they can be readily moulded and fashioned at will. They have taken an important place as structural materials both in useful and artistic applications. The acetates of cellulose have recently been perfected, and are used in coating fine wires for electrical purposes, especially in instrument-making; this use depends upon their electrical properties of high insulation and low inductive capacity. Hydrated forms of cellulose, which result from treatment with various reagents, are the bases of the following industries: vegetable parchment results from the action of sulphuric acid upon cellulose (cotton) in the form of paper, followed by that of water, which precipitates the partially colloidalized cellulose. This industry is carried out on "continuous" machinery, the cellulose, in the form of paper, being treated in rolls. Vulcanized fibre is produced by similar processes, as for instance by treating paper with zinc chloride solvents and cementing together a number of sheets when in the colloidal hydrated state; the goods are exhaustively washed to remove, last traces of soluble electrolytes; this is necessary, as the product is used for electrical insulation. The solvent action of cupro-ammonium is used in treating cellulose goods, cotton and paper, the action being allowed to proceed sufficiently to attack the constituent fibres and convert them into colloidal cupro-ammonium compounds, which are then dried, producing a characteristic green-coloured finish of colloidal cellulose and rendering the goods impervious to water. The important industry of mercerization has been mentioned above; this is carried out on both yarns and cloth of cotton goods chiefly composed of Egyptian cottons. A high lustrous finish is produced, giving the goods very much the appearance of silk.

Of special importance are the more recent developments in the production of artificial fibres of all dimensions, by spinning or drawing the solutions of cellulose or derivatives. Three such processes are in course of evolution, (1) The first is based on the nitrates of cellulose which are dissolved in ether-alcohol, and spun through fine glass jets into air or water, the unit threads being afterwards twisted together to constitute the thread used for weaving (process of Chardonnet and Lehner). These processes were developed in the period 1883 to 1897, at which later date they had assumed serious industrial proportions. (2) The cupro-ammonium solution of cellulose is similarly employed, the solution being spun or drawn into a strong acid bath which instantly regenerates cellulose hydrate in continuous length. (3) Still more recently the "viscose" solution of cellulose, *i.e.* of the cellulose xanthogenic acid, has been perfected for the production of artificial silk or lustra-cellulose; the alkaline solution of the cellulose derivative being drawn either into concentrated ammonium salt solutions or into acid baths. This product, known as artificial silk, prepared by the three competing processes, was in 1908 an established textile with a total production in Europe of about 5000 tons a year, a quantity which bids fair to be very largely increased by the advent of the viscose process, which will effect a very considerable lowering in the cost of production. The viscose solution of cellulose is also used for a number of industrial effects in connexion with paper-sizing, paper-coating, textile finishes, and the production of book cloth and leather cloth, and, solidified in solid masses, is used in preparing structural solids which can be moulded, turned and fashioned.

For the special literature of cellulose treated from the general point of view of this article, the reader may consult the following works by C.F. Cross and E.J. Bevan:*Cellulose* (1895, 2nd ed. 1903), *Researches on Cellulose*, i. (1901), *Researches on Cellulose*, ii. (1906).

(C. F. C.)

1C.F. Cross and E.J. Bevan, *Jour. Chem. Soc.*, 1895, 67, p. 449; C.R. Darling, *Jour. Faraday Soc.* 1904; A. Campbell, *Trans. Roy. Soc.* 1906.

CELSIUS, ANDERS (1701-1744), Swedish astronomer, was born at Upsala on the 27th of November 1701. He occupied the chair of astronomy in the university of his native town from 1730 to 1744, but travelled during 1732 and some subsequent years in Germany, Italy and France. At Nuremberg he published in 1733 a collection of 316 observations of the aurora borealis made by himself and others 1716-1732. In Paris he advocated the measurement of an arc of the meridian in Lapland, and took part, in 1736, in the expedition organized for the purpose by the French Academy. Six years later he described the centigrade thermometer in a paper read before the Swedish Academy of Sciences (seeTHERMOMETRY). His death occurred at Upsala on the 25th of April 1744. He wrote: *Nova Methodus distantiam solis a terra determinandi* (1730); *De observationibus pro figura telluris determinanda* (1738); besides many less important works.

See W. Ostwald's *Klassiker der exacten Wissenschaften*, No. 57 (Leipzig, 1904), where Celsius's memoir on the thermometric scale is given in German with critical and biographical notes (p. 132); Marie, *Histoire des sciences*, viii. 30; Poggendorff s *Biog.-literarisches Handwörterbuch*.

CELSUS (c. A.D. 178), a 2nd-century opponent of Christianity, known to us mainly through the reputation of his literary work, *The True Word* (or *Account*; ἀληθὴς λόγος), published by Origen in 248, seventy years after its composition. In that year, though the Church was under no direct threat of attack, owing to the inertia of the emperor Philip the Arabian, the atmosphere was full of conflict. The empire was celebrating the l000th anniversary of its birth, and imperial aspirations and ideas were naturally prominent. Over against the state and the worship of the Caesar stood as usual the Christian ideal of a rule and a citizenship not of this world, to which a thousand years were but as a day. A supernatural pride was blended with a natural anxiety, and it was at this juncture that Origen brought to light again a book written in the days of Marcus Aurelius, which but for the great Alexandrian might have been lost for ever. Sometimes quoting, sometimes paraphrasing, sometimes merely referring, he reproduces and replies to all Celsus's arguments. His work shows many signs of haste, but he more than compensates for this by the way in which he thus preserves a singularly interesting memorial of the 2nd century. When we remember that only about one-tenth of the *True Word* is really lost and that about three-quarters of what we have is verbatim text, it would be ungracious to carp at the method.

Celsus opens the way for his own attack by rehearsing the taunts levelled at the Christians by the Jews. Jesus was born in adultery and nurtured on the wisdom of Egypt. His assertion of divine dignity is disproved by his poverty and his miserable *The argument* end. Christians have no standing in the Old Testament prophecies, and their talk of a resurrection that was only revealed to some of their own adherents is foolishness. Celsus indeed says that the Jews are almost as ridiculous as the foes they attack; the latter said the saviour from Heaven had come, the former still looked for his coming. However, the Jews have the advantage of being an ancient nation with an ancient faith. The idea of an Incarnation of God is absurd; why should the human race think itself so superior to bees, ants and elephants as to be put in this unique relation to its maker? And why should God choose to come to men as a Jew? The Christian idea of a special providence is nonsense, an insult to the deity. Christians are like a council of frogs in a marsh or a synod of worms on a dunghill, croaking and squeaking, "For our sakes was the world created." It is much more reasonable to believe that each part of the world has its own special deity; prophets and supernatural messengers had forsooth appeared in more places than one. Besides being bad philosophy based on fictitious history, Christianity is not respectable. Celsus does not indeed repeat the Thyestean charges so frequently brought against Christians by their calumniators, but he says the Christian teachers who are mainly weavers and cobblers have no power over men of education. The qualifications for conversion are ignorance and childish timidity. Like all quacks they gather a crowd of slaves, children, women and idlers. "I speak bitterly about this," says Celsus, "because I feel bitterly. When we are invited to the Mysteries the masters use another tone. They say, 'Come to us ye who are of clean hands and pure speech, ye who are unstained by crime, who have a good conscience towards God, who have done justly and lived uprightly.' The Jews say, 'Come to us ye who are sinners, ye who are fools or children, ye who are miserable, and ye shall enter into the kingdom of Heaven.' The rogue, the thief, the burglar, the poisoner, the spoiler of temples and tombs, these are their proselytes. Jesus, they say, was sent to save sinners; was he not sent to help those who have kept themselves free from sin? They pretend that God will save the unjust man if he repents and humbles himself. The just man who has held steady from the cradle in the ways of virtue He will not look upon." He pours scorn upon the exorcists—who were clearly in league with the demons themselves—and upon the excesses of the itinerant and undisciplined "prophets" who roam through cities and camps and commit to everlasting fire cities and lands and their inhabitants. Above all Christians are disloyal, and every church is an illicit collegium, an insinuation deadly at any time, but especially so under Marcus Aurelius. Why cannot Christians attach themselves to the great philosophic and political authorities of the world? A properly understood worship of gods and demons is quite compatible with a purified monotheism, and they might as well give up the mad idea of winning the authorities over to their faith, or of hoping to attain anything like universal agreement on divine things.

Celsus and Porphyry (*q.v.*) are the two early literary opponents of Christianity who have most claim to consideration, and it is worth noticing that, while they agree alike in high aims, in skilful address and in devoted toil, their *The philosophy of Celsus* religious standpoints are widely dissimilar. Porphyry is above all a pure philosopher, but also a man of deep religious feeling, whose quest and goal are the knowledge of God; Celsus, the friend of Lucian, though sometimes called Epicurean and sometimes Platonist, is not a professed philosopher at all, but a man of the world, really at heart an agnostic, like Caecilius in Minucius Felix (*q.v.*), whose religion is nothing more or less than the Empire. He is keen, positive, logical, combining with curious dashes of scepticism many genuine moral convictions and a good knowledge of the various national religions and mythologies whose relative value he is able to appreciate. "His manner of thought is under the overpowering influence of the eclectic Platonism of the time, and not of the doctrine of the Epicurean school. He is a man of the world, of philosophic culture, who accepts much of the influential Platonism of the time but has absorbed little of its positive religious sentiment. In his antipathy to Christianity, which appears to him barbaric and superstitious, he gives himself up to the scepticism and satire of a man of the world through which he comes in contact with Epicurean tendencies." He quotes approvingly from the *Timaeus* of Plato: "It is a hard thing to find out the Maker and Father of this universe, and after having found him it is impossible to make him known to all." Philosophy can at best impart to the fit some notion of him which the elect soul must itself develop. The Christian on the contrary maintained that God is known to us as far as need be in Christ, and He is accessible to all. Another sharp antithesis was the problem of evil. Celsus made evil constant in amount as being the correlative of matter. Hence his scorn of the doctrine of the resurrection of the body held then in a very crude form, and his ridicule of any attempt to raise the vulgar masses from their degradation. The real root of the difficulty to Platonist as to Gnostic was his sharp antithesis of form as good and matter as evil.

Opinion at one time inclined to the view that the *True Word* was written in Rome, but the evidence (wholly internal) points much more decisively to an Egyptian, and in particular an Alexandrian origin. Not only do the many intimate **Place and date.** references to Egyptian history and customs support this position, but it is clear that the Jews of Celsus are not Western or Roman Jews, but belong to the Orient, and especially to that circle of Judaism which had received and assimilated the idea of the Logos.

The date also is clearly defined. Besides the general indication that the Empire was passing through a military crisis, which points to the long struggle waged by Marcus Aurelius against the Marcomanni and other Germanic tribes, there is a reference (*Contra Celsum*, viii. 69) to the rescript of that emperor impressing on governors and magistrates the duty of keeping a strict watch on extravagances in religion. This edict dates from 176-177, and inaugurated the persecution which lasted from that time till the death of Marcus Aurelius in 180. During these years Commodus was associated with Marcus in the imperium, and Celsus has a reference to this joint rule (viii. 71).

Celsus shows himself familiar with the story of Jewish origins. Any pagan who wished to understand and criticize Christianity intimately had to begin by learning from the Jews, and this accounts for the opening chapters of his argument. **Value in the history of Christianity.** He has a good knowledge of Genesis and Exodus, refers to the stories of Jonah, Daniel (vii. 53) and Enoch (v. 52), but does not make much use of the Prophets or the Psalter. As regards the New Testament his position is closely in agreement with that reflected in the contemporary *Acts of the Martyrs of Scili*. He speaks of a Christian collection of writings, and knew and used the gospels, but was influenced less by the fourth than by the Synoptics. There is more evidence of Pauline ideas than of Pauline letters.

The gnostic sects and their writings were well known to him (viii. 15 and vi. 25), and so was the work of Marcion. There are indications, too, of an acquaintance with Justin Martyr and the Sibylline literature (vii. 53, op. v. 61). "He is perfectly aware of the internal differences between Christians, and he is familiar with the various stages of development in the history of their religion. These are cleverly employed in order to heighten the impression of its instability. He plays off the sects against the Catholic Church, the primitive age against the present, Christ against the apostles, the various revisions of the Bible against the trustworthiness of the text and so forth, though he admits that everything was not really so bad at first as it is at present."

The *True Word* had very little influence either on the mutual 611 relations of Church and State, or on classical literature. Echoes of it are found in Tertullian and in Minucius Felix, and then it lay forgotten until Origen gave it new life. A good deal of the neo-Platonic polemic naturally went back to Celsus, and both the ideas and phrases of the *True Word* are found in Porphyry and Julian, though the closing of the New Testament canon in the meantime somewhat changed the method of attack for these writers.

Of more importance than these matters is the light which the book sheds on the strength of the Church about the year 180. It is of course easy to see that Celsus had no apprehension of the spiritual needs even of his own day which it was the Christian purpose to satisfy, that he could not grasp anything of the new life enjoyed by the poor in spirit, and that he underrated the significance of the Church, regarding it simply as one of a number of warring sections (mostly Gnostic), and so seeing only a mark of weakness. And yet, there is all through an undercurrent which runs hard against his surface verdicts, and here and there comes to expression. He is bound to admit that Christianity has been stated reasonably; against the moral teaching of Jesus he can only bring the lame charge of plagiarism, and with the Christian assertion that the Logos is the Son of God he completely accords. Most suggestive, however, is his closing appeal to the Christians. "Come," he says, "don't hold aloof from the common regime. Take your place by the emperor's side. Don't claim for yourselves another empire, or any special position." It is an overture for peace. "If all were to follow your example and abstain from politics, the affairs of the world would fall into the hands of wild and lawless barbarians" (viii. 68). Forced to admit that Christians are not *infructuosi in negotiis*, he wants them to be good citizens, to retain their own belief but conform to the state religion. It is an earnest and striking appeal on behalf of the Empire, which was clearly in great danger, and it shows the terms offered to the Church, as well as the strength of the Church at the time. Numerically, Christians may have formed perhaps a tenth of the population, *i.e.* in Alexandria there would be fifty or sixty thousand, but their power in a community was out of all proportion to their mere numbers.

LITERATURE.—Th. Keim, *Celsus' Wahres Wort* (1873); Pélagaud, *Étude sur Celse*(1878); K.J. Neumann's edition in *Scriptores Graeci qui Christianam impugnaverunt religionem*, and article in Hauck-Herzog's *Realencyk. fur prot. Theol.*, where a very full bibliography is given. See also W. Moeller, *Hist, of the Chr. Church*, i. 169 ff.; A. Harnack, *Expansion of Christianity*, ii. 129 ff.; J.A. Froude, *Short Studies*, iv.

CELT, or KELT, the generic name of an ancient people, the bulk of whom inhabited the central and western parts of Europe. (For the sense of a primitive stone tool, see the separate article, later.) Much confusion has arisen from the inaccurate use of the terms "Celt" and "Celtic." It is the practice to speak of the dark-complexioned people of France, Great Britain and Ireland as "black Celts," although the ancient writers never applied the term "Celt" to any dark-complexioned person. To them great stature, fair hair, and blue or grey eyes were the characteristics of the Celt. The philologists have added to the confusion by classing as "Celtic" the speeches of the dark-complexioned races of the west of Scotland and the west of Ireland. But, though usage has made it convenient in this work to employ the term, "Celtic" cannot be properly applied to what is really "Gaelic."

The ancient writers regarded as homogeneous all the fair-haired peoples dwelling north of the Alps, the Greeks terming them all *Keltoi*. Physically they fall into two loosely-divided groups, which shade off into each other. The first of these is restricted to north-western Europe, having its chief seat in Scandinavia. It is distinguished by a long head, a long face, a narrow aquiline nose, blue eyes, very light hair and great stature. Those are the peoples usually termed Teutonic by modern writers. The other group is marked by a round head, a broad face, a nose often rather broad and heavy, hazel-grey eyes, light chestnut hair; they are thick-set and of medium height. This race is often termed "Celtic" or "Alpine" from the fact of its occurrence all along the great mountain chain from south-west France, in Savoy, in Switzerland, the Po valley and Tirol, as well as in Auvergne, Brittany, Normandy, Burgundy, the Ardennes and the Vosges. It thus stands midway not only geographically but also in physical features between the "Teutonic" type of Scandinavian and the so-called "Mediterranean race" with its long head, long face, its rather broad nose, dark brown or black hair, dark eyes, and slender form of medium height. The "Alpine race" is commonly supposed to be Mongoloid in origin and to have come from Asia, the home of round-skulled races. But it is far more probable that they are the same in origin as the dark race south of them and the tall fair race north of them, and that the broadness of their skulls is simply due to their having been long domiciled in mountainous regions. Thus the "Celtic" ox (*Bos longifrons*), from remote ages the common type in the Alpine regions, is characterized by the height of its forehead above the orbits, by its highly-developed occipital region, and its small horns. Not only do animals change their physical characteristics in new environment, but modern peoples when settled in new surroundings for even one or two centuries, *e.g.* the American of New England and the Boer of South Africa, prove that man is no less readily affected by his surroundings.

The northern race has ever kept pressing down on the broad-skulled, brown-complexioned men of the Alps, and intermixing with them, and at times has swept right over the great mountain chain into the tempting regions of the south, producing such races as the Celto-Ligyes, Celtiberians, Celtillyrians, Celto-Thracians and Celto-Scythians. In its turn the Alpine race has pressed down upon their darker and less warlike kindred of the south, either driven down before the tall sons of the north or swelling the hosts of the latter as they swept down south.

As the natives of the southern peninsula came into contact with these mixed people, who though differing in the shape of the skull nevertheless varied little from each other in speech and colour of their hair and eyes, the ancient writers termed them all "Keltoi." But as the most dreaded of these Celtic tribes came down from the shores of the Baltic and Northern Ocean, the ancients applied the name Celt to those peoples who are spoken of as Teutonic in modern parlance. The Teutons, whose name is generic for Germans, appear in history along with the Cimbri, universally held to be Celts, but coming from the same region as the Guttones (Goths) by the shores of the Baltic and North Sea. Again, the Germani themselves first appear in the Celtic host destroyed by Marcellus at Clastidium in 225 B.C. All the true Celtae or Galatae in France had come across the Rhine; the Belgic tribes in northern France were Cimbri, who also had crossed the Rhine: in Caesar's day the Germans were still constantly crossing that river, and so-called Gauls who lived near the Germans, *e.g.* the Treveri, closely resembled the latter in their habits, while in later times were to come Goths and Franks from beyond the great river. It is then not strange that the Gallic name for a henchman (*ambactus*) is the same as the Gothic (*ambahts*).

The earliest invaders, under the name of Celtae, had occupied all central Gaul, doubtless mixing with the aboriginal Ligurians and Iberians, who, however, maintained themselves respectively in the later Provence and in Aquitania. The Celts had firmly established themselves by the 7th century B.C. and we know not how long before, the Bituriges (whose name survives in Berri) being the dominant tribe. In the Alps and the Danube valley some of the Celts had dwelt from the Stone Age; there they had developed the working of copper, discovered bronze (an alloy of copper and tin), and the art of smelting iron (see HALLSTATT). The Umbrians, who were part of the Alpine Celts, had been pressing down into Italy from the Bronze Age, though checked completely by the rise of the Etruscan power in the 10th century B.C. The invention of iron weapons made the Celts henceforth irresistible. One of the earliest movements after this discovery was probably that of the Achaeans of Homer, who about 1450 B.C. invaded Greece (see ACHAEANS), bringing with them the use of iron and brooches, the practice of cremating the dead, and the style of ornament known as Geometric. Later the Cimmerians (see SCYTHIA and CIMMERII) passed down from the 612Cimbric Chersonese, doubtless following the amber routes, and then turned east along the Danube, some of their tribes, *e.g.* the Treres, settling in Thrace, and crossing into Asia; others settled in southern Russia, leaving their name in the Crimea; then when hard pressed by the Scythians most of them passed round the east end of the Euxine into Asia Minor, probably being the people known as Gimirri on Assyrian monuments, and ravaged that region, the relics of the race finally settling at Sinope.

At the beginning of the 6th century B.C. the Celts of France had grown very powerful under the Biturigian king Ambigatus. They appear to have spread southwards into Spain, occupying most of that country as far south as Gades (Cadiz), some tribes, *e.g.* Turdentani and Turduli, forming permanent settlements and being still powerful there in Roman times; and in northern central Spain, from the mixture of Celts with the native Iberians, the population henceforward was called Celtiberian. About this time also took place a great invasion of Italy; Segovisus and Bellovisus, the nephews of Ambigatus, led armies through Switzerland, and over the Brenner, and by the Maritime Alps, respectively (Livy V. 34). The tribes who sent some of their numbers to invade Italy and settle there were the Bituriges, Arverni, Senones, Aedui, Ambarri, Carnuti and Aulerci.

Certain material remains found in north Italy, *e.g.* at Sesto Calende, may belong to this invasion. The next great wave of Celts recorded was that which swept down on north Italy shortly before 400 B.C. These invaders broke up in a few years the Etruscan power, and even occupied Rome herself after the disaster on the Allia (390 B.C.). Bought off by gold they withdrew from Rome, but they continued to hold a great part of northern Italy, extending as far south as Sena Gallica (*Sinigaglia*), and henceforward they were a standing source of danger to Rome, especially in the Samnite Wars, until at last they were either subdued or expelled, *e.g.* the Boii from the plains of the Po. At the same time as the invasion of Italy they had made fresh descents into the Danube valley and the upper Balkan, and perhaps may have pushed into southern Russia, but at this time they never made their way into Greece, though the Athenian ladies copied the style of hair and dress of the Cimbrian women. About 280 B.C. the Celts gathered a great host at the head of the Adriatic, and accompanied by the Illyrian tribe of Autariatae, they overthrew the Macedonians, overran Thessaly, and invaded Phocis in order to sack Delphi, but they were finally repulsed, chiefly by the efforts of the Aetolians (279 B.C.). The remnant of those who returned from Greece joined that part of their army which had remained in Thrace, and marched for the Hellespont. Here some of their number settled near Byzantium, having conquered the native Thracians, and made Tyle their capital. The Byzantines had to pay them a yearly tribute of 80 talents, until on the death of the Gallic king Cavarus (some time after 220 B.C.) they were annihilated by the Thracians. The main body of the Gauls who had marched to the Hellespont crossed it under the leadership of Leonnorius and Lutarius. Straightway they overran the greater part of Asia Minor, and laid under tribute all west of Taurus, even the Seleucid kings. At last Attila, king of Pergamum, defeated them in a series of battles commemorated on the Pergamene sculptures, and henceforth they were confined to a strip of land in the interior of Asia Minor, the Galatia of history. Their three tribes—Trocmi, Tolistobogians and Tectosages—submitted to Rome (189 B.C.), but they remained autonomous till the death of their king Amyntas, when Augustus erected Galatia into a province. Their descendants were probably the "foolish Galatians" to whom St Paul wrote (see GALATIA).

Ancient writers spoke of all these Gauls as Cimbri, and identified them with the Cimmerians of earlier date, who in Homeric times dwelt on the ocean next to the Laestrygones, in a region of wintry gloom, but where the sun set not in summer. Nor was it only towards the south and the Hellespont that the Celtic tide now set. They passed eastward to the Danube mouth and into southern Russia, as far as the Sea of Azov, mingling with the Scythians, as is proved by the name Celto-scyths. Mithradates VI. of Pontus seems to have negotiated with them to gain their aid against Rome, and Bituitus, a Gallic mercenary, was with him at his death.

The Celts had continually moved westwards also. The Belgae, who were Cimbric in origin, had spread across the Rhine and given their name to all northern France and Belgium (*Gallia Belgica*). Many of these tribes sent colonies over into south-eastern Britain, where they had been masters for some two centuries when Caesar invaded the island (see BRITAIN). But there is evidence that from the Bronze Age there had been settlers in northern Britain who were broad-skulled and cremated their dead, a practice which had arisen in south Germany in the early Bronze Age or still earlier. It is not unlikely that, as tradition states, there were incursions of Celts from central Gaul into Ireland during the general Celtic unrest in the 6th century B.C. It is certain that at a later period invaders from the continent, bringing with them the later Iron Age culture, commonly called La Tène, which had succeeded that of Hallstatt, had settled in Ireland. Not only are relics of La Tène culture found in Ireland, but the oldest Irish epics celebrate tall, fair-haired, grey-eyed heroes, armed and clad in Gallic fashion, who had come from the continent. The Celts in Italy, in the Balkan, in France and in Britain, overspread the Indo-European peoples, who differed from themselves but slightly in speech. The Celts represented Indo-European q by p, whilst the Greeks, Illyrians, Thracians, Ligurians, and aborigines of France, Britain and Ireland represented it by k, c or qu. The Umbrian-Sabellian tribes had the same phonetic peculiarity as the Celts. Thus Gallic *petor(petor-ritum*, "four-wheeler"), Umbrian *petur*, Homeric πίσυρες, Boeotian (Achaean)πέτταρες, Welsh *pedwar*, but Gaelic *cethir*, Lat. *quatuor*. The Celts are thus clearly distinguished from the Gaelic-speaking dark race of Britain and Ireland, and in spite of usage it must be understood that it is strictly misleading to apply the term Celtic to the latter language.

See also Ridgeway, *Early Age of Greece*, vol. i., and *Oldest Irish Epic*; Ripley, *The Races of Europe*; Sergi, *The Mediterranean Race*.

(W. RI.)

CELTIC LANGUAGES

Introduction.—The Celtic languages form one group of the Indo-European family of languages. As might be expected from their geographical distribution, they hold a position between the Italic and Teutonic groups. They are distinguished from these and other branches of the family by certain well-marked characteristics, the most notable of which are the loss of initial and inter-vocalic *p*, cf. Ir. *athair* with Lat. *pater*; Ir. *lān*, "full," Welsh *llawn*, Breton *leun*, with Lat. *plenus*; Gaulish *are-*, "beside," Ir. *ar*. Welsh, Breton *ar*, with Gr.περί, παρά; and the change of I. E. *ē* to *ī*, cf. Ir. *fīr*, "true," Welsh *gwir*, Breton *gwir*, Lat. *verus*. We may further mention that the I. E. labialized velar *gv* is represented by *b*, e.g. Ir. *bo*, "cow," Welsh *buwch*, Gr. βοῦς, Sanskr. *gāus*; Ir. *ben*, "woman," Gr. γυνή, whilst the medial aspirates *bh, dh, gh* result in simple voiced stops. I. E. sonant *r* and *l* become *ri, li*. Other distinctive features of the modern dialects are not found in Gaulish, partly owing to the character of the monuments. Such are the -ss- preterite and the fusion of simple prepositions with pronominal elements, e.g. Ir. *fri-umm*, "against me," Welsh *wrth-yf*, Breton *ouz-inn*. The initial mutations which are so characteristic of the living languages did not arise until after the Romans had left Britain. The Celtic languages betray a surprising affinity with the Italic dialects. Indeed, these two groups seem to stand in a much closer relationship to one another than any other pair. As features common to both Celtic and Italic we may mention: (i) the gen. sing, ending *-ī* of masc. and neut. stems in *o*; (2) verbal nouns in *-tion*; (3) the *b*-future; (4) the passive formation in *-r*.

The various Celtic dialects may be divided as follows:—(1) Gaulish; (2) Goidelic, including Irish, Scottish Gaelic, and Manx; (3) Brythonic, including Welsh, Breton and Cornish. Gaulish and Brythonic, like Oscan and Umbrian among the Italic dialects, change the I. E. labialized velar guttural *qv* to *p*, whilst the Goidelic dialects retain the *qv* which later gives up the labial element and becomes *k*, e.g. Gaulish *petor-*, "four," Ir. *cethir*, Welsh *petguar*, Breton *pevar*, Lat. *quattuor*; Ir. *cia*, "who," Welsh *pwy*, Lat. *quis*; Gaulish *epo-*, "horse," Welsh *eb-ol*, Breton *eb-eul*, Ir. *ech*, Lat. *equus*. Several attempts have been made to prove the existence of Celtic dialects with *qv* on the continent. Forms containing *p* occur in the Coligny calendar, discovered in 1897, by the side of others with *qv*, a state of affairs not yet satisfactorily accounted for. The Rom tablets, discovered in 1898, have not been interpreted as yet, but *p* forms are found on them exclusively. In an excursus we shall deal with the language of the Picts.

No comprehensive handbook of the Celtic languages on the lines of Gröber's *Grundriss der romanischen Philologie* or Paul's *Grundriss der germanischen Philologie* was available in 1909. The reader may refer to Windisch's article "Keltische Sprachen" in Ersch und Gruber's *Allgemeine Encyklopädie der Wissenschaften und Künste*, and V. Tourneur, *Esquisse d'une histoire des études celtiques* (Liége, 1905; vol. ii. with full bibliography). Also H. Zimmer, "Die kelt. Litteraturen" in *Die Kultur d. Gegenwart*, T. i. Abh. xi. I, Berlin and Leipzig, 1909. The materials for the study of the older forms of the languages are to be found in Zeuss's *Grammatica Celtica* as revised by Ebel. A comparative grammar of the Celtic dialects has been prepared by H. Pedersen (Göttingen, 1908). See also Whitley Stokes and A. Bezzenberger, *Wortschatz der keltischen Spracheinheit* (Göttingen, 1894).

I. GAULISH.—Celtic place-names are found as far east as the Dniester and Dobrudja, and as far north as Westphalia. The language of the Galatians in Asia Minor must have stood in a very close relation to Gaulish. Indeed few traces of dialectical differences are to be observed in continental Celtic. Unfortunately no literary monuments written in the ancient speech of Gaul have come down to us, though Caesar makes mention of religious poems orally transmitted by the Druids, and we also hear of *bardi* and *vates*. But a large number of personal and place-names have been preserved. The classical writers have, moreover, recorded a certain number of Gaulish words which can generally be identified without difficulty by comparing them with words still living in the modern dialects, e.g. *pempedula*, "cinquefoil," cf. Welsh *pump*, "five," and *deilen*, "leaf"; *ambactus*, Welsh *amaeth*; *petorritum*, "four-wheeled chariot," cf. Welsh *pedwar*, "four," and Ir. *roth*, "wheel," or *rith*, "course." We have further between thirty and forty inscriptions (three in north Italy) which we may without hesitation ascribe to the Gauls. These inscriptions are written in either N. Etruscan or Greek or Latin characters. We are thus in a position to reconstruct much of the old system of declension, which resembles Latin very closely on the one hand, and on the other represents the forms which are postulated by the O. Ir. paradigms. Hence Gaulish is particularly valuable as preserving the final vowels which have disappeared in early Irish and Welsh. The few verb-forms which occur in the remains of Gaulish are quite obscure and have not hitherto admitted of a satisfactory explanation. The statements of ancient authors with regard to the Belgae are conflicting, but there cannot be much doubt that the language of the latter was substantially the same as Gaulish. Caesar observes that there was little difference between the speech of the Gauls and the Britons in his day, and we may regard Gaulish as closely akin to the ancestor of the Brythonic dialects. It is difficult to say when Gaulish finally became extinct. It disappeared very rapidly in the south of France, but lingered on, possibly till the 6th century, in the northern districts, and it seems unnecessary to discredit Jerome's statement that the speech of the Galatians in Asia Minor bore a strong resemblance to the language he had heard spoken in the neighbourhood of Trier. There is no evidence that Breton has been influenced by continental Celtic. The number of Gaulish words which have come down in the Romance languages is remarkably small, and though at first sight the sound-changes of French and Welsh seem to bear a strong likeness to one another, any influence of Gaulish pronunciation on French is largely discounted when we find the same changes occurring in other dialects where there is little or no question of Celtic influence.

The proper names occurring in classical writers, on inscriptions and coins, have been collected by A. Holder in his monumental *Altceltischer Sprachschatz* (Leipzig, 1896-1908). The inscriptions have been most recently treated by J. Rhys in the *Proceedings of the British Academy*, vol. ii. See also a paper in this volume entitled "Celtae and Galli" by the same author for the text of the Coligny and Rom inscriptions. The value of Gaulish for grammatical purposes is set forth by Whitley Stokes in a paper on "Celtic Declension" in the *Proceedings of the London Philological Society* (1885-1886). For the extent over which Gaulish was spoken, its relation to Latin and its influence on Romance, see E. Windisch's article on "Keltische Sprache" in the section "Die vorromanischen Volkssprachen" in Gröber's *Grundriss der romanischen Philologie²*, vol. i. pp. 373 ff. Cf. further the introduction to J. Loth's *Chrestomathie bretonne* (Paris, 1890); G. Dottin, *Manuel pour servir à l'étude des antiquités celtiques* (Paris, 1906); R. Thurneysen, *Keltoromanisches* (Halle, 1884).

II. GOIDELIC AND BRYTHONIC.—When the monuments of the Celtic dialects of the British Islands begin to appear, we find a wide divergence between the two groups. We can only mention some of the more important cases here. The Brythonic dialects have gone very much farther in giving up inflectional endings than Goidelic. In Irish all final syllables in general disappear except long vowels followed by *s* or *r* and *u* < *ō* preceded by *i*. But these reservations do not hold good for Brythonic. Thus, whilst O. Irish possesses five cases the Brythonic dialects have only one, and they have further lost the neuter gender and the dual number in substantives. In phonology there are also very striking differences, apart from the treatment of the labialized velar *qv* already mentioned. The sonant *n* appears in Brythonic as *an*, whereas in Goidelic the nasal disappears before *k*, *t* with compensatory lengthening of the vowel, *e.g.* I. E. **kmtom*, Ir. *cét*, "hundred," W. *cant*, Bret. *kant*; Prim. Celt. **joṇko-*, O. Ir. *óac*, Mod. Ir. *óg*, "young," W. *ieuanc*, Bret, *iaouank*. *t*, *k* standing after a vowel and preceding *l*, *n* (and also *r* if *k* precede) disappear in Goidelic with compensatory lengthening of the vowel, *e.g.* Prim. Celt. **stātlā-*, Ir. *sál*, "heel," W. *sawdl*; Prim. Celt. **petno-*, Ir. *én*, "bird," O. W. *etn*, Mod. W. *edn*. Similarly *b*, *d*, *g* disappear in Goidelic when standing after a vowel and preceding *l*, *r*, *n* with compensatory lengthening of the vowel, but in Welsh they produce a vowel forming a diphthong with the preceding vowel, *e.g.* Prim. Celt. **neblo-*, Ir.*nél*, "cloud," W. *niwl*; Prim. Celt. **ogno-*, cf. Lat. *agnus*, Ir. *uan*, "lamb," from **ōn*, W. *oen*; Prim. Celt. **vegno-*, cf. Ger. *Wagen*, Ir. *fén*, "wagon," O. W. *guein*, Mod. W. *gwain*. The Goidelic dialects have preserved the vowels of accented syllables on the whole better than Brythonic. Thus Brythonic has changed Prim. Celt, *ā* (= I. E. *ā*, *ō*) to *ō* (W. *aw*, Bret. *eu*); and Prim. Celt. *ū* to *ī*, *e.g.* Ir. *bráthir*, "brother," W. *brawd*, Bret. *breur*; Gaulish *dūnum*, Ir.*dún*, "fort," W. *din*. Already in Gaulish the I. E. diphthongs show a tendency to become simple long vowels and the latter are treated differently by Goidelic and Brythonic. In early times I. E. *eu*, *ou* both became *ō* and I. E. *ei* gave *ē*. In Goidelic *ō*, *ē*, in accented syllables were diphthongized in the early part of the 8th century to *ua*, *ia* if the next syllable did not contain the vowels *e* or *i*, whereas in Brythonic *ō* gave *ü* (written *u*) and *ē* became in W. *ui(wy)*, and in Bret. *oe (oue)*, e.g. Gaulish *Teuto-, Toutius*, Ir. *tuath*, "people," W., Bret. *tud*; Brythonic *Lēto-cētum*, Ir. *tuath*, "grey," W. *llwyd*, Bret, *loued*. Similarly in loan-words, Ir.*céir, fial*, W. *cwyr*, O. Corn. *guil*, from Lat. *cēra, vēlum*. Further I. E. *ai, oi* are preserved in Irish as *ai (ae), oi (oe)*, Mod. Ir. *ao*, but in Welsh I. E. *ai* gave either *ai* or *oe*, whilst *oi*changed to *ü* (written *u*), Ir. *toeb*, "side," W., Bret. *tu*; I. E. **oinos*, Ir. *óen*, "one," W., Bret.*un*; Prim. Celt. **saitlo-*, cf. Lat. *saeculum*, W. *hoedl*, "age," Bret. *hoal*. In Goidelic accented *e* changes to *i* before *i*, *u* in the following syllable, cf. Ir. *fid*, "wood," gen. sing, *fedo*, O. H. G. *witu*, and *i* changes to *e* before *a* or *o* under similar conditions. In like manner *u* becomes *o* before *a* or *o*, whilst *o* changes to *u* before *i*, *u*, cf. Ir. *muir*, "sea," Prim. Celt. **mori*, gen. sing. *mora*. Of Brythonic finals which disappear, *ā*, *ī*, *(ō)*, *j* alone influence preceding vowels, whilst an *i* (y) which received the stress in O. W. was also able to modify vowels which went before it. In Goidelic the combinations *sqv*, *sv* appear respectively as *sc*, *s*(medially, *f*), but in Brythonic they both give *chw*; Prim. Celt. **sqvetlon*, Ir. *scél*, "story," W.*chwedl*; Prim. Celt. **svesor*, Ir. *siur*, "sister," but *mo fiur*, "my sister" (whence Scottish*piuthar* by false de-aspiration), W. *chwaer*, Bret. *c'hoar*. In 614Brythonic initial *s* becomes *h* in the 7th century, but this is unknown in Goidelic, e.g. Ir. *salann*, "salt," W. *halen*, Cornish*haloin*, Bret, *holenn*; Lat. *sé-men*, Ir. *síl*, "seed," W. *hil*. Initial *v* gives *f* in Goidelic in the course of the 7th century, whereas in Brythonic it appears as *gu*, *gw*, cf. Lat. *vérus*, Ir. *fír*, W., Bret. *gwir*. We may also mention that in Goidelic initial *j* and medial *v* disappear, e.g.Gaulish *Jovincillus*, W. *ieuanc*, "young," Bret, *iouank*, Ir. *óac*, *óc*; W. *bywyd*, "food," Ir.*biad*. Post-consonantic *j* in Brythonic sometimes gives *-id* (Mod. W. -*ydd*, Mod. Bret. -*ez*),e.g. Gaulish *nevio-, novio-*, O. Bret, *nowid*, W. *newydd*, Bret, *nevez*, Ir. *núe*. I.E. -*kt* and -*pt*both appear in Goidelic as -*cht* but in Brythonic as -*ith*, cf. Lat. *septem*, O. Ir. *secht*, W. *seith*, Bret. *seiz*.

We unfortunately know very little about the position of the stress in ancient Gaulish. According to Meyer-Lübke in place-names the penult was accented if the vowel was long, otherwise the stress lay on the preceding syllable, e.g. *Augustodūnum*, O. Fr. *Ostedun*, now*Autun; Cataláunos* (Châlons), *Trícasses* (Fr. Troyes), *Bitúriges* (Fr. Bourges). In Goidelic the stress, which is strongly expiratory, is always placed on the first syllable except in certain cases in verbs compounded with prepositional prefixes. In Old Welsh and Old Breton, on the other hand, the final syllable, *i.e.* the primitive penult, received the stress, but in both languages the stress was shifted in the middle period to the penultimate. The Goidelic dialects, like the Slavonic, distinguish between palatalized and nonpalatalized consonants, according as the consonant was originally followed by a front (*e*, *i*) or back vowel (*a*, *o*, *u*), a phenomenon which is entirely unknown to Brythonic.

Finally, the two groups differ radically in the matter of initial mutation or, as it is often called, aspiration. These mutations are by no means confined to initial consonants, as precisely the same changes have taken place under similar conditions in the interior of words. The Goidelic changes included under this head probably took place for the most part between the 5th and 7th centuries, whilst in Brythonic the process seems to have begun and continued later. It is easier to fix the date of the changes in Brythonic than in Goidelic, as a number of British names are preserved in lives of saints, and it is possible to draw conclusions from the shape that British place-names assumed in the mouths of the Anglo-Saxons. In Goidelic, we find two mutations, the vocalic and the nasal. Initial mutation only takes place between words which belong together syntactically, and which form one single stress-group, thus between article, numeral, possessive pronoun or preposition, and a following substantive; between a verbal prefix and the verb itself.

1. When the word causing mutation ended in a vowel we get the vocalic mutation, called by Irish grammarians aspiration. The sounds affected are the tenues *k* (c), *t*, *p*; the mediae *g*, *d*, *h*; the liquids and nasals *m*, *n*, *r*, *l*, *s*, and Prim. Celt. *v* (Ir. *f*, W. *gw*). At the present day the results of this mutation in Irish and Welsh may be tabulated as follows. Where the sound is at variance with the traditional orthography, the latter is given in brackets. In the case of *n*, *r*, *l* in Goidelic we get a different variety of *n*, *r*, *l* sound. In Welsh in the case of *r*, *l*, the absolute initial is a voiceless *r*, *l* written *rh*, *ll*, which on mutation become voiced and are written *r*, *l*. In Irish *s* becomes *h* written *sh* and the mutation of *f* is written *fh*, which,

however, is now silent. Examples:—Irish, *cú*, "hound," *do chú*, "thy hound"; Welsh *ci*, *dy gi* (*do, dy* represent a Prim. Celt. **tovo*); Irish *máthair*, "mother," *an mháthair*, "the mother," Welsh *mam, y fam* (the feminine of the article was originally **sentā, sendā*).

Original sound						b	m
Irish	(ch)	(th)	(ph)	(gh)	(dh)	,w(bh)ᵛ	,w(mh)ᵛ
Welsh				il	(dd)	(f)ᵛ	(f)ᵛ

2. When the word causing mutation originally ended in a nasal, we get the nasal mutation called by Irish grammarians eclipse. The sounds affected are *k* (c), *t, p; g, d, b*; Prim. Celt. *v* (Ir. *f*, W. *gw*). In mod. Irish and mod. Welsh the results are tabulated below. Irish *f* becomes *w* written *bh*, whilst W. *gw* gives *ngw*. Examples:—Irish *bliadhna*, "year," *seacht m-bliadhna*, "seven years," cf. Latin *septem*, Welsh *blynedd, saith mlynedd*; Irish *tir*, "country," *i d-tir*, "in a country," Welsh *tref*, "town," *yn nhref*, "in a town," cf. Latin *in*.

Original Sound						
Irish			g			
Welsh	gh	h	h	g		

3. In Welsh *k* (c), *t, p* undergo a further change when the word causing mutation originally ended in *s*. There is nothing corresponding to this consonantal mutation in Goidelic. In this case *k* (c), *t, p* become the spirants χ (*ch*), *th, f* (*ph*), e.g. *tad*, "father," *ei thad*, "her father," *ei* represents a primitive **esiās*. In the interior of words in Brythonic, *cc, pp, tt* give the same result as initial *k, t, p* by this mutation.

The relation in which the other Celtic dialects stand to this system will be mentioned below in dealing with the various languages. It will be noted from what has been said above that, with the exception of the different treatment of the labialized velar *qv*, and the nasal sonant *n̥*, the features which differentiate the Brythonic from the Goidelic dialects first appear for the most part after the Romans had left Britain. At the beginning of the Christian era the difference between the two groups can only have been very slight. And Strachan has shown recently that Old Irish and Old Welsh agree in a very striking manner in the use of the verbal particle *ro* and in other syntactical peculiarities connected with the verb.

(i.) *Goidelic*.—The term Goidelic is used to embrace the Celtic dialects of Ireland, Scotland and the Isle of Man. In each case the national name for the speech is *Gaelic* (Ir. *Gaedhlig*, Scottish *Gaidhlig*, Manx *Gailck*), from Ir. Scottish *Gaodhal, Gaedheal*, Mid. Ir. *Góedel*, W. *Gwyddel*, "a Gael, inhabitant of Ireland or Scotland." Old Irish may be regarded as the ancestor of Scottish and Manx Gaelic, as the forms of these dialects can be traced back to Old Irish, and there are practically no monuments of Scottish and Manx in the oldest period. Scottish and Irish may be regarded as standing to one another in much the same relation as broad Scottish and southern English. The divergences of Scottish and Manx from Irish will be mentioned below. The language of the Ogam inscriptions is the oldest form of Goidelic with which we are acquainted. Some 300 inscriptions have up to the present been discovered in this alphabet, the majority of them hailing from the south-west of Ireland (Kerry and Cork). In Scotland 22 are known, whilst in England and Wales about 30 have turned up. Most of the latter are in South Wales, but odd ones have been found in North Wales, Devon and Cornwall, and one has occurred as far east as Hampshire. The Isle of Man also possesses two. The letters in the oldest inscriptions are formed by strokes or notches scored on either side of the edge of an upright stone. Thus we obtain the following alphabet:—

This system, which was eked out with other signs, would seem to have been framed in the south-west of Ireland by a person or persons who were familiar with the Latin alphabet. Some of the inscriptions probably go back to the 5th century and may even be earlier. As illustrations of the simplest forms of Ogam inscriptions we may mention the following:*Doveti maqqi Cattini, i.e.* "(the stone) of Dovetos son of Cattinos"; *Trenagusu Maqi Maqi-Treni* is rendered in Latin *Trenegussi Fili Macutreni hic jacit; Sagramni Maqi Cunatami,* "(the stone) of Sagramnos son of Cunotamos"; *Ovanos avi Ivacattos,* "(the stone) of Ovanus descendant of Ivacattus." It will be seen that in the oldest of these inscriptions *q* is still kept apart from *k* (c), and that the final syllables have not disappeared (cf. *maqqi,* O. Ir. *maicc*), but it appears certain that in Ogamic writing stereotyped forms were used long after they had disappeared in ordinary speech. Several stones contain bilingual inscriptions, but the key to the Ogam alphabet is supplied by a treatise on Ogamic writing contained in the Book of Ballymote, a manuscript of the late 14th century. It should be mentioned that the Welsh 615stones are early whilst the Scottish ones are almost without exception late, and several of the latter have so far defied interpretation. In addition to the Irish Ogams there are a number of Christian inscriptions in Latin character, but, with one exception, they are not older than the 8th century.

See R.R. Brash, *The Ogam Inscribed Monuments of the Gaedhil* (London, 1879); R.A. Stewart Macalister, *Studies in Irish Epigraphy* (London), vol. i. (1897), vol. ii. 1902, vol. iii. 1907. The Welsh inscriptions are contained in J. Rhys, *Lectures on Welsh Philology*[2] (London, 1879). The Scottish stones have also been treated by Rhys in the*Proceedings of the Scottish Society of Antiquaries* (Edinburgh, 1892). See also G.M. Atkinson for the tract in the Book of Ballymote, *Kilkenny Journal of Archaeology*(1874). The Irish Christian inscriptions were published by Margaret Stokes as the annual volumes of the Roy. Hist, and Archaeol. Association of Ireland (1870-1877), and have been republished by R.A. Stewart Macalister.

(a) *Irish.*—We are able to trace the history of the Irish language continuously for a period of 1200 years, and from the time that the literary documents begin we are better supplied with linguistic material for the study of the language than is the case with any other Celtic dialect. At the same time that form of Irish which is to be found in the oldest documents has preserved a number of features which have entirely, or almost entirely, disappeared from the Brythonic languages. For this reason scholars have largely occupied themselves with Irish, which for purposes of comparative philology may be regarded as the classic Celtic language.

The history of Irish is divided into three periods:—Old Irish (700-1100), the documents mainly representing the language of the 8th and 9th centuries; Middle Irish, extending roughly from 1100 to 1550; Modern Irish from 1550 to the present day. These periods merge into one another to such an extent that no firm division can be made. The language of some manuscripts of the 14th century contains forms which are really Old Irish, and Middle Irish orthography was partly employed by historians and antiquarians in the middle of the 17th century. Old Irish, as compared with Brythonic, preserves a wealth of inflectional forms in declension and conjugation, but many of these tend to disappear very early. In the modern dialects of Ireland and Scotland there is a rigid rule of orthography that a palatalized, or, as it is termed, slender consonant in medial or final position, must be preceded by a palatal vowel (i), and a non-palatalized consonant by a non-palatal or broad vowel (*a, o, u*). This is the famous rule of the grammarians known as *caol le caol agus leathan le leathan* ("slender to slender and broad to broad"), but it is not so strictly adhered to in the spoken language as is commonly stated. In the older language the quality of medial and final consonants is only denoted very imperfectly, thus non-palatalized final consonants are regularly not denoted as such, *e.g.* O. and Mid. Ir. *fir,* Mod. Ir. *fior.* In Old and Mid. Irish the initial mutations are only regularly denoted in the case of the vocalic mutation of *c, p, t, s, f,*and the nasal mutation of *b, d, g.* The vocalic mutation of *c, p, t, s, f* was denoted by writing *ch, ph, th, sh, fh,* the first three symbols of which were derived from the Latin alphabet. Another method of denoting the mutation was to write a dot over the letter, originally the punctum delens, which was justified in the case of mutated *f* as the latter early became silent. But no such devices were ready at hand in the case of the medial *b, d, g,* and the mutated forms of these consonants were consequently not represented at all in the orthography. The same remark holds good in the case of the nasal mutation (eclipse) of the tenues. But it is easy to demonstrate that the same condition of affairs as we find in the modern language must have obtained in Old Irish. This insufficiency of symbols renders the orthography of the early stages of the language very complicated. We find that *b, d, g* were used initially to denote the voiced stops, but medially and finally they represent spirants, the voiced stops in this case being denoted by *c, p, t*. It is not until much later times that the *h* in the mutated forms of the tenues, or the use of the dot, was extended to the mediae. Thus in Mid. Irish we find *do bochtaib in choimded*(Mod. Ir. *dobhochtaibh*), Mid. Ir. *ro-gab* = Mod. Ir. *do ghabh*. The nasal mutation of *c, p, t* was first denoted by writing these sounds double and finally in the 18th century by writing *gc, bp, dt*. The spirants arising out of Prim. Celt. *g, d, b* came in Old Irish to be confused with those which developed out of Prim. Celt, *p, t, k*, in other than initial positions. In final positions in polysyllables we commonly find *d* and *b* written but medially *th* and *ph, e.g. didnad,* "consolation," gen. sing, *dithnatha.* For the ending -*ad*cp. Lat. -*ātu*-. On the other hand we find *g* written medially and *ch* finally. These rules, however, are not yet applied in the oldest documents.

When we turn to the inflections we find that most of the old terminations have disappeared, but that their influence on preceding consonants is still felt and serves to distinguish one form from another; thus in the declension of *fer,* "man," nom. sing. *fer,* gen. sing. *fir,* dat. sing, *fiur,* acc. sing, *fer n-,* nom. pl. *fir,* gen. pl. *fer n-,* corresponding to Prim. Celt. (Gaulish) *viros, virī, virō, viron, virī, viron,* the influence of the following sound still differentiates the cases from one another. In the later language the initial mutations come more and more to be used for this purpose. In Middle Irish the declensions and conjugations are much simplified and the neuter gender is given up in substantives. In the verb the athematic conjugation has disappeared and the distinction of primary and secondary endings is not observed. On the other hand Irish has developed a peculiar system of absolute and conjoint inflection with different sets of endings. The conjoint endings are always used in the case of compound verbs, and in simple verbs they are employed after certain proclitics, *e.g.* the negative particles. Thus*berid,* "he bears," is an absolute form; *do-beir,* "he gives," *ni beir,* "he does not bear," are conjoint forms. Further, the verb system is partly dominated by the various devices employed to express relative function. There are three main types of conjugation in Old Irish corresponding to the Latin first, third and fourth conjugations, the Latin types*moneo* and *audio* being difficult to distinguish in Irish. In the modern language there is in reality but one conjugation. The old Irish verb system comprises present and imperfect indicative, imperative, pres. subjunctive in -*ā*- or -*s*- with corresponding past subjunctive, future in -*f*- or -*s*- or -*ē*- or with reduplication along with corresponding secondary future, -*s*- preterite, -*t*- preterite, reduplicated preterite, a preterite containing a long stem-vowel, together with deponential and passive forms in -*rd.* This system is eked out with the verbal prefix *ro,* which among other functions changes a preterite into a perfect or a present into a perfect. Such a cumbrous system was bound to fall to pieces. A number of isolated forms have come down, but the only tenses which have survived into the modern period are the present and imperfect indicative, the imperative, the present subjunctive, the -*s*- preterite, the -*b*- and -*ē*- future with corresponding secondary forms, and some of the passive forms in -*r.* At the same time in the modern language there is an increasing tendency to use analytical forms. Two noteworthy features of the Irish verb remain to be mentioned. The one is the use of pronouns as objects infixed between particle and verb, or in a verb compounded with a preposition between preposition and verb. There are two sets of forms according as to whether the verb occurs in a relative clause or not. Thus -*m*- is the ordinary infixed pronoun of the 1st pers. sing., whilst -*dom*- is the corresponding relative form. In the 3rd pers. sing. aspiration may be employed, *e.g. ní ceil,* "he does not hide," *ní cheil,* "he does not hide it." This has been given up in the modern language. Secondly in verbs compounded with prepositions the accent of the verb varies according as to whether the verb is used enclitically or not—thus after the negative *ní* or in the infinitive and imperative. Hence we have *do-béir,* "he gives," by the side of *ní tábair,* "he does not give," infin. *tabairt;do-gníu,* "I do," *ní dĕnim,* "I do not do," infin. *dĕnum.* The changes caused by this alternation in addition to others due to the working of the Irish accent and to

245

the initial and internal mutations have played havoc with the verb system and render it exceedingly difficult to reconstruct the paradigms. In the later periods of the language analogy naturally plays a great part, and many of the complicated forms are done away with, but even in the modern dialects the alternation between enclitic and orthotonic forms still survives in the commonest verbs, *e.g.* Irish *bheir sé* "he gives," *ní thabhair sé*, "he does not give," infin. *tabhairt*; Scottish *bheir e, cha toir, toirt*; Manx *ver eh, cha der, coyrt*; Irish *ní sé*, "he does," *ní dheanann sé*, "he does not do," infin. *deanamh*; Scottish *nì e*, "he does," *cha dean e*, "he will not do," infin. *deanamh*; Manx *nee eh, cha jean eh, jannoo*.

In the early period Irish borrowed a number of words from Latin. These are mainly connected with the church or with articles of civilization which would be imported from Roman Britain. Some of these show traces of British pronunciation, *e.g.* O. Ir. *trindóit*, from Latin *trinitātem* with *ō* for *ā*. In others again Lat. p is represented in Ir. by c, which may be due to the substitution of q as being the nearest Irish sound to the foreign p. Thus we find Ir. *corcur*, "purple," *casc*, "Easter"; *cenciges*, "Whitsuntide"; *cruimther*, "presbyter." In addition to these several loans were received from Norse. In the Mid. Irish period many French words came in, and during the middle and modern periods the number of English words introduced is legion. Pedersen has tried to show in his *Vergl. Gramm.* that a considerable number of words were borrowed from Brythonic (Welsh) at an early date.

[For the Latin loan-words, see J. Vendryès, *De hibernicis vocabulis quae a latina lingua originem duxerunt* (Paris, 1902); Kuno Meyer has collected a number of loan-words from Norse, Anglo-Saxon, Early English, Latin and Early French in *Revue celtique*, xii. 460 and xiii. 505. See also Whitley Stokes, *Bezzenberger's Beiträge*, xviii. 56 ff. For Celtic names in Norse see W. Stokes, *Revue celtique*, iii. 186 ff., and W.A. Craigie, *Zeitschr. f. celt. Phil.* i. 439 ff.]

With regard to the dialects of Irish, there is a well-known rhyme which states the peculiarities of the speech of the four provinces, and dialectical differences must have existed at an early period, though they do not make their appearance in the literary language until the 18th century. At the present day the Irish of Leinster has vanished entirely, and we have unfortunately no records of it. But in the other three provinces the vernacular still lives, and we find the Irish of Munster, Connaught and Ulster marked off from one another by well-defined peculiarities. In general it may be stated that the south of Ireland is more conservative than the north. In Munster there is a tendency to shift the word-stress from the initial syllable to a heavy derivative syllable, *e.g.* *-án*. This does 616not take place in Connaught, whilst in Ulster the tendency is to shorten the vowel. Again in monosyllables ending in *ll, nn, m*, and under certain other conditions a short vowel becomes a diphthong in the south, in Connaught it is merely lengthened, but in Ulster the original length is retained, *e.g.* Ulster *ball*, "member, limb," Connaught *bāll*, Munster *baull*. Final *dh, gh* in Munster are sounded as *g*. In certain cases the north prefers the vocalic mutation where the west and south have the nasal, thus notably in the dative singular after preposition and article, *e.g.* Munster-Connaught *do'n bhfear*, "to the man," Ulster *do'n fhear*. In the south synthetic verb-forms are employed to a much larger extent than in the north.

In the early part of the 19th century Irish was still the speech of more than half the inhabitants of Ireland. A German traveller reckoned that out of a total population of seven millions in 1835 four millions spoke Irish as their mother-tongue. The famine of 1846-1847 was felt most in those districts that were purely Irish, and these were the parts that were and still are chiefly affected by the tide of emigration. Add to this the fact that the influence of O'Connell and his satellites, and above all that of the Roman Catholic clergy, was against the language. In spite of the efforts of the Gaelic League (founded 1893), which have met with considerable success, the language is rapidly dying of internal decay. The speakers of Irish are chiefly confined to the following counties, where over 20% of the population speak Gaelic:—Waterford, Cork, Kerry, Clare, Galway, Mayo, Sligo, Donegal. The following figures will illustrate the decay of the language since the famine:—

Year	Monoglots.	Bilinguists.
185 1	319,602	1,204,684

186	163,275	942,261
1		
187	103,562	714,313
1		
188	64,167	885,765
1		
189	38,192	642,053
1		
190	20,953	620,189
1		

According to the 1901 census report the speakers of Irish were distributed as follows:—Leinster, 26,436; Munster, 276,268; Connaught, 245,580; Ulster, 92,858. The Gaelic movement, which has thriven largely on account of its anti-English character, would have a much better chance of galvanizing the ancient language of Ireland if it were not for the supreme difficulties of Irish spelling and phonetics. Of the hundreds of thousands of persons who attend the classes of the League not more than one or two per cent. at the outside arrive at any state of proficiency. Presbyterian Gaels in Scotland are taught to read the Bible but Irish Catholics are not encouraged to do so. The result of this is seen in the fact that, whilst many, if not all, of the local Nationalist newspapers under the pressure of the League publish badly-printed and little-read columns in Irish, there are only two regularly appearing periodicals which contain any large amount of Irish. Half the contents—and those the most important—of the weekly organ of the league, *An Claidheamh Soluis* ("the flaming sword"), are in English. The latter was started in 1898 under the title of *Fáinne an Lae* ("the ring of day," *i.e.* the dawn). The other periodical is the monthly *Gaelic Journal* (*Irisleabhar na Gaedhilge*), a would-be literary magazine of very inferior quality which has led a precarious existence since 1882. In 1898 it was decided to hold a festival called the *Oireachtas* ("hosting, gathering") on the lines of the Welsh *Eisteddfod*. The venture was a great success and similar meetings have been held every year since, whilst each province and many of the counties have their annual local Gaelic *feis* (festival). The literary output of the movement has been prodigious, consisting in the main of a number of short stories and dramas (mostly propagandist), but nothing of any particular merit has as yet been forthcoming. The best-known writers are Dr Douglas Hyde (collector of folk-stories—*Beside the Fire*, 1890, *An Sgeulaidhe Gaedhealach*, 1895 (reprinted from vol. x. of the *Annales de Bretagne*), *Love Songs of Connaught*, 1893, *Religious Songs of Connaught*, 1905); P. O'Leary (author of two lengthy stories, *Seadna*, 1904, *Niamh*, 1907); P. Dinneen (author of an historical tale, *Cormac Ua Connaill*, 1901); P. O'Shea, better known as "Conan Maol," author of a collection of short stories entitled *An Buaiceas*, 1903.

AUTHORITIES ON IRISH LANGUAGE.—For the study of Old Irish—Zeuss, *Grammatica Celtica*2 (Berlin, 1871); B. Güterbock and R. Thurneysen, Indices to the Irish words treated in Zeuss (Leipzig, 1881); E. Windisch published the first grammar of Old Irish in 1879 (trans. by N. Moore, Pitt Press, 1882), but Windisch's treatment of the verb was rendered obsolete by the discovery of the laws of the Irish accent by H. Zimmer,*Keltische Studien* (Berlin, 1884), and R. Thurneysen, *Revue celtique*, vi. 309, J. Vendrèys, *Grammaire du Vieil-Irlandais* (Paris, 1908); R. Thurneysen, *Handbuch des Alt-Irischen* (Heidelberg, 1909). Mention should also be made of J. Strachan, *Selections from the Old Irish Glosses* (Dublin, 1904); and the same writer's *Old Irish Paradigms*(Dublin, 1905), *Stories from the Táin* (Dublin, 1908). See also various papers on the Irish verb in the *Transactions of the London Philological Society* by Strachan (1895-1902); H. Pedersen, *Aspirationen i Irsk* (Copenhagen, 1898); C. Sarauw, *Irske Studier*(Copenhagen, 1901); G.J. Ascoli, *Archivio glottologico italiano*, vols. v. and vi. For the study of Middle Irish—E. Windisch, *Irische Texte mit Wörterbuch* (Leipzig, 1880). (Other volumes in conjunction with W. Stokes.)

Editions of texts by W. Stokes, Kuno Meyer and others in the *Revue celtique, Zeitschrift für celtische Philologie, Ériu.* K. Meyer has issued an exhaustive Mid. Irish glossary (A-D) as a supplement to the *Archiv für celtische Lexikographie.* The remainder is being published under the auspices of the Royal Irish Academy. The first grammar of Modern Irish was published by Francis Molloy in 1677 at Rome under the title of *Grammatica Latino-Hibernica*. Molloy was followed by Jeremiah Curtin in 1728 with a book called *Elements of the Irish Language*. Numerous other grammars were published towards the end of the 18th and at the beginning of the 19th century, but few of them have any value. The more important of them are enumerated in the introduction to O'Donovan's *Grammar* and to Windisch's *Kurzgefasste irische Grammatik*, and in Pedersen's *Aspirationen i Irsk*, pp. 29-47. We may mention W. Neilson's *Grammar* (1808) as it is important for the Irish of E. Ulster. But the greatest native grammarian was John O'Donovan, who traversed Ireland in connexion with the Ordnance Survey, and published in 1854 a comprehensive grammar noting the differences between the various dialects. A little grammar published by Molloy in 1867 is instructive on account of the author's peculiar point of view. The most useful books for the study of the living language are the series of booklets (five) published by Father O'Growney, one of the chief promoters of the present movement. Mention should also be made of J.P. Henry's *Handbook of Modern Irish*, pts. i.-iv., and of the grammars by P.W. Joyce (Dublin, 1896) and the Christian Brothers (Dublin, 1901). For the northern form of Irish J.P. Craig's *Grammar of Modern Irish* is useful (^{2} Dublin, 1904). The phonetics of a Munster dialect have been investigated by R. Henebry, *A Contribution to the Phonology of Desi Irish* (Greifswald, 1901). The dialect of the Aran Islands off the coast of Galway has been described by F.N. Finck, *Die Araner Mundart*, i. *Lautlehre und Grammatik*, ii.*Wörterbuch* (Marburg, 1899). G. Dottin has given an account of a dialect of North Connaught (Mayo) in the *Revue celtique*, xiv. pp. 97-137. A study of the speech of the north was published by E.C. Quiggin under the title of *A Dialect of Donegal, Phonology and Texts* (Cambridge, 1906). For an account of the decay of Irish see H. Zimmer, "Die keltische Bewegung in Irland," *Preussische Jahrbücher* for 1898, vol. 93, p. 59 ff., and the last chapter of Douglas Hyde's *Literary History of Ireland* (London, 1901).

The work of the earlier compilers of glosses will be mentioned in the literature section below. The first dictionary of the modern language of any importance was that published by J. O'Brien in 1768. Next came E. O'Reilly with his *Irish-English Dictionary* (Dublin, 1817). This book contains a vast store of words gathered on no principle whatever from all manner of sources, and has therefore to be used with caution, but even at the present day it renders considerable service. A second edition with a supplement by O'Donovan was published after the latter's death in 1864. The first trustworthy dictionary of the modern language was published under the auspices of the Irish Texts Society by P.J. Dinneen (London, 1904). English-Irish dictionaries have been compiled by D. Foley (Dublin, 1855); E.E. Fournier (Dublin, 1903); T. O'Neill Lane (Dublin, 1904).

(b) *Scottish Gaelic.*—Scottish Gaelic is the form of Goidelic speech which was introduced into Scotland by the Dalriadic Scots who came over from Ireland in the early centuries of our era. We possess practically no early monuments of the language. We have one or two inscriptions in Latin characters, such as that at St Vigeans and the Ogams mentioned above, which have not yet been solved. In the *Book of Deir* there is a colophon of a few lines probably written by an Irish scribe in the 9th century, and as the language of these lines differs in no wise from the Irish of the period, we do not know if they accurately represent the Gaelic of Scotland or if they may not be pure Irish. In the same MS. there are further Gaelic scraps belonging to the 11th and 12th centuries. The word-forms in these entries are identical with those current at the time in Ireland, but the historical orthography seems to show more signs of decay than is the case in Irish. The medieval Scottish MSS. in the Advocates' Library at Edinburgh are only just being published, but they seem either to hail from Ireland or to be written in pure Irish. The end of the 15th century brought a change. The Lordship of the Isles, the great bond between Ireland and Scotland, was broken up. The Gaels of Scotland, thrown on their own resources, advanced their own dialect to the position of a literary language and tried to discard the Irish orthography. The *Book of the Dean of Lismore*, compiled about 1500, is written in a kind of phonetic orthography which has not as yet been sufficiently investigated. The language of those poems which are not directly ascribed to Irish poets, and which may therefore be regarded as representing the literary language of the Highlands at the time, seems to occupy a position midway between Irish and Scottish Gaelic. But until the beginning of the 18th century the Highlands were 617under the literary dominion of Ireland, so much so that Bedell's Irish version of the Scriptures was circulated in Scotland with a glossary from 1690 to 1767, and Bishop Carsewell's version of Knox's Prayer-book (1567) is pure Irish. The language of the people is poorly represented in the 16th and 17th centuries, and the orthography is not fixed until we reach the 18th century.

Irish and Scottish Gaelic differ considerably in point of vocabulary, but there are also important divergences in phonetics and inflections. In the first place, Scottish Gaelic as written has entirely given up the nasal mutation (eclipse), e.g. Scottish *ar bò*, "our cow," Irish *ar m-bó*; Scottish *nan tìr*, "of the countries," Irish *na d-tír*. It should, however, be observed that in Skye and the Outer Isles the nasal mutation has been partly restored and in some places there are even parallels to the Welsh nasal mutation of *c, p, t* to *ngh, mh, nh*. Secondly, post-vocalic *c, p, t* are commonly preceded by a breathed sound not represented in writing, thus *mac* "son," is pronounced *mahk*; *slat*, "rod," as *slaht*. Again there is a tendency to insert a sibilant in the group *rt*, thus *ceart*, "right," is sounded *kearst*, and the distinction between palatalized and non-palatalized sounds is not so rigidly observed as in Irish. The group *cht* is in Scotland pronounced as if *chk*. We may also mention that Scottish Gaelic preserves an old *ĕ* in a number of words where Irish now has *ă*, thus, Old Ir. *fer*, Scottish G. *fĕr*, Irish *făr*, but in both cases the spelling is *fear* (in this respect Scottish Gaelic goes hand in hand with Manx and the almost extinct Irish of Down). Similarly, we find that in Scottish Gaelic and Manx stressed vowels preceding a palatalized consonant have not undergone palatalization to the same extent as in Irish, e.g. in Ireland *duine*, "man," < **dunjo-*, is pronounced *din'ò*, but in Scotland *dun'ò* (in Manx written *dooinney*). A further peculiarity of Scottish Gaelic is that it substitutes lenes or voiceless mediae for the voiced stops, and even *l, r, n* sounds show a great tendency to give up the voice. Scottish Gaelic goes farther even than Irish in the confusion of vowel-sounds, e.g. Lat. *coxa*, Ir. *cos*, "foot," Sc. *cas*; Ir. *codal*, Sc. *cadal*. When we turn to the inflections we find that analogy has here played a much greater part than in Irish. There is a tendency to make the plural of all substantives except masculine monosyllables end in *-an*. In the conjugation the synthetic forms have with one or two exceptions entirely disappeared and the present forms have become momentary in force. Hence in ordinary grammars it is stated that the present has become a future, thus *ni mi* means "I shall do." The past participle chiefly ends in *-te* as against Irish *-the, -te*, or *-tha, -ta*, according to the quality of the preceding sound. The present (future) and past subjunctive (conditional, representing both the imperfect indic. and secondary future of Irish) supply the place of the Irish consuetudinal forms. In idiom also Scottish has diverged very considerably from Irish, e.g. in the use of *tha* (Ir. *tá*) for *is*.

It seems now to be agreed that the various dialects of Scottish Gaelic fall into two main divisions—northern and southern. Mackinnon states that the boundary between the two passes roughly up the Firth of Lorne to Loch Leven, then across country from Ballachulish to the Grampians. The country covered by the northern dialect was of old the country of the Northern Picts, whilst the portion of Argyllshire south of the boundary line, together with Bute and Arran, made up the kingdom of Dalriada. The Gaelic district south of the Grampians belonged to the Southern Picts. The southern dialect is commonly regarded as the literary language. It approaches more nearly to Irish and preserves the inflections much better than the speech of the north.

The following characteristics of the northern dialects may be mentioned:—(1) The diphthongization of open *ē* to *ia* is carried much farther in the north than in the south. (2) The vowel *ao* in the north is more regularly the high-back-narrow-unrounded vowel-sound, whereas the south in many cases has a low-front-wide-round sound. (3) The north has *str* in initial position where the south prefers *sr*. Further, the northern dialects go very far in dropping unaccented final vowels. It may be remarked that in the reduction of derivative endings containing long vowels Scotland goes hand-in-hand with Ulster Irish, thus Connaught *arān*, "bread," is in Ulster and Scotland *arăn*. Again, Scottish agrees with North Irish in the loss of synthetic verb-forms and in using as negative *cha*, Mid. Ir. *nico, nocha*. But, on the other hand, Scotland, with the exception of South Argyll and some of the Isles, diphthongizes accented *a, ɔ, e*, in monosyllables, before *ll, nn, m*, thus resembling the speech of Munster. In South Argyll the original short vowel is half lengthened.

As to the southern limits of Gaelic speech in Scotland, the boundary between Gaelic and English in medieval times was the so-called Highland line, and at the War of Independence it is probable that it extended to Stirling, Perth and the Ochil and Sidlaw Hills, the Inglis being limited to a very narrow strip along the coast. Dr J.A.H. Murray traced the linguistic frontier in 1869-1870 with the following results. The line started about 3 m. west of the town of Nairn on the Moray Firth and ran in a south-east direction to the Dee, 4 m. above Ballater. On the other side of the Dee it began 4 m. above Balmoral and followed the boundary of Perth and Forfar as far as Glen Shee, where it went off to the south-west as far as Dunkeld. After passing Birnam Hill it turned due west until the upper part of Glen Almond was reached, where it bent to the southward, passing through Comrie and along the braes of Doune to the Teith, 3 or 4 m. below Callander. Thence it ran along the north shore of Lake Monteith to Gartmore, and from there to Rowardennan on the east side of Loch Lomond. On the west side it passed through Glen Douglas down Loch Long and the Firth of Clyde, leaving Bute and Arran to the west. At the present day this boundary has probably receded to the extent of several miles, and even in 1870 there were districts such as Bute and the region round Dunoon where Gaelic was only spoken by the oldest natives and the immigrant population. The language is not found in the north-east of Caithness, the boundary running, according to Murray, roughly from a little north-east of Lybster to the mouth of the Forss. Celtic was driven out of Shetland and Orkney by Scandinavian some time during the middle ages. (See further J.A.H. Murray, *The Dialect of the Southern Counties of Scotland*, London, 1875; *Revue celtique*, vol. ii. pp. 180-187.)

Until the 18th century Gaelic was spoken in Galloway and on the uplands of Ayr and Lanark. The following figures from the census returns illustrate the decrease in the number of persons who speak Gaelic:—

	Monolinguists.	Bilinguists.
1881	No return	231,594 (this includes Gaelic monolinguists)
1891	43,738	210,677
1901	28,106	202,700

In the last-mentioned year it appears that nearly one-half of the speakers of Gaelic are reported from the counties of Inverness and Ross (23,893 monolinguists and 82,573 bilinguists). From about 1300 we find Scottish emigrants filtering into the glens of Antrim, where the Gaelic that is spoken is still unmistakably Scottish. There have long been local societies of Highlanders for the cultivation of their native tongue, the most important one being *An Comunn Gàidhealach* (founded 1891). This society holds an annual gathering called the *Mòd* (= Eng. "moot") on the lines of the Welsh Eisteddfod, and recently the Scottish Education Department has countenanced the teaching of Gaelic in Highland schools. But the political element plays little or no part in the language movement in Scotland, and the latter is not likely to assume the proportions of the Gaelic League in Ireland. As a rule, however, Highlanders are better able to read their own language than Irish Gaels, for, the majority being Protestants, they are encouraged to read their Bibles. There are only two periodicals which devote half their space to Gaelic. The one is *An Deo-Greine* ("the sunbeam"), founded October 1905; and the other is the Catholic propagandist quarterly *Guth na Bliadhna* ("the voice of the year"), started in 1904. Up to 1905 a fortnightly newspaper printed wholly in Gaelic appeared in Prince Edward Island, under the title of *An Mactalla* ("the echo"), and efforts have been made to revive it. A weekly newspaper wholly in Gaelic was started in 1908 by R. Stuart Erskine under the title of *Alba*.

AUTHORITIES ON SCOTTISH GAELIC.—The first grammar of Scottish Gaelic was compiled by W. Shaw (*An Analysis of the Galic Language*, 1778). The most useful one was that published by Alexander Stewart, *Elements of Gaelic Grammar* (Edinburgh, 1801). A revised edition of this work with many additions and corrections was published by H.C. Gillies, London, 1902. This book is rather spoilt by the author's attitude, and requires to be supplemented and corrected. G. Henderson and C.W. Robertson have published important papers on the modern dialects in the *Zeitschrift für celtische Philologie*, the *Celtic Review* and the *Transactions of the Gaelic Society of Inverness*. The most useful work on Gaelic philology is Alexander Macbain's *Etymological Gaelic Dictionary* (Inverness, 1896) (a later edition by W.J. Watson). The chief dictionaries are *Dictionarium Scoto-Celticum*, published by the Highland Society of Scotland (Edinburgh, 1828); R.A. Armstrong, *Gaelic Dictionary* in two parts (London, 1825); N. McAlpine, *Pronouncing Gaelic Dictionary* (Edinburgh, 1847) (this book gives the pronunciation of Islay); Macleod and Dewar, *Gaelic and English Dictionary* (latest edition, Edinburgh, 1901); *Faclar Gàidhlig*, published by E. Macdonald, Herne Bay, appearing in parts since 1902.

(c) *Manx.*—Our sources of information with regard to the language of the Isle of Man are even more scanty in the early period than they are in the case of Scotland. There are a number of references to the island in Irish literature, but the earliest monument of the vernacular we possess is the version of the Book of Common Prayer made by Bishop Phillips in 1610. In this translation the traditional Irish orthography is not followed. The spelling resembles the orthography which was employed in Scotland by the compiler of the *Book of the Dean of Lismore*. How far this system was used is a question which it is difficult to decide. In Scotland the Irish orthography has prevailed in a slightly modified form, but Manx writers adhered to a mode of spelling which was as phonetic as any system based on English, or, probably more correctly Anglo-Scottish, orthography could be. This fact, combined with the rapid phonetic decay of the 618 language, makes it extremely difficult to discover what sound-values are to be attached to the various symbols. At the beginning of the 18th century English was not understood by two-thirds of the natives, and in 1764 the S.P.C.K. issued a paper containing this statement: "The population of the Isle is 20,000, of whom the far greater number are ignorant of English." But from this time English gradually crept in. The last edition of the Manx Bible was issued in 1819, and of the New Testament in 1840. The present writer's great-grandmother refused to speak English, his grandfather (b. 1815) preached in Manx and English, and his father (b. 1844) only spoke English. The following figures illustrate the rapid decline of the language:—

	Monolinguists.	Bilinguists.
1875	190	12,340 (out of a population of 41,084 exclusive of Douglas)
1901	None	4,419

Manx stands in a much closer relation to Scottish Gaelic than Irish, and fishermen state that they could understand a good deal of what is said in South Argyll, though they are quite at a loss at Kinsale. Manx exhibits the same tendency as Scottish to use analytical and periphrastic forms in the verb, thus *jannoo*, "to do," is used like Scottish *deanamh* with an infinitive to express the past and future. The present has acquired a momentary (future) signification, and the past participle ends in *-it* (Scottish *-te*). The negative is *cha* as in Scotland and Ulster. Manx goes as far as northern Scottish in dropping unstressed final vowels, *e.g. chiarn*, "lord," Irish, *tighearna*; *-yn* is the favourite plural ending in substantives. The nasal mutation has been partly given up. Old Irish stressed *ĕ* is frequently retained, *e.g. fĕr*, "man," Irish *făr* (spelt *fear*), and the vowels *ŏ* and *ă* are confused as in Scottish, *e.g.* Manx *cass*, "foot," Scottish *cas*, Irish *cos*. Manx is divided in itself about the treatment of short accented vowels before *ll, nn, m*. According to Rhys the south side lengthens, whilst the north side diphthongizes; *e.g.* Irish *crann*, "tree," *clann*, "offspring," S. Manx *krōn, klōn*, N. Manx, *kroun, kloun* (written *croan, cloan*). In the matter of stress Manx is quite original, going farther even than the dialects of the south of Ireland. Not only does it shift the stress in the case of heavy derivative suffixes like *-ān* and reduce the preceding vowel, *e.g.* Ir. *fuarān*, Sc. *fuaran*, Manx *frān*, "spring," but even in cases like *caghláa*, "variety," Sc. Ir. *caochladh*, O. Ir. *coimmchloud*; *coráa*, "voice," Ir. *comhradh*. The Mid. English stress on the final is further retained in words from the French such as *ashóon*, "nation," *livréy*, "deliver."

As other features peculiar to Manx we may mention the following. An intervocalic *s* or *sh* shows a tendency to become lisped and voiced to *d*. In monosyllables post-vocalic final *m, n,* are often preceded by an intrusive *b, d* respectively, thus *ben* "woman," may be heard as *bedn.* Ir. *a* becomes more palatal and is often *æ.* Ir. *sc* becomes *st, sht,* e.g.Ir. *fescor,* "evening," Manx *fastyr;* Ir. *uisce,* "water," Manx *ushtey.*

AUTHORITIES ON MANX.—The place and personal names of the Isle of Man have been collected by A.W. Moore in *Manx Names²* (London, 1903) (33% of the proper names are Scandinavian). The chief source of information about the spoken language is J. Rhys, *The Outlines of the Phonology of Manx Gaelic* (London, 1895) (the book has unfortunately no index and no texts). The only serious attempt to represent spoken Manx graphically is the transcription of a song by J. Strachan in the *Zeitschr. für celtische Philologie,* vol. i. p. 54. The native grammarian is J. Kelly, who in 1803 published *A Practical Grammar of the Ancient Gaelic or Language of the Isle of Man, usually called Manks.* This book was republished by W. Gill for the Manx Society in 1859, and a facsimile reprint of this latter was made for Quaritch, London, 1870. A useful little book entitled, *First Lessons in Manx* was published by Edwin Goodwin (Dublin, 1901). There are two dictionaries, one by A. Cregeen, Douglas 1835, which is now being reprinted for *An Cheshaght Gailckagh,* a Douglas society which is endeavouring to encourage the use of Manx and to get it introduced into the schools. The other dictionary is by J. Kelly in two parts—(i) Manx and English, (2) English and Manx, published by the Manx Society in 1866. Kelly also prepared a Triglot of Manx, Irish and Gaelic, based upon English, which has never been published. A useful paper on the language appeared in the *Transactions of the London Philological Society* for 1875 by H. Jenner, "The Manx Language: Its Grammar, Literature and Present State."

(E. C. Q.)

(ii). *Brythonic.* The term Brythonic is used to denote the Celtic dialects of Wales, Brittany and Cornwall. Unlike the Goidels the Brythonic peoples have no common name for their language. Forms of Brythonic speech were doubtless current throughout England and Wales and the Lowlands of Scotland at the time of the Saxon invasion. The S.E. of Britain may have been extensively Romanized, and it is not impossible that remnants of Goidelic speech may have lingered on in out-of-the-way corners. No literary documents dating from this period have been preserved, but some idea of the character of Brythonic may be gathered from the numerous inscriptions which have come to light. In the middle of the 6th century Brythonic was confined to the western half of Britain south of the Clyde and Forth. The colonization of Britannia minor or Armorican Brittany during the 5th and 6th centuries will be described later. In the latter part of the 6th century the W. Saxons pushed their conquests as far as the estuary of the Severn, and from that time the Brythons of S.W. Britain were cut off from their kinsmen in Wales. Early in the 7th century the Brythons of Strathclyde were similarly isolated by the battle of Chester (613). The kingdom of Strathclyde maintained a separate existence until the 10th century, and it is generally stated that Brythonic speech did not die out there until the 12th century. The question as to how far Brythonic names and words have survived in these districts has never been properly investigated. Certain it is that Brythonic numerals survived amongst shepherds in Cumberland, Westmorland and N.W. Yorkshire down to the second half of the 19th century, just as herrings are still counted in Manx by Manx fishermen otherwise quite innocent of the language. Accordingly, from the 7th century onwards Brythonic became gradually limited in Great Britain to three districts—Strathclyde, Wales, and Cornwall and Devon. During the 7th century the Brythons of Wales and Strathclyde often fought side by side against the Angles, and it is from this period that the name by which the Welsh call themselves is supposed to date, *Cymro* < **Combrox,* pl.*Cymry* < **Combroges, i.e.* "fellow-countrymen" as opposed to W. *allfro,* Gaul. *Allobroges,* "foreigners." We have no means of determining when Celtic speech became extinct in the petty states of the north which retained their independence longest.

The chief features which distinguish the Brythonic from the Goidelic dialects have already been enumerated. In the course of the 6th and 7th centuries final short vowels disappeared. In compound names the final vowel remains in the first component until the 7th century. Short vowels in other than initial syllables when immediately preceding the stress (on the historical penultimate) disappear, whilst long ones are

252

shortened, *e.g.* Welsh *cardawt* from Lat.*caritātem*. Other vowels in unstressed position are apt to be reduced, thus *ŏ*, *ŭ*, give *i* in O.W. (Mid. W. *y*). A marked characteristic of Welsh as distinguished from Cornish and Breton is the treatment of *ă* under the influence of a following *ī*. In Welsh the result is *ei*, in Corn. and Bret. *e*, *e.g.* Welsh *seint*, "saints," Bret. *sent*, sing. *sant*. The mutations seem to have started in the second half of the 6th century in the case of the tenues.

See J. Loth, *Les Mots latins dans les langues Brittoniques* (Paris, 1892); J. Loth,*Chrestomathie bretonne* (Paris, 1890).

(a) *Welsh (Cymraeg).*—It is usual to divide the history of the Welsh language into three periods—Old, Middle and Modern. To the oldest period belong the collections of glosses, the earliest of which go back to about 800. The middle period extends from 1100 to 1500.

As a rule the medial mutation of the tenues and mediae is not denoted in O. Welsh. Intervocalic *g* is sometimes retained but generally it has disappeared, whilst after *r* and *h*t is still written. In the course of the 9th century initial *w* (v) becomes *gu* (later *gw*). As the O. Welsh documents consist almost entirely of isolated words, we know scarcely anything about the morphology of the language during this period. To the middle period belong the ancient poems from the Black Book of Carmarthen, but the language of these compositions is evidently much older than the date of the manuscript (12th century), as it preserves a number of very archaic features. Other important sources of information for this period are the O. Welsh Laws contained in a MS. of the 12th century. To a somewhat later date belong the Mabinogion (14th century MS.), and the prose versions of French romances published by R. Williams (15th century). In Middle Welsh the consonant mutations are in general denoted in writing, though not consistently, and from this period dates the introduction of *w* and *y* (O.W. *u*, *i*) to denote vowel sounds. The symbol *ll* to denote a voiceless *l* was already employed in Mid. W. but *rh* (= voiceless *r*), *dd* (= Eng. *th* in "thou") and *f* (= *v*) either do not appear or only become regular during the modern period In Mod. W. the orthography is regularized and does not differ 619materially from that of the late medieval documents. In O.W. the old stress on the final syllable (the historical penult) appears to have been preserved, but during the middle period the accent was shifted to the penult. In consequence of this change *aw* (< *ā*) in final syllables is reduced to *o* in Mod. W., *e.g.* Mid. W. *pechawt* < Lat. *peccātum*, Mod. W. *pechod.*

The comparative wealth of inflection preserved by O. Ir. has almost entirely disappeared in Welsh. There are only the faintest traces of the case forms, the dual and the neuter gender. Compared with the Irish nominal declension according to *-o-* (*-jo-*), *-ā-*, *-i-*, *-u-*, *-s-*, guttural, dental and nasal stems, Welsh only distinguishes the nom. sing. and plur., the latter sometimes retaining an old formation. Thus masc. *-o-* stems show palatal modification, *e.g. corn*, "horn," plur. *cyrn* < *kornī*; the plural ending of *-u*-stems, O. Gaulish *-oves*, gives O.W. *-ou*, Mid. W. *-eu*, Mod. W. *-au*, *e.g. penneu*, "heads." The termination *-ones* of the *-n-* stems appears as *-on*. The infixation of pronominal objects between a verbal particle and the verb itself continues in use down to the present day as in Breton. In the third person sing. of the pres. ind. there are instances in the oldest Welsh of the peculiar alternation between orthotonic and absolute forms which characterize the Irish paradigms, *e.g. pereid*, "it endures," but *ny phara*. The several types of conjugation represented in Irish have become obscured, traces remaining only in the endings of the third sing. of the pres. ind., the pret. ind. (Mid. W. *-as*, *-es*, *-is*) and the pret. passive (Mid. W. *-at*, *-et*, *-it*). The verb system of Welsh comprises the following tenses: indic. present (also used as future), imperative, imperfect, preterite (in Mid. W. forms with *s* have become prevalent as in Irish, but forms corresponding to the Irish preterites in *t* or with reduplication or unreduplicated with long vowel are not infrequent in the early poetry), pluperfect (a new formation), pres. and pret. passive. In the subj. early W. distinguishes pres. and past, but the latter comes to be replaced by the pluperfect indicative. The sign of the subj. is *-h-* < *s*, which reminds one of the Irish *s*-subj., though the formation is somewhat different. There are also traces of a future formation containing *h* < *s*. (See also under <u>WALES</u>.)

We have seen already that Wales began to exist as a separate entity roughly at the end of the 6th and beginning of the 7th centuries. In the second half of the 8th century the

Welsh were confined in pretty much their present limits by **History and extent.** Offa, king of Mercia, who constructed the Dyke going by his name, which has approximately remained the political boundary between England and Wales ever since. From this time onwards the bitter feeling against England which we find expressed in the fervid compositions of Iolo Goch and other political bards served to prevent any serious inroads of English on Welsh-speaking territory. With the advent of the Tudors, however, there came a great change. Henry VII. owed his throne in large measure to the support he had received from Wales and he prided himself on his Welsh ancestry. A consequence of this was that throughout the 16th century Wales received exceptionally favourable treatment at the hands of the English sovereign and parliament. In 1562 a decree was issued ordering a translation of the Bible to be made into Welsh. All this could naturally not be without effect on the attitude of the leaders of the people towards England. The change is already apparent in the poems of Lewis Glyn Cothi and others. And the striking difference in the manner in which the Reformation was regarded in Ireland and Wales is worthy of remark. During the Stuart wars the Welsh nobles fought invariably on the Royalist side, and there is plenty of other evidence that the aristocracy of Wales was becoming thoroughly anglicized both in sentiment and language. At the same time the practice of the Tudors was reversed in many particulars. Thus it became the custom to appoint Englishmen ignorant of the national language to the Welsh bishoprics. In this manner it is not a matter for surprise that a feeling of estrangement should grow up between the bulk of the population, who only knew Welsh, and the clergy and nobles, their intellectual leaders. The neglect of the national language is evident from the large number of English words which have even crept into such classical works as Prichard's *Canwyll y Cymry* and Ellis Wynn's *Gweledigaethau y Bardd Cwsg*. It is stated that, of the 269 works published by Welshmen between 1546 and 1644, 44 were in Latin, 184 in English and only 41 in Welsh, and of these 37 consist of works of piety. Thus at the beginning of the 18th century there seemed a fair chance that Welsh would soon become extinct like Cornish.

An extraordinary change was brought about by the Methodist movement in Wales. The preachers, in order to get hold of the masses, addressed them in the vernacular, and their efforts were crowned with enormous success. At the same time a minister of the Established Church, Griffith Jones, went about Wales establishing lay schools to which young and old might come to learn to read the Welsh Bible. Between 1737 and 1761 3395 such schools sprang up, at which no fewer than 158,238 persons of all ages learned to read their native language. After Griffith Jones's death this work was carried on by others, notably by Charles of Bala (1755-1814), who passed over to Calvinistic Methodism and whose schools were transformed after the model of the Sunday schools instituted in 1782 by Robert Raikes. Charles of Bala was largely instrumental in the founding of the British and Foreign Bible Society, and Wales was provided with 100,000 copies of the Bible and Testament at very moderate prices. Bishop's Morgan's version of the Scriptures made in 1588 (final revision 1620) represents the speech of North Wales which had remained more or less free from English influence, so that the language of the Welsh Bible is rightly regarded as the literary model. Three-fourths of the inhabitants of Wales belong to the various Nonconformist sects, and therefore pass almost without exception through the Sunday school, where they are drilled in its sole object of study, the Welsh Bible.

With the increasing employment of Welsh owing to the Nonconformist movement there was also awakened a new interest in the past history of the principality. A society calling itself the *Cymdeithas y Cymmrodorion* was founded in London in 1751, and during the succeeding half-century two periodicals exclusively in Welsh were started, the one, *Trysorfa y Gwybodaeth*, in 1770, the other, *Cylchgrawn Cymraeg*, in 1793. The year 1792 witnessed the creation of an important society, the *Cymdeithas y Cymreigyddion*, in London, in which the moving spirits were William Owen (Pughe), Owen Jones and Edward Williams. The results of their indefatigable search for ancient Welsh manuscripts were published in three volumes under the title *Myvyrian Archaiology* (London, 1801-1807). Owen further published an edition of the greatest medieval Welsh poet Dafydd ap Gwilym, and also the first copious dictionary. But this was not all. In Goronwy Owen (1722-1769) a poet had arisen whose works could stand comparison with the compositions of the medieval writers, and it was owing to the efforts of the three men above mentioned that the national Eisteddfod (=

session, from *eistedd*, "to sit") was revived. The origin of these literary festivals is shrouded in obscurity. It is recorded that a S. Welsh prince, Gruffydd ap Rhys, held a festival lasting forty days in 1135 to commemorate a victorious campaign at which poets and minstrels competed for gifts and other rewards. Gruffydd's son Rhys ap Gruffydd is reported to have instituted a similar contest in 1176, at which the successful competitors received a chair whilst the others were given presents. It would seem that after the loss of Welsh independence a carefully graded order and a system of jealously guarded rules came into existence. Similar national festivals were held under royal patronage under Henry VIII. in 1523 and again under Elizabeth in 1568. From 1568 until 1819 no general eisteddfod for all Wales was held. Since 1819 the national festival has been held annually and every little town has its own local celebration. Hence the Nonconformist Sunday school, the pulpit and the eisteddfod may be regarded as the most potent factors in resisting the inroads of English. The whole question of the vitality of Welsh and what may be called the political and social history of the language is treated in great detail by H. Zimmer, "Der Pan-Keltismus in Gross-britannien und Irland," i., in *Preussische Jahrbücher*, vol. xcii. (1898). In elementary schools in Wales the use of Welsh has been permitted since 1893.

With regard to the extent over which Welsh is spoken a detailed map is given in J.E. Southall's *Welsh Language Census of 1891* (Newport, 1895). A line drawn from the southern end of the estuary of the Dee about 2 m. W. of Connah's Quay to Aberthaw in Glamorgan would practically include all those districts where Welsh is spoken by 60% of the population, and considerable deductions would have to be made for parts of Flint, Montgomery, most of Radnor and the N. part of Brecon. Little is spoken in the southern half of the Gower peninsula or in S. Pembrokeshire. Over much of Anglesey 97½% of the population spoke Welsh and in parts of Cardiganshire 98.3%. Of a total population in 1901 of 2,012,876, 929,824 were returned as speakers of Welsh, of whom 280,905 were monoglots. That Welsh is a very living language may be gathered from the following statistics. Between 1801 and 1898 no fewer than 8425 volumes were published in the vernacular, whilst in 1895 there were appearing regularly 2 quarterlies, 2 bi-monthlies, 28 religious and literary monthlies and 25 weekly papers. In 1909 the number was probably greater. The danger for Welsh lies rather in the direction of internal decay. The speech of the people is saturated with English words and idiom, and modern writers like Daniel Owen submit to the same influence instead of returning to the classical models of the 17th century.

Much remains to be done as regards the classification of the modern Welsh dialects. It is usual to divide them into four groups—(1) Powys (N.E.); (2) Gwynedd (N.W.); (3) Dyfed (S.W.); (4) Gwent (S.E.). One of the chief points on which N. and S. diverge is the pronunciation of the vowels *i, u, y*, which in the S. all tend to become *i*. The difference between N. and S. was noticeable as early as the time of Giraldus Cambrensis. See M. Nettlau, *Beiträge zur cymrischen Grammatik* (Leipzig, 1887), also *Rev. celt.* ix. pp. 64 ff., 113 ff.; T. Darlington, "Some Dialectal Boundaries in Mid-Wales," *Trans, of the Hon. Soc. of Cymmrodorion*, 1900-1901. The only scientific description of a living dialect is "Spoken N. Welsh," by H. Sweet, *Trans, of the London Phil. Soc.*, 1882-1884.

AUTHORITIES ON WELSH LANGUAGE.—For the study of older Welsh:—J.C. Zeuss, *Grammatica Celtica* (Berlin[2], 1871)—an index to the O. Welsh glosses cited in this work was compiled by V. Tourneur, *Archiv f. celt. Lexikographie*, iii. 109-137; J. Strachan, *An Introduction to Early Welsh*, with a Reader (Manchester, 1909); J. Rhys, *Lectures on Welsh Philology* (London[2], 1879). Editions of texts—*The Black Book of Carmarthen*, facsimile edition by J. Gwenogvryn Evans (Pwllheli, 1906); J. Rhys and J. Gwenogvryn Evans, *The Text of the Mabinogion* (Oxford, 1887); *The Myvyrian Archaiology of Wales* (1801-1807); reprinted Denbigh, 1870); W.F. Skene, *The Four Ancient Books of Wales* (2 vols., Edinburgh, 1868); Aneurin Owen, *Ancient Laws and Institutes of Wales* (London, 1841); facsimile edition by A.W. Wade-Evans, *Welsh Medieval Law* (Oxford, 1909); K. Meyer, *Peredur ap Efrawc* with glossary (Leipzig, 1887); R. Williams, *Selections from the Hengwrt Manuscripts* (London, 1876-1892); J.E. Southall, *Wales and Her Language* (Newport, 1892). The earliest Welsh grammar was published as long ago as 1567 in Milan by Griffiths Roberts, reprinted in facsimile as supplement to the *Revue celtique* (Paris, 1883). An account of the language was prefixed to Owen Pughe's Dictionary (1803). During the 19th century many manuals of indifferent value saw the light of day. The most authoritative works are:—T. Rowland, *A Grammar of the Welsh Language* (Wrexham, 18531, 18764), (still the most complete work), the same author also published a companion volume of *Welsh Exercises*(Wrexham, n.d.); W. Spurrell, *A Grammar of the Welsh Language* (Carmarthen3, 1870); E. Anwyl, *A Welsh Grammar for Schools, (i.) Accidence, (ii.) Syntax* (London2, 1898). Other useful manuals for the beginner:—T. Jones, *A Guide to Welsh*, pts. i. ii. new ed. (Wrexham, n.d.); S.J. Evans, *The Elements of Welsh Grammar* (Newport3, 1903). Dictionaries:—The first Welsh dictionary was compiled by William Salesbury (London, 1547; facsimile reprint, London, 1877); W. Owen Pughe, *A Dictionary of the Welsh Language* (2 vols., London, 1803; reprinted Denbigh, 1870); W. Spurrell, *Welsh-English and English-Welsh Dictionary* (Carmarthen6, 1904); a smaller one by W. Richards in 2 vols. (Wrexham, n.d.), and many others. A dictionary on a large scale was planned by D. Silvan Evans and subsidized by the government. Only A-Dd has, however, appeared (Carmarthen, 1893-1906), cp. J. Loth in *Archiv. f. celt. Lex.* vol. i. for additions and corrections. A survey of Welsh periodical literature is contained in T.M. Jones's *Llenyddiaeth fy Ngwlad* (Treffynnon, 1893). For Welsh folklore see J. Rhys, *Celtic Folklore, Welsh and Manx* (Oxford, 1901). H.H. Vaughan, *Welsh Proverbs*(London, 1889), also *Rev. celt.* iii. 419 ff. See also G. Dottin, *Revue de synthèse historique*, vi. 317 ff.; H. Zimmer and L.C. Stern in *Kultur der Gegenwart*, Teil 1, Abt. xi. 1.

(E. C. Q.)

(b) *Breton.*—Breton (*Brezonek*) is the name given to the language spoken by those Britons who fled from the south-west of England to Armorica (see <u>BRITTANY</u>) in the 5th and 6th centuries of our era to avoid being harassed by the Saxons. The first migration probably took place about 450. The Dumnonii and Cornovii founded small states in Brittany, or Britannia Minor, as it was termed, and were followed in the second half of the 6th and into the 7th century by a long stream of refugees (cf. J. Loth, *L'Émigration bretonne*, Paris, 1883; A. de la Borderie, *Histoire de la Bretagne*2, vol. i., 1905).

In the earliest stages it is difficult to distinguish Breton from Welsh. The history of the language may be divided into Old Breton from the 7th to the 11th centuries, Middle Breton from the 11th to the 17th centuries, and Modern Breton. In Old Breton the only material we possess consists of glosses and names occurring in lives of saints, Frankish authors, and charters. However, we find a few characteristics which serve to show that the old glosses are really Breton and not Welsh. Thus, an original $\bar{a}$ never becomes a diphthong (*au*, *aw*) in Old Breton, but remains $\bar{o}$. In Bret, *gn* becomes *gr*. Further, in O.W. pretonic $\breve{u}$ is weakened to an indeterminate sound written *i* and later *y*, a phenomenon which does not occur in Breton, *e.g.* Lat. *culcita* appears in O.W. as *cilcet*, but in O. Br. as *colcet*. A marked characteristic of Breton is the confusion of $\bar{i}$ and $\breve{e}$, *e.g.*Ir. *lis*, "court," W. *llys*, Br. *les*. In Old Breton as in Old Welsh neither the initial nor the medial mutations are expressed in writing, whilst in Middle Breton only the latter are regularly denoted. In this period the language diverges very rapidly from Welsh. As prominent features we may mention the following. Stressed $\bar{o}$ (= Prim. Celt. and Ir. $\bar{a}$) becomes *eu*, in unstressed syllables *e*; thus the suffix -$\bar{a}co$ becomes *-euc* and later *-ec*, but in Welsh *-auc* and later *-oc*, *-og*. Postvocalic *-tr*, *-tl* become *-dr*, *-dl* as in Welsh, but in Middle Breton they pass into *-zr*, *-zl*, which in the modern language appear as *-er*, *-el*; *e.g.* Mid. Br. *lazr*, Mod. Br. *laer*, "robber," W. *lleidr*, Lat. *latro*. Further, -*lt* becomes *-ot,-ut*, *e.g.* Br. *aot, aout*, "cliff," W. *allt*; Br. *autrou*, "lord," Ir. *altram*, W. *alltraw, athraw*, Corn. *altrou*; and, more important still, *th*, $\mathring{a}$ (W. *dd*) become *s*, *z*, *e.g.* Mid. Br. *clezeff*, "sword," Mod. Br. *kleze*, W. *cleddyf*. The orthography only followed the pronunciation very slowly, and it is not until 1659 that we find any attempt made to reform the spelling. In this year a Jesuit priest, Julien Maunoir (Br. Maner), published a manual in which a new spelling is employed, and it is usual to date Modern Breton from the appearance of this book, although in reality it marks no new epoch in the history of the language. It is only now that the initial mutations are consistently denoted in writing (medially they are already written in the 11th century), and the differences between the dialects first come into view at this time. As in Welsh the accent is withdrawn during the middle period from the final to the penultimate (except in the Vannes dialect), which causes the modern unstressed vowel to be reduced in many cases. Again, in Old Welsh and Old

Breton a short stressed vowel in words of one syllable was lengthened, *e.g. tãd*, "father," pl. *tãdau*, but in Modern Breton the accent tends to lengthen all stressed vowels. Breton has gone its own way in the matter of initial mutation. The nasal mutation has been entirely given up in the initial position, whilst a new mutation, called medial provection, has arisen in the case of *b, d, g,* which become *p, k, t* after a few words which originally ended for the most part in *z* or *ch.* The vocalic mutation of initial *g* in Breton is *c'h.* We may also make mention of one or two other points on which Breton differs widely from Welsh. Breton has given up the combination *ng, e.g.* Mid. Br. *moe,* Mod. Br. *moue,* "mane," W. *mwng,* Ir. *mong.* The language betrays a fondness for nasalized vowels, and in this connexion it may be noted that *v* representing an original *m* (W. *f,* Ir. *mh*), though generally written *ff* in Middle Breton, now frequently appears as *nv;* Mid. Br. *claff,* Mod. Br. *klanv,* "sick, ill," W. *claf,* M. Ir. *clam.* Final *g* after *r* and *l* and sometimes in monosyllables after a vowel is represented in Breton by *c'h,* whilst in Welsh in the one case we find a vowel and in the other nil, *e.g.* Br. *erc'h,* "snow," W. *eiry, eira;* Br. *lec'h,* "place," W. *lle.* In Welsh *mb, nd* immediately preceding the stress appear in the modern language as *mm, nn* but in Breton we find *mp,nl, e.g.* Br. *kantol,* "candle," W. *cannwyll,* Lat. *candela;* Br. *kemper,* "confluence" (in place names), W. *cymmer,* Ir. *combor.*

With regard to the extent of country over which Breton is spoken we shall do well to note the seats of the old Breton bishoprics. These were Quimper, St Pol de Léon, Tréguier, St Brieuc, St Malo, Dol and Vannes. Under Count Nominoe the Bretons succeeded in throwing off the Frankish yoke (841-845) and founded an independent state. At this time of greatest political expansion the language boundary was formed by a line which started roughly a little to the west of Mont St Michel at the mouth of the Couesnon, and stretched to the mouth of the Loire. During the next three centuries, however, in consequence of political events which cannot be enumerated here, we find French encroaching rapidly on Breton, and the old dioceses of Dol, St Malo, St Brieuc, and in part Vannes became Romance-speaking (cp. J. Loth, *Revue celtique,* xxviii. 374-403). So that since the 13th and 14th centuries the boundary between French and Breton begins in the north about Plouha (west of St Brieuc Bay), and stretches to the mouth of the Vilaine in the south. That is to say, the Breton speakers are confined to the department of Finistère and the west of the departments Côtes-du-Nord and Morbihan. Lower Brittany contains a population of 1,360,000, of whom roughly 1,250,000 speak Breton. The number of monoglot Bretons is stated to have been 768,000 in 1878, 679,000 in 1885, and over 500,000 in 1898. There is an infinity of dialects and subdialects in Brittany, but it is usual to divide them into four groups. These are the dialects of (1) Léon in Finistère; (2) Cornouailles in Finistère, the Côtes-du-Nord and a part of Morbihan; (3) Tréguier in the Côtes-du-Nord and Finistère; (4) Vannes in Morbihan and a portion of the Côtes-du-Nord. The first three resemble one another fairly closely, but the speech of Vannes has gone its own way entirely. The dialect of Léon is regarded as the literary dialect, thanks to Legonidec.

The modern language is unfortunately saturated with words borrowed from French which form at least a quarter of the whole vocabulary. The living speech is further characterized by innumerable cases of consonantal metathesis and by parasitic nasalization. Loth gives specimens of the most important varieties of Breton in his *Chrestomathie bretonne,* pp. 363-380, but here we must confine ourselves to pointing out the two most salient differences between the speech of Vannes and the rest of Brittany. In Vannes the stress has not been shifted from the final syllable. In Haute-Cornouailles and Goelo there is a tendency to withdraw the stress on to the antepenultimate, whilst in Tréguier certain enclitics attract the accent to the final. *s, z* of the other dialects representing Welsh *th* become *h* in Vannes, *e.g.* W. *caeth,* Br. *keaz, kez,* "poor, miserable," Vannes *keah, keh.* This phenomenon occurs sporadically in other dialects. It may also be mentioned that Prim. Celt, non-initial *d,* W. *dd,* is retained as *z* in Léon but disappears when final or standing between vowels in the other dialects, *e.g.* O. Br. *fid,* W. *ffydd,* "faith," Léon *feiz,* in Cornouailles, Tréguier and Vannes, *fé.* It is doubtful if the most serious differences between the dialects are older than the 16th century.

In the middle ages the language of the Breton aristocracy was French. Upper Brittany was politically more important than the western portion. The consequence was that no patronage was extended to the vernacular, and Breton sank to the level of a patois with no unity for literary purposes. But a new era dawned with the beginning of the 19th century. The national consciousness was awakened at the time of the Revolution, when the Bretons became aware of the difference between themselves and their French neighbours. It may be mentioned by the way that the Breton language was regarded with suspicion by the leaders of the First Republic and attempts were made to suppress it. A Breton named Legonidec had to flee to England for fighting against the Republic. He came under the influence of the movement in Wales, and on his return sought to create a Breton literary language. He published an excellent grammar (*Grammaire celto-bretonne*, Paris, 1807) and a dictionary (*Dictionnaire breton-français*, Paris, 1821), from which he omitted the numerous French words which had crept into the language and for which native terms already existed. Legonidec's 621example fired a number of writers with zeal for their native tongue and the clergy became interested. Under their auspices manuals of Breton were published and the language was utilized in a number of schools. A society called the *Association Bretonne* was founded in the year 1844. But under the Second Empire, for reasons which are not easy to discover, this Breton awakening was declared to be contrary to the interests of the state, and all the means at the disposal of a highly centralized government like that of France were employed to throttle the movement. Down to the present day the use of Breton is strictly forbidden in all the state schools, and the influence of the Roman Catholic clergy has for the most part been hostile to the language. However, the attitude of the government aroused considerable dissatisfaction in the early 'nineties, and in 1896 the *Association Bretonne* (disbanded in 1859 and reconstructed in 1873) appointed a permanent committee with the object of preserving and propagating the national language. At the same time some of the clergy headed by Abbé Buléon began to move, and Breton was introduced into many of the schools not under state control. In 1898 was founded the*Union Régionaliste Bretonne*, the most important section of which endeavours to foster the native speech in conjunction with the *Comité de préservation du breton* (founded 1896). In 1899 the annual meeting of the U.R.B. was modelled on the lines of the Irish Oireachtas, the Welsh Eisteddfod and the Scottish Mod, and festivals of this kind have been held ever since. Many Breton newspapers publish columns in Breton, thus *Ar Bobl*(a weekly newspaper founded in 1904 and published at Carhaix) frequently devotes half its columns to the language. But there is also a weekly four-page newspaper which is wholly in Breton. This is *Kroaz ar Vretoned*, edited by F. Vallée and published at St Brieuc. In addition to this there are three monthly magazines wholly in Breton. The first is *Ar Vro*, edited by the poet Jaffrennou, and in 1908 in its fifth year. The second is*Dihunamb*, written in the dialect of Vannes and started in 1905. The third is *Feiz ha Breiz*, started 1899.

AUTHORITIES FOR BRETON.—For the external history of Breton see H. Zimmer, "Die keltische Bewegung in der Bretagne," *Preussische Jahrbücher* for 1899, xcix. 454-497. For Old and Middle Breton, J. Loth, *Chrestomathie bretonne* (Paris, 1890), and the same writer's *Vocabulaire vieux-breton* (Paris, 1884). Loth and E. Ernault have been indefatigable in investigating the history of the language. Their numerous contributions are mainly to be found scattered through the *Revue celtique, Zeitschrift für celtische Philologie* and the *Annales de Bretagne*. Ernault has also published *Glossaire moyen-breton* in 2 vols. (Paris, 1895-1896); *Dictionnaire étymologique du moyen-breton*(Paris, 1888). Another etymological dictionary was published by V. Henry (Paris, 1900). Grammars, &c.:—Dialect of Léon: Legonidec, *Grammaire celto-bretonne* (Paris, 1807, 1838², also contained in H. de la Villemarqué's edition of Legonidec's Dictionary); F. Vallée, *Leçons élémentaires de grammaire bretonne* (St Brieuc, 1902); E. Ernault, *Petite Grammaire bretonne* (St Brieuc, 1897, the latter also takes account of the dialects of Tréguier and Cornouailles). Dialect of Tréguier: L. le Clerc, *Grammaire bretonne* (St Brieuc, 1908); J. Hingant, *Éléments de la grammaire bretonne* (Tréguier, 1868); P. le Roux, "Mutations et assimilations de consonnes dans le dialecte armoricain de Pleubian," *Annales de Bretagne*, xii. 3-31. Dialect of Vannes: A. Guillevic and P. le Goff, *Grammaire bretonne du dialecte de Vannes* (Vannes, 1902); *Exercises sur la grammaire bretonne* (Vannes, 1903); H. d'Arbois de Jubainville, "Étude phonétique sur le dialecte breton de Vannes," *Revue celtique*, i. 85 ff. 211 ff.; E. Ernault, "Le Dialecte vannetais de Sarzeau," *Rev. celt.* iii. 47 ff., 232 ff.; J. Guillome, *Grammaire française-bretonne* (Vannes, 1836). As a curiosity we mention P. Treasure, *An Introduction to Breton Grammar* (Carmarthen, 1903). Dictionaries: Legonidec, *Dictionnaire français-breton* (St Brieuc, 1847), *Breton-Français* (St Brieuc, 1850), both republished by de la Villemarqué and representing the Léon dialect; A. Troude, *Nouveau Dictionnaire pratique français et breton du dialecte de Léon avec les acceptations diverses dans les dialectes de Vannes, de Tréguier, et de Cornouailles* (Brest, 1869), and *Nouveau Dictionnaire pratique breton-français* (Brest, 1876); E. Ernault, "Supplément aux dictionnaires bretons-français," *Revue celtique*, iv. 145-170. The Breton words in Gallo, the French patois of Upper Brittany, were collected by E. Ernault, *Revue celtique*, v. 218 ff.

(c) *Cornish.*—The ancient language of Cornwall (*Kernûak, Carnoack*) stood in a much closer relation to Breton than to Welsh,1 though in some respects it sides with the latter against the former.

It agrees with Breton on the following points:—It has given up the nasal mutation of initials but provects the mediae. Prim. Celt. *ā* is not diphthongized, but becomes *ē*, *e.g.*Corn, *ler*, "floor," Br. *leur*, W. *llawr*, Ir. *lār*. *Ng* is lost as in Breton, *e.g. toy*, "to swear," Br. *toui*, W. *tyngu*, Ir. *tongu; nd* becomes *nt* before the stress and not *nn* as in Welsh,*e.g.* Corn. Br. *hanter*, W. *hanner*. Cornish like Breton does not prefix a vowel to words beginning with s + consonant, *e.g.* Corn. *spirit*, later *spyrys*, Br. *spered*, W.*yspryd*. On the other hand, O. Cornish does not confuse *ī* and *ĕ* to the same extent as Bret., *e.g.* W. *helyg*, "willow," O. Cornish *heligen*, Br. *halek*. Further, Cornish does not change *th, d* to *s, z* as in Breton, *e.g. beth*, "grave," Br. *bez*, W. *bedd*, and initial *g* disappears in the vocalic mutation as in Welsh. Peculiar to Cornish is the change of non-initial *t, d* to *s, z*. This occurs in the oldest Cornish after *n, l, e.g.* O. Corn, *nans*, "valley," W. *nant;* Corn. *tâs*, "father," W. *tad*. A feature of later Cornish is the introduction of a *d* before post-vocalic *m, n, e.g. pedn*, "head," W. *pen*. In later Cornish the accent seems to have fallen on the penultimate as in Modern Welsh and Breton.

In 936 the "Welsh" were driven out of Exeter by Æthelstan, and from that time the Tamar appears to have formed a general boundary between English and Cornish, though there seems to be evidence that even as late as the reign of Elizabeth Cornish was spoken in a few places to the east of that river. The decay of Cornish has been largely attributed to the Reformation. Neither the Prayer-book nor the Scriptures were translated into the vernacular, and we find the same apathy on the part of the Church of England in Cornwall as in Wales and Ireland. Unfortunately the Methodist movement came at a time when it was too late to save the language. By 1600 Cornish had been driven into the western parts of the duchy and in 1662 we are informed by John Ray that few of the children could speak it. Lhuyd gives a list of the parishes in which Cornish was spoken, but goes on to state that every one speaks English. In 1735 there were only a few people along the coast between Penzance and Land's End who understood Cornish, and Dolly Pentreath of Mousehole, who died in 1777, is commonly stated to have been the last person who spoke it, though Jenner seems to show that there were others who lived until well into the 19th century who were able to converse in the dialect. However, the modern English speech of West Cornwall is full of Celtic words, and nine-tenths of the places and people from the Tamar to Land's End bear Cornish names. Celtic words still in use are to be found in Jago's *Dialect of Cornwall* (Truro, 1882); thus the name for the dog-fish is *morgy*, "sea-dog."

AUTHORITIES FOR CORNISH.—A mass of details about Cornish is collected in H. Jenner's*Handbook of the Cornish Language* (London, 1904). (Cf. J. Loth's review in the *Revue celtique*, xxvii. 93.) Lhuyd's *Archaeologica Britannica* (1707) contains a grammar of the language as spoken in his day, and a *Sketch of Cornish Grammar* is to be found as an appendix to Norris's *Ancient Cornish Drama*. A dictionary was published by R. Williams entitled *Lexicon Cornu-Britannicum* (Landovery, 1865), to which W. Stokes published a supplement of about 2000 words in the *Transactions of the London Philological Society* for 1868-1869. We may also mention the *English-Cornish Dictionary*, by F.W.P. Jago (Plymouth, 1887), and a *Glossary of Cornish Names*, by J. Bannister (Truro, 1871). W. Stokes published a Glossary to *Beunans Meriasek* in the*Archiv für celtische Lexikographie*, i. 101, and important articles by J. Loth have appeared in the *Revue celtique*, vols. xviii. to xxiv. W.S. Lach-Szyrma, "Les Derniers Échos de la langue cornique," *Revue celtique*, iii. 239 ff. H. Jenner, "Some Rough Notes on the Present Pronunciation of Cornish Names," *Rev. celt.* xxiv. 300-305.

III. THE LANGUAGE OF THE ANCIENT PICTS.—The evidence from which we can draw any conclusions as to the affinities of the language of the Picts is so extremely scanty that the question has been the subject of great controversy. The Picts are first mentioned by Eumenius (A.D. 297), who regarded them as having inhabited Britain in the time of Caesar. In the year 368 they are described by Ammianus Marcellinus as invading the Roman province of Britain in conjunction with the Irish Scots. In Columba's time we find the whole of Scotland east of Drumalban and north of the Forth divided into two kingdoms—north and south Pictland—and it is reasonable to identify the Picts, at any rate in part, with the Caledonians of the classical authors. Galloway and Co. Down were also inhabited by Picts. Bede in enumerating the languages of Britain mentions those of the Britons, Picts, Scots and the English. The names by which the Picts are known in history have aroused considerable discussion. It seems natural to connect Lat. *Picti* with the *Pictones* and *Pictavi* of Gaul, but in Irish they are known as *Cruithne*, which appears in Welsh as *Prydyn*, "Pict"; cp. *Prydein*, "Britain," forms corresponding to the earliest Greek name for these islands, νῆσοι πρετανικαί.

Three conflicting theories have been held as to the character of the Pictish language. Rhys, relying on the strange character of the Scottish Ogam inscriptions, pronounces it to be non-Celtic and non-Indo-European. In this he has been followed by Zimmer, who bases his argument on the Pictish rule of succession. Skene maintained that the Picts spoke a language nearly allied to Goidelic, whilst Stokes, Loth, Macbain, D'Arbois and Meyer are of opinion that Pictish was more closely related to Brythonic. Of personal names mentioned by classical writers we have Calgacus and Argentocoxus, both of which are certainly Celtic. The names occurring in Ptolemy's description of Scotland have a decidedly Celtic character, and they seem, moreover, to bear a greater resemblance to Brythonic than to Goidelic, witness such tribal designations as Epidii, Cornavii, Damnonii, Decantae, Novantae. In the case of all these names, however, it should be borne in mind that they probably reached the writers of antiquity through Brythonic channels. Bede mentions that the east end of the Antonine Wall terminated at a place called in Pictish *Pean-fahel*, and in Saxon *Penneltun*. *Pean* resembles Old Welsh *penn*, "head," Old Irish *cenn*, and the second element may possibly be connected with Gaelic *fàl*, Welsh *gwawl*, "rampart." The names of the kings in the Pictish chronicles are not an absolutely trustworthy guide, as owing to the Pictish rule of succession the bearers of the names may in many cases have been Brythons. The names of some of them occur in one source in a Goidelic, in another in a Brythonic form. It is of course possible that the southern part of Pictish territory was divided between Goidels and Brythons, the population being very much mixed. On the other hand there are a number of elements in place-names on Pictish ground which do not occur in Wales or Ireland. Such are *pet*, *pit*, "farm" (?), *for*, *fother*, *fetter*, *foder*, "lower" (?). *Aber*, "confluence," on the contrary, is pure Brythonic (Gaelic *inver*). Though the majority of scholars are of opinion that Pictish was nearly akin to the Brythonic dialects, we are entirely in the dark as to the manner in which that language was ousted by the Goidelic speech of the Dalriadic Scots. In view of the comparatively unimportant part played for a considerable period in Scottish affairs by the colony from Ireland, it is well-nigh incredible that Pictish should have been supplanted by Gaelic.

AUTHORITIES.—J. Rhys, *Celtic Britain* (London², 1905), *The Welsh People* (London3, 1902), "The Language and Inscriptions of the Northern Picts," in *Proceedings of the Society of Antiquaries of Scotland* (1892); H. Zimmer, "Das Mutterrecht der Pikten," in *Savignys Zeitschrift* (1895); also trans. by G. Henderson in *Leabhar nan Gleann* (Inverness, 1898); W.F. Skene, *Celtic Scotland* (Edinburgh, 1876); A. Macbain in appendix to reprint of Skene's *Highlanders of Scotland* (Stirling, 1902); A. Macbain, "Ptolemy's Geography of Scotland," in *Transactions of the Gaelic Society of Inverness*, xviii. 267-288; W. Stokes, *Bezzenbergers Beiträge*, xviii. 267 ff.; H. d'Arbois de Jubainville, *Les Druides et les dieux celtiques à forme d'animaux* (Paris, 1906). The various theories have been recently reviewed and criticized by T. Rice Holmes in an appendix to his *Caesar's Invasion of Britain* (London, 1907).

IV. History of Celtic Philology.—For many centuries the affinities of the Celtic languages were the subject of great dispute. The languages were in turn regarded as descended from Hebrew, Teutonic and Scythian. The first attempt to treat the dialects comparatively was made by Edward Lhuyd in his *Archaeologia Britannica* (Oxford, 1707), but the work of this scholar seems to have remained unnoticed. A century later Adelung in Germany divided the dialects into true Celtic (= Goidelic) and Celtic influenced by Teutonic (= Brythonic). But it took scholars a long time to recognize that these languages belonged to the Indo-European family. Thus they were excluded by Bopp in his comparative grammar, though he did not fail to notice certain resemblances between Celtic and Sanskrit. James Pritchard was the first to demonstrate the true relationship of the group in his *Eastern Origin of the Celtic Nations* (London, 1831), but his conclusions were not accepted. As late as 1836 Pott denied the Indo-European connexion. A year later Pictet resumed Pritchard's arguments, and Bopp himself in 1838 admitted the languages into the charmed circle, showing in an able paper entitled *Über die keltischen Sprachen* that the initial mutations were due to the influence of terminations now lost. But it was reserved to a Bavarian historian, J.C. Zeuss (1806-1856), to demonstrate conclusively the Indo-European origin of the Celtic dialects. Zeuss, who may worthily rank with Grimm and Diez among the greatest German philologists, rediscovered the Old Irish glosses on the continent, and on them he reared the magnificent structure which goes by his name. The *Grammatica Celtica* was first published in 1853. The material contained in this monumental work was greatly extended by a series of important publications by Whitley Stokes and Hermann Ebel, so much so that the latter was commissioned to prepare a second edition, which appeared in 1871. Stokes has rendered the greatest service to the cause of Celtic studies by the publication of countless texts in Irish, Cornish and Breton. In 1870 the *Revue celtique* (vol. xxviii. in 1908) was founded by Henri Gaidoz, whose mantle later fell upon H. d'Arbois de Jubainville. In 1879 E. Windisch facilitated the study of Irish by publishing a grammar of Old Irish, and a year later a volume of important Middle Irish texts with an exhaustive glossary, the first of its kind. Since then Windisch and Stokes have collaborated to bring out some of the greatest monuments of Irish literature in the series of *Irische Texte*. The text of the Würzburg glosses was published by Zimmer (1881) and by Stokes (1887), and that of the Milan glosses by Ascoli. An important step forward was the discovery of the laws of the Irish accent made simultaneously by Zimmer and Thurneysen. This discovery led to a thorough investigation of the difficult verb system of Old Irish—a task which has largely occupied the attention of Strachan in England, Thurneysen and Zimmer in Germany, and Pedersen and Sarauw in Denmark. In a sense the publication of the *Thesaurus Palaeohibernicus* (Cambridge, 1901-1903) may be regarded as marking the close of this epoch. The older stages of Irish have hitherto so monopolized the energies of scholars that other departments of Celtic philology save Breton have been left in large measure unworked. J. Strachan had begun to tap the mine of the Old Welsh poems when his career was cut short by death. J. Loth and E. Ernault have concentrated their attention on Breton, and can claim that the development of the speech of Brittany has been more thoroughly investigated than that of any other Celtic language. The number of periodicals devoted entirely to Celtic studies has increased considerably of recent years. In 1896 K. Meyer and L. C. Stern founded the *Zeitschrift für celtische Philologie* (now in its 7th volume), and in 1897 the *Archiv für celtische Lexikographie* began to appear under the direction of K. Meyer and W. Stokes. As a supplement to the latter Meyer has been publishing his invaluable contributions to Middle Irish lexicography. In Ireland a new periodical styled *Ériu* was started by the Irish School of Learning in 1904. The Scottish*Celtic Review*, dealing more particularly with Scottish and Irish Gaelic, began to appear in 1903, and the *Transactions of the Gaelic Society of Inverness* are in the 26th volume. For Wales we have *Y Cymmrodor* since 1877, and the *Transactions of the Hon. Society of Cymmrodorion* since 1892, and for Brittany the *Annales de Bretagne*, published by the Faculty of Letters at Rennes (founded 1886).

See V. Tourneur, *Esquisse d'une histoire des études celtiques* (Liége, 1905).

(E. C. Q.)

CELTIC LITERATURE

I. IRISH LITERATURE.—In the absence of a native coinage it is extremely difficult to say when the use of letters was introduced into Ireland. It is probable that the Latin alphabet first came in with Christianity. With the exception *Ogam inscriptions.* of the one bilingual Ogam inscription as yet discovered in Ireland (that at Killeen Cormac) all the inscriptions in Roman letters are certainly later than 500. Indeed, apart from the stone reading "LIE LUGUAEDON MACCI MENUEH," they are all contemporary with or later than the Old Irish glosses. With regard to the Ogam inscriptions we cannot make any confident assertions. Owing to the lack of criteria for dating certain Irish sound-changes accurately it is impossible to assign chronological limits for the earlier stones. The latter cannot be later than the 5th century, but there is nothing to show whether they are Christian or not, and if pagan they may be a century or two earlier. It is true that the heroes and druids of the older epics are represented in the stories as making constant use of Ogam letters on wood and stone, and as the state of civilization described in the oldest versions of the Ulster sagas seems largely to go back to the beginning of the Christian era, it is not impossible that this peculiar system of writing had been 623framed by them. The Ogam system is certainly based on the Latin and not the Greek alphabet, and was probably invented by some person from the south of Ireland who received his knowledge of the Roman letters from traders from the mouth of the Loire. It may, however, be regarded as certain that the Ogam script was never employed in early times for literary purposes. We are told that the Gaulish druids disdained to commit their lore to writing, although they were familiar with the use of Greek letters, and their Irish confrères probably resembled them in this respect. Tradition connects the codification of the Brehon Laws with the name of Patrick, and there is reason for believing, as we shall see later, that the greatest Irish epic was first committed to writing in the 7th century.

The great bulk of Irish literature is contained in MSS. belonging to the Middle Irish period (1100-1550), and in order to be able to treat this literature as a whole it will be convenient for us to deal first with those documents which are **Old Irish MSS.** termed Old Irish, especially as the contemporary remains of the literature of the earlier period are almost exclusively of a religious nature. Most of the Old Irish documents have been printed by Stokes and Strachan in the *Thesaurus Palaeohibernicus*, and where no reference is given the reader is referred to that monumental work. The extraordinary outburst of intellectual activity in Ireland from the 6th to the 9th centuries and the compositions of Irishmen in the Latin language, belong to the history of medieval European literature and fall outside the scope of this article. For the *Confession of St Patrick* and his "Letter to the Subjects of Coroticus" see PATRICK. The only Irish document ascribed to the saint is the strange so-called "Hymn," the *fáeth fiada*, more properly *fóid fiada*, "the cry of the deer." This is a rhythmical incantation which is said **Hymns.** to have rendered the saint and his companions invisible to King Loigaire and his druids. The Trinity and powers of nature are invoked to help him to resist spells of women and smiths and wizards. The hymn, which contains a number of strange grammatical forms, is undoubtedly referred to in the Book of Armagh, and may very well go back to the 5th century. The Latin hymns contained in two MSS. dating from the end of the 11th or beginning of the 12th century, a Trinity College, Dublin, MS., and a MS. belonging to the Franciscan monastery in Dublin, are of interest to us as exhibiting the influence of the native metrical system. Quantity and elision are ignored, and rhymes, assonances, alliterations and harmonies abound in true Irish fashion. The line consists of two units which commonly contain either seven or eight syllables apiece. The earliest and best-known of these religious poems are the Hymn of Secundinus (Sechnall d. 447) on St Patrick, and the two hymns attributed to St Columba (d. 597) beginning "*Noli pater*" and "*Altus prosator*," the latter of which exhibits some of the peculiarities of the so-called Hibernian Latin of the *Hisperica Famina* and the *Lorica* of Gildas. The date of the Irish hymns in the*Liber Hymnorum* ranges, according to Stokes and Strachan, from the 7th to the 11th centuries. Ultán's hymn on St Brigit beginning "*Brigit bé bithmaith*," which is by far the most artistic of the collection, was perhaps composed in the 7th century. Definite metrical laws had evidently been elaborated when this poem was written. The beat is iambic, but the natural accent of the words is rigidly observed. The long line consists of two units of five syllables each. The rhymes are dissyllabic and perfect. Alliteration is always observed in the latter half of each line and assonances are found knitting up the half-lines. The short prayer ascribed to Ninine or to Fiacc is a highly alliterative piece without rhyme, the date of which cannot be fixed. The well-known hymn on St Patrick traditionally ascribed to Fiacc, bishop of Sletty, and the piece beginning *"Sén Dé,"* traditionally ascribed to Colmán, are assigned on linguistic grounds to the beginning of the 9th century. The lines going by the name of "Sanctán's Hymn" probably belong to the same century, whilst the metrical catalogue of marvels performed by St Brigit contains such a medley of older and later forms, probably due to interpolation, that it is impossible to determine its age. The few lines entitled "Mael-Ísu's Hymn" are the most recent of all and probably belong to the 11th century (Mael-Ísu d. 1086). The Patrician documents by Muirchu Maccu Machthéni, who professed to write at the command of Bishop Aed of Sletty (d. 698), and by Tirechán, who is said to have received his information from Bishop Ultán (d. 656), are contained in the Book of Armagh, a MS. compiled by Ferdomnach in 807. These documents, like the *Life of St Columba* by Adamnan, the MS. of which was written by Dorbbéne, abbot of Hi (d. 713), contain a number of names and forms of great importance for the study of the language.

The earliest pieces of connected prose in Irish are three:—(1) the Cambray Homily, contained in an 8th-century codex at Cambray copied by a continental hand from a MS. in the Irish character; the language is very archaic and ***Earliest prose.*** dates from the second half of the 7th or the beginning of the 8th century; (2) the additions to the notes of Tirechán on the life of St Patrick in the Book of Armagh; these seem to go back to the early 8th century; (3) the tract on the Mass in the Stowe Missal, which is in all probability nearly as old as the Cambray Homily, though contained in a 10th or 11th century MS. Of especial interest are the spells and poems found in the Stowe Missal and two continental MSS. The Stowe MS. (now deposited in the Royal Irish Academy) contains three rather badly preserved spells for a sore eye, a thorn and disease of the urine. A St Gall codex has preserved four Irish incantations of the 8th and 9th centuries. These are respectively against a thorn, urinary disease, headache and various ailments. Another charm, which is partly obscure, occurs in the 9th-century codex preserved at the monastery of St Paul in Carinthia. The same MS. also contains (1) a humorous poem treating of the doings of a bookish writer and his favourite cat Pangur Bán; (2) a riddling poem ascribed to Suibne Geilt, a king who is said to have lost his reason at the battle of Moira (A.D. 637); (3) verses extracted from a poem ascribed to St Moling (d. 697), who may very well have been the actual author; (4) a poem in praise of some Leinster princeling called Aed.

For our knowledge of the older language, however, we have to rely mainly on the numerous glosses scattered about in a large number of MSS., which it is impossible to enumerate here. Indeed, such an enumeration is now rendered ***Old glosses.*** superfluous owing to the publication of the *Thesaurus Palaeohibernicus*, in which all the various glosses have been collected. For our purpose it will be sufficient to mention the three most important codices containing Old Irish glosses. These are as follows:—(1) The Codex Paulinus at Würzburg, which contains the thirteen epistles of St Paul, and the Epistle to the Hebrews, with a great mass of explanatory glosses, partly in Latin, partly in Irish, partly mixed. The chief source of the commentary is the commentary of Pelagius, who is often cited by name. The date of this highly important MS. is much disputed; part of the Irish glosses seem to date from about 700, whilst the rest may be placed a little before 800. (2) The Codex Ambrosianus, formerly at Bobbio, now at Milan, which contains a commentary on the psalter with a large number of Irish glosses. In their present state these glosses were copied in the first half of the 9th century. (3) Glosses on Priscian contained in four MSS., of which the most important is the Codex Sangallensis, dating from the middle of the 9th century. Apart from the biblical glosses and scholia the other chief texts or authors provided with Irish glosses are Augustine, Bede, the Canons, the Computus, Eutychius, Juvencus, Philargyrius, Prudentius and Servius.

The Milan and the St Gall codices just mentioned both contain several short poems in Irish. In two stanzas in the Swiss MS. we find expressed for the first time that keen sympathy with nature in all her moods which is so marked a feature of Irish and Welsh verse.

Two ponderous religious poems have now to be noticed. To Oengus the Culdee is attributed the lengthy *Félire* or Calendar of Church Festivals, consisting of 365 quatrains in *rinnard* metre, one for each day in the year. The language of this dry compilation, which is heavily glossed and annotated, points to 800 as the date of composition, and Oengus, who is stated to have 624lived about that time, may well have been the author. This calendar has been twice edited by W. Stokes with an English translation, the first time for the Royal Irish Academy (Dublin, 1880), and again for the Bradshaw Society (London, 1905).

It may perhaps be as well to enumerate here the later Irish martyrologies. (1) The*Martyrology of Tallaght* (Tamlacht), founded on an 8th-century calendar, but containing additions down to 900 (ed. D.H. Kelly, Dublin, 1857). (2) The metrical *Martyrology of O'Gorman*, c. 1166-1174, edited by Stokes for the Bradshaw Society (London, 1895). (3) The *Martyrology of Donegal*, an important compilation in prose made by Michael O'Clery in 1630, edited by J.H. Todd (Dublin, 1864). A composition which is wrongly assigned to Oengus the Culdee is the *Saltair na Rann* or Psalter in Quatrains, contained in an Oxford MS. (Rawlinson B 502) and published without a translation by Stokes (Oxford, 1883). The work proper consists of 150 poems corresponding to the number of Psalms in the psalter, but 12 poems have been added, and in all it contains 2098 quatrains, chiefly in *deibide* metre of seven syllables. The poems are mainly based on biblical (Old Testament) history, but they preserve a large measure of medieval sacred lore and cosmogony. The psalter received additions as late as 998, and the Oxford MS. belongs to the 12th century. We should perhaps also mention here the famous *Amra* or Eulogy of St Columba, commonly attributed to Dallán Forgaill, a contemporary of the saint, but Stokes takes the view that it was written in the 9th century, and is intentionally obscure. The oldest but not the best copy of the *Amra* is preserved in the Trinity College, Dublin, MS. of the *Liber Hymnorum*, but it also occurs in LU. and elsewhere. It invariably appears heavily gloss-laden, and the glosses and commentary added thereto are out of all proportion to the text. This piece, which is not extant in its integrity, was probably intended as artificial alliterative prose, but, as we have it, it is a medley of isolated phrases and irrelevant comment.

During the 9th and 10th centuries Ireland was harassed by the Vikings, and a host of scholars seem to have fled to the continent, carrying with them their precious books, many of which are preserved in Italy, Switzerland, Germany **Old collectors.**and elsewhere. Hence very few early Irish MSS. are preserved in Ireland itself. When the fury of the storm was past, Irish scholars showed increased interest in the old literary documents, and copied all that they could lay hands on into miscellaneous codices. The earliest of these collections, such as the *Cin of Druim Snechta*, the *Yellow Book of Slane*, the *Book of Dubdaleithe*, the *Psalter of Cashel*, exist no longer, though their names have come down and certain of them were known in the 17th century. However, copies of a goodly portion of the contents of these old books are preserved to us in one form or another, but mainly in a series of huge miscellaneous codices **Book of the Dun Cow.**ranging in date from the 12th to the 16th century. The oldest is *Lebor na h-uidre*, or Book of the Dun Cow, preserved in the Royal Irish Academy and published in facsimile (Dublin, 1870). This MS. was compiled in part in the monastery of Clonmacnoise by Moelmuire MacCelechair, who was slain in 1106. The Book of the Dun Cow (where necessary we shall abbreviate as LU.) derives its name from a legend that Ciaran of Clonmacnoise (d. 544) took down the story of the *Táin Bó Cualnge* on a parchment made from the hide of his favourite cow. The name seems to have been wrongly applied to the 12th-century MS. in the 15th century. LU. is almost entirely devoted to romance, the stories which **Book of Leinster.**it contains belonging mainly to the Ulster cycle. The next MS. in point of age is the Book of Leinster (abbreviated LL.) now in Trinity College, Dublin. It was transcribed by Finn, son of Gorman, bishop of Kildare (d. 1160). LL. also contains a large number of romances in addition to other important matter, mainly historical and*Yellow Book of Lecan.*genealogical, bearing more particularly on the affairs of Leinster. The Yellow Book of Lecan (YBL.), also in Trinity College, Dublin, was written at different times by the MacFirbis family, but chiefly by Gilla Isa, son of Donnchad Mór MacFirbis about 1391. The MacFirbises were hereditary scribes and genealogists to the O'Dowds, chiefs of the Hy Fiachrach (Co. Sligo). YBL. contains a vast amount of romance, and is indispensable as supplementing and checking **Book of Ballymote.**the contents of LU.

and LL. The most extensive collection of all is the Book of Ballymote (BB.), now belonging to the Royal Irish Academy, which was compiled about the beginning of the 15th century by various scribes. The book was in the possession of the chiefs of Ballymote for more than a century. In 1522 it was purchased by the O'Donnells for 140 milch cows. BB. only contains little romantic matter but it has preserved much valuable historical and *Speckled Book.* genealogical material. The contents of the *Leabhar Breac* (LB.), or Speckled Book, now in the Royal Irish Academy, are chiefly ecclesiastical and religious. LB. seems to have been compiled in large measure before 1544. All these five codices have been published in facsimile by the Royal Irish Academy with a description of their contents. Two important Mid. Ir. MSS. in the Bodleian (Rawlinson B 512 and Laud 610), containing a good deal of romantic material, are also published in facsimile by Henry Frowde.

Other MSS. which require special mention are (1) The Great Book of Lecan, compiled in the year 1417 by Gilla Isa Mór MacFirbis, in the Royal Irish Academy; (2) The Book of Lismore, the property of the duke of Devonshire at Lismore *Other MSS. material.* Castle. This codex was compiled in the latter half of the 15th century from the lost book of Monasterboice and other MSS. Its contents are described in the introduction to Stokes's *Lives of Saints from the Book of Lismore* (Oxford, 1890). (3) The Book of Fermoy in the Royal Irish Academy. The contents are described in the introduction to O'Beirne Crowe's edition of the *Táin Bó Fraich* (Dublin, 1870). (4) The Book of Hy Maine recently acquired by the Royal Irish Academy. The scribe who wrote it died in 1372. O'Curry, O'Longan and O'Beirne Crowe drew up a MS. catalogue of the Irish MSS. in the Royal Irish Academy, and O'Donovan performed the same service for the Trinity College, Dublin, collection. A briefer account of the Irish MSS. in TCD. will be found in Abbott's Catalogue of the MSS. in that library. O'Curry also drew up a list of the Irish MSS. in the British Museum, and S.H. O'Grady has printed part i. of a descriptive catalogue of this collection (London, 1901), part ii. by T. O'Maille. The twenty-six MSS. in the Franciscan monastery in Dublin are described by J.T. Gilbert in the *Fourth Report of the Royal Commission on Historical MSS.* W.F. Skene catalogued the collection of MSS. in the Advocates' Library, Edinburgh, a printed catalogue of which has been issued by D. Mackinnon (Edinburgh, 1909; see also *Trans. Gaelic Soc. of Inverness*, xvi. 285-309).

In order to give some idea of the enormous extent of Irish MS. material we may quote some calculations made by O'Curry, who states that if the five oldest vellum MSS. were printed the result would be 9400 quarto pages. Other vellum MSS. ranging in date from 1300 to 1600 would fill 9000 pages of the same size, whilst the innumerable paper MSS. belonging chiefly to the early 18th century would cover no less than 30,000 pages. The well-known French scholar, D'Arbois de Jubainville, published in 1883 a tentative catalogue of Irish epic literature. His work is by no means complete, but his figures are instructive. He mentions 953 Irish MSS containing epic matter preserved in Irish and English libraries. To these have to be added another 56 in continental libraries. Of this mass of material 133 Irish and British MSS. and 35 continental MSS. were written before 1600. It should, however, be stated that the same subject is treated over and over again, and much of the later material is absolutely valueless.

Before we pass on to the consideration of the literature itself, it will be well to make a few preliminary observations on the nature of the language in which the pieces are written and on the status of the poet in medieval Ireland. *Character of Middle Irish.* The language in which the huge miscellaneous codices enumerated above are contained is called by the general name of Middle Irish, which is a very wide term. Irish scribes often copied their original somewhat mechanically, without 625 being tempted to change the language to that of their own time. Thus in many parts of LU. we find a thin Middle Irish veneer on what is largely Old Irish of the 8th or 9th century. Hence such a MS. often preserves forms which had been current several centuries before, and it may even happen that a 14th or 15th century MS. such as YBL. contains much older forms than a corresponding passage in LL. Of recent years several scholars—notably Strachan—have devoted much attention to the Old Irish verb-forms, so that we have now safe criteria for establishing with some degree of certainty the age of recensions of stories and poems preserved in late MSS. In this way a number of compositions have been assigned to the 9th, 10th and 11th centuries, though actual written documents belonging to this period are comparatively rare.

It remains for us to say a few words about the *fili*, the professional literary man in Ireland. The *fili* (from the stem *vel-*, "to see," Welsh, Breton, *gwelet*, "to see") appears to have been originally a diviner and magician, and corresponds **The "fili."** to the *vates*,οὐάτεις, of the ancient Gauls mentioned by classical writers. In Ireland he is represented as sole possessor of three methods of divination: the *imbas forosnai, teinm lóida* and *díchetal di chennaib cnáime*. The first two of these were forbidden by Patrick, but they seem to have survived as late as the 10th century. Part of the tremendous influence exercised by the *fili* was due to the belief in his powers of satire. By reciting a satirical poem or incantation he was able to raise blotches on the face of and so disfigure any person who aroused his displeasure. Numerous cases of this occur in Irish literature. The origin of the science of the *fili* is sometimes traced back to the *Dagda*, one of the figures of the Irish pantheon, and they were held in such esteem that the annalists give the obituaries of the head-ollams as if they were so many princes. With the introduction of Christianity they seem to have gradually superseded the druid, and their functions are therefore very wide. We are told that they acted in three capacities: (i) as story-tellers (*fer comgne* or *scélaige*); (2) as judges (*brithem*), including the professions of arbiters, legislators and lawyers; (3) as poets proper (*fercerte*). We are here only concerned with the *fili* in his capacity of story-teller and poet. In accordance with the minute classification of the various ranks of society in early Ireland, the social status of the literary man was very carefully defined. The degrees vary slightly in different documents, but the following list of ten from the *Senchus Mór* is very instructive: (1) The highest degree is the *ollam* (ollave), who knows 350 stories; (2) the *ánruth*, 175 stories; (3) the *clí*, 80 stories; (4) the *cana*, 60 stories; (5) the *doss*, 50 stories; (6) the *macfuirmid*, 40 stories; (7) the *fochlocon*, 30 stories; (8) the *drisac*, 20 stories; (9) the *taman*, 10 stories; (10) the *oblaire*, 7 stories. In LL. we are told that the stories (*scél*) are divided into primary and secondary, and that the latter are only obligatory on the first four of the grades enumerated. Again, certain styles of composition seem to have been the monopoly of certain grades. Thus the poem which was most highly rewarded and demanded the highest technical skill was called the *anomain*, and was the exclusive right of the *ollam*. A notable instance of this kind of composition is the *Amra* of Columba, attributed to Dallán Forgaill. The higher grades were allowed a number of attendants, whom the kings had to support along with the poet himself. Thus the *fochlocon* had two and the *doss* four attendants. In the 6th century Dallán Forgaill, the chief *fili* of Ireland, claimed the right to be attended by thirty *filid*, which was the number of the train allowed to the supreme king. The reigning monarch, Aed MacAinmirech, weary of the pretensions of the poets, attempted to banish them, which led to the famous assembly of Druim Ceta, where Columba intervened and reduced the number to twenty-four (the train of a provincial king). In the plan of the hall of Tara, preserved in LL. and YBL., the *sui littre* or doctor in theology has the seat of honour opposite the king. The *ollam brithem* or supreme judge or lawyer ranks with the highest rank of nobility, whilst the *ollam fili* is on a footing with the nobleman of the second degree.

We have already stated that the stories which formed the stock-in-trade of the poets were divided into primary and secondary stories. Of the latter there were 100, but little is known of them. However, several more or less complete lists of the primary stories have come down to us. The oldest catalogue (contained in LL.) gives the titles of 187 of these tales arranged under the following heads—destructions, cow-spoils, courtships, battles, caves, navigations, violent deaths, expeditions, elopements and conflagrations; together with the following, which also reckon as prime-stories—irruptions, visions, loves, hostings and migrations. Of these stories sixty-eight have been preserved in a more or less complete form. The tales enumerated in these catalogues, which in their substance doubtless go back to the 8th or even to the 7th century, fall into four main categories: (1) the mythological cycle, (2) the Cúchulinn cycle, (3) the Finn cycle, (4) pieces relating to events of the 5th, 6th and 7th centuries. Meyer has estimated that of the 550 titles of epic tales in D'Arbois's *Catalogue* about 400 are known to us, though many of them only occur in a very fragmentary state; and about 100 others have since been discovered which were not known in 1883.

The course of training undergone by the *fili* was a very lengthy one. It is commonly stated to have extended over twelve years, at the end of which time the student was thoroughly versed in all the legendary, legal, historical and topographical lore of his native country, in the use of the innumerable and excessively complicated Irish metres, in Ogam writing and Irish grammar. The instruction in the schools of poetry seems to have been entirely oral, and the course consisted largely in learning by heart the verses in which the native lore was enshrined. These schools of learning existed in one form or another down to the 17th century. In the early days the *fili* is represented as employing a mysterious archaic form of speech—doubtless full of obscure kennings—which was only intelligible to the initiated. An instance of this *bérla féine*, as it was termed, is the piece entitled *Acallam an Dá Shuad*(Colloquy of the Two Sages, *Rev. celt.* xxvi. 4 ff.). In this piece two *filid* of the 1st centuryA.D. are represented as contending in this dialect for the office of chief *ollam* of Ireland, much to the chagrin of King Conchobar, to whom their speeches were unintelligible. It was in consequence of this that Conchobar ruled that the office of *fili* should no longer carry with it of necessity the office of judge (*brithem*). It ought to be observed that the church never showed itself hostile to the *filid*, as it did to the druids. Dubthach, chief *fili* of Ireland in the time of St Patrick, is represented as the saint's constant companion, and the famous Flann Mainistrech (d. 1056), though a layman and *fili*, was head of the monastery school at Monasterboice.

Before leaving the subject of the literary classes, we must notice an inferior grade of poet—the bard. Like the official *filid*, the bards were divided into grades. There were both patrician and plebeian bards, each subdivided into **The bard.** eight degrees, having their own peculiar metres. Like the *fili* the bard had to go through a long course of study, and he was generally attached to the house of some chieftain whose praises he had to sing. In course of time the office of *fili*became extinct, owing to a variety of causes, and from the 13th to the 16th century we find the hitherto despised family bard stepping into the place of the most influential literary man in Ireland. His importance was fully realized by the English government, which did its best to suppress the order.

The medieval romances form by far the most attractive part of Irish literature, and it is to them that we shall first turn our attention. Two main groups of stories have to be distinguished. The one is the Ulster cycle, with **Medieval romances.**Conchobar and Cúchulinn as central figures. The other is the Southern or Leinster-Munster cycle, revolving round Finn and Ossian. Further stories dealing with mythological and historical personages will be mentioned in their turn.

The Ulster cycle may be regarded as Ireland's most important contribution to the world's literature. The chief and at the same time the lengthiest romance in which the heroes of this group figure is the great epic, the *Táin Bó Cualnge* or the **Ulster cycle.**626Cattle-raid of Cooley (Co. Louth). Here we find ourselves in a world of barbaric splendour, and we are constantly reminded of the Iliad, though the Irish epic from a purely literary point of view cannot bear comparison with the work of Homer. The main actors in the drama are Conchobar, king of Ulster, the great warrior Cúchulinn (seeCÚCHULINN), Ailill and Medb, king and queen of Connaught, **The "Táin."**and Fergus, Conchobar's predecessor as king of Ulster, now in exile in Connaught. These persons may or may not have actually lived, but the Irish annalists and synchronists agree in placing them about the beginning of the Christian era. And there cannot be any doubt as to the antiquity of the state of civilization disclosed in this great saga. It has been repeatedly pointed out that the Irish heroes are equipped and conduct themselves in the same manner as the Gauls described by the Greek traveller Posidonius, and Prof. W. Ridgeway has shown recently that several articles of dress and armour correspond exactly to the La Tène types of the continent. To mention a few primitive traits among many—the Irish champions of the *Táin* still fight in chariots, war-dogs are employed, whilst the heads of the slain are carried off in triumph and slung round the necks of the horses. It may also be mentioned that Emain Macha, Conchobar's residence, is reported by the annalists to have been destroyed in A.D. 323, and that portions of Meath, which is stated to have been made into a separate province in the 2nd century A.D., are in the*Táin* regarded as forming part of Ulster. Noteworthy is the exalted position occupied by the druid in the Ulster sagas, showing how little the romances were influenced by Christianity. No Roman soldier ever set foot in Ireland, and this early epic literature is of supreme value as a monument of primitive Celtic civilization. Ireland has always been a pastoral country. In early times no native coins were in circulation: the land belonged to the tribe. Consequently a man's property consisted mainly of cattle. Cattle-raids were an event of daily occurrence, and Sir Walter Scott has made us familiar with similar expeditions on the part of the Scottish Highlanders in the 18th century. Hence it is not a matter for surprise that the theme of the greatest Irish epic is a cattle-raid. At the time there were two wonderful bulls in Ireland, the Bond or Brown Bull of Cualnge, and the Findbennach or White-horn, belonging to Medb. These two animals are of no ordinary nature. Other stories represent them as having existed under many different forms before they were reborn as bulls. First they appear as swineherds belonging to the supernatural people of the *síd* of fairy mounds; then they are metamorphosed successively as ravens, warriors, sea-monsters and insects. It was Queen Medb's ambition to gain possession of the Brown Bull of Cualnge, and for this purpose she collected the united hosts of Ireland to raid the province of Ulster and carry him off. Medb chooses the season when she knows the Ulstermen are all incapacitated as the result of a curse laid upon them by a fairy woman. Cúchulinn alone is exempt from this debility.

The story is divided into a number of sections, and has been summarized by Miss Hull as follows:—(1) the prologue, relating, in the form of a night dialogue between Ailill and Medb, the dispute between them which brought about the raid; (2) the collecting of Medb's hosts and the preliminary movements of the army, during which period she first became aware of the presence and powers of Cúchulinn. Her inquiry of Fergus as to who this formidable foe is leads to a long section called (3) Cúchulinn's boy-deeds, in which Fergus relates the remarkable prodigies of Cúchulinn's youth, and warns Medb that, though the hero is but a beardless youth of seventeen, he will be more than a match for all her forces. (4) A long series of single combats, of which the first part of the tale is made up; they are at first gay and bombastic in character, but become more grave as they proceed, and culminate in the combat of Cúchulinn with his old companion, Fer Diad. This section contains the account of Cúchulinn's "distortion" or frenzy, which always occurred before any great output of the hero's energy, and of the rout of the hosts of Medb which followed it. (5) The general awakening of the warriors of Ulster from their lethargy, and their gathering by septs upon the Hill of Slane, clan by clan being described as it comes up in order. (6) The final Battle of Gairech and Ilgairech, followed (7) by the rout of Medb's army and (8) the tragic death of the bulls.

The text of the *Táin* has come down to us as a whole or in part in nearly a score of MSS., most of which, however, are modern. The most important MSS. containing the story are LU., LL. and YBL. Of these LU. and YBL. are substantially the same, whilst LL. contains a longer and fuller text later in both style and language. LL. attempts to give a complete and consistent narrative in more polished form. In ancient times there were doubtless other versions now lost, but from the middle of the 12th century the scribes seem to have taken few liberties with the text, whilst previously the *filid* were constantly transforming the material and adding fresh matter. The YBL. version preserves a number of forms as old as the O. Ir. glosses (*i.e.* 8th century or earlier), and a curious story contained in LL. seems to point to the fact that the *Táin* was first committed to writing in the 7th century. Senchán Torpeist, who lived in the first half of the 7th century and succeeded Dallán Forgaill as chief *ollam* of Ireland, summoned the *filid* to inquire which of them knew the *Táin* in its entirety. As they were only familiar with fragments he despatched them to discover it. One of them seated himself at the grave of Fergus MacRoig, who appeared to him in a mist and dictated the whole story to him in three days and three nights.

At this point it will be well to say a few words about the form of the *Táin*. The old Irish epic is invariably in prose with poems of varying length interspersed. The narrative and descriptive portions are in prose and are frequently followed by a brief epitome in verse. Dialogues, eulogies and laments also appear in metrical form. The oldest poems, termed rhetoric, which are best represented in LU., seem to be declamatory passages in rhythmical prose, not unlike the poetical passages in the Old Testament, and the original *Táin* may have consisted of such rhetorics bound together with short connecting pieces of prose. At a later date poems were inserted in the metres of the *filid* (particularly the quatrain of four heptasyllabic lines) which Thurneysen and Windisch consider to have been developed out of medieval Latin verse. When in course of time the old rhetorics became unintelligible they were often omitted altogether or new poems substituted. Thus the LL. version contains a larger number of poems than the LU.-YBL. copy, whilst LU. preserves a number of rhetorics which do not appear in the later MS. The prose portions in LU. are very poor from a literary point of view. These passages are abrupt, condensed and frequently obscure, with no striving after literary effect such as we find in LL. The form in which many episodes are cast is not unlike a mnemonic, leaving the story-teller to fill in the details himself. In the 11th century certain portions of the theme possessing great human interest were vastly extended, new poems were added, and in this manner such episodes come to form sagas complete in themselves. The most notable instance of this is the "Fight with Fer Diad," which is not contained in LU. The genesis of the *Táin* may thus be briefly summarized as follows. The story was first committed to writing in the 7th or 8th century, after which it was worked up by the *filid*. Extended versions existing in the 10th or 11th century form the basis of the copies we now possess.

Though the sagas of the Ulster cycle are eminently Irish and pagan in character and origin, it cannot be denied that traces of foreign influence are to be observed. A number of Latin and Norse loan-words occur in them, and there can be little doubt that the monkish scribes consciously thrust the supernatural element into the background. However, although figures of Vikings are unmistakable in a few cases, and in one story Cúchulinn is made to fight with Hercules, such foreign elements can easily be detected in the older tales. They only affect minor details, and do not influence the body of the romances.

From what we have already said it will be plain that the Irish epic is in a fluid state. The *Táin* is of interest in the history of literature as representing the preliminary stage through which the great verse epics of other nations have had to pass, but its 627value as a work of art is limited by its form. We must now say a few words about the character and style of these romances. As already stated, the atmosphere is frankly pagan and barbaric, with none of that courtly element which we find in the Arthurian epics. The two features which strike one most forcibly in the medieval Irish romances are dramatic force and humour. The unexpected and weird is always happening, the effect of which is considerably heightened by the grim nature of the actors. In particular the dialogues are remarkably brilliant and clever, and it is a matter for surprise that this gifted race never developed a drama of its own. This is doubtless partly due to the political conditions of the island. And, moreover, we are constantly struck by the lack of sustained effort which prevented the *filid* from producing great epics in verse. Dramatic material is abundantly present in the old epics, but it has never been utilized. As one might expect from the vernacular literature of Ireland, these romances are pervaded by a keen sense of humour. We feel that the story-teller is continually expecting a laugh and he exaggerates in true Irish fashion, so that the stories are full of extravagantly grotesque passages. In the later LL. version we notice a tendency to linger over pathetic situations, but this is unknown in the earlier stage. Perhaps the most serious defect of all Irish literary products is the lack of any sense of proportion, which naturally goes hand in hand with the love of the grotesque. Far too much attention is paid to trivial incidents and minute descriptions, however valuable the latter may be to the antiquarian, to the detriment of the artistic effect. Further, the story-teller does not know when to stop. He goes meandering on long after the main portion of the story is finished, with the result that Irish romances are apt to end in a most uninteresting anticlimax. Finally we are wearied with a constant repetition of the same epithets and similes, and with turgid descriptions; even the grotesque exaggerations pall when we find them to be stereotyped. But the early epics do not offend our sense of propriety in expression to the same extent as the later Finn cycle.

The *Táin Bó Cualnge* formed a kind of nucleus round which a number of other tales clustered. A number of these are called *remscéla* or introductory stories to the *Táin*. Such are the "Revealing of the Táin" (already mentioned), the "Debility of the Ultonians" (giving the story of the curse), "The Cattle-Driving of Regamon, Dartaid and Flidais," "*Táin bó Regamna*," "The Cattle-Driving of Fraech," "The Dispute of the Swineherds," telling the previous history of the Bulls, "The Capture of the Fairy Mound," "The Dream of Mac óc," the "Adventures of Nera," the "Wooing of Ferb." Other stories form a kind of continuation of the *Táin*. Thus the "Battle of Rosnaree" ("*Cath Ruis na Ríg*") relates how Conchobar, as a result of the loss of the Bull, sends an army against the kings of Leinster and Tara, and would have been routed but for the prowess of Cúchulin. The "Great Rout of the Plain of Murthemne" and "Cúchulinn's Death" tell how the hero's downfall is compassed by a monstrous brood of ill-shapen beings whose father and brothers had been slain by him during the *Táin*. He finally meets with his end at the hands of Lugaid, son of Curói mac Daire (the central hero of a Munster cycle which has not come down to us), and Erc, king of Tara. We are also told of the terrible vengeance taken on the murderers by Conall Cernach. Other stories deal with the "Conception of Conchobar," the "Conception of Cúchulinn," "The Glories of Conchobar's Reign," with an account of how he acquired the Throne from Fergus, "The Wooing of Emer and the Hero's Education in Scotland under Scathach," "The Siege of Howth," "Bricriu's Feast and the Exile of the Sons of Doel Dermait," "The Battle of the Boyne" (*Ériu*, vol. ii.), "The Deaths of Ailill, Medb and Conall Cernach," "Destruction of Bruden Dá Choca," "The Tragical Death of Conlaech at the hands of Cúchulinn his father," "The Deaths of Goll and Garbh," "The Sickbed of Cúchulinn," in which the hero is lured away for a time into the invisible land by a fairy, Fand, wife of Manandán, "The Intoxication of the Ultonians," telling of a wild raid by night across the entire extent of the island from Dún-da-Benn near Coleraine to the fort of Curói MacDaire at Temair-Luachra in Kerry, "The Death of Conchobar," "The Phantom Chariot of Cúchulinn," in which the hero is brought up from the grave to witness before St Patrick and King Loigaire to the truth of the Christian doctrine.

Four other stories in connexion with the Ulster cycle remain to be mentioned. The first is "*Scél mucci Maic Datho*" ("The Story of MacDatho's Pig"). Various writers of antiquity inform us that at the feasts of the Gauls the champion received the best portion of meat, which frequently led to brawls. In this savage but picturesque Irish story we find the Ulstermen vaunting their achievements against the Connaughtmen, until at last the contest lies between Conall Cernach and Cet MacMagach. Nowhere, perhaps, is the dramatic element better brought out.

Apart from the *Táin* the greatest and at the same time the longest saga in which Cúchulinn figures is *Fled Bricrend* (Bricriu's Feast). Bricriu is the mischief-maker among the Ulstermen, and he conceives the idea of building a banqueting hall in order to invite Conchobar and his nobles to a feast. After much hesitation they consent. Bricriu in turn incites the three chief heroes, Cúchulinn, Conall Cernach and Loigaire Buadach, to claim the champion's portion. He does the same thing with the spouses of the three warriors, who declaim in obscure verse the achievements and excellences of their several husbands in a passage entitled the "Women's War of Words." Loosely attached to this story follows a wild series of adventures in which the powers of the three champions are tested, Cúchulinn always proving his superiority. In order to decide the dispute, visits are paid to Medb at Rath Cruachan and to Curói in Kerry, and the story ends with the "beheading incident," which occurs in the romance of "Sir Gawayne and the Green Knight." *Fled Bricrend* presents a number of textual difficulties. The text of the oldest MS. (LU.) shows signs of contamination, and several versions of the story seem to have been current.

But the story of the Ulster cycle which is better known than any other, is the story of the "Tragical Death of the Sons of Usnech, or the Life and Death of Deirdre," one of the "Three Sorrows of Story-telling." This is the only tale of the group which has survived in the minds of the common people down to the present day. It is foretold of Deirdre, a girl-child of great beauty, that she will be the cause of great misfortunes, but Conchobar, having lost his wife, determines to have her brought up in solitude and marry her himself. However, the maiden chances to see a noble youth named Naisi, one of the three sons of Usnech, and persuades him to carry her off to Scotland, where they live for many years. At length they are induced to return after several of the most prominent Ulster warriors have gone bail for their safety. But Conchobar resorts to treachery, and the three sons of Usnech are slain, whilst the account of Deirdre's end varies. The oldest version of the story is found in LL., and the characters are as rugged and unsophisticated as those of the *Táin*. But in the later versions the savage features are toned down.

Before passing on, we must mention several old stories which are independent of the Ulster cycle, but which deal with events which are represented as having taken place before the Christian era. Few of the old romances deal directly with what we may call Irish mythology. The "Battle of Moytura" tells of the tremendous struggle between the Tuatha Dé Danann and their enemies, the Fomorian pirates. Connected with the events of this saga is the story of the "Tragic Deaths of the Sons of Tuirenn," which, though mentioned in Cormac's glossary, is not found in any MS. older than the 18th century. The three sons of Tuirenn have slain Cian, father of Lug Lamfhada, who lays upon them a huge eric-fine. They go through terrific ordeals and accomplish their task, but return home to die. This is the second of the "Three Sorrows of Story-telling." An old story dealing with Tuatha Dé Danann personages, but having a certain bearing on the Cúchulinn cycle, is the "Courtship of Étáin," who, though of supernatural (*síd*) birth, is wedded to Eochaid Airem, a mortal king. In her previous existence she was the wife of the supernatural personage Midir of Brí-leith, who wins back Étáin from her mortal husband in a game of chess and carries her off to his fairy mound.

For sake of completeness we may add the titles of two other 628well-known stories here. The one is the "Story of Baile the Sweet-spoken," which tells of the deaths of two lovers for grief at the false tidings of each other's death. The other is the "Fate of the Children of Lir," the third of the "Three Sorrows of Story-telling," which is only known in a modern dress. It relates how the four daughters of Lir (father of the sea-god Manandán and the original of Shakespeare's Lear) were changed into swans by a cruel stepmother, and how, after 900 years of wandering on the ocean, they at length regain their human form through the instrumentality of St Mochaomhog.

A large number of sagas, which claim to be founded on historical events, present a great similarity to the tales of the Ulster cycle. Most of them are mentioned in the old catalogues. We can only name the more important here. The "Destruction of Dind-Rig and Exile of Labraid Loingsech" relates how the kingdom of Leinster was snatched by one brother from another in the 6th century B.C., and how the son of the murdered prince with the aid of a British force sacked Dind-Rig, the fortress of the usurper. The story of the visit of the pigmies to the court of Fergus MacLeite, king of Ulster in the 2nd century B.C., is only contained in a 15th-century MS. This tale is commonly stated to have given Swift the idea of his *Gulliver's Travels to Lilliput*. "*Caithréim Chonghail Claringnigh*," which only occurs in a modernized 17th-century version, deals with a revolution in the province of Ulster, supposed to have taken place before the Christian era.

The most important Old Irish saga after the *Táin* is beyond doubt the *Destruction of Dá Derga's Hostel*, contained in LU. It deals with events in the reign of the High-King Conaire Mór, who is said by the annalists to have been slain in 43 B.C. after a reign of seventy years. Conaire, who was a descendant of the Étáin mentioned above, was a just ruler, and had banished among other lawless persons his own five cousin brothers. These latter devoted themselves to piracy and made common cause with one Ingcel, a son of the king of Britain, who had been outlawed by his father. The high-king was returning from Co. Clare when he found the whole of Meath in flames. He turned aside into Leinster and made for Dá Derga's hostel. The pirates perceive this, and Ingcel is sent to spy out the hostel and discover the size of Conaire's force. This gives the story-teller a chance for one of those lengthy minute descriptions of persons in which his soul delighted. This catalogue occupies one-half of the whole story. The pirates make their attack, and the king and most of his followers are butchered.

We can do no more than enumerate the titles of other historical tales: The "Destruction of the Hostel of MacDareo," describing the insurrection of the Aithech-Tuatha (1st centuryA.D.), "The Expulsion of the Déisi" and the "Battle of Mag Lemna" (2nd century A.D.), "Battle of Mag Mucrime" (A.D. 195 or A.D. 218), "Siege of Drom Damgaire" (3rd century), "Adventures of the Sons of Eochaid Muigmedóin, father of Niall Nóigiallach" (4th century), "Death of Crimthann" (reigned 366-378), "Death of Dathi" (d. 428), "Death of Murchertach, son of Erc," and "Death of Diarmait, son of Cerball" (6th century)

"Wooing of Becfola, who became the wife of Diarmait, son of Aed Slane" (reigned 657-664), "Battle of Mag Rath" (637), "Battle of Carn Conaill" (c. 648), "Death of Maelfothartaig MacRonain" (7th century), who was a kind of Irish Hippolytus, "Battle of Allen" (722).

It will be well to deal here with another class of story in its various stages of development. We have seen that in the older romances there is a close connexion between mortals and supernatural beings. The latter are represented as either inhabiting the *síd* mounds or as dwelling in islands out in the ocean, which are pictured as abodes of bliss and variously called *Mag Mell* (Plain of Delight), *Tír na n-Óc* (Land of Youth) and *Tír Tairngiri* (Land of Promise). The visits of mortals to the Irish Elysium form the subject of three romances which we must now examine. The whole question has been exhaustively dealt with by Kuno Meyer and Alfred Nutt in the *Voyage of Bran* (London, 1895-1897). Condla Caem, son of Conn Cétchathach, was one day seated by his father on the hill of Usnech, when he saw a lady in strange attire approaching invisible to all but himself. She describes herself, as coming from the "land of the living," a place of eternal delight, and invites the prince to return with her. Conn invokes the assistance of his druid to drive away the strange visitor, who in parting throws an apple to Condla. The young man partakes of no food save his apple, which does not diminish, and he is consumed with longing. At the end of a month the fairy-maiden again makes her appearance. Condla can hold out no longer. He jumps into the damsel's skiff of glass. They sail away and were seen no more. This is the *Imram* or Adventure of Condla Caem, the oldest text of which is found in LU. A similar story is entitled *Imram Brain maic Febail*, contained in YBL. and Rawlinson B 512 (the end also occurs in LU.), only with this difference that Bran, with twenty-seven companions, puts to sea to discover *tír na mban* (the land of maidens). After spending some time there, one of his comrades is seized with home-sickness. They return, and the home-sick man, on being set ashore, immediately turns to dust. A later story preserved in BB., YBL. and the Book of Fermoy, tells of the visit of Cormac, grandson of Conn Cétchathach, to Tír Tairngiri. These themes are also worked into tales belonging to the Ossianic cycle, and Finn and Ossian in later times become the typical warriors who achieve the quest of the Land of Youth. The romances we have just mentioned are almost entirely pagan in character, but a kindred class of story shows us how the old ideas were transformed under the influence of Christianity. A typical instance is *Imram curaig Maelduin*, contained in YBL. and in part in LU. Maelduin constructs a boat and sets out on a voyage with a large company to discover the murderer of his father. This forms the framework of the story. Numerous islands in the ocean are visited, each containing some great marvel. *Imram ua Corra* (Book of Fermoy) and *Imram Snedgusa ocus Mac Riagla*(YBL.) contain the same plan, but in this case the voyage is undertaken as an expiation for crime. In the 11th century an unknown monkish writer compiled the *Navigatio S. Brendani*, drawing the material for his episodes from *Imram curaig Maelduin*. This famous work only appears in an Irish dress in a confused and disconnected "Life of St Brendan" in the Book of Lismore. The same MS. contains yet another voyage, the "Adventure of Tadg MacCéin."

We must now turn our attention to the later heroic cycle, commonly called the Fenian or Ossianic. Unfortunately the origin of the stories and poems connected with Finn and his warriors is obscure, and scholars are by no **Fenian or Ossianic cycle.** means agreed over the question (see FINN MAC COOL). In the earlier cycle the figures and the age in which they live are sharply drawn, and we can have no hesitation in assuming that the *Táin* represents in the main the state of Ireland at the beginning of the Christian era. Finn and his companions are nebulous personages, and, although it is difficult to discover the actual starting-point of the legend, from the 12th century onwards we are able to trace the development of the saga with some degree of certainty. A remarkably small amount of space is devoted to this cycle in the oldest MSS. Of the 134 pages contained in LU. only half-a-dozen deal with Finn as against 58 with Cúchulinn. In LL. the figures are, Ulster cycle 100 pp., Ossianic 25 pp., the latter being mainly made up of short ballads, whilst in 15th-century MSS., such as the Book of Lismore and Laud 610, the proportion is overwhelmingly in favour of the later group. Again in Urard MacCoisi's list of tales, which seems to go back to the 10th century, only two appear to deal with subjects taken from the Ossianic cycle. In the first instance Finn seems to have been a poet, and as such he appears in the 12th-century MSS., LU. and LL. Thus the

272

subjects of the Ossianic cycle in the earliest MSS. appear in a new dress. The vehicle of the older epic is prose, but the later cycle is clothed in ballad form. Of these ballads about a dozen, apart from poems in the *Dindsenchus* are preserved in LU., LL. and YBL., and none of these poems are probably much older than the 11th century. In the commentary to the *Amra* of Columbkille a beautiful poem on winter is attributed to Finn. At the same time we do find a few prose tales, *e.g.* "*Fotha catha* 629 *Cnucha*" in LU., describing the death of Cumall, Finn's father, and in LL. and Rawlinson B 502, part of which Zimmer assigns to the 7th century, we have the first story in which Finn actually occurs. But it is remarkable that in no case do tales belonging to the Finn cycle contain any of the old rhetorics which occur in the oldest of the Ulster romances. Already in LL., by the side of Finn, Ossian, Cáilte and Fergus Finnbel are represented as poets, and the strain of lament over the glories of the past, so characteristic a feature of the later developments of the legend, is already sounded. Hence by the 12th century the stories of the Fiann and their destruction at the battle of Gabra must have been fully developed, and from this time onward they appear gradually to have supplanted the Cúchulinn cycle in popular favour. Several reasons have been assigned for this. In the first place until the time of Brian Boroime the high-kings of Ireland had almost without exception been drawn from Ulster, and consequently the northern traditions were pre-eminent. This exclusiveness on the part of the north was largely broken down by the Viking invasions, and during the 11th century the leading poets were attached to the court of Brian and his descendants. In this manner an opportunity was afforded to the Leinster-Munster Fenian cycle to develop into a national saga. John MacNeill has pointed out Finn's connexion with a Firbolg tribe, and maintains that the Fenian cycle was the property of the subject race. Zimmer has attempted to prove with great plausibility that Finn and his warriors were transformed on the model of the Ulster heroes. Thus one text deals with the boyish exploits of Finn in the manner of Cúchulinn's youthful feats recorded in the *Táin*. And it is possible that the *Siaburcharpat Conchulainn* gave rise to the idea of connecting Ossian and Cáilte with Patrick. As Cúchulinn was opposed to the whole of Ireland in the *Táin*, so Finn, representing Ireland, is pitted against the whole world in the *Battle of Ventry*.

We have already stated that the form assumed by the stories connected with Finn in the earliest MSS. is that of the ballad, and this continued down to the 18th century. But here again the Irish poets showed themselves incapable of rising from the ballad to the true epic in verse, and in the 14th century we find the prose narrative of the older cycle interspersed with verse again appearing. The oldest composition of any length which deals with the Ossianic legends is the *Acallam na Senórach* or Colloquy of the Old Men, which is mainly preserved in three 15th-century MSS., the Book of Lismore, Laud 610 and Rawlinson 487. In this text we have the framework common to so much of the later Ossianic literature. Ossian and Cáilte are represented as surviving the battle of Gabra and as living on until the time of Patrick. The two warriors get on the best of terms with the saint, and Cáilte is his constant companion on his journey through Ireland. Patrick inquires the significance of the names of the places they visit, and Cáilte recounts his reminiscences. In this manner we are given nearly a hundred stories, the subjects of some of which occur in the short ballads in older MSS., whilst others appear later as independent tales. A careful comparison of the *Acallam* with the Cúchulinn stories, whether from the point of view of civilization or language or art, discloses that the first lengthy composition of the Ossianic cycle is but a feeble imitation of the older group. All that had become unintelligible in the Ulster stories, owing to their primitive character, is omitted, and in return for that the reminiscences of the Viking age play a very prominent part.

With the 16th century we reach the later treatment of the legend in the *Battle of Ventry*. In this tedious story Daire, the king of the whole world, comes to invade Ireland with all his forces, but is repulsed by Finn and his heroes. The *Battle of Ventry*, like all later stories, is a regular medley of incidents taken from the writers of antiquity and European medieval romance. The inflated style to which the Irishman is so prone is here seen at its worst, and we are treated to a nauseous heaping up of epithet upon epithet, *e.g.* we sometimes find as many as twenty-seven adjectives accompanying a substantive running in alliterating sets of three.

Of greater literary interest are the later ballads connected with Finn and Ossian. The latter has become the typical mouthpiece of the departed glory of the Fenian warriors, and Nutt has pointed out that there is a striking difference in spirit between the *Acallam na Senórach* and the 15th-16th century poems. In the latter Ossian is represented as a "pagan, defiant and reckless, full of contempt and scorn for the howling clerics and their churlish low-bred deity," whilst Patrick is a sour and stupid fanatic, harping with wearisome monotony on the damnation of Finn and all his comrades. The earliest collection of these later Ossianic poems is that made in Scotland by James Macgregor, dean of Lismore, early in the 16th century. Another miscellany is the *Duanaire Finn*, a MS. in the Franciscan monastery in Dublin, compiled from earlier MSS. in 1627. This "song-book," which has been edited for the Irish Texts Society by John MacNeill (part i. 1908), contains no less than sixty-nine Ossianic ballads, amounting in all to some ten thousand lines. Other Ossianic poems of dates varying from the 15th to the 18th century have been published in the *Transactions of the Ossianic Society* (Dublin, 1854-1861), including amongst others "The Battle of Gabhra," "Lamentation of Oisin (Ossian) after the Fenians," "Dialogue between Oisin and Patrick," "The Battle of Cnoc an Air," and "The Chase of Sliabh Guilleann." These ballads still survive amongst the peasants at the present day. We further possess a number of prose romances, which in their present form date from the 16th to the 18th century; *e.g.* *The Pursuit of Diarmaid and Gráinne, Finn and Gráinne, Death of Finn, The Clown in the Drab Coat, Pursuit of the Gilla Decair, The Enchanted Fort of the Quicken-tree, The Enchanted Cave of Ceis Corann, The Feast in the House of Conan.*

At the present moment it is impossible to give a complete survey of the other branches of medieval Irish literature. The attention of scholars has been largely devoted to the publication of the sagas to the neglect of other portions of the wide field. An excellent survey of the subject is given by K. Meyer, *Die Kultur der Gegenwart*, i. xi. 1. pp. 78-95 (Berlin-Leipzig, 1909).

We have already pointed out that as early as the Old Irish period nameless Irish poets were singing the praises of nature in a strain which sounds to our ears peculiarly modern. At the present time it is difficult to say how much of **Nature poetry.** what is really poetic in Irish literature has come down to us. Our MSS. preserve whole reams of the learned productions of the *filid* which were so much prized in medieval Ireland, but it is, generally speaking, quite an accident if any of the delightful little lyrics entered in the margins or on blank spaces in the MSS. have remained. The prose romances sometimes contain beautiful snatches of verse, such as the descriptions of Mag Mell in *Serglige Conculaind, Tochmarc Étáine,* and the *Voyage of Bran* or the *Lament of Cúchulinn over Fer Díad.* Mention has also been made of the exquisite nature poems ascribed to Finn, which have been collected into a pamphlet with English renderings by Kuno Meyer (under the title of "Four Old Irish Songs of Summer and Winter," London, 1903). The same writer points out that the ancient treatise on Irish prosody published by Thurneysen contains no less than 340 quotations from poems, very few of which have been preserved in their entirety. To Meyer we also owe editions of two charming little texts which sufficiently illustrate the lyrical powers of the early poets. The one is a poem referred to the 10th century in the form of a colloquy between Guaire of Aidne and his brother Marban. Guaire inquires of his brother why he prefers to live in a hut in the forest, keeping the herds and swine of the king, to dwelling in the king's palace. The question calls forth so wonderful a description of the delights of nature as viewed from a shieling that Guaire exclaims, "I would give my glorious kingship to be in thy company, Marban" (*King and Hermit*, ed. with trans. by K. Meyer, London, 1901). Another text full of passionate emotion and tender regret ascribed to the 9th century tells of the parting of a young poet and poetess, who after plighting their troth are separated for ever (*Liadain and Curithir*, ed. with trans. by K. Meyer, London, 1902). In the *Old Woman of Beare* (publ. K. Meyer in *Otia Merseiana*) an old hetaira laments her departed youth, comparing her life to the ebbing of the tide (10th century).

630

We must now step aside from pure literature and turn our attention to the various productions of the professional learned classes of Ireland during the middle ages. The range of subjects coming under this heading is a very wide one, comprising history, genealogies,

274

hagiology, topography, grammar, lexicography and metre, law and medicine. It will perhaps be as well first of *Professional literature.*all to deal with the learned *filid* whose works have been preserved. Irish tradition preserves the names of a number of antiquarian poets of prehistoric or early medieval times, such as Amergin, one of the Milesian band of invaders; Moran Roigne, son of Ugaine Mór, Adna and his successor Ferceirtne, Torna (c. 400), tutor to Niall Nóigiallach, Dallán Forgaill, Senchán Torpéist, and Cennfaelad (d. 678), but the poems attributed to these writers are of much later date. We can only enumerate the chief of those whose works have been preserved. To Maelmura (d. 887) is attributed a poem on the Milesian migrations. About the same time lived Flanagan, son of Cellach, who wrote a long composition on the deaths of the kings of Ireland, preserved in YBL., and Flann MacLonáin (d. 918), called by the Four Masters the Virgil of Ireland, eight of whose poems have survived, containing in all about 1000 lines. Cormacan, son of Maelbrigde (d. 946), composed a vigorous poem on the circuit of Ireland performed by Muirchertach, son of Niall Glúndub. A poet whose poems are most valuable from an antiquarian point of view is Cinaed Ua h-Artacáin (d. 975). Some 800 lines of his have been preserved in LL. and elsewhere. Contemporary with him is Eochaid O'Flainn (d. c. 1003), whose chief work is a long chronological poem giving a list of the kings of Ulster from Cimbaeth down to the destruction of Emain in 331. A little later comes MacLiac (d. 1016), who celebrated in verse the glories of the reign of Brian Boroime. His best-known work is a lament over Kincora, the palace of Brian. Contemporary with MacLiac is MacGilla Coim Urard MacCoisi (d. 1023). To Cúán ua Lothcháin (d. 1024), chief poet in the reign of Maelsheachlainn II., are ascribed poems on the antiquities of Tara. Sixteen hundred lines of his have come down to us. A writer who enjoyed a tremendous reputation in medieval Ireland was Flann Mainstrech (d. 1056), who in spite of his being a layman was head of the monastery school at Monasterboice. He is the author of no fewer than 2000 lines in LL., and many other poems of his are contained in other MSS. His best-known work is a *Book of Synchronisms* of the kings of Ireland and those of the ancient world. We have also poems from his pen on the monarchs descended from Niall Nóigiallach and on the chronology of the high-kings and provincial kings from the time of Loigaire. Flann's successor, Gilla Coemgin (d. 1072), gives us a chronological poem dealing with the annals of the world down to A.D. 1014. He also is the author of the Irish version of Nennius which contains substantial additions dealing with early Ireland. Minor writers of the same nature whose works have come down to us are Colmán O'Sesnáin (d. 1050), Néide ua Maelchonaire (d. 1136), Gilla na noem ua Duinn (d. 1160), Gilla Moduda O'Cassidy (1143). In the 13th century these historical poems become very rare. In the next century we again find antiquarian poets of whom the best-known is John O'Dugan (d. 1372). His most valuable composition treats of the tribes of the northern half of Ireland at the time of the northern conquest. This work, containing 1660 lines in all in debide metre, was completed by his younger contemporary Gilla na naem O'Huidhrin. From the beginning of the 13th century the official poets began to give way to the hereditary bards and families of scribes. Among the chief bardic families we may mention the O'Dalys, the MacWards, the O'Higinns, the MacBrodys and the MacDaires. We must here content ourselves with glancing at a few of the more prominent names. Muiredach Albanach (c. 1214-1240), whose real name was O'Daly, has left behind in addition to the religious verses a considerable number of poems in praise of various patrons in Ireland and Scotland. He is said by Skene to be the first of the Macvurrichs, bards to Macdonald of Clanranald. A number of his compositions are preserved in the Book of the Dean of Lismore. Gilla Brigde MacConmidhe was a contemporary of the last-mentioned bard. He wrote a number of poems in praise of the O'Neills and O'Donnells. We may next mention the name of an abbot of Boyle, Donnchad Mór O'Dálaig (d. 1244), a writer whose extant poems are usually of a religious character. Many of them are addressed to the Virgin. Most of them appear in late MSS., but some few are preserved in the Book of the Hy Maine. Donnchad Mór is said to be the greatest religious poet that Ireland has produced. Many other members of the O'Daly family belonging to the 14th and 15th centuries have left poems behind them, but we cannot mention them here. Angus O'Daly, who lived in the second half of the 16th century, was employed by the English to satirize the chief Gaelic families in Ireland. Two members of the O'Higinn family deserve mention, Tadg mór O'Higinn (d. 1315). and Tadg

Óg O'Higinn (d. 1448), a voluminous writer who eulogized the O'Neills, O'Connors and O'Kellys. Tadg Óg also composed a number of religious poems, which enjoyed enormous popularity in both Ireland and Scotland. A *duanaire* was inserted into YBL., which contains some forty poems by him.

Closely connected with the compositions of the official poets are the works of native topography. Most of the sagas contain a number of explanations of the origins of place-names. The *Dindsenchus* is a compilation of such etymologies. But its chief value consists in the amount of legendary matter it contains, adduced in support of the etymologies given. The *Dindsenchus* has come down to us in various forms both in prose and in verse. Irish tradition ascribes it to Amergin MacAmalgaid, who lived in the 6th century, but if the kernel of the work goes back as early as this it must have been altered considerably in the course of the centuries. Both prose and verse forms of it are contained in LL. A kindred compilation is the *Cóir Anmann* (Fitness of Names), which does for personal names what the *Dindsenchus* does for geographical names. We further possess a versified compendium of geography for educational purposes dealing with the three continents, from the pen of Airbertach MacCosse-dobráin (10th century).

No people on the face of the globe have ever been more keenly interested in the past of their native country than the Irish. This will already have been patent from the compositions of the *filid*, and now we may describe briefly **History.** the historical works in prose which have come down to us. The latter may be divided into two classes, (1) works containing a connected narrative, (2) annals. Closely allied to these are the sagas dealing with the high-kings. Even in the serious historical compositions we often find the manner of the sagas imitated, *e.g.* the supernatural plays a prominent part, and we are treated to the same exaggerated descriptions. The earliest of these histories is the wars of the Gael and Gall (*Cogad Gaedel re Gallaib*), which gives an account of the Viking invasions of Ireland, the career of Brian Boroime and the overthrow of the Norsemen at the battle of Clontarf. This composition, a portion of which is contained in LL., is often supposed to be in part the work of MacLiac, and it is plain from internal evidence that it must have been written by an eye-witness of the battle, or from materials supplied by a person actually present. Numerous shorter tracts dealing with the same period exist, but as yet few of them have been published. *Caithreim Cellacháin Caisil* treats of the conflicts between the Vikings and the Irish, and the *Leabhar Oiris* gives an account of Irish history from 979 to 1027. Compilations relating to local history are the Book of Fenagh and the Book of Munster. Another ancient work also partly preserved in LL. is the Book of Invasions (*Leabhar Gabhála*). This deals with the five prehistoric invasions of Ireland (see IRELAND: *Early History*) and the legendary history of the Milesians. The most complete copy of the *Leabhar Gabhála* which has been preserved was compiled by Michael O'Clery about 1630. The *Boroma* or History of the Leinster Tribute contained in LL. belongs rather to romance. Another history is the *Triumphs of Turlough O'Brian*, written about the year 1459 by John MacCraith, a Munster historian (edited by S.H. O'Grady, Camb. Press). This inflated composition is an important source of information on Munster history from the landing of the Normans to the middle of the 14th century. We also possess 631several documents in Irish concerning the doings of the O'Neills and O'Donnells at the close of the 16th century. A life of Hugh Roe O'Donnell, by Lughaidh O'Clery, has been published, and a contemporary history of the *Flight of the Earls*, by Tadhg O'Cianan, was being prepared in 1908. But the most celebrated Irish historian is certainly Geoffrey Keating (c. 1570-1646), who is at the same time the greatest master of Irish prose. Keating was a Munster priest educated in France, who drew down upon himself the displeasure of the English authorities and had to go into hiding. He travelled up and down Ireland examining all the ancient records, and compiled a history of Ireland down to the Norman Conquest. His work, entitled *Forus Feasa ar Eirinn*, was never published, but it circulated from end to end of Ireland in MS. Keating's history is anything but critical. Its value for the scholar lies in the fact that the author had access to many important sources of information now lost, and has preserved accounts of events independent of and differing from those contained in the Four Masters. In addition to the history and a number of poems, Keating is also the author of two theological works in Irish, the Defence of the Mass

(*Eochairsgiath an Aifrinn*) and a collection of sermons entitled the Three Shafts of Death (*Trí biorghaoithe an Bháis*), which are models of Irish prose.

From the writers of historical narrative we turn to the annalists, the most important sources of information with regard to Irish history. We have already mentioned the *Synchronisms* of Flann Mainistrech. Apart from this work the earliest collection of annals which has come down to us is the compilation by Tigernach O'Braein (d. 1088), abbot of Clonmacnoise. Tigernach, whose work is partly in Latin, partly in Irish, states that all Irish history previous to 305 B.C. is uncertain. No perfect copy is known of this work, but several fragments are in existence. The *Annals of Innisfallen* (a monastery on an island in the Lower Lake of Killarney), which are also in Latin and Irish, were perhaps compiled about 1215, though they may have begun two centuries earlier. The invaluable *Annals of Ulster* were compiled on Belle Isle on Upper Lough Erne by Cathal Maguire (d. 1498), and afterwards continued by two different writers down to 1604. This work, which deals with Irish affairs from A.D. 431, exists in several copies. The *Annals of Loch Cé* (near Boyle in Roscommon) were copied in 1588 and deal with Irish events from 1014 to 1636. The *Annals of Connaught* run from 1224 to 1562. The *Chronicon Scotorum*, one copy of which was transcribed about 1650 by the famous antiquary Duald MacFirbis, deals with Irish affairs down to 1135. The *Annals of Boyle* extend down to 1253. The *Annals of Clonmacnoise*, which come down to 1408, only exist in an English translation made by Connell MacGeoghegan in 1627. The most important of all these collections is the *Annals of the Four Masters* (so christened by Colgan), compiled in the Franciscan monastery of Donegal by Michael, Conary and Cucogry O'Clery and Ferfesa O'Mulconry. The O'Clerys were for a long period the hereditary ollams to the O'Donnells. Michael O'Clery (1575-1643), the greatest of the four, was a lay brother in the order of St Francis, and devoted his whole life to the history of Ireland. He collected all the historical MSS. he could find, and was encouraged in his undertaking by Fergal O'Gara, prince of Coolavin, who paid all expenses. The great work, which was begun in 1632 and finished in 1636, begins with the arrival in Ireland of Ceasair, granddaughter of Noah, and comes down to 1616. Nearly all the materials from which O'Clery drew his statements are now lost. O'Clery is also the author of a catalogue of the kings of Ireland, the genealogies of the Irish saints, and the Martyrology of Donegal and the Book of Invasions.

Of less interest, but every whit as important, are the lists of genealogies which occupy a great deal of space in LL., YBL. and BB., and two Trinity College, Dublin, MSS. (H. 3.18 and H. 2.4). But by far the most important collection of all is that made by the last great shanachie Duald MacFirbis, compiled between 1650 and 1666 in the college of St Nicholas at Galway. The only portions of any considerable length which have as yet been published deal with two Connaught tribes; viz. the Hy Fiachrach from Duald mac Firbis and the Hy Maine (O'Kellys), and a Munster tribe, the Corcalaidhe, both from YBL. Valuable information with regard to early Irish history is often contained in the prophecies or, as they are sometimes termed, *Baile* (*raptures, visions*), a notable example of which is *Baile in Scáil* (Vision of the Phantom).

When we turn from secular to religious themes we find that Ireland is also possessed of a very extensive Christian literature, which is extremely valuable for the comparative study of medieval literature. Apart from the martyrologies **Religious literature.** already mentioned in connexion with Oengus the Culdee, a number of lives of saints and other ecclesiastical literature have come down to us. One of the most important documents is the Tripartite Life of St Patrick, which cannot very well have been composed before the 10th or 11th century, as it is full of the extravagant miracles which occur in the later lives of saints. The work consists of three separate homilies, each complete in itself. A later version of the Tripartite Life was printed by Colgan in 1647. The *Leabhar Breac* contains a quantity of religious tracts, most of which have been published. R. Atkinson issued a number of them under the title of *Passions and Homilies from Leabhar Breac* (Dublin, 1887). These are not original Irish compilations, but translations from Latin lives of saints. Nor do they deal with the lives of any Irish saints. Stokes has published nine lives of Irish saints from the Book of Lismore, including Patrick, Brigit, Columba, Brendan, Findian (Clonard), Ciaran, Senan, Findchua and Mochua. They are written in the form of homilies preceded by short explanations of a text of scripture. These lives also occur in the *Leabhar Breac*. Other lives of saints have been published by O'Grady in *Silva Gadelica*. The longest life of St Columba was compiled in 1536 at the command of Manus O'Donnell. This tedious work is a specimen of hagiology at its worst. The *Leabhar Breac* further contains a number of legends, such as those on the childhood of Christ, and scattered through many MSS. are short anecdotes of saints which are very instructive.

But the most interesting Irish religious text is the *Vision of Adamnan* (preserved in LU.), which Stokes assigns to the 11th century. The soul of Adamnan is represented as leaving his body for a space to visit heaven and hell under the conduct of an angel. The whole treatment of the theme challenges comparison with Dante's great poem, but the Irish composition contains many ideas peculiar to the land of its origin. Later specimens of this kind of literature tend to develop into grotesque buffoonery. We may mention the *Vision of Fursae*, the *Vision of Tundale* (Tnugdal), published by V. Friedel and K. Meyer (Paris, 1907), Laisrén's *Vision of Hell* and the *Vision of Merlino*. A further vision attributed to Adamnan contains a stern denunciation of the Irish of the 11th century. Another form of religious composition, which was very popular in medieval Ireland, was the prophecy in verse, but scarcely any specimens have as yet been published. Kuno Meyer edited a tract on the Psalter in his *Hibernica Minora* from a 15th century Oxford MS., but he holds that the text goes back to 750. A number of collections of monastic rules both in prose and verse have been edited in *Ériu*, and the MSS. contain numerous prayers, litanies and religious poems.

In LU. are preserved two sermons, *Scéla na esergi* (Tidings of Resurrection) and *Scéla lái brátha* (Tidings of Doomsday); and a number of other homilies have been published, such as the "Two Sorrows of the Kingdom of Heaven," "The Penance of Adam," the "Ever-new Tongue," and one on "Mortals' Sins." All the homilies contained in LB. have been published by R. Atkinson in his *Legends and Homilies from Leabhar Breac* (Dublin, 1887), and E. Hogan, *The Irish Nennius* (Dublin, 1895). The popular "Debate of the Body and the Soul" appears in Ireland in the form of a homily. A collection of maxims and a short moral treatise have been published by K. Meyer.

For the religious literature in general the reader may refer to O'Curry, *Lectures on the MS. Materials of Ancient Irish History* (pp. 339-434), and G. Dottin, "Notes bibliographiques sur l'ancienne littérature chrétienne de l'Irlande," in *Revue d'histoire et de litterature religieuses*, v. 162-167. See also *Revue celtique*, xi. 391-404. ib. xv. 79-91.

632

Here we may perhaps mention an extraordinary production entitled *Aisling Meic Conglinne*, the Vision of Mac Conglinne, found in LB. and ascribed to the twelfth century (ed. K. Meyer, London, 1892). Cathal MacFinguine, king of Munster (d. 737), was possessed by a demon of gluttony and is cured by the recital of a strange vision by a vagrant scholar named MacConglinne. The composition seems to be intended as a satire on the monks, and in particular as a travesty of medieval hagiology. Another famous satire, entitled the Proceedings of the Great Bardic Institution, holds up the professional bards and their extortionate methods to ridicule. This curious work contains the story of how the great epic, the *Táin bó Cualnge*, was recovered (see *Transactions of the Ossianic Society*, vol. v.).

Collections of pithy sayings in the form of proverbs and maxims must have been made at a very early period. Not the least remarkable are the so-called Triads (publ. K. Meyer, Dublin, 1906), which illustrate every statement with **Gnomic literature.**3 examples. Over 200 such triads were brought together in the 9th century. There are also two documents attributed to 1st-century personages, "The Testament of Morann MacMóin to his son Feradach," which is quoted as early as the 8th century, and "The Instructions of Cúchulinn to his foster-son Lugaid." K. Meyer has published *Tecosca Cormaic* or the Precepts of Cormac MacAirt to his son Cairpre (Dublin, 1909). Other collections such as the *Senbriathra Fithail* still await publication.

With that enthusiasm for the classics which is characteristic of the Irish, it is not strange that we should find medieval versions of some of the better-known authors of antiquity. It is interesting to note that only those works are **Classical stories.**translated that could be utilized by the professional story-teller. So much so, that in the ancient (10th century) catalogue of sagas enumerated by Urard MacCoisi we find mention of *Togail Troi* and *Scéla Alexandir maic Pilip*. We get descriptions of battle weapons and clothing similar to those occurring in the native sagas. *Togail Troi* is taken from the medieval prose version, *Historia de Excidio Troiae* of Dares Phrygius. The oldest Irish copy is found in LL. This version is exceedingly valuable, as it enables us to determine the meaning of words and formulas in the sagas which are otherwise obscure. An Irish abstract of the *Odyssey*, following an unknown source, and part of the story of Theseus have been published by K. Meyer. *Scéla Alexandir* is preserved in LB. and BB. *Imthechta Aeniusa*, taken from the *Aeneid*, is contained in BB. A number of MSS. contain the *Cath Catharda*, a version of books vi. and vii. (?) of Lucan's *Pharsalia*, which has been published by Wh. Stokes. There is further at least one MS. containing a version of Statius's *Thebaid* and of Heliodorus's *Aethiopica*. Somewhat later, the medieval literature of western Europe comes to be represented in translations. Thus we have Irish versions, amongst others of the *Gesta Romanorum*, the *Historia Brittonum*, the Wars of Charlemagne, the History of the Lombards, Sir John Maundeville's Travels (trans. by Fingin O'Mahony in 1475), the Book of Ser Marco Polo (abridged), Guy Earl of Warwick, Bevis of Southampton, the Quest of the Holy Grail, Octavian, the chronicle of Turpin, Barlaam and Josaphat, and the story of Fierabras. The Arthurian cycle is developed in independent fashion in the Adventures of the Eagle Boy and the Adventures of the Crop-eared Dog. For translation literature see M. Nettlau, *Revue celtique*, x. pp. 184, 460-461.

Hand in hand with the interest of the medieval Irish scholars in the history of their island goes the cultivation of the native tongue. Owing to the profound changes produced by the working of the Irish laws of accent and initial **Philology.** mutation, it is doubtful if any other language lends itself so well to wild etymological speculation. By the beginning of the Middle Irish period a good part of the cumbrous Old Irish verb-system had become obsolete, and texts which were at all faithfully copied had to be plentifully supplied with glosses. Moreover, if, as is probable, all the historical and legal lore was in verse, a large part of it must have been unintelligible except to those who knew the *bérla féne*. But even before this Cormac mac Cuillenáin, the bishop-king of Cashel (d. 903), had compiled a glossary of archaic words which are accompanied by explanations, etymologies, and illustrative passages containing an amount of invaluable information concerning folk-lore and legendary history. This glossary has come down to us in various recensions all considerably later in date than the original work (the oldest copy is in LB.). Later collections of archaic words are O'Mulconry's Glossary (13th century), the Lecan Glossary (15th century), which draws principally from the glosses in the *Liber Hymnorum*, O'Davoren's Glossary (16th century), drawn principally from the Brehon Laws, a 16th century list of Latin and Irish names of plants employed in medicine, and O'Clery's Glossary (published at Louvain, 1643). BB. contains a curious tract on Ogamic writing. An Irish treatise on grammar, called *Uraicept na n-éces*, the Poet's Primer, traditionally ascribed to Cennfaelad and others, is contained in BB. and YBL. It appears to be a kind of medley of Donatus and the notions of the medieval Irish concerning the origin of their language. The St Gall glosses on Priscian contain Irish terms for all the nomenclature of the Latin grammarians, and show how extensive was the use made of Irish even in this department of learning.

Thurneysen had edited from BB., Laud 610 and a TCD. MS. three treatises on metric which give an account of the countless metres practised by the *filid*. It is impossible for us here to enter into the question of Irish prosody in any **Prosody.** great detail. We have seen that there is some reason for believing that the primitive form of Irish verse was a kind of rhythmical alliterative prose as contained in the oldest versions of the sagas. The *filid* early became acquainted with the metres of the Latin church hymns, whence rhyme was introduced into Ireland. (This is the view of Thurneysen and Windisch. Others like Zeuss have maintained that rhyme was an invention of the Irish.) In any case the *filid* evolved an intricate system of rhymes for which it is difficult to find a parallel. The medieval metres are called by the general name of *Dán Dírech*, "Direct Metre." Some of the more general principles were as follows. The verses are grouped in stanzas of four lines, each stanza being complete in itself. Each line must contain a fixed number of syllables, whilst the different metres vary as to the employment of internal and end rhyme, assonance and alliteration. The Irish elaborated a peculiar system of consonantal correspondence which counted as rhyme. The consonants were divided with a considerable degree of phonetic accuracy into six groups, so that a voiceless stop (c) rhymes with another voiceless stop (t, p), a voiced stop (b) with another voiced stop (d, g), and so forth. The commonest form of verse is the four-line stanza of seven syllables. Such a verse with rhymes *abab* and monosyllabic or dissyllabic finals belongs to the class *rannaigecht*. A similar stanza with *aabb* rhymes is the basis of the so-called *debide* (cut in two) metres. A peculiarity of the latter is that the rhyming word ending the second line must contain at least one syllable more than the rhyming word which ends the first. Another frequently employed metre is the *rindard*, consisting of lines of six syllables with dissyllabic endings. In the metrical treatises examples are given of some 200 odd metres. The result of the complicated technique evolved in Ireland was an inclination to sacrifice sense to musical harmony. See K. Meyer, *A Primer of Irish Metrics* (Dublin,1909).

We can conclude this survey of medieval Irish literature by mentioning briefly two departments of learning to which much attention was paid in Ireland. These are law and medicine. The so-called Brehon Laws (*q.v.*) are **Law.** represented as having been codified and committed to writing in the time of St Patrick. There is doubtless some grain of truth in this statement, as a fillip may have been given to this codification by the publication of the Theodosian Code, which was speedily followed by the codes of the various Teutonic tribes. The Brehon Laws were no doubt originally transmitted from teacher to pupil in the form of verse, and traces of this are to be found in the texts which have been preserved. But the Laws as we have them do not go back to the 5th century. In our texts isolated phrases or portions of phrases are given with a commentary, and this commentary is further explained by some 633later commentators. Kuno Meyer has pointed out that in the commentary to one text, *Críth Gablach*, there are linguistic forms which must go back to the 8th century, and Arbois de Jubainville, who apart from Sir Henry Maine is the only scholar who has dealt with the subject, has attempted to prove from internal evidence that part of the oldest tract, the one on *Athgabáil* or Seizure, cannot, in its present form, be later than the close of the 6th century. Cormac's Glossary contains a number of quotations from the commentary to *Senchus Mór*, which would therefore seem to have been in existence about 900. The Irish Laws were transcribed by O'Donovan and O'Curry, and have been published with a faulty text and translation in five volumes by the government commissioners originally appointed in 1852. A number of other law tracts must have existed in early times, and several which have been preserved are still unedited. Kuno Meyer has published the *Cáin Adamnáin* or Adamnan's Law from an Oxford MS. Adamnan succeeded in getting a law passed which forbade women to go into battle. An interesting but little-investigated text in prose and verse called *Leabhar na gCeart* or Book of Rights was edited with an English translation by O'Donovan (1847). It deals with the rights to tribute of the high-king and the various provincial kings. The text of the Book of Rights is preserved in YBL. and BB. In its present form it shows distinct traces of the influence of the Viking invasions, and cannot go back much beyond the year 1000. At one time it was incorporated in a larger work now lost, the Psalter of Cashel. We also possess a 9th-century treatise on Sunday observance (*Cáin Domnaig*).

The medical profession in Ireland was hereditary in a number of families, such as the O'Lees (from Irish *liaig*, "a leech"), the O'Hickeys (Irish *icide*, "the healer"), the O'Shiels, the O'Cassidys, and many others. These families each **Medicine.** had their own special leech-books, some of which are still preserved. In addition to these there are many others. The medical literature which has come down to us is contained in MSS. ranging from the 13th to the 18th centuries. The Irish MSS. are translations from the Latin with the invariable commentary, and they further contain additions derived from experience. YBL. contains four of these tracts, and amongst others we may mention the Book of the O'Hickeys, a translation of the *Lilium Medicinae* of Bernard Gordon (written 1303), the Book of the O'Lees (written in 1443), the Book of the O'Shiels, transcribed in 1657, and the Book of MacAnlega, transcribed in 1512. Of these texts only two have been published as yet from MSS. in Edinburgh. O'Curry drew up a MS. catalogue of the medical MSS. in the Royal Irish Academy, and many more are described in O'Grady's catalogue of Irish MSS. in the British Museum. Some few MSS. deal with the subject of astronomy, but up to the present no description of the texts has been published.

With the steady advance of the English power after 1600 it was only natural that the school of bardic poets should decline. But at the beginning of the 17th century for the last time they gave a great display of their resources. ***Later Irish literature.*** Tadhg MacDaire, the ollam of the earl of Thomond, composed a poem in elaborate verse exalting the line of Eber (represented by the reigning families of Munster) at the expense of the line of Eremon (represented by the reigning families of the other provinces). In a body of verse attributed to Torna Éces (c. 400), but obviously of more recent origin, the Eremonian, Niall Noigiallach, is lavishly praised, and Tadhg's attack takes the form of a refutation of Torna's pretensions. The challenge was immediately taken up by Lughaidh O'Clery. The recriminations of the two bards extend to nearly 3000 lines of verse, and naturally drew down the attention of the whole Irish world of letters. Soon all the hereditary poets were engaged in the conflict, which raged for many years, and the verses of both parties were collected into a volume of about 7000 lines in *debide* metre, known as the *Contention of the Poets*. Amongst the prominent poets of the period may be mentioned Tadhg Dall O'Higinn (d. shortly before 1617) and Eochaidh O'Hussey, who between them have left behind nearly 7000 lines in the classical metres, Bonaventura O'Hussey and Ferfesa O'Cainti. The intricate classical measures gradually broke down. Dr Douglas Hyde gives it as his opinion that the exceedingly numerous metres known in Middle Irish had become restricted to a couple of dozen, and these nearly all heptasyllabic. Nevertheless they continued to be employed till into the 18th century. However, during the 17th century we find a new school arising with new principles and new methods. These consisted in (1) the adoption of vowel rhyme in place of consonantal rhyme, (2) the adoption of a certain number of accents in each line in place of a certain number of syllables. Thus, according to what we have just said, the accented syllables in a line with four accents in one line will fall on, say, the following vowels *e, u, u, e,* and the line rhyming with it will have the same sounds in the same or a different sequence. (For English imitations see Hyde, *A Literary History of Ireland,* pp. 548 ff.)

The consequences of the changed political conditions were of the greatest importance. The bards, having lost their patrons in the general upheaval, threw behind them the old classical metres and turned to the general public. At the same time they had to abandon the countless chevilles and other characteristics of the old bardic language, which were only understood by the privileged few. But to compensate for this much more freedom of expression and naturalness were possible for the first time in Irish verse. The new metres made their appearance in Ireland about 1600, and the learned Keating himself was one of the first to discard the ancient prosody. During the latter half of the 17th century and throughout the 18th century the body of verse produced in Ireland voices the sorrows and aspirations of the whole nation, and the literary activity in almost every county was correspondingly great. It is only during the last few years that the works of any of the poets of this period have been published. Pierce Ferriter was the last chieftain who held out against Cromwell's army, and he was hanged in 1653. His poems have been edited by P.S. Dinneen (Dublin, 1903). The bard of the Williamite wars was David O'Bruadar (d. 1697-1698). From this period date three powerful satires on the state of affairs in Munster, and in particular on the Cromwellian settlers. They are of a coarse and savage nature, for which reason they have never been printed. Their titles are the Parliament of Clan Thomas, the Adventures of Clan Thomas, and the Adventures of Tadhg Dubh (by Egan O'Rahilly). A description of the parliament of Clan Thomas is given by Stern in the *Zeitschr. f. celt. Phil.* v. pp. 541 ff.

A little later we come across a band of Jacobite poets. The gallant figure of Charles Edward was so popular with Irish bards that a conventional stereotyped form arose in which the poet represents himself as wandering in a wood and meeting a beautiful lady. We are treated to a full description of all her charms, and the poet compares her to all the fair heroines of antiquity. But she replies that she is none of these. She is Erin seeking refuge from the insults of foreign suitors and looking for her mate. The idea of such poems is a beautiful one, but they become tedious when one has read a dozen of them only to find that there are scores of others in exactly the same strain. Besides the Visions (*Aisling*), as they are termed, there are several noteworthy war-songs, whilst other poems are valuable as giving a picture of the state of the country at the time. We can do no more than mention the names of John O'Neaghtan (d. c. 1720; edition of his poems by A. O'Farrelly, Dublin, 1908), Egan O'Rahilly, who flourished between 1700 and 1726; Tadhg O'Naghten, Andrew MacCurtin (d. 1479), Hugh MacCurtin, author of a grammar and part editor of O'Begley's *Dictionary*;

John Clárach MacDonnell (1691-1754), John O'Tuomy (d. 1775); Andrew Magrath, Tadhg Gaolach O'Sullivan (d. c. 1795), author of a well-known volume of religious poems, a valuable source of information for the Munster dialect; and Owen Roe O'Sullivan (d. 1784), the cleverest of the Jacobite poets (his verses and *bons mots* are still well known in Munster). These poets hailed mostly from the south, and it is chiefly the works of the Munster poets that have been preserved. Ulster and Connaught also produced a number of writers, but very little beyond the mere names has been preserved except in the case of the Connaught poet Raftery 634(1784-1835), whose compositions have been rescued by Hyde (*Abhráin an Reachtúire*, Dublin, 1903). Torlough O'Carolan (1670-1738), "the last of the bards," was really a musician. Having become blind he was educated as a harper and won great fame. His poems, which were composed to suit his music, are mostly addressed to patrons or fair ladies. His celebrated "Ode to Whisky" is one of the finest bacchanalian songs in any language. Michael Comyn (b. c. 1688) is well known as the author of a version based upon older matter of "Ossian in the Land of Youth." This appears to be the only bit of deliberate creation in the later Ossianic literature. Comyn also wrote a prose story called "The Adventures of Torlogh, son of Starn, and the Adventures of his Three Sons." Brian MacGiolla Meidhre or Merriman (d. 1808) is the author of perhaps the cleverest sustained poem in the Irish language. His work, which is entitled the *Midnight Court*, contains about 1000 lines with four rhymes in each line. It describes a vision in which Aoibhill, queen of the Munster fairies, is holding a court. A handsome girl defends herself against an old man, and complains to the queen that in spite of all her charms she is in danger of dying unwed. Merriman's poem, which was written in 1781, has recently been edited with a German translation by L.C. Stern (*Zeitschrift für celtische Philologie*, v. 193-415). Donough MacConmara (Macnamara) (d. c. 1814) is best known as the author of a famous lyric "The Fair Hills of Holy Ireland," but he also wrote a mock epic describing his voyage to America and how the ship was chased by a French cruiser. He is carried off in a dream by the queen of the Munster fairies to Elysium, where, instead of Charon, he finds Conan, the Thersites among the Fenians, acting as ferryman (*Eachtra Ghiolla an Amaráin, or The Adventures of a Luckless Fellow*, edited by T. Flannery, Dublin, 1901).

During the first half of the 19th century nothing new was produced of a high order, though the peasants retained their love for poetry and continued to copy the MSS. in their possession. Then came the famine and the consequent drain of population which gave Irish the death-blow as a living literary force. The modern movement has been dealt with above in the section on Irish language.

It remains for us to glance briefly at the later religious literature and the collections of folk-tales. The translation of the New Testament made by William O'Donnell and published in 1603 was first undertaken in the reign of Queen Elizabeth, who sent over to Dublin the first fount of Irish type. Bishop Bedell, one of the very few Protestant clergymen who undertook to learn Irish, translated the remainder of the Scriptures with the help of a couple of natives, but the whole Bible was not translated and published until 1686. This version naturally never became popular, but it is a valuable source of information with regard to Modern Irish. It is perhaps of interest to note that the earliest specimen of printing in Irish is a ballad on Doomsday (Dublin, 1571). A version of the English Prayer Book was published in 1716.

The scholars of the various Irish colleges on the continent were particularly active in the production of manuals of devotion mainly translated from Latin. We can mention only a few of the more important. *Sgathán an chrábhaidh* (The Mirror of the Pious), published in 1626 by Florence Conry; *Sgathán sacramente na h-Aithrighe* (Mirror of the Sacrament of Penance), by Hugh MacCathmhaoil, published at Louvain, 1618; *The Book of Christian Doctrine*, by Theobald Stapleton (Brussels, 1639); *Párrthas an Anma, or The Paradise of the Soul*, by Anthony Gernon (Louvain, 1645); a book on *Miracles*, by Richard MacGilla Cody (1667); *Lochrán na gcreidmheach, or Lucerna Fidelium*, by Francis O'Mulloy (Louvain, 1676); O'Donlevy's *Catechism* (1742). O'Gallagher, bishop of Raphoe, published a collection of sermons which went through twenty editions and are still known at the present day. He is one of the earliest writers in whom the characteristics of the speech of the north are noticeable. The only Catholic version of any considerable portion of the Scriptures up till quite recently was the translation of the Pentateuch by Archbishop MacHale, who also turned six books of the *Iliad* into Irish. It is only within recent years that attention has been paid to the collection of folk-songs and tales in Irish, although as long ago as 1825 Crofton Croker published three volumes of folk-lore in the south of Ireland which attracted the attention of Sir Walter Scott. Nor do the classic stories of Carleton fall within our province. We may mention among others Patrick O'Leary's *Sgeuluidheacht Chuige Mumhan* (Dublin, 1895); Hyde's *Beside the Fire* (London, 1890) and *An Sgeuluidhe Gaedhealach*, reprinted from vol. x. of the *Annales de Bretagne* (London, 1901); Daniel O'Fogharta's *Siamsa an Gheimhridh* (Dublin, 1892); J. Lloyd's *Sgéalaidhe Óirghiall* (Dublin, 1905); and Larminie's *West Irish Folk-Tales* (London, 1893). The most important collections of folk-songs are *Love-Songs of Connaught* (Dublin, 1893) and *Religious Songs of Connaught* (Dublin, 1906), both published by Hyde. The most extensive collection of proverbs is the one entitled *Seanfhocla Uladh* by Henry Morris (Dublin, 1907). See also T. O'Donoghue, *Sean-fhocail na Mumhan* (Dublin, 1902).

AUTHORITIES.—In the absence of a comprehensive history, the best manual is Eleanor Hull's *Text Book of Irish Literature* (2 parts, London, 1904-1908; vol. 2 contains a bibliographical appendix). D. Hyde's larger *History of Irish Literature* (London, 1899) is only trustworthy as regards the more *modern* period. A full bibliography of all published material is contained in G. Dottin's article "La littérature gaélique de l'Irlande" (*Revue de synthèse historique*, vol. iii. pp. 1 ff.). Dottin's article has been translated into English and supplemented by Joseph Dunn under the title of *The Gaelic Literature of Ireland* (Washington, 1906, privately printed). The following are important works:—W. Stokes and J. Strachan, *Thesaurus Palaeohibernicus* (2 vols., Cambridge, 1901-1903); J.H. Bernard and R. Atkinson, *Liber Hymnorum* (London, 1895); E. O'Curry, *Lectures on the MS. Materials of Ancient Irish History* (Dublin, 1873) and *Lectures on the Manners and Customs of the Ancient Irish* (3 vols., Dublin, 1873); P.W. Joyce, *A Social History of Ancient Ireland* (2 vols., London, 1903); E. O'Reilly, *Irish Writers* (Dublin, 1820); S.H. O'Grady, *Catalogue of Irish MSS. in the British Museum* (London, 1901); H. d'Arbois de Jubainville, *Introduction à l'étude de la littérature celtique* (Paris, 1883), *Essai d'un catalogue de la littérature épique de l'Irlande* (Paris, 1883), *L'Épopée celtique en Irlande* (Paris, 1892), *La Civilisation des Celtes et celle de l'épopée homérique* (Paris, 1899); E. Windisch, *Táin Bó Cualnge*, ed. with an introd. and German trans. (Leipzig, 1905); L. Winifred Faraday, *The Cattle-Raid of Cualnge* (London, 1904); the Irish text according to LU. and YBL. has been published as a supplement to *Ériu*, Eleanor Hull, *The Cuchulinn-saga* (London, 1899); W. Ridgeway, "The Date of the First Shaping of the Cuchulinn Cycle," *Proceedings of the British Academy*, vol. ii. (London, 1907); A. Nutt, *Cuchulin, the Irish Achilles* (London, 1899); H. Zimmer, "Keltische Beiträge" in *Zeitschrift f. deutsches Altertum*, vols. 32, 33 and 35, and "Über den compilatorischen Charakter der irischen Sagentexte in sogenannten Lebor na hUidre," Kuhn's *Zeitschr.* xxviii. pp. 417-689. We cannot here enumerate the numerous heroic texts which have been edited. For texts published before 1883 see d'Arbois's *Catalogue*, and the same writer gives a complete list in *Revue Celtique*, vol. xxiv. pp. 237 ff. The series of *Irische Texte*, vols. i.-iv. (Leipzig, 1880-1901), by E. Windisch (vols. ii.-iv. in conjunction with W. Stokes), contains a number of important texts. Others, more particularly those belonging to the Ossianic cycle, are to be found in S.H. O'Grady's *Silva Gadelica* (2 vols. London, 1892). See also R. Thurneysen, *Sagen aus dem alten Irland* (Berlin, 1901); P.W. Joyce, *Old Celtic Romances* (London², 1901).

For the Ossianic cycle see H. Zimmer, "Keltische Beiträge III." in vol. 35 of the *Zeitschr. f. deutsches Altertum*, also *Gottinger Gelehrte Anzeigen*, 1887, pp. 153-199; A. Nutt, *Ossian and the Ossianic Literature* (London, 1899); L.C. Stern, "Die ossianischen Heldenlieder," in *Zeitschr. f. vergleichende Litteraturgeschichte* for 1895, trans. by J.L. Robertson in *Transactions of the Inverness Gaelic Society*, vol. xxii.; J. MacNeill, *Duanaire Finn* (London, 1908); *Book of the Dean of Lismore*, ed. by T. Maclauchlan (Edinburgh, 1862), and in vol. i. of A. Cameron's *Reliquiae Celticae* (Edinburgh, 1892); *Transactions of the Ossianic Society* (6 vols., Dublin, 1854-1861); Miss Brooke, *Reliques of Ancient Irish Poetry* (Dublin, 1789).

Keating's *History* was translated by John O'Mahony (New York, 1866). The first part was edited with Eng. trans. by W. Halliday (Dublin, 1811) and the whole work in 3 vols. for the Irish Texts Society by D. Comyn and P. Dinneen (London, 1901-1908). Comparatively few specimens have been published of the older bards. Several from a Copenhagen MS.

were printed by Stern in the *Zeitschr. f. celt. Phil.* vol. ii.; J. Hardiman,*Irish Minstrelsy* (2 vols., Dublin, 1831); J.C. Mangan, *The Poets and Poetry of Munster*(Dublin4, no date); G. Sigerson, *The Bards of the Gael and Gall* (Dublin, 1906). Editions of the poems of Ferriter, Geoffrey O'Donoghue, O'Rahilly, John O'Tuomy, Andrew Magrath, John Claragh MacDonnell, Tadhg Gaolach and Owen Roe O'Sullivan by Dinneen, Gaelic League, Dublin, and Irish Texts Society, London, 1900-1903.

(E. C. Q.)

635

II. SCOTTISH GAELIC LITERATURE.—It is not until after the Forty-five that we find any great manifestation of originality in the literature of the Scottish Highlands. The reasons for this are not far to seek. Just as the dialects of Low German in the middle ages were overshadowed by the more brilliant literary dialect of the south, so Scotch Gaelic was from the outset seriously handicapped by the great activity of the professional literary class in Ireland. We may say that down to the beginning of the 18th century the literary language of the Highlands was the Gaelic of Ireland. During the dark days of the penal laws and with the extinction of the men of letters and their patrons in Ireland, an opportunity was given to the native Scottish muse to develop her powers. Another potent factor also made itself felt. After Culloden the causes of the clan feuds and animosities of the past were removed. The Highlands, perhaps for the first time in history, formed a compact whole and settled down to peace and quietude. A remarkable outburst of literary activity ensued, and the latter half of the 18th century is the period which Scottish writers love to call the golden age of Gaelic poetry. But before we attempt to deal with this period in detail, we must examine the scanty literary products of Gaelic Scotland prior to the 18th century.

The earliest document containing Gaelic matter which Scotland can claim is the *Book of Deer*, now preserved in the Cambridge University Library. This MS. contains portions of the Gospels in Latin written in an Irish hand with **"Book of Deer."** illuminations of the well-known Irish type. At the end there occurs a colophon in Irish which is certainly as old as the 9th century. Inserted in the margins and blank spaces are later notes and memoranda partly in Latin, partly in Gaelic. The Gaelic entries were probably made between 1000 and 1150. They relate to grants of land and other privileges made from time to time to the monastery of Deer (Aberdeenshire). The most interesting portion deals with the legend of Deer and its traditional foundation by St Columba. The language of these entries shows a striking departure from the traditional orthography employed in contemporary Irish documents. The Advocates' Library in Edinburgh contains a number of MSS. probably written in Scotland between 1400 and 1600, but with one exception the language is Irish.

The solitary exception just mentioned is the famous codex known as the *Book of the Dean of Lismore*. The pieces contained in this volume are written in the crabbed current Roman hand of the period, and the orthography is **"Book of the Dean of Lismore."** phonetic, both of which facts render the deciphering of this valuable MS. a task of supreme difficulty. The contents of this quarto volume of 311 pages are almost entirely verse compositions collected and written down by Sir James Macgregor, dean of Lismore in Argyllshire, and his brother Duncan, between the years 1512 and 1526. A disproportionate amount of space is allotted to the compositions of well-known Irish bards such as Donnchadh Mór O'Daly (d. 1244), Muiredhach Albanach (c. 1224), Tadhg Óg O'Higgin (d. 1448), Diarmaid O'Hiffernan, Torna O'Mulconry (d. 1468). But native bards are also represented. We can mention Allan Mac Rorie, Gillie Calum Mac an Ollav, John of Knoydart, who celebrates the murder of the young lord of the isles by his Irish harper in 1490, Finlay MacNab, and Duncan Macgregor, the transcriber of the greater part of the volume. The poems of the last-mentioned writer are in praise of the Macgregors. A few other poems are by Scottish authors such as Campbell, Knight of Glenorchy (d. 1513), the earl of Argyll and Countess Isabella. A number consist of satires on women. These Scottish writers are still under the influence of Irish metric, and regularly employ the four-lined stanza. They do not appear to adhere to the stricter Irish measures, but delight rather in the freer forms going by the name of *óglachas*. The Irish rules for alliteration and rhyme are not rigidly observed.

The linguistic peculiarities of the Dean's Book await investigation, but among the pieces which represent the Scottish vernacular of the day are the *Ossianic Ballads*. These, twenty-eight in number, extend to upwards of 2500 lines, and form by far the most important part of the collection. Thus the Dean's Book was compiled a full hundred years before the earliest similar collection of heroic ballads was made in Ireland. In Scotland the term Ossianic is used loosely of both the Ulster and the Fenian cycles, and it may be as well to state that three of the pieces in the volume deal with Fraoch, Conlaoch and the Bloody Rout of Conall Cearnach. It is interesting to note that nine of the poems are directly attributed to Ossian, two to Ferghus File, one to Caoilte Mac Ronan, and one to Conall Cearnach, whilst others are ascribed to Allan MacRorie, Gillie Calum Mac an Ollav and Caoch O'Cluain, who are otherwise unknown. The Dean's Book was first transcribed by Ewen MacLachlan in 1813. Thomas MacLauchlan published the text of the Ossianic ballads with modern Gaelic and English renderings in 1862. In the same volume W.F. Skene gave a useful description of the MS. and its contents. Alexander Cameron revised the text of the portion printed by MacLauchlan, and his amended text is printed in his *Reliquiae Celticae*, vol. i. (See also L.C. Stern, *Zeitschr. f. celt. Phil.* i. 294-326.)

Between the Book of the Dean and the Forty-five we find another great gap, which is only bridged over by a collection which presents many points of resemblance to Macgregor's compilation. The *Book of Fernaig*, which is also written in a **"Book of Fernaig."** kind of phonetic script, was compiled by Duncan Macrae of Inverinate between 1688 and 1693. The MS. contains about 4200 lines of verse of different dates and by different authors. The contents of the collection are mainly political and religious, with a few poems which are termed didactic. As in the Dean's Book love-songs and drinking-songs are conspicuously absent, whilst the religious poetry forms about one-half of the contents. In state politics the authors are Jacobite, and in church politics Episcopalian. The Ossianic literature is represented by 36 lines. There are a number of poems by 16th-century writers, among whom is Bishop Carsewell. Mackinnon has pointed out that the language of the *Book of Fernaig* corresponds exactly to the dialect spoken in Kintail at the present day. The text of the *Book of Fernaig* is printed in its entirety in vol. ii. of Cameron's *Reliquiae Celticae*, and many of the poems are to be found in standard orthography in G. Henderson's *Leabhar nan Gleann*. The metres employed in the poems show the influence of the English system of versification. (See Stern, *Zeitschr. f. celt. Phil.* ii. pp. 566 ff.)

Two other Highland MSS. remain to be noticed. These are the *Red* and *Black Books of Clanranald*, which are largely taken up with the histories of the families of Macdonald and with the achievements of Montrose, written in the **"Red and Black Books of Clanranald."** ordinary Irish of the period by the Macvurichs, hereditary bards to the Clanranald chiefs. The *Red Book* was obtained by Macpherson in 1760 from Neil Macvurich, nephew of the last great bard, and it figured largely in the Ossianic controversy. In addition to poems in Irish by Neil Macvurich, who died at a great age some time after 1715, and other bardic matter, the MSS. now contain only three Ossianic poems, and these are in Irish. During the Ossianic controversy the *Red Book of Clanranald* was supposed to contain the originals of much of Macpherson's famous work; but, on the book coming into the hands of the enthusiastic Gaels of the closing years of the 18th century, and on its contents being examined and found wanting, the MS. was tampered with.

Mackenzie's *Beauties of Gaelic Poetry* contains poems written by a number of writers who flourished towards the end of the 17th century and at the beginning of the 18th. These are Mary Macleod, John Macdonald (Iain Lom), Archibald **Mary Macleod.** Macdonald, Dorothy Brown, Cicely Macdonald, Iain Dubh Iain 'Ic. Ailein (b. c. 1665), the Aosdan Matheson (one of his poems was rendered in English by Sir Walter Scott under the title of "Farewell to Mackenzie, High Chief of Kintail"), Hector Maclean (also known through a translation by Scott called "War-song of Lachlan, High Chief of Maclean"), Lachlan Mackinnon, Roderick Morrison (an Clarsair Dall), and John Mackay of Gairloch, but we can here only notice the first two. The famous Mary Macleod, better known as Mairi Nighean Alastair Ruaidh 636(c. 1588-1693), was family bard to Sir Norman Macleod of Bernera, and later to John "Breac" Macleod of Macleod, in honour of whom most of her poems were composed. Like very many of the Highland poets Mary had little or no education, and it would seem that none of the poems which have come down to us were composed before 1660. Her pieces are composed in the modern Irish metres with the characteristic vowel rhymes of the accented syllables. As might perhaps be expected it was only the Macvurichs (the professional bards of the Clanranald) who went on practising the classical *debide* metre. This they still continued to do during the first quarter of the 18th century. Mary Macleod's best-known pieces comprise a dirge on the drowning of Iain Garbh (Mac'Ille Chalum) in the Minch, a song "An Talla 'm bu ghnath le MacLeoid," and an ode to Sir Norman Macleod of Bernera, produced during her exile in Mull, which begins "'S mi'm shuidhe air an tulaich." For the details of her career, which are the subject of some dispute, the reader may be referred to a paper by Alexander Mackenzie in the *Transactions of the Gaelic Society of Inverness*, vol. xxii. pp. 43-66. Mary Macleod is accounted one of the most musical and original of the Highland bards.

John Macdonald, better known as Iain Lom (d. c. 1710), was a vigorous political poet whose verses exercised an extraordinary influence during his lifetime. He is said to have received a yearly pension from Charles II. for his **"Iain Lom.** "services to the Stuart cause. His best-known poems are *Mort na Ceapach*, on the murder of the heir of Keppoch, who was eventually avenged through the poet's efforts, and a piece on the battle of Inverlochay (1645). However great the inspiration of Mary Macleod and Iain Lorn, they were after all but political or family bards. In succession to them there arose a small band of men with loftier thoughts, a wider outlook and greater art. The literature of the Scottish Highlands culminates in the names of Alexander Macdonald, Duncan Ban MacIntyre and Dugald Buchanan.

Alexander Macdonald, commonly called Alasdair MacMaighstir Alasdair (b. c. 1700), was the son of an Episcopalian clergyman in Moidart. He was sent to Glasgow University to fit himself for a professional career. But an imprudent **Alexander Macdonald.** marriage caused him to abandon his studies, and about 1729 he received an appointment as a Presbyterian teacher in his native district. He was moved from place to place, and from 1739 to 1745 he taught at Corryvullin on the Sound of Mull, the scene of some of his most beautiful lyrics. About 1740 he was invited to compile a Gaelic vocabulary, which was published in 1741. Macdonald has thus the double distinction of being the author of the first book printed in Scotch Gaelic and of being the father of Highland lexicography. The news of the landing of the Pretender brought visions of release to the poverty-stricken poet, who was by this time heartily sick of teaching and farming. He turned Roman Catholic, and was present at the unfurling of the Stuart standard. He was given the rank of captain, but rendered greater services to the Jacobite cause with his stirring poems than with the sword. After Culloden he suffered great privations. But in 1751 he visited Edinburgh and brought out a collection of his poetry, which has the honour of being the first original work printed in Scotch Gaelic. His volume was therefore entitled *Ais-eiridh na Seann Chanain Albannaich* (Resurrection of the Ancient Scottish Tongue). Till the day of his death he led a more or less wandering life, as he was dependent on the generosity of Clanranald. Only a small part of Macdonald's compositions have been preserved (thirty-one in all). These naturally fall into three groups—love-songs, descriptive poems and patriotic and Jacobite poems. In his love-songs and descriptive poems Macdonald struck an entirely new note in Gaelic literature. His *Moladh Mòraig* and *Cuachag an Fhasaich* (also called *A'Bhanarach Dhonn*) are his best-known compositions in the amatory style. But he is distinctly at his best in the descriptive poems. We have already seen that even as early as the 8th century the poets of Ireland gave expression to that intimate love of nature which is perhaps the most striking feature in Celtic verse. Macdonald had a wonderful command of his native Gaelic. His verse is always musical, and his skilful use of epithet, often very lavishly strewn, enables him to express with marvellous effect the various aspects of nature in her gentler and sterner moods alike. His masterpiece, the *Birlinn of Clanranald*, which is at the same time, apart from Ossianic ballads, the longest poem in the language, describes a voyage from South Uist to Carrickfergus. Here Macdonald excels in describing the movement of the ship and the fury of the storm. In *Allt an t-Siucair* (The Sugar Brook) we are given an exquisite picture of a beautiful scene in the country on a summer morning. Other similar poems full of melody and colour are *Failte na Mòr-thir* (Hail to the Mainland), *Oran an t-Sambraidh* (Ode to Summer), and *Oran an Gheamhraidh* (Ode to Winter). When this gifted son of the muses identified himself with the Stuart cause he poured forth a stream of inspiring songs which have earned for him the title of the Tyrtaeus of the Rebellion. Among these we may mention *Oran nam Fineachan Gaelach* (The Song of the Clans),*Brosnachadh nam Fineachan gaidhealach* (A Call to the Highland Clans), and various songs to the prince. But incomparably the finest of all is *Oran Luaighe no Fucaidh*(Waulking Song). Here the prince is addressed as a young girl with flowing locks of yellow hair on her shoulders, and called Morag. She had gone away over the seas, and the poet invokes her to return with a party of maidens (*i.e.* soldiers) to dress the red cloth, in other words, to beat the English red-coats. The song contains forty-seven stanzas in all, with the characteristic refrain of the waulking-songs. *Am Breacan Uallach* is a spirited poem in praise of the kilt and plaid, which had been forbidden by the English government Macdonald is also the author of a number of poems in MS. which have been called the quintessence of indecency. His works have gone through eight editions, the last of which is dated 1892.

In connexion with Macdonald's Jacobite songs it will be well to mention here the name of a kindred spirit, John Roy Stuart (Iain Ruadh Stiubhart). Stuart was a gallant soldier who was serving in Flanders with the French against the English when the rebellion broke out. He hurried home and distinguished himself on the field of battle. After Culloden he gave vent to his dejection in two pathetic songs, one on the battle itself, while the other deals with the sad lot of the Gael.

The only poet of nature who can claim to rival Macdonald is a man of a totally different stamp. Duncan Bàn MacIntyre (Donnachadh Bàn, 1724-1812) was born of poor parents in Glenorchy, and never learned to read and **Duncan Bàn.**write or to speak English. He was present on the English side at the battle of Falkirk, on which he wrote a famous ode, and shortly afterwards he was appointed gamekeeper to the earl of Breadalbane in Coire Cheathaich and Ben Dorain, where he lived for many years until he accepted a similar appointment from the duke of Argyll in Buachaill-Eite. Stewart of Luss is credited with having taken down the 6000 lines of verse of his own composition which MacIntyre had carried about with him for many years, and his works were published in 1768. In his later years he was first a volunteer and afterwards a member of the city guard in Edinburgh. In addition to his poems descriptive of nature MacIntyre composed a number of Jacobite martial songs, songs of love and sentiment, and comic and satiric pieces. The poem *Mairi bhàn òg* addressed to his wife is, on account of its grace and delicate sentiment, generally held to be the finest love-song in the language. But it is above all as the poet of ben and corrie that MacIntyre is remembered. He has been called the Burns of the Highlands, but the bitterness and intellectual power of the Ayrshire poet are absent in MacIntyre. Duncan Bàn describes fondly and tenderly the glories of his native mountains as only one can who spends his life in daily communion with them. His two great compositions are styled *Ben Dorain* and *Coire Cheathaich*. The former is a long poem of 550 lines divided into eight parts, alternating with a sort of strophe and antistrophe, one slow called *urlar* in stately trochees, the other swift called *siubhal* in a kind of galloping anapaests; the whole ending with the *crunluath* or final quick motion. It is said to reproduce very accurately the lilt of a pipe-tune. The poem, which might be called the "Song of the Deer," has been well done into English by J. S. Blackie. *Coire Cheathaich* (The Misty Corrie), a much shorter poem than Ben Dorain, gives a loving description of all the prominent features in the landscape—the flowers, the bushes, the stones, the hillocks with the birds and game, and the whirling eddies with the glistening salmon. MacIntyre's works went through three editions in his lifetime, and a twelfth was issued in 1901.

From Duncan Bàn we pass on to consider the compositions of two men who hailed from the outlying parts of Gaeldom. Robert Mackay, or, as he is generally called, Rob Donn (1714-1778), was a native of Strathmore, Sutherlandshire, **Rob Donn.**who, like Duncan Bàn, never learned to read or write. His life, which was uneventful, was spent almost entirely within the confines of the county of his birth. He left behind a large number of poems which may be roughly classified as elegiac, love and satiric poems. His elegies are of the typical Highland kind. The singer is overwhelmed with sadness and despairing in his loss. His best-known composition in this style is "The Death-Song of Hugh." Having just heard of the death of Pelham, the prime minister, Mackay finds a poor friend of his dying alone amid squalor in the heart of the mountains. In a poem composed on the spot the poet contrasts the positions of the two men and reflects on the vanity of human existence. Among his love-poems the "Shieling Song" is deservedly famous. But it was above all as a satirist that Mackay excelled during his lifetime. Indeed he seems to have had the sharpest tongue of all the Highland bards. We have already seen what powers were attributed to satirical poets in Ireland in medieval times, and though bodily disfigurements were no longer feared in the 18th century, nothing was more dreaded, both in Ireland and Scotland, than the lash of the bard. Hence many of Rob Donn's compositions have lost their point, and opinions have been greatly divided as to his merits as a poet. His collected poems were first published in 1829, a second edition appeared in 1871, and in 1899 two new editions were issued simultaneously, the one by Hew Morrison, the other by Adam Gunn and Malcolm Macfarlane. Another satirical poet who enjoyed a tremendous ***John MacCodrum.*** reputation in his own day was John MacCodrum, a native of North Uist and a contemporary of the men just mentioned. It is related of MacCodrum that the tailors of the Long Island refused to make any clothes for him in consequence of a satire he had directed against them. He was encountered in a ragged state by the Macdonald, who on learning the cause of his sorry condition promoted him to the dignity of bard to his family. Consequently a number of his compositions are addressed to his patrons, but one delightful poem entitled *Smeòrach Chlann-Domhnuill* (The Mavis of Clan Donald) describes in verses full of melody the beauties of his beloved island home.

In the lyrical outburst which followed the Forty-five it was only to be expected that religious poetry should be represented. We have seen that much of the space in the Dean's Book and in the *Book of Fernaig* is allotted to verse of a pious order, though apart from the works of such Irish singers as Donnchadh O'Daly the poems do not reach a very high pitch of excellence. The first religious poem to be printed in Scotch Gaelic was a long hymn by David Mackellar, published in 1752. But incomparably the greatest writer of hymns and sacred poems is Dugald Buchanan (1716-1768). Buchanan was born in Strathyre in Perthshire and was the son of a miller. He ***Dugald Buchanan.*** received a desultory kind of education and tried his hand at various trades. In 1753 he was appointed schoolmaster at Drumcastle near Kinloch Rannoch. He was selected to assist Stewart of Killin in preparing the first Highland version of the New Testament for the Society for Propagating Christian Knowledge (published 1767), and at the same time he issued an edition of his own poems. Of all Gaelic books this has been far and away the most popular, having gone through no less than forty editions. Buchanan seems to have been very susceptible to religious influences, and the stern Puritan doctrines of retribution and eternal damnation preached around him so worked on his mind that from his ninth to his twenty-sixth year he was a prey to that mental anguish so eloquently described by Bunyan. The awful visions which presented themselves to his vivid imagination find expression in his poems, the most notable of which are "The Majesty of God," "The Dream," "The Sufferings of Christ," "The Day of Judgment," "The Hero," "The Skull," "Winter" and "Prayer." In the "Day of Judgment," a poem of about 120 stanzas, we are given in sublime verses a vivid delineation of the crack of doom as the archangel sounds the last trumpet. The poet then goes on to depict the awful scenes consequent upon the wreck of the elements, and pictures the gathering together of the whole human race before the Throne. But Buchanan's masterpiece is admittedly "The Skull." Traces of the influence of English writers have been observed in all the poet's writings, and it seems certain that the subject of his greatest poem was suggested by Shakespeare. The poet seated by a grave espies a skull. He takes it up and muses on its history. This poem in 44 stanzas concludes with a picture of the torments of hell and the glories of heaven.

The writers whom we have been discussing are practically unknown save to those who are able to read them in the original. Now we have to turn our attention to a man whose works have never been popular in the Highlands, but ***Macpherson's "Ossian."*** who nevertheless plays a prominent part in the history of European literature. Though the precise origin of the Fenian cycle may remain a moot-point to all time, the development of the literature centring in the names of Finn and Ossian is at any rate clear from the 11th century onwards. The interest taken in Celtic studies since the middle of the 19th century in Ireland

and Scotland and elsewhere has accumulated a body of evidence which has settled for all time the celebrated dispute as to the authenticity of Macpherson's Ossian. James Macpherson (1736-1796), a native of Kingussie, showed a turn for versification whilst yet a student at college. Whilst acting as tutor at Moffat he was asked by John Home as to the existence of ancient Gaelic literature in the Highlands. After some pressing Macpherson undertook to translate some of the more striking poems, and submitted to Home a rendering of "The Death of Oscar." Blair, Ferguson and Robertson, the foremost men in the Edinburgh literary circles of the day, were enthusiastic about the unearthing of such unsuspected treasures, and at their instance Macpherson published anonymously in 1760 his *Fragments of Ancient Poetry, collected in the Highlands of Scotland and translated from the Gaelic or Erse Language*. This publication contained in all fifteen translations, preceded by a preface from the pen of Blair. Published under such auspices, Macpherson's venture was bound to succeed. In the preface it was stated that among other ancient poems an epic of considerable length existed in Gaelic, and that if sufficient encouragement were forthcoming the author of the versions would undertake to recover and translate the same. A subscription was raised at once, and Macpherson set out on a journey of exploration in the Highlands and islands. As the result of this tour, on which he was accompanied by two or three competent Gaelic scholars, Macpherson published in London in 1762 a large quarto containing his epic styled *Fingal* with fifteen other smaller poems. In the following year a still larger epic appeared with the title of *Temora*. It was in eight books, and contained a number of notes in addition to *Cath-Loda* and other pieces, along with the seventh book of *Temora* in Gaelic as a specimen of the original. Ten years later a new edition of the whole was issued. The authenticity of Macpherson's translations was soon impugned by Dr Johnson, Hume and Malcolm Laing, and the author was urged by his friends to publish the originals. Macpherson prevaricated, even though the Highlanders of India sent him a cheque for £1000 to enable him to vindicate the antiquity of their native literature. Macpherson at different times, and particularly towards the end of his life, seems to have had some intention of publishing the Gaelic of his Ossian, but he was naturally deterred by the feeling that his knowledge of Gaelic was becoming shakier with his continued absence from the Highlands. At any rate he left behind a quantity of Gaelic matter in MS. which was ultimately 638published by the Highland Society of London in 1807. This MS., however, was revised and transcribed by Ross and afterwards destroyed, so that we are ignorant of its nature. The Highland Society also instituted an inquiry into the whole question, but their conclusions were somewhat negative. They succeeded in establishing that the characters introduced by Macpherson were familiar in the Highlands and that Ossianic ballads really existed, which Macpherson had utilized. Macpherson's claims still found ardent advocates, such as Clark, in the 'seventies, but the question was finally disposed of in papers by Alexander Macbain (1885) and L.C. Stern (1895). We can here only summarize briefly the main lines of argument. (1) Macpherson's Ossian is full of reminiscences of Homer, Milton and the Hebrew prophets. (2) He confuses the Ulster and the Fenian heroic cycles in unpardonable fashion. (3) The Gaelic text of 1807 only represents one-half of the English versions (11 poems out of 22 poems). Some Gaelic fragments from different pens appeared prior to 1807, but these differ considerably from the "official" version. (4) In the Gaelic text of 1807 the version of the passage from *Temora* is quite different from that published in 1763. (5) Macpherson's Gaelic is full of offences against idiom and unnaturally strained language. (6) The names Morven and Selma are entirely of his own invention (see also MACPHERSON, JAMES). As a result of the stir caused by Macpherson's work a number of men set about collecting the genuine popular literature of the Highlands. A few years before the appearance of *Fingal*, Jeremy Stone, a schoolmaster at Dunkeld, had collected ten Ossianic ballads and published one of them in an English versified translation. For this collection see a paper by D. Mackinnon in the *Transactions of the Gaelic Society of Inverness*, vol. xiv. pp. 314 ff. Unfortunately other persons were led to follow Macpherson's example. The chief of these imitators were (1) John Clark, who in 1778 published, along with several others, an English poem *Mordubh*, later translated into Gaelic by Gillies; (2) R. Macdonald, son of Alexander Macdonald, who is the author of *The Wish of the Aged Bard*; (3) John Smith of Campbeltown (d. 1807), author of fourteen Ossianic poems styled *Seandàna*, published in English in 1780 and in Gaelic in 1787; (4) D.

MacCallum of Arisaig, who in 1821 published *Collath* and a complete *Mordubh* "by an ancient bard Fonar."

We have now reviewed in turn the greatest writers of the Scottish Highlands. The men we have dealt with created a kind of tradition which others have attempted to carry on. Ewen Maclachlan (1775-1822), the first transcriber of **Later poets.** the Dean's Book, was assistant librarian of King's College and rector of the grammar school of Aberdeen. Amongst other things he translated the greater part of seven books of Homer's *Iliad* into Gaelic heroic verse, and he also had a large share in the compilation of the Gaelic-English part of the Highland Society's *Dictionary.* A number of Gaelic poems were published by him in 1816. These consist of poems of nature, *e.g. Dàin nan Aimsirean, Dàn mu chonaltradh, Smeòrach Chloinn-Lachuinn,* and of a well-known love-song, the *Ealaidh Ghaoil.* William Ross (1762-1790), a schoolmaster at Gairloch, is the typical Highland poet of the tender passion, and he is commonly represented as having gone to an early grave in consequence of unrequited affection. His finest compositions are *Feasgar Luain* and *Moladh na h-òighe Gaelich.* Another exquisite song *Cuachag nan Craobh,* is usually attributed to this poet, but it seems to go back to the beginning of the 18th century. A fifth edition of Ross's poems appeared in 1902. The most popular writer of sacred poems after Buchanan is undoubtedly Peter Grant, a Baptist minister in Strathspey, whose *Dàin Spioradail* (first published in 1809) reached a twentieth edition in 1904, Sweetness, grace and simplicity are the characteristics which have endeared him to the heart of the Gael. Two other well-known hymn-writers spent their lives in Nova Scotia—James Macgregor (1759-1830) and John Maclean, a native of Tiree. The compositions of the latter have been published under the title *Clarsach na Coille* (Glasgow, 1881). But John Morrison (1790-1852), the poet-blacksmith of Rodel, Harris, is the most worthy of the name of successor to Buchanan. His works have been carefully edited in two volumes by George Henderson (2nd edition, 1896). His poems are remarkably musical and imaginative. Two of the most characteristic are *An Iondruinn* and *Tha duin' òg agus seann duin' agam.* William Livingston or MacDhunleibhe (1808-1870) was a native of Islay. He received scarcely any education, and was apprenticed as a tailor, but he early made his way to the mainland. He was ever a fierce Anglophobe, and did his best to make up for the deficiencies of his early training. He published in English a *Vindication of the Celtic Character,* and attempted to issue a *History of Scotland* in parts. His poems, which have been at least twice published (1858, 1882), are equally powerful in the expression of ruthless fierceness and tearful sorrow. In *Fios thun a' Bhaird* he sings pathetically of the passing of the older order in Islay, and another powerful poem entitled *Duan Geall* deals with the campaign of the Highlanders under Sir Colin Campbell in the Crimea. Livingston's contemporary, Evan Maccoll (1808-1898), the son of a small farmer on Lochfyneside, in his early years devoured eagerly all the English literature and Gaelic lore that came in his way. In 1836 he issued a volume of songs called the *Mountain Minstrel,* containing his productions in Gaelic and English. Two years later two volumes appeared, one entirely in Gaelic, styled *Clarsach nam Beann,* the other in English under the old title. A third edition of the Gaelic collection was published in 1886. Maccoll acted for many years as clerk in the custom-house at Liverpool, and afterwards he filled a similar post at Kingston, Canada. He has been called the Moore of Highland song. His spirit is altogether modern, and his poems are much nearer the Lowland type than those of the older bards. Among his best-known pieces are *Bàs Mairi* and *Duanag Ghaoil.* We can do no more than mention the names of John Maclachlan of Rahoy (1804-1874), James Munro (1794-1870), well known as a grammarian, Dugald Macphail (b. 1818), Mrs Mary Macpherson, Angus Macdonald (1804-1874), Mrs Mary Mackellar (1834-1890) and Neil Macleod (b. 1843), author of a popular collection *Clarsach an Doire* (1st ed., 1883; 3rd ed., 1904). Neil Macleod is also the writer of the popular song *An Gleann's an robh mi òg.* Others whom we cannot mention here are known as the authors of one or more songs which have become popular. It is natural to compare the state of affairs at the beginning of the 20th century with that obtaining in 1800. In the dawn of the 19th century every district in the Highlands had its native poet, whilst a century later not a single Gaelic bard of known reputation existed anywhere within its borders. It is only too evident that the new writers prefer English to Gaelic as a medium of literature, partly because they know it better, but also because in it they appeal to a far wider public.

It will have been observed that we have said nothing about prose works written in Gaelic. Original Gaelic prose is conspicuous by its absence. The first printed work is the translation of Knox's *Liturgy* by Bishop Carsewell, **Prose writers.** published in 1567 (reprinted in 1873). Calvin's Catechism is said to have been issued in 1631. The Psalms and Shorter Catechism appeared in 1659, while two other psalters saw the light before the end of the century, one by Kirke (1684), the other issued by the Synod of Argyll (1694). The language of all these publications may, however, be termed Irish. Apart from reprints of the catechism and psalter, the only other Gaelic matter which appeared in print before 1750 were Kirke's Irish version of the Bible in Roman type with a vocabulary (1690), and the *Vocabulary* by Alexander Macdonald (1741). But from the middle of the 18th century translations of the works of English religious writers streamed from the various presses. Alleine, Baxter, Boston, Bunyan, Doddridge and Jonathan Edwards were all prime favourites, and their works have gone through many editions. Apart from a well-meant but wholly inadequate version of Schiller's *Tell*, the only non-religious work which can be termed literature existing in a Gaelic translation is a portion of the *Arabian Nights*, though fragments of other classics such as Lamb's *Tales from Shakespeare* have appeared in magazines. The one-sided character of Gaelic literature, in addition to exercising a baneful influence on Highland character, has in the 639 long run of necessity proved adverse to the vitality of the language. The best standard of Gaelic is by common consent the language of the Scriptures. James Stewart of Killin's version of the New Testament, published by the Society for Propagating Christian Knowledge, was followed by a translation of the Old Testament in four parts (1783-1801), the work of John Stewart of Luss and John Smith of Campbeltown. The whole Gaelic Bible saw the light in 1807. But the revision of 1826 is regarded as standard. The translators and revisers had no norm to follow, and it is difficult to say how far they were influenced by Irish tradition. Much in the Gaelic version seems to savour of Irish idiom, and it is a pity that some competent scholar such as Henderson has not investigated the question. Of original prose works we can mention two. The one is a *History of the Forty-five (Eachdraidh a' Phrionnsa, no Bliadhna Thearlaich)*, published in 1845 by John Mackenzie, the compiler of the *Beauties of Gaelic Poetry* (1806-1848). A second edition of this book appeared in 1906. The other is the more famous *Caraid nan Gaedheal*, by Norman Macleod (new edition, 1899). This volume consists mainly of a number of dialogues dealing with various departments of Highland life, which were originally contributed to various magazines from 1829 to 1848. Macleod's style is racy and elegant, and his work is deservedly popular.

In conclusion we must take notice of the more important collections of folklore. Gaelic, like Irish, is extraordinarily rich in proverbs. The first collection of Gaelic proverbs was published in 1785 by Donald Macintosh. This work was supplemented and enlarged in 1881 by Alexander Nicolson, whose book contains no fewer than 3900 short sayings. A large collection of Gaelic folk-tales was gleaned and published by J.F. Campbell under the title of *Popular Tales of the West Highlands* (4 vols., Edinburgh, 1862). Alexander Carmichael published a version of the *Táin Bó Calnge*, called *Toirioc na Táine*, which he collected in South Uist (*Transactions of the Gaelic Society of Inverness*, ii. 25-42), also the story of Deirdre and the sons of Uisneach in prose taken down in Barra (ib. xiii. 241-257). Five volumes of popular stories, collected by J.G. Campbell, D. MacInnes, J. Macdougall and Lord Archibald Campbell, have been published (1889-1895) by Nutt under the title *Waifs and Strays of Celtic Tradition*. These collections contain a good deal of matter pertaining to the old heroic cycles. Seven ballads dealing with the Ulster cycle were collected and printed by Hector Maclean under the title *Ultonian Hero-ballads* (Glasgow, 1892). Macpherson gave a fillip to collectors of Ossianic lore, and a number of MSS. going back to his time are deposited in the Advocates' Library at Edinburgh. J.F. Campbell spent twelve years searching for variants, and his results were published in his *Leabhar na Feinne* (1872). This volume contains 54,000 lines of heroic verse. The Edinburgh MSS. were transcribed by Alexander Cameron, and published after his death by Alexander Macbain and John Kennedy in his *Reliquiae Celticae*. This work is therefore a complete corpus of Gaelic heroic verse. Finally the charms and incantations of the Highlands have been collected and published by Alexander Carmichael in two sumptuous volumes under the title *Carmina Gadelica* (1900).

AUTHORITIES.—The standard work is Magnus Maclean, *The Literature of the Highlands* (London, 1904); see also various chapters in the same writer's *Literature of the Celts* (London, 1902); L.C. Stern, *Die Kultur der Gegenwart*, i. xi. 1, pp. 98-109; Nigel MacNeill, *The Literature of the Highlanders* (Inverness, 1892); J.S. Blackie, *The Language and Literature of the Scottish Highlands* (Edinburgh, 1876); P.T. Pattison,*Gaelic Bards* (1890); L. Macbean, *Songs and Hymns of the Scottish Highlands*(Edinburgh, 1888); John Mackenzie, *Sàrobair nam Bàrd Gaelach*, or *The Beauties of Gaelic Poetry* (new ed., Edinburgh, 1904); A. Sinclair, *An t-Oranaiche* (Glasgow, 1879); *The Book of Deer*, edited for the Spalding Club by Dr Stuart (1869); Alexander Macbain, *Transactions of the Gaelic Society of Inverness*, vols. xi. and xii.; *The Book of the Dean of Lismore*, edited by T. Maclauchlan (1862); Alexander Cameron, *Reliquiae Celticae* (Inverness, 1892-1894); John Reid, *Bibliotheca Scoto-Celtica* (Glasgow, 1832); *Catalogue* of the books in the Celtic department, Aberdeen University Library (1897); George Henderson, *Leabhar nan Gleann* (Inverness, 1898); D. Mackinnon, "The Fernaig MS." in *Transactions of the Gaelic Society of Inverness*, xi. 311-339; J.S. Smart, *James Macpherson, An Episode in Literature* (London, 1905); L.C. Stern, "Die Ossianischen Heldenlieder" in *Zeitschrift für vergleichende Litteraturgeschichte* (1895), translated by J.L. Robertson in *Transactions of the Gaelic Society of Inverness*, xxv. 257-325; G. Dottin, *Revue de synthèse historique*, viii. 79-91; M.C. Macleod, *Modern Gaelic Bards* (Stirling, 1908).

(E. C. Q.)

III. MANX LITERATURE.—The literary remains written in the Manx language are much slighter than those of any other Celtic dialect. With one small exception nothing pertaining to the saga literature of Ireland has been preserved. The little we possess naturally falls under two heads—original compositions and translations. With regard to the first category we must give the place of honour to an Ossianic poem contained in a MS. in the British Museum (written in 1789), which relates how Orree, Finn's enemy, was tormented by the women of Finn's household when the latter was away hunting, how he in revenge set fire to the house, and how Finn had him torn in pieces by wild horses. Most of the existing literature of native origin, however, consists of ballads and carols, locally called carvels. These used to be sung on Christmas eve in the churches, the members of the congregation each bringing a candle. Any one who pleased could get up and sing one. These carvels deal largely with the end of the world, the judgment-day and the horrors of hell. About eighty of them were published under the title of *Carvalyn Gailckagh* (Douglas, 1891). An attempt is being made by *Yn Cheshaght Gailckagh* to revive the *Oiel Voirrey* (=Irish *Oidhche Fhéile Mhuire*), "the feast of Mary," as the festival used to be called, and gatherings in the old style have been held in Peel for the last two or three years. Apart from the carvels there are other ballads in existence, the most important of which were printed in vol. xvi. of the *Publications of the Manx Society*. The earliest is an 18th-century song of Manannan Mac y Lheir, traditionally supposed to have been written in the 16th century, and which tells of the conversion of the island by St Patrick. Then comes *Baase Ittiam Dhône* (The Death of Brown William), dealing with the death of William Christian, who was shot as a traitor in 1662. The best-known Manx song is*Mylecharaine* (= Irish *Maolchiarán*). It is directed against a man of this name who was the first to give a dowry to his daughter, the custom having previously been for the bridegroom to pay money to the father of the bride. Others are *Ny Kirree fo Sniaghtey* (The Sheep under the Snow), a song about the loss of the Douglas herring fleet in 1787 (reprinted at Douglas, 1872), and *O Vannin Veg Veen* (Dear little Mona). A further ballad was taken down by J. Strachan and is published in the *Zeitschrift für celtische Philologie*, i. 79. In 1760 Joseph Bridson wrote a "Short Account of the Isle of Man" in Manx (*Coontey Ghiare jeh Ellan Vannin ayns Gailck*), which was reprinted in vol. xx. of the *Publications of the Manx Society*. The translated literature is almost entirely of a religious character. Jenner prints a list of twenty-three volumes in his article referred to below, but we can only here mention the most important. The first is the translation of the English Prayer-Book by Bishop Phillips, 1610 (published by A.W. Moore, Oxford, 1895). The *Sermons* of Bishop Wilson in 3 vols. (1783) are a very rare work, highly important for our knowledge of Manx prose, and it is to be hoped that *Yn Cheshaght Gailckagh* will see their way to reprint it. A translation of parts of Milton's *Paradise Lost* (*Pargys Caillit*) by Thomas Christian, 1796, is reprinted in vol. xx. of the *Publications of the Manx Society*. The later translation of the Church of England

292

Prayer-Book was printed in 1765 and again in 1777 and 1840. But by far the most important of all is the translation of the Bible. The energetic Bishop Wilson managed to get parts of the Scriptures translated and the Gospel of St Matthew was printed in 1748. Wilson's successor, Bishop Hildesley, completed the work, and in 1775 the whole Bible appeared. The last reprint of the Bible appeared in 1819, that of the New Testament in 1810 (?). As a curiosity it may be mentioned that recently *Aesop's Fables* have been translated into the vernacular (Douglas, 1901).

AUTHORITIES.—H. Jenner, "The Manx Language: its Grammar, Literature and Present State," *Transactions of the London Philological Society* (1875), pp. 172 ff.; *Publications of the Manx Society*, vols. xvi., xx., xxi.; L.C. Stern, *Die Kultur d. Gegenwart*, i. xi. 1, pp. 110-11.

640

IV. WELSH LITERATURE.—The oldest documents consist of glosses of the 9th and 10th centuries found in four MSS.—Oxoniensis prior and posterior, the Cambridge Juvencus and Martianus Capella. These glosses were published **Early MSS.** by J. Loth in his *Vocabulaire vieux-breton* (1884), but their value is entirely philological. In addition, we possess two short verses, written in Irish characters, preserved in the Juvencus Manuscript in the University Library at Cambridge (printed in Skene's *Four Ancient Books of Wales*). This manuscript is a versification of the Gospels dating from the 9th century. The value of these two verses is threefold: they give us, in the first place, a specimen of the Welsh language at a time when the modern laws of euphony were in a comparatively elementary stage; secondly, they are of the utmost importance to the historian tracing the development of Welsh versification, and, in future research, they must be taken into account by the historian of modern metres in other languages; and, thirdly, the similarity of their form and diction to other verses, attributed to Llywarch Hen, and preserved in a much later orthography, will be a serious consideration to the higher critic in Welsh literature.

All the prose and verse of the succeeding centuries, that is to say from the 10th to the beginning of the 14th, is preserved in four important manuscripts, written during the latter half of the period. The first of these manuscripts is **"Black Book of Carmarthen."** the *Black Book of Carmarthen*, a small quarto vellum manuscript of fifty leaves, written in Gothic letters by various hands during the reign of Henry II. (published in facsimile by Gwenogvryn Evans, Oxford, 1907). This book belonged originally to the priory of Black Canons at Carmarthen, from whom it passed to the church of St David; at the suppression of the monasteries in the reign of Henry VIII. it was presented by the treasurer of that church to Sir John Price, one of the king's commissioners, and from him it passed eventually into the hands of Sir Robert Vaughan, the owner of the famous **"Book of Aneirin."** Hengwrt collection. It is now among the Peniarth Manuscripts, undoubtedly the most valuable collection of Welsh manuscripts in the United Kingdom. The second manuscript is the *Book of Aneirin*, a small quarto manuscript of nineteen leaves of vellum, written about 1250. It was at one time in the possession of Sir Thomas **"Book of Taliessin."** Phillips of Middlehill, and now belongs to the free library of the city of Cardiff. The third is the *Book of Taliessin*, in the Hengwrt and subsequently in the Peniarth collection. It is a small quarto manuscript containing thirty-eight leaves, written in Gothic letters, about the early part of the 14th century. The fourth manuscript, and in some respects the most important, is the *Red Book* **"Red Book of Hergest."** *of Hergest*, so called from Hergest Court, one of the seats of the Vaughans. It is a folio volume of 360 leaves written by different hands between the beginning of the 14th and the middle of the 15th century. This manuscript, which is the most extensive compilation of the medieval prose and verse of Wales, is now in the possession of Jesus College, Oxford, and is kept in the Bodleian Library of that university. The main body of the poems contained in these four MSS. was printed by W. F. Skene with a tentative English version in his *Four Ancient Books of Wales*.

The other Welsh manuscripts, ranging down from the 15th to the 18th century, are far too numerous to notice, and it is outside the scope of this article to deal minutely with the original sources of the text of Welsh writings.

We will now only endeavour to sketch the history of Welsh literature from these early centuries down to our own times, and to show how the Celtic people of Wales have developed a literature true to their own genius, and how that literature stands to this day both a minister to the culture of the Welsh people and a sure indication of it.

1. *Early Latin Writers.*—The works now known as those of Gildas (*q.v.*) and Nennius (*q.v.*) are written in Latin; they throw considerable light on the origin of Welsh romantic literature and on the history of the earlier poems. Gildas was born at Ailclyd, the modern Dumbarton, that part of Britain which is called by Welsh writers *Y Gogledd*, or the North. Several dates have been assigned for his birth and death, but he probably flourished between 500 and 580, and his book, *De Excidio Britanniae* seems to have been written about 560. This work is **Gildas** sketch of British history under the Romans and in the period after their withdrawal from the country, and includes the period of the wars of the Britons with the Picts, Scots and Saxons. Mr Skene suggests very reasonably that the well-known letter of the Britons to Aetius, asking for Roman aid, is misplaced, and that if put in its own place some of the anachronisms of Gildas will disappear. This work, which contains some spirited attacks on the leaders of the Britons for their sins, is strangely full of contradictions. It seems to be the work of some person well versed in the facts of that part of British history, to which he had an easy access, but who supplemented them with traditional details and with dates which were mere guess-work. Mr Skene thinks that the work of Nennius was originally written in Welsh in the north and was afterwards translated into Latin. To this nucleus was added the genealogies of the Saxon kings down to 738. Afterwards some person, called Marc in the Vatican manuscript, appended probably about 823 the life of St Germanus and the legends of St Patrick, which were subsequently incorporated with the history. Some South Welshman added to the oldest manuscript of the history in these countries, about 977, a chronicle of events from 444 to 954, in which there are genealogies beginning with Owain, son of Hywel Dda, king of South Wales. This chronicle, which is not found in other manuscripts, has been made the basis of two later chronicles brought down to 1286 and 1288 respectively. It is consequently not the work of one author. A learned Irishman named Gilla Coemgin, who died in 1072, translated it into Irish and added many things concerning the Irish and the Picts. The *Historia Britonum* is more valuable for the legendary matter which it contains than for what may be accepted as history, for it gives us the British legends of the colonization of Great Britain and Ireland, the exploits of King Arthur and the prophecies of Merlin, which are not found elsewhere before the 12th century. The date of the book is of the greatest importance to the history of medieval romance, and there can be no doubt that it is earlier than the Norman Conquest and that the legends themselves are of British origin.

2. *The Epic Period, 700-950.*—The higher criticism of the early poetry of Wales contained in the four ancient manuscripts already mentioned has undergone a good many changes since their contents first excited the curiosity of English scholars. In turn Welshmen, with more zeal than discretion, have displayed an amazing charlatanism in the extraordinary theories which they put forth, and Englishmen have shown an utmost meanness in belittling what is undoubtedly a most valuable monument of the past. But now the labours of Zeuss and others who have made a study of Celtic philology furnish us with much safer canons of criticism than existed in 1849, when even a learned Welshman, the late Thomas Stephens, who did more than any one else to establish the claims of his country to a real literature, doubted the authenticity of a large number of the poems said to have been written by Taliessin, Aneirin, Myrddin and Llywarch Hen, who are supposed to have lived in the 5th century. A great service was done to Welsh literature by the publication of the texts of those poems from the four ancient manuscripts by W.F. Skene. In addition to the text, translations of the poems were furnished by Dr Silvan Evans and the Rev. Robert Williams, but the translation, though on the whole a very creditable work, is full of mistakes which few men, writing at that time, could have avoided. The publication of the text of the Black Book, with notes by Dr Gwenogvryn Evans, will be of great service towards clearing up the mist which envelops this older literature.

Most of the poems in these four manuscripts are attributed to four poets, Aneirin, Llywarch Hen, Taliessin and Myrddin, who are said to have lived and written in Cumbria or Y Gogledd, where the actors in the events referred to also lived. The greater part of this region enjoyed substantial independence down to the end of the 9th century, with the exception of the 641 interval from 655, when they were subjected to the kingdom of

Northumbria by Oswy after the defeat of Cadwallawn and Penda, to the battle of Dunnichen in 686, when Ecfrid, king of Northumbria, was defeated. From the 7th to the 9th century Cumbria, including under that name all the British territory from the Ribble to the Clyde, was the principal theatre of British and Saxon conflict. The rise of the dynasty of Maelgwn Gwynedd, who, according to Welsh tradition, was a descendant of Cunedda Wledig, one of the Picts of the north, brought Wales into close connexion with the Cumbrian kingdom, and prepared both North and South Wales for the reception of the northern traditions and the rise of a true Welsh literature.

Whether the poets of the north really wrote any of the poems which in a modified form have come down to us or not, there can be no doubt that a number of lays attributed to them lived in popular tradition, and that under the sudden burst of glory which the deeds of Cadwallawn called forth and which ended in the disastrous defeat of 655, a British literature began to spring up, and was nourished by the hopes of a future resurrection under his son Cadwaladr, whose death was disbelieved in for such a long time. These floating lays and traditions gradually gathered into North Wales, brought thither by the nobility and the bards who fled before advancing hosts of the victorious Saxon kings of the north. The heroes of the north became now the heroes of Wales, and the sites of the battles they fought were identified with places of similar name in Wales and England.

By far the longest and the most famous poem of this series is attributed to Aneurin. This spelling of his name is comparatively modern, and in the old manuscripts it is given as Aneirin. The later form seems to have been affected *Aneurin* by the form *eurin*, "golden," and to owe the continuation of the misspelling to a belief that the poet and Gildas, whose name is supposed to be the Latin form of the Old English *gylden*, were one and the same person. This poem, called the *Gododin* (with notes by T. Stephens and published by Prof. Powel for the Cymmrodorion Society, London, 1888), is extremely obscure, both on account of its vocabulary and its topography and allusions. It deals mainly with "the men who went to Cattraeth," which is supposed to have been fought between the Britons and the Scots under Aedan, king of Dalriada, and the pagan Saxons and their British subjects in *Devyr* (Deira) and *Bryneich* (Bernicia), and the half-pagan Picts of Guotodin, a district corresponding to the northern half of the Lothians along the Firth of Forth. Critics have attempted with partial success to cast some light on its obscurity by supposing that the poem as a whole is made up of two parts dealing with two distinct battles. This may or may not be, but there is no doubt that many of the stanzas of the poem as found in the manuscript are not in their proper places, and a critical readjustment of the different stanzas and lines would do much towards solving its problem. It seems probable, too, that the original nucleus of the poem was handed down orally, and recited or sung by the bards and minstrels at the courts of different noblemen. It thus became the common stock-in-trade of the Welsh rhapsodist, and in time the bards, using it as a kind of framework, added to it here and there pieces of their own composition formed on the original model, especially when the heroes named happened to be the traditional forefathers of their patrons, and occasionally introduced the names of new heroes and new places as it suited their purpose; and all this seems to have been done in early times. Older fragments dealing too with the legendary heroes of the Welsh were afterwards incorporated with the poem, and some of these fragments undoubtedly preserve the orthographical and grammatical forms of the 9th century. So that, on the whole, it seems as fruitless to look for a definite record of historical events in this poem as it would be to do so in the Homeric poems, but like them, though it cannot any longer be regarded as a correct and definite account of a particular battle or war, it still stands to this day the epic of the warriors of its own nation. It matters not whether these heroes fought at far Cattraeth or on some other forgotten field of disaster; this song still reflects, as a true national epic, the sad defeats and the brave but desperate rallies of the early Welsh. Like the music of the Welsh, its dominant note is that of sadness, expressing the exultation of battle and the very joy of life in minor notes. To a great extent Welsh poets are to this day true and faithful disciples of this early master.

Many of the poems attributed to Taliessin are undoubtedly late. Indeed, both Taliessin and Myrddin,2 the one as the mythological chief of all Welsh bards and the other as a great magician, seem pre-eminently suited to attract a great *Taliessin.* deal of later Welsh poetry under their aegis; but the older poems attributed to them are worthy of any literature. Sometimes, as in the verses attributed to Llywarch Hen beginning *Stafell Cynddylan*, an early specimen of poetic grief over departed glory, we find that gentle elegiac note which is so common in early English poetry. In the Taliessinic poems, the *Battle of Argoed Llwyvain* and others, we have that boldness of portraiture which is found in the *Gododin*, whilst in many a noble line we seem to hear again the ravens screaming shrilly over their sword-feasts, and the strong strokes of the advancing warriors.

It was but natural that all the pseudo-prophetic poems, written of course after the events which they foretold, should be attributed to the chief among seers, Myrddin, or, as **Merlin.** his name is written in English, Merlin; so that all the poems accredited to him, with the exception perhaps of the *Avallenau*, were not written before the 12th century.

In most of the poems attributed to Llywarch Hen and in some of the Myrddin poems, the verses begin with the same line, which, though it has no direct reference to the subject of the poem itself, is used as a refrain or catch-word, exactly like the refrains employed by Mr Swinburne and others in their ballads. These lines generally refer to some natural object or objects, as, for instance, "the snow of the mountain" or "bright are the tops of the broom."

The first period, then, of Welsh literature lies between 700 and 950. It is in most respects the epic period, the period in which poets wrote of great men and their deeds, the legendary and the historic heroes of the Cymry, men like Urien Rheged, and heroes like Hyveidd Hir. Even in the next period the epic note had not quite died out.

3. *The Prose Romances and the Poet Princes, 1100-1290.*—It will be seen that there is a considerable gap between the first and second period of Welsh literature. It must not be supposed, however, that nothing was composed or written during these years. Indeed, it may well be that some of the poetry attributed to the minor bards of the last period was composed between 900 and 1100, and that some other poetry too was written and lost. But there are abundant reasons for believing that Welsh poetry was at a very low ebb during those years. The progress of Wales as a political unit had suffered a check after the battle of Chester in 613. The effects of this defeat were not immediate, as the Welsh had still enough of their characteristic hopefulness to expect ultimate victory; we therefore have reasons for believing **The Gododin series.** that the Gododin series of poems were still used—or perhaps used then for the first time—to spur on "the hawks of war" to greater efforts. Gradually, however, the Angles, hemming them in on all sides from the Clyde to the Severn, began to press nearer and nearer; the Welsh at last seem to have lost heart, and no one any longer "had the desire of song." Content with their old epics and their older myths, which owe perhaps to these years a darker and more sombre tinge, they allowed their song to be hushed. The great lords had hardly chosen their final abodes; the smaller lords had all been killed in war and their places taken now by one, now by another, so that the warrior prince himself had not the leisure, and hardly the inspiration necessary, for song, and the bards found but scanty patronage among such a diminished and poverty-stricken nobility. The only order that seemed to prosper was that of the monks, and we owe them our gratitude for 642preserving the ancient writings and the ancient traditions; but they were simply copyists, though they had undoubtedly some hand in giving the *Gododin* its final form and in setting in its convenient framework the names of the forefathers of their aristocratic abbots.

In the year 1044 Gruffydd ab Llewelyn conquered Hywel ab Edwin and became king of Wales. By means of his diplomacy and his arms he succeeded in stemming the tide of Saxon invasion that was threatening to overflow even the little remnant of land that was left to the Welsh, and his strong rule gave the Welsh muse another opportunity. Gruffydd, however, died in 1063, and was eventually succeeded in 1073 by Trahaern in North Wales, and Rhys ab Owen in South Wales. The rule of these two princes was destined to be the last period of literary inertness in the long interval following the confinement of Wales to her inaccessible highlands.

During these years a man was hiding in Ireland, called Gruffydd ab Cynan, a scion of the old branch of Welsh kings. In Brittany, too, Rhys ab Tewdwr, a claimant to the throne of South Wales, had sought the protection of his Breton kinsmen. In 1073 Rhys ab Tewdwr obtained the throne of Rhys ab Owen, and, after many years of hard fighting, Gruffydd ab

Cynan, with the help of Rhys ab Tewdwr, defeated Trahaern at the battle of Myrydd Carn in 1081. On the accession of these two powerful princes the whole country broke forth into songs of praise and jubilation, and the long night was at an end.

It is important to remember that both Gruffydd and Rhys had a direct personal influence on the literary revival of their times. Gruffydd ab Cynan while in exile had seen how the Irish *Oenach* was held, and had seen prizes given for poetry and song. We have it on the authority of Welsh writers that he reorganized the bards and improved the music, and in many other ways gave a great and beneficial impulse to Welsh literature. He may have brought over some of the later Irish legends which have had such a powerful effect on the literature of Wales.

Rhys ab Tewdwr, too, brought with him from Brittany an enthusiasm for the old Celtic tales, and perhaps some of the tales themselves which had been by that time forgotten in Wales, tales of the Round Table, and Arthur "begirt with British and Armoric knights," of knightly deeds and magical metamorphoses, which were destined to influence profoundly all the literatures of the West. We find, therefore, in this period that poetry flourished mostly in the North under Gruffydd ab Cynan, and prose in the south under Rhys ab Tewdwr, where the new enthusiasm for the old Welsh legends resulted in the **Geoffrey of Montmouth.** *History of Britain* of Geoffrey of Monmouth, which is an expansion of the books attributed to Gildas and Nennius. It was written in Latin sometime before 1147, and is dedicated to Robert, earl of Gloucester, the grandson of Rhys ab Tewdwr. In the introductory epistle, Geoffrey states that Walter, archdeacon of Oxford, had given him a very ancient book in the British tongue, giving an account of the kings of Britain from Brutus to Cadwaladr, and that he had translated it into Latin at the archdeacon's request. The book, however, is a compilation and not a translation, but the materials were probably drawn from British sources. In this history Geoffrey asserts that the deeds of Arthur "were commonly related in a pleasing manner." He was perhaps originally but the hero of some popular ballad, or of a forgotten stanza of the *Gododin*, and the importance of his name in the literature of the world seems to be due to an accident. We cannot, however, in this article consider the Arthurian Legend (*q.v.*) as a whole; we must be content with dealing with the most important of the romantic tales which are contained in the *Red Book of Hergest*. They may be divided into four classes:—

(i.) The *Mabinogi* proper, containing (1) *Pwyll*, prince of Dyvet; (2) *Branwen*, daughter of Llyr; (3) *Manawyddan*, son of *Llyr*; (4) *Math*, son of Mathonwy.

(ii.) Old British tales referring to Roman times, viz. (1) *Lludd* and *Llevelys*; (2) The Dream of *Macsen Wledic*.

(iii.) British Arthurian tales, viz. (1) *Kilhwch* and *Olwen*; (2) The Dream of *Rhonabwy*.

(iv.) Later tales of chivalry, viz. (1) The Lady of the Fountain; (2) *Peredur*, son of *Evrawc*; (3) *Geraint*, son of *Erbin*.

The group of four romances in the first class forms a cycle of legends and is called in the manuscript *Pedeir Keinc y Mabinogi*—the Four Branches of the Mabinogi; so it is only these four tales that can, strictly speaking, be called **The Mabinogion.** *Mabinogion*. In these stories we have the relics of the ancient Irish mythology of the *Tuatha Dé Danann*, sometimes mixed with later myths. The *Caer Sidi*, where neither disease nor old age affects any one, is the *Sid* of Irish mythology, the residence of the gods of the *Aes Side*. It is called in one of the old poems the prison of *Gweir*, who no doubt represents *Gaiar*, son of Manandán MacLir, the Atropos who cut the thread of life of Irish mythology. *Llyr* is the Irish sea-god Lir, and was called *Llyr Llediaith*, or the half-tongued, implying that he spoke a language only partially intelligible to the people of the country. *Bran*, the son of Llyr, is the Irish Bran MacAllait, Allait being one of the names of Lir. *Manawyddan* is clearly the Manandán or Manannán MacLir of Irish mythology. These tales contain other characters which may not have been borrowed from Irish mythology but which are common to both mythologies; for example, Rhiannon, the wife of Pwyll who possessed marvellous birds which held warriors spellbound for eighty years by their singing, comes from *Annwn*, or the unseen world, and her son Pryderi gives her, on the death of Pwyll, as a wife to Manawyddan.

Of the second class the first story relates to Lludd, son of Beli the Great, son of Manogan, who became king after his father's death, while his brother Llevelys becomes king of France and shows his brother how to get rid of the three plagues which devastated Britain:—first, a strange race, the Coranians, whose knowledge was so great that they heard everything no matter how low soever it might be spoken; second, a shriek which came into every house on May eve, caused by the fighting of two dragons; and third, a great giant who carried off all the provisions of the king's palace every day. The second tale relates how Maxen, emperor of Rome, has a dream while hunting, in which he imagines that he visits Britain, and in *Caer Seint* or Carnarvon sees a beautiful damsel, Helen, whom he ultimately finds and marries. Both tales are British in origin and are founded on traditions referring to Roman times.

The most important of these tales are undoubtedly those contained in the first class, and the story of *Kilhwch* and *Olwen*. The form in which they are found in the *Red Book of Hergest* is, as we have already said, comparatively speaking, modern. But it is apparent to any one reading these tales that the writers or compilers, as Matthew Arnold has suggested, are "pillaging an antiquity, the secret of which they do not fully possess." The foundations of the tales are the old Celtic traditions of the gods and the older heroes, and they clearly show Goidelic influence both in the persons they introduce and in their incidents. The tales would at first exist only in oral tradition, and after the advent of Christianity the characters they contain lost their title of divinity and became simply heroes—warriors and magicians. In time the monks began to write these ancient traditions, embellishing them and suppressing no doubt what they considered to be most objectionable. These then are the tales which we now possess—the traditional doings of the old heroes as set in order by Christian writers.

The changes which these later copyists wrought in the substance of the tales fall into two main divisions. In the first place, they attempted to find some connexion between tales or cycles of tales which originally had no connexion whatever, and were therefore forced to invent new incidents or to introduce other incidents from the outside in order to establish this connexion; and secondly, as in the case of the *Gododin*, the tales were twisted and altered to support references to and explanations of names known to the writer. So we find in the tale of *Math vab Mathonwy* the incident of the pigs is expanded to explain some place-names which the writer knew. It is this also that gives a local interest to the tales; for instance, *Dyvet*, the land of *Pwyll*, has come to be regarded as the home of *Hud a Lledrith*, of magic and 643enchantment. Some places in North Wales, especially in the vicinity of Carnarvon, seem to be well known to the writers, and, therefore, to have associated with them to all time the glamour of the Mabinogion.

Besides the scholastic efforts of the monks, which in course of time so greatly changed these old legends, there was another class of men who had no little influence on the form and matter of Welsh, and consequently of European, romance. These were the Welsh jongleurs—the professional story-tellers, against whom the bards proper nursed a deadly hatred because, presumably, their tales drew larger audiences and won greater rewards than the *awdlau* of the poets. There is little doubt that this order existed in Wales at a very early period, being quite a natural evolution of the older poet who sang in comparatively free metres of the deeds of the great dead. It is these men who invented the term *Mabinogi*, which is supposed to mean a "tale for young people"; but whatever the word may mean, the fact that they were the stock-in-trade of the professional story-teller will explain a good many of their structural peculiarities.

Thus there existed two distinct classes of tales, though it is to be supposed that the subject matter of both was more or less common; there are, in the first place, the "four branches" and the tales of the second class, and, secondly, tales like those of the third class. With the exception of the Irish influence, which we have already referred to, and some later additions from early continental romance in the third class, we may take it that these three classes are of purely British origin. The *pedair cainc* are the old tales which were first committed to writing at an early period before the influence of the Armoric Arthur began to be felt, that is to say, about the beginning of the reign of Rhys ab Tewdwr in 1073. The other tales, that is those we have put in the third class, remained for a much longer time unwritten and were not set in writing before the early Arthur of Armoric and British romance had been evolved. This will account for the fact that Arthur is not mentioned in the first class of tales, and that in the third class he is simply a British Arthur. The third class is, therefore, in a sense later than the first and second, but its materials are as old as the oldest of the Mabinogion proper, and they show the influence of Irish mythology to the same extent. In the first class Irish names like *Penardim*, which have not been assimilated, show conclusively that the tale is a written one, while the eloquence of the descriptions in *Kilhwch ac Olwen* seem to point to the fact that it was up to a late period a *spoken* tale. Other such tales there were once, but they have now been lost.

The romances of the fourth class do not claim much notice. They are mostly imitations or translations of Norman French originals, and they belong to the history of European chivalry rather than to the history of Welsh literature.

As literature the Mabinogion may rank among the world's classics. We cannot here point out their beauties, but it will be sufficient to notice that the unknown writer who gave them their final form was a true artist in every sense of the word. In *Branwen verch Lyr*, for instance, the whole setting of the story is that of a great tragedy, a tragedy neither Hellenic nor Shakespearean, but the strong and ruthless tragedy of the Celts,—the tragedy of nature among unnatural surroundings, the tragedy which in our times Mr Thomas Hardy has so successfully developed. In this tale, Branwen is introduced as the sister of Manawyddan, the king of all Britain, and as the "fairest maid in the world." But as the tragedy deepens we read how this woman, dowered with beauty and goodness and nobility of lineage, is simply used as a pawn in a political game, and the full force of the tragedy falls on her own undeserving head. She is subjected to all kinds of indignities in her husband's court in Ireland, but throughout all her severe trials she preserves the cold and detached haughtiness which characterizes the full-bosomed heroines of the northern sagas; and, in the end, when her brother has delivered her and punished the Irish, and when she has safely reached the shores of her own Môn, she raises her eyes and beholds the two islands, Britain and Ireland. "'Ah God!' said she, 'is it well that two islands have been made desolate for my sake?' And she gave a deep groan and died." So was her tragedy consummated, and the writer, with a superb tragic touch, mentions the very shape of the grave in which they left her on the bank of the Alaw in Môn.

One of the earliest poets of this period whose productions we can be certain of is Meilir, bard of Trahaern, whom Gruffydd ab Cynan defeated at the battle of Carn, and afterwards of the conqueror Gruffydd himself. His best piece is the *Death-bed of the Bard*, a semi-religious poem which is distinguished by the structure of the verse, poetic feeling and religious thought. Meilir was the head of a family of bards; his son was Gwalchmai, one of the best Welsh poets; the latter had two sons, Einion and Meilir, some of whose poetry has reached us. In *Gorhoffedd Gwalchmai*, Gwalchmai's Delight, there is an appreciation of the charms of nature, medieval parallels to which are only to be found in Ireland. His *Arwyrain i Owain* is an ode of considerable beauty and full of vigour in praise of Owain Gwynedd, king of North Wales, on account of his victory of Tal y Moelvre, part of which has been translated by Gray under the name of "The Triumphs of Owen." Kynddelw, who lived in the second half of the 12th century, was a contemporary of Gwalchmai, and wrote on a great number of subjects including religious ones; indeed some of his eulogies have a kind of religious prelude. He had a command of words and much skill in versification, but he is pleonastic and fond of complicated metres and of ending his lines with the same syllable.

Among the other poets of the second half of the 12th century may be mentioned Owain Kyveiliog and Howel ab Owain Gwynedd. The first named was prince of Powys, and was distinguished also as a soldier. The *Hirlas*, or drinking-horn, is a long poem where the prince represents himself as carousing in his hall after a fight; bidding his cup-bearer fill his great drinking-horn, he orders him to present it in turn to each of the assembled warriors. As the horn passes from hand to hand he eulogizes each in a verse beginning *Diwallaw di venestr*, "Fill, cup-bearer." Having thus praised the deeds of two warriors, Tudyr and Moreiddig, he turns round to challenge them, but suddenly recollecting that they had fallen in the fray, and listening, as it were, to their dying groans, he bursts into a broken lamentation for their loss. The second was also a prince; he was the eldest of the many sons of Owain Gwynedd, and ruled for two years after his father until he fell in a battle between himself and his step-brother Dafydd. He was a young man of conspicuous merit, and one of the most charming poets of Wales, his poems being especially free from the conceits, trivial commonplaces, and complicated metres of the professional bards, while full of a gay humour, a love of nature and a delicate appreciation of women. The Welsh poets went on circuit like their Irish brethren, staying in each place according as hospitality was extended to them. When departing, a bard was expected to leave a sample of his versification behind him. In this way many manuscripts came to be written, as we find them in different hands. Llywarch ab Llywelyn has left us one of those departing eulogies addressed to Rhys Gryg, prince of South Wales, which affords a favourable specimen of his style.

The following are a few of the poets of the 13th century whose poems are still extant. Davydd Benvras was the author of a poem in praise of Llywelyn ab Iorwerth; his works, though not so verbose or trite as bardic poems *13th century poets.* of this class usually are, do not rise much above the bardic level, and are full of alliteration. Elidir Sais was, as his name implies, able to speak the English language, and wrote chiefly religious poetry. Einiawn ab Gwgawn is the author of an extant address to Llywelyn ab Iorwerth of considerable merit. Phylip Brydydd, or Philip the poet, was household bard to Rhys Gryg (Rhys the hoarse), lord of South Wales. One of his pieces, an apology to Rhys Gryg, is a striking example of the fulsome epithets a household bard was expected to bestow upon his patron, and of the privileged domesticity in which the bards lived, which, as in Ireland, must have been fatal to genius. Prydydd Bychan, the Little Poet, was a South Wales bard whose extant work consists of short poems all addressed to his own princes. The chief feature of his *Englynion* is the use of a 644kind of assonance in which in some cases the final vowels agreed alternately in each quatrain, and in others each line ended in a different vowel, in both cases with alliteration and consonance of final consonants or full rhyme. Llygad Gŵr is known by an ode in five parts to Llywelyn ab Gruffydd, written about the year 1270, which is a good type of the conventional flattery of a family bard. Howel Voel, who was of Irish extraction, possessed some poetical merit; his remonstrance to Llywelyn against the imprisonment of his brother Owain is a pleasing variety upon the conventional eulogy. It has many lines beginning with the same word, *e.g. gŵr,* man. The poems of Bleddyn Vardd, or Bleddyn the Bard, which have come down to us are all short eulogies and elegies. One of the latter on Llywelyn ab Gruffydd is a good example of the elaborate and artificial nature of Welsh versification.

The most illustrious name among the poets of this century is Gruffydd ab yr Ynad Coch, "Gruffydd, son of the Red Justice," who wrote many religious poems of great merit. His greatest work, however, is the elegy to Llywelyn ab Gruffydd, the last prince of Wales. It is easily first among all the elegies written in the Welsh language. We do not find in it that artficial grief which is too evident in the *Marwnadau* of the Welsh poets; it re-echoes an intense personal grief, and throughout the whole piece the poet feels that he stands at the end of all things,—the end of his own ideals, the extinction of all Cymric hopes. So poignant is his grief, and in so universal a manner does the catastrophe of Llywelyn's death present itself to him, that he imagines that all the natural features of the Welsh fatherland know that the last great Welshman is dead; the winds howl over the mountains, the rain-clouds gather thick, the waves rage with grief against the Welsh coasts, and far away on the hills the giant oak-trees beat against each other in the fury of their passion. Sadly, in this manner, closes the second period of Welsh literature.

4. *The Golden Age of the Cywydd, 1340-1440.*—Just as, after the loss of the North, the Welsh muse was hushed, so after the final subjugation of Wales in 1282, hardly a note was heard for many a long year. The ancient patrons of literature were dead, and the country had not yet settled down to the steady rule of England. Indeed, the conquest of Wales effectively put an end to the older Welsh poetry of that type which we noticed in the last period. These older bards were without exception subjects of the princes of North Wales, where the old heroic poetry was still popular, and when the power of these princes came to an end the old poetry too ceased. When the Welsh muse emerges again from the darkness of this interval she is no longer of the North; the new poets are drawn from the Welshmen of the South, a land which had practically ceased to be a part of an independent Wales shortly after the Norman conquest of England. We find, too, that the poetry which poured forth from the Welsh bards of the south is of an altogether different type, it is modern in all its essentials, in

diction, in language, and, comparatively speaking, in sentiment. Indeed, there is an infinitely greater difference between Dafydd ab Gwilym and Gruffydd ab yr Ynad Coch than there is between him and any poet writing in the alliterative metres in the 19th century. So that we must suppose that at the time when the poets of North Wales still sang of war and mead-drinking in a style and diction that was an inheritance from the times of the *Gododin*, the poets of the South, unharassed by wars, were developing a new poetry of their own, a poetry that had relinquished for ever the Old Welsh models and was at last in line with the great poetical movements of Europe. And, judging from the fact that the earliest of these poets whose works are accessible to us are in the full zenith of their poetical development, we must believe that their work is the consummation of a period, that is to say, that they must have had a long line of predecessors whose works were lost during the period intervening between the loss of Welsh independence and the rise of Dafydd ab Gwilym. These men wrote, as we have already said, in South Wales, a country which was then under the rule of the Norman lords, who, with the lapse of years and the rise of new systems, were fast becoming Welsh. It is no wonder, then, that the poets who wrote under their patronage should show unmistakable traces of Norman influence. Most of the barons still spoke French, and it was only natural that they should be well versed in French poetry. The poets followed the lead of their patrons, and their work was modelled to a very great extent on French and Provençal poetry. Nor does this account altogether for the wonderful similarity between Welsh *cywyddau* and other poems of this period and the French lays; we must remember that the Welsh poets lived under conditions similar to those under which the troubadours and the trouvères lived, and it was natural that the same environments should produce the same kind of work. The Provençal *alba* and the French *aube*, the *serenade* and other forms, became well known in South Wales and were of course read by the Welsh poets. We find continual references in the poets to "books of love" under the name of *llyfr Ofydd*, or the "book of Ovid," and a reference in one of Dafydd ab Gwilym's poems shows conclusively that one particular *llyfr Ofydd* was a work of the French poet Chrestien de Troyes. Indeed, one of the commonest names among the poets of this period—the *llatai*,[3] or love-messenger—may be a Romance word borrowed through the Norman-French from the Italian *Galeotto*, originally the name of the book of the loves of Galahaad, but afterwards the ordinary word for a go-between. This book of Galeotto, by the way, was the book which taught Paolo and Francesca da Rimini, in Dante's *Divina Commedia*, the tragic secret of love.

Another movement also was favourable to the rise of the new Welsh poetry. The iron hand of the church, which had been the censor of poetry for so many centuries, was slowly relaxing its grasp, and the men who a few years before would have sung religious hymns to the Virgin, now laid their tributes at the feet of divine womanhood as they saw it in the Welsh maidens and matrons living among them. The pale queen of heaven no longer held hearts captive; they had transferred their allegiance to the "brow that was as the snow of yesternight," and "the cheeks that were like the passion-flower." The Iolo MSS. assert that some time between January 1327 and November 1330 there were held, under the patronage of Ivor Hael, Dafydd ab Gwilym's patron, and others, the three *Eisteddfodau Dadeni*, or the Eisteddfods of the Revival of the Muse, to reorganize the bards, and to set in order all matters pertaining to Welsh poetry. The most important bards who are reported as present at some or all of these meetings were Dafydd ab Gwilym, Sion Cent, Rhys Goch of Eryri, and Iolo Goch. It is now, however, generally agreed that this account is a fabrication and that the date of all the poets is later.

Dafydd ab Gwilym is certainly the most distinguished of all the Welsh poets, and were it not for the absolute impossibility of adequately translating his *cywyddau* he would rank amongst the greatest poets of medieval times. By **Dafydd ab Gwilym.** far the greater part of his poetry is written in the metre called *cywydd*, with heptasyllabic lines rhyming in couplets. It was he who imparted so much lustre to this metre that it became the vehicle of all the most important poetry from his time to the 19th century, and he is generally referred to by his contemporaries as the special poet of the cywydd—*Dafydd gywydd gwin*, "Dafydd of the wine-sweet cywydd." Most of his poems deal with love in the spirit of the medieval writers of France and of Provence, but with this very important difference, that the French writers must base their reputation on their treatment of love as a theme, whereas Dafydd's claim to fame is based on his treatment of nature and of out-door life. In many cases, indeed, love is only a conventional peg whereon he may hang his observations on nature, and Welsh literature may claim the distinction of having had its Wordsworth in the 14th century. His treatment of nature is not merely realistic and objective, it has a certain quaint and elusive symbolism and a subjectiveness which come as a revelation to those who are acquainted with the medieval poetry of other nations. Many 645of the poems attributed to him are undoubtedly the work of later hands, but even after making all possible deductions, there is still an infinite variety among what remains, ranging as his poems do from a sturdy denunciation of monkish fraudulence to the most delicate and pathetic recollections of departed joys. He has, besides, considerable importance as a teacher, as when, for instance, he invites the nun "to leave her watercress and paternosters of Romish monks," and to come with him "to the cathedral of the birch to listen to the cuckoo's sermons," for, "were it not an equally worthy deed to save his (Dafydd's) soul in the birch-grove as to do so by following the ritual of Rome and St James of Compostella"? Even in his old age, when he is beginning to repent of his rash and merry youth, nature has not deserted him,—the very tree under which in the old days he used to meet his sweetheart has become bent and withered in sympathy with him. Though Dafydd yields not the palm to any poet of his class throughout the world, and though his influence is still a potent factor in the literature of Wales, we are certain of hardly a single fact about his life. He flourished between 1340 and 1390. His works were published in London in 1789. This edition was reprinted by Ffoulkes of Liverpool in 1870. See L.C. Stern, *Zeitschr. f. celt. Phil.* vol. vii.

Sion Cent was chaplain to the Scudamores of Kentchurch in Herefordshire, and though, therefore, in orders, was a most bitter opponent of the pretentious and the evil life of the monks of his time. All his writings show signs of the influence of the moralists of the middle ages, and treat of religious or of moral subjects. His poetry is strong and austere, interfused here and there with the most biting satire. He died about 1400. Like many of his contemporaries, Dunbar, Villon, Menot and Manrique, his dominant note is that of sadness and regret.

Rhys Goch Eryri had a sprightly muse which deals with fanciful subjects. His themes are often similar to those of Dafydd ab Gwilym, but whereas the subject of Dafydd's muse was nature and his treatment universal, Rhys Goch's are simply natural objects which he treats in a vigorous but narrow and cold manner.

Iolo Goch, that is, Iorwerth the Red, deserves a special mention as the poet who voiced the aspirations of a new Wales when Owen Glyndwr began to rise into power, and it is to one of his poems that we owe a most minute description of Sycharth, Owen Glyndwr's home. His poetry is slightly more archaic in diction than that of his contemporaries, as his subject—war and the glory of Welsh heroes—belonged more properly to the age before his own. In one very striking *cywydd* composed after Glyndwr's downfall, he calls upon this hero to come again and claim his own, and addresses himself fancifully to all the countries of the world where his hero may be in hiding. He died after 1405, and, if the dates generally given for his birth be even approximately correct, he must have lived to a prodigious age (cf. *Gweithiau Iolo Goch*, by Charles Ashton, London, 1896).

Rhys Goch ap Rhiccert claims to be named with Dafydd ab Gwilym as a writer of lyrics in praise of beautiful women. He has one advantage, however, over his more famous contemporary in the variety of his metres. The musical lilt and the delicate workmanship of his poems, with their recurring refrain, give him a unique position among his medieval contemporaries as the first purely lyrical poet. His *floreat* is probably a little later than that of Dafydd ab Gwilym, for we must not be misled by the late orthography of his poems.

Dafydd Nanmor is chiefly famous for two exquisite cywyddau, *Cywydd Marwnad Merch*, or Elegy of a Maiden, and *Cywydd i wallt Llio*, or Cywydd to Llio's Hair. In both these poems he shows elegance rather than depth, and a fancy as bold as that of his great master Dafydd. In the first of these cywyddau his grief is so great that he wishes that he were but the shroud around his dead sweetheart, and, in the second, Llio Rhydderch's golden hair over her white brow is compared to the refulgence of lightning over the fine snow. He is supposed to be a younger contemporary of Rhys Goch Eryri, but there are many facts to warrant a supposition that he lived much later, even as late as 1490.

Llywelyn Goch ap Meurig Hen deserves to be mentioned as the author of the famous *Marwnad Lleucu Llwyd*, an elegy which is far more convincing in its sincerity than Dafydd Nanmor's *cywydd*. Few of his compositions are extant, but the one already mentioned is sufficient to place him in the first rank of the poets of the period. He lived approximately from 1330 to 1390.

The other poets of this period who deserve some mention are Dafydd Ddu o Hiraddug, who wrote poems on religious subjects, and who is supposed to have translated part of the *Officium Beatae Mariae* into Welsh; Gruffydd Grug, between whom and Dafydd ab Gwilym a most fierce poetic quarrel raged, but who is the author of a beautiful elegy on his opponent; Gruffydd Llwyd ab Dafydd, who was the poet of Owen Glyndwr, and whose cywydd in praise of his patron is one of the best of that type; Hywel Swrdwal and Gwilym ab Ieuan Hen.

5. *The Silver Age of the Cywydd, 1440-1550.*—The insurrection of Owen Glyndwr, though originally the result of a private quarrel, was the general revolt of a nation against the conquerors whom it hated, and the English king knew well enough that the discontent with his rule was fanned by the older and more national Welsh institutions, and by none more than by the system of wandering bards. The conditions which had given rise to this system were fast dying out, but the noblemen, who fortunately were still intensely Welsh, were loth to give up their family bards, and the bards themselves, never a too industrious class, were too glad of their freedom and easy life to turn to more profitable work. We find, therefore, that a law was passed in 1403, the fourth year of Henry IV.'s reign, prohibiting bards "and other vagrants" from exercising their profession in Gwynedd or North Wales. This law, however, like its predecessor in the reign of Edward I., failed utterly in its purpose. By prohibiting the Welsh noblemen from giving their patronage to the bards, and, therefore, from distinguishing between the real bards and the mendicant rhymesters, this law took away the only safeguard against the latter class, with the result that by about 1450 they had become a pest to the country. About that time there flourished a poet called Llawdden, who, noticing the very unsatisfactory state of poetry in Wales, induced his kinsman, Gruffydd ab Nicolas, a nobleman living in Y Drenewydd (Newtown), to petition Henry VI. for permission to hold an eisteddfod similar in purpose to the three *Eisteddfodau Dadeni* of the last period. This famous eisteddfod **Eisteddfod of 1451.** was held at Caerfyrddin (Carmarthen) in 1451, and shortly before the actual eisteddfod was held a "statute" was drawn up under the direction of Llawdden, regulating the different orders of bards and musicians and setting in order the *cynghaneddion a mesurau*, the different kinds of alliterative verse to be presented to the assembled bards at the meeting. Among those present at that eisteddfod the most distinguished was Dafydd ab Edmwnd, who then made famous the dictum that the purpose of an eisteddfod was "to bring to mind the past, to consider the present, and to deliberate about the future." He, therefore, proposed emendations in "the rules of Welsh verse," making them more strict, so as to keep the unlearned rhymesters from the privileged bardic class. This measure had a most important effect on Welsh literature. It effectively put an end to the charming spontaneity which distinguishes the poetry of Dafydd ab Gwilym and his contemporaries, and by introducing an arbitrary set of rules gave an artificial tone to almost all the poetry of the next two hundred years. It had, indeed, exactly the same retarding effect on Welsh poetry as the Unities had on the French drama. So that, whereas the poems of Dafydd ab Gwilym, though written in the difficult alliterative metres, are nearly all light and have a sweet lyrical re-echo, the poetry of Dafydd ab Edmwnd and his successors is often heavy and nearly always artificial. After making, however, all these deductions, it is a debatable point whether the hard and fast rules which now regulated Welsh poetry did not eventually justify their existence. They have helped, by inciting to carefulness, to keep the idiom and the language pure and undefiled, and to this day style in Welsh 646 poetry is not necessarily a striving after the uncommon as it too often is in English.

There are some poets included in this period who belong more properly to the last, but even these show signs of the attempt at correctness and distinction which was supplanting the old simplicity. Ieuan ap Rhydderch ab Ieuan Llwyd, who is supposed to be a brother of the Llio Rhydderch of Dafydd Nanmor's poem, is the author of some cywyddau and other poems addressed to the Virgin, the structure of which shows great skill accompanied by force and clearness. He flourished about 1425. Dafydd ab Meredydd ap Tudur, who flourished about 1420, is the author of a cywydd "to Our Saviour." About the same time lived Rhys Nanmor, Ieuan Gethin ab Ieuan, and Ieuan Llwyd ab Gwilym. Among the earliest of the poets who belong properly to this period is Meredydd ap Rhys, whose cywyddau are a fair specimen of the generality of poems written in these years. Among the most famous of his works is a cywydd "begging for a fishing-net," and another giving thanks for the same. We shall find that many of his contemporaries were able to write long and interesting poems on such seemingly dry and uninteresting subjects, but it is vain to look for anything beyond good verse in such compositions. Of poetry, as generally understood, there is none.

The commanding figure in this period is, of course, Dafydd ab Edmwnd, who was a disciple of Meredydd ap Rhys. He bears somewhat the same relation to his contemporaries as Dafydd ab Gwilym does to his, and to strain an *Dafydd ab Edmwnd*analogy, we might say that as Dryden was to Milton, so Dafydd ab Edmwnd was to Dafydd ab Gwilym. He was regarded by his contemporaries as the greatest poet that North Wales had ever produced, and some would set him up as a rival even to Dafydd ab Gwilym himself. He would probably have produced much greater poetry had he understood that the cywydd and the other metres were strait and shackled enough without the *cymeriadau* and other devices which he introduced, or at least sanctioned and made popular. He begins many of his cywyddau and odes with the same letter; he is the chief among Welsh formalists, but in spite of his self-imposed restrictions he is a great poet also. His most famous poems are three *Cywyddau Merch* or "Poems to a Lady," and his*Cywydd i Wallt Merch*, "cywydd to a lady's hair." He is the author of the lines already quoted: "thy brow," he sings, "is as the snow of yesternight, and thy cheeks like a shower of roses." He died about 1480. Dafydd ab Edmwnd's disciples were Gutyn Owain and Tudur Aled, who was also his nephew. Gutyn Owain lived between 1420 and 1500, and was one of the men appointed by the king's commissioners to trace, or perhaps to manufacture, the Welsh pedigree of Henry VII. He belonged entirely to the school inaugurated by Dafydd ab Edmwnd, and though he was by no means wanting in imagination, the highest distinction of his verse is its intricacy of form and very often the felicity of his couplets.

Just as the rise of Owen Glyndwr in the beginning of the century had given a new impulse and a new interest to poetry, so in 1485, when Henry VII.—the "little bull" as he is called by the poets—ascended the throne of England, a particular kind of poetry called *brud*, half history and half prophecy, became popular, and we have in the manuscripts much writing of this description, a good deal of it worthless as poetry. Occasionally, however, some of these "bruts" may claim to be called poetry, especially the compositions of Robin Ddu o Fon, who wrote poems in praise of the Tudors and hailed them as the deliverers of the nation, even before Henry VII. had landed in England, and Dafydd Llwyd ab Llywelyn, whose works deserve to be much better known than they are at present. One of the best cywyddau among his works is the "Address to the Raven," to whom he promises a right royal feast when the hero whom all Wales is expecting has met his royal enemy. Tudur Aled, too, was a zealous partisan of Henry VII. and wrote many cywyddau in praise of Sir Rhys ap Thomas, the great champion of Henry's cause in South Wales. He is also famous as having supplemented and made a new recension of Dafydd ab Edmwnd's rules of poetry in the eisteddfod held at Caerwys in 1524. Tudur Aled has always been more widely known in Wales than almost any other of the earlier poets except Dafydd ab Gwilym. This is perhaps due to the quotability and sententiousness of his couplets. There is a certain refreshing dryness about his poetry which partly makes up for his want of imagination. One of the most interesting poets of this century is Lewis Glyn Cothi, who lived between 1410 and 1490. During the Wars of the Roses he was a zealous Lancastrian, and his bitterest enemies were the men of Chester, who had treated him scurvily while he was there in hiding, and his *awdl*, satirizing the men of that city, is one of the most vigorous compositions in the language. Indeed, among so many *cywyddau* of this period in conventional praise of different patrons, it is most refreshing to find such an outburst of sincere personal feeling, boldly and fiercely expressed. He wrote an *awdl* also rejoicing in the victory of Henry VII. Most of his work, however, consists of *cywyddau mawl*—praise of patrons—containing weary and unpoetical pedigrees. Gruffydd Hiraethog, who flourished about 1540, was a disciple of Tudur Aled. A fierce poetical dispute raged between him and Sion Brwynog of Anglesey, who was a contemporary of his. About this time there were many poets in Wales who were imitators of Dafydd ab Gwilym, and who did not follow implicitly the lead of Dafydd ab Edmwnd, like those whom we have mentioned. Much of their poetry is feeble, but Bedo Brwynllysg especially stands out from among the rest, and his poetry, though highly imitative and often over fanciful, is of a much higher order than the genealogical poems of Lewis Glyn Cothi and others. In the same way the only poem of any merit of Ieuan Denlwyn printed in the *Gorchestion* is written in this imitative strain. Other poets of the middle of this period are Deio ap Ieuan Du, Iorwerth Fynglwyd, Lewys Morganwg, Ieuan Brydydd Hir, and Tudur Penllyn, who wrote a superb *cywydd* to Dafydd ab Siencyn, the outlaw.

Towards the end of the period we begin to breathe a literary atmosphere that is gradually but surely changing,—it is the change from the misty Wales of Roman Catholic times to the modern Wales after the Reformation. The poetical incoherencies of the old metres and the tricks of fancy of the old stylists occasionally form a somewhat incongruous dress for the thoughts of later poets. The old spirit and the glamour were gradually wearing away, only to be momentarily revived in the poetry of Goronwy Owen, nearly two centuries later. Two or three figures, indeed, stand out prominently during these years, among whom are some of the bards ordained *penceirddiaid* (master-poets) in the second Caerwys Eisteddfod held in 1568, viz. William Llŷn, William Cynwal, Sion Tudur, and Sion Phylip. William Llŷn (1530?-1580) was a pupil of Gruffydd Hiraethog. His complicated *awdlau* are marvels of ingenuity, but many of them are on that very account almost unintelligible. He was, however, a complete master of the *cywydd*, in which he sometimes displays a sense of style and a sweetness of imagery allied to a melodiousness of language unequalled by the other poets of the period. His best-known work is the famous *marwnad* to his master, Gruffydd Hiraethog. Sion Tudur (d. 1602), also a disciple of G. Hiraethog, was connected in some capacity or other with the cathedral at St Asaph. He is a realist, and delights in giving vivid word pictures in a less fanciful strain than his predecessors. Sion Phylip (1543-1620) wrote a famous *marwnad* to his father and a *cywydd* "to a sea-gull," which is a superb piece of nature-painting in the style of Dafydd ab Gwilym. While dealing with this second Eisteddfod at Caerwys, we may note that Simwnt Fychan's "Laws of Poetry" were accepted at this festival.

Two poets of this period, whom an English writer describes as "the two filthy Welshmen who first smoked publicly in the streets," were captains in Queen Elizabeth's navy, viz. Thomas Prys (d. 1634) of Plas Iolyn, and William Myddleton (1556-1621), called in Welsh Gwilym Canoldref. The former wrote, among other things, humorous *cywyddau* descriptive of life in London and in the English navy of those days, in a style which was afterwards attempted by Lewys Morys. The work of 647Myddleton, by which he is best known, is his translation of the Psalms (1603) into Welsh *cywydd* metre, a difficult and profitless experiment.

With Edmwnd Prys (1541-1624), the famous archdeacon of Merioneth, we come to distinctly modern times. He is hardly a great poet, if we judge him by the canons which are now popular. His gift was a gift of terse and biting statement, and his *cywyddau* on the whole have more of literary than of poetical merit. He was a man of vast learning, and his works are full of scholastic and often difficult allusions. His most famous *cywyddau* are those written in the literary quarrel between him and Wiliam Cynwal. "Wiliam Cynwal," says Goronwy Owen, "though the greater poet, was like a man fighting with bare fists against complete armour," and it may be freely granted that in this, the most famous quarrel in Welsh literature, the palm of victory rested with the contentious old ecclesiastic. We shall deal with the rest of Edmwnd Prys's literary work in the section on the rise of popular poetry.

Here the age of the *cywydd* and the *awdl*, as the chief forms of verse, ends. They appear again in the succeeding centuries, but as aliens among a nation that no longer paid them homage. The distinctly Welsh fashion in song was dying out.

6. *Prose, 1550-1750.*—One of the most striking features of Welsh literature is the almost entire absence of prose between 1300 and 1550. The genius of the people has always been an eminently poetical and imaginative one, and the history of Wales, politically and

socially, has always been a fitter subject for poetry than for prose. During this period, Wales enjoyed a rest from propagandists and revolutionaries which has seldom been the happy lot of any other nation—they lay content with their own old traditions, acquiescing proudly in their separation from the other nations of Europe, and in their aloofness from all the movements which shook England and the continent during those years. Dynasties came and went, one religion ousted another religion, a new learning exposed the absurdities of the old, but the Welsh, among their hills, knew nothing of it; and when new ideas began to brood over the consciousness of the nation, they never got beyond the stage of providing new subjects for *cywyddau*. The Peasant Revolt, for instance, had but little effect on Welsh history, its most important contribution to the heritage of the nation being Iolo Goch's superb "*Cywydd* to the Labourer." Even the Reformation, which helped to change the whole fabric of English literature, had little effect on that of Wales, and the age of the *cywydd* dragged out wearily its last years without experiencing the slightest quickening from the great movement which was remaking Europe. Hardly a prophet or reactionary raised his voice in defence or condemnation, and the Welsh went on serenely making and reading poetry. The two political movements in which Wales was really interested, the revolt of Glyndŵr and the accession of Henry VII., paid their tribute to its poetry alone, and both enterprises had sufficient of romance in them to repel the historian and to capture the poet. Naturally, therefore, we have no prose in this period, because there was no cause strong enough to produce it. What prose the nation required they found in the tales of romance, in the legends of Arthur and Charlemagne and the Grail, and, as for pedigrees and history, were they not written in the *cywyddau* of the poets?

The little prose that was produced during this period (1300-1550) was of an extraordinary kind. It was simply an exercise in long sentences and in curiously built compounds, and therefore more nearly allied to poetry. It generally took the form of *dewisbethau*, a list of the "choice things" of such and such a person, or of the later triads (*trioedd*), which, starting from an ancient nucleus, gradually grew till, at the present day, Wales has a gnomic literature out of all proportion to the rest of its prose. Modern Welsh prose, however, is only very indirectly connected with these compositions. It is almost altogether a product of the Biblical literature which began to appear after the Reformation, and we shall proceed to give here the main facts and dates in its development. The first Welsh book was printed in 1546. It consisted of extracts in Welsh from the Bible and the Prayer Book, and a calendar. The author was Sir John Prys (1502-1555). The most important name in the early part of this period is William Salesbury (1520?-1600?). His chief books were, *A Dictionary in Englyshe and Welshe* (printed in 1547, and published in facsimile reprint by the Cymmrodorion Society), *Kynniver Llith a Ban* (1551), the Prayer Book in Welsh (1567), and the most important of all his works, the translation of the New Testament (1567). It is difficult to form any estimate, at this distance of time, of the impetus which William Salesbury gave to Welsh prose, but it must be regretfully admitted that his great work was marred by many defects. He had a theory that Welsh ought to be written as much like Latin as possible, and the result is that his language is very poor Welsh, both in spelling and idiom; it is an artificial dialect. It is a striking testimony, however, to his influence that many of the constructions and words which he manufactured are found to this day in correct literary Welsh.

In 1567 was published a *Welsh Grammar* by Dr Gruffydd Roberts, a Roman Catholic priest living at Milan (reprinted in facsimile, Paris, 1883), and in 1583, under the direction of Dr Rhosier Smyth, his *Drych Cristionogawl* was published at Rouen. Many other important Welsh books were produced during these years, but the work which may be regarded as having the greatest influence on the subsequent literature of Wales was the translation of the *Welsh Bible* (1588) by Dr William Morgan (1547?-1604), bishop of Llandaff, and afterwards of St Asaph. The Authorized Version (1620) now in use is a revision of this work by Dr Richard Parry, bishop of St Asaph (1560-1623). In 1592 the *Welsh Grammar* of Sion Dafydd Rhŷs (1534-1609) was published—a most valuable treatise on the language and on the rules of Welsh poetry. It was followed in 1621 by the *Welsh Grammar*, and in 1632 by the *Welsh Dictionary* of Dr John Davies o Fallwyd (1570?-1644).

There are two prose compositions which stand entirely by themselves in this period of Bibles and grammars—the *History* of Ellis Gruffydd, and Morris Kyffin's *Deffyniad y Ffydd*. The former was a soldier in the English army during the reign of Queen Elizabeth, and wrote a long history of England from the earliest times to his own day. This document, which has never been published, and which lies hidden away among the Mostyn MSS., is a most important and valuable original contribution to the history of the author's contemporaries, and it sheds considerable light on the inner life of the court and the army. It is written in a delightfully easy style, contrasting favourably with the stiff diction of this period of translations. The work of Morris Kyffin (1555?-1598?) which we have mentioned is a translation of Bishop Jewel's *Apologia Ecclesiae Anglicanae* (1562) and was published in 1595. This work is the first piece of modern Welsh prose within reach of the ordinary reader, written in the rich idiom of the spoken Welsh. It is a precursor of many other books of its kind, a long series culminating in the immortal *Bardd Cwsc*. In this sense Morris Kyffin may with perfect justice be hailed as the father of modern Welsh prose.

Most of the works which were afterwards written in the strong idiomatic Welsh of Morris Kyffin were on religious subjects, and many of them were translated from the English. The first was *Ymarfer o Dduwioldeb* (1630) by Rowland Vychan o Gaergai (a translation of Bailey's *Practice of Piety*), which was followed in 1632 by Dr John Davies's *Llyfr y Resolution*, and in 1666 by *Hanes y Ffydd Ddiffuant* (A History of the True Faith) by Charles Edwards. All these authors and many of their successors were strong adherents of the Established Church, which was then intensely Welsh in sentiment. But in the midst of these churchmen, a flame-bearer of dissent appeared—Morgan Llwyd o Wynedd, who published in 1653 "a mystery to be understood of some, and scorned of others"—*Llyfr y Tri Aderyn* (The Book of the Three Birds). It is in the form of a discussion between the eagle (Cromwell), the dove (Dissent) and the raven (the Established Church). This book is certainly the most important original composition published during the 17th century, and to this day remains one of the widely-read classics of the Welsh 648tongue. Morgan Llwyd wrote many other books in Welsh and English, all more or less in the vein of the first book.

During the remaining years of this period, the prose output of the Welsh press consisted mainly of devotional books, written or translated for or at the instigation of the Society for Promoting Christian Knowledge. The Established Church, with the help of this society, made a gallant attempt to lighten the darkness of Wales by publishing books of this description, and it is mainly due to its exertions that the lamp of Welsh prose was kept burning during these years. Among the clergy who produced books of this description were Edward Samuel (1674-1748), who published among other works *Holl Ddyledswydd Dyn*, a translation of *The Whole Duty of Man* (1718); Moses Williams (1684-1742), a most diligent searcher into Welsh MSS. and translator; Griffith Jones of Llanddowror (1683-1761), the father of Welsh popular education; Iago ab Dewi (1644?-1722) and Theophilus Evans (1694-1769), the famous author of *Drych y Prif Oesoedd* (1716 and 1740). This book, like *Llyfr y Tri Aderyn* and *Y Bardd Cwsc*, has an established position for all time in the annals of Welsh literature.

We come now to the greatest of all Welsh prose writers, Ellis Wyn o Lasynys (1671-1734). His first work was a translation of Jeremy Taylor's *Holy Living*, under the title of *Rheol Buchedd Sanctaidd* (1701). His next work was the immortal *Gweledigaethau y Bardd Cwsc* (1703). The foundation of this work was L'Estrange's translation of the *Suenos* of the Spaniard Quevedo. Ellis Wyn has certainly followed his original closely, even as Shakespeare followed his, but by his inimitable magic he has transmuted the characters and the scenery of the Spaniard into Welsh characters and scenery of the 17th century. No writer before or after him has used the Welsh language with such force and skill, and he will ever remain the stylist whom all Welsh writers will strive to imitate. The magic of his work has endowed the stately idiom of Gwynedd with such glamour that it has now become the standard idiom of Welsh prose. See Stern, *Z. f. celt. Phil.* iii. 165 ff.

7. *The Rise of Popular Poetry, 1600-1750.*—When Henry VII. ascended the throne, the old hostility of the Welsh towards the English disappeared. They had realized their wildest hope, that of seeing a Welshman wearing "the crown of London." Naturally enough, therefore, the descendants of the old Welsh gentry began to look towards England for

recognition and preferment, and their interest in their own little country necessarily began to wane. The result was that the traditional patrons of the Welsh muse could no longer understand the language of the poets, and the poets were forced to seek some more profitable employment. Besides, the old conditions were changing; the medieval traditions were indeed dying hard, but it gradually and imperceptibly came about that the poets of the older school had no audience. The only poets who still followed the old traditions were the rich farmers who "sang on their own land," as the Welsh phrase goes. A new school, however, was rising. The nation at large had a vast store of folk-poetry, full of all the poetical characteristics of the Celt, and it was this very poetry, despised as it was, that became ultimately the groundwork of the new literature.

The first landmark in this new development was the publication in 1621 of Edmwnd Prys's metrical version of the Psalms (followed by later editions in 1628, 1630, 1638 and 1648), and of the first poem of the *Welshmen's Candle* (*Cannwyll y Cymry*) of Rhys Pritchard, vicar of Llandovery (1569-1644). This was published in 1646. These works were not written in the old metres peculiar to Wales, but in the free metres, like those of English poetry. The former work is of the utmost importance, as these Psalms were about the first metrical hymns in use. They are often rugged and uncouth, but many of the verses—such as the 23rd Psalm—have a haunting melody of their own, which grips the mind once and for ever. The second work, the first complete edition of which was published in 1672, consisted of moral verses in the metres of the old folk-songs (*Penillion Telyn*), and for nearly two centuries was the "guide, philosopher and friend" of the common people. Many other poets of the early part of this period wrote in these metres, such as Edward Dafydd o Fargam (fl. 1640), Rowland Fychan, Morgan Llwyd o Wynedd and William Phylip (d. 1669). Poetry in the free metres, however, was generally very crude, until it was given a new dignity by the greatest poet of the period, Huw Morus o Bont y Meibion (1622-1709). Most of his earlier compositions, which are among his best, and which were influenced to a great extent by the cavalier poetry of England, are love poems, perfect marvels of felicitous ingenuity and sweetness. He fixed the poetic canons of the free metres, and made what was before homely and uncouth, courtly and dignified. He wrote a *cywydd marwnad* to his contemporary, Edward Morus o'r Perthi Llwydion (d. 1689), who was also a poet of considerable merit. Most of his work is composed of "moral pieces" and carols. Other poets of the period were Sion Dafydd Las (1650-1691), who was among the last of the family bards, and Dafydd Jones o Drefriw (fl. 1750). Towards the end of the period comes Lewys Morys (1700-1765). His poetry alone does not seem to warrant his fame, but he was the creator of a new period, the inspirer and the patron of Goronwy Owen. According to the lights of the 18th century, he was, like his brothers Richard and William, a scholar. His poetry, except a few well-known pieces, will never be popular, because it does not conform to modern canons of taste. His greatest merit is that he wrote the popular poetry then in vogue with a scholar's elegance.

8. *The Revival, 1750-1830.*—The two leading figures in this period are Goronwy Owen (1722-1769) and William Williams, Pantycelyn (1717-1791). Goronwy Owen wrote all his poetry in the *cynghanedd*, and his work gave the old metres a new life. He raised them from the neglect into which they had fallen, and caused them to be, till this day, the vehicle of half the poetical thought of Wales. But he was in no way a representative of his age; he, like Milton, sang among a crowd of inferior poets themes quite detached from the life of his time, so that he also, like his English brother, lacks "human interest." After Dafydd ab Gwilym, he is the greatest poet who sang in the old metres, and the influence of his correct and fastidious muse remains to this day. William Williams, however, wrote in the free metres in a way that was astoundingly fresh. It is not enough to say of him that he was a hymnologist; he is much more, he is the national poet of Wales. He had certainly the loftiest imagination of all the poets of five centuries, and his influence on the Welsh people can be gauged by the fact that a good deal of his idiom and dialect has fixed itself indelibly on modern literary Welsh. Besides the hymns, he wrote a religious epic, *Theomemphus*, which is to this day the national epic of evangelical Wales. Even as Goronwy Owen is the father of modern Welsh poetry in the old metres, so William Williams is the great fountain-head of the free metres, because he set aflame the imagination of every poet that succeeded him. With two such pioneers, it is natural that the rest of this period should contain many great

names. Thomas Edwards (Twm o'r Nant) (1739-1810) has been called by an unwarrantably bold hyperbole, "the Welsh Shakespeare." Most of his works are interludes and ballads, and he used to be very popular with the common people; he is, to this day, probably the oftenest quoted of all the Welsh poets. William Wynn, rector of Llangynhafal (1704-1760), is the author of a "*Cywydd* of the Great Judgment," which bears comparison with Goronwy Owen's masterpiece. Evan Evans (Ieuan Brydydd Hir) (1731-1789) was famous both as a poet and as a scholar and antiquarian. Edward Rhisiart (1714-1777), the schoolmaster of Ystradmeurig, was a scholar and a writer of pastorals in the manner of Theocritus. Most of the other poets who flourished towards the end of this period—Dafydd Ddu Eryri (1760-1822), Gwallter Mechain (1761-1849), Robert ab Gwilym Ddu (1767-1850), Dafydd Ionawr (1751-1827), Dewi Wyn o Eifion (1784-1841)—were brought into prominence by the Eisteddfod, which began to increase in influence during this period until it has become to-day the national festival. They all wrote for the most part in *cynghanedd*, and the work of nearly all of them is marked by correctness rather than by poetical inspiration.

649

9. *Prose after 1830.*—In the preceding periods, we have seen that Welsh prose, though abundant in quantity, had a very narrow range. Few writers rose above theological controversy or moral treatises, and the humaner side of literature was almost entirely neglected. In this period, however, we find a prose literature that, with the exception of scientific works, is as wide in its range as that of England, and all departments are well and competently represented, though by but few names. Dr Lewis Edwards (1809-1887) struck a new note when he began to contribute his literary and theological essays to the periodicals, but, though many have equalled and even surpassed him as theological essayists, few, if any, of his followers have attempted the literary and critical essays on which his fame as writer must mainly rest. Together with Gwilym Hiraethog (1802-1883), the author of the inimitable*Llythyrau Hen Ffarmwr*, he may be regarded as the pioneer of the new literature. Samuel Roberts (1800-1885), generally known as S.R., wrote numerous tracts and books on politics and economics, and as a political thinker he was in many respects far in advance of his English contemporaries. It was in this period, too, that Wales had her national novelist, Daniel Owen (1836-1895). He was a novelist of the Dickens school, and delighted like his great master "in writing mythology rather than fiction." He has created a new literary atmosphere, in which the characters of Puritanical and plebeian Wales move freely and without restraint. He can never be eclipsed just as Sir Walter Scott cannot be eclipsed, because the Wales which he describes is slowly passing away. He has many worthy disciples, among whom Miss Winnie Parry is easily first. Indeed, in her finer taste and greater firmness of touch, she stands on a higher plane than even her great master. The inspiring genius of the latter part of this period is Owen M. Edwards (b. 1858), and, as a stylist, all writers of Welsh prose since Ellis Wynn have to concede him the laurel. His little books of travel and history and anecdote have created, or rather, are creating a new school of writers, scrupulously and almost pedantically careful and correct, an ideal which, on its philological side is the outcome of the scientific study of the language as inaugurated by Sir John Rhŷs and Professor Morris Jones. One of the earliest, if not the ablest writer of this "new Welsh" was the independent and original Emrys ap Iwan (d. 1906), whose *Homiliau* was published in 1907.

10. *Poetry after 1820.*—The origins of this period are really placed in the last period. Its great characteristics are the development of the lyric, and the influence of English and continental ideas. Just as the *cywydd* was among the older writers the favourite form of poetry, so the lyric becomes now paramount, almost to the exclusion of other forms. The first great name, after those already mentioned in the development of this form of poetry, is that of Anne Griffiths (1776-1805). Her poetry is exclusively composed of hymns, but to the English mind, the word "hymn" is entirely inadequate to give any idea of the passion, the mysticism and the rich symbolistic grace of her poems. She gave to the Welsh lyric the depth and the rather melancholy intensity which has always characterized it. Evan Evans (Ieuan Glan Geirionydd) (1795-1855) was also a hymnologist, but he wrote many secular lyrics and*awdlau*—among the former being the famous *Morfa Rhuddlan*. Ebenezer Thomas (Eben

Fardd) (1802-1863) was a famous *Eisteddfodwr*, his best work is his *awdlau*, and no one will deny him the distinction of being the master poet of the *awdl* in the 19th century. Gwilym Cawrdaf (1795-1848), also a writer of *awdlau*, has the gift of simple and direct expression, well exemplified in *Hiraeth Cymro am ei wlad*. Daniel Ddu (1792-1846) was a scholar who wrote some touching lyrics and hymns. Gwilym Hiraethog (1802-1883) attempted an epic, *Emmanuel*, with indifferent success. His shorter works and some of his *awdlau* are of a much higher order. Caledfryn (1801-1869) was a direct successor of Dewi Wyn and the earlier writers of *awdlau*, but his *Drylliad y Rothsay Castle* is superior to anything which his master wrote. Similar in genius, though not on quite as high a plane, were Nicander (1809-1874), Cynddelw (1812-1875), Gwalchmai (1803-1897) and Tudno (1844-1895).

John Blackwell (Alun) (1797-1840) was a lyricist of the first order. With Ieuan Glan Geirionydd, he is the pioneer of the secular lyric of the 19th century. Succeeding to this group of lyricists, we have another later group, Ceiriog (1832-1887), Talhaiarn (1810-1869) and Mynyddog (1833-1877), who certainly had the advantage over their predecessors in freshness, in vigour and in human interest, but they lacked the scholastic training of the earlier group, and so their work is often uneven, and cannot therefore be fairly compared with that of the earlier poets. Ceiriog, of course, is the greater name of the three, and is to Wales what Robert Burns was to Scotland, sharing with him his poetical faults and merits. He is called the national poet of Wales, because he was the first to sing of the land and the nation he knew, and he cast the glamour of his genius over the life of the *gwerin*, the peasants of Wales.

Somewhat higher flights were essayed by Gwilym Marles (1834-1879) and Islwyn (1832-1878). Their poetry is Wordsworthian and mystical, and well exemplifies the love of metaphysics and speculation which is growing in Wales. Islwyn's *Y storm*, though uneven, is full of powerful passages, and he was a master of blank verse. Of the remaining poets of the period living in 1908, the most distinguished was the Rev. Elvet Lewis in the older generation, and Eifion Wyn in the younger—both writers of lyrics. Other lyrical poets of the first class are Gwylfa and Silyn Roberts. In the old metres, two poets stand out prominent above all others—J. Morris Jones and T. Gwynn Jones. The *Awdl i Famon* of the former, and the *Ymadawiad Arthur* of the latter, gave reason to believe that Welsh poetry was only entering on its golden period.

AUTHORITIES.—*General.*—T. Stephens, *Literature of the Kymry* (London[2], 1876); L.C. Stern in *Die Kultur d. Gegenwart*, i. xi. 1 pp. 114-130; Gweirydd ap Rhys. *Hanes Llenyddiaeth Gymreig, 1300-1650* (London, 1885); C. Ashton, *Hanes Llenyddiaeth Gymreig, 1651-1850* (Liverpool, 1893); J. Loth, *Les Mabinogion* (2 vols., Paris, 1889); E. Anwyl, *Prolegomena to Welsh Poetry* (London, 1905), also on the Mabinogi in *Zeitschr. f. celt. Phil.* i. 277 ff.; I.B. John, *The Mabinogion* (London, 1901); T. Shankland, *Diwygwyr Cymru*, reprinted from *Seren Gomer* (1899); W.J. Gruffydd, *Foreign Influences on Welsh Literature in the XIV. and XV. Centuries*, Guild of Welsh Graduates (1908); Gwilym Lleyn, *Llyfryddiaeth y Cymry* (Llanidloes, 1867); Robert Williams, *Enwogion Cymru* (Llandovery, 1852); Owen Jones, *Cymru* (2 vols., London, 1875); D.W. Nash, *History of the Battle of Cattraeth* (Tenby, 1861); *Encyclopaedia Cambrensis* (10 vols[2]., 1889-1896); C. Ashton, *Bywyd ac amserau yr Esgob Morgan* (Treherbert, 1891); J. Foulkes, *J. Ceiriog Hughes, ei fywyd a'i waith* (Liverpool, 1887); J.M. Jones, *Llenyddiaeth fy ngwlad* (Holywell, 1893); H. Elvet Lewis, *Sweet Singers of Wales* (London, 1889); H.W. Lloyd, *Welsh Books Printed Abroad in the XVI. and XVII. Centuries* (London, 1881).

Anthologies, Selected Prose and Verse, &c.—W.F. Skene, *The Four Ancient Books of Wales* (2 vols., Edinburgh, 1868); W. Owen (Pughe), Iolo Morganwg and Owen Jones (Myfyr), *Myvyrian Archaiology of Wales* (3 vols., London, 1801;[2] Denbigh, 1870, in 1 vol.); Dr John Davies (o Fallwyd), *Flores Poetarum Britannicorum* (Shrewsbury, 1710; Swansea, 1814; reprinted London, 1864); Iolo Morganwg, *Iolo Manuscripts* (Llandovery, 1848); E. Evans, *Some Specimens of the Poetry of the Antient Welsh Bards translated into English, &c.* (London, 1764); Hugh Jones, *Dewisol Ganiadau yr Oes Hon* (Shrewsbury, 1759;5 Merthyr, 1827), *Diddanwch Teuluaidd* (London, 1763); David Jones, *Blodeugerdd Cymry* (Shrewsbury[2], 1779); Owen Jones, *Ceinion Llenyddiaeth Gymreig* (2 vols., London, 1876); W. Lewis Jones, *Caniadau Cymru* (Bangor[2], 1908); W. Jenkyn Thomas, *Penillion Telyn* (Carnarvon, 1894); Myrddin Fardd, *Cynfeirdd Lleyn* (1905); *Cyfres Llen Cymru*, vols. i.-vi. (Cardiff, 1900-1906); W.J.

Gruffydd, *Y Flodeugerdd Newydd* (Cardiff, 1908); O.M. Edwards, *Beirdd y Berwyn* (Conway, 1903).

Versification, &c,—Dafydd Morganwg, *Yr Ysgol Farddol* (Cardiff3, 1887); Iolo Morganwg, *Cyfrinach Beirdd Ynys Prydain* (Merthyr, 1829²; Carnarvon, 1874); *Simwnt Vychan and Dafydd Ddu Athraw, Dosparth Edeyrn Davod Aur*, ed. by J. Williams ab Ithel (Llandovery, 1856); J. Morris Jones, "Welsh Versification," *Zeitschr.f. celt. Phil.*iv. pp. 106-142.

Collected Works, Editions and Reprints,—J. Gwenogvryn Evans and John Rhys, *Y Llyvyr Coch o Hergest* (2 vols. Oxford, 1887-1890), *Pedeir Kainc y Mabinogi* (Oxford, 1897); J. Gwenogvryn Evans, *The Black Book of Carmarthen* (Oxford, 1907; also in facsimile, Oxford, 1888), *Llyvyr Job trans. by Dr Morgan, 1558* (reprinted 1888), *Oll Synwyr pen* [Salesbury] (Bangor, 1902); J. Morris Jones and John Rhys, *Llyvyr Agkyr Llandewivrevi* (Oxford, 1894); Aneurin Owen, *Ancient Laws and Institutes of Wales* (2 vols., London, 1841), *Brut y Tywysogion* (London, 1863); J. Williams ab Ithel, *Gododin with Notes and Translation* (Llandovery, 1852); T. Stephens, 650*Gododin with Notes and Translation*, ed. by T. Powel (London, 1888); R. Williams, *Selections from the Hengwrt MSS.* (2 vols., London, 1876-1892); T. Powel, *Ystorya de Carolo Magno* (London, 1883); *Psalmau Dafydd trans. by W. Morgan* (facsimile, 1896); Owen Jones (Myfyr) and W. Owen (Pughe), *Barddoniaeth Dafydd ab Gwilym* (London, 1789); Walter Davies and J. Jones, *Poetical Works of Lewis Glyn Cothi* (1837); Prince Louis Bonaparte, *Athrawaeth Gristnogavl by Morys Clynoc* (facsimile London, 1880); Walter Davies, *Caniadau Huw Morus* (2 vols., 1823); *Psalmau Dafydd gan W. Middleton*(Llanfair, 1827); J. Morris Jones, *Gweledugaethai y Bardd cwsg gan Elis Wynne*(Bangor, 1898); R. Jones, *The Poetical Works of Goronwy Owen* (2 vols. London, 1876); W.J. Gruffydd, *Cywyddau Goronwy Owen* (Newport, 1906); T.E. Ellis,*Gweithiau Morgan Llwyd* (Bangor, 1899); J.H. Davies, *Yn y Llyvyr hwn* (Bangor, 1902); S.J. Evans, *Drych y Prif Oesoedd gan Th. Evans* (Bangor, 1902); W.P. Williams,*Deffyniad Ffydd Eglwys Loegr gan Morys Kyffin* (Bangor, 1908); N. Cynhafal Jones,*Gweithiau W. Williams Pantycelyn* (2 vols., 1887-1891); O.M. Edwards, *Gweithiau Islwyn* (1897).

(W. J. G.)

V. BRETON LITERATURE.—Unlike the literature of Wales, the literature of Brittany is destitute of originality, and we find nothing to compare with the *Mabinogion*. Till the 19th century all the monuments which have come down to us are copies of French models, though the retention down to the 17th century of that intricate system of versification found in Welsh and Cornish may indicate that what was really Breton in spirit has not been preserved (v. J. Loth, *La Métrique galloise*, ii. 177-203). It is usual to divide the literature into three periods in conformity with the language in which the monuments are written—Old, Middle, and Modern Breton. No connected monuments of the first period (8th to 11th centuries) have come down to us. For our knowledge of the language of this period we must have recourse to the manuscripts containing glosses and the names occurring in ancient documents. The chief collections of glosses are (1) the Oxford glosses on Eutychius; (2) the Luxemburg glosses; (3) the Bern glosses on Virgil; (4) the glosses on Amalarius (Corpus Christi, Cambridge); (5) five *Collationes Canonum*, the chief manuscripts being at Paris and Orleans. All these glosses have been published in one volume by J. Loth (*Vocabulaire Vieux-Breton*, Paris, 1884). From a linguistic point of view the Breton names in the Latin lives of saints are very important, particularly those of St Samson, St Paul, Aurelian, St Winwaloe, St Ninnoc, St Gildas and St Brieuc. Of even greater value are the names in the Charter of Redon, which was written in the 11th century, but dates largely from the 9th (published by A. de Courson, 1865); we may also mention the Charter of Landevennec (11th century). In the Middle Breton period, which extends from the 11th to the 17th centuries, we are obliged, down to the 15th century, to rely on official documents such as the Charter of Quimperlé. French seems to have been the language of the aristocracy and the medium of culture. Hence the oldest connected texts are either translated or imitated from French, and are full of French words. We might mention a Book of Hours belonging to the 16th century, published by Whitley Stokes, and three religious poems bound up with the *Grand Mystère de Jésus*; further, the *Life of St Catherine* (1576) in prose (published by Ernault, *Revue celtique*, viii. 76), translated from the *Golden Legend*, the *Mirror of Death*, containing 3360 verses, which was composed in 1519 and printed in 1576, the *Mirror of Confession*, a translation from the French

311

in prose (1621), the *Christian Doctrine*, a translation in verse (1622), a collection of carols (*An Nouelou ancien*, 1650, *Rev. celt.* vols. x.-xiii.) and the *Christian Meditations* of J. Cadec, 1651 (*Rev. Celt.* xx. 56). The earliest Breton printed work is the *Catholicon* of Jean Lagadeuc, a Breton-Latin-French dictionary, dated 1464 but printed first in 1499 (reprinted by R.F. Le Men, Lorient, 1867). Modern Breton begins with the orthographical reforms of the Jesuit, Julien Maunoir, whose grammar (*Le Sacré Collège de Jésus*) and dictionary appeared in 1659. Throughout the modern period we find numerous collections of religious poems and manuals of devotion in prose and verse, which we cannot here attempt to enumerate. But the bulk of Breton literature before the 19th century consists of mysteries and miracle plays. This class of literature had a tremendous vogue in Brittany, and the native stage was only killed about 1850. It is stated, for instance, that no less than 15,000 copies were sold of the *Tragedy of the Four Sons of Aymon*, first published in 1815. It is impossible to give the titles of all the dramas which have come down to us (about 120). The manuscript collection of the Bibliothèque Nationale in Paris is described in the *Revue celtique*, xi. 389-423 (many since published) and Le Braz gives a useful list of other manuscripts in the bibliographical appendix to his *Théâtre celtique*. A few of these plays belong to the Middle Breton period. The *Life of St Nonn*, the mother of St David, belongs to the end of the 15th century, and follows the Latin life (published by Ernault in the *Revue celtique*, viii. 230 ff., 405 ff.). *Le Grand Mystère de Jésus* (1513) follows the French play of Arnoul Gresban and Jean Michel (published by H. de la Villemarqué, Paris, 1865). A French original is also followed in the *Mystère de Sainte Barbe* (1st ed., 1557, 2nd ed., 1647, reprinted by Ernault, Nantes, 1885). These mystery plays may be divided into four categories according to the subjects with which they deal: (1) Old Testament subjects; (2) New Testament subjects; (3) lives of saints; (4) romances of chivalry. There is occasionally a dash of local colouring in these plays; but the subject matter is taken from French sources or, in the case of the third category, from Latin lives. Even when the life of a Breton saint, *e.g.* St Gwennolé, is dramatized, the treatment is the traditional one accorded to all saints of whatever origin. Amongst the most favourite subjects in addition to those already mentioned we may note the following: *Vie des quatre fils Aymon, Ste Tryphine et le roi Arthur, Huon de Bordeaux, Vie de Louis Eunius, Robert le Diable*. These mysteries commonly contain from 5000 to 9000 lines of either 12 or 8 syllables apiece. For the sake of completeness we may add the names of three farces, described by Le Braz: *Ar Farvel goapaer* (*Le bouffon moqueur*), *Ian Melargé* (*Mardi-gras*), *La Vie de Mardi-gras, de triste Mine, sa femme, et de ses enfants*. The actors, who were always peasants, came to be regarded with an unfavourable eye by the clergy, who finally succeeded in killing the Breton stage.

We look in vain for any manifestation of originality in Breton literature until we reach the 19th century. The consciousness of nationality then awakened and found expression in verse.

The movement led by Le Gonidec (described above in the section on Breton language) caused ardent patriots to endeavour to create a national literature, more especially when the attention of the whole world of letters was directed to Brittany after the publication of the *Barzas Breiz*. The most prominent of these pioneers were Auguste Brizeux, F.M. Luzel and Prosper Proux. Brizeux (1803-1858), better known as a French poet, wrote a collection of lyrics entitled *Telen Arvor*, or the *Armorican Harp* (Lorient, 1844, reprinted Paris, 1903). Luzel's original compositions were published under the title of *Bepred Breizad, Toujours Breton* (Morlaix, 1865), and Prosper Proux is known as the author of *Canaouenno grét gant eur C'hernewod* (1838) and *Ar Bombard Kerne*, or *The Hautboy of Cornouailles* (Guingamp, 1866). Dottin also mentions *Telenn Remengol*, by J. Lescour (Brest, 1867); *Telenn Gwengam*, by the same writer (Brest, 1869), a volume of *Chansoniou* by Y.M. Thomas (Lannion, 1870), and another by C. Rannou. This was a very creditable beginning, but the themes of these writers are apt to be somewhat conventional and the constant recurrence of the same situation or the same idea grows monotonous. An anthology of poems connected with this movement appeared at Quimperlé in 1862 under the title of *Bleuniou Breiz, Poésies anciennes et modernes de la Basse-Bretagne* (reprinted, Paris, 1905). Several of La Fontaine's fables were published in a Breton dress by P.D. de Goesbriand (Morlaix, 1836), and a collection of fables in verse which is thought very highly of by cultivated Bretons appeared under the title of *Marvaillou Grac'h koz* by G. Milin (Brest, 1867). A book of Georgics in the dialect of Vannes appeared under the title of *Levr al labourer* (The Farmer's Book) by l'Abbé Guillome (Vannes, 1849), and Le Gonidec prepared a translation of the Scriptures, which was revised by Troude and Milin, and published at St Brieuc in 1868. But the real literature of Brittany consists of legends, folk-tales and ballads. The first to tap this source was 651Hersart de la Villemarqué (1815-1895), who issued in 1839 his famous collection of ballads entitled *Barzas Breiz*, but which cannot be regarded as an anthology of Breton popular poetry. The publication of this work gave rise to a controversy which is almost as famous as that caused by Macpherson's forgeries. De la Villemarqué was endowed with considerable poetic gifts, and, coming as he did at a time when folk-poetry was the fashion, he determined to collect the popular literature of his own country. However, he was not content to publish the poems as he found them circulating in Brittany. With the aid of several collaborators he transformed his material, eliminating anything that was crude and gross. The poems included in his collection may be divided into three classes: (1) Poems rearranged by himself or others. These consist mainly of love-songs and ballads. (2) Modern poems transferred to medieval times. (3) Spurious poems dealing with such personages as Nominoe and Merlin. The compiler of the *Barzas Breiz* unfortunately laboured under the delusion that these Breton folk-songs were in the first instance the work of medieval bards corresponding to Taliessin and Llywarch Hen in Wales, and that it was possible to make them appear in their primitive dress. The very title of the collection indicates the artificial nature of the contents. For *Barzas* (in the 2nd edition of 1867 spelt *Barzaz*) is not a Breton word at all but is formed on Welsh *barddas* (bardic poems). For the whole controversy the reader may consult H. Gaidoz and P. Sébillot, "Bibliographie des traditions et de la littérature populaire de la Bretagne" (*Revue celtique*, v. 277 ff., and G. Dottin in the *Revue de synthèse historique*, viii. 95 ff.). In Brittany it is usual to divide the popular poetry into *gwerziou* and *soniou*. The *gwerziou* (complaintes) deal with local history, folk-lore, religious legends and superstitions, and are in general much more original than the other class. The *soniou* consist of love-songs, satires, carols and marriage-lays, as well as others dealing with professional occupations, and seem in many cases to show traces of French influence. The first scholar who published the genuine ballad literature of Brittany was F.M. Luzel, who issued two volumes under the title of *Gwerziou Breiz-Izel, chants populaires de la Basse-Bretagne* (Lorient and Paris, 1868, 1874). This collection contains several of the originals of poems in the *Barzas Breiz*. Luzel is also the author of a collection of Breton tales in French translation, *Contes bretons recueillis et traduits par F.M. Luzel* (Quimperlé, 1870). The same author published *Les Légendes chrétiennes de la Basse-Bretagne* (Paris, 1881) and *Veillées bretonnes, moeurs, chants, contes et récits populaires des Bretons-Armoricains* (Morlaix, 1879). Another indefatigable collector of Breton legends was Anatole le Braz, who was commissioned by the minister of public instruction to investigate the stories current with reference to *An Ankou* (death). Le Braz's results are to be found in his *La Légende de la mort* (1902). A well-known collection of stories with a French translation was issued by the lexicographer Troude under the title of *Ar marvailler brezounek* (Brest, 1870), and one of the most popular books at the present day is *Pipi Gonto*, by A. le Moal (St Brieuc, vol. i. 1902, vol. ii. 1908). A recent collection of stories with a religious tendency is C.M. le Prat's *Marvailhou ar Vreuned* (Brest, 1907). The modern movement, which started in the 'nineties of last century, has already produced numerous dramas and volumes of lyrics, and it may now be affirmed in all seriousness that Brittany is producing something really national. The scope of the writers of the earlier movement was very limited and little originality was displayed in their productions. The literary output of the last ten years in Brittany may truly be termed prodigious, and much of it reaches quite a high level. The dramas which are being produced are mainly propagandist in the interests either of the *Union Régionaliste Bretonne* or of temperance reform. These are for the most part very crude, but they have been received with great enthusiasm, and this has led to the revival of the old mysteries, though in a somewhat modified form. The foremost living writer is Fanch Jaffrennou, who writes under the name of "*Taldir*" (Brow of Steel) and is the author of two very striking volumes of lyrics—*An Hirvoudou* or *Sighs* (St Brieuc, 1899) and *An Delen Dir* or *The Harp of Steel* (St Brieuc, 1900). The latter is the most interesting outcome of the modern movement. Among other poets we may mention N. Quellien (*Annaïk*, Paris, 1880; *Breiz, Poésies bretonnes*, Paris, 1898), Erwan Berthou (*Dre an Delen hag ar c'horn-boud, Par la harpe et par le cor de guerre*, St Brieuc, 1904), C.M.

le Prat, who writes under the name of Klaoda (*Mouez Reier Plougastel,* "The Voice of the Cliffs of Plougastel," St Brieuc, 1905), J. Cuillandre (*Mouez an Aochou, La Voix des grèves,* Rennes, 1903), abbé Lec'hvien, *Gwerziou ha soniou* (St Brieuc, 1900), and, further, two anonymous volumes of verse, *An Tremener, Gwerziou ha soniou* (Brest, 1900), and *Kanaouennou Kerne* (Brest, 1900). Two older collections are mentioned by Dottin—J. Cadiou, *En Breiz-Izel* (Morlaix, 1885) and *Ivona*(Morlaix, 1886). An anthology of latter-day lyrics appeared at Rennes in 1902 under the title of *Bleuniou Breiz-Izel, Dibab Barzoniezou.* Of the numerous plays those most deserving of mention from a literary point of view are perhaps *Ar Vezventi* by T. le Garrec; the comedy*Alanik al Louarn* by J.M. Perrot (Brest, 1905) based on the farce of Pathelin; Tanguy Malmanche, *Le Conte de l'âme qui a faim,* in which Breton superstitions connected with the spirits of the dead are introduced with strange effect; J. le Bayon, *En Eutru Keriolet* (Vannes, 1902), which deals with the life and death of a blaspheming Breton nobleman of the early part of the 17th century; F. Jaffrennou, *Pontkallek* (Brest, 1903), which tells of the betrayal of a noble Breton who was put to death by the French in 1720; and the farce *Eur Pesk-Ebrel*by L. Rennadis (Morlaix, 1900).

AUTHORITIES.—A history of Breton literature does not exist, though we possess ample materials for such a work. The following works and articles may be consulted: G. Dottin. *Revue de synthèse historique,* viii, 93-104, contains a full bibliography; J. Loth,*Chrestomathie bretonne* (Paris, 1890); L.C. Stern in *Die Kultur d. Gegenwart,* i. xi. 1, pp. 132-137; A. le Braz, *Le Théâtre celtique* (Paris, 1904); H. Gaidoz and P. Sébillot, "Bibliographie des traditions et de la littérature populaire de la Bretagne" (*Revue celtique,* v. 277-338; supplement by P. Sébillot, *Revue de Bretagne, de Vendée, et d'Anjou,* 1894); F.M. Luzel, "Formules initiates et finales des conteurs en Basse-Bretagne" (*Revue celtique,* iii. 336 ff.); L.F. Sauvé, "Formulettes et traditions diverses de la Basse-Bretagne" (*Revue celtique,* v. 157 ff.); *Charmes,* "Oraisons et conjurations magiques," *ib* vi. 66 ff.; "Devinettes bretonnes," *ib.* iv 60 ff.; "Proverbes et dictons de la Basse-Bretagne," *ib.* i-iii. For Breton proverbs see also A. Brizeux, "Furnez Breiz," in*Oeuvres de A. Brizeux* (Paris, 1903); J. Loth, "Chansons en bas-vannetais" (*Revue celtique,* vii. 171 ff.); N. Quellien, *Chansons et danses des Bretons* (Paris, 1889); E. Ernault, "Chansons populaires" (*Revue celtique,* xxiii. 121 ff.); P. le Roux, "Une Chanson bretonne du xviiie siècle" (*Revue celtique,* xix. 1). Since 1901 a complete bibliography of modern works pertaining to Breton language and literature appears from time to time in the *Annales de Bretagne.*

(E. C. Q.)

VI. CORNISH LITERATURE.—The literature of Cornwall is more destitute of originality and more limited in scope than that of Brittany, and it is remarkable that the medieval drama should occupy the most prominent place in both. The earliest Cornish we know consists of proper names and a vocabulary. About 200 Cornish names occur among the manumissions of serfs in the Bodmin Gospels (10th century). They were printed by Whitley Stokes in the*Revue celtique,* i. 232. Next comes the Cottonian Vocabulary, which seems to follow a similar Anglo-Saxon collection and is contained in a 12th-century MS. at the British Museum. It consists of seven pages and the words are classified under various headings, such as heaven and earth, different parts of the human body, birds, beasts, fishes, trees, herbs, ecclesiastical and liturgical terms. At the end we find a number of adjectives. This vocabulary was printed by Zeuss[2], p. 1065, and again in alphabetical order by Norris in the *Ordinalia.* The language of this document is termed Old Cornish, although the forms it contains correspond to those of Mid. Welsh and Mid. Breton.

The first piece of connected Cornish which we know consists of a poem, or portion of a play(?), of forty-one lines discovered by Jenner in the British Museum. This fragment was probably written about 1400 and deals with the subject of marriage (edited by W. Stokes in the *Revue celtique,* iv. 258). A little later is the *Poem of Mount Calvary* or *the Passion,* of which five MSS. are in existence. The poem has been twice printed, 652first by Davies Gilbert with English translation by John Keigwin (1826), and again by W. Stokes for the London Philological Society in 1862. It consists of 259 stanzas of eight lines of seven syllables apiece, and contains a versified narrative of the events of the Passion made up from the Gospels and apocryphal sources, notably the Gospel of Nicodemus. But the bulk of Cornish literature is made up of plays, and in this connexion it may be noted that there still exist in

314

the west of Cornwall the remains of a number of open-air amphitheatres, locally called *plan an guari*, where the plays seem to have been acted. The earliest representatives of this kind of literature in Cornwall form a trilogy going under the name of *Ordinalia*, of which three MSS. are known, one a 15th-century Oxford MS. from which the two others are copied. The *Ordinalia* were published by Edwin Norris under the title of *The Ancient Cornish Drama*(Oxford, 1859). The first play is called *Origo Mundi* and deals with events from the Old Testament down to the building of Solomon's temple. The second play, the *Passio Domini*,goes on without interruption into the third, the *Resurrectio Domini*, which embraces the Harrowing of Hell, the Resurrection and Ascension, the legend of St Veronica and Tiberius, and the death of Pilate. Here again the pseudo-Gospel of Nicodemus is drawn upon, and interwoven with the Scriptural narrative we find the Legend of the Cross. As the title*Ordinalia* indicates, these plays are of learned origin and are imitated from English sources. The popular name for these dramas, *quari-mirkle*, is a literal translation of the English term miracle play, and Norris shows that whole passages were translated word for word. Many of the events are represented as having taken place in well-known Cornish localities, but apart from this scarcely any traces of originality can be discovered. The same remark holds good in the case of another play, *Beunans Meriasek* or the *Life of St Meriasek*. This deals in an incoherent manner with the life and death of Meriasek (in Breton *Meriadek*), the son of a duke of Brittany, and interwoven with this theme is the legend of St Silvester and the emperor Constantine, quite regardless of the circumstance that St Silvester lived in the 4th and St Meriasek in the 7th century. The MS. of this play was written by "Dominus Hadton" in the year 1504, and is preserved in the Peniarth library. The language is more recent than that of the *Ordinalia*, and there is a certain admixture of English. The *Life of St Meriasek* falls into two parts, and at the end of each the spectators are invited to carouse. St Meriasek was in earlier times the patron saint of Camborne, where his fountain is still to be seen and pilgrims to it were known by the name of *Merra-sickers*. In this play, consequently, we might expect to find something really Cornish. But le Braz has shown that the author of this motley drama was content to draw his materials from Latin and English lives of saints. The story of Meriasek himself was taken from a Breton source and closely resembles the narrative of the 17th-century Breton hagiographer, Albert le Grand. The last play we have to mention is*Gwreans an Bys* (The Creation of the World), of which five complete copies are known. Two of these are in the Bodleian and one in the British Museum, which also possesses a further fragment. The oldest text was revised by William Jordan of Helston in 1611, but there are indications that parts of it at any rate are older than the Reformation. This play bears a great resemblance to the first part of the *Origo Mundi*, and may have been imitated from it. It was printed first by Davies Gilbert in 1827 with a translation by John Keigwin, and again by W. Stokes in the *Transactions of the London Philological Society* for 1864. The language shows considerable signs of decay, and Lucifer and his angels are often made to speak English. The only other original compositions of any length written in Cornish are *Nebbaz Gerriau dro tho Carnoack* (A Few Words about Cornish), by John Boson (printed in the*Journal of the Royal Institution of Cornwall*, 1879), and the *Story of John of Chy-an-Hur*(Ram's House), a folk-tale which appears in Ireland and elsewhere. The latter was printed in Lhuyd's *Grammar* and in Pryce's *Archaeologia*. Andrew Borde's *Booke of the Introduction of Knowledge* (1542) contains some Cornish conversations (see *Archiv f. celt. Lexikographie*,vol. i.), and in Carew's *Survey of Cornwall* a number of words and phrases are to be found. Apart from the Cornish preface to Lhuyd's *Grammar*, the other remains of the language consist of a few songs, verses, proverbs, epigrams, epitaphs, maxims, letters, conversations, mottoes and translations of chapters and passages of Scripture, the Lord's Prayer, the Creed, the Commandments, King Charles's Letter, &c. These fragments are to be found (1) in the Gwavas MS. in the British Museum, a collection ranging in date from 1709 to 1736; (2) in the Borlase MS. (1750); (3) in Pryce's *Archaeologia Cornu-Britannica* (1790); (4) in D. Gilbert's editions of the *Poem of the Passion* (1826) and the Creation of the World (1827). They are enumerated, classified and described by Jenner in his *Handbook*.

AUTHORITIES.—H Jenner, *Handbook of the Cornish Language* (London, 1904); A. le Braz, *Le Théâtre celtique* (Paris, 1905); E. Norris, *The Ancient Cornish Drama* (2 vols., Oxford,

1859); T.C. Peter, *The Old Cornish Drama* (London, 1906); L.C. Stern, *Die Kultur d. Gegenwart*, i. xi. 1, pp. 131-132.

(E. C. Q.)

1J. Loth gives it as his opinion that as late as 1400-1600 a Cornishman and a Breton might have been able to understand one another.

2It is indeed probable that Myrddin is a purely fictitious character, whose name has been made up from Caer Fyrddin (= Maridunum), which was certainly not a personal name.

3Another derivation of this word is from *llad*, "profit" + *hai*, a suffix denoting the agent. Others derive it from or connect it with the Irish *slad-*.

CELT, a word in common use among British and French archaeologists to describe the hatchets, adzes or chisels of chipped or shaped stone used by primitive man. The word is variously derived from the Welsh *cellt*, a flintstone (that being the material of which the weapons are chiefly made, though celts of basalt felstone and jade are found); from being supposed to be the implement peculiar to the Celtic peoples; or from a Low Latin word *celtis*, a chisel. The last derivation is more probably correct. The word has come to be somewhat loosely applied to metal as well as stone axe-heads. The general form of stone celts is that of blades approaching an oval in section, with sides more or less straight and one end broader and sharper than the other. In length they vary from about 2 to as much as 16 in. The largest and finest specimens are found in Denmark: one in an English collection being of beautiful white flint 13 in. long, 1½ in. thick and 3½ in. broad. Those found in Denmark are sometimes polished, but usually are left rough. Those found in north-western Europe are ground to a more or less smooth surface. That some were held in the hand and others fixed in wooden handles is clear from the presence of peculiar polished spaces produced by the friction of the wood. In the later stone adzes holes are sometimes found pierced to receive the handles.

The bronze celts vary in size from an inch to a foot in length. The earlier specimens are much like the stone ones in shape and design, but the later manufactures show a marked improvement, the metal being usually pierced to receive the handles. It is noteworthy that the celtmakers never cast their axes with a transverse hole through which the handle might pass. Bronze celts are usually plain, but some are ornamented with ridges, dots or lines. That they were made in the countries where they are found is proved by the presence of moulds.

A point worthy of mention is the position which stone celts hold in the folk-lore and superstitious beliefs of many lands. In the West of England the country folks believe the weapons fell originally from the sky as "thunderbolts," and that the water in which they are boiled is a specific for rheumatism. In the North and Scotland they are preservatives against cattle diseases. In Brittany a stone celt is thrown into a well to purify the water. In Sweden they are regarded as a protection against lightning. In Norway the belief is that, if they are genuine thunderbolts, a thread tied round them when placed on hot coals will not burn but will become moist. In Germany, Spain, Italy, the same beliefs prevail. In Japan the stones are accounted of medicinal value, while in Burma and Assam they are infallible specifics for ophthalmia. In Africa they are the weapons of the Thunder-God. In India and among the Greeks the hatchet appears to have had a sacred importance, derived, doubtless, from the universal superstitious awe with which these weapons of prehistoric man were regarded.

See Sir J. Evans's *Ancient Stone Implements of Great Britain*; Lord Avebury's *Prehistoric Times* (1865-1900) and *Origin of Civilization* (1870); E.B. Tylor's *Anthropology, and Primitive Culture*, &c. For the history of polished stone axes up to the 17th century see Dr Marrel Bandouin and Lionel Bonnemère in the *Bulletin de la Société d'Anthropologie de Paris*, April-May 1905.

www.ingramcontent.com/pod-product-compliance
Lightning Source LLC
Chambersburg PA
CBHW070104290526
45789CB00005B/1920